Global Perspectives on Youth Gang Behavior, Violence, and Weapons Use

Simon Harding
Middlesex University, UK

Marek Palasinski
Liverpool John Moores University, UK

A volume in the Advances in Psychology, Mental Health, and Behavioral Studies (APMHBS) Book Series

An Imprint of IGI Global

Published in the United States of America by
     Information Science Reference (an imprint of IGI Global)
     701 E. Chocolate Avenue
     Hershey PA, USA 17033
     Tel: 717-533-8845
     Fax: 717-533-8661
     E-mail: cust@igi-global.com
     Web site: http://www.igi-global.com

Library of Congress Cataloging-in-Publication Data

Names: Harding, Simon (Criminologist) editor.| Palasinski, Marek, 1981- editor.
Title: Global perspectives on youth gang behavior, violence, and
  weapons use / Simon Harding and Marek Palasinski, editors.
Description: Hershey : Information Science Reference, 2016. | Includes
  bibliographical references and index.
Identifiers: LCCN 2015046878| ISBN 9781466699380 (hardcover) | ISBN
  9781466699397 (ebook)
Subjects: LCSH: Violence in adolescence. | Youth and violence. | Gangs--Case
  studies.
Classification: LCC HQ799.2.V56 P79 2016 | DDC 303.60835--dc23 LC record available at http://lccn.loc.gov/2015046878

This book is published in the IGI Global book series Advances in Psychology, Mental Health, and Behavioral Studies (APMHBS) (ISSN: pending; eISSN: pending)

British Cataloguing in Publication Data
A Cataloguing in Publication record for this book is available from the British Library.

For electronic access to this publication, please contact: eresources@igi-global.com.

Advances in Psychology, Mental Health, and Behavioral Studies (APMHBS) Book Series

Bryan Christiansen
PryMarke, LLC, USA

ISSN: pending
EISSN: pending

MISSION

The complexity of the human mind has puzzled researchers and physicians for centuries. While widely studied, the brain still remains largely misunderstood.

The **Advances in Psychology, Mental Health, and Behavioral Studies (APMHBS)** book series presents comprehensive research publications focusing on topics relating to the human psyche, cognition, psychiatric care, mental and developmental disorders, as well as human behavior and interaction. Featuring diverse and innovative research, publications within APMHBS are ideally designed for use by mental health professionals, academicians, researchers, and upper-level students.

COVERAGE

- Human Behavior
- Cognition
- Developmental Disorders
- Psychiatry
- Personality Disorders
- Treatment & Care
- Anxiety
- Counseling & Therapy
- Eating Disorders
- Mental Health & Disorders

IGI Global is currently accepting manuscripts for publication within this series. To submit a proposal for a volume in this series, please contact our Acquisition Editors at Acquisitions@igi-global.com or visit: http://www.igi-global.com/publish/.

Titles in this Series

For a list of additional titles in this series, please visit: www.igi-global.com

Psychosocial Studies of the Individual's Changing Perspectives in Alzheimer's Disease
Cordula Dick-Muehlke (University of California, Irvine, USA) Ruobing Li (University of California, Irvine, USA) and Myron Orleans (California State University, Fullerton, USA)
Medical Information Science Reference • copyright 2015 • 434pp • H/C (ISBN: 9781466684782) • US $225.00 (our price)

Psychological and Social Implications Surrounding Internet and Gaming Addiction
Jonathan Bishop (Centre for Research into Online Communities and E-Learning Systems, Swansea, UK)
Information Science Reference • copyright 2015 • 335pp • H/C (ISBN: 9781466685956) • US $195.00 (our price)

Handbook of Research on Innovations in the Diagnosis and Treatment of Dementia
Panagiotis D. Bamidis (Aristotle University of Thessaloniki, Greece) Ioannis Tarnanas (Aristotle University of Thessaloniki, Greece) Leontios Hadjileontiadis (Aristotle University of Thessaloniki, Greece) and Magda Tsolaki (Aristotle University of Thessaloniki, Greece)
Medical Information Science Reference • copyright 2015 • 511pp • H/C (ISBN: 9781466682344) • US $245.00 (our price)

Exploring Implicit Cognition Learning, Memory, and Social Cognitive Processes
Zheng Jin (Zhengzhou Normal University, China & University of California, Davis, USA)
Information Science Reference • copyright 2015 • 371pp • H/C (ISBN: 9781466665996) • US $195.00 (our price)

DISSEMINATOR OF KNOWLEDGE
www.igi-global.com

701 E. Chocolate Ave., Hershey, PA 17033
Order online at www.igi-global.com or call 717-533-8845 x100
To place a standing order for titles released in this series, contact: cust@igi-global.com
Mon-Fri 8:00 am - 5:00 pm (est) or fax 24 hours a day 717-533-8661

List of Reviewers

Lorraine Bowman-Grieve, *Waterford Institute of Technology, Ireland*
Ami Carpenter, *University of San Diego, USA*
Barbara Cooke, *Texas A&M University – Kingsville, USA*
Sarah E. Daly, *Rutgers University – Newark, USA*
Laura Dunbar, *University of Ottawa, Canada*
Claire Hanlon, *University of Manchester, UK*
Laura L. Hansen, *Western New England University, USA*
Sukdeo Ingale, *DES's Navalmal Firodia Law College, India*
Ronn Johnson, *University of San Diego, USA*
Tim Lauger, *Niagara University, USA*
Dev Rup Maitra, *University of Cambridge, UK*
Andrej Naterer, *University of Maribor, Slovenia*
Angus Nurse, *Middlesex University, UK*
Don Pinnock, *University of Cape Town, South Africa*
Birau Ramona, *University of Craiova, Romania*
Kier Southcott, *Middlesex University, UK*
Rob White, *University of Tasmania, Australia*
Qianwei Zhao, *University of Southern California, USA*

Table of Contents

Detailed Table of Contents

Section 1
North America

Chapter 1

    Laura L. Hansen, Western New England University, USA
    Melissa E. Freitag, Bowling Green State University, USA

Violent initiation rites directed at new members or potential members of an organization are not recent phenomena and not exclusive to joining street gangs or crews. This chapter will explore the origins of violent initiation through history and how contemporary rites used to "welcome" new members in youth gangs mirror other entries into exclusively male enclaves. These rituals include controlled, choreographed patterns of violent behavior, including participants vs. voyeurs and number of blows directed at the initiate before the rite is considered to be completed. In additional to taking a historical perspective, recognized predictive risk factors for gang recruitment are listed, including those identified by Hill et al. (1999) in their Seattle study of juvenile delinquency and how it leads down the slippery slope to gang affiliation.

Chapter 2

    Laura L. Hansen, Western New England University, USA

With gang initiation starting as early as the primary school grades, the challenge to educators and administrators is to identify and suppress gang activities within the confines of school grounds. Taking into consideration the impotence of school systems to control the neighborhood and family environments, understanding the important role of schools to keep students engaged in scholarship to prevent gang membership cannot be stressed enough. Taking an applied approach, this chapter identifies what educators, administrators, and staff can do to identify behavior that might be on the surface mere imitation of gang membership (e.g. throwing gang signs), but could be symptomatic of close contact with known gang members and possibly exposure to the violence associated with gangs. The more school personnel can be cognizant of behavior that is indicative of exposure to gangs, curriculum planning and after school programs can be designed more efficiently to counter delinquent influences within the community, beyond "just say no" strategies.

Gang-related violence in schools can have a number of negative effects on the school environment, student achievement, and perceptions of fear. Schools that report a gang presence among students often report higher rates of victimization on school property. In response, many schools have focused on both physical and procedural safety measures to enhance security and prevent violence. However, attempts at maintaining order and ensuring safety often fall short in preventing violence and may actually enhance feelings of fear at schools. As such, schools face the difficult task of addressing violence with effective safety measures while also minimizing and balancing the prison-like feeling that comes with many of the options. This chapter aims to describe the effects of violence in schools and examine a variety of safety measures in terms of cost, effect on perceptions of fear, and effectiveness.

Chapter 4

Weapons and violence are both real and mythic elements of gang life. Though violence is a real element of gang life, public perceptions about gangs may be exaggerated, invoking the idea of dangerous youth roaming the streets. The image of violent gang members is also embraced and used by youth on the streets to navigate their social world. Gang members often create personal and group-based myths by exaggerating their use of weapons and violence. This chapter examines the division between myth and reality in gang life. It reviews research to establish that weapons and violence are real elements of gang members' lives throughout the world. It further explores how myths emerge among gang members who have ample motivation for fictionalizing violence and weapons use. This chapter relies on the social psychological ideas of social constructionism, interpretive socialization, and identity to explain the existence of myths in gang life.

The purpose of this chapter is to explore issues related to gang-affiliated youth's use of JFSB behavior as a weapon. Too often, the critical analysis of JFSB is circumscribed to the act with little or no consideration of a clinical forensic weapons use motivation. In this case, successful efforts to identify and isolate the origins of such events are more contingent upon a deeper understanding of the subtle processes that explain this particular kind of weapons use by juvenile gang members.

Chapter 6

The present chapter takes a social psychological approach to understanding hate groups and how hate groups use hate as a promotional tool and as an implement of aggression. As a promotional tool, hate groups use hate to attract new members to their organizations and to promote their beliefs to the mainstream public. Hate also serves as an incendiary, to fuel the emotions of their members, to incite them into action, and to wield against their targets. In this chapter we will attempt to explain why people hate and how they justify their hatred and resulting actions through a number of social psychological theories including realistic group conflict (Bonacich, 1972; Sherif et al., 1961/1988) relative deprivation (Catalono et al., 1993; Hepworth & West, 1988; Hovland & Sears, 1940), social identity theory (Abrams & Hogg, 1990; Festinger, 1954; Tajfel & Turner, 1986; Thoits & Virshup, 1997) and terror management (Pyszczynski, Solomon, & Greenberg, 1997; 2005; Solomon, Greenberg, & Pyszczynski, 1991; 2004).

Youth gangs and their members have been studied in a variety of contexts; however the issue of desistance has received less attention. This chapter seeks to address this gap. In order to situate the material to be covered, the chapter begins with an introduction to the topic of youth gangs. Next, an overview of the concept of desistance and how it is measured is provided. Following that is a review of some prominent criminological perspectives demonstrating that leaving the gang is a complex process involving the interaction of a combination of factors. The process of desistance and methods for leaving the gang are also briefly discussed. Several approaches have been developed to address youth gangs and their members. These approaches are reviewed and different interventions under these headings are discussed with Canadian examples provided. Finally, an argument for the development of a comprehensive strategy for youth gang exit is presented.

Section 2
Latin America

This chapter examines how gender dynamics shape violent acts among Mexican American young adult males with a history of adolescent gang membership. We use the concept of hegemonic masculinity to examine the various ways that gender is performed in acts of violence (Connell, 1995). Masculinity is not a fixed entity or individual personality traits, masculinities are "configurations of practice that are accomplished in social action and, therefore, can differ according to the gender relations in a particular setting" (Connell & Messerschmidt, 2005:836). In other words, "gender identity is never a completed project, but always a developmental process which unfolds within a social context" (Messner, 1990:209). Nevertheless, the tendencies for aggression and violence are central to what it means to be masculine (Messerschmidt, 2000; Crowley, Foley et al., 2008) because "real men" must show others that they are not afraid (Kimmel, 2010). We examine the unfolding of masculine identity among disadvantaged Mexican American men in two different yet related contexts: violent acts with other men and the retelling of these violent acts. Among disadvantaged men, in general, social class is central to masculinity because these men are likely to have limited options in accomplishing their masculinity compared to men with more advantages (Britton, 2011; Messerschmidt, 1993; Stretesky & Pogrebin, 2007). The type of masculinity expressed by Mexican American males, more specifically, varies depending on a constellation of variables related to social class including income, generational status, education, and association with the criminal justice system (Rios, 2011; Valdez, 2007).

Chapter 9

This chapter interrogates the nature and function of weapons in Latino gang culture, and is divided into three parts. It begins by defining Latino gangs in the Americas, and classifying them into Mexican-American gangs, Mexican gangs, and Central American gangs. Despite differences in region, economic situation, generations and cultural characteristics, I draw broad similarities by focusing specifically on large, organized gangs within each of the three classifications. The second section interrogates the logics and motivations driving gangs' use of weapons, along with the psychological and instrumental functions of weapons use for Latino gangs. The chapter's third section is a substantial conclusion which argues for approaches to gang-violence which derive from the field of peace and conflict studies, including short-term approaches to violence reduction (gang ceasefires and truces) and longer term, ecological approaches based on the theoretical framework of community resilience.

Section 3
Europe

Chapter 10

This chapter explores the activities and characteristics of street gangs and organised crime groups in contemporary British society. Although numerous studies exist which investigate youth delinquency and group violence in Britain, there is less research which specifically investigates contemporary British criminal gangs - carrying out such an exploration is the organising principle of this chapter. Through conducting qualitative research at an adult men's prison in England and its surrounding area, this chapter attempts to articulate the experiences of prisoners and street-offenders on this subject. The results illustrate the entrenched role street gangs and organised crime groups hold in certain areas of England; not only are they seen as viable alternatives to gainful employment, but their activities are often sanctioned by the communities within which they are based. Subsequently, a high level of violence is normalised within such communities, including heightened levels of weapon usage by gang members, both within and outside prison.

Chapter 11

This chapter investigates the composition of prison gangs, their effects on the prison environment, and their relationships with street gangs. Through conducting an ethnographic study of an adult men's prison in England, the chapter attempts to articulate the experiences of prison gang members, as well as prisoners exposed to high levels of gang activity. The results illustrate the established role gangs play within English prisons, but also the relevance of other groups, collectives and "sets" within the penal environment. Through analysing the gathered data, I aim to show the important - but not defining - role gangs play within an English prison. Moreover, when compared to the American prison system, gangs are far less entrenched in English prisons; this can partly be attributed to the deeper historical roots of American prison gangs, as well as their highly racialized dimensions. The chapter begins with two case-studies, the subjects of which are prisoners from the research site.

Chapter 12
Andrej Naterer, University of Maribor, Slovenia

The chapter explores the subculture of street children in Makeevka, Ukraine. Drawing upon qualitative and quantitative data gathered during longitudinal anthropological field research their surviving strategies along with social structures, economic activities and substance abuse are presented. In addition, extra-, intra- and inter-group violence is analyzed with an emphasis on the child's situational interpretation and adoption of the code of the street through subsequent code/identity switching and subcultural reactions.

Section 4
Africa

Chapter 13
Don Pinnock, University of Cape Town, South Africa

Almost all gang studies throughout the 20th century and most in the 21st locate the reasons for both gang membership and a tendency to violence in the environments within which young people are raised: family, neighbourhood, school, poverty, access to drugs and general deprivation. In Cape Town all these were present under apartheid and still persist 20 years after the country became a democracy. The reasons for this persistence have to do with global and local economics, skills shortages, corruption, political mismanagement and neglect of certain neighbourhoods and are beyond the scope of this chapter. Rather, acknowledging these influences, this study looks at how gangs are defined and examines them from a more finely grained perspective.

Section 5
Asia

Chapter 14
Simon Harding, Middlesex University, UK

This chapter considers youth offending and youth justice in contemporary China noting significant changes due to the rapid economic transformation. Once famous for its low crime rates, the apparent rapid rise in Chinese juvenile delinquency has left the media 'wondering what transformed these little "flowers of the motherland" into "carnivorous plants". The chapter charts changes from the yanda (hard strikes) crackdown in 1983 to the highly publicised anti-crime crackdown in Chongqing. Despite limited data, a picture is emerging of changing influence of triads and altered relationships between organised crime and street gangs, noting street gangs are increasing due to an influx of rural migrants to the mega-cities. The chapter touches upon the risk factors and emergent arguments of this contemporary phenomenon, noting that Zhang et al (1997:299) has suggested that 'China is in an early stage of gang development' possibly equivalent to the USA from 1930s to the 1960s.

Section 6
Pacifica

Chapter 15
Rob White, University of Tasmania, Australia

This chapter provides an introduction and overview of issues pertaining to youth gangs and youth violence in Australia. The first part features the voices of young people from around Australia describing their experiences of youth gang violence. The second part provides a broad overview of biological, psychological and social factors that together shape the propensities for young people, and young men in particular, to join gangs and to engage in youth violence. The final part of the chapter provides more detailed exposition of two gang members, 'Mohammad' and 'Tan', and the everyday complexities of their lives. The chapter concludes by noting that the gang does not have to be seen as an overwhelming influence in the lives of young people, and that their activities and behaviours are more diverse, and include positive elements, than generally given credit in mainstream youth gangs research and analysis.

Chapter 16
Jarrod Gilbert, University of Canterbury, New Zealand

The first decade of the new century has seen significant changes among the gangs of New Zealand. Facing a changing cultural climate in which rebellious young people see membership in traditional 'patch'-wearing gangs as less desirable, New Zealand's established gangs have become starved for recruits. Rather than precipitating a straightforward decline in the country's gang scene, however, what we are seeing is a reorganisation of the gangs. This chapter examines the problems facing the outlaw motorcycle clubs and the patched street gangs, and the numerous and complex nature of the issues facing these groups. It also explores the rise of LA-style street gangs and the similarities and difference that exist between them and New Zealand's traditional gangs.

Foreword

The United Nations estimates that by 2020 half the world's population will be living in urban slums of one sort or another. Moreover, they calculate that around half of the inhabitants will be aged under 15. This is a population whose problems in gaining access to legitimate opportunity will be exacerbated by burgeoning income polarization and the effective withdrawal of state services from the poorest. In these circumstances, it is probable that the gang phenomenon will not only grow, but become more deeply entrenched. As Elijah Anderson (1999) has written:

In some of the most economically distressed and drug and crime-ridden pockets of the city, the rules of civil law have been severely weakened, and in their stead a 'code of the streets' often holds sway ... The code of the streets emerges where the influence of the police ends and personal responsibility for one's safety is felt to begin, resulting in a kind of 'people's law' based on street justice. (p. 29)

However, the more conventional North American accounts of the origins of the youth gang, that suggest they are the product of the 'social disorganisation' of a culturally deficient urban underclass or a consequence of the globalization of 'gangster rap' don't really get to grips with the complexity of the problem.

Moreover, much of the U.S. research locates the origins of the gang form in the migration of disadvantaged social, ethnic and religious groups to the host country and the consequent cultural dislocation they experience. This type of analysis does not dwell for long on the relationship between migration, the social and economic circumstances encountered by the migrant groups. However, in his chapter 'From Little flowers', about gangs in China, Harding points to the fact that it is the children of poor, sometimes disposed, rural workers who come to the major Chinese cities to find work who are becoming involved in gangs. Here it is not so much cultural dislocation as social exclusion and lack of access to legitimate opportunity that is propelling these young people into these new groupings.

Clearly, anybody writing about 'gangs' today would be unwise to ignore the huge body of research and scholarship devoted to the gang phenomenon by North American academics. However, the contributors to Global Perspectives on Youth Gang Behaviour, Violence, and Weapons Use, who are drawn from several different developed countries, have moved beyond the traditional accounts of the aetiology of gangs in order to analyse the contemporary constellation of social, economic and cultural forces which have either brought these groupings into being or caused them to change.

Dev Maitra's account of an Exploratory Study of Prison Gangs in Contemporary British Society, for example, breaks new ground because while the prison gang is an established feature of imprisonment in the United States, it is only in the past few years that they have come to be recognised as a feature of the UK penal system. This chapter has particular relevance at the moment as both research and the Prisons Inspectorate in the UK have revealed a sharp escalation in prison violence in the recent period Indeed, in March 2013 the UK Parliamentary Public Accounts Committee (PPAC, 2013) indicated that spending cuts had increased the level of risk in prisons, noting that:

We are concerned about safety and decency in some prisons and the fact that more prisoners are reporting that they do not feel safe. Assaults on staff, self-harm and escapes from contractor escorts have all increased. The agency should ensure that savings plans have regard to the potential impact on risks to standards of safety, decency and respect in prisons and in the community.

Similarly, the contributions from Ukraine, South Africa, New Zealand and Australia illustrate significant cultural differences which underpin the presentations of gangs. The relationships with violence and weapons within gangs, and how this differs across the globe, are key issues for research and academia and it is considerable value that different perspectives have been assembled together for this book.

Whereas in both the UK and the USA it has become a 'taken-for-granted' that effective intervention with youth gangs should involve a pincer movement, with tough enforcement on the one side and educational, vocational, welfare and therapeutic intervention on the other. However, this collection suggests that a one-size-fits-all response which fails to address the deep rooted origins of the 'gang phenomenon' are unlikely to succeed.

John Pitts
University of Bedfordshire, UK

REFERENCES

Anderson, E. (1999). *Code of the street: Decency, violence, and the moral life of the inner city.* New York: W. W. Norton & Company, Inc.

UK Parliamentary Public Accounts Committee (PPAC). (2013). *Restructuring the national offender management service.* Retrieved from http://www.publications.parliament.uk/pa/cm201213/cmselect/cmpubacc/717/71704.htm

Preface

THE GLOBALIZED GANG

Gangs are no longer solely associated with run-down inner-city American cities but are now effectively a worldwide phenomenon with activities stretching from street corner drug deals to regional, or even countrywide, violence which can threaten the existence and survival of the political state. As renowned gang scholar John Hagedorn (2008) has so clearly set out, gangs find their genesis in poverty, immigration, urbanisation and weakened states. Whilst globalisation itself does not cause gangs, it reproduces the conditions which allow gangs to generate and then thrive. These global conditions of structural unemployment, dis-investment, socio-political marginalisation, find their expression in a concentration of disadvantage and high-crime neighbourhoods (Pitts, 2008). Familiar to us as projects, estates, banlieus, slums, favelas, ghettos, barrios, townships, shantytowns these communities then find themselves further excluded and ultimately discredited and abandoned by the State. The discredited populations become stigmatised (Baum, 1996) and subject to racism and ethnic oppression which exacerbates and inflames marginalization and hopelessness (van Gemert, Peterson, & Lien, 2008; Vigil, 2002).

Diego Vigil says that the youth of such communities know that they live in neighborhoods which are 'physically inferior' and needy and this generates a sense of being social outcasts, 'a psychological state of bitterness and resentment often becomes another burden' (Hazan & Rogers, 2014, p. 54).

This, in conjunction with the neo-liberal restructuring of world economies, generates the conditions which present a bleak outlook: a Planet of Slums (Davis, 2006) increasingly populated by urban outcasts (Wacquant, 2008) which in turn generates a World of Gangs (Hagedorn, 2008). Such phenomena are increasingly reported and recognised all over the world. These features of globalization and convergent evolution were recognized as two of several factors helping to generate gangs in the recent edited collection, Global Gangs by Hazan and Rogers (2014). In his chapter on the migratory origins of Chicano gangs in Los Angeles, Diego Vigil (2002, p. 49) identifies a further critical factor in the development of gangs - the continuous migration and 'adaptation and adjustment to urban society', which is passed down as 'inter-generational marginalisation'. For Vigil, this issue, best expressed as 'multiple marginality' (Vigil, 2007) underlies the creation of street gangs, especially when co-joined with high impact issues which are socio-economic, social-cultural, psychological, and ecological. As he points out, at the very least, multiple marginality reduces the effectiveness of family, school and law enforcement for young people. As such the mechanisms of social control are eroded, diluted or even absent, it seems inevitable that many young people join the 'pool of availability' which then leads many to affiliate to urban street gangs.

Within these discredited communities there inevitably is a lessening of social control and increasingly 'law enforcement disconnects from low-income communities' (Vigil in Hazan & Rogers, 2014, p. 50). In such ways street socialization becomes the central focus and orientation of youth offering both the answers and outcomes they seek. This is best witnessed through the global appeal and expansion of Hip Hop as a shared global culture, which itself has become an immersive cultural experience for many street oriented young people. For some it has moved beyond a poetic cultural reflection of lived experience and instead becomes a credo or template for how to experience life.

John Hagedorn argues that within these forms of social exclusion it becomes a goal to create 'identities to protect their personality and community' (Hagedorn, 2008, p. 60). In this way Hip Hop both articulates this world and provides a counterbalance to what is otherwise a world of ultra-violence, misogyny and nihilism, which has a global appeal to the youth caught up in this expanding net. It offers a cultural response which articulates stories of survival offering life lessons to those who recognise themselves and their predicament.

A further issue of globalized expansion of street gangs, and one which might be a cause for serious concern, is the geographical spread of gangs through transplantation, which has given rise to the 'transnational gang'. This form of gang has largely evolved from migratory movements of people from Central America to the USA and then notably through the subsequent attempts to reverse this via an extensive programme of deportations. Consequently, gang and prison hierarchies established, formalised and codified in the mega-penitentiaries of the USA, were frequently replicated and then transplanted back to Central American states. This has resulted in increased gang activity and violence in the original domestic communities. These transplanted gangs were then well placed to link up with the emergent narco-gangs and cartels from Mexico and Columbia. Such issues now present a considerable and growing threat to the political stability of several Latin American states. The question for all of us is how are such issues now to be addressed?

The key challenge for the future is to address the depth of alienation of some marginalised communities and the consequent potential for gangs to institutionalise. Considering this phenomena, Hagedorn warns of 'institutionalised gangs and other armed young men [that] have become permanent fixtures in many ghettos, barrios and favelas across the globe are an ever present option for marginalized youth. Gangs are unmistakeable signs that all is not well and that millions of people are being left out of the marvels of a globalised economy' (Hagedorn, 2008, p. xxiv).

If true, then gangs can be viewed as simply logical conclusions to the need to survive and adapt to these changing social and global conditions. Where conditions of marginalisation, poverty and deprivation persist, urban street gangs will thrive whether it be in local housing neighborhoods, prison, secondary schools, in India, Kenya, France, Ukraine, New Zealand, Mexico or the USA. Here neglected populations will find both protection and opportunity for social and economic advancement in these alternative social institutions. Increasingly this search for protection and social advancement is inter-generational with the struggle and also the various adopted techniques for survival handed down from one generation to the next. Gangs are now increasingly embedded in these communities and their predicament is often made worse by grinding poverty and racism. As Klein (1971) and Vigil (1998) note, Mexican gangs have operated in Los Angeles since the 1940s and there local youths have to engage with what are now both 2nd and 3rd generation gangs. For this reason, Hagedorn describes gangs as institutionalised 'living organisms'. I would argue they are also adaptive, evolving and regenerative. The result of which means - gangs are here to stay!

A NEW RESEARCH AGENDA?

The concept of urban street gangs as a logical adaptation to local, and global, conditions is not universally acknowledged, but does seem to be gathering ground.

Sudhir Venkatesh also suggests that, 'gangs are a logical and inevitable expression of local social structure' (Hazan & Rogers, 2008, p. 281) and more recently has posed an interesting question which jumps to the heart of a new approach in gang scholarship - *why shouldn't gangs exist?* (Hazan & Rogers, 2014).

This query echoes recent developments in gang scholarship in the UK (Pitts, 2008; Densley, 2013; Deuchar, 2009; Harding, 2014) which similarly argue that gangs are a logical development of the local expression of social-structural inequities (though each with a different cultural flavour and situational context). These arguments are advanced through new research which advocates analysis of the social field, (Bourdieu, 1985). Thus future research should perhaps consider how the localised gang context is first generated and then how this social field interacts with the structural factors which bring them about through poverty. This analytical form might then allow for issues of local, or regional, variation and diversity to be explored in greater depth.

The majority of gang studies, whether in the US, Europe or beyond, often remains a highly fragmented and disparate discipline. In places it is overly positivist in its approach. Almost certainly it fails to effectively engage with other disciplines which impact upon it including macro issues such as geography, economics, transport, migration patterns, or more localised issues such as child safeguarding, child sexual exploitation, missing children, etc. On a brighter note, prison studies and mental health issues have more recently begun to intrude into these debates generating fresh perspectives, though they too often remain thematically silo'd.

The advent and impact of social media has similarly generated fresh developments, both within gang life, and within gang studies in the form of social network analysis. It is likely that such new analytical developments will prove influential and insightful. Other new developments in gang research are now considering aspects of gang embeddedness and depth of engagement in gangs and importantly how this relates to policy development for models of desistance. These newly emerging issues are awaited with keen interest and they may permit gang studies to move in new directions; whilst perhaps side-stepping some of the more intransigent and thorny issues, yet to be fully resolved.

Gang studies have, in places, been somewhat hindered by definitional challenges and at times this has dogged the development of international perspectives on street gangs across the globe. For some, the term gang should only ever appear as 'gang'. The term often then evokes colourful imagery, covering an all too expansive spectrum ranging from local schoolyard groups or street corner youths, via neighbourhood street gangs, to organized crime syndicates and narco–cartels. Despite globalisation and the global proliferation of such groups, a shared global typology and definition remains elusive.

Whilst the study of youth delinquency in the United Kingdom has a rich sociological background of inquiry, studies into urban street gangs are on the whole, much more recent. Here definitional concerns have undoubtedly hindered scholarly inquiry, as has a reluctance, if not an outright denial by some academics, to believe that street based youth groups, or 'gangs', even exist. This has created, in some localities, an impediment to local recognition, research and policy development.

I would argue that part of this problem relates to people's point of entry into the gangs debate and its discussions. This then serves to influence their subsequent perspective.

Many people only experience or learn about gangs via negative and alarmist media – or through global gang imagery via manipulated portrayals of street gangs in Hollywood movies. Such cultural or mediated imagery portray strong cultural representations of their subject such as the Bloods and Crips or the Maras and pandillas. These accounts are highly context specific but nevertheless, often widely reported. There can be few scholars or communities who remain unfamiliar with the advance of narco-cartels or the deadly impact of street gangs in Chicago – a city now pejoratively renamed Chi-Raq by filmmaker Spike Lee. This endonym can be heard by some Chicago residents who see a resemblance in high local death rates and endemic violence which for many equates to other recent war zones.

This constructed symbolism becomes highly recognizable and symbolic of gang life. As a result of this it is usually the Bloods or Crips, or the violent drug gangs of Rio's favelas, which are immediately conjured up by the public whenever the topic of 'gangs' is raised. The strong symbolism of gang colours, masking, gang signs, tattoos and prison segregation creates an instant default image of the 'gang' and the 'gangster' in the public mind. It becomes easy to situate this culturally and thus deny their existence in your own locality if your own local gangs are clearly nothing like them.

This imagined reality then provides ample opportunity for those unfamiliar with gangs to simply overlook the home-grown street gangs on their door-step. Emerging from local neighborhood concentrations of poverty and deprivation these localised street gangs may be less colourful, less obvious or less violent than the Hollywood portrayals of the Gangs of Compton, but they may nonetheless be destructive, controlling and dangerous. In this way localised home-grown gangs can be dismissed as not the real thing.

Thus when people in England are asked do gangs exist in the UK many refer to these globally mediated cultural representations by default and then claim such issues do not exist in the UK. Domestic representations of local street gangs can be more difficult to recognise, identify or even, in the case local politicians, to accept. It requires undertaking localised research, keeping your nose to the ground and working with local practitioners and authorities to determine if gangs are in fact emerging locally; to identify how they may present; to understand how they are organised or to determine which criminal activates they might be actively involved in.

Whilst this contention was prevalent, even predominant for the first few years of the century in the UK, recent empirical work by Pitts (2008), Deuchar (2009), and Firmen (2010), and ethnographic work by Densley (2013) and Harding (2014) have successfully laid such divisive views to rest by clarifying and evidencing the increasingly violent behavioural world of urban street gang-affiliated youth in the UK. Similar debates are underway across Europe, notably in France, but also in Canada, Australia and New Zealand.

If this book teaches us anything, it is that gangs come in many shapes and sizes with many different forms of behaviour, expression and violence and we should, both as academics and the public, be accepting of this diversity. Perhaps to overcome this we need effective and accurate localised descriptions of street-oriented gangs rather than continue to search for a globally accepted definition.

THE BOOK

The original intention of the book was to consider youth gang behaviour in relation to weapons and the psychological functions served by these weapons and indeed the initial call for contributions reflected this objective. This call however only generated a limited number of responses and thus a slightly wider brief was determined for the publication. This is suggestive of two factors: firstly, the chapters on gang weaponisation came only from the Americas, indicative perhaps of the centrality of firearms in the USA, but also that gang scholarship there is sufficiently advanced that scholars are able to isolate and focus on this detailed topic.

Secondly the chapters from other global regions were broader and more generalised in their approach to gangs or the topic aired, focusing more perhaps on neighbourhood context, communities and issues of cultural change, immigration and different forms of violence within their localised contexts. This reflects the likelihood that gang scholarship outside north America is still developing with the arguments articulated being broader and not yet focussed on specific details such as weaponisation. It was felt therefore that it is important to give room to these different broader perspectives and to only consider the issues of weapons as part of a broader grouping of chapters. This decision proved a useful way forward in terms of grouping the book as it generated some new thinking as well as new chapters. Reading across the submitted works, clearly some chapters provided detailed specifics on violence and behavioural dynamics of street gangs. Others, by contrast, articulated these broader themes of immigration, incarceration, poverty, ethnicity and social deprivation as the dominant discursive agenda for that region.

Interestingly this permits the confluence of two different types of chapter in the book: those geared towards weapon use within an established gang context, and those articulating emerging trends or changing gang dynamics. This confluence in turn highlights both the similarities and differences of urban street gangs in different socio-economic and socio-cultural contexts across the globe.

In this way then this book generates a particular perspective and provides a platform for the reader to consider, through detailed discussion and presentation, both the localised and globalised nature of gangs and how they present in various world regions. Setting the chapters side by side in a global context best illustrates the commonalities of experience of gang-affiliated youth as well as the challenges faced in addressing this complex issue.

In reading the book as a whole it is compelling how similar conditions of poverty, racial inequality, marginalisation and immigration co-exist in neighborhoods throughout the developed and the developing world. That regardless of the continent, these conditions find expression in localised neighbourhood contexts which are remarkably similar in that they become the well-spring of emergent local street gangs. The type of gang, how it presents and its relation to the community or to the local policing authorities might differ significantly; however, the core issues remain the same.

Often it is how these globalised experiences of the urbanised poor find their expression in localised community contexts which are the most enlightening. Examination of this process can lead scholars to consider the cultural diversification of gangs and the unique, and shared, forms of cultural and violent expression. Whilst this appreciation of globalised influences marks a relatively new perspective on gang scholarship, the focus on the local is a long-standing aspect of gang studies, i.e. the work of the Chicago School of Sociology rightly identified community and neighbourhood context as critical in developing an understanding of delinquency and social control.

As gang studies increasingly becomes an international discipline, these localised neighbourhood contexts can sometimes be overlooked in pursuit of broader globalised themes. It is therefore an aim of this book that both global and localised themes are juxtaposed. In this context, the term Global references not only the proliferation and geo-spread of street gangs around the globe, but the global nature of poverty, deprivation and marginalisation as a prolific element of our urbanised environments.

The essays collated in the book also demonstrate that gangs present in many different forms. Gang research can often focus on single issues, or upon single groups situated within their own regional context. Thus comparative analysis in gang studies is often very difficult. For example, researchers comparing US and UK gangs often claim that domestic or situated features dilute the applicability of any comparisons. Whilst key issues might be context specific, there may nonetheless be commonalties worth exploring. In a similar way the global practices of the urban street are not fully explored. Hazan and Rogers suggest a failure to undertake such comparative analysis is a failing, or at least a limitation, in our understandings of gangs. However, comparative analysis quickly stumbles at the door of definitional problems. Hazan and Rogers (2014) argue caution is required with any international comparisons, noting that 'variability is one of the major challenges to developing shared definitions' (p. 5). It is important therefore to avoid making assumptions.

Furthermore, it is important that any comparative analysis seeks to identify differences not only in context but in presentation of gangs and group offending. This is important to help us develop more nuanced understandings of how gangs present, form, dissolve or transmogrify. Only then can we begin to map, chart, and explain aspects of commonalities, globalisation and the shared practice.

In consideration of these points we follow work by eminent scholars in this field. Decker and Pyrooz (2010) previously examined the prevalence of gangs internationally and found them located in many urbanised centres of population across the globe. Levels of violence varied however depending upon access to and use of, firearms.

Such findings have been supported by international comparative work including that of Gatti et al. (2005, 2011). The conclusions of a proliferation of urban street gangs across the globe is more specifically supported and revealed in an increasing number of country or region specific studies which offer insight in localised and neighbourhood contexts. For example, the work of Thale and Falkenburger (2006), Juttersonke, Muggah, and Rogers (2009), and Papachristos (2005, 2009) considering gangs in Latin America; the work of Jose Cruz (2007, 2010) and the central American maras; the work of Rob White in considering youth gangs in Australia (2013); the emergence of gang studies from Russia in the work of Salagaev et al. (2005); and a developing picture of gangs in China (Zhang et al., 1997, 2008; Pyrooz & Decker, 2012; Broadhurst & Wa, 2009). Whilst gang scholarship in Africa and India is still in its infancy (with the exception of the growing body of work in the Republic of South Africa by Don Pinnock), indications are that this issue is increasingly of public concern and academic focus. Gangs in the European context are similarly the focus of increased research by international scholars such as Decker and Weerman (2005), Decker et al. (2009), Gatti et al. (2005), and through the work of the Eurogang Network (Esbensen & Maxson, 2012).

Our present collaborative work was conceived by Marek Palasinski and Simon Harding who sought to contribute to these debates in gang studies by grouping together a range of essays from established or emerging gang scholars across the world. The approach offered to authors was as broad as could be. No definitional criteria on gangs were set, thus allowing contextualisation and differing definitions to be offered or challenged. As such the contributions offered here range across a broad spectrum from the challenges of schools in addressing gang behaviour on their premises, to prison gangs, and street children. It considers group offending and violence by youth groups that may, or may not, always be included in the gang definition, to those who clearly fit the concept of urban street gangs.

Despite what appears as a disparate collection of essays, common trends quickly become identifiable. The essays illuminate commonalities and differences, global and local phenomena; contextual similarities and how the behavioural dynamics of gangs are shaped by global or local contexts.

This book therefore offers a global gallery of street gangs as they present and operate in multiple different ways across the globe.

ORGANIZATION OF THE BOOK

The book is organized into 16 chapters which in turn are grouped into global continental regions, notably; North America, Latin America, Europe, Africa, Asia and Pacifica.

The first section presents a group of essays which considers gangs in North America. The first chapter by Laura Hansen and Melissa Freitag, "'Come on Now, I Want to See Blood!': Choreographed Violence in Gang Initiation Rites," considers the often violent initiation rites directed at new members or potential members of an organization noting this is not a recent phenomenon nor is it exclusive to joining street gangs or crews. This chapter explores the origins of violent initiation through history and how contemporary rites are used to "welcome" new members in youth gangs mirror other entries into exclusively male enclaves. These rituals include controlled, choreographed patterns of violent behaviour, including participants vs. voyeurs and number of blows directed at the initiate before the rite is considered to be completed. In addition to taking a historical perspective, recognized predictive risk factors for gang recruitment are listed, including those identified by Hill et al. (1999) in their Seattle study of juvenile delinquency and how it leads down the slippery slope to gang affiliation.

Chapter 2, "Baby Steps: Urban Violence, Gangs, and School Safety," takes a different perspective on gang initiation, focusing this time on the primary school grades. It considers the challenges experienced by educators and administrators in identifying and suppressing gang activities within schools. Author Laura Hansen highlights the impotence of school systems in controlling the neighbourhood and family environments whilst striving to keep students engaged. Taking an applied approach, this chapter identifies what educators, administrators, and staff can do to identify behaviour which on the surface might simply be imitation of gang membership (e.g. throwing gang signs), but could be symptomatic of closer contact or possibly exposure to gang violence. She argues that the more school personnel can be cognizant of behaviour indicative of exposure to gangs, curriculum planning and after school programs can be effectively designed to counter delinquent influences within the community, beyond "just say no" strategies.

Chapter 3, "Gang Violence in Schools: Safety Measures and Their Effectiveness," is also located within the school environment. Here author Sarah Daly reports on how gang-related violence in schools can have numerous negative effects on the school environment, student achievement, and perceptions of fear. Schools reporting a gang presence often report higher rates of victimization on school property. In response, many schools have focused on both physical and procedural safety measures to enhance security and prevent violence. However, attempts at maintaining order and ensuring safety often fall short in preventing violence and may actually enhance feelings of fear at schools. This presents schools with a difficult task of addressing violence with effective safety measures while also minimizing and balancing the prison-like feeling that is often the end result. This chapter aims to describe the effects of violence in schools and examine a variety of safety measures in terms of cost, effect on perceptions of fear, and effectiveness.

Chapter 4 by Tim Lauger looks at the "Reality and Myth of Weapons and Violence in Gang Life." This chapter examines the division between myth and reality in gang life. Here the author addresses the image of the violent gang and the perception of gang members prepared to use ultra-violence. Lauger notes that the image of violent gang members is usefully embraced and used by youth on the streets to navigate their social world. He argues that in peer on peer groups, gang members often create personal and group-based myths by exaggerating their willingness and ability to use weapons and violence. This chapter offers an exploration of the boundaries between reality and fantasy or mythic representations of gang violence. Whilst weaponised violence is a reality amongst global gangs, myths about gang violence can emerge among gang members who have ample motivation for fictionalizing both violence and the use of weapons. To better understand the development of myths, this chapter also briefly reviews the social psychological ideas of social constructionism, interpretive socialization, and identity.

The focus of Chapter 5 switches to different types of weapons potentially used by gang. Here Ronn Johnson considers "Forensic Perspectives on Youth Gang Involvement in Juvenile Fire Setting and Bomb Making Weapons (JFSB)." Taking a Forensic psychological perspective, Ronn Johnson, explores issues related to gang-affiliated youth's use of JFSB behaviour as a weapon. This essay argues that too often, the critical analysis of JFSB is circumscribed to the act with little or no consideration of a clinical forensic weapons use motivation. In this case, successful efforts to identify and isolate the origins of such events are more contingent upon a deeper understanding of the subtle processes that explain this particular kind of weapons use by juvenile gang members.

The following chapter considers a different form of gang – that of the hate group where the weapon of choice used is frequently that of words. Chapter 6 takes a social psychological approach to understanding hate groups and how hate groups use hate as a promotional tool and as an implement of aggression. In "Sticks and Stones: When the Words of Hatred Become Weapons," Robin Valeri and Kevin Borgeson detail how hate groups use hate speech to attract new members to their organizations and to promote their beliefs to the mainstream public. Here hate also serves as an incendiary, to fuel member's emotions and incite them to action against their targets. This chapter offers a rich interpretative background of theories as to how and why certain groups or gangs act as hate groups and how they justify their resulting actions through a number of social psychological theories including realistic group conflict, relative deprivation, social identity theory and terror management.

Chapter 7 sees us move north to consider "Youth Gang Exit from a Canadian Perspective." Laura Dunbar contends that the issue of desistance has received little research attention and seeks to address this gap with an overview of desistance and how it is measured. Having set out the desistance landscape she then reviews some prominent criminological perspectives to demonstrate that leaving the gang is a complex process involving the interaction of multiple factors. Several approaches to desistence are developed with different types of intervention, including some Canadian examples, discussed. Laura concludes by arguing for the development of a comprehensive strategy for youth gang exit.

The next section takes us to Latin America. In Chapter 8, Nowonty, Zhao, Kaplan, Cepeda, and Valdez, examine the "Gender Dynamics of Violent Acts among Gang Affiliated Young Adult Mexican American Men." Using the concept of hegemonic masculinity to examine the various ways that gender is performed in acts of violence they consider how tendencies for aggression and violence are central to masculine identity. Among this sub-population of street-oriented disadvantaged former gang members, there are limited options to express their masculinity. As a result engaging in personal violence becomes a means to gain social status and respect within the context of racial segregation and community disadvantage. Whilst this essay resonates across all the chapters, it enhances our understanding of the way that cultural constructions of gender influence violent acts. This in turn is important for constructing interventions for violence.

Chapter 9, "In Hand, Out of Hand: Weapons and Violence Culture in Large Latino Gangs," interrogates the nature and function of weapons in Latino gang culture. Author, Ami Carpenter has divided the chapter into three parts. It begins by defining Latino gangs in the Americas, and classifying them into Mexican-American gangs, Mexican gangs, and Central American gangs. Despite differences in region, economic situation, generations and cultural characteristics, Carpenter draws broad similarities by focusing specifically on large, organized gangs within each of the three classifications. She then moves on to interrogate the logics and motivations driving gangs' use of weapons, along with the psychological and instrumental functions of weapons use for Latino gangs. The chapter's third section is a substantial conclusion which argues for approaches to gang-violence which derive from the field of peace and conflict studies, including short-term approaches to violence reduction (gang ceasefires and truces) and longer term, ecological approaches based on the theoretical framework of community resilience.

The subsequent section moves the gang's debate to Europe. In Chapter 10, "'It's a Vicious Game': Youth Gangs, Street Violence, and Organised Crime in Modern Britain," Dev Maitra, explores the activities and characteristics of street gangs and organised crime groups in contemporary British society. Maitra acknowledges there is scant research which specifically investigates contemporary British criminal gangs before offering findings from his qualitative research at an adult men's prison in England. The chapter attempts to articulate the experiences of prisoners and street-offenders and illustrates the entrenched role street gangs and organised crime groups hold in certain areas of England. Here gangs are often considered viable alternatives to gainful employment and their activities are often sanctioned by their host communities. Subsequently, Maitra reports that a high level of violence is normalised within such communities, including heightened levels of weapon usage by gang members, both within and outside prison.

In a second chapter by Maitra, Chapter 11, the focus now shifts to the composition of UK prison gangs, their effects on the prison environment, and their relationships with street gangs. Titled "An Exploratory Study of Prison Gangs in Contemporary British Society," the author conducts an ethnographic study of an adult men's prison in England. The chapter attempts to articulate the experiences of prison gang members, as well as prisoners exposed to high levels of gang activity. The results illustrate the established role gangs play within English prisons, but also the relevance of other groups, collectives and "sets" within the penal environment. Through analysing the gathered data Maitra shows the important - but not defining - role gangs play within an English prison. Interestingly he concludes that when compared to the American prison system, gangs are far less entrenched in English prisons; this can partly be attributed to the deeper historical roots of American prison gangs, as well as their highly racialized dimensions.

The final chapter on Europe draws upon some unique research from the Ukraine. In Chapter 12, "Surviving the Streets of Makeevka: A Study of Subculture of Street Children in Ukraine," Andrej Naterer, explores the subculture of street children in Makeevka, Ukraine. Drawing upon qualitative and quantitative data gathered during longitudinal anthropological field research he articulates their survival strategies whilst commenting upon the social structures, economic activities and substance abuse which are prevalent. Naterer also analyses the extra-, intra- and inter-group violence with an emphasis on the child's situational interpretation and adoption of the code of the street through subsequent code/identity switching and subcultural reactions.

The next section focusses on Africa with a chapter by Don Pinnock investigating the underlying causes of gang formation in Cape Town. Chapter 13, "Cape Town Gangs: The Other Side of Paradise," begins by setting the unique context and historical underpinnings in apartheid and post-apartheid South Africa. Pinnock then explores various aspects of violent gang life on the city including firearms, marginalized masculinity, the impact of toxic stress and substance abuse on prenatal development. Finally he concludes with an examination of drug usage (and the impact on epigenetic damage), and poverty on the increasingly violent youth culture in the city's low-income, high-risk areas.

In the section on Asia, Simon Harding considers youth offending and youth justice in contemporary China which has witnessed considerable changes over the past two decades. In Chapter 14, "From 'Little Flowers of the Motherland' into 'Carnivorous Plants': The Changing Face of Youth Gang Crime in Contemporary China," he considers how youth offending is broadly similar to that in the West. However, he argues recent rapid economic transformation has initiated rapid changes in the nature and presentation of youth offending. Once famous for its low rates of crime and juvenile delinquency, the apparent rapid rise in Chinese juvenile delinquency has left the media 'wondering what transformed these little "flowers of the motherland" into "carnivorous plants". He charts changes from 1983 to the contemporary and highly publicised anti-crime crackdowns in Chongqing. Despite challenges of obtaining Chinese data, a picture is now emerging of changing influence of triads and altering relationships between organised crime and street gangs. The chapter offers a typology of Asian gangs before considering how street gangs appear to be on the rise in China as a result of large scale immigration from rural China to the rapidly urbanised mega cities.

The final section of the book is Pacifica. Here two chapters focus on group offending in both Australia and New Zealand. In Chapter 15, "Youth Gangs and Youth Violence in Australia," Rob White provides an overview of issues pertaining to youth gangs and youth violence in Australia. The first part features the voices of young people from around Australia describing their experiences of youth gang violence. The second part of the chapter provides a broad overview of biological, psychological and social factors that together shape the propensities for young people, and young men in particular, to join gangs and to engage in youth violence. The final part of the chapter provides more detailed exposition of two gang members, 'Mohammad' and 'Tan', and the everyday complexities of their lives. The chapter concludes by noting that the gang does not have to be seen as an overwhelming influence in the lives of young people, and that their activities and behaviours are more diverse, and include positive elements, than generally given credit in mainstream youth gangs research and analysis.

The last essay presented in Chapter 16 by Dr. Jarrod Gilbert, is titled "The Reorganisation of Gangs in New Zealand." This chapter considers the significant changes among the gangs of New Zealand since the turn of the century. Facing a changing cultural climate in which rebellious young people see membership in traditional 'patch'-wearing gangs as less desirable, New Zealand's established gangs have become starved for recruits. Rather than precipitating a straightforward decline in the country's gang scene, however, Gilbert argues that we are seeing a reorganisation of the gangs. This chapter examines the problems facing the outlaw motorcycle clubs and the 'patched' street gangs, and the numerous and complex nature of the issues facing these groups. It also explores the rise of LA-style street gangs, the influence of drug misuse and the similarities and difference that exist between them and New Zealand's traditional gangs.

REFERENCES

Baum, D. (1996). Can integration succeed? Research into urban childhood and youth in a deprived area of Koblenz. *Social Work in Europe*, *3*(2), 30–35.

Bourdieu, P. (1985). The genesis of the concept of habitus and field. *Sociocriticism*, *2*(2), 11–24.

Broadhurst, R., & Wa, L. K. (2009). The transformation of triad 'dark societies' in Hong Kong: The impact of law enforcement, socio-economic, and political change. *Security Challenges*, *5*(4), 1–38.

Cruz, J. (2007). Factors associated with juvenile gangs in Central America. In J. M. Cruz (Ed.), *Street gangs in Central America* (pp. 13–65). San Salvador: UCA.

Cruz, J. (2010). Central American Maras: From youth gangs to transnational protection rackets. *Global Crime*, *11*(4), 379–398. doi:10.1080/17440572.2010.519518

Davis, M. (2006). *Planet of slums*. London: Verso Press.

Decker, S., & Pyrooz, D. (2010). Gang violence worldwide: Context, culture, and country. In G. MacDonald & E. LeBrun (Eds.), *Small arms survey 2010: Gangs, groups and guns* (pp. 128–155). Cambridge, UK: Cambridge University Press.

Decker, S., van Gemert, F., & Pyrooz, D. (2009). Gang, migration and crime: The changing landscape in Europe and the United States. *Journal of International Migration and Immigration*, *10*(4), 393–408. doi:10.1007/s12134-009-0109-9

Decker, S. H., & Weerman, F. M. (Eds.). (2005). *European street gangs and troublesome youth groups*. Lanham, MD: Altamira Press.

Densley, J. (2013). *How gangs work: An ethnography of youth violence*. London: Palgrave Macmillan. doi:10.1057/9781137271518

Deuchar, R. (2009). *Gangs: Marginalised youth and social capital*. Stoke on Trent, UK: Trentham.

Esbensen, F., & Maxson, C. (2012). *Youth gangs in international perspective: Results from the Eurogang program of research*. New York: Springer. doi:10.1007/978-1-4614-1659-3

Firmin, C. (2010). *Female voice in violence project: A study into the impact of serious youth and gang violence on women and girls*. London: ROTA.

Gatti, U., Angelini, F., Marengo, C., Melchiorre, N., & Sasso, M. (2005). An old-fashioned youth gang in Genoa. In S. Decker & F. Weerman (Eds.), *European street gangs and troublesome youth groups*. Lanham, MD: Altamira Press.

Gatti, U., Haynoz, S., & Schadee, H. (2011). Deviant youth groups in 30 countries: Results from the second international self-report delinquency study. *International Criminal Justice Review*, *21*(3), 208–224. doi:10.1177/1057567711418500

Hagedorn, J. (2008). *A world of gangs: Armed young men and gangsta culture*. Minneapolis, MN: University of Minnesota Press.

Harding, S. (2014). *The street casino: Survival in violent street gangs*. Bristol, MA: The Policy Press. doi:10.1332/policypress/9781447317173.001.0001

Hazan, J., & Rogers, D. (2014). *Global gangs: Street violence across the world*. Minneapolis, MN: University of Minnesota Press. doi:10.5749/minnesota/9780816691470.001.0001

Juttersonke, O., Muggah, R., & Rogers, D. (2009). Gangs, urban violence and security interventions in Central America. *Security Dialogue*, *40*(4-5), 373–397. doi:10.1177/0967010609343298

Klein, M. (1971). *Street gangs and street workers*. Englewood Cliffs, NJ: Prentice Hall.

Papachristos, A. (2005). Interpreting inkblots: Deciphering and doing something about modern street gangs. *Criminology & Public Policy*, *4*(3), 643–651. doi:10.1111/j.1745-9133.2005.00301.x

Papachristos, A. (2009). Murder by structure: Dominance relations and the social structure of gang homicide. *American Journal of Sociology, 115*(1), 74–128. doi:10.1086/597791 PMID:19852186

Pitts, J. (2008). *Reluctant gangsters: The changing face of youth crime.* Cullompton: Willan Publishing.

Pyrooz, D., & Decker, S. (2012). Delinquent behaviour, violence and gang involvement in China. *Journal of Quantitative Criminology, 29*(2), 251–272. doi:10.1007/s10940-012-9178-6

Salagaev, A., Shaskin, A., Sherbakova, I., & Touriyanskiy, E. (2005). Contemporary Russian gangs: History, membership and crime involvement. In S. H. Decker & F. M. Weerman (Eds.), *European street gangs and troublesome youth groups.* Lanham, MD: Altamira Press.

Thale, G., & Falkenburger, E. (2006). *Youth gangs in Central America: Issues on human rights, effective policing, and prevention.* Washington, DC: Washington Office on Latin America.

Thrasher, F. M. (1927). *The gang: A study of 1,313 gangs in Chicago.* Chicago: University of Chicago Press.

Van Gemert, F., Peterson, D., & Lien, I. L. (2008). *Street gangs, migration and ethnicity.* Cullompton: Willan Publishing.

Venkatesh, S. (2014). The inevitable gang. In *Global gangs: Street violence across the world.* Minneapolis, MN: University of Minnesota Press. doi:10.5749/minnesota/9780816691470.003.0014

Vigil, D. (1988). *Barrio gangs: Street life and identity in Southern California.* Austin, TX: University of Texas Press.

Vigil, D. (2002). *A rainbow of gangs: Street cultures in the mega-city.* Austin, TX: University of Texas Press.

Wacquant, L. (2008). *Urban outcasts.* Cambridge, MA: Polity Press.

White, R. (2013). *Youth gangs, violence and social respect.* Basingstoke, UK: Palgrave Macmillan. doi:10.1057/9781137333858

Zhang, L., Messner, S. F., & Liu, J. (2008). A critical review of recent literature on crime and criminal justice in China: Research findings, challenges and prospects (introduction). *Crime. Law and Social Change: An Interdisciplinary Journal, 50*(3), 125–130. doi:10.1007/s10611-008-9134-4

Zhang, L., Messner, S. F., Lu, Z., & Deng, X. (1997). Gang crime and its punishment in China. *Journal of Criminal Justice, 25*(4), 289–302. doi:10.1016/S0047-2352(97)00014-7

Acknowledgment

The editors would like to acknowledge the help of all the people involved in this project and, more specifically, to the authors and reviewers that took part in the review process. Without their support, this book would not have become a reality.

First, the editors would like to thank each one of the authors for their contributions. Our sincere gratitude goes to the chapter's authors who contributed their time and expertise to this book.

Second, the editors wish to acknowledge the valuable contributions of the reviewers regarding the improvement of quality, coherence, and content presentation of chapters. Most of the authors also served as referees; we highly appreciate their double task.

Simon Harding
Middlesex University, UK

Marek Palasinski
Liverpool John Moores University, UK

Section 1
North America

Chapter 1
"Come on Now, I Want to See Blood!":
Choreographed Violence in Gang Initiation Rites

Laura L. Hansen
Western New England University, USA

Melissa E. Freitag
Bowling Green State University, USA

ABSTRACT

Violent initiation rites directed at new members or potential members of an organization are not recent phenomena and not exclusive to joining street gangs or crews. This chapter will explore the origins of violent initiation through history and how contemporary rites used to "welcome" new members in youth gangs mirror other entries into exclusively male enclaves. These rituals include controlled, choreographed patterns of violent behavior, including participants vs. voyeurs and number of blows directed at the initiate before the rite is considered to be completed. In additional to taking a historical perspective, recognized predictive risk factors for gang recruitment are listed, including those identified by Hill et al. (1999) in their Seattle study of juvenile delinquency and how it leads down the slippery slope to gang affiliation.

INTRODUCTION

Violent initiation rites directed at new members or potential members of an organization are not recent phenomena and not exclusive to joining street gangs or crews. This chapter explores the origins of initiation through history and how contemporary rites used to "welcome" new members in youth gangs mirror other entries into almost exclusively male enclaves. Commonly termed "blood in, blood out", the ritual implies that there is no easy way to enter or exit gang life.

Most discussions, research, media items on gang ritual ride on the side of extremes, including commitment of horrific crimes like drive-by-shootings, or wholesale homicide (Best and Hutchinson, 1996).

DOI: 10.4018/978-1-4666-9938-0.ch001

This chapter is about the less explored nuances of "beating in" initiation ceremonies, where the neo-phyte gang member receives controlled, physical abuse at the hands of members of a gang one wishes to become a part of.

These rituals include controlled, choreographed patterns of violent behavior, including participants vs. voyeurs and number of blows directed at the initiate before the rite is considered to be finished. In additional to taking an anthropological, interactionist perspective, recognized predictive risk factors for gang recruitment are examined, including those identified by Hill et al. (1999) in their Seattle study of juvenile delinquency and how these lead down the slippery slope to gang affiliation.

Using a grounded theory approach, we examined 22 gang initiations posted to youtube.com between June 2007 and April 2014. Except in the case of one posting attributed to a 1985 gang initiation, we do not know exactly when the initiations took place. As the motivation of this chapter is to explore reinforced masculinities through gang ceremonies, we will be focusing primarily on the 15 videos collected and coded where males were exclusively present. However, for contrast, we are including the deconstruction of 5 gang initiations that were coed and 2 that were exclusively female gang initiations.

In addition to examining gang initiations for themes of controlled violence, we include an analysis of 14 videos (Males = 7; Females = 7) posted to youtube.com that document public fights that are not part of gang initiation rites. In these cases, the blows exchanged were bilateral, messy, and unorganized, leading us to believe that there is a distinct difference between the violence involved in gang initiation, though it might be described as a "beating in", that on the surface to have some semblance of rules and civility, as compared to garden variety altercations that come to blows. Admittedly we were observing these rituals from the safety of our homes or university offices and we acknowledge that the selection is subjective in that these were self-reported incidents, and are limited to small world analysis. We cannot assume generalization of our findings, nor do we seek it.

In coding these videos, we developed the following framework: In the face of being blocked from normative routes to expressions of masculine hegemony (e.g. education, subsequent "legitimate" career), are new recruits looking to gangs as a means by which to be accepted into a class of hyper-masculine, modern day warriors?

We are not passing judgment, but rather explore this in the direction that anthropologists and sociologists are currently headed. We view members of gangs as an underclass, victims of economic disadvantage and marginalization. As Stoll (2013) questions in his review of gang literature,[1] should gangs be viewed as a general threat to society, or the fact that they are threats to themselves warrants suppression? Either way, the anatomy of gang initiation rites, when individuals are assumed to fully committed to joining, whether by choice or by coercion, is worth exploring.

MICRO/MACRO PROCESSES

One can point to a number of risk factors for why juveniles are attracted to gang life, many of which are listed within the pages of this book, including this chapter. In the extreme, children are subjected to pressures on the local and global level that make it near impossible to imagine a "normal" life or realization of the "American Dream" of gainful employment, "normal" family life (spouse, children), home ownership. There is no one smoking gun variable to explain away gang membership, but rather the additive effect of a number of social ills that contribute to the compulsion to join.

Table 1. Sample dialogue during gang initiation*

Setting	No. of Participants	No. of Initiates	Verbal Instructions
Bathroom, School	6	1	"Don't get him in his head."
Basement/laundry room	6	1	"Let him get up."
Outdoors (Park?)	7	1	"No headshots, no knees, no fucking hitting dicks."
Backyard of home	1	1	"It is over with, man. It is after two minutes, man."
Front yard of home	4	1	"No face shots and you can't fight back."

*Source: youtube.com, postings, May 2011-May 2014

On the micro-level, some children are damned from the start, born into a family that already possesses intergenerational gang membership ties. This is not unlike the mafia or any other long established organized crime group. For others, they will join even in the face of strong family disapproval. Though it is disconcerting to note that in one of the pre-initiation discussions on a video data we collected that showed female gang initiation, a parent resigns himself to the inevitability of gang membership, stating In either case, the rites of passage into a gang happen only after a protracted period of time, where the individual vets the gang and is vetted by the gang. On the most part, one does not simply walk up to a member of an established street gang (e.g. Bloods, Crips) and ask, "Where do I sign up?"

As Collins contends (2004; 1981), it may be more realistic to begin at the situational level, rather than at the individual level. In introducing his theory of Interaction Ritual Chains (1981), with Goffmanian and Durkheimian influences, rituals are viewed as social action that create material and nonmaterial symbols with collective meaning. In the case of gang initiation, as argued in this chapter, the actions of established gang members "welcoming" a new recruit become institutionalized with highly organized proceedings. This controlled orchestration is mirrored across gangs and across geography by similar nonmaterial, verbal cues. A sample of verbal instructions demonstrating control within the instructions on how to deliver blows to the initiate is offered in Table 1.

Gang membership lends itself to material symbols in membership as well. Members of the same gang will don gang "colors", at times camouflaged in fandom attire of sports teams or famous clothing designers. As we witnessed in the videos we reviewed, in a number of cases, the new member immediately puts on his new family's costume provided to him by one his or her "brother" or "sister". Along with the new clothing will come the inevitable gang hand signs, more openly displayed than the secret handshakes of honor societies. These are not individuals who wish to hide their membership. Rather even minute details of hairstyle, jewelry, and shoelace color can be used to separate the "wannabes" or "posers" from the truly initiated.

More germane to this study, the verbal instructions given during gang initiation, though seemingly not formalized, are repeated patterns of scripted dialogue that we found to be consistent in one fashion or another in each of the videos we reviewed that depict alleged gang initiation. As Collins (2005) contends, each encounter serves as a marketplace where meanings are negotiated. Just in the fact that these rituals have definitive beginnings and endings, unlike ad hoc altercations, the script itself is fairly institutionalized, even when theorists argue that at least in the case of Chicano street gangs, there is a specialized culture specific to ethnic identity (Valdez, 2003). In the case of our own research on gang initiation, we did not find there to be clearly distinct differences down racial or ethnic lines.

The purpose is not to annihilate the initiative, but to prove their worthiness. One must also asked if in the process of broadcasting these staged events, if this likewise enforces the commitment of those who are not present at the initiation or for those who might be on the verge of joining. Certainly there is an element of voyeurism within and outside of the context of the publicized videos, discussed in more depth later in this chapter.

The macro forces that have allowed for an ever-ready pool of gang recruits include failed schools, failed economy, and failed family lives, risk factors that are further exploited within the next section of this chapter. Merton's Strain Theory (and subsequent "strain-like" theories) produced a template by which to understand why juveniles are likely to be at risk to join gangs. In the face of blocked institutional means by which to achieve accepted cultural goals (e.g. wealth, power), individuals, and in many cases, collectives may become innovative by way of criminality (Agnew and Brezina, 2010). As Rodriguez shares in his study of East Los Angeles street gangs, "I've talked to enough gang members and low-level dope dealers to know they would quite today if they had a productive, livable wage job." (Rodriquez, 2005, p. 251)

Evidence of social strain providing catalyst for gang initiation is not limited to the United States. The construction of marginalized masculinity for Black males is evident in South Africa, where protection in groups is inevitably within the context of gang life, forcing them into patterns of criminal behavior (Jensen, 2014). Escaping post-war torn countries, in the past few decades recent immigrants to large cities throughout Europe are finding gang problems growing at an alarming rate, with their children experiencing risk factors common in American urban poor that lead some to gang life: disrupted communities and fractured families (Hazen and Rodgers, 2014; Hazelhurst and Hazelhurst, 1998).

RISK FACTORS

As in the case of micro/macro processes, risks factors can be measured at the individual and community level. When scaled, as in the case of Seattle, Washington study (Hill, et al., 1999), there are a multitude of variables that contribute to risk of gang recruitment, when in combination, make gang membership an enticing alternative to the status quo (see Table 2). Though sounding like a broken record for several decades now, juveniles who are exposed to violence in and out of their homes, coupled with substance abuse and poor school performance, attachment to school, are at greatest risk of entering lives of crime and possibly gang membership.

Some focus should be made on the absence of fathers, positive male role models in helping prevent general juvenile delinquency. Again, poor family management and low bonding to family repeatedly show themselves to be key factors in general delinquency for gang and non-gang members (Hansen, 2005; Hill et al., 1999). Specifically, Dishion et al. (2005, p. 63) assert that, "the general assumption is that the family context can be influential in the development of antisocial behavior.... Conditions such as parent psychopathology, substance use, and marital distress can disrupt parenting practices."

More recently the Office of Juvenile Justice and Delinquency Prevention (OJJDP) has adopted a pared down, five-fold scale of risk factors similar to the Seattle study: community, individual, family, peer, and school (Ebensen et al., 2010). This is far from a departure from earlier pioneers in gang research, including Thrasher who was strongly influenced by the Chicago School of urban sociology (Howell, 2012; Thrasher, 1927/2000).

Table 2. Factors present ages 10-12 that predict gang recruitment between ages 13 and 18*

Neighborhood	Family	Schools	Peers	Individual
Availability of Marijuana	Structure	Low academic aspirations	Friends with problem behaviors	Anti-social beliefs
Youth in Trouble	Poverty	Low commitment		Alcohol
Low attachment	Anti-social siblings	Low attachment		Marijuana initiation
	Poor management	Low academic achievement, elementary		Violence
	Pro-violent attitudes	Learning disabled		Externalizing
				Hyperactivity
				Poor refusal skills

*SCALE:
NO RISK: 0-1 RISK FACTORS
LOW RISK: 2-3 RISK FACTORS
MEDIUM RISK: 4-6 RISK FACTORS
HIGH RISK: 7+ RISK FACTORS
(Source: Hill, 1999)

Certainly for most gang initiates, their first exposure to violence is not when they are initiated into the gang. Many are coming from streets that are already riddled with violence, as demonstrated by the recent events witnessed in Ferguson, Missouri.[2] If juveniles are living in gang-infested neighborhoods, it is inevitable that they will be aware of the commonality of violent acts either by word-of-mouth or by direct witness of violence on the streets (Sanchez, 2000).

Prevalence alone of gangs within major metropolitan areas put urban youth at risk for recruitment. Urban cities other than the usual suspects (e.g. Los Angeles, Chicago, New York City) have dangerously high numbers of gang members living within their borders, as noted in Esbensen et al.'s study of youth violence (Table 3).

SOCIOLOGICAL EXPLANATIONS FOR RITUAL: MAKING THE MACRO/MICRO BRIDGE

We may immediately prescribe Strain Theory (Merton) to explain the social forces that lead to recruitment, retention, and motivations for advancement within gang culture. However, a synthesis of strain theories, incorporating Collin's interaction ritual chains (1981, 2004) offers a micro-macro bridge through which to explain the recursive nature of recruitment, including secrecy and powerful homo-social bonds for which participants are willing to subject themselves to physical harm to demonstrate their commitment to divorcing themselves forever from mainstream society. Like a recovering alcoholic, even if one does leave gang life, they will be self-labeled or labeled by others as "former gang members."

Rational-choice approaches cannot be ignored as well. From a social psychological level, rather than from economic theory, weighing the probability of punishment for not joining a gang must be taken into consideration, particularly when taking a microscope to prison populations. Gangs can be highly

Table 3. Prevalence of gang membership*

Town/City	Population (2012)**	% Gang Membership
Milwaukee, WI	598,916	15.4
Phoenix, AZ	1,488,755	12.6
Omaha, NE	421,570	11.4
La Cruces, NM	101,047	11
Kansas City, MO	464,310	10.1
Orlando. FL	249,662	9.6
Philadelphia, PA	1,547,607	7.7
Torrance, CA	147,027	6.3
Providence, RI	178,432	6
Pocatello, ID	54,777	5.6
Will County, IL	682,518	3.8

*Source: Adopted from Esbensen et al., 2010, p. 74
**Source: http://www.city-data.com/

organized enterprises and rational-choice theory allows for better understanding of how order comes out of chaos in criminal underground networks (Skarkek, 2014). This married to network effects provides one of the best-synthesized models of social action within the context of gangs.

Whatever forms that these societies, and in this case, gangs, find themselves, their secrets and rituals have similar purposes and can be examined by returning to classical social theory, as well as the inclusion of contemporary theories (e.g. Collins' Interaction Ritual Chains, 2004). The basic properties of emotional impact based on group density, as a concept of cohesive bonding through ritual can be applied to gang initiation.

Borrowing from 19th century sociology, though Durkheim's study of ritual was in religious context, it is no less useful in explaining secular rituals. The central theme of Durkheim's interpretation of ritual is the idea of the "social" (Nagendra, 1971). This is represented by his argument that there must be equally weighted importance placed on both experience and reason (Nagendra, 1971). Thus the repetitive characteristic of ritual, including initiation, can be interpreted as an experience that overrides any predisposed idea that the ritual itself is beyond reason, as in the case of the violence associated to gang initiation.

In order to reinforce newly acquired relations, there generally is some effort to "thicken" ties by way of ritualized interaction. Rather than viewing Collin's theory of Interaction Rituals as being dyadic, gang initiation ceremonies may be perceived as collective reinforcement of social ties. The question comes from meaning. Those of us in possession of doctoral degrees certainly had our own initiation rites to pass, with generalized meaning. Comprehensive and qualifying exams are not unlike boot camp, where the graduate student recruit is intellectually humbled and only the strong survive. Academic programs and gangs alike do not look to shore up recruits who may degrade the reputation of the collective by way of letting a perceived inferior "wannabe" into the fold, and in some respects, initiation into exclusive clubs can be degrading or coercive. Certainly this can be said about the prisonization process after incarceration. You either join the "cool group" or die a symbolic (and in some cases, real) death trying.

In Collins' genesis of interaction ritual chains (1981, 996), he proposes that repetitive behavior is desirable, "routine occurs because the world is too complex for us to renegotiate all of it (or even very much of it) all the time. Most of the time it is easier to stay where one is familiar." It doesn't take a far stretch of the imagination to couple this with labeling theories (including Becker's *Outsiders*, 1997; Goffman's *Stigma*, 1986), where deviant behavior in the form of violent initiation rites becomes an inevitable part of gang life.

It is the repetitive, simplistic, yet violent ritual of gang initiation that perhaps provides the sanity needed in an every-growing complicated society where the disenfranchised are being left ever further behind. It is the emotional rejuvenation that occurs with the assemblage of likeminded others. Collins (1975) argued that normative control through ritual is a viable alternative to material rewards in order to obtain allegiance to an organization. This is demonstrated by the exclusivity of some organized crime groups, including gangs. As Collins points out in his conflict theory of organizations, some groups are expressively built around conflict with others (1975). Gangs are inherently in battle with the subjective other, including rival gangs and law enforcement.

SOCIAL PSYCHOLOGICAL PURPOSES OF INITIATION

Whether we are reviewing Native American, Meso-American, Australian, Polynesian, African, or Caribbean indigenous people, all have had their kinship and clan rituals disrupted with colonialism, including forced religious conversion. In the case of Native Americans, these rituals solidified family cohesion and clan unity (Duran et al. 1998). Covert membership in not so secret societies of gangs may serve the same purpose of solidifying kinship-like ties along ethnic and racial lines, particularly in prison populations.

For what little we know of gang initiation on the streets, there is less known about the process in prison. But prison gang politics cannot be ignored; "Racially segregated prison gangs rule over the inmate population." (Skarbek, 2014, p. 2) What is interesting to note is that prison is the one place where middle-aged men will join gangs (Skarbek, 2014), unlike the risk of recruitment into gangs dropping exponentially by mid- to late-twenties.

Yet initiation rites, violent or otherwise, are significantly powerful events that seal individuals to a group or culture. Even in the face of the prohibition of rituals, groups will find a way to continue them in secret, disguising the steps in seemingly innocuous ways. Afro-Caribbeans masked gods and goddesses within saints as a means to continue rituals and beliefs banned by the Catholic Church and forbidden by coercive slave owners, resulting in creation of Santeria religion (Brown, 2003).

Ritualistic behavior is not exclusive to illegitimate (and in the case of gangs, not so secretive) groups. Ritual practices, ceremonies perpetuate organizational solidarity. Even historically respected organizations, including the Boy Scouts and Girl Scouts of America have initiation practices that promote exclusivity. Some of these rituals are held in within limited public circles. This halo of secrecy is not unique to contemporary society. As Whalen (1966, 1) noted, "From primitive times to the present day men and women have sworn the solemn oaths, preserved the secrets, and worked the rituals of secret societies."

What is key to why the need for initiation rites, rather than simply saying, "I'd like to be part of your group; where do I sign up?" is two-fold: First, individuals feel a need to seek out individualism in the face of the impersonal space of metropolitan life, as observed by Simmel (Wolff, 1950). Second, marginalized populations, in particular young, minority males, have few positive role models, largely due to economic disparity, as well as political neglect by civic leaders, as witnessed by the aftermath of Los Angeles riots in 1992 (Davis, 1999). How enticing is it, then, to be brought into the fold of a gang by way of ritualized beating? And how far removed is this from the hazing rituals of college fraternities and sororities, where first year students are willing to weather humiliation in order to feel a sense of belonging?

DEFINING VIOLENCE

Violent acts can be subjectively defined, based on intent. For the purposes of this study, we are defining violence as being controlled acts by which the victim is placed in some physical, if not psychological fear for their own safety.

Violence functions as social glue, much as Durkheim suggested that religion does, albeit to a lessor degree. Though as a society, we give lip service to abhorring violence, we are known to walk to the edge of it as fans of violent movies, television shows and literature. Though we claim necrophobic proclivity and most of us possess a natural fear of death as part of our survival instincts, it is the collective experience of facing death together, even figuratively in initiation rituals. However, faced with the intergroup violence that permeates gang life, violence offers, in the collective, reinforcement that "they" are bad, whoever "they" might be, (Dunbar et al., 2014) and must be vanquished in some fashion when "they" threaten the group's wellbeing. This is part and parcel of the culture of gang violence.

It then comes as no surprise that for some gangs, it requires being a willing victim of violence in order to join. Violence is a given in gang life when taking into consideration that one motivation is territorial competition in geographic space, whether in a neighborhood or in prison (Brantingham et al., 2012). Nonetheless, based on the cowering of many of the initiates that we observed in the videos, compared to individuals engaged in spontaneous fights, most of what we could see on the part of the supposed victim are defensive moves. In fact in all of the initiation rites, male, coed, or female, the initiates were discouraged from fighting back. "Earn your strips, Bro."

VIOLENT MEMBERSHIP CEREMONIES

Initiation into gangs is not wholly different than initiation into fraternities. Or into military organizations or sport teams, for that matter. Hazing, from a symbolic interactionist perspective, serves to manipulate symbols and guide the pledges' reframing of self (Sweet, 1999). As in the case of gangs, there is greater attention being made to street violence in any form as being a public health issue, warranting notice if for no other reason than the cost to taxpayers.

As noted in fraternity hazing rituals, as well in our observations noted in the opening paragraph of this chapter, excessive alcohol consumption plays a part in escalation of violence and accidents in initiations, including alcohol being present 94% of the time in fights (Finkel, 2002). Whether alcohol was present or not in the videos we collected, in no case did we witness anything that appeared to warrant immediate medical attention, but we can speculate that at the very least, there were lacerations and/or head injuries should, under normal circumstances, would suggest a trip to the emergency room of a hospital would be a wise move. Again, this may be because of the subjectivity of this type of research and the limitations of these type of data sources that we don't explore this topic further.

That is not to say that some of these ceremonies won't result in hospitalization. There is greater evidence that violence associated with gangs has more to do with revenge and victimization. In Los

Angeles, California, the end of gang truces result in escalated gun violence, in particularly in the rise of drive-by shootings, as witnessed in Level 1 trauma centers (Ordog et al., 1995).

There is no corresponding literature that suggests that initiations the require "jumping in" rather than shooting rival gang members results in a disproportionate number of emergency room visits. This could also be a function of self-diagnosis and treatment of injuries, and may be the resulting fear of detection. Not to mention the lack of health care benefits in an already disadvantaged population. However, if we expand our scope beyond the limitations of our data and include international differences, dental loss, certainly a condition that can affect health over time, where missing teeth is an indication of gang initiation or membership in South Africa (Russell et al., 2013), we cannot ignore the possibility that real physical harm is done in these ceremonies.

There are some practical purposes in requiring a violent initiation into a gang. There is a toughness quotient that is being tested, even in the case of female gang members who are becoming increasingly more willing to resort to violence when conflict arises with rival gangs (Hansen, 2005). The "street" baptism of taking a beating serves to screen the fighting capabilities of potential new members, as well as testing courage (Vigil, 1996).

Perhaps Barbara Ehrenreich (1998) is correct: humanity loves blood rites. Those who have spent any time on the front lines in a war have stories to tell, forever bonding them to others who have been on the battlefield. In the absence of war, where might young men find a means by which to express their aggressive proclivities? Certainly those who are critics of professional sports might argue that outside of wartime, the soccer or football field offers a means by which to indulge hyper-masculine tendencies, both as participant and as fan.

On the other hand, domestic violence as a predictor of paradigm shift from being the victim to being an abuser, initiator of violence is well documented. Critical to our argument here as to why violent gang initiation, while serving the purpose of demonstrated masculinities, also may be a byproduct of child abuse and neglect appearing to be normative in some families. Whether juveniles witness violence on the streets or within their own homes, they are at just as much risk as children who experience violence and may suffer from low self-esteem, poor impulse control, higher risk of alcohol and/or drug abuse, and running away, all factors leaving them vulnerable to gang recruitment (McNamara and Bucher, 2012). Violence, in this instance is normative, and it is no surprise if this extends itself to gang initiation.

We focus here less on the violence associated with gang recruitment per se, but rather on the meaning of promising and completion of ritual boasts within a hyper-masculinized environment (micro processes) in contemporary gang culture, without ignoring the historical roots of violent initiation. As convergent social development is occurring, organisms, including gangs, will evolve in the face of similar social structures, including environmental constraints (macro processes).

Unlike their male counterparts who appear to be enacting age old male initiation rites, the purposes of female initiation ceremonies has drastically changed from the intentions of pre-industrial society through to late 20th century. Female rites of passage were generally celebrated between ages 8 and 20, coincided with onset of menses (Brown, 1963), and in some cultures, mimics a marriage ceremony (e.g. Quinceañeras). From what we could observe of female gang initiation rites by way of youtube.com postings, there was as much, if not more levels of violence inflicted on the initiate.

During one of the videos we studied, three girls piled onto a 16-year-old who allegedly spent a year committing petty crimes (of which, we assume, she was not adjudicated, based on her presence in the video) her worthiness before her "jumping in" ceremony. In this particular initiation the beating lasted to the count of 30, an amount of time that was on average, longer than similar ceremonies with males.

Though decidedly violent, this is still carefully organized, with the abuse immediately ending after the count.

In contrast, a video (posted on youtube.com, April 2013) of an argument between four girls in the middle of street is laced with profanities, threats of "ass beatings" with more bravado than blows exchanged. When they do begin to become violent, it results in slapping, hair pulling, and shoving and less organized, with no clear conclusion to the.

But at no time is there the same level of fisticuffs as witnessed in the gang initiations involving males or females.

One argument for describing these initiations as being violent, but choreographed, controlled events is the absence of weapons. Whether this is a function of not wanting to be caught on video in possession of illegal firearms or other weapons, we did not observe any weapons in the hands of individuals, either in the gang initiations or ad hoc street fights. That is not to say that these individuals were not carrying weapons and possibly used them off camera. Even administrators at some inner city schools will confide off the record that half their school populations carry weapons to school each day (Devine, 1996).

What does appeared to be mirrored from ancient societal rituals is the number of participants in male and female initiation rites. Whereas historically males have group-centered highly visible rituals, female initiation ceremonies were more frequent and on a smaller scale, abet with neglect in research: "When attention is paid to female initiation, moreover, that attention is too often an analytical afterthought – as though female initiation were merely appendage to, or imitation of, male initiation." (Lutkehaus and Roscoe, 2013, xiv)

We, however, would argue that whether it is a function of feminism or that economic necessity results in increased willingness to resort to necessity, as in the case of protecting oneself in the course of selling drugs, females are, nonetheless, becoming increasingly violent in gangs and their initiation rites are no less bloody (Hansen, 2005). In many respects, they are trying to find their own place in the streets, outside of being ancillary to male gang members. As one woman stated in our video data, "The homeboys think they own the homegirls...they're jealous of us...I guess they think they own us. I guess they want us for themselves, but that is not the way it should be."

An exception to violent initiation rites in joining most street gangs, the Almighty Latin King and Queen Nation (ALKQN), membership comes by way of birth or by protracted entry into the gang. Brotherton and Barrios (2004, p. 202) observed that individuals enter ALKQN in stages, "each stage is carefully administered by the respective leadership of the tribes, and finally, when members have passed all the different trials they are welcomed into the organization." But with few exceptions, most gangs require some violent entry, either by "jumping in" or by committing a violent crime.

CONTROLLED, ORCHESTRATED BLOWS

In the videos we reviewed, the most common type of contacts with the initiates' bodies were by kicking and punching to the full body, including the head. This is close up, personal violence. In a few of the ceremonies, other objects were used, including whipping of the body with belts, squeezing lemon juice into the eyes, and lit cigarettes. Even in the case of the use of objects other than fists, knees and feet, the dialogue exchanged between both deliverers of blows and voyeurs indicated that there was duality between watching out for the initiate and making sure that they received a serious dose of abuse (Examples, Table 4).

Table 4. Examples of dialogue exchanges

No. of Participants*	Dialogue
9	n/a**
7	"Don't get him in his head"
9	"Let him get up"
6	at the end, "Stop"
7	"That's it, he's down man"
8	n/a
3	"Nig, do something." "Tell this dude to swing"
2	"No headshots, no knees, no fucking hitting dicks.", "Stand it", "Don't run"
4	n/a
3	"You better lie down on that ground and cover your head, lay down like a bitch."
3	"Get Up.", "Hold it"
n/a	"This guy want to be in my club.", "Open up the eyes", "This is initiation test for you.", "Start squeezing"
3	"Hell Yeah", "Do it again"
3	"Don't let 'em get up.", "Kick her!", "Slug her in the face!"
3	"No don't do that.", "That's the bad part you don't want to back away.", "Don't do it, back out.", "It feels pretty good"
2	n/a
2	n/a, "nigger in the hood"
3	"Come on, get up.", "Keep fighting.", "It is overwith man, it is after two minutes man.", "Oh you all doing the double IN"
9	"Take that bag off Bro.", "Woop his ass.", "Crach his ass.", "You don't want to get caught my nigga."
12	"oh, here we go" "Earn your stripe Bro.", "You better not lose.","Knock his ass out.", "Bust his ass.", "knee that Nigga in the face.", "Back off."
9	"Do that over.", "Get closer.", "Hit man!", "Come on now I wanna see blood!", "Get yo' ass up Nigga.", "Now you're a motherfucking blood."
8	"Put your hands up niggas.", "No face shots and you can't fight back.", "Hey you about to get it Bro."

* Participants include the initiates, the members delivering blows, and voyeurs.

** n/a – unable to determine due to video quality

(Source: Youtube.com, May 2011-May 2014)

VOYEUR VS. VIOLENT PARTICIPANT

It would be too easy to say that the willingness to be a willing witness to or perpetrator of violence is a purely a function of hyper-, hegemonic masculinities. Certainly in the videos we examined we saw evidence of males and females being equally violent in gang initiations. We may be alone in our criticism, as much of what we see in dissection of gender differences is found in gender literature, proposing that hyper-masculinity is exclusive a function of being "male" (Connell and Messerschmidt, 2005). Even the earlier work of one of this chapter's authors (Hansen, 2005) proposed that the purposes of joining gangs were distinctly different for males and females, with females being more purposely nurturing.

Instead of using the term "witness" in our description of gang members who are part of the gang initiation, but are not actually engaging in the direct violence against the initiates, we are describing them at "voyeurs." This suggests that willingly watching violent rituals is seductive and reinforces their own membership: "I had to go through this, so do you, if you want to be part of this group." Those of us who ran the gauntlet of graduate school can certainly attest to this type of mentality taken on by those who are on the other side of gatekeeping exams, ourselves included. At least in our data set, in all but 5 cases, all took part in delivering blows to the initiate. For the 5 exceptions, there was, on average, five other individuals who acted as bystanders, giving verbal instructions.

As in the case of "peeping" at sexual acts (e.g. pornographic materials), watching violent acts for enjoyment is not exclusively within the confines of gang life, as in the case of the sport of boxing. Violence for entertainment sake, including violent video game exposure, has been argued to be a contributor to violent behavior and aggression (Engelhardt et al., 2011). Desensitization, at the very least has been linked to increased aggression: ".... For individuals whose prior exposure to video game violence was low, playing a violent video game caused a reduction in the brain's response to depictions of real-life violence, and this reduction, in turn, predicted an increase in aggression." (Engelhardt et al., 2011, p. 1036)

The irony of membership is that it robs the individual of the very individuality that they might be seeking. Though one might be personally opposed to violence on legal or religious grounds, individuality is difficult to maintain in the face of overwhelming social forces (Wolff, 1950). Hence even though individuals within a gang may deem violence abhorrent, in the heat of the moment of initiation, group cohesiveness overrules any sympathy that they might have for the initiate.

POST-INITIATION CHOREOGRAPHY

Whether examining the post-initiation rituals of fraternities and sororities or those of gangs, the new member is not left to deal with the post-traumatic stress on their own. One of the authors here once heard a story of how new aviators in the Navy were held up against a wall and their wings (a pin that is part of the uniform) were beaten into their chest by the older, experienced flyers. Afterwards, the ritual ends with a few rounds of drinks at the Officers' Club, with the expected backslapping and congratulations passed around.

In the videos that we reviewed, the end of the beating in ceremony inevitably ends with the initiate being help up off the ground and/or helped with straightening up their clothing, pats on the back and in some cases, bear hugs. Some were given their new gang colors, generally a shirt. These adornments ("colors") are a reflection of meaning beyond the face value of the attire. By this means, the new members can distinguish themselves from one another bypassing the need to establish common ground in any other meaningful way. By means of symbolic adornment, there is a greater opportunity for cohesiveness within the gang. What is perplexing are the new reported trends in gangs: in order to escape labeling and detection by law enforcement, some gangs will change their name, colors, hand signs, and other markers on a regular basis (NGCRC, 2014).

There is also the inevitable peek behind the curtain of gang life that the initiate may not be privileged to witness in advance of membership. Though in this day and age of media and instant, if not always accurate information available on the Internet, the mysticism and language of gangs may not be so secretive as they once were. It is crucial to the process for members to return to meetings, however loosely structured, in order to reinforce the goals of the group. And in identifying who is part of the gang, further choreography is used, including "throwing" or "stacking" gang signals as a means of communication. Again, due to prevalence of gang references in media, including gang hand signs, one cannot assume that anyone using them is really part of a gang. However, inevitably, new initiates will have to learn this means of communication specific to their gang in order to be recognized as a member from time of initiation onward. There is perhaps no better example of the separation of the sacred (secret hand signs, gang colors) and the profane (economic enterprises of gangs, including drugs), than greeting rituals of gang members.

BLOOD OUT

There is little research beyond the ethnographic to describe gang initiation; far less is known about the process by which one extracts oneself from a gang, short of being killed by rival or fellow gang members. What we do know is that gang members, in general, are fatalistic in their views of death, to the extent that, "They see death as ever present, forever in their future, and nothing to hide from or fear." (Coenen, 2013, p. 133) Exiting gang life then is presumed to happen feet first, by way of a morgue.

What we do know is that due to the range of types of gangs, from the short-lived neighborhood oriented youth crew to the well-established, highly organized street gangs, membership, to some extent, can be transient. It is a challenge to researchers, as well as to law enforcement, who exactly is in or out of a gang (Bolden, 2012).

One option in leaving gang life is to physically leave the geographic location of the gang. Ethnographies confirm this, as in the case of Bolden's (2013) study of former gang members: gang desistance is additionally dependent on support systems. This is easier said than done, particularly if one has the customary markings of a gang member in tattooing, sometimes crudely drawn images created in prison or by amateur tattoo artists. The second challenge in moving to a new community is in the economic means to do so, as well as prospects for employment. Last, as a good portion of gang members, as in the case of prison populations, have drug and alcohol use that is difficult to get away from. The Youth Violence Survey indicates that gang members experiment with drugs, drug selling, and alcohol at a far younger age than non-gang member juveniles (Swahn et al., 2010). The risk is in simply transporting the same social issues with you in what can amount to, in many cases, a failed escape.

SYNTHESIZED THEORETICAL MODEL

Taking into consideration all the theories within this chapter that we proposed are apropos to gang initiation, as well as evidence to support the use of those theories from our data, a synthesized process model in the form of a timeline with feedback loops would look something like the model we provide in Figure 1.

As in the first law of motion in Newtonian physics, our model suggests that the initiation rite itself is embedded in a process that results in a feedback loop, until the individual or a sizable portion of the gang hits the proverbial wall of either exit from the gang, prison (where the cycle may begin again), or death. We take into consideration the micro-processes of family disruption, layered with the resulting social disorder in school and community and proposed these are the catalysts by which legitimate opportunities are blocked (think Merton). Gang recruitment and initiation becomes an inevitable option for some (not all) individuals living under these conditions, which in turn thicken criminal network ties (Hansen and Movahedi, 2010). Membership requires recommitment to the organization and is reinforced by either being an active participant delivering blows in a gang initiation or watching the proceedings (voyeurism).

Figure 1.

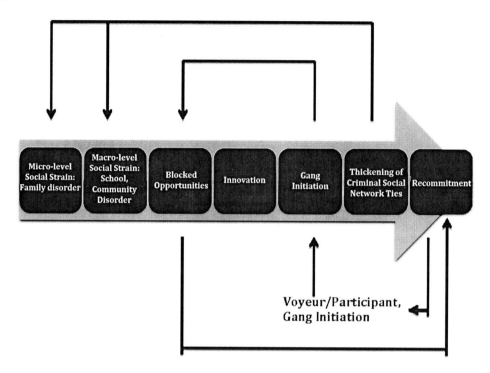

Unfortunately the continued reinforcement of criminal network ties feeds back to family, school, and community disorder. There are few definitive answers to how to successfully intervene after individuals have committed themselves to gang life. Admittedly, many become disillusioned afterwards, when faced with the constant threat of danger with substantial material reward be actualized only by the few and the most brazen of gang members. It is because of this that preventative measures are suggested to be the best strategy in combating gang recruitment, though there is realistically little funding for these types of projects.

CONCLUSION

Based on language spoken (English) and locations, the videos are assumed to have been filmed in the United States. It is interesting to note that as we found that there were no international videos readily available, it begs the question: Are Americans more demonstrative in their membership or are other parts of the world not caught up as yet to the gang initiation video "selfie"?

We have a number of questions that come out of this current research. For instance, is location symbolic in any fashion? In one of the videos we examined, the initiation takes place on church property – is this a form of defiance, or perhaps some distorted version of "God's eyes are on us?" In another case, the beating takes place in what appears to be a school bathroom. Was this for convenience, secrecy, or to humiliate the initiative further? We also question the authenticity of the events as they unfolded, as in one of the videos, it appeared to be a second take, based on a comment, "How did you manage to do that again?"

Non-judgmental as we have tried to be in this exploration of gang rituals, we do acknowledge that the violence associated with gang membership, either within initiation rituals or in gang rivalry, is a serious public health issue. At the height of gang violence in Los Angeles County in the 1990s, the cost in medical treatment alone due to gang violence was estimated to be $23.1 million per year (Friedrichs, 1999).

Even if violence between rival gang members can be reduced, will initiation rites follow suit? With more attention on reducing fraternity and sorority hazing rituals, including alcohol abuse, sexual assaults and in the extreme, physical harm, stories continue to come out of college campuses of initiations going terribly wrong (Nuwer, 2001). Likewise violent American football rituals on the field have become "softer" (at least in the American and National Football Leagues) in the face of new medical evidence on concussions. Should we not also be equally concerned with the violence associated with gang initiation rites?

It is impossible to predict whether gangs will ever witness a reduction in violence within initiation ritual…. from what we can gather from our research, there appears to be little to no concern for safety, even with the controlled choreography of these ceremonies. At the very least, we should be concerned that gang violence that is perpetuated on each other, rival gangs, or innocent bystanders is a public health problem that warrants further research.

REFERENCES

Agnew, R., & Brezina, T. (2010). Strain theories. In E. McLaughlin & T. Newburn (Eds.), *Sage handbook of criminological theory*. London: Sage Publications. doi:10.4135/9781446200926.n6

Becker, H. S. (1997). *Outsiders: Studies in the sociology of deviance*. New York: Free Press.

Best, J., & Hutchinson, M. M. (1996). The gang initiation rite as a motif in crime discourse. *Justice Quarterly*, *13*(3), 383–404. doi:10.1080/07418829600093021

Bolden, C. (2013). Tales From the hood: An emic perspective on gang Joining and gang desistance. *Criminal Justice Review*, *38*(4), 473–490. doi:10.1177/0734016813509267

Bolden, C. L. (2012). Liquid soldiers: Fluidity and gang membership. *Deviant Behavior*, *33*(3), 207–222. doi:10.1080/01639625.2010.548655

Brantingham, P. J., Tita, G. E., Short, M. B., & Reid, S. E. (2012). The ecology of gang territorial boundaries. *Criminology*, *50*(3), 851–885. doi:10.1111/j.1745-9125.2012.00281.x

Brown, D. H. (2003). *Santería enthroned: art, ritual, and innovation in an Afro-Cuban religion*. Chicago: University of Chicago Press.

Brown, J. K. (1963). A Cross-cultural study of female initiation rites. *American Anthropologist*, *65*(4), 837–853. doi:10.1525/aa.1963.65.4.02a00040

Coenen, I. (2013) Blood out: Nihilism in gang culture. In Confronting Death: College Students on the Community of Mortals. Bloomington, IN: iUniverse LLC.

Collins, R. (1981). On microfoundations of macrosociology. *American Journal of Sociology*, *86*(5), 984–1014. doi:10.1086/227351

Collins, R. (2005). *Interaction ritual chains*. Princeton University Press.

Connell, R. W., & Messerschmidt, J. W. (2005). Hegemonic masculinity rethinking the concept. *Gender & Society, 19*(6), 829–859. doi:10.1177/0891243205278639

Davis, M. (1999). *Ecology of fear: Los Angeles and the imagination of disaster*. New York: Vintage Books.

Devine, J. (1996). *Maximum security: The culture of violence in inner-city schools*. Chicago: University of Chicago Press.

Dishion, T. J., Nelson, S. E., & Yasui, M. (2005). Predicting early adolescent gang involvement from middle school adaptation. *Journal of Clinical Child and Adolescent Psychology, 34*(1), 62–73. doi:10.1207/s15374424jccp3401_6 PMID:15677281

Dunbar, E., & Blanco, A. (2014). *Psychological perspectives on culture, violence, and intergroup animus: Evolving traditions in the bonds that tie and hate. APA Handbooks in Psychology* (pp. 377–399). Washington, DC: American Psychological Association.

Duran, B., Duran, E., & Yellow Horse Brave Heart, M. (1998). The trauma of history. In R. Thornton (Ed.), *Studying Native America: Problems and perspectives* (pp. 60–78). Madison, WI: University of Wisconsin Press.

Ehrenreich, B. (1998). *Blood rites: Origins and history of the passions of war*. New York: Holt and Company.

Engelhardt, C. R., Bartholow, B. D., Kerr, G. T., & Bushman, B. J. (2011). This is your brain on violent video games: Neural desensitization to violence predicts increased aggression following violent video game exposure. *Journal of Experimental Social Psychology, 47*(5), 1033–1036. doi:10.1016/j.jesp.2011.03.027

Esbensen, F., Peterson, D., Taylor, T. J., & Freng, A. (2010). *Youth violence: Sex and race differences in offending, victimization, and gang membership*. Philadelphia: Temple University Press.

Finkel, M. A. (2002). Traumatic injuries caused by hazing practices. *The American Journal of Emergency Medicine, 20*(3), 228–233. doi:10.1053/ajem.2002.32649 PMID:11992345

Friedrichs, M. (1999). *Poverty and prejudice: Gang intervention and rehabilitation*. Edge: Ethics of Development in a Global Environment. Available at https://web.stanford.edu/class/e297c/poverty_prejudice/ganginterv/gangsproblems.htm

Goffman, E. (1986). *Stigma: Notes on the management of spoiled identity*. New York: Simon and Schuster, Touchstone.

Hansen, L. L. (2005). Research Note: Girl "crew" members doing gender, boy "crew" members doing violence: An ethnographic and network analysis of Maria Hinojosa's New York gangs. *Western Criminology Review, 6*(1), 134–144.

Hansen, L. L., & Movahedi, S. (2010) Wall Street scandals: The myth of individual greed. *Sociological Forum, 25*(2), 367-374.

Hazlehurst, K. M., & Hazlehurst, C. (1998). Gangs and youth subcultures: International explorations. Transaction Publishers.

Hill, K. G., Howell, Hawkins, & Battin-Pearson. (1999). Childhood risk factors for adolescent gang membership: Results from the Seattle Social Development Project. *Journal of Research in Crime and Delinquency, 36*(3), 300-322.

Howell, J. C. (2012). *Gangs in America's communities.* Thousand Oaks, CA: Sage Publications, Inc.

Lutkehaus, N., & Roscoe, P. (Eds.). (2013). *Gender rituals: Female initiation in Melanesia.* Routledge.

McNamara, R. H. (2012). *Problem children: Special populations in delinquency.* Durham, NC: Carolina Academic Press.

Nagendra, S. P. (1971). *The concept of ritual in modern sociological theory.* New Delhi: The Academic Journals of India.

Nuwer, H. (2001). *Wrongs of passage: Fraternities, sororities, hazing, and binge drinking.* Bloomington, IN: Indiana University Press.

Ordog, G. J., Shoemaker, W., Wasserberger, J., & Bishop, M. (1995). Gunshot wounds seen at a county hospital before and after a riot and gang truce: Part two. *The Journal of Trauma Injury Infection and Critical Care, 38*(3), 417–419. doi:10.1097/00005373-199503000-00024 PMID:7897730

Rodriquez, L. J. (2005). *La vida loca: Gang Days in L.A., always running.* New York: Simon & Schuster.

Russell, S. L., Gordon, S., Lukacs, J. R., & Kaste, L. M. (2013). Sex/gender differences in tooth loss and edentulism: Historical perspectives, biological factors, and sociologic reasons. *Dental Clinics of North America, 57*(2), 317–337. doi:10.1016/j.cden.2013.02.006 PMID:23570808

Sanchez, R. (2000). *My bloody life: The making of a Latin King.* Chicago: Chicago Review Press.

Shakur, T., Young, Cocker, Cunningham, Durham, Hooks, Hudson, … Troutman. (1995). *California love.* (Recorded by T. Shakur, Dr. Dre, & L. Troutman). Los Angeles, CA: Death Row Records.

Skarbek, D. (2014). *The social order of the underground: How prison gangs govern the American penal system.* New York: Oxford University Press. doi:10.1093/acprof:oso/9780199328499.001.0001

Stoll, D. (2013) Book review: Gangsters without borders: An ethnography of a Salvadoran gang. *Social Forces, 91*(4), 1549-1551.

Swahn, M. H., Bossarte, R. M., West, B., & Topalli, V. (2010). Alcohol and drug use among gang members: Experiences of adolescents who attend school. *The Journal of School Health, 80*(7), 353–360. doi:10.1111/j.1746-1561.2010.00513.x PMID:20591101

Sweet, S. J. (1999). Understanding fraternity hazing: Insights from symbolic interactionist theory. *Journal of College Student Development, 40*(4), 355–364.

Thrasher, F. M. (1927/2000). *The gang: A study of 1,313 gangs in Chicago.* Chicago: New Chicago School Press.

Valdez, A. (2003). Toward a typology of contemporary Mexican American youth gangs. In L. Kontos, D. Brotherton, & L. Barrios (Eds.), *Gangs and society: Alternative perspectives.* New York: Columbia University Press.

Vigil, J. D. (1996). Street baptism: Chicago gang initiation. *Human Organization, 55*(2), 149–152. doi:10.17730/humo.55.2.3358547x86552mg4

Whalen, W. J. (1966). *Handbook of secret organizations.* Milwaukee, WI: Bruce Publishing Co.

Wolff, K. H. (1950). *The sociology of Georg Simmel.* New York: The Free Press.

ENDNOTES

[1] Includes Ward, T. W., & Brenneman, R. (2012). Gangsters without borders: An ethnography of a Salvadoran street gang.

[2] On August 9, 2014, Michael Brown, an unarmed Black teenager had an altercation with law enforcement officer, Darren Wilson that resulted in Brown's death (CNN. com, http://www.cnn.com/interactive/2014/08/us/ferguson-brown-timeline/). There is considerable controversy surrounding this case, particularly after the November 2014 Grand Jury decision not to prosecute Officer Wilson for the shooting death of Brown, resulting in city-wide violent protests after the announcement.

Chapter 2
Baby Steps:
Urban Violence, Gangs, and School Safety

Laura L. Hansen
Western New England University, USA

ABSTRACT

With gang initiation starting as early as the primary school grades, the challenge to educators and administrators is to identify and suppress gang activities within the confines of school grounds. Taking into consideration the impotence of school systems to control the neighborhood and family environments, understanding the important role of schools to keep students engaged in scholarship to prevent gang membership cannot be stressed enough. Taking an applied approach, this chapter identifies what educators, administrators, and staff can do to identify behavior that might be on the surface mere imitation of gang membership (e.g. throwing gang signs), but could be symptomatic of close contact with known gang members and possibly exposure to the violence associated with gangs. The more school personnel can be cognizant of behavior that is indicative of exposure to gangs, curriculum planning and after school programs can be designed more efficiently to counter delinquent influences within the community, beyond "just say no" strategies.

INTRODUCTION

It's a typical Friday evening in fall, in Holyoke, Massachusetts. The air is crisp, the promise of cold nights to come and most are tucked in for the night, in their residences. Filing out of Morgan Elementary School around 8 p.m. are cheery family groups, chatting with the uniformed police officers and saying goodnight to the South Holyoke Safe Neighborhood Initiative volunteers. Standing out from these families leaving the school is a group of young teen boys, wearing what appears to be local gang colors. No adults accompany them as they leave the "Family Fun Night" event and they walk down the poorly lit streets in search of who knows what. Can we assume them to be gang members, or on the cusp of initiation?

Whether teaching in an inner city school district or in a rural community, few newly minted teachers, fresh from university with credential in hand, are equipped for the realities of the presence of gangs. Save

DOI: 10.4018/978-1-4666-9938-0.ch002

in sociology or criminal justice courses, there is little attention to the challenges of teaching students whose daily reality includes negotiating gang territories. In the case of some children, they have been born into gang life, whether due to an older sibling who is involved, or parents who are active members, as in the example of the Almighty Latin King and Queen Nation (ALKQN).

For more seasoned veterans in teaching, school policies may not include strategies to address the issues that can arise in the classroom that are a direct effect of the exposures their students have to gang violence. Bullying has gained greater attention in recent years and addressing bullying behavior should include being cognizant of intimidation in ritualized gang recruitment. In fact, for some individuals, joining gangs is perceived to be a means by which to be protected from bullying (Forber-Pratt et al., 2014).

Beyond bullying, youth gangs, including those in schools, have gained attention as well from media and academic researchers (Esbensen et al., 2013). In California alone, billions of dollars (USD) have been spent towards gang suppression on the streets and in schools since the 1990s (Friedrichs, 1999; Steinhart, 2008). However, few programs have demonstrated to be successful, in spite of the vast amounts of financial resources that have been thrown at the problem.

For those of us in the trenches of applied social science, preventing juveniles from joining gangs is the Achilles' heel of violence prevention policy. Even with the best intentions, families living in gang-infested communities are challenged to find solutions to limit the exposure their children have to violence within their neighborhood. As witnessed in Moreno Valley, California, a bedroom community about 60 miles east of Los Angeles, families who move to other cities believed to be "gang-free" will find that gang membership and criminality will be imported to the new neighborhood, particularly if ease of transportation is available, including easy access highways and mass transit.

Key to finding solutions lies in the joint efforts of parents, schools and law enforcement, many times a teetering 3-legged stool with little stability when these three entities do not effectively, formally collaborate to bring about changes in communities. This chapter explores the macro (community-level) and micro (family-level) exogenous variables that contribute to the risk of youth gang recruitment, including active recruitment in schools. Recommendations include taking "baby steps" to educate parents, teachers, and administrators on the risks of gang violence in schools, as well as looking at evidence-based programs to address it.

This chapter also introduces as case study the valiant grassroots efforts of one community to combat gang violence and recruitment, particularly in school-age juveniles. Since 2011, South Holyoke Safe Neighborhood Initiative (SHSNI) in South Holyoke, Massachusetts, has taken a "weed and seed" approach adopted from the Massachusetts State Police C3 model, outlined later in this chapter. Through a grassroots campaign, SHSNI has worked with the community, including Morgan School Elementary School, to provide afterschool and family programs to offer positive alternatives to gang life.

URBAN VIOLENCE

In a recent National Public Radio (NPR) story, Los Angeles, California reportedly is experiencing the lowest homicide rate in four decades, this in spite of a particularly bloody holiday season in 2010 (del Barco, Jan. 6, 2011). Homicide has been cited as the number one cause of death in America among young African American males, many of which live in urban settings (Robinson et al., 2009; Sweatt et al., 2002; Center for Disease Control, United States).

Table 1. Urban violence: Intersection of economy and social variables

Category of Crime	Types of Violence by Perpetrators and/or Victims	Manifestations
Economic	• Organized crime • Business interests • Delinquents • Robbers	• Intimidation and violence as means of resolving economic disputes • Street theft, robbery and crime • Kidnapping • Armed robbery • Drug-trafficking • Car theft and other contraband activities • Small-arms dealing • Assaults including killing and rape in the course of economic crimes • Trafficking in prostitutes • Conflict over scarce resources
Economic/social	• Gangs • "Street children" (boys and girls) • Ethnic violence	• Territorial or identity-based "turf" violence • robbery, theft • Petty theft • Communal riots
Social	• Intimate partner violence inside the home • Sexual violence (including rape) in the public arena • Child abuse: boys and girls • Inter-generational conflict between parent and children • Gratuitous/routine daily violence	• Physical or psychological male–female abuse • Physical and sexual abuse, particularly prevalent in the case of stepfathers but also uncles • Physical and psychological abuse • Incivility in areas such as traffic, road rage, bar fights and street confrontations • Arguments that get out of control

Source: Adapted from Moser, C and A Winton (2002); Moser (2004)

Urban violence is generally defined as "street crime," committed out in public, including assault and homicide. However, the variables contributing to urban violence spill over into public school systems and into homes. Likewise, domestic violence and problems in schools spill over into the streets. Whether discussion of urban violence includes violence that occurs outside the public eye, it is complex. This is best represented by an adaptation of Moser's (2002; 2004) urban crime/violence classifications, focusing on the intersection of economic and social variables (Table 1). Urban violence is not solely an "American Problem" nor is it restricted to the Black American community. Urban violence has increasingly become a global issue.

A number of factors, including structural and social explanations have been argued as the causes of urban violence. Poverty continues to be the front-runner as a reason given for why cities continue to be centers of racial/ethnic tensions and violence. High unemployment rates, intergenerational poverty and higher than average high school drop out rates have contributed to high numbers of urbanites living in poverty.

One explanation for perpetuation of Black poverty in the inner city has been U.S. immigration policies since the 1960s, that has allowed for increasing numbers of Latinos/Latinas to compete with Blacks for low skill-skilled jobs in agriculture, manufacturing and construction (Shihadeh & Barranco, 2010). Urban violence becomes a function of the indirect effect of increased economic deprivation (Shihadeh & Ousey, 1998). Randall Collins (2009) contradicts economic explanations for violence, theorizing that violence is exceptional and goes against human nature, in spite of the media perceptions (films, television, and news shows) to the contrary. It is important to note that Collins' views are controversial and do not reflect the majority of research findings on the causes of urban violence.

Explanations for poverty within urban Black populations include the disappearance of low-skilled, as well as white-collar, middle-class jobs altogether in cities that have increased investment in global transactions, or as Elsinger and Smith (2000) succinctly noted, "export jobs or die." Another argument is that in our new global economy, jobs have been exported overseas to peripheral and semi-peripheral countries that provide a cheaper labor force, as compared to the more costly, historically unionized work-force in the United States. Due to our current global economic recovery, even the most vibrant urban cities have suffered massive unemployment, whether they have been active participants in the global economy or not, as exemplified by Detroit, Michigan.

Most of what we know to be urban violence is associated with gang activity, as well as related drug enterprises and prevalence of guns. Lesser-known and misunderstood is the concept of gangs as protective agents from urban violence. Adolescents in particular join gangs in response to violent crimes within their community (Sobel & Osoba, 2009), even though gangs are key contributors to urban violence, creating a distressing tautology. It is too simple to propose that gang activity of any kind, per se, is exclusively responsible for urban violence. Density of gangs within a small urban area appears to play an additional role (Robinson et al., 2009).

Other explanations for urban violence are more anthropological than sociological or psychological, and propose that the culture of marginalized inner city groups, including young Black males, has lead to violence in the streets. One of the best-known theorists of recent decades to address the issues sur-rounding urban violence is Elijah Anderson (University of Pennsylvania). In his seminal works, *A Place on the Corner* (1978; 2003), *Code of the Streets: Decency, Violence, and the Moral Life of the Inner City* (1999), and more recently, *The Cosmopolitan Canopy: Race and Civility in Everyday Life* (2012), Anderson argues that urban violence is a function of the culture that emerges out of the stresses of living in violent, impoverished communities. In this model, violence is perpetuated by cultural transmission. This supports the earlier theories of Edwin H. Sutherland (1947) who suggested that deviance and crime, in this case urban violence, are learned through intimate peers.

Yet other explanations for urban violence include social disorganization, where urban dwellers are viewed as being less tethered to their community, particularly in more impoverished areas of cities where there are greater numbers of renters, less owner-occupied homes and more government-subsidized hous-ing. Breakdown of social controls, including community investment, results in individuals feeling free to commit violent acts (Robinson et al., 2009). This runs counter to theories of racial/ethnic identity and solidarity within urban communities.

Some theorists have asked why there have not been more riots in American cities as have increas-ingly been the experience in France within the past decade. The same structural problems exist in France within African and other immigrant populations: poverty and joblessness (Katz, 2007). However, as Katz (2007, p 23) observed, "….American cities do not burn. Urban violence has not disappeared; it has been transformed [since the 1960s]. Anger and frustration turn inward, exploding in gang war-fare, homicide, and random killing in drive-by shootings."

Malcontent has not manifested itself in targeted retaliation against law enforcement personnel, as in the case of European cities plagued with urban violence. Though we should mention that recent incidents of police officers as targeted victims themselves, would argue conditions are otherwise. The criminal justice reaction to urban violence in the U.S., nevertheless, has largely been perceived and portrayed as being racist and contentious, as demonstrated by the growing interest in racial profiling research (Higgins et al., 2008). More positive responses to urban violence, though met with mixed results, have included creation of partnerships between urban communities and law enforcement, including citizen taskforces and community policing (Brown, 2010).

Urban violence appears to be, on the most part, a function of the intersection of several factors, including poverty, population (and gang) density, and community disorganization as well as social culture. Urban violence in general will continue to be the major challenge for law enforcement and other criminal justice professionals in the coming decades, if not centuries. Causes for urban violence have been exhaustively explored, but there have been no easy solutions. Unfortunately, urban violence spills over into schools, leaving challenges for teachers, students, parents, and law enforcement.

Urban violence associated with gangs is not limited to the United States. Though not viewed as critically an issue in Europe (Klein et al., 2006), street violence has none-the-less been on the rise in European cities. It is important to not impose a United States model of gang life on that witnessed elsewhere. However, the social problems that contribute to youth gangs are similar: divisions by race and ethnicity, poverty, disorganized/transient neighborhoods, and disrupted family life.

THE ANATOMY OF STREET GANGS

No doubt through the pages of this book, the reader will find inconsistencies in contemporary definitions of what constitutes a gang. As Klein and Maxson (2006, p 3) have questioned, "does it really matter how we define it?" The percentages of juveniles supposed to be gang members varies by definition, from a low of 6% to as high as 30% (Estrada et al., 2013).

Urban gangs and suburban gangs, for that matter, are not new to the streets of the United States or other countries. Originally simply a word to describe groups that gather on city streets, "gangs" first operated as a derogatory term to label groups of highway robbers as early as seventeenth century England (Howell, 2015). The genesis of street gangs as an observed growing regional problem in the United States began first in the Northeast moving south and west, lastly identified as a problem in southern states (Howell, 2015) primarily within the nineteenth century on the heels of the Industrial Revolution. This is not to suggest that gang activity migrated from one region to another. Rather recognition of "gangs" as a new social and criminal justice problem did not come emerge simultaneously as cities in the Northeast United States were vastly more populated than those in the Southwest, including Los Angeles, California, until the mid-twentieth century.

There is a hazard in pronouncing any gathering of alleged troublesome youth on city streets. The concern lies in Labeling Theory: if it walks like a duck and talks like a duck, it might not be a duck (yet). Particularly in the discussions of youth gangs (or perceived youth gangs), being told over and over again that certain behaviors are "troublesome" may result in self-identification with delinquency, even if that delinquency is marginal in nature (e.g. minor offensives, including infrequent marijuana use). This is analogous to a spouse who is suspected of cheating, when in actuality they are not, and begins an extramarital affair with an attitude of "as long as I'm being accused of this, I may as well become what my spouse thinks I am already" if the suspicions continue. Labeling of students is not unheard of by teachers and staff who may jump to conclusions about a student's possible gang affiliation on the basis of attire that could just as easily be associated with urban hip hop or rap culture. As noted in the introductory paragraph of this chapter, we do not know for sure if the young men leaving the South Holyoke event indeed were gang-affiliated or imitative.

As it is critical to have a template by which to review the activities of a questionable juvenile group to determine if it indeed constitutes a street gang, Klein and Maxson (2006) offer a 5-point list of characteristics (p 3):

Point 1: *Durability* of at least several months; most "gang-like" groups dissipate within a few months.
Point 2: The group should be spending group time outside of home, work or school, or are believed to be *street-oriented*.
Point 3: As most street gangs, at least those that have not become intergenerational (e.g. Crips, Bloods, ALKQN), consist of juveniles and therefore are *youth-oriented*.
Point 4: At least some of the activities that the members are involved with are *illegal*, not merely "bothersome".
Point 5: The group self-identifies (*identity*) as a gang; not based on individuals' self-image.

Without creating a Weberian typology that requires formalization by definition (i.e. written rules, hierarchy), Klein and Maxson's list allows the expansion of the definition of what constitutes a gang to include groups that have the characteristics, without institutionalization of structure. This is particularly useful in the case of youth gangs, where membership has fluidity based on a number of variables, including family transience.

Recruitment into gangs is poorly understood, save ethnographic accounts and logistics (e.g. "blood in, blood out"). What we do know is that gang recruitment is a process that occurs over time and that commitment to join may take up to a year, for those who are not already born into gang life (Miller, 2000). It is presumptuous to assume that a juvenile has joined a gang, solely on the basis of appearances and in the absence of overt criminal or delinquent behavior.

What we do know is that gangs are seductive, within the contexts of disorganized communities. Some of the monikers themselves are suggestive of sex, excitement, and danger: Sexy Boys (1970s, 80s), Asbestos Boys (1980s, 90s), Ready to Die (2010s, Holyoke, MA). Hazen and Rodgers (2014) reduce the attraction to one of protection. "To survive on the streets, young men sought protection in groups that were invariably interpreted through the lens of the gang." (Hazen & Rodgers, 2014, p. 37) Hence gang membership may be viewed as a means to cope with the conditions of poverty and fractured families.

Key conduits into gang life are social networks. Sutherland's Differential Association theory (1947) compliments the dynamics of social network theories on transmission of culture, in regards to how seductive gang membership can appear. In many respects, it is a recursive relationship. Networks can serve the purposes of *incubators* or *bridges* for social influence (Mische, 2011), and in turn can influence the culture of the social network. In the absence of normatively accepted, positive alternatives, or reward for acceptance of the alternatives, the opinions of delinquent peers will generally prevail. Within this context, we can view gangs and the violence associated with them as contagion, particularly in the petri dish of a dysfunctional, distrusted school system and absence of empathetic parents (Lenzi et al., 2015).

The most common places for recruitment are on the streets and in prison. Increasingly, schools are seeing signs of recruitment within their walls (Hansen, 2011a). When youth do join gangs, they may lose their normative family and cultural ties. For indigenous juveniles in Canada who join gangs, they take on Black American gangster personae and lose connection to their Aboriginal identities (Grekul & LaBoucane-Benson, 2008). Imitation of mannerisms and dress should not make us jump to the conclusion that groups of seemingly delinquent juveniles are partaking in the level of violence and crime of organized street gangs.

There are alarming research findings on the type of schools that are most vulnerable to gang recruitment. We ordinarily associate juvenile delinquency exclusively with poor urban schools. However what appear to be more critical independent variables are the degree to which the school is perceived to be a safe environment and the *type* of school. Schools that on average attract more gang membership are special education, vocational, or alternative schools[1] (Lenzi et al., 2015). And as larger towns and cities, including those in suburbia, must offer these types of schools in lieu of traditional education, we can conclude that the risk for gang membership in schools is not limited to urban settings.

This begs the question as to whether the condition is recursive: Does the non-traditional school produce the gang member or is the gang member more likely to end up in a non-traditional school? Important to note that on the basis of the Youth Risk Behavior Survey, it is suggested that gang membership should be operationalized as a predictor variable rather than as a dependent variable (Gebo & Sullivan, 2014); gangs do not as a general rule form within the confines of the school, but rather this is happening outside school hours. Whether the genesis discussion is centered on Importation Theory (Zamble & Porporino, 1988)[2] or Differential Association (Sutherland), gangs are often disruptive to the administrative needs of schools, as more resources are spent on public safety rather than educational materials.

Though not distinctly the focus of this chapter, the purposes for joining gangs differ between boys and girls. Crucial to both are social network ties, however boys are more transient in their membership and more prone to violence, though girls are becoming increasingly so (Hansen, 2005). The attraction to gangs for pubescent boys is to "get girls" or to make money to purchase material goods, as demonstrated by the personal accounts of former gang members (Sanchez, 2000). As Merton prescribed (1957), in the absence of positive institutional means by which to achieve societal goals, individuals (or in the case of the collective, a gang) will seek delinquent innovation to achieve them.

Female gang members have been historically ancillary to male gangs. However, since the 1970s, female gangs and their members have been more seriously viewed as a public safety threat, including in schools (Grover et al., 2009). And females are more willing to resort to violence, more willing to use guns in recent decades and moving away from their roles as "gun-holders" to "gun totters" (Peterson, 2012; Hansen, 2005). None-the-less, their structures are distinctly different and motivation to join female gangs is sharply different than reasons given by males for joining gangs, even in the face of strives for parity (Hansen, 2005).

For females, gang formation more resembles establishment of pseudo-families, substitutes for the dysfunctions of family life that they are experiencing at home, including absentee fathers, unwed mothers who gave birth to them when they were teens themselves (Hansen, 2005). Using school-based data, De La Rue and Espelage (2014) found that young girls who were involved in gangs had significantly greater history of running away from home, family gang involvement (again, intergenerational), and greater levels of aggression and delinquency, as compared to girls who did not have gang affiliation. Sexual abuse prior to recruitment also is a consistent variable in girls who join gangs or live on the peripheral of gangs (De La Rue & Espelage, 2014; Wiemann et al., 2000). Sadly, girls and women who join gangs are more likely to be sexually exploited and/or assaulted by male gang members, the very types of abuses that they are trying to escape in the first place by joining a gang.

GANGS IN SCHOOLS

The middle school experience, the juncture at which gang membership may become the exceptionally attractive, is a unique one. Including grades 7-8, 6-8, or 7-9 in the United States, juveniles are generally between the age of 11 and 14, ages that are fraught with the developmental stages of puberty and the cusp of adolescence, young adulthood. Add the attention to media icons, some that glamorize gang lifestyles, schools are challenged to close Pandora's box. In comparison to the 19% of U.S. school-aged students who report that gangs exist in their schools (Roberts et al., 2013), the *National Survey of American Attitudes on Substance Abuse XV* (2010) revealed, "that 35% of middle school students reported that there were gangs in their schools or students who consider themselves [sic] to be part of a gang." (Estrada et al., 2013, p 626)

Two key variables in gang recruitment at any grade level, including elementary, are poor school performance and low attachment to learning. Coupled with large class sizes, fewer resources for schools in low-income communities, violence spilling into schools from the surrounding community may be an inevitable outcome in the absence of prevention and intervention measures.

As students with special needs, including those with learning disabilities, are at greater risk for poor school performance, in addition to children who have emotional challenges, this population cannot be ignored for their risks for gang recruitment. Juveniles who do not do well in school, particularly those with undiagnosed learning disabilities, face an uphill battle to graduation and ultimately to gainful employment (Winters, 1997). In a credentialed society, the 4-year college degree will be (and is) increasingly viewed in the same vein as the high school diploma was considered 50 years ago (Collins, 1979). For juveniles faced with little prospect of succeeding in school, much less any hope of attending university without intensive intervention, gangs become attractive, lucrative alternatives to normative societal goals, including material wealth.

The crime statistics in U.S. schools are alarming, when taking into account the school to prison pipeline policies of recent decades, as well the prevalence of unreported crimes. The U.S. Bureau of Justice Statistics (BJS), in partnership with the Institute of Education Sciences, offer in their Indicators of School Crime and Safety Report the following school environment statistics (Roberts et al., 2013):

- 85% of public schools reported one or more crime incidents taking place, accounting for and estimated 1.9 million crimes in 2009-2010.
- 74% of public schools reported incidents of violent crimes, with 16% reporting serious offenses in 2009-2010.
- 16% of public schools reported that gang activities took place in their schools in 2009-2010. This translates to nearly 16,000 schools nationwide, based on the number of public schools in the U.S. in 2009-2010, as reported by the National Center for Education.

As school administrators come and go, they may not be cognizant of the specific risks for gang recruitment within the walls of their institution. Reasons to take a macro-micro approach to gang issues in schools is that many inner city schools (and increasingly, suburban schools), are faced with highly organized gangs that represent an isolated urban underclass that have strong, longstanding cohesive ties, making it difficult to separate the student from the neighborhood environment once they reach the steps of the school. Though the culture of violence within gangs is varying, as well as the racial/ethnic makeup, the end result is the same: if schools do not provide an alternative to gang life, aggressive recruitment into gangs or self-selection for membership becomes almost inevitable by middle school (Hansen, 2005).

Reports of serious, violent offending in schools are not new phenomena. In the 1980s, schools were progressively deteriorating, most notably in the inner city. As teaching salaries stagnated and instances of violence in schools increased, teacher morale deteriorated as well (Price, 2009). Within two decades of the 1980s, most public schools throughout the U.S. were living under the cloud of punitive discipline with zero tolerance procedures and policies for a broader range of behavioral problems (Skiba & Peterson, 2000).

Zero tolerance policies in schools may be an extension of the general movement towards militarism in the United States since 9/11. As police departments attempt to move away from the impression of being invading armies (e.g. community policing), American culture, in general, is increasingly becoming more tolerant of strong punitive actions for social problems. The "war on drugs" has segued to a "war on violence" and by extension, a "war on gangs". As Bacevich (2005, p. 36) proposes, using the construct "war" allows for "'wartime' prerogatives by expanding the police powers of the state and circumscribing constitutional guarantees of due process."

Increasingly the media began reporting stories of grade school age children that were being thrown out of school for what had historically been considered minor offenses. In one extreme instance in Colorado Springs, Colorado, a 6-year-old boy who had a history of discipline problems was suspended from school for "sexual harassment" for kissing one of his classmates' hands (Wallace, CNN, December 2013). These stories take attention from the real issues of serious, violent offenses that warrant zero-tolerance policies.

According to the U.S. BJS report, juveniles are particularly vulnerable between the ages of 12 and 18 for violent offending and gang recruitment (Roberts et al., 2013). A strong argument for adoption of anti-gang recruitment strategies in elementary (primary) schools is that by the time students reach middle school (junior high school, secondary education), if they are at risk to join a gang, in absence of prevention or intervention, it is almost too late to stop them from becoming a statistic.

There have been few, if any, anti-gang programs in schools that are universally successful. Yet policy, as in most cases of tackling social problems, tend to take a one-size fits all stance. An example of a school-based program with mix results is Gang Resistance Education and Training (G.R.E.A.T.) first introduced in the 1990s. Until academics began to independently evaluate the program, primarily program developers conducted program evaluations that, on the surface, imply biases towards significant changes as a result of the program. In a 2013 longitudinal study (Esbensen et al., p 399), students who participated in the G.R.E.A.T. Program "expressed more positive attitudes to the police and [had] lower odds of gang membership.... more use of refusal skills.... [but] The effect sizes are small" in comparison to the control group that did not participate in the program. In some cities, the results were null, as in the cases of Chicago and Philadelphia (Esbensen et al., 2013), offering further evidence that school anti-gang programs have not historically been found to be transportable. Yet it is not uncommon for a school program to become the new shiny policy object that becomes universally implemented without thorough vetting to determine if these programs will work elsewhere beyond the pilot study site.

A more effective response is a grassroots preventative model like the one described in the case study in this chapter (South Holyoke Safe Neighborhoods Initiative), as challenging as it might be. A program that addresses potential discipline problems, including the suspicion of students living on the fringes of gang involvement, allows for diversion rather than punishment. One alternative to zero tolerance policies is early response, where students are taught to solve interpersonal and intrapersonal problems with more socially acceptable, positive strategies than resorting to violence (Skiba & Peterson, 2000).

Whole family approaches are also gaining momentum, where not only the child is "diagnosed" and "treated" for problems within the confines of the school, but the issues in the home are addressed as well. Unfortunately the alternative strategies offered here are labor intense for school and community departments, agencies, and may be dependent on grants to sustain programs. Plus it requires the continued commitment of parents, a particular issue within more transient populations. The other weakness in these programs is that many do not begin until middle school, when the problem may already be beyond repair for both students and their families.

One means by which schools have attempted to stem gang influences within them is to implement mandatory school uniform policies. This is not a new concept. Certainly these policies have always been in effect within private and/or parochial schools, albeit not initially for the purposes of preventing gang activities. Uniforms have tentatively been found to have a positive effect on school behavior (Stanley, 1996). It is ironic, though, to observe school-aged children walking to school in polo-style shirts that are in the very colors that are co-opted by the gangs within their neighborhoods. Worse yet, when a school adopts the colors of a rival gang, though there has been little research to suggest that this may have a negative effect off site of the school setting.

Beyond the esthetics of mandatory uniforms, the argument for institutionalizing a policy at the secondary school level is that it improves academic performance, student safety, discipline, and morale, while reducing clothing costs for parents (Caruso, 1996). In comparative studies, uniforms unto themselves appear to be less a determining factor in the rates of delinquency than the culture of the institution itself (Tanioka & Glaser, 1991). It may possibly be reflexive in that the culture of schools may be changed by the implementation of mandatory uniform policies, just as clothing uniformity within the military de-emphasizes individuality.

In discussions with elementary school staff and teachers, they report that uniforms do not squash the urges for individuality (Hansen, 2011a). Students may collude in adopting new hairstyles, color shoelaces or shoe brands, even chose to wear their uniforms in un-ironed, untidy ways to demonstrate either individuality or group/gang affiliation (Hansen, 2011a). Of greater concern is when gang graffiti shows up on homework assignments and other handed in schoolwork. Teachers will either jump to conclusions that the student is gang-affiliated or be oblivious of the warning signs of student interest in gangs, without educators and school staff receiving extensive training on how to recognize these signs in the classroom or on the school grounds (Hansen, 2011a, 2011b).

Of graver concern are the economic enterprises that come off of the streets and into schools as a direct result of gang affiliation. Gang members are more likely to be involved in selling drugs than non-gang juveniles (Hill et al., 2001). This is also true in comparison to other at-risk youth who are not gang members (Huff, 1998). We should also note that schools have little control over the drug activities, including distribution, that takes place within the surrounding neighborhoods, but directly effect the school-aged population as they walk or commute to and from school.

One counter measure to gangs in schools and the illegal activities that come with them is insertion of resource officers. The presence of resource officers in schools is increasingly becoming controversial, particularly with the inclusion of metal detectors at school entrances, creating a penitentiary atmosphere. Already alarmed by the acceleration of the school to prison pipeline with zero tolerance policies, there is advocacy that if resource officers are to be utilized, then they should be police department employees rather than school district personnel. The argument is that resource officers should be trained in conducting investigations and interrogations for criminal activities at the same level of professionalism that police officers on the street are held to (in theory) (Price, 2009). Again, this gives the alarming impression of an invading army despite the softening of the appearance of police presence by substituting khakis and polo shirts for traditional police uniforms.

When students do attempt to be part of normative life, either due to need to supplement family income or to be able to afford some of the luxuries that teens covet (e.g. smartphones), they may find that the only legitimate means of employment is in a minimum wage job. As in the case of fast food employees, it may require working late hours that are not conducive to maintaining passing grades in school (Hansen, 2005; Hernandez, 1998). Again, this makes gangs appear to be the more attractive and lucrative alternative.

There have been a number of studies to indicate that gang members commit violent crimes at higher rates than non-gang members. What is becoming more apparent in recent research is that gang members experience higher rates of violent victimization (Estrada et al., 2013; Katz et al., 2011), which unto itself creates another dimension in attempting to prevent students from dropping out of school.

Beyond the extent to which violent victimization, gang related and otherwise, is a public health issue, it becomes an additional factor in poor school performance. Students cannot learn with the added fear of personal safety. Contrary to perceptions, gangs are not found to have protective value (Peterson et al., 2004). With the growing focus on bullying in schools, it also begs attention to the additional risk of gang recruitment on school grounds, if the victimized student believes that joining a gang is the only alternative to being tormented. However, this sets up a dangerous tautology, where there is strong evidence that it is critical for schools to establish programs that dispel the myth that gangs provide safe havens (Peterson et al., 2004).

CASE STUDY: SOUTH HOLYOKE SAFE NEIGHBORHOODS INITIATIVE AND MORGAN SCHOOL

Schools cannot be the first line of defense for gang prevention. School populations are a reflection of the surrounding neighborhoods that feed into them. In South Holyoke in Western Massachusetts, community members including social agencies, law enforcement, and the school district personnel are attempting to take matters in their own hands to reduce gang presence in their schools and neighborhood. The challenges are multi-faceted, from higher rates of unemployment, greater numbers of young, single female-head of households, to a disproportionate number of children living in poverty. Add to that an elementary school that has been downgraded to "Level 5" for underperformance on standardized tests (see http://www.doe.mass.edu/apa/sss/turnaround/level5/schools/), the outlook, on the surface, appears to be grim.

For those unfamiliar with American pedagogy, in a controversial move to improve teaching and the quality of education, standardized testing mutated from "leave no child behind" to school failures increasing across the country. There are approximately 4% of public schools in receivership in the United States, with the number growing every year (CREDO, 2013). In doing so, education is further stratified between those communities with funding to bring excellence in personnel and resources to better prepare students for standardized exams (e.g. higher property values with the associated higher property taxes funding schools) and those with depressed home property values, fewer homeowners, and more transient populations. The later is an apt description of the target area of South Holyoke around Morgan School.

South Holyoke, a mid-size city, has historically been a disadvantaged neighborhood with a disproportionate number of families living in poverty, high rates of teen pregnancy, and in more recent years, a center of gang activity. Inspired by the Massachusetts State Police C3 Policing (MSPC3) approach adopted by neighboring Springfield, Massachusetts, a grassroots organization was formed in South Holyoke to customize the approach to the specific needs of a targeted neighborhood that was experiencing the worst of gang activity (shsni.org).

As described by the MSPC3 website (mspc3policing.com), C3 policing or Counter Criminal Continuum Policing incorporates a strategic program to extract criminal gangs and drug dealers out of the community. While MSPC3 does not abandon traditional community policing, SHSNI in South Holyoke takes this one step further to a "weed and seed" philosophy of removing criminal elements, while simultaneously encouraging community members into self-efficacy, with collaboration with social service agencies, law enforcement, and the public schools.

In 2012 and 2013, SHSNI conducted door-to-door surveys of residents in order to collect data on perceptions of public safety, crime, social service needs, and availability of afterschool programs that target prevention of gang recruitment. While only 35% of households reported that their children were in afterschool programs in 2012, this number increased to 63% by 2013 (Hansen & Morin, 2012; Hansen et al., 2013). The greatest interest was in sports programs, followed by arts and craft programs, all of which had become casualties of cash-strapped school districts since the 1970s.

Of value to the school community from the SHSNI survey reports are the statistics on perceptions of safety. Though domestic violence is admittedly under-reported, as compared to agencies' perceptions of how big a problem it is within Holyoke (Hansen et al. 2013), the most pressing issue for residents was the drug activities around the housing projects, followed for concerns of gang presence (Hansen & Morin, 2012).

Parents are an integral part of SHSNI's strategy. Offering a "Family Fun Night" each month that encourages families to participate in a number of activities with subliminal and not so subliminal anti-violence messages, a no judgment safe zone is established, where parents can make contact with needed social services. The initiative has used the data from the 2012 and 2013 surveys to create programs that are tailored to specific community needs.

An additional benefit of the "Family Fun Night" is that the initiative works with community partners to provide much needed school supplies. As schools are less able to provide the materials students need to have to succeed in school (pens, pencils, notebooks, backpacks, etc.), the initiative has a "Back to School" event every fall to provide children within this financially depressed neighborhood with school supplies. As well as offering much needed materials to succeed in the classroom, a latent function of these family-oriented events is that they serve to provide meals that feel more communal than charity.

Though SHSNI is in its infancy, it shows great promise in supplementing services where Morgan School is deficient. Currently the initiative is dependent on using Holyoke school facilities for many of their programs. Ultimately the initiative would like to establish a multi-agency community center in the neighborhood that can provide afterschool programs, as well as direct access to social services that take a whole family approach to violence and gang prevention, intervention, reaching residents who would otherwise go underserved due to transportation constraints.

SUMMARY

The problem of violence and gangs in school is a complex one. Because of the violence and criminal activities associated with gangs, inner city schools become contested terrains between school personnel, parents, law enforcement, and the neighborhoods in which they dwell. Add the pressure of schools to preform well in standardized testing, without necessarily having the resources to do so, juveniles will continue to slip through the cracks and be at risk for gang recruitment. It appears to be a losing battle, one that has been ongoing since the 1960s when deindustrialization created far fewer legitimate opportunities for parents and their offspring, particularly those with limited education.

For all the pessimism introduced here, there do appear to be solutions. Collaborative, multi-agency initiatives are beginning to find traction, as in the case of SHSNI. Prevention continues to be the greatest challenge, as there is little research on what the variables are that prevent juveniles from becoming gang members, when faced with the same risk factors as those who do join.

The first "baby step" in addressing the gang problems that spill into schools is to educate school administrators, staff, and faculty on the risks. This can be met with resistance (as this author has found) as the responsibilities that school personnel must attend to constitute well beyond a 40-hour workweek, even in the supposed freedom of summer vacations. Requiring additional in-service training in anything beyond classroom instruction does result in the message not being heard. Understanding gangs and general violent behavior should be part of every education curriculum in universities, particularly for future educators and administrators who intend to be employed in urban school districts.

Either way, if juveniles are not receiving the direction and attention they need to succeed in school from home or the community, then schools become the last line of defense in the prevention of juvenile delinquency. As one former gang member reported in his autobiography, school was a retreat from his abusive home life: "Back in school I was in heaven…. I was a model student, always on time, my homework neatly completed…." (Sanchez, 2000, p 11) It is important to recognize that for some, school can offer a means by which to escape gang life, as well as a vicious cycle of poverty and delinquency (Hansen, 2005).

The answer does not lie in across the board zero tolerance procedures and policies for a range of offenses. On the other hand, violence and felonious criminal behavior should never be tolerated in schools, as they are massively disruptive to the learning process. The key is to avoid throwing out the proverbial baby with the bathwater, where the marginally juvenile delinquent (e.g. truancy) should be given ample opportunity to stay in mainstream schooling. To segregate them into populations of more serious juvenile offenders in alternative schools or in the juvenile criminal justice system only increases their risk of joining gangs by way of differential association and delinquent networks (think Sutherland).

The real fear is that the three-legged stool, described in the introduction of this chapter, is teetering. Unless school, parents, and law enforcement join as a united front against gang recruitment and gangs in schools without overt militarization, there will always be communities that will be faced with sending their children to school that are essentially environments ripe with risks for gang recruitment.

REFERENCES

Bacevich, A. J. (2005). The real World War IV. *The Wilson Quarterly, 29*(1), 36–61.

Brown, E. (2010). Race, urban governance, and crime control: Creating model cities. *Law & Society Review, 44*(3/4), 769–804. doi:10.1111/j.1540-5893.2010.00422.x PMID:21132958

Caruso, P. (1996). Individuality vs. conformity: The issue behind school uniforms. *National Association of Secondary School Principals (NASSP) Bulletin, 80*, 83–88.

Center for Research on Education Outcomes. (2013). *National charter school study, executive summary.* Stanford University. Retrieved from: http://credo.stanford.edu/documents/NCSS%202013%20 Executive%20Summary.pdf

Collins, R. (1979). *The credentialed society: A historical sociology of education and stratification.* Waltham, MA: Academic Press.

Collins, R. (2009). *Violence: a Micro-sociological Theory.* Princeton, NJ: Princeton University Press.

De La Rue, L., & Espelage. (2014, July). Family and abuse characteristics of gang-involved, pressured-to-join, and non-gang involved girls. *Psychology of Violence,* 253-65.

Del Barco, M. (2011, January 6). L.A.'s homicide rate lowest in four decades. *National Public Radio.*

Elsinger, P. S., & Smith, C. (2000). Globalization and metropolitan well-being in the U.S. *Social Science Quarterly,* (June), 634–644.

Esbensen, F., Osgood, Peterson, Taylor, & Carson. (2013). Short- and long-term outcome results from a multisite evaluation of the G.R.E.A.T. Program. *Criminology and Public Policy, 12*(3), 375-411.

Estrada, J. N., Gilbreath, T. D., Astor, R. A., & Benbenishty, R. (2013). Gang membership of California middle school students: Behaviors and attitudes as mediator of school violence. *Health Education Research, 28*(4), 626–639. doi:10.1093/her/cyt037 PMID:23525778

Forber-Pratt, A., Aragon, S. R., & Espelage, D. L. (2014). The influence of gang presence on victimization in one middle school environment. *Psychology of Violence, 4*(1), 8–20. doi:10.1037/a0031835

Gebo, E., & Sullivan. (2014). A statewide comparison of gang and non-gang youth in public high schools. *Youth Violence and Criminal Justice, 12*(3), 191-208.

Grekul, J., & LaBoucane-Benson. (2008). Aboriginal gangs and their (dis)placement: Contextualizing recruitment, membership, and status. *Canadian Journal of Criminology and Criminal Justice, 5,* 59-82.

Grover, A. R., Jennings, W. G., & Tewksbury, R. (2009). Adolescent male and female gang members' experiences with violent victimization, dating violence, and sexual assault. *American Journal of Criminal Justice, 34*(1-2), 103–115. doi:10.1007/s12103-008-9053-z

Hansen, L., & Morin. (2012). *Survey report, first wave.* South Holyoke Safe Neighborhood Initiative.

Hansen, L., Simpson, & Morin. (2013). *Survey report, Residents and Agencies.* South Holyoke Safe Neighborhood Initiative.

Hansen, L. L. (2005). Girl "crew members doing gender, boy "crew" members doing violence: An ethnographic and network analysis of Maria Hinojosa's New York gangs. *Western Criminology Review, 6*(1), 134–144.

Hansen, L. L. (2011a, June 11). *Recognizing the signs of gang recruitment.* Workshop, Western New England College.

Hansen, L. L. (2011b). *"Baby Steps": Educating educators on the risks of gang recruitment.* Annual Conference, American Society of Criminology, Chicago, IL.

Hernandez, A. (1998). *Peace in the streets: Breaking the cycle of gang violence*. Washington, DC: Child Welfare League of America.

Higgins, G. E., Vito, G. F., & Walsh, W. F. (2008). Searches: An understudied area of racial profiling. *Journal of Ethnicity in Criminal Justice, 6*(1), 23–39. doi:10.1300/J222v06n01_03

Hill, K. G., Lui, & Hawkins. (2001, December). Early precursors of gang membership: A study of Seattle youth. *Office of Juvenile Justice and Delinquency Prevention (OJJDP) Bulletin,* 1-5.

Howell, J. C. (2015). *The history of gangs in the United States: Their origins and transformations.* Lanham, MD: Lexington Books.

Huff, R. C. (1998). Comparing the criminal behavior of youth gangs and at-risk youth. Research brief. Washington, DC: Department of Justice. doi:10.1037/e507882006-001

Katz, C. M., Webb, V. J., Fox, K., & Shaffer, J. N. (2011). Understanding the relationship between violent victimization and gang membership. *Journal of Criminal Justice, 39*(Jan-Feb), 48–59. doi:10.1016/j.jcrimjus.2010.10.004

Katz, M. B. (2007). Why aren't U.S. cities burning? *Dissent, 54*(3), 23–29. doi:10.1353/dss.2007.0069

Klein, M. W., & Maxson, C. (2006). *Street Gang Patterns and Policies*. New York: Oxford University Press, Inc. doi:10.1093/acprof:oso/9780195163445.001.0001

Klein, M. W., Weerman, F. M., & Thornberry, T. P. (2006). Street gang violence in Europe. *European Journal of Criminology, 3*(4), 413–437. doi:10.1177/1477370806067911

Lenzi, M., Sharkey, Vieno, Mayworm, Doughety, & Nylund-Gibson. (n.d.). Adolescent gang involvement: The role of individual, peer, and school factors in a multilevel perspective. *Aggressive Behavior, 41*(4), 386-397.

Merton, R. K. (1957). *Social Theory and Social Structure*. New York: Free Press.

Miller, J. (2000). *Getting into gangs. In One of the Guys: Girls, Gangs, and Gender* (pp. 35–63). New York: Oxford University Press.

Moser, C. (2004). Urban violence and insecurity: An introductory roadmap. *Environment and Urbanization, 16*(3), 3–16. doi:10.1177/095624780401600220

Moser, C., & McIlwaine, C. (2004). *Encounters with Violence in Latin America: Urban Poor Perceptions from Colombia and Guatemala*. London: Routledge.

Moser, C., & Winton, A. (2002). *Violence in the Central American region: towards an integrated framework for violence reduction*. ODI Working Paper No. 171. ODI.

Peterson, D. (2012). Girlfriends, gun-holders, and ghetto-rats? Moving beyond narrow views of girls in gangs. In S. Miller, L. D. Leve, & P. K. Kerig (Eds.), *Delinquent girls: Contexts, relationships, and adaption*. Switzerland: Springer International Publishing. doi:10.1007/978-1-4614-0415-6_5

Peterson, D., Taylor, T. J., & Esbensen, F. (2004). Gang membership and violent victimization. *Justice Quarterly, 21*(4), 793–815. doi:10.1080/07418820400095991

Price, P. (2009). When is a police officer an officer of the law? The status of police officers in schools. *Journal of Criminal Law and Criminology, 99*(2), 541-70.

Roberts, S., Kemp, J., Rathburn, A., Morgan, R. E., & Snyder, T. D. (2013). Indicators of School Crime and Safety: 2013. Bureau of Justice Statistics (BJS) and Institute of Education Sciences, National Center for Education Statistics.

Robinson, P. L., Boscardin, W. J., George, S. M., Teklehaimanot, S., Heslin, K. C., & Bluthenthal, R. N. (2009). The effect of urban street gang densities on small area homicide incidences in a large metropolitan county, 1994-2002. *Journal of Urban Health Bulletin of the New York Academy of Medicine, 86*(4), 511–523.

Sanchez, R. (2000). *My bloody life: The making of a Latin King.* Chicago: Chicago Review Press.

Shihadeh, E. S., & Barranco, R. (2010). Latino employment and black violence: The unintended consequences of U.S. immigration policy. *Social Forces, 88*(3), 1393–1420. doi:10.1353/sof.0.0286

Shihadeh, E. S., & Ousey, G. C. (1998). Industrial restructuring and violence: The link between entry-level jobs, economic deprivation, and Black and White homicide. *Social Forces, 77*(1), 185–207. doi:10.1093/sf/77.1.185

Skiba, R. J., & Peterson. (2000) School discipline at a crossroads: From zero tolerance to early response. *Exceptional Children, 66*(3), 335-47.

Sobel, R. S., & Osoba, B. J. (2009). Youth gangs as pseudo-governments: Implications for violent crime. *Southern Economic Journal, 75*(4), 996–1019.

Stanley, S. M. (1996). School uniforms and safety. *Education and Urban Society, 28*(4), 424–435. doi:10.1177/0013124596028004003

Sutherland, E. H. (1947). *Principles of criminology.* Philadelphia: J.B. Lippincott Co.

Sweatt, L. C., Harding, Knight-Lynn, Rasheed, & Carter. (2002). Talking about the silent fear: Adolescent's experiences of violence in an urban high-rise community. *Adolescence, 37*(145), 109–121. PMID:12003284

Tanioka, I., & Glasier. (1991). School uniforms, routine activities, and social control of delinquency in Japan. *Youth and Society, 23*(1), 50-75.

Wallace, K. (2013). 6-year-old suspended for kissing girl, accused of sexual harassment. *CNN.* Retrieved from: http://www.cnn.com/2013/12/11/living/6-year-old-suspended-kissing-girl/

Wiemann, C. M., Agurcia, C. A., Berenson, A. B., Volk, R. J., & Rickert, V. L. (2000). Pregnant adolescents: Experiences and behaviors associated with physical assault by an intimate partner. *Maternal and Child Health Journal, 4*(2), 93–101. doi:10.1023/A:1009518220331 PMID:10994577

Zamble, E., & Porporino, E. (1988). *Coping behavior and adaptation in prison inmates.* New York: Springer-Verlag. doi:10.1007/978-1-4613-8757-2

ENDNOTES

[1]   In the United States, students who have been expelled from traditional public school are generally educated in alternative high schools.

[2]   Importation Theory was intended to apply to the behavior of prisoners, but is argued here as being generalizable to the delinquency that is brought into schools off of the streets.

Chapter 3
Gang Violence in Schools:
Safety Measures and Their Effectiveness

Sarah E. Daly
Rutgers University – Newark, USA

ABSTRACT

Gang-related violence in schools can have a number of negative effects on the school environment, student achievement, and perceptions of fear. Schools that report a gang presence among students often report higher rates of victimization on school property. In response, many schools have focused on both physical and procedural safety measures to enhance security and prevent violence. However, attempts at maintaining order and ensuring safety often fall short in preventing violence and may actually enhance feelings of fear at schools. As such, schools face the difficult task of addressing violence with effective safety measures while also minimizing and balancing the prison-like feeling that comes with many of the options. This chapter aims to describe the effects of violence in schools and examine a variety of safety measures in terms of cost, effect on perceptions of fear, and effectiveness.

CASE STUDY

In an urban Northeastern public high school, there have been multiple gang-related incidents. Rival gangs have been feuding in the neighborhood, and the violence has carried over into the school with its juvenile, low-level members. More graffiti and tagging has appeared around the school in the bathrooms and on lockers, while increased tension has resulted in fist fights, threats, and general disruption to the school and classroom environment. The school administrators have worked with local police to punish the culprits and prevent further incidents by carrying out "random" locker searchers, staging interventions between students, and monitoring surveillance cameras more closely. Principals have confiscated three knives and two guns in the past month, and they are fearful that more weapons are entering the school. In response, the school board has approved a new zero-tolerance policy that ensures mandatory expulsion for students involved in gang-related violence or those who bring weapons on the property. The students and staff at the school are well aware of the problems, and many fear for their personal safety on a daily basis. Parents and teachers who are concerned are calling for increased security measures

DOI: 10.4018/978-1-4666-9938-0.ch003

such as metal detectors or police officers in school, but administrators and the school board assert that with an already strapped budget, they do not have the financial or staffing resources to carry out these requests.

INTRODUCTION

In the past decade, youth violence in schools has come to the forefront of public and academic attention as a result of horrific displays of violence, most notably at Columbine High School and Sandy Hook Elementary. While tragic and shocking, these shootings may not necessarily serve as an accurate representation of youth violence in schools. School violence can range from the more frequent fist fight or minor altercation to the sensationalized school shooting and mass violence. While the latter is more publicized and documented, the former still has the potential to affect the school environment and have long term consequences for the school, the victims and the perpetrators, teachers, and society at large. More specifically, gang violence in urban schools can disrupt the learning environment, create a dangerous space for students and staff, and intimidate students or lure them into joining gangs. While not all students will be directly affected or victimized by violence in schools, they will all experience the school culture that is shaped by violent activities and fear. This chapter aims to discuss the scope of the problem of both gang-related violence in schools and the effectiveness of safety measures designed to prevent and decrease such violence. While the chapter aims to address many of these measures and outline the effect of violence in schools, it is important that the reader note that the same measures may also be used to address other non-gang issues in school such as general violence or mass violence prevention. However, a school faced with gang-related problems may look to any or all of these to address issues of gang violence for prevention and intervention.

WHY IS IT IMPORTANT TO CRIMINAL JUSTICE?

While some may imagine that seemingly minor violence that occurs in the school realm may be outside of the criminal justice spectrum, these incidents and the school environment in which they occur can and should serve as a strong indicator of the neighborhoods, town, or geographic areas that encompass the larger environment of the children involved. The students and the school itself are a reflection of the town and a microcosm of the people who live in the area. Often, underprivileged, high-crime areas are associated with dangerous, failing schools that neglect to offer their students a safe and secure environment in which they can learn. For this reason, school and gang violence has remained a priority area of research in child and adolescent psychology, school administration and public health, and counseling or social work fields. Yet, it has major implications and ties for criminal justice research as well.

Rather than examining schools solely for their explanatory power of understanding the effects of the larger environment (e.g. community, neighborhood or census tract), a look through an optimistic lens allows researchers, practitioners, and educators to view schools as an opportunity to create long-term change in a given area. If violence, gang membership, and harassment have the potential for negative, life-altering consequences, schools should similarly present the prospect of positive change as well. Changing the face of youth violence in the environment in which they can spend the vast majority of their time can change generations of children in the coming years, thus changing the community and the adults who will likely face the same problems that their parents faced. Strong life lessons learned in schools have the power to carry out into the community and break the cycle of violence and crime on which criminologists and criminal justice scholars focus so many of their studies.

GANGS IN SCHOOLS

As Burnett (1999) notes, "Although many gang members acknowledge the importance of the educational objectives of a school, school is much more important to them as a place for gathering with fellow gang members for socializing and other more violent activities" (2). Researchers, administrators, and educators cannot ignore the presence of gangs and gang violence in schools. The 2011 School Crime Supplement (SCS) to the National Crime Victimization Survey (NCVS) noted that 17.5 percent of students ages 12 through 18 reported a gang presence at school (U.S. Department of Education, 2013). While this may seem like a relatively low percentage that may have minimal effects, Trump (1993) found that students in schools with gangs feel an increased likelihood of becoming victims of violence.

The scope of the problem of juvenile gang membership lies in many areas. One must realize that there exist many difficult, often intertwined problems in defining, identifying, classifying, measuring, and assisting gang-involved juveniles. Only when all relevant parties can agree upon common definitions, policies and systems (that are not only similar across towns, but counties and states as well), can everyone create a multi-agency plan of action. Crimes committed by and against children in schools need to be addressed by a myriad of people. Psychologists, counselors, school administrators, social workers, criminologists, and law and government officials (federal, state, and local) must collaborate in order to create a consistent, effective method of protecting communities and victims of gang-related crimes, lowering crime rates, and reducing the prevalence and influence of gangs throughout the country.

Schools can also contribute to the decision to join a gang or participate in gang activities. If a student fails to succeed academically—thus separating him from peers who may have opportunities to attend college or seek gainful employment—drug sales and delinquent activity present entrepreneurial opportunities for success. Many students in at-risk, low-income areas are inadequately equipped to meet school and teacher expectations when measured with Cohen's (1955) notion of "the middle class measuring rod." When they are unable to achieve success in the classroom and faced with the prospect of legal personal and professional success, these students may choose to subscribe to a delinquent subculture.

Moreover, the "pulls" of gang life can provide the child with a sense of hope, the promise of protection and support, or the prospect of financial gain. Without teacher role models or a belief that a student can succeed, students can feel disjointed within the school system or labeled as a low achiever. This, in conjunction with aggression, desire for belonging, protection, or companionship, and prior delinquency can easily lead a child down a path toward gang life[1].

GANG VS. NON-GANG VIOLENCE

One of the most difficult aspects of understanding violence in schools is parsing out gang-related violence from non-gang related violence. In research studies that have examined violence in schools and gang membership, students are often asked to self-identify, leading to wide ranges of estimates (Estrada, Gilreath, Astory & Benbenishty, 2013). Further complicating the matter, research has found that gang members in schools do not necessarily form their own subset of students. Instead, they are mixed in with a larger population that includes non-gang youth. As Gebo and Sullivan (2014) assert, "gang members, particularly those in public schools, cannot be set apart from others in terms of addressing their risks and needs. They are part of a larger group of high-risk youth with multiple problems…especially given the high probability of both mental health and victimization in this class" (202).

Supporting this notion, Estrada, Gilreath, Astor, & Benbenishty (2013) found that "the direct effects of gang members on school violence perpetration and school victimization were very weak" (635), but when they engage in risk behaviors, they are at increased risk for perpetration of offenses and victimization. Thus, to address these issues (and attempt to indirectly reduce the prospect of gang-related victimization), schools should look to research, policies, and procedures that address the nature of violence and victimization rather than solely examining gang membership as an independent variable.

As such, this chapter will address issues of violence in school in a comprehensive way that is designed to understand the effectiveness of school safety measures. While many may be general in nature, they still attempt to prevent gang-related violence while also trying to create a safer environment for all students and school personnel. This is directly in line with calls from researchers who assert that, "Rather than focusing on gang membership as a separate major issue, schools should spend more energy addressing the risk behaviors and attitudes that are related to school violence perpetration and victimization" (Estrada, Gilreath, Astor, & Benbenishty, 2013, p. 637).

VIOLENCE IN SCHOOLS: THE EFFECTS

Extensive research in a variety of fields has shown that violence in schools can have grave consequences at both the macro and micro levels. Violence can be measured through a variety of different behaviors, including physical violence, delinquency, bullying[2], and weapon carrying (Blosnich & Bossarte, 2011; Johnson, 2009; Salmivalli, Kaukiainen, & Voeten, 2005). Research studies have often examined violence as an independent variable and measured its effects through consequences on physical and social environments (Johnson, Burke, & Gielen, 2011; Allen, 2010; Sprott, 2004; Felson, Liska, South, & McNulty, 1994), perceptions of victimization and safety (Karna, Voeten, Psokiparta, & Salmivalli, 2011; Flaspohler, Elfstrom, Vanderzee, Sink, & Birchmeier, 2009), and responses from teachers and school personnel (Allen, Cornell, Lorek, & Sheras, 2008; Behre, Astor, & Meyer, 2001). Largely, three categories of effects can explain the consequences of violence in school: effects on students, effects on teachers and school personnel, and effects on the school environment.

On Students

Without a doubt, school violence and violent incidents can have short- and long-term effects on the students involved and on other students in the school. Research shows that involvement in and ongoing exposure to violence and has significant effects for all students in the school environment. As Johnson, Burke, & Gielen (2011) note, "Violence in US schools is hindering the educational, psychological, and social development of students" (331). For all students, but especially those who already live in high-risk areas, the school should serve as a safe, protected area for students to learn and grow. Yet, schools and the violence that occurs within them can exacerbate the community effects that violence has on developing children.

Direct Violence

Children who are bullied, harassed, victimized, and/or attacked at school report feelings of lower self-esteem, increase violent acts, depression, frustration, and poorer school attachment (Blosnich & Bossarte, 2011; Lopez & DuBois, 2005; Juvonen, Nishina, & Graham, 2000). Bullying and violence can take a variety of forms including staged fights, humiliation, pushing, shoving, hair pulling, and slapping. As a student reported on a bullying blog, "…kids starting outcasting me. Then came the verbal attacking along with physical. They would punch, kick, throw things and beat me up…Then kids started pushing me into lockers" (Eisenberg, 2012). Clearly, the short- and long-term consequences of direct victimization in schools should send a message about the severity and the seriousness of school violence and bullying. In terms of gang-related violence in schools, gang members may threaten other non-member students or intimidate them in a variety of ways. DeVoe and Kaffenberger (2005) note that "students who reported the presence of street gangs at school were more likely to report being bullied in any way (21 percent) than those who reported that street gangs were not present (13 percent)" (6).

As Burnett (1999) describes, "Both 'willing' and 'unwilling' members are drawn into gangs" (2). Of the thousands of students interviewed for the 1995 School Crime Supplement of the National Crime and Victimization Survey, 50 percent recognized violence as indicating gang presence at school, while 80 percent of the students also recognized time spent with other gang members as indicative of gang presence at school (Howell & Lynch, 2000).

However, engaging in and being the victim of bullying and violence (both gang-related and non-gang related) can have similar negative outcomes. Victims and bullies are not mutually exclusive categories; rather, they may overlap, creating a unique type of "bully-victims" who are at the highest risk for negative psychological, social, and behavioral outcomes (Olweus, 1993). Flaspohler, Elfstrom, Vanderzee, Sink, & Birchmeier (2009) stated that "the experiences of bullying and being bullied have both been linked to later development of negative consequences" (638). Directly engaging in violence or bullying, even at young ages, can predict other troubling life events and behaviors in the future, including gang membership and delinquency. Kupersmidt & Coie (1990) found that among their independent variables, only preadolescent aggression toward peers can be a significant predictor of juvenile delinquency.

Indirect Violence and Exposure

Though many students in schools characterized as being violent will not experience direct victimization, the existence and prevalence of violent incidents can affect those students as well. As Johnson (2009) found in a review of the literature, continued exposure to and observations of violence can affect fear of victimization, fear of attending school, and perceptions of school safety. Despite the lack of direct violence, the potential for violence and the possibility of victimization can lead to a sense of dread and a negative belief about the safety of the school.

On Teachers and School Personnel

Teachers, school administrators, and other school workers may often witness or engage in the school violence. As Sela-Shayovitz (2009) notes, "Teachers and principals encounter on a daily basis violent behaviour at various levels—among students, against property, and between staff members and students" (1061). Like students, continued exposure to violence and the fear of victimization or personal injury at work can negatively affect their personal well-being as well as their professional performance. Galand, Lecocq, & Phillipot (2007) found that "the construct of school violence, including student misbehaviour, perceived violence at school and verbal victimization, is strongly related to teacher report of anxious, depressive and somatic symptoms" (473). Professionally, Johnson (2009) found that "school violence disrupts the working environment for teachers. By having to handle behavioral problems and quell potentially violent situations, teachers cannot devote as much time to instruction" (452).

Furthermore, school administrators, who often spend the majority of their time addressing student misbehavior and reacting to school violence, may feel that little can be done to address issues in need of improvement or to create preventative school policies. The daily struggle of addressing the myriad of problems related to school violence can essentially make school personnel and teachers less effective and lead to a snowballing of ongoing difficulties and an overall decrease in school safety and effectiveness.

Overall, the personal and professional effects of exposure to school violence and decreased perceptions of school violence can contribute to higher teacher turnover and attrition rates. Smith & Smith (2006) found that "attrition itself seemed to play a role in the continued violence (or at least the perception of it) as it stymied school reform efforts that targeted violence" (36). Adding in the cycle of teacher attrition in violence is the quality of teachers who are often employed in low-income urban school districts; naïve, unqualified teachers "are given the most demanding teaching loads with the greatest number of extra duties, and receive few curriculum materials and no mentoring" (Aaronson, 199, p. 335). Combined with fear of victimization, dissatisfaction in protective school factors, and an overwhelming burden on one's professional well-being, the effects of school violence clearly take a negative toll on teachers and school personnel, and therefore affect the students and the school environment.

On the School Environment

Shade (2006) argues that "violence in schools generates fear and distrust that are just as debilitating to the educational process as are the disconnection and despair associated with poverty" (215). For this reason, the school environment should be considered its own entity when examining school violence[3]. Though the environment will be discussed in greater depth later in the paper, one must understand that the general atmosphere and occurrences within the school "[influence] students' academic success indirectly, by impacting students' behaviors" (Johnson, Burke, & Gielen, 2011, p. 331). This macro-level notion of the school environment presents an overarching picture of perceptions of school safety, "the nature of interactions between students and between students and school staff" (Johnson, Burke, & Gielen, 2011, p. 337), and classroom and school culture.

In Johnson's (2009) review of the literature on the school environment, she found that research studies using violence-related as the dependent variable measured the school environment using a variety of constructs including peer relationships; school norms about violence; success in the school environment; school culture; and school disorder. Norms about violence was the most prevalent measure of environment, and her findings stated that "all studies found that school norms against violence were associated with a decrease in student-reported perpetration and victimization" (Johnson, 2009, p. 463). Similarly, Felson, Liska, South, and McNulty (1994) found that "a boy's violence and delinquency are related to the values prevalent in his school, independent of his own values" (168). Thus, the school environment has the potential to shape the beliefs, attitudes, and actions of its students, creating a more urgent need to address school violence in relation to the environment, situations, and context in which they occur.

UNDERSTANDING PERCEPTIONS OF FEAR

While experiencing actual victimization can have a significant negative effect on students (including isolation, depression, frustration, and decreased school attachment), student perceptions can affect can affect the both the school social environment and the school physical environment (Johnson, 2009). Juvonen, Nishina, & Graham (2000) found that perceptions of victimizations affected student achievement, absenteeism, and social adjustment. The importance of understanding student perceptions of fear is highlighted by the inclusion of the School Crime Supplement (SCS) of the National Crime Victimization Survey (NCVS) beginning in 1989. The 2009 report shows that students' perceptions of fear lead them to avoid school/class or specific places inside of the building (DeVoe, Bauer, & Hill, 2012).

Other studies, however, have evaluated the fear of being attacked while at school; traveling to and from campus; perceptions based on previous victimizations; the fear of potential victimization; and the relationship between school safety measures and fear (Alvarez & Bachman, 1997; May & Dunaway, 2000; Mayer & Leone, 1999; Schreck & Miller, 2003). Such research aims to address the effects of student fear on the individual students and the school. Specifically, the research examining the relationship between safety measures and perceptions of fear attempts to unpack the nature of school security and its unintended effects that may actually negatively impact schools and students. Student perceptions of fear can be affected by any number of school safety measures individually or collectively, including metal detectors, school resource officers, identification card policies, surveillance cameras, and stricter discipline policies.

Students are not the only individuals who may experience fear of gangs and victimization while in school. Forber-Pratt, Aragon, & Espelage (2014) utilized qualitative research methods and observed a middle school in an area surrounded by gang activity. Through observations and interviews, they found that administrators and teachers felt helpless while students felt trapped in an unsafe environment. They also noted that gang violence in schools is affected by the long history of gangs and bystander fear. Gang-related incidents were more violent, and fear in school affects the entire school environment.

A simple scan of American newspapers demonstrates the concern about gang activity in major cities such as Chicago or Los Angeles to smaller cities like Camden, New Jersey to suburbs and rural areas. Parents, students, teachers, and administrators are demanding that action be taken in order to protect the learning environment and the schools. In some cases, conflicts from neighborhoods are spilling into the schools and school-related events. In Summerville, South Carolina, "drones, metal detectors, and a SWAT presence were just a few of the security measures taken…at [a] Homecoming game after threats of gang violence" (Mallia, 2014). Additionally, many schools are often aware of threats of gang-related violence toward their students even outside of school. In Maryland, a high school principal communicated that parents not should not send their children to a local theme park because a of a fight reports of a gang fight planned as retaliation that left a 15-year-old student in a coma (Wiggins & Bui, 2014).

FOUNDATIONS IN THEORY

Two main theories emerge as the foundation for safety measures when considering school violence and gang membership: social control and deterrence. First, the school serves as an entity that enforces rules, insists on conformity and obedience, and requires students to act in a specific manner. In addition to teaching academic lessons, schools often strive to teach character lessons, morality, and citizenship. Their role in that sense is to create an environment in which students are encouraged to follow rules and avoid unlawful or violent behavior. Beyond the notion of social bonds that can be forged in school with positive peers and teachers (see Hart & Mueller, 2013), the highly protected and almost militarized school environment also exerts a specific level of formal social control. Much like prison design, schools must consider the visibility of all students and the goals of such control. As Hope (2009) explains, "the keeping of registers, filing of reports, wearing of standardised uniforms, observance of rules, strict use of timetables, regimented examinations and ostentatious punishments can all be seen as fashioning a discourse of control" (896)[4].

Visible safety measures such as metal detectors, surveillance cameras, and police officers or school resource officers also provide general deterrence in the school. By implement highly observable and noticeable measures, school administrators and police aim to prevent gang violence from entering into the school. If presented with the notion of being caught with a gun at a metal detector upon arrival at school, students would be less likely to bring one to school. Similarly, surveillance cameras should not only identify students engaging in violence, but also their mere presence would remind them that they would likely be caught and punished, thus dissuading them from doing so. Yet, for more policy-oriented approaches such as zero tolerance or increased punishment for gang-related infractions, students need to be aware that the policies exist. More specifically, in order for deterrence to be effective, there need to be three main components: severity, certainty, and celerity of punishment. Students in school who may commit a crime must be certain that the punishment will be severe, certain, and swift, which (as in the criminal justice system) may not always be the case. Combined with a psychological understanding of adolescent development and awareness of consequences, deterrence-based school safety measures may not always be effective[5].

As a result, it becomes necessary to evaluate school safety measures, their cost, and their effectiveness individually.

SPECIFIC SCHOOL SAFETY MEASURES AND EFFECTS ON VIOLENCE

In order to prevent gang-related violence in schools, schools and police rely on a number of different methods. There a variety of theoretical and functional justifications for the use of school safety measures, including social control, prevention, intervention, and punishment. The National Institute of Justice (1999) describes school security measures as being most effective when "(1) the opportunities for security infractions should be eliminated or made more difficult to accomplish, (2) the likelihood of being caught must be greatly increased, and (3) consequences must be established and enforced" (1). School security measures can be used to modify situations in schools through target hardening and intervention facilitation (Hope, 2009) while simultaneously creating a culture in which social control is enforced to create a safer environment for students. In terms of punishment, many of these security measures can be used to evaluate and identify student offenders after a violent incident has occurred. Using these goals, the most common specific security measures will be evaluated in terms of benefits and effectiveness, cost (when applicable), and potential unintended consequences on student perceptions of fear in schools[6].

Metal Detectors

In an effort to prevent weapons from entering the premises and offsetting gang-related violence, many schools nationwide have invested in metal detectors. Reports from the past decade estimate that approximately five to fifteen percent of schools utilize metal detectors to discourage and apprehend students who attempt to bring weapons to school (Addington, 2009; Hankin, Herzy & Simon, 2011; Mayer & Leone, 1999; National Institute of Justice, 1999; Robers, Zhang, Truman, & Snyder, 2011).

Cost

Metals detectors, however, can be costly for schools. In addition to the necessary hardware and installation, metal detectors require trained personnel for operation. Hankin, Hertz, & Simon (2011) note that "the Cleveland public school system estimated a cost of $3.7 million to incorporate walk-through metal detectors and X-ray scanners in each of the 111 public schools. This estimate includes 1 detector per 500 students, and the hiring of 50 full-time armed security guards and 150 part-time security guards" (101). With limited resources and funding available for schools and education, the costly installation and use of metals detectors should be justified through effective practices and a reduction in school violence and weapon carrying.

Effectiveness

Metal detectors, while effective in identifying students carrying weapons and serving as a deterrent for those who would, still do not address issues of non-weapon related school violence. Such security measures would be ineffective in preventing fights using fists, clubs, or other non-weapon objects. In addition, Mayer & Leone (1999) found that schools that utilize physical means such as metal detectors indicated a presence of increased school disorder. Similarly, Cheurprakobkit & Bartsch (2005) found that in Texas schools, the presence of metal detectors was correlated with an increase in interpersonal crimes. Conversely, in a more hopeful study, however, a survey of high school students in New York City indicated that students who attended schools with metal detectors were less likely than students in schools without metal detectors to carry weapons in school or in transit to or from school (Ginsberg & Loffredo, 1993). Yet, in an extensive review of the literature from the past fifteen years, Hankin, Hertz, & Simon (2011) found a "mixed, complex, and sometimes contradictory picture of the impact of metal detector use in schools" (104). This could be attributed to a number of limitations, including measurement tactics, research design issues (e.g. Are more disordered schools more likely to use metal detectors or do metal detectors create more disorder?), and a lack of pre- and post-testing when completing evaluations. Most importantly, however, most evaluations of school safety include metal detectors as any number of physical security measures, making the direct effects of metal detectors alone difficult to parse out from other measures (Hankin, Hertz, & Simon, 2011).

Effect on Perceptions of Fear

Mayer & Leone (1999) suggest that certain physical security measures (including metal detectors) that "[create] an unwelcoming almost jail-like, heavily scrutinized environment, may foster the violence and disorder school administrators hope to avoid" (349). Supporting this hypothesis, Hankin, Hertz, & Simon (2011) cite a study in which schools with average level student problems (as reported by principals) had a significant negative association with perceived safety given the presence of metal detectors. Gagnon & Leone (2001) note that "schools should be a nurturing environments promoting children's intellectual and social development" (101). The presence of such overt security measures may affect the perceptions of school as potentially dangerous area necessitating weapons detection, thus leading to perceptions of fear and potential violent victimization.

School Resource/Security Offices

A more human element of physical school safety is the presence of school resource officers (SROs) or security officers in schools. Addington (2009) utilized the SCS from the NCVS and found that in 2005, students surveyed reported security guards or police in 72% of their schools.

Cost

In response to large-scale violence such as Columbine and ongoing victimization in schools, lawmakers, politicians, and administrators have looked to SROs to reduce school violence. Addington (2009) noted that President Clinton allotted $60 million for SROs in schools with other federal programs and organizations providing hundreds of million dollars for security training and law enforcement planning. Schools have options in hiring SROs in that they can hire guards from private organizations or directly hire their own guards who may also be active or retired police or corrections officers. Garcia (2003) found that in school districts included in her survey, "78% used a proprietary model (i.e. guards were employees of the district), and 22% contracted with private security firms" (33).

DeMitchell and Cobb (2003) assert that the cost of security personnel can range from $60,000 to $100,000 for an officer and $15,000 to $30,000 for an aide. Given the significant cost for SROs and the need for multiple officers in larger schools, the effectiveness of SROs in reducing violence and perceptions of fear should be a serious consideration in hiring and retaining them as a valuable part of school safety measures.

Effectiveness

As with metal detectors, the findings on effectiveness of SROs are mixed. In conducting qualitative interviews with students, Bracy (2011) found a variety of opinions about the SROs. Some students reported feeling that the SRO prevented crime, while others felt that school was not dangerous enough to warrant his presence. Others point out that "the officer can't be everywhere in the school all the time to prevent all crimes that might occur on campus" (374). While Mayer & Leone (1999) found that SROs are often associated with more school violence, Jennings, Khey, Maskaly, & Donner (2011) found mixed results of SROs but concluded that they were generally effective in reducing crime and enhancing police-student relations. Little evaluative research has been done, however, and like the research on metal detectors, there are an abundance of research design issues that lead to questions about causality and pre- and post-test issues. More research, however, has focused on the effect of SROs on perceptions of fear and safety in schools.

Effect on Perceptions of Fear

Addington (2009) claims that SROs may actually create a false sense of security in schools through the implementation of a policy that may make students feel better as opposed to actually addressing problem behaviors in schools. However, most research yields positive results about perceptions of effectiveness and safety. Addington (2009) notes studies that find students have a positive view of their SRO and felt comfortable reporting crimes while feeling safe at school. Kupchik & Ellis (2008) found that students who attend schools with SROs had positive appraisals of their security guards, but speculate that these students are accustomed to this security measure as they may have never attended a school without them in their lifetime. Perhaps this is an indication of a generational change in school safety and perceptions of violence. Overall, though, as an independent security measure, SROs seem to be least detrimental to student perceptions of fear.

Surveillance Cameras

Surveillance cameras represent a shift from school safety measures to social control in schools. Not only do they serve to gather evidence, but they also aim to facilitate direct observation and self-surveillance and deter deviancy. Additionally, they may be used for access control to identify visitors or intruders at the school. Hope (2009) found that in eight British schools, CCTV surveillance cameras were installed throughout the school, but no one was assigned to monitor any of them continuously. Rather, they point to the fact the primary function of surveillance cameras may be to alert students to the presence of social control and serve as a form of conduct control, deterrence, and prevention. In Garcia's (2003) study of school security administrators, 90% reported using some type of security cameras in their school.

Cost

There is little research available describing the cost of surveillance camera installation, monitoring, and upkeep, but a report from a Massachusetts high school describes spending $76,000 for 36 cameras in a high school with approximately 1,100 students (Fletcher, 2012). In Napa Valley, the school district paid nearly $3 million to install cameras through the district's eight schools (Dills, 2012). And in Bridgeport, Connecticut, the school district spent $6,000 each for 18 surveillance cameras to monitor the school and the areas in the neighborhoods around the school (Lockhart, 2012). Garcia (2003) noted that school safety administrators paradoxically reported that surveillance cameras "reduced the number of personnel needed; however, the same number argued that cameras increased staffing needs" (43). As with metal detectors, with the costly nature of surveillance cameras, the need for their effectiveness in terms of prevention, deterrence, and social control must be evaluated in order to justify their purchase and use.

Effectiveness

Theoretically, the presence of school surveillance cameras should lead to students monitoring and altering their own behavior through enhanced social control measures. Given the knowledge that their activities and behaviors are being monitored, they should refrain from violent acts knowing that they could be apprehended and punished for their actions. More importantly, though, Garcia (2003) found that in her survey that "cameras and recorders were considered to be the most effective school safety technologies utilized by districts in the sample" (40). Moreover, they found them effective in addressing disordered behavior, drug crimes, and violent crimes through their function as a "visual deterrent" (Garcia, 2003, p. 40). While this study is informative, it provides no evidence that surveillance cameras actually prevent gang-related violence or other problem behavior in schools. There is little other evidence and research that examines the direct effects of security cameras in schools and their effect on actual violence. Cheur-prakobkit & Bartsch (2005) analyzed data from Texas schools and found that a positive correlation between surveillance equipment and both interpersonal and drug crimes; yet, neither relationship was statistically significant, indicating that security cameras provided any significant deterrent or preventative function in the schools surveyed. Hope (2009), however, noted that in order for school security cameras to be a preventative measure against school violence and crimes, students must be aware of their presence. Additionally, he discussed cameras and their importance in collecting evidence. Thus, given the post-facto nature of cameras in this case, they may do little to actually prevent crime. Rather, they may be best suited to apprehend perpetrators of school crimes after they happen.

Effect on Perceptions of Fear

In addition to limited research about the direct effects of cameras on actual school violence, little research is available about the effects of school security cameras and their effect on student perceptions of fear. In qualitative interviews, when asked about how to change anything about school security, a student who had frequently been disciplined suggested, "...more cameras, somebody actually paying attention to surveillance" (Bracy, 2011, p. 379). In this vein, he felt that more cameras and monitoring would improve the school environment, even despite his own misbehavior in school. Amidst the research collected, however, none discussed the potential for positive or negative effects of school cameras on student perceptions of fear.

Increased Teacher Presence in Hallways and Unstructured Areas

While many schools have moved to formal, physical safety measures to prevent victimization, they have also looked to policy changes with preexisting resources. Similar to hot spots in neighborhoods, identifying locations for disorder and violence against students and responding appropriately has been an asset to many school safety administrators. To address concerns about less structured areas, schools have implemented policies in which teachers are asked to monitor students in the hallways between classes and in unstructured locations in school, such as the bus areas before or after school and in the cafeterias. By posting authority figures in high-traffic areas where students are more likely to come into close contact with others and potentially be victimized in a fight or altercation, schools hope that teachers and staff members can be a deterrent to bullying, violence, and general misbehavior.

Effectiveness

Using the SCS to the NCVS, Blosnich & Bossarte (2011) found that only teacher presence in the hallways had a statistically significant effect on victimizations at school. Other school safety measures that were evaluated were identification badges, security guards, security cameras, and a clearly stated code of conduct. Despite the perceived effectiveness of these other measures, none even approached significance, whereas teachers in the hallways had a negative coefficient (in terms of reducing victimization) at the .000 level.

In a related study, Behre, Astor, & Meyer (2001) interviewed teachers about their willingness to intervene in violence-prone contexts. By examining their judgments and reasoning about their roles in school fights, the authors contribute to the body of knowledge by unpacking the teachers' role in violence, which could affect the way they behave when monitoring hallways or intervening in conflicts. As they note, "The ways teachers perceive, judge, and respond to acts of school violence could have implications for school climate, perceptions of school safety and individual students' aggressive behaviors" (Behre, Astor, & Meyer, 2001, p. 132). Through qualitative interviews with teachers, researchers found

a hesitancy to intervene in areas outside of their classrooms. Even those teachers who said they would intervene outside of the classroom viewed this behaviour as 'above and beyond the call of duty' and would not necessarily expect their colleagues to intervene in a similar manner. (Behre, Astor, & Meyer, 2001, p. 135)

Thus, even if teacher presence alone is effective in preventing victimization and student violence, one must question their willingness to intervene and their effectiveness in the event that a violent incident occurs.

Effect on Perceptions of Fear

Again, there is little evidence of the direct effect of teacher presence on perceptions of fear, but Blosnich & Bossarte (2010) suggest "having teachers/adults in the hallways allows for greater cohesion/interaction between students and adults that would facilitate prosocial behaviors" (111). Creating relationships between teachers and students may in fact reduce perceptions of fear if teachers are seen as supportive and concerned. Connors-Burrow et al. (2009) found that students at schools "showed fewer signs of depression when they reported having social support from teachers" (602), perhaps indicating a reduced perception of fear at school. Similarly, Bosworth, Ford, & Hernandaz (2011) found in focus groups that "students often reported feeling unsafe in locations where no adults were present" (197). High teacher visibility appeared to enhance feelings of safety in the school.

Enhanced Punishment Policies

In response to student misbehavior and violence in schools, many districts have created increasingly punitive punishment policies to both deter potential student offenders and adequately address their actions. While some districts have moved to zero-tolerance policies that punish serious offenders with expulsion or mandatory suspension, others have focused on creating clear rules and consequences for violent behaviors. While the cost of expulsion may be high (due to loss of funding for a student who leaves the district), stricter enforcement of rules and consequences bears little cost to districts, so neither program/policy will discuss cost. Rather, the following section will include a brief overview of the rationale for such policies, the research on effectiveness of each policy, and the effect that both can have on school climate and perceptions of fear and safety in school.

Zero-Tolerance Policies

Similar to a *get tough* approach to crime, many schools nationwide have enacted zero-tolerance policies in response to weapons, violence, and bullying. This new wave of punitive punishment in schools may have begun with President Clinton's Gun-Free School Act (GFSA) which mandated "at least a one-year expulsion for students who are caught with a gun at school" (Rice, 2009, p. 559). Rice (2009) also notes potential problems with zero-tolerance policies:

Schools have also sought to control drugs, alcohol, sexual harassment, bullying, teasing, and disrespectfulness through the application of zero tolerance policies; and each of these categories of offense covers vast territory. In this worldview, aspirin appears in the same class as methamphetamine, and mouthwash the same as whiskey. (559)

Given the broad definitions for zero tolerance policies, the logical and theoretical foundation of zero-tolerance policies can be lost amidst the absurd applications of the idea. Moreover, if zero-tolerance policies are implemented in such a way that students are unaware of harsh consequences for any number of violations of rules, the potential preventative and deterrent benefits of such policies are meaningless. Martinez (2009) asserts that school administrators now use the policy to justify suspending students despite the fact that suspensions serve no beneficial purpose for students or schools. She further argues that implementation of this policy focuses on street-level bureaucrats who do not evaluate environmental factors in the application of zero tolerance laws, and instead manipulate and use the policies as they deem appropriate.

Effectiveness

The APA (2008) notes that zero tolerance policies are designed to reduce future problematic behavior. Yet, in a review of the literature, they found that "school suspension in general appears to predict higher future rates of misbehavior and suspension" (854). Moreover, the same review found that zero tolerance school districts appear to have less satisfactory ratings of school climate and misbehavior. If zero tolerance policies are in fact effective, one would expect a decrease in suspensions, deviance, and violence, but there have been no research studies to support this theory. Cheurprakobkit & Bartsch (2005) concluded that "punishment (stricter punishment and zero-tolerance policies…) is ineffective in solving school crime and violence, and should focus more on activities that foster norms against violence, aggression, and bullying" (248). Similarly, Chen's (2008) analysis of school violence data indicated that "higher numbers of penalties [as related to zero tolerance policies] is associated with higher numbers of criminal incidents" (314).

The APA (2008) even suggests implementing a cost-benefit analysis by examining the perceived benefits students from school and the cost to society "in terms of student alienation, dropout, or juvenile incarceration" (858). If the unintended consequences are that much graver than the ill-understood benefits of removal from the school environment, zero-tolerance policies cannot be considered an effective method of addressing student violence in schools.

Moreover, the long-term consequences of removing a troubled or violent student from school may contribute further to the gang problem. If a student who has few academic or professional opportunities is already seeking out gang membership as a place to belong or find comfort, the prospect of a gang would seem like an even better option when expelled from school.

Consistent Enforcement of Clearly Established Rules

The consistent enforcement of clear rules that address violence and student misbehavior in schools is repeated in much of literature and studied extensively. The literature constantly noted the effect that this can have on school climate and thus on student victimization. As D. Gottfredson & DiPietro (2011) assert, "When students recognize the moral authority of adults in the school and internalize school rules as just and fair, they are more likely to abide by them" (70). Such application of a basic notion of legitimacy can affect the school culture and create appropriate behavioral norms. As Felson, Liska, South, & McNulty describe, "If boys are expected to retaliate when provoked, it appears that they are more likely to engage in violence" (170). Thus, a school culture that does not clearly state the consequences for violations of rules (such as fighting, gang-related violence, etc.) will create the perfect breeding ground for violence and victimization. Conversely, if consistent application of rules and consequences creates a school culture in which violent behaviors are not acceptable, violence can be reduced. The rules and regulations, however, should be fair and students should feel as though they can express themselves in order to effectively implement such a policy. Bracy (2011) found that in disciplinary practices "students [can feel] alienated and powerless and disconnected from their school" (381). Additionally, students can feel as they are treated unfairly or that other students are given preferential treatment which would undermine the legitimacy of the rules and consequences.

Effectiveness

Of all of the safety measures that were evaluated in this literature review, the most promising of all was the enforcement of rules (e.g. consistent application of clearly stated consequences for misbheavior). Mayer & Leone (1999) used a construct called System of Law to measure "the understanding that students have of rules and consequences for breaking rules along with their understanding of the nature of and degree to which the system of rules is implemented in the school" (338). They found that compared to other constructs of school safety (including safe building and self-protection), the system of law construct was more effective and led to less disorder, which suggests that "schools should concentrate more on communicating individual responsibility to students" (351).

Johnson (2009) also found that "schools with less violence tend to have students who are aware of school rules and believe that they are fair" (451). In examining the literature, she concluded that all studies included in her metanalysis found that there is a clear negative relationship between norms against violence and student-reported victimization and perpetration. Increased belief in norms and school rules led to less violence.

In another evaluation data from secondary schools, G. Gottfredson et al. (2005) found that "schools in which students report that rules are fair and the discipline is consistently managed experience less disorder, regardless of the type of school and community" (435).

Effect on Perceptions of Fear

If applied appropriately, this method of rule enforcement can lead to decreased levels of school disorder, thus affecting students' perceptions of fear. Conversely, zero tolerance policies which do not reduce school violence, suspensions, or school disorder, can negatively impact students and their experiences at school. Because zero tolerance policies are often applied unfairly or in a way that students do not understand, their impact on perceptions of fear is more than likely ineffective. Moreover, the American Psychological Association (APA) (2008) even noted that unfair zero tolerance practices can lead to students with feelings of "alienation, anxiety, [and rejection]" (855) which can all similarly be consequences of fear in schools. Additionally, the APA (2008) suggests that schools that utilize zero tolerance policies may also engage in profiling, "a method of prospectively identifying students who may be at risk of committing violence or disruption by comparing their profiles to those of others who have engaged in such behavior in the past" (856). If profiled this would clearly affect students negatively and affect their perceptions of fear in schools, not necessarily from other students, but perhaps from school administrators, teachers, or safety officers.

COLLECTIVE EFFECTS OF SCHOOL SAFETY MEASURES

Overall, it appears that many school safety measures are ineffective in addressing matters of school violence and victimization. Moreover, they may even be more detrimental in that they negatively impact students' perceptions of fear and safety in the schools. Heavily policing and militarizing schools or creating a prison-like feel to "protect" students will most likely create a negative environment in which they will feel alienated, untrusted, and more than likely still victimized. Other students in schools felt that security strategies were unnecessary (Bracy, 2011). Most importantly, though, such safety measures may create an atmosphere of fear and low expectations about behavior. Hope (2009) posited, "If students are expected to misbehave, then deviancy may become perceived as a mundane, inevitable, everyday occurrence" (903).

Perhaps the most important point of this chapter is the importance of relationships and people in schools. Rather than focusing on physical features of the school such as cameras or metal detectors to prevent or deter violence, school resources officers and teachers emerged as having positive effects on perceptions of safety in schools. Additionally, the clear communication and application of rules has a distinctly human element that requires active involvement of all school personnel. The research appears to be clear in that the relationships and clear communication with students has a much more beneficial impact on at-risk students and their feelings about safety and victimization at school.

Instead of a quick fix method designed to simply stop or address violence quickly, more individual and personal methods need to be implemented in order to make children feel safer in schools. As Gagnon & Leone (2001) describe, "The evidence suggested that [metal detectors, surveillance cameras, and perimeter fencing] were ineffective in suppressing gang activity and student violence in the schools" (116). Likewise, Mayer & Leone (1999) concluded that reactive, school based policies are simply not effective in solving school violence problems. School administrators and safety officers should look to more humane, interpersonal methods of creating a safe school environment for all students rather than demonizing students and normalizing the militarization of schools that are supposed to foster innocence and learning. Communicating with students is much less costly and more effective than securing the building through physical means.

EFFECTS OF SCHOOL SAFETY MEASURE ON STUDENTS OF COLOR

This chapter would be remiss if it did not discuss the differences in school safety perceptions between students of color and white students when addressing issues of gang-related violence. There has been a long history of educational research that points to students of color, particularly African American students, being disciplined more harshly and more often than non-minority students. Some researchers attribute this to racism of teachers and administrators or general fear of African American students (Bracy, 2011).

The findings appear to be mixed regarding race and perceptions of fear and fairness. In their study, Bachman, Randolph, & Brown (2011) found that security measures did not affect groups of gender and race differently. Metal detectors increased levels of fear for all groups, but security guards only increased levels of fear for white students, but not black students.

While the importance of clearly communicated rules has been proven effective as described earlier, administrators, teachers, and school safety officials should take caution when applying these policies to students of color. Similar to Bachman, Randolph, & Brown (2011), Kupchik & Ellis (2008) found that physical school security measures such as metal detectors and surveillance cameras did not affect perceptions of fear negatively for students of color, but they did find that "African American students perceive less fairness and consistency of school rules and their enforcement than do White students" (549). This is an important element to consider when planning and implementing school policies and disciplinary measures to create a culture of communication and positive behavioral norms.

Lastly, the APA (2008) notes that "African American youth have been found to be two to three times more likely than White youth to be suspended and or expelled for infractions, and such disparities cannot be attributed to differences in socioeconomic status or to racial/ethnic differences in rates of misbehavior" (858). Given this knowledge, one can only conclude that black students would be disproportionately affected by zero tolerance policies. Amidst the myriad of problems with zero tolerance policies, discrimination against students of color should be yet another reason to completely remove such policies from the discourse about school safety measures.

Given the concern about gang membership and violence and the role that the school plays, the notion of alienating already at-risk students using policies that may reflect racism and fear, administrators and research must examine the long-term effects of such punitive measures. If the school essentially becomes "a push" toward gang life, the need for reevaluation and a new remedy is clear.

IMPLICATIONS FOR SCHOOLS

To address the problems caused by youth gangs and gang members in school, efforts must include all parties and be collaborative in nature. In order to prevent and address issues of gang membership and violence, everyone must strive to fill in the missing pieces in the lives of at-risk children. Classroom teachers must understand the effects of violence and fear of violence on all students, while administrators and support personnel need to evaluate best practices for addressing students who may create problems in the school environment. While tactical and physical safety measures may be a symbolic gesture to present the illusion of security, they may also serve as physical reminders of the unsafe nature of the school. Parents, teachers, administrators, and law enforcement must work together to create a safe environment while also address root causes of the issue and focus on prevention programs while consider potential outcomes. Cost-effective prevention strategies may include evidence-based programs such as Gang Resistance Education and Training (GREAT). Early prevention models such as this can provide insight to children who suffer from the pushes and seek out the pulls of gang life.

Even more, community-based efforts have the power to affect more people on a much larger scale. By offering programs that enhance the lives of families and community members (such as programs for incentive-based parenting, GED and educational opportunities, job training, and mentoring), the enticing aspects of gang life may prove unnecessary.

Inter-agency collaboration (though seemingly utopian) serves as a key model for any type of prevention or intervention program for gang-affiliated youth. If police can identify at-risk youth, they can then notify the appropriate agencies that can best assist in seeking out positive alternatives to gang life. The Comprehensive Community-Wide Approach to Gang Prevention, Intervention, and Suppression Program (Spergel & Grossman, 1997), known also as The Little Village Project, calls for collaboration between "police, prosecutors, judges, probation and parole officers, corrections officers, school officials, employers, [and] community-based agency staff." By including all stakeholders within the community, everyone views gang violence and victimization as a shared responsibility. The program aims to prevent children from joining gangs, assisting those who are currently gang affiliated in safely leaving, and then rehabilitating offenders and offering support to victims.

The research and the literature call upon schools to create safer environments by interacting with students and creating positive relationships with students. This more than likely is an unattractive option for schools, as the process to change the school environment, culture, and norms is not one that can occur overnight. It requires participation and buy-in from teachers, administrators, students, communities, and families while demanding consistency and fairness for all students. Though it seems tedious, idealistic, and cumbersome, the long- and short-term effects of a successful transition would be worth the effort.

IMPLICATIONS FOR FUTURE RESEARCH

While there exists a significant amount of research on student perceptions of fear and violence in schools, academics and researchers must examine the effects of school safety measures on gang violence and the school environment. Though certain measures may seem necessary for deterrence and violence-reduction, we still know little about their effectiveness and consequences on teachers, students, and perceptions of fear. In a time when kneejerk reactions are common, especially in response to crimes in which the victims are children, the need for evidence-based practices and research-driven policy is clear. Schools have a responsibility to its students and teachers to take every measure to effectively evaluate the effects of safety practices in a rigorous manner in order to protect students and utilize waning resources in a productive way. They should implement risk assessments, cost-benefit analyses, and survey data from students, parents, and teachers to best understand the wide spectrum of effects that physical school safety measures have on the school environment.

REFERENCES

Aaronson, J. U. (1999). Recruiting, supporting, and retaining new teachers: A retrospective look at programs in the District of Columbia public schools. *The Journal of Negro Education, 68*(3), 335–342. doi:10.2307/2668105

Addington, L. A. (2009). Cops and cameras: Public school security as a policy response in Columbine. *The American Behavioral Scientist, 52*(10), 1426–1446. doi:10.1177/0002764209332556

Addington, L. A., & Yablon, Y. (2011). How safe do students feel at school and while traveling to school?: A comparative look at Israel and the United States. *Journal of American Education, 117*(4), 465–493. doi:10.1086/660755

Allen, K., Cornell, D., Lorek, E., & Sheras, P. (2008). Response of school personnel to student threat assessment training. *School Effectiveness and School Improvement, 19*(3), 319–332. doi:10.1080/09243450802332184

Allen, K. P. (2010). Classroom management, bullying, and teacher practices. *Professional Educator, 34*(1), 1–16.

Alvarez, A., & Bachman, R. (1997). Predicting fear of assault at school and while going to and from school in an adolescent population. *Violence and Victims, 12*(1), 69–86. PMID:9360289

American Psychological Association. (2008). Are zero tolerance policies effective in the schools? An evidentiary review and recommendations. *The American Psychologist, 63*(9), 852–862. doi:10.1037/0003-066X.63.9.852 PMID:19086747

Bachman, R., Randolph, A., & Brown, B. L. (2011). Predicting perceptions of fear at school and going to and from school for African American and White students: The effects of school security measures. *Youth & Society, 43*(2), 705–726. doi:10.1177/0044118X10366674

Beher, W. J., Aston, R. A., & Meyer, H. A. (2001). Elementary- and middle-school teachers' reasoning about intervening in school violence: An examination of violence-prone school subcontexts. *Journal of Moral Education, 30*(2), 131–153. doi:10.1080/03057240120061388

Blosnich, J., & Bossarte, R. (2011). Low-level violence in schools: Is there an association between school safety measures and peer victimization? *The Journal of School Health, 81*(2), 107–113. doi:10.1111/j.1746-1561.2010.00567.x PMID:21223278

Bosworth, K., Ford, L., & Hernandaz, D. (2011). School climate factors contributing to student and faulty perceptions of safety in select Arizona schools. *The Journal of School Health, 81*(4), 194–201. doi:10.1111/j.1746-1561.2010.00579.x PMID:21392011

Bracy, N. L. (2011). Student perceptions of high-security school environments. *Youth & Society, 43*(1), 365–305. doi:10.1177/0044118X10365082

Bradshaw, C. P., Waasdorp, T. E., Goldweber, A., & Johnson, S. L. (2013). Bullies, gangs, drugs, and school: Understanding the overlap and the role of ethnicity and urbanicity. *Journal of Youth and Adolescence, 42*(2), 220–234. doi:10.1007/s10964-012-9863-7 PMID:23180070

Burnett, G. (1999). *Gangs in Schools*. ERIC Digest [Online]. Retrieved from: http://eric-web.tc.columbia.edu/digests/dig99.html

Chen, G. (2008). Communities, students, schools and school crime: A confirmatory study of crime in U.S. high schools. *Urban Education, 43*(3), 301–318. doi:10.1177/0042085907311791

Cheurprakobkit, S., & Bartsch, R. A. (2005). Security measures on school crime in Texas middle and high schools. *Educational Research, 47*(2), 235–250. doi:10.1080/00131880500104366

Cohen, A. K. (1955). *Delinquent boys: The culture of the gang*. New York: Free Press.

Conners-Burrow, N., Johnson, D., Whiteside-Mansell, L., McKelvey, L., & Gargus, R. A. (2009). Adults matter: Protecting children from the negative impacts of bullying. *Psychology in the Schools, 46*(7), 593–604. doi:10.1002/pits.20400

DeMitchell, T. A., & Cobb, C. D. (2003). Policy responses to violence in our schools: An exploration of security as a fundamental value. *B.Y.U. Education and Law Journal*, 459–484.

DeVoe, J., Bauer, L., & Hill, M. (2011). *Student victimization in U.S. schools: Results from the 2009 School Crime Supplement from the National Crime Victimization Survey. U.S. Deparment of Education, National Center for Education Statistics*. Washington, D.C.: U.S. Government Printing Office.

DeVoe, J., & Kaffenberger, S. (2005). *Student reports of bullying: Results from the 2001 School Crime Supplement to the National Crime Victimization Survey* (NCES 2005-310). U.S. Department of Education, National Center for Education Statistics.

Dills, I. (2012, August 16). Napa schools installing security cameras. *Napa Valley Register*. Retrieved from: http://napavalleyregister.com/news/local/napa-schools-installing-security-cameras/article_f7a30be2-e823-11e1-8c5c-001a4bcf887a.html

Eisenberg, A. (2012, 25 April). *Bullying stories: Dealing with bullying from an adult perspective*. [Web log entry.] Retrieved from: bullyinglte.wordpress.com

Estrada, J. N., Gilreath, T. D., Astor, R. A., & Benbenishty, R. (2013). Gang membership of California middle school students: Behaviors and attitudes as mediators of school violence. *Health Education Research, 28*(4), 626–639. doi:10.1093/her/cyt037 PMID:23525778

Felson, R. B., Liska, A. E., South, S. J., & McNulty, T. L. (1994). The subculture of violence and delinquency: Individuals vs. school context factors. *Social Forces, 73*(1), 155–173. doi:10.1093/sf/73.1.155

Flaspohler, P. D., Elfstrom, J. L., Vanderzee, K. L., Sink, H. E., & Birchmeier, Z. (2009). Stand by me: The effects of peer and teacher support in mitigating the impact of bullying on quality of life. *Psychology in the Schools, 46*(7), 636–649. doi:10.1002/pits.20404

Fletcher, S. (2012, February 29). *35 security cameras debut in high school*. Retrieved from: http://www.gloucestertimes.com/local/x952196953/36-security-cameras-debut-in-high-school

Forber-Pratt, A. J., Aragon, S. R., & Espelage, D. L. (2014). The influence of gang presence on victimization in one middle school environment. *Psychology of Violence, 4*(1), 8–20. doi:10.1037/a0031835

Foucault, M. (1995). *Discipline and punish: The birth of the prison*. New York: Vintage Books.

Gagnon, J. C., & Leone, P. E. (2001). Alternative strategies for school violence prevention. *New Directions for Youth Development, 92*(92), 101–125. doi:10.1002/yd.23320019207 PMID:12170826

Galand, B., Lecocq, C., & Philippot, P. (2007). School violence and teacher professional disengagement. *The British Journal of Educational Psychology, 77*(2), 465–477. doi:10.1348/000709906X114571 PMID:17504557

Garcia, C. (2003). School safety technology in America: Currect use and perceived effectiveness. *Criminal Justice Policy Review, 14*(1), 30–54. doi:10.1177/0887403402250716

Ginsberg, C., & Loffredo, L. (1993). Violence-related attitudes and behaviors of high school students--New York City. *Journal of Student Health, 63*(10), 438–439. PMID:8133649

Gottfredson, D. C., & DiPietro, S. M. (2011). School size, social capital, adn student victimization. *Sociology of Education, 84*(1), 69–89. doi:10.1177/0038040710392718

Gottfredson, G. D., Gottfredson, D. C., Payne, A. A., & Gottfredson, N. C. (2005, November 01). (2050). School climate predictors of school disorder: Results from a national study of delinquency prevention in schools. *Journal of Research in Crime and Delinquency, 42*(4), 412–444. doi:10.1177/0022427804271931

Hankin, A., Hertz, M., & Simon, T. (2011). Impacts of metal detector use in schools: Insights from 15 years of research. *The Journal of School Health, 81*(2), 100–106. doi:10.1111/j.1746-1561.2010.00566.x PMID:21223277

Hart, C. O., & Mueller, C. E. (2013). School delinquency and social bond factors: Exploring gendered differences among a national sample of 10th graders. *Psychology in the Schools, 50*(2), 116–133. doi:10.1002/pits.21662

Holmes, S. R., & Brandenburg-Ayres, S. J. (1998). Bullying behavior in school: A predictor of later gang involvement. *Journal of Gang Research, 5*(2), 1–6.

Hope, A. (2009). CCTV, school surveillance and social control. *British Educational Research Journal, 35*(6), 891–907. doi:10.1080/01411920902834233

Howell, J. C. (1998). Youth gangs: An overview. *Juvenile Justice Bulletin.* Retrieved from: https://www.ncjrs.gov/pdffiles/167249.pdf

Howell, J. C., & Lynch, J. P. (2000). Youth gangs in schools. *Juvenile Justice Bulletin.* Retrieved from: https://www.ncjrs.gov/pdffiles1/ojjdp/183015.pdf

Jennings, W. G., Khey, D. N., Maskaly, J., & Donner, C. N. (2011). Evaluating the relationship between law enforcement and school security measures and violent crime in schools. *Journal of Police Crisis Negotiations, 11*(2), 109–124. doi:10.1080/15332586.2011.581511

Johnson, S. L. (2009). Improving the school environment to reduce school violence: A review of the literature. *The Journal of School Health, 79*(10), 451–465. doi:10.1111/j.1746-1561.2009.00435.x PMID:19751307

Johnson, S. L., Burke, J. G., & Gielen, A. C. (2011). Prioritizing the school environment in school violence prevention efforts. *The Journal of School Health, 81*(6), 311–340. doi:10.1111/j.1746-1561.2011.00598.x PMID:21592128

Jones, S., & Lynam, D. R. (2009). In the eye of the impulsive beholder: The interaction between impulsivity and perceived informal social control on offending. *Criminal Justice and Behavior, 36*(3), 307–321. doi:10.1177/0093854808328653

Juvonen, J., Nishina, A., & Graham, S. (2000). Peer harassment, psychological wellbeing, and school adjustment in early adolescence. *Journal of Educational Psychology, 92*, 349–359. doi:10.1037/0022-0663.92.2.349

Kärnä, A., Voeten, M., Poskiparta, E., & Salmivalli, C. (2010). Vulnerable children in varying classroom contexts: Bystanders' behaviors moderate the effects of risk factors on victimization. *Merrill-Palmer Quarterly, 56*(3), 261–282. doi:10.1353/mpq.0.0052

Kupchik, A., & Ellis, N. (2008). School discipline and security: Fair for all students. *Youth & Society, 39*(4), 549–574. doi:10.1177/0044118X07301956

Kuperschmidt, J. B., & Coie, J. D. (1990). Preadolescent peer. *Child Development, 61*, 1350–1362. PMID:2245729

Lockhart, B. (2012, November 17). Cameras watch over Bridgeport chools. *CTPost.com*. Retrieved from: http://www.ctpost.com/local/article/Cameras-watch-over-Bridgeport-schools-4047135.php

Lopez, C., & DuBois, D. L. (2005). Peer victimization and rejection: Investigation of an integrative model of effects on emotional, behavioral, and academic adjustment in early adolescence. *Journal of Clinical Child and Adolescent Psychology, 34*(1), 25–36. doi:10.1207/s15374424jccp3401_3 PMID:15677278

Mallia, R. (2014, October 24). Drones, SWAT surround Summerville game after gang threats. *ABC News 4*. Retrieved from: http://www.abcnews4.com/story/26888495/drones-swat-surround-summerville-game-after-gang-threats

Martinez, S. (2009). A system gone bezerk: How are zero-tolerance policies really affecting schools? *Preventing School Failure, 53*(3), 153–157. doi:10.3200/PSFL.53.3.153-158

Mateu-Galabert, P., & Lune, H. (2003). School violence: The bidirectional conflict flow between neighborhood and school. *City & Community, 2*(4), 353–368. doi:10.1046/j.1535-6841.2003.00060.x

May, D., & Dunaway, G. (2000). Predictors of fear of criminal victimization at school among adolescents. *Sociological Spectrum, 20*(2), 149–168. doi:10.1080/027321700279938

Mayer, M. J., & Leone, P. E. (1999). A structural analysis of school violence and disruption: Implications for creating safer schools. *Education & Treatment of Children, 22*(3), 333–365.

National Institute of Justice. (1999). *The appropriate use of security technology in U.S. schools: A guide for schools and law enforcement agencies*. Washington, DC: National Institude of Justice.

Olweus, D. (1993). *Bullying at school: What we know and what we can do*. Malden, MA: Blackwell Publishing.

Rice, S. (2009). Education for toleration in an era of zero tolerance school policies: A Deweyan analysis. *Educational Studies, 45*(6), 556–571. doi:10.1080/00131940903338308

Robers, S., Kemp, J., Rathbun, A., & Morgan, R. E. (2014). *Indicators of School Crime and Safety: 2013. (NCES 2014-042/NCJ 243299).* Washington, DC: U.S. Department of Justice.

Robers, S., Zhang, J., Truman, J., & Snyder, T. D. (2011). *Indicators of school crime and safety: 2011 (NCES 2011-002/NCJ 230812).* Washington, DC: U.S. Department of Justice.

Romer, D. (2009). Adolescent risk taking, impulsivity, and brain development: Implications for prevention. *Developmental Psychobiology, 52*(3), 263–276. PMID:20175097

Salmivalli, C., Kaukiainen, A., & Voeten, M. (2005). Anti-bullying intervention: Implementation and outcome. *The British Journal of Educational Psychology, 75*(3), 465–487. doi:10.1348/000709905X26011 PMID:16238877

Schreck, C. J., & Miller, J. (2003). Sources of fear of crime at school: What is the relative contribution of disorder, individual characteristics, and school security? *Journal of School Violence, 2*(4), 57–79. doi:10.1300/J202v02n04_04

Sela-Shayovitz, R. (2009). Dealing with school violence: The effect of school violence prevention training on teachers' perceived self-efficacy in dealing with violent events. *Teaching and Teacher Education, 25*(8), 1061–1066. doi:10.1016/j.tate.2009.04.010

Shade, P. (2006). Educating hopes. *Studies in Philosophy and Education, 25*(3), 191–225. doi:10.1007/s11217-005-1251-2

Smith, D. L., & Smith, B. J. (2006). Perception of violence: The views of teachers who left urban schools. *High School Journal, 89*(3), 34–42. doi:10.1353/hsj.2006.0004

Spergel, I. A., & Grossman, S. F. (1997). The Little Village Project: A community approach to the gang problem. *Social Work, 42*(5), 456–470. doi:10.1093/sw/42.5.456 PMID:9311304

Sprott, J. B. (2004). The development of early delinquency: Can classroom and school climates make a difference? *Canadian Journal of Criminology and Criminal Justice, 46*(5), 553–572. doi:10.3138/cjccj.46.5.553

Trump, K. S. (1993). *Youth gangs and schools: The need for intervention and prevention strategies.* Cleveland, OH: Urban Child Research Center.

U.S. Department of Education. (2013). *Student reports of bullying and cyber-bullying: Results from the 2011 School Crime Supplement to the National Crime Victimization Survey. NCES Publication No. 329.* Washington, DC: National Center for Education Statistics.

Wiggins, O., & Bui, L. (2014, October 22). Rumors about possible violence at Fright Fest prompt principal to send warning. *The Washington Post.* Retrieved from: http://www.washingtonpost.com/local/education/rumors-about-possible-violence-at-fright-fest-prompts-principal-to-send-warning/2014/10/22/c4ecfd56-5a23-11e4-bd61-346aee66ba29_story.html

ENDNOTES

[1]   For further information on school-based risk factors, see Howell (1998).

[2]   While it can certainly be gang-related (especially when pressuring teens to join a gang), bullying is such a grand topic with extensive research that it would need its own chapter. Bullying is discussed briefly in this chapter, but it is a serious issue in all schools, and should be considered when evaluating school violence and safety measures. For further reading on bullying, see Bradshaw, Waasdorp, Goldweber, & Johnson, 2013; Holmes & Brandenburg-Ayres, 1998; and DeVoe & Kaffenberger, 2005.

[3]   Other studies have examined school-related safety matters such as traveling to and from school and the effect of neighborhood conflict on school violence. Though the focus of this chapter is on the physical school environment and safety measures taken to protect students and school, the author encourages readers to examine the importance of other school-related activities and effects that may be created by external factors such as neighborhoods. For further reading, see Mateu-Gelabert & Lune (2003) or Addington & Yablon (2011).

[4]   The notion of Foucauldian panopticonism and social control in schools is an extremely interesting topic when considering school safety measures and deterrence. While applied to prisons, many of the same principles apply when exerting social control in schools. For further reading, see Foucault (1995) and Hope (2009).

[5]   The influence of adolescent development should be taken into consideration when addressing issues of deterrence. For example, "it is argued that the [prefrontal cortex] has not yet matured to the point where risks can be adequately assessed and control over risk taking can be sufficiently exerted to avoid unhealthy outcomes" (Romer, 2009, p. 264). Additionally, Jones and Lynam (2009) found that lack of premeditation (a conceptualization of impulsivity) was strongly related to offending among young adults who perceived their neighborhoods as lacking in informal social control. As such, it can be concluded that a number of factors should be considered when examining the function and effectiveness of deterrence measures.

[6]   This safety measures should be considered as most common for middle and high schools. As, Kemp, Rathbun, and Morgan (2013) found, "primary schools recorded lower percentages of these types of crimes [violent crime, serious violent crime, theft, and other incidents] than middle schools and high schools" (28). As such, it can be concluded that the focus on violent school crimes and related safety measures should lie in those schools with older adolescents.

Chapter 4
The Reality and Myth of Weapons and Violence in Gang Life

Timothy R. Lauger
Niagara University, USA

ABSTRACT

Weapons and violence are both real and mythic elements of gang life. Though violence is a real element of gang life, public perceptions about gangs may be exaggerated, invoking the idea of dangerous youth roaming the streets. The image of violent gang members is also embraced and used by youth on the streets to navigate their social world. Gang members often create personal and group-based myths by exaggerating their use of weapons and violence. This chapter examines the division between myth and reality in gang life. It reviews research to establish that weapons and violence are real elements of gang members' lives throughout the world. It further explores how myths emerge among gang members who have ample motivation for fictionalizing violence and weapons use. This chapter relies on the social psychological ideas of social constructionism, interpretive socialization, and identity to explain the existence of myths in gang life.

BACKGROUND

At approximately 9:30 p.m. on July 17, 2010, during a large public event in downtown Indianapolis, a seventeen-year-old gang member affiliated with the Ratchet Boyz fired multiple shots on a crowded street. He wounded eight individuals who were all between the ages of ten and eighteen. Local news teams covering the event captured the sound of gunshots and the ensuing chaos for the public to view during the nightly newscast. Media outlets also reported that witnesses observed gang-related clothing and heard people shout the name of a rival gang before the perpetrator fired the gun. Police revealed the shooting stemmed from a conflict between two local street gangs. Officers found nine .40 caliber cartridges at the scene. A search of the shooter's home found a box of eight unused cartridges that matched those at the scene and officers found another cartridge on the shooter at the time of arrest (State v. Patton, 2010).

DOI: 10.4018/978-1-4666-9938-0.ch004

On July 23, 2011, at about 4:30 in the afternoon, a few gang members in the Seattle suburb of Kent, WA shot twelve individuals at a low-rider car show/concert held in a strip mall parking lot. Court documents indicate a rapper performing at the car show encouraged attenders to proclaim their gang affiliations. Members of the Little Valley Lokates, Varrios Locos, and Playboy Surenos were in attendance. The latter two gangs were rivals and a confrontation between the groups quickly ensued. Shortly before the shooting, witnesses at another car show a few miles away noticed members of the Surenos gang quickly drive off in three cars. They arrived at the strip mall a few minutes later. During this time a member of the Varrios Locos began punching a member of the Surenos. One of the cars that had just arrived circled the lot, opened fire, and fled the scene. Two individuals exited another car, approached on foot, shot into the crowd, and returned to their car leaving a chaotic scene behind. Police found seventeen shell casings from five different guns at the scene. About eight hours later, in an apparent retaliation, a member of the Surenos gang was shot in the shoulder at his apartment by a .45 caliber handgun that was also fired one time during the earlier incident. The ensuing investigation led police to confiscate multiple .9mm handguns, a .380 caliber handgun, and a .223 rifle (State v. Moreno et al., 2011).

INTRODUCTION

Weapons and violence are both real and mythic elements of gang life. High profile and widely reported incidents of gun violence, like those from Indianapolis and Seattle, influence perceptions about gangs and gang violence. Yet such stories rarely include information that places these incidents within the context of crime trends over time, the nature and prevalence of gang violence, and the frequency of violence in the daily lives of gang members. Public perceptions about gangs may be skewed or exaggerated, raising fears about the prevalence of dangerous youth roaming the streets. The image of gun-toting, violent gang members is not just created by outsiders. It is also embraced and used by youth on the streets to navigate their social world. When gang members interact with peers, they often create personal and group-based myths by exaggerating their willingness and ability to use weapons and violence. The division between myth and reality is sometimes hard to discern in gang life.

To argue that weapons and violence become part of a fictional, alternative reality about street gangs is not to deny their presence in gang members' lives. It does force one to carefully examine how reality can become distorted to influence both perceptions and behaviors. Hacking (1999) makes the important distinction between an object, which is an indisputable element of reality, and the ideas people have about an object. Ideas about objects (or events) can become alternative and influential forms of reality. The shootings in Indianapolis and Seattle are objects of gun violence grounded in real events. They accounted for twenty victims, multiple shooters, and numerous guns. No one would argue the wounds suffered by victims were anything less than real. These events are, however, connected to exaggerated ideas about gang violence that can fuel public fear. They can also be used by members of those gangs to develop group-based myths about violence that influences their status in the streets. This chapter argues that weapons and violence are prominent features of gang life, yet social processes in and outside of gang life produce powerful myths about gangs. It also relies on social constructionism, interpretive socialization, and the concept of identity to explain the existence of myths in gang life.

THE REALITY OF WEAPONS AND VIOLENCE IN GANG LIFE

To identify this gap between myth and reality, researchers must try to measure the reality of violence and weapons in gang life. They strive to accurately account for gang member participation in real events by carefully measuring gang membership, weapons carrying, and participation in violence. What researchers measure and observe becomes part of an empirical reality, which, in ideal circumstances, resembles actual reality (Sayer, 1999). For example, multiple studies have found that asking individuals to self-report gang membership is a viable approach for identifying gang members (Decker, Pyrooz, Sweeten, & Moule, 2014; Esbensen, Winfree, Ne, & Taylor, 2001). This gives researchers confidence that their methods measure part of social reality and provide useful insights about gangs and gang members. An abundance of research in the United States, and a growing body of research in other countries, specifically in Great Britain, finds that weapons are real elements of gang life.

Gangs, Weapons, and Violence in the United States

The majority of careful research in multiple cities throughout the United States finds that self-reported gang members also report unusually high levels of violence and gun carrying. (Battin, Hill, Abbott, Catalano, & Hawkins, 1998; Bjerregaard & Lizotte, 1995, Esbensen & Weerman, 2005; Thornberry, Krohn, Lizotte, Smith, & Tobin, 2003). According to a study using data from eleven cities, 76 percent of gang members in eighth grade have hidden a weapon and 27 percent of gang members have shot at someone in their lifetime (Esbensen & Lynskey, 2001). Gang members are also more prone to handling weapons than their peers. Thornberry and colleagues (2003) find gang members in Rochester, NY to be 7-to-12 times more likely to carry guns than their non-gang counterparts. This research indicates that guns and violence are real fixtures of gang life in America.

Although discerning the extent to which gang members are responsible for weapons-related violence throughout the country is challenging, as accurate data is difficult to attain (Harrell, 2005), studies indicate gangs can account for a high percentage of gun violence within some cities. Gang members represented 1 percent of the population in Lowell, MA but were the known offenders in 46 percent of gun-aggravated assaults and 75 percent of murders (Braga, Pierce, McDevitt, Bond, & Cronin, 2008). These findings do not always translate to other cities. Gang-related murders accounted for 40-42 percent of murders in Los Angeles and Long Beach, CA, but only 22 percent in San Antonio, TX and 10 percent in Oakland, CA and Newark, NJ (McDaniel, Egley, & Logan, 2014). Despite these disparate findings, gang-related homicides in all of the cities were more likely to involve a gun. Ninety-two to 96 percent of gang-related homicides involved a firearm, whereas guns were used in 57-86 percent of non-gang homicides (McDaniel et al., 2014). Guns remain prominent in gang-related murders even when such murders are not common.

Gangs, Weapons, and Violence across the World

There is a growing body of research that measures the association between gangs, weapons, and violence throughout the world. Research in Singapore, the United Kingdom, Germany, The Netherlands, and China also indicates that gang members are more heavily involved in violence and are more likely to carry weapons than nongang members (Ang, Huan, Chua, & Lim, 2012; Bennett & Holloway, 2004; Chu, Daffern, Thomas, & Lim, 2012; Esbensen & Weerman, 2005; Huizinga & Schumann, 2001; Klein, Weerman, & Thornberry, 2006; Pyrooz & Decker, 2013). Gang members surveyed in Russia are almost two times more likely than nongang peers to carry weapons and more than three-and-a-half times more likely to attack someone with a weapon (see Klein et al., 2006). Similar disparities in the handling and use of weapons have also been found in Singapore and England (Bennett & Holloway, 2004; Chu et al., 2012). This trend is not just an American phenomenon.

Despite such consistency in research findings, the type of weapons commonly used in violent events varies by region and country. According to the United Nations (2011), guns are used more often during violent encounters in the United States, Central America, South America, and select African countries than they are in other parts of the world. They are used in 71 percent of all homicides in the Americas but are used in only 21 percent of homicides in European countries. However, knives or other sharp objects account for 36 percent of homicides in European countries but only 16 percent of homicides in the Americas (United Nations, 2011). The general findings in gang research mirror these worldwide trends. Guns have a strong presence in the lives of American gang members (Bjerregaard & Lizotte, 1995; Decker & Van Winkle, 1996), but they are not as prominent in European gangs (Klein et al., 2006).

Research in Britain reveals that knives have a pronounced role on British streets, but most youth do not carry knives or carry them sparingly and do not intend to use them during an act of violence. One study estimated that only 4 percent of youth carried a knife specifically for protection, to commit a crime, or to use during a fight (Eades, C., Brimshaw, R., Silvestri, A., & Solomon, E., 2011). Gang members seem to carry knives more frequently. In Scotland Gang members were three times more likely than their nongang peers to carry a knife (McVie, 2010). Over 60 percent of surveyed gang members in London reported carrying a knife at least once during an offense (Golding, McClory, & Lockhart, 2008). Densely (2013) reported that 28 of the 69 London gang members included in his study had been stabbed, and stories about knife violence are well represented throughout his data. Like gun carrying in the United States, knife carrying may be relatively common among gang members in Britain.

THE MYTH OF WEAPONS AND VIOLENCE IN GANG LIFE

Although weapons have a real presence in gang members' lives, the idea of weapons is also important for how outsiders perceive gang members, how gang members present themselves to their peers, and how peers view other gang members. Incidents like those in Indianapolis and Seattle can create localized myths about the extent and nature of gang life in both cities. Gang members can also use these incidents to develop group lore and increase their stature on the street. Myths are exaggerated or distorted counter realities that are widely embraced and disseminated within and outside of gang life. They can be born out of ignorance, misinformation, political agendas, and/or developed for self-serving purposes. The construction of myths about gangs and violence can occur among any interested parties, ranging from policy makers to gang members themselves.

Mythmaking among Gang Outsiders

Scholars from varying backgrounds have bemoaned a tendency among criminal justice practitioners and the general public to distort and misunderstand street gangs. Most researchers identify a gap between perception and reality about street gangs while also advocating that research should have a more prominent role in informing policy makers and the public about gangs. Klein and Maxson (2006) argue that inaccurate conventional wisdom about gangs often guides public policy. Howell (2007) identified numerous widely accepted myths about gangs that contradict research but influence public policy. These scholars challenge beliefs that street gangs are highly organized, entrepreneurial entities that purposely migrate to set up gang franchises in other cities. They accept that gang members are more likely to carry weapons and engage in violence.

Other scholars embrace a more radical stance by arguing that myths about gangs are disseminated not only by policy makers and the general public, but also by researchers who accept an exaggerated notion of the violent gang. Gangs are "folk devils," demonized and unfairly blamed for the evils plaguing urban areas (Duran, 2013; Hallsworth, 2013; Hallsworth & Young, 2008). According to Katz and Jackson-Jacobs (2004), even the idea that gangs exist is a myth and perceptions of the connection between gangs and violence may be caused by flawed research methods. This position has led to a vibrant debate among British scholars about the extent to which gang members are involved in riots and knife violence. Some scholars deny gang involvement in these problems and claim media and public officials have cultivated myths to suggest otherwise (Hallsworth, 2013). Critics of these denials respond that political ideology and an agenda to minimize the relationship between gangs and crime cause some scholars to ignore the reality of the gang problem (Pitts, 2012). The distinction between myth and reality can create disagreements even when trying to assess current problems.

Research on Mythmaking in the Media and Criminal Justice Organizations

Research provides some evidence that perceptions among gang outsiders exaggerate the prevalence of gangs and their role in local crime. Studies in Honolulu, HI and Las Vegas, NV found dramatic increases in gang-related news stories even though juvenile crime and gang related crime remained stable or increased at a much lower rate than the attention it received (McCorkle & Meithe, 1998; Perrone & Chesney-Lind, 1997). Duran (2013) argued that public hysteria in both Denver, CO and Ogden, UT led official to overestimate the role of gang members in local crime, utilize aggressive suppression-based police tactics, and mislabel of many Latino youth as gang members. However, studies in other cities have found that public officials estimate local gang problems to be less serious than what gang members and local youth report (St. Cyr, 2003; Decker & Kempf-Leonard, 1991). Youths in the streets may actually perceive the gang problem to be more severe than public officials.

Scholars have historically questioned the accuracy of police records and perceptions about street gangs (Klein, 1995). Inconsistent definitions of "street gang" produce differences in how police record gang members and gang activity, which creates challenges when using police data for research (Maxson & Klein, 1990). Studies in the United States and England identify how errors in record keeping cause police to overestimate the number of gang members in communities (Fraser & Atkinson, 2014; Meehan, 2000). Some researchers also suggest that police generate myths by altering their records and exaggerating the gang presence in their communities to receive more funding for gang control programs, (Duran, 2013; Fraser & Atkinson, 2014; Zatz, 1987). Not all studies are negative. Gang lists from the gang intelligence unit and probation offices in Mesa, AR accurately identified crime prone youth and were useful to the police (Katz, Web, & Shaeffer, 2000). Other researchers are beginning to suggest police records of gang-related homicides are relatively accurate (Decker & Pyrooz, 2010). Katz (2001) also demonstrated how one department in the Midwest created a gang unit in response to expectations of some community members. Local perceptions still influenced police actions, but they were not the byproduct of efforts to create and take advantage of myths about gangs.

Mythmaking within the Gang

Exaggerated ideas about gangs, weapons, and violence are not limited to the public or policy makers. Gang members exaggerate their willingness and ability to use weapons and engage in extreme violence, which perpetuates a false reality within their peer environment. Gang members are notorious for talking about violence more often than they engage in violence (Klein, 1971; 2005). They also embellish violent events so that the gap between what is real and what is presented to others can, at times, be substantial (Lauger, 2014). Street gangs operate in a social environment that emphasizes violence as means for building respect and authenticating one's rightful place among peers (Anderson, 1999; Matsueda, Melde, Taylor, Freng, & Esbensen, 2013). Thus gang members have ample motivation for fictionalizing violence and weapons use. Real acts of violence occur and contribute to the reputation of an individual or group, but exaggerated accounts can further enhance reputations. Carefully constructed myths that are accepted by peers can become powerful realities in the lives of gang members.

The Social Setting of Gang Members

Gang members occupy a unique and influential social setting within their local community. Harding (2014) describes the gang environment in London as a social field that establishes rules and behavioral expectations for how to negotiate interpersonal conduct. This environment operates like a casino. Gang members must compete with peers to accumulate street capital, which consists of cultural knowledge, social connections, and status. Street capital is similar to casino chips that can be won, lost, or traded during elaborate social contests with other players in the competitive game of the streets. Gang members are players in this system and must compete with others to increase social and economic power. Strategies ranging from gossiping about peers, to manipulating information, to developing tough public personas generate advantage in this environment (Harding, 2014).

Violence is another tool that allows gang members to gain or maintain street capital within this competitive social arena. Research in the United States and Britain indicates that violence allows individuals to negotiate interpersonal relationships through the establishment of reputations that merit respect among peers (Anderson, 1999; Densely, 2013; Lauger, 2012; Harding, 2014; Stretesky & Pogrebin, 2007). Well-known reputations for violence demand widespread respect, which allows individuals or groups to increase their influence on the streets (Lauger, 2012). Such reputations increase access to social and economic opportunities while also generating a large number of deferential peers. Individuals lacking the necessary social capital to compete struggle to navigate a potentially violent social world. Individuals seeking to build reputations may target weaker peers through violent victimization or intimidation (Anderson, 1999; Jones, 2010). The consequences for losing in the competitive social environment of street life can be severe.

Social Performance and the Added Pressure to "Do Gang"

Public interactions within street life are opportunities to build street capital through image-enhancing performances that communicate one's toughness and public identity to peers (Anderson, 1999). Developing such an image can involve wearing expensive, desirable cloths and jewelry, embracing physical mannerisms that communicate toughness to observers, and talking loudly in public (e.g. Anderson, 1990). For gang members it can also include wearing gang apparel. Public settings also allow individuals to challenge peers with threats of violence. Confrontations force a targeted individual to either respond aggressively or back down and appear weak to peers. Routine interactions can transform into contests that enhance or diminish reputations. Gang members have acknowledged, for example, the power of slapping a person in a public setting. A public slap takes away the manhood of the victim. It also communicates to peers the aggressor is willing to humiliate others in public without fear of reprisal, which elevates his or her status on streets (see Lauger, 2012, 2014). Not all contentious interactions in the streets produce dramatic changes in personal status (Garot, 2009), but all interactions have the potential to enhance or diminish a person's reputation.

The social pressures of street life also influence nongang members who are similarly concerned with developing reputations to increase their respect and street capital (Anderson, 1999). Yet, Matsueda and colleagues (2013) find that gang members in seven cities report stronger adherence to the code of the street and are more likely than their nongang peers to associate violence with respect. These researchers contend gangs provide a unique social setting that alters or intensifies members' attitudes and beliefs. According to Lauger (2012), gang members face a crisis of legitimacy. Peers in their social setting often dismiss or challenge the authenticity of membership claims, and individuals must prove to peers that they are real gang members. They face an added pressure to "do gang," or perform according to the expectation that gang members are capable of violence. Failure to perform properly causes peers to reject or dismiss an individual as a wannabe, which substantially reduces street capital and undermines credibility in the streets. Developing a well-known reputation for violence alleviates this problem.

The Symbolic Value of Weapons

Within this cultural setting, weapons have practical and symbolic significance for accumulating street capital. Weapons inflict serious injury. They also signify a person's fondness for violence and authenticate masculinity or another desired street identity (Kubrin, 2005). Wilkinson (2001) argues street life involves a hierarchy of identities and individuals labeled as "crazy," "wild," or "killers" are considered to be in elite standing among peers and granted a level of respect that is difficult to attain. Such reputations are attained through extreme acts of violence, and using a gun enhances public performances. Gang members have also reported that handling a gun creates a sense of power and bolsters street reputations (Stretesky & Pogrebin, 2007). This effect also occurs in situations that do not involve a direct conflict or threat. Gang members frequently use the Internet to post pictures or videos of themselves holding guns. They are apparently more concerned with maintaining a proper image to peers than they are with the prospect that police also view the images. Even without being used, guns can send a message to peers and enhance status on the streets.

Research on knife carrying and violence in Britain also reveals how the symbolic power of knives contributes to their role in the streets. Some youth claim to carry knives only for protection, but others carry them to gain respect (Palansinski, 2013; Palansinski & Riggs, 2012). The small percentages of London gang members who are willing to stab another person achieve the elevated status of being a "hyped cat" (Densely, 2013, p. 86). Stabbing another person dramatically increases a gang member's street capital through the development of a violent reputation (Harding, 2014). Gang members accumulate street capital more efficiently when stab wounds are potentially fatal rather than just injurious (Harding,

2014). Peers observe these acts of violence and become aware of a person's proclivity for violence. The symbolic role of knives in Britain is similar to that of guns in the United States.

Fictional Weapons and Violence in Gang Life

Not all violence is real, as gang members often develop reputations based on a mixture of real and fictitious exploits. Klein (1971) argued that violence is less of a prominent way of life and more of an established myth system that permeates group life. Gang members commonly talk about violence and tell personal stories about violent encounters, but actual violence occurs infrequently. Much of gang life is mundane (Decker & Van Winkle, 1996; Lauger, 2012). When talking with peers, however, gang members exaggerate the role of weapons and the intensity of violence used during conflicts with other groups. They embellish their roles in violent events by incorporating extreme and unrealistic details into personal stories of violence (Lauger, 2014). If peers accept these accounts, they enhance the gang's reputation by reinforcing members' willingness and ability to engage in extreme gun violence. Even fictionalized violence has real consequences for gang members.

Fictionalized accounts of weapons and violence proliferate in a peer environment characterized by complex and overlapping social relationships that transmit information to a broad audience. Observers of and participants in violence communicate the details of these events to people who are unfamiliar with what actually happened. Storytellers alter the events in a self-serving way to either appear favorably to the listening audience or diminish the contributions of an adversary (Shuman, 1986). They also tell stories that become part of the gang's lore. This contributes to the establishment of a group identity, which is then presented to gang outsiders. Each person listening to the story is a potential transmitter of information that can further disseminate and reinforce a gang member's or gang's reputation. These fictionalized stories about weapons and violence become real if the broader audience of peers accepts them as such. In the pursuit of street capital, the fictitious use of weapons can be just as effective for building a reputation as the actual use of weapons. However, if peers view these accounts to be false, they will dismiss the individual as a fake gang member, which will lead to a reduction in street capital and, possibly, future victimization.

The social environment of gang members is saturated with a blend of real and fictitious accounts about the use of weapons and violence. Discerning where reality ends and myth begins is a challenge for both researchers and gang members. To ensure that data accurately represents reality, researchers must determine if stories of violence are factual retellings or exaggerated, even fictitious accounts. Gang members must assess if the reputations of their peers are based on fallacies, exaggerations, or real events. As they engage other peers and other gangs, this assessment influences how they negotiate their pursuit of street capital. Gang members threaten adversaries assuming they are unwilling to use extreme violence. They develop reputations through their exaggerated stories of violence believing that peers will not see them as false. They gamble to increase their street capital and sometimes pay with their lives.

SOCIAL PSYCHOLOGICAL PERSPECTIVES

Identifying the existence of myths within gang life provides researchers with an opportunity to examine how group life contributes to the social realities of gang members. Scholars have both argued that examining group processes is integral to understanding gang life and developed numerous ideas about the process of socialization within gangs (e.g. Goldman, Giles, & Hogg, 2014; Klein & Maxson, 2006; Vigil, 1991; Wood, 2014). The remainder of this chapter will briefly cover three social psychological ideas that help explain the coexistence of myth and reality. *Social constructionism* examines the creation and consequences of meaning within social life. It helps explain how the meanings of real objects and events can change to become powerful counter realities. *Interpretive socialization* provides insight into how social interactions can amend and create meaning through routine communications. Gang members negotiate the meaning of violence and exaggerate their role in violence events during routine conversations with peers. *Identity* allows scholars to examine how one's sense of self is connected to group life and contributes to social performances. Exaggerating one's capacity for violence may be a performance linked and individual's temporary identity as a gang member.

Social Constructionism

Social constructionism questions the reality of objects and events in everyday life. People encounter and respond to meaning rather than established, nonnegotiable elements of reality. These meanings arise and become accepted through social processes (Searle, 1995; Smith, 2010). Searle (2006), for example, argues that the object of money has no inherent value beyond the meaning society has attached to it. Yet this meaning is incredibly powerful for inducing behavior, and the idea of money is more important than the object representing it. Similarly, the meaning given to a collection of people can become more important than the actual characteristics of those people. "Street gang" is a meaningful label often connected to crime, violence, and danger. Even when such conduct does not adequately describe a collection of individuals, the label of gang invokes meaning that becomes more prominent than the actual behavior of the group. Outsiders may mislabel a group as a gang and treat them unfairly according to the label. Or, a group may purposely cultivate a fictional image consistent with a gang label, which appeals to others in their immediate social setting. These social constructions become part of social reality even if they have little to no foundation in actual events.

Maintaining Reality within the Constructionist Perspective

Although constructionist positions differ (Smith, 2010), many constructionists maintain that aspects of reality exist independent of human awareness (Hacking, 1999; Luckman, 2008; Searle, 1995; Smith, 2010). Not everything is a social construction. A mountain exists even if we are not aware of it. This is part of the natural world (Searle, 1995). People create other elements of reality, like guns and knives, but our knowledge of them clearly indicates they are real (Searle, 1995). One cannot reasonably argue a gun is a window. Similarly, the shootings in Indianapolis and Seattle involved real guns, actual bullets, and inflicted serious harm on victims. People cannot dispute the factual foundations of these incidents. Ideas about weapons or violence may distort reality and become engrained in society, but these objects and events are firmly grounded in reality.

Other facets of reality are more complex because they do not produce widespread agreement about their meaning (Searle, 1995). Knowledge is based on impressions that are heavily influenced by prior experiences and socialization (Luckman, 2008). Constructionists must be careful to distinguish clear and agreed upon elements of reality from those that are more uncertain (Smith, 2010). Sometimes the distinction between the two is challenging. For example, the label of "killer" may initially seem like a clear description of someone who has killed. The label merits further description because someone may be a killer of deer, mosquitos, dreams, or people. Even when "killer" is applied only to individuals who kill another person, it can still mean different things to different people. In one setting it may invoke strong appraisals of moral disgust in the murderous nature of a person but produce admiration in another setting. The label of killer in street life is reserved for high status individuals who have demonstrated a unique fondness for violence and the use of weapons (Wilkinson, 2001). This varies from most other social settings. The idea of a killer is a social construction even when the object of the killer (one who kills another person) is an accurate description of real events.

Constructionism in Everyday Life

Constructionists often question the reality of social problems and suggest public concerns reflect fictional or exaggerated evils (Hacking, 1999). Scholarly arguments questioning the severity of the "gang problem" typically disagree with the meaning of gang and reject how media and public officials present the idea of gangs to the public. Such disagreement merits a closer examination into the possible division between myth and reality. Denying the influence of either real or fictionalized violence will only lead to a limited understanding of issue. Yet, constructionist ideas need not be limited to examining how media outlets and public officials create exaggerated or fictionalized realities, they can also be applied to the development of meaning on the streets and within gangs. Gang members actively make sense of their social worlds. They use, alter, and even create meaning during the day-to-day interactions with peers. They can also exaggerate the prevalence and intensity of violence in their lives.

Without careful consideration of how social processes produce meaning, constructionist arguments lose potency for explaining social life (Hacking, 1999; Hollander & Gordon, 2006; Smith, 2010). The construction of reality occurs daily, as people apply categories to what they observe and then attach symbolic meanings to them (Hollander & Gordon, 2006). Individuals in the streets use meaningful terms like killer, wannabe, and/or gang member to describe people in their social environment (Wilkinson, 2001; Lauger, 2012). They then give these labels meaning by explaining them to peers or incorporating them into stories (Hollander & Gordon, 2006; Lauger, 2014). They also connect these meanings to positive and negative statuses and emotions (Hollander & Gordon, 2006). Even the boundary between "real" gang members and "wannabes" can be a social construction partially molded by member's reputation for violence (Lauger, 2012). As peers interact, their understanding of meaning in social life forms so that aspects of social reality varies and, at times, reflects myths rather than actuality.

Public Violence, Meaning, and Alternate Realities

The shootings in Indianapolis and Seattle can mean different things to different groups, even if everyone can agree about the facts of the cases. Concerned citizens and criminal justice officials may apply labels like "thug," "killer," and "gang member" to an incident. They can use the facts of the case without any context about the nature and prevalence of gangs or violence to create a reality that may or may not accurately reflect the nature of the problem. This happens during conversations at social or workplace gatherings. Local news coverage and criminal justice or political rhetoric about the incident also influences perceptions. People involved in street life similarly apply meaning to various versions of these incidents. They use labels to describe the shooters and victims. They communicate the justices or injustices of the shootings, which is largely dictated by one's perspective. They then act according their version of reality.

The notion of divergent realities does not deny the reality of events. It merely suggests myths can emerge from real events, which forces researchers to examine how social interactions contribute to this process.

Interpretive Socialization

The construction of ideas about weapons and violence in gang life is a social endeavor, as individuals collectively communicate the logic of local gang and street culture. According to some scholars, culture acts as a social filter that influences how people both interpret situations and anticipate the consequences of their behavior (e.g. Corsaro, 1983, 1992; Harding, 2010). It is a lens through which people view the world. It simplifies social life by categorizing and providing meaning for social events. Social interactions establish a working understanding of when to apply specific meanings to daily life. For example, youth in the street talk about "killers" and provide ample context so everyone understands the meaning of the label. When individuals lack an understanding of local meanings, they will be confused during even the most mundane social situations, unable to anticipate consequences of their behavior. Interactions between gang members contribute to how they understand the role of violence and weapons in social life. What makes sense to the gang member may seem senseless to an outsider.

Although socialization theories are numerous and varied, some researchers argue social routines contribute to the development and maintenance of cultural ideas. Corsaro (1992) calls this process the interpretive reproduction culture. As individuals spend time with peers, they develop social routines that create and become a part of local, group-based culture (Fine & Kleinman, 1979). Together, youth take established elements of their broader culture and accept, reject, or subtly alter them during social routines (Corsaro, 1992). Everyone is involved in this process so that no person passively accepts what other group members preach. Some individuals may be more influential than others, but everyone is free to contribute to a given cultural setting. Group life involves the constant negotiation of meaning, as group members make sense of events and other people in their social environment.

Socialization and Methods of Communication

Social routines vary and change as people age, but adolescents typically engage peers through various forms of conversation (Kyratzis, 2004). These conversations allow peers to use, apply, and explain cultural ideas that influence how they perceive social situations. When gossiping, for example, youth discuss undesirable behavior in detail and then apply meaningful labels to the individuals involved in such behavior (Fine, 1986; Goodwin, 1980). They also establish, apply, and reinforce expectations for proper and improper conduct. Gossip among gang members highlights the negative traits of other groups, which clarifies and helps establish group identity (Campbell, 1987). It also allows gang members to enhance personal reputations and disparage peers by applying culturally specific labels to individuals who are unwilling and unable to engage in violence (Lauger, 2012). As gang members apply these labels to people and events, the listening audience becomes more familiar with the meanings, applications, and consequences of these labels.

Youth similarly communicate, clarify, or amend important cultural ideas by telling stories. Storytellers restructure events to appeal to the audience, which means stories are often fictionalized (Ochs & Capps, 1996; Shuman, 1986). Events unfold in scripted, predictable patterns that reflect and reinforce expectations for proper conduct within the local social setting. Stories frequently involve a struggle between contrasting characters that exemplify despised or admired traits within local culture (Ewick & Silbey, 1995).

This is especially true when stories focus on fights or open conflicts. Storytellers reconstruct personal experiences with fights so that their actions always appear justified in response to their adversary (Shuman, 1986). These stories elevate the status of the storyteller while also highlighting both the sequence of events leading to violence and the intensity of violence to be used in the situation (Lauger, 2014).

Storytelling and Embellished Violence

Stories allow gang members and street offenders to communicate criminal or violent behavior in culturally appropriate ways (Copes, Hochstetler, & Forsyth, 2013; Sandberg, 2009). Local expectations for public behavior influence how storytellers describe and explain their role in violent or criminal events (Brookman, Copes, & Hochstetler, 2011; Lauger, 2014). These expectations function like a script that unfolds in a predictable manner. Research among armed robbers and violent offenders in Britain suggests personal stories of violence are formulaic and predictably reference important cultural ideas like respect or a given violent identity (Brookman, Copes, & Hochstetler, 2011). These stories communicate both the meaning of respect and how events unfold to produce violence, which contributes to a specific identity. Gang members in Indianapolis, IN tell stories in which extreme violence is the inevitable response to another person's improper conduct. They often exaggerate these accounts to enhance their reputation on the streets (Lauger, 2014). These stories communicate local expectations for how personal conduct can or should lead to violence.

Mythic violence and weapons use is partially caused by the storytelling routines of gang members. As they tell personal stories of violence, gang members embellish key elements that resonate with the audience and reinforce their ability to use violence (Lauger, 2014). The desire to build reputations provides the underlying motivation for embellishing stories, yet gang members are also concerned with performing adequately in the moment they tell the story. Storytellers rarely revisit or highlight events that make them look bad, regardless of the cultural setting. Even when a gang member is assaulted, he or she may exaggerate the number of people responsible for the assault (Lauger, 2014). This provides a justification for their victimization while also depicting the aggressors as being unfair and worthy of violent retaliation. Exaggerations saturate stories of violence within gang life, which can create the general perception that violence is both routine and severe.

Matters of Identity

The notion of identity also offers insight into the intersection between mythic and real violence in gang life. Scholars generally agree one's sense of self is complex, composed of many roles or identities (Stryker, 1980). Yet, theoretical development on the idea of identity varies so that numerous disagreements exist. Although some scholars argue personal identity is relatively stable, others view it to be more fluid (see Athens, 1994). Some align personal identity with group identity, while others argue personal interactions within groups are influential but individuals participate in multiple overlapping, contrasting, or independent groups (Hogg, Terry, & White, 1995; Stets & Burke, 2000). Personal identity, therefore, contains multiple roles stemming from varying sets of social relationships that may or may not conflict with each other (Stryker, 1980). The remainder of this chapter briefly covers how some researchers have applied these ideas to gangs and how such insights can help explain gang myths.

Vigil's Theory on Identity in Gang Life

According to Vigil (1988, 1991), adolescent gang members are in a phase of life when personal identity is especially sensitive to change, and their social and economic environments limit their options for socialization. Their negotiation of identity occurs within gangs and involves the interplay between four types of self-concepts. The *ideal self* refers to who a person would like to be. The *feared self* is who a person desires not to become. The *claimed self* is how one would like to be perceived by others. And the *real self* refers to who a person actually is. Individuals work to match the real self with the ideal self and perform so the claimed self appears ideal. They also actively work to avoid becoming or being perceived as their feared self. Group participation, especially during adolescence, influences an individual's understanding of the ideal and feared self, which influences how one performs in social settings.

A gang member's understanding of the ideal and feared self is influenced by his or her interactions with other gang members. Not all gangs are alike, which produces variations in what one wants to become or how a person desires to be perceived by peers. If a gang embraces toughness or violence as central to the group's identity, members may develop ideal self-concepts that focus on toughness. They will then fear being weak and act in ways to align their real selves with their idealized selves. This can directly lead to violence and the use of weapons, but members may also navigate the elements of identity through fictionalized violence. Gang members must maintain a claimed self that convinces peers of their toughness. Fictitious violence helps develop a reputation closer to an idealized identity rather than a real or feared identity. Gang members often exaggerate their involvement in violence and their capacity to use weapons, especially when their gang embraces a violent group identity. Their claimed self must align with group ideals or the ideal self. When large numbers of gang members generate claimed selves that do not match their real selves, the role of violence and weapons in the entire social environment of gang members can become exaggerated or mythical.

Social Identity Theory

Hennigan and Spanovic (2012) use *social identity theory* to reexamine the influence of gang membership on personal identity (see also Goldman, Giles, & Hogg, 2014; Wood, 2014). From this orientation, social life involves an array of categories (e.g. gang member) that informs people how they should think or behave in specific circumstances. When internalized, these categories become social identities that guide public behavior (Hogg, Terry, & White, 1995). People fit into multiple categories, and so they have an array of social identities to perform during different social events. However, one's commitment to these social identities varies according to the degree of their participation in groups. The stronger one is connected to a group the more prominent that social identity will become. When individuals are heavily involved in gang life, their social identity of gang member, which comes from the group, will be more prominently displayed in public behavior than if they are tangentially connected to a gang.

The social identity of a gang member is also connected to group characteristics. Cohesive groups that experience external conflict tend to foster strong group identities and social identities among members (Hennigan & Spanovic, 2012). Street gangs vary in both their cohesiveness and level of conflict with other gangs. Individual gang identities may be more prominent in some gangs than others. Some gang members may be heavily invested in performing their gang identity in public when others are not. Substantial differences are likely to occur in how gang members fictionalize violence and weapons during these performances, which is an issue largely unexplored in gang research.

Garot's Nonessentialism

Other perspectives on identity question the importance of gang membership to a person's sense of self. They argue gang membership lacks a true essence, or a fixed and identifiable set of traits. Garot (2007, 2010) emphasizes the instability of gang identity. Many individuals perform like a gang member in specific social situations, but these performances are temporary and activated only when perceived beneficial. Gang identity is accomplished in the moment but is fleeting as the need vanishes. So-called gang members do not internalize gang as part of their sense of self. These temporary performances, which can sometimes involve violence or the threat of violence, are not representative of normalcy on the streets or in the lives of "gang members." Much of the violence associated with gang members is mythic, the byproduct of how individuals strategically negotiate interactions with peers. Strategies invoking the threat of violence are relatively uncommon in daily lives of youth who can more effectively manage social interactions without activating their gang identity. Yet outsiders often fixate on the less common encounters when violence or the threat of violence occurs. Thus myths about weapons and violence proliferate.

CONCLUSION: REALITY AS A FOUNDATION FOR MYTH?

Weapons have severe consequences for both gang members and communities. Research findings account for part of the observable, measurable world, and scholars have made great efforts to ensure that research methods closely, though not perfectly, measure reality. Researchers can examine the events in Seattle and Indianapolis and accurately categorize them as incidents of gun violence between conflicting groups that are widely known as gangs. They can further simplify this description to either "gun violence between gangs" or "gang violence". These incidents provide no context to the prevalence of gangs or the nature of violence in Seattle of Indianapolis. They do not speak to the association between gangs, weapons, and violence in these cities and beyond. They do demonstrate that researchers can accurately describe and categorize events, which allows them to both measure incidents of gang violence in multiple locations and determine the extent to which gang members carry weapons and engage in violence.

Ironically, research findings can provide the foundation for gang myths while also limiting the extent to which people can claim the gang problem is purely mythical. Research findings provide a foundation for myths because they can easily fuel exaggerated stereotypes. People can misinterpret good research and perceive statistical associations between gangs, weapons, and violence to be an indication all gang members are excessively violent. Or they read studies describing the use of weapons and violence by gang members and assume gang members routinely engage in extreme violence. Both assertions are exaggerated. Research findings also limit the extent to which people can claim the image of a violent gang or gang member is only a myth. One can argue that perceptions of weapons and violence about gang life are exaggerated, but rejecting the reality of weapons and violence altogether dismisses the majority of careful research on the topic.

Myths about weapons and violence in gang life are powerful because they are partially grounded in reality. The naïve public embraces an exaggerated image of violent gang members because gang members engage in violence, and events like those in Indianapolis and Seattle occur. They accept high profile events as being normal and never contemplate that such incidents may be exceptional. The same is true on the streets among gang members. Group-based myths about violence evolve through exaggeration or when members routinely talk about a few violent incidents that happened over the course of a few years. Without perceiving the exaggeration or realizing the timeline of events, one can misperceive a gang or gang member to be routinely involved in excessive violence. Yet, if gang members do not ground mythic violence in real events, they risk exposure and public humiliation. When their stories are not believable, gang members severely undermine their ability to compete in the streets. Myths are more powerful when grounded in real events.

REFERENCES

Anderson, E. (1990). *Streetwise: Race, class, and change in an urban community*. Chicago: University of Chicago Press.

Anderson, E. (1999). *Code of the street: Decency, violence, and the moral life of the inner city*. New York: W.W. Norton & Company.

Ang, R. P., Huan, V. S., Chua, S. H., & Lim, S. H. (2012). Gang affiliation, aggression, and violent offending in a sample of youth offenders. *Psychology, Crime & Law, 18*(8), 703–711. doi:10.1080/10 68316X.2010.534480

Athens, L. (1994). The self as soliloquy. *The Sociological Quarterly, 35*(3), 521–532. doi:10.1111/j.1533-8525.1994.tb01743.x

Battin, S. R., Hill, K. G., Abbott, R. D., Catalano, R. F., & Hawkins, J. D. (1998). The contribution of gang membership to delinquency beyond delinquent friends. *Criminology, 36*(1), 93–115. doi:10.1111/j.1745-9125.1998.tb01241.x

Bennett, T., & Holloway, K. (2004). Gang membership, drugs and crime in the UK. *The British Journal of Criminology, 44*(3), 305–323. doi:10.1093/bjc/azh025

Bjerregaard, B., & Lizotte, A. J. (1995). Gun ownership and gang membership. *The Journal of Criminal Law & Criminology, 86*(1), 37–58. doi:10.2307/1143999

Braga, A. A., Pierce, G. L., McDevitt, J., Bond, B., & Cronin, S. (2008). The strategic prevention of gun violence among gang-involved offenders. *Justice Quarterly, 25*(1), 132–162. doi:10.1080/07418820801954613

Brookman, F., Copes, H., & Hochstetler, A. (2011). Street codes as formula stories: How inmates recount violence. *Journal of Contemporary Ethnography, 40*(4), 397–424. doi:10.1177/0891241611408307

Campbell, A. (1987). Self definition by rejection: The case of gang girls. *Social Problems, 34*(5), 451–466. doi:10.2307/800541

Chu, C. M., Daffern, M., Thomas, S., & Lim, J. Y. (2012). Violence risk and gang affiliation in youth offenders: A recidivism study. *Psychology, Crime & Law, 18*(3), 299–315. doi:10.1080/106831 6X.2010.481626

Copes, H., Hochstetler, A., & Forsyth, C. J. (2013). Peaceful warriors: Codes for violence among adult male bar fighters. *Criminology, 51*(3), 761–794. doi:10.1111/1745-9125.12019

Corsaro, W. A. (1983). Script recognition, articulation and expansion in children's role play. *Discourse Processes*, 6(1), 1–19. doi:10.1080/01638538309544551

Corsaro, W. A. (1992). Interpretive reproduction in children's peer cultures. *Social Psychology Quarterly*, 55(2), 160–177. doi:10.2307/2786944

Decker, S. H., & Kempf-Leonard, K. (1991). Constructing gangs: The social definition of youth activities. *Criminal Justice Policy Review*, 5(4), 271–291. doi:10.1177/088740349100500401

Decker, S. H., & Pyrooz, D. C. (2010). On the validity and reliability of gang homicide: A comparison of disparate sources. *Homicide Studies*, 14(4), 359–376. doi:10.1177/1088767910385400

Decker, S. H., Pyrooz, D. C., Sweeten, G., & Moule, R. K. Jr. (2014). Validating self-nomination in gang research: Assessing difference in gang embeddedness across non-current, and former gang members. [online first]. *Journal of Quantitative Criminology*, 30(4), 577–598. doi:10.1007/s10940-014-9215-8

Decker, S. H., & Van Winkle, B. (1996). *Life in the gang*. Cambridge, England: Cambridge University Press. doi:10.1017/CBO9781139174732

Densely, J. A. (2013). *How gangs work: An ethnography of youth violence*. Oxford: Palgrave MacMillan. doi:10.1057/9781137271518

Duran, R. J. (2013). *Gang Life in Two Cities*. NY: Columbia University Press.

Eades, C., Brimshaw, R., Silvestri, A., & Solomon, E. (2011). *'Knife Crime:' A review of evidence and policy* (2nd ed.). London: Center for Crime and Justice Studies.

Esbensen, F.-A., & Lynskey, D. P. (2001). Youth gang members in a school survey. In M.W. Klein, H.-J. Kerner, C.L. Maxson & E.G.M. Weitekamp (Eds.), The European paradox: Street gangs and youth groups in the U.S. and Europe, (pp. 93-114). Dordecht: Kluwer Academic Publishers.

Esbensen, F.-A., & Weerman, F. M. (2005). Youth gangs and troublesome youth groups in the United States and the Netherlands: A cross-national comparison. *European Journal of Criminology*, 2(1), 1477–3708. doi:10.1177/1477370805048626

Esbensen, F.-A., Winfree, L. T. Jr, Ne, H., & Taylor, T. J. (2001). Youth gangs and definitional issues: When is a gang a gang, and why does it matter? *Crime and Delinquency*, 47(1), 105–130. doi:10.1177/0011128701047001005

Ewick, P., & Silbey, S. S. (1995). Subversive stories and hegemonic tales: Toward a sociology of narrative. *Law & Society Review*, 29(2), 197–226. doi:10.2307/3054010

Fine, G. A. (1986). The social organization of adolescent gossip: The rhetoric of moral evaluation. In J. Cook-Gumperz, W. A. Corsaro, & J. Streeck (Eds.), *Children's worlds and children's language* (pp. 405–423). Berlin: Mouton. doi:10.1515/9783110864212.405

Fine, G. A., & Kleinman, S. (1979). Rethinking subculture: An interactionist analysis. *American Journal of Sociology*, 85(1), 1–20. doi:10.1086/226971

Fraser, A., & Atkinson, C. (2014). Making up gangs: Looping, labeling and the new politics of intelligence-led policing. *Youth Justice*, 14(2), 154–170. doi:10.1177/1473225414529047

Garot, R. (2007). "Where you from?": Gang identity as performance. *Journal of Contemporary Ethnography, 36*(1), 50–84. doi:10.1177/0891241606287364

Garot, R. (2009). Reconsidering retaliation: Structural inhibitions, emotive dissonance, and the acceptance of ambivalence among inner-city young men. *Ethnography, 10*(1), 63–90. doi:10.1177/1466138108099587

Garot, R. (2010). *Who you claim: Performing identity in school and on the streets.* New York: New York University Press.

Golding, B., McClory, J., & Lockhart, B. (2008). *Going ballistic: Dealing with guns, gangs, and knives.* London: The Policy Exchange.

Goldman, L., Giles, H., & Hogg, M. A. (2014). Going to extremes: Social identity and communication processes associated with gang membership. [forthcoming – online first]. *Group Processes & Intergroup Relations, 17*(6), 813–832. doi:10.1177/1368430214524289

Goodwin, M. H. (1980). He-said-she-said: Formal cultural procedures for the construction of a gossip dispute activity. *American Ethnologist, 7*(4), 674–695. doi:10.1525/ae.1980.7.4.02a00050

Hacking, I. (1999). *The social construction of what?* Cambridge, MA: Harvard University Press.

Hallsworth, S. (2013). *The Gang & Beyond: Interpreting violent street worlds.* Oxford: Palgrave Macmillian. doi:10.1057/9781137358103

Hallsworth, S., & Young, T. (2008). Gang talk and gang talkers: A critique. *Crime, Media, Culture, 4*(2), 175–195. doi:10.1177/1741659008092327

Harding, D. J. (2010). *Living the drama: Community, conflict, and culture among inner city boys.* Chicago: University of Chicago Press. doi:10.7208/chicago/9780226316666.001.0001

Harding, S. (2014). *The street casino: Survival in violent street gangs.* Bristol, UK: Policy Press. doi:10.1332/policypress/9781447317173.001.0001

Harrell, E. (2005). Violence by gang members, 1993-2003. U.S. Department of Justice. Office of Justice programs.

Hennigan, K., & Spanovic, M. (2012). Gang dynamics through the lens of social identity theory. In F. A. Esbensen & C. L. Maxson (Eds.), *Youth Gangs in international perspective: Results from the eurogang program of research* (pp. 127–149). New York: Springer. doi:10.1007/978-1-4614-1659-3_8

Hogg, M. A., Terry, D. J., & White, K. M. (1995). A tale of two theories: A critical comparison of identity theory with social identity theory. *Social Psychology Quarterly, 58*(4), 255–269. doi:10.2307/2787127

Hollander, J. A., & Gordon, H. R. (2006). The process of social construction in talk. *Symbolic Interaction, 29*(2), 183–212. doi:10.1525/si.2006.29.2.183

Howell, J. C. (2007). Menacing or mimicking? Realities of youth gangs. *Juvenile & Family Court Journal, 58*(2), 39–50. doi:10.1111/j.1755-6988.2007.tb00137.x

Huizinga, D., & Schumann, K. F. (2001). Gang membership in Bremen and Denver: Comparative longitudinal data. In M. W. Klein, H.-J. Kerner, C. L. Maxson, & E. G. M. Weitekamp (Eds.), *The Eurogang paradox: Street gangs and youth groups in the U.S. and Europe, 231–46*. Dordrecht: Kluwer Academic Publishers. doi:10.1007/978-94-010-0882-2_18

Jones, N. (2010). *Between good and ghetto: African American girls and inner-city violence*. New Brunswick, NJ: Rutgers University Press.

Katz, C. M. (2001). The establishment of a police gang unit: An examination of organizational and environmental factors. *Criminology, 39*(1), 37–74. doi:10.1111/j.1745-9125.2001.tb00916.x

Katz, C. M., Web, V. J., & Shaeffer, D. R. (2000). Gang intelligence lists: Examining differences in delinquency between documented gang members and nondocumented delinquent youth. *Police Quarterly, 3*, 413–437.

Katz, J., & Jackson-Jacobs, C. (2004). The Criminologists' Gang. In C. Sumner (Ed.), *Blackwell Companion to Criminology*. Malden, MA: Blackwell Publishers.

Klein, M. W. (1971). *Street gangs and street workers*. Englewood Cliffs, NJ: Prentice Hall, Inc.

Klein, M. W. (1995). *The American street gang: Its nature prevalence and control*. Oxford: Oxford University Press.

Klein, M. W. (2005). The value of comparisons in street gang research. *Journal of Contemporary Criminal Justice, 21*(2), 135–152. doi:10.1177/1043986204272911

Klein, M. W., & Maxson, C. (2006). *Street gang patterns and policy*. New York: Oxford University Press. doi:10.1093/acprof:oso/9780195163445.001.0001

Klein, M. W., Weerman, F. M., & Thornberry, T. P. (2006). Street gang violence in Europe. *European Journal of Criminology, 3*(4), 413–437. doi:10.1177/1477370806067911

Kubrin, C. E. (2005). Gangstas, thugs, and hustlas: Identity and the code of the street in rap music. *Social Problems, 52*(3), 360–378. doi:10.1525/sp.2005.52.3.360

Kyratzis, A. (2004). Talk and interaction among children and the co-construction of Peer groups and peer culture. *Annual Review of Anthropology, 33*(1), 625–649. doi:10.1146/annurev.anthro.33.070203.144008

Lauger, T. R. (2012). *Real gangstas: Legitimacy, reputation, and violence in the intergang environment*. New Brunswick, NJ: Rutgers University Press.

Lauger, T. R. (2014). Violent stories: Personal narratives, street socialization, and the negotiation of street culture among street-oriented youth. *Criminal Justice Review, 39*(2), 182–200. doi:10.1177/0734016814529966

Luckman, T. (2008). On social interaction and the communicative construction of personal identity, knowledge and reality. *Organization Studies, 29*(2), 277–290. doi:10.1177/0170840607087260

Matsueda, K. N., Melde, C., Taylor, T. J., Freng, A., & Esbensen, F.-A. (2013). Gang membership and adherence to the "code of the street.". *Justice Quarterly, 30*(3), 440–468. doi:10.1080/07418825.2012.684432

Maxson, C. L., & Klein, M. W. (1990). Street gang violence: Twice as great, or half as great? In C. R. Huff (Ed.), *Gangs in America* (pp. 71–100). Newbury Park, CA: Sage.

McCorkle, R. C., & Meithe, T. D. (1998). The political and organizational response to gangs: An examination of a "moral panic" in Nevada. *Justice Quarterly, 15*(1), 41–64. doi:10.1080/07418829800093631

McDaniel, D., Egley, A. Jr, & Logan, J. (2014). Gang homicides in five U.S. cities, 2003-2008. *Morbidity and Mortality Weekly Report, 61*, 46–51. PMID:22278158

McVie, S. (2010). *Gang membership and knife carrying: Findings from the Edinburgh study of youth transitions and crime.* The Scottish Centre for Crime and Justice Research.

Meehan, A. J. (2000). The organizational career of gang statistics: The politics of policing gangs. *The Sociological Quarterly, 41*(3), 337–370. doi:10.1111/j.1533-8525.2000.tb00082.x

Ochs, E., & Capps, L. (1996). Narrating the self. *Annual Review of Anthropology, 25*(1), 19–43. doi:10.1146/annurev.anthro.25.1.19

Palansinski, M. (2013). Security, respect and culture in British teenagers' discourses of knife-carrying. *Safer Communities, 12*(2), 71–78. doi:10.1108/17578041311315049

Palansinski, M., & Riggs, D. W. (2012). Young white British men and knife-carrying in public: Discourses of masculinity, protection and vulnerability. *Critical Criminology, 20*(4), 463–476. doi:10.1007/s10612-012-9161-4

Perrone, P. A., & Chesney-Lind, M. (1997). Representations of gangs and delinquency: Wild in the streets? *Social Justice (San Francisco, Calif.), 24*, 96–116.

Pitts, J. (2012). Reluctant criminologists: Criminology, ideology and the violent youth gang. *Youth & Policy, 109*, 27–45.

Pyrooz, D. C., & Decker, S. H. (2013). Delinquent behavior, violence, and gang involvement in China. *Journal of Quantitative Criminology, 29*(2), 251–272. doi:10.1007/s10940-012-9178-6

Sandberg, S. (2009). A narrative search for respect. *Deviant Behavior, 30*(6), 478–510. doi:10.1080/01639620802296394

Sayer, A. (1999). *Realism and social science.* Thousand Oaks, CA: Sage.

Searle, J. R. (1995). *The construction of social reality.* New York: The Free Press.

Searle, J. R. (2006). Social ontology: Some basic principles. *Anthropological Theory, 6*(1), 12–29. doi:10.1177/1463499606061731

Shuman, A. (1986). *Storytelling rights: The uses of oral and written texts by urban adolescents.* New York: Cambridge University Press. doi:10.1017/CBO9780511983252

Smith, C. (2010). *What is a person?* Chicago: University of Chicago Press. doi:10.7208/chicago/9780226765938.001.0001

St. Cyr, J. L. (2003). The folk devil reacts: Gangs and moral panics. *Criminal Justice Review, 28*(1), 26–46. doi:10.1177/073401680302800103

State v. Moreno et al. (2011). Washington, King County. *Information*. Retrieved October 29, 2014 from http://blog.seattlepi.com/seattle911/files/2011/09/Kent Car-Show-Charges.pdf

State vs. Patten. (2010). Indiana, Marion. *Probable Cause Affidavit*. Retrieved October 29, 2014 from http://media2.wishtv.com/_local/pdf/pattonPC.pdf

Stets, J. E., & Burke, P. J. (2000). Identity theory and social identity theory. *Social Psychology Quarterly*, *63*(3), 224–237. doi:10.2307/2695870

Stretesky, P. B., & Pogrebin, M. R. (2007). Gun-related gun violence: Socialization, identity, and self. *Journal of Contemporary Ethnography*, *36*(1), 85–114. doi:10.1177/0891241606287416

Stryker, S. (1980). *Symbolic Interactionism: A social structural version*. Menlo Park, CA: The Benjamin/Cummings Publishing Company.

Thornberry, T. P., Krohn, M. D., Lizotte, A. J., Smith, C. A., & Tobin, K. (2003). *Gangs and Delinquency in Developmental Perspective*. New York: Cambridge University Press.

United Nations. (2011). *Global Study on Homicide*. United Nations Office on Drugs and Crime.

Vigil, J. D. (1988). Group processes and street identity: Adolescent Chicano gang members. *Ethos (Berkeley, Calif.)*, *14*(4), 421–445. doi:10.1525/eth.1988.16.4.02a00040

Vigil, J. D. (1991). *Barrio gangs: Street life and identity in Southern California*. Austin: University of Texas Press.

Wilkinson, D. L. (2001). Violent events and social identity: Specifying the relationship between respect and masculinity in inner city youth violence. *Sociological Studies of Children and Youth*, *8*, 231–265. doi:10.1016/S1537-4661(01)80011-8

Wood, J. L. (2014). Understanding gang membership: The significance of group processes. [in press, online first]. *Group Processes & Intergroup Relations*, *17*(6), 710–729. doi:10.1177/1368430214550344

Zatz, M. (1987). Chicano youth gangs and crime: The creation of a moral panic. *Contemporary Crises*, *11*(2), 129–158. doi:10.1007/BF00728588

KEY TERMS AND DEFINITIONS

Identity: A person's sense of self.

Interpretive Socialization: A social psychological theory of socialization that emphasizes the collaborative negotiation of meaning through routine interactions.

Myth: A widely accepted idea or story that is grossly exaggerated or not true.

Social Constructionism: A sociological perspective that posits social processes generate elements of accepted reality.

Street Gang: A durable group of street-oriented youths that embraces crime as part of its group identity.

Violence: The intentional use of physical force to harm someone.

Weapon: A device intentionally used to harm someone.

Chapter 5
Forensic Psychological Perspectives on Youth Gang Involvement in Juvenile Fire Setting and Bomb Making Weapons Cases:
Forensic Perspective Youth Gangs Fire Setting and Weapons

Ronn Johnson
University of San Diego, USA

ABSTRACT

The purpose of this chapter is to explore issues related to gang-affiliated youth's use of JFSB behavior as a weapon. Too often, the critical analysis of JFSB is circumscribed to the act with little or no consideration of a clinical forensic weapons use motivation. In this case, successful efforts to identify and isolate the origins of such events are more contingent upon a deeper understanding of the subtle processes that explain this particular kind of weapons use by juvenile gang members.

INTRODUCTION

The media accounts of juvenile gang use of juvenile fire setting behavior (JFSB) have been around for decades. There is periodical documentation in a 1958 Denver, Colorado newspaper that arson was being used as a means to initiate juvenile gang members. Juvenile gang members admitted that "in order to gain gang membership they were told to set a fire (Ludington Daily News, 1958)." Despite widespread media attention and the high risk to life and property, juvenile fire setting and bomb making is an area of that has received very little professional consideration from law enforcement and forensic psychology.

DOI: 10.4018/978-1-4666-9938-0.ch005

There is clear and convincing evidence that criminal justice and forensic psychological experts must engage in an informed dialogue that is aimed at helping communities better understand the full scope of the issues accompanying this juvenile justice population.

The purpose of this chapter is to explore issues related to gang-affiliated youth's use of fire and bombs as weapons. Too often, the critical analysis of JFSB, particularly gang related juvenile fire setting and bomb making behavior (GR-JFSB) is circumscribed to the act itself with little or no consideration of a clinical forensic weapons use motivation. In this case, successful efforts to identify and isolate the origins of such events are more contingent upon a deeper understanding of the subtle processes that explain this particular kind of weapons use by juvenile gang members.

OVERVIEW OF A CASE INVOLVING GANG RELATED JUVENILE FIRE SETTING AND BOMB MAKING BEHAVIOR

Tuco, aka "Pyro," is a 14-year-old male of mixed ethnicity. His mother is first generation Mexican-American and his father is of European ancestry. He has been identified as a member of a local neighborhood gang WSV. He is currently residing in juvenile hall, but prior to the instant offense for which he was detained, he was residing in a two-bedroom apartment with his mother and extended family members. Tuco was referred for a psychological evaluation focused on his use of fire as a weapon; fire was used during the attempted homicide of a rival gang member from the local neighborhood gang NSD. The fire resulted in the deaths of three individuals, and as such this case may be tried under the California special circumstances for capital murder, and the street gang-sentencing enhancement. Due to his age, this case is not eligible for a death penalty sentence, even if Tuco stands trial as an adult.

The records indicate at 2am, on a Thursday morning during the summer, Tuco met with four members of WSV to plan a retaliation against Anthony, a 13-year-old-male member of NSD. Members of WSV had attempted to assault Anthony earlier in the day, but were driven off by bystanders in the park across from Anthony's home. The members of WSV collectively decided that Tuco should be the one to exact revenge because he had initiated the first altercation. The previous week Tuco and Anthony had a verbal altercation when Anthony had ridden his bicycle across WSV territory to visit his relative. The other four members stood lookout as Tuco snuck into the backyard of Anthony's family home, a two-story duplex with wood siding and shake shingle roof.

As California was in the middle of a drought, the yard was dry and scrub had grown up in dense patches around the 6' wooden privacy fence surrounding the back of the property. Tuco brought a small plastic jug of gasoline and a lighter with him. In the back yard he found an empty beer bottle and a rag, with which he fashioned a crude Molotov cocktail. Tuco poured the gasoline on the wooden back porch, and some patio furniture, and then used a discarded newspaper as a torch to set fire to the porch. As soon as the porch ignited, he ran. Tuco set the rag in the beer bottle on fire as he came around the front of the house, then threw the device at the front door of the duplex apartment. He stated later, he did this "because [he] needed them [the WSV at the park] to see I really did it."

The fire engulfed both sides of the duplex within minutes. Anthony's uncle was able to get Anthony and Anthony's niece out of the house. Anthony's 85-year-old grandmother, his 42-year-old mother, and a 5-year-old girl in the next-door residence perished in the fire. Two firefighters were severely injured in the process of attempting to rescue the three remaining victims.

Tuco's gang moniker of "Pyro" was bestowed prior to this incident. Tuco frequently burned small objects out of boredom, and bragged that he was never without a lighter. He had set multiple nuisance fires in trashcans at the park, and was suspended twice from school for setting fires in the boy's bathroom. The fire setting behavior was never addressed in a psychological setting, as all services were focused on Tuco's diagnoses of Conduct Disorder and ADHD. The first forensic psychological evaluation, conducted by an experienced clinical psychologist, found Tuco to be at "low risk" for future fire setting. This finding was based primarily on clinical assessments and a structured interview instrument developed by FEMA for use by the fire service.

The second forensic psychological evaluation, conducted by a more experienced clinical forensic evaluation team with extensive research and training experience in juvenile fire setting and bomb-making behaviors, found Tuco to be at "extreme risk" of future fire setting. The second forensic evaluation explained this risk as the product of Tuco's motivation for the fire setting, and his historical evolution of fire setting. Tuco's early fire setting (at age 6) began as a reaction to crisis in the home where he witnessed chronic domestic violence and drug use. The frequent use of fire fed Tuco's irrational belief that he could control fire. There was a well-entrenched cognitive schema that led to the instrumental use of fire as a weapon of choice. Tuco's schema regarding retribution was supported by Anthony's pain and suffering as a result of the fire-related and fire-caused deaths. Without clinical treatment targeted specifically at Tuco's fire setting behavior, that challenge of his beliefs regarding fire on a cognitive level, he will most likely continue to use fire as both a tool for coping with internal distress, and a weapon against others. There were also concerns about his ability to complete therapeutic enhancement activities (TEAs) and other noncompliance matters (i.e., risk for No Show behavior).

A HISTORY OF GANG RELATED FIRE SETTING AND BOMB MAKING

Man is the only creature that dares to light a fire and live with it. The reason? Because he alone has learned to put it out. ~ Henry Jackson Vandyke, Jr.

Due to their destructive powers, fire and explosive devices have long been used as weapons. As early as the eighth-century there is documentation that fire and explosive devices were used in warfare. In the United States, fire and explosive devices were used extensively as weapons in early wars such as the revolutionary war and the civil war. The use of fire and explosive devices as weapons has not been limited to warfare. Arson and bombs have been used as weapons by organized gangs in the facilitation of criminal activity all over the world.

Early 20th Century United States

In the early twentieth century United States arson catalyzed by explosive devices was a prevalent and common crime. This was a particularly prevalent behavior during the era of prohibition (1920-1933) when organized crime groups operated illegal bars known as speakeasies. These organized crime groups would utilize Molotov Cocktails to start fires in rival gangs' speakeasies in order to eliminate competition. These fires would often be started when the speakeasies were full of people. Not only did starting a fire eliminate the existence of a competing speakeasy, it also sent a strong message and was an effective way to eradicate evidence. Thus, the early twentieth century gave rise to arson and bomb related crimes as the use of fire became an efficient and effective way for gangs to gain power and assert dominance (National Gang Crime Research Center, 2005). Arson, particularly arson catalyzed by the use of explosive devices, continues to be a tool employed by gangs to demonstrate power and convey messages of dominance within their territories (National Gang Crime Research Center, 2005; FEMA, 2012). Since the early twentieth century there have been hundreds of documented incidents involving the use of arson and bombs by street gangs and organized crime groups. (National Gang Crime Research Center, 2005).

An Understudied Area

Despite the documented prevalence of this issue, the use of arson and bombs by gangs remains an understudied area. In 2005 the National Gang Crime Research Center conducted a study addressing the use of arson and bombs as weapons in gang related criminal activity, the report produced after the study stated, "the issue of bomb and arson activity, among gang members, has been a totally neglected area of gang research" (Bomb and Arson Crimes Among American Gang Members, p. 4). The use of arson and bombs as weapons in gang related criminal activity is not only an issue in adult gang member populations, juvenile gangs and juvenile gang members also use arson and explosive devices either because they are imitating adult gangs or because they are juvenile members of gangs carrying out orders from their superiors (FEMA, 2012).

The 2005 study completed by the National Gang Crime Research Center remains the most comprehensive and empirically based source of information regarding the use of arson and bombs as weapons by gangs in the United States. The sample examined in this study consisted of 1,042 adult and juvenile gang affiliated offenders. Unfortunately, the study did not separate juvenile and adult participant data and therefore it is impossible to distinguish similarities and/or differences between adult and juvenile gang affiliated offenders and their respective use of bombs and arson as weapons.

What is clear is that arson and bombs are being utilized as weapons by both adult and juvenile gang members in gang related criminal activity. What is unclear is whether or not the reasons for the use of arson and bombs as weapons are the same in both juvenile and adult contexts.

Contributing Factors to the Use of Fire and Bombs by Gang Members

In the report generated as a result of this 2005 study, entitled, "Bomb and Arson Crimes Among American Gang Members: A Behavioral Science Profile", it is noted that completing a literature review on the subject is a difficult task due to the limited amount of previous research regarding the use of arson and bombs by gangs. The literature review in this particular study is thus primarily anecdotal and based on media and periodical reports, not empirically supported literature.

Although the literature review in this particular publication is qualitative in nature, it does demonstrate that the use of arson and bombs as weapons by gangs seems to be based on either one or a combination of the following factors; gang member initiation, facilitation of a crime, the cover up or elimination of evidence, and vengeance based retribution. There are other less common factors that could play a role in a gang's choice to utilize a bomb or arson as a weapon.

It is helpful, particularly for law enforcement and criminologists, to consider the motivation behind a gangs' use of arson and/or bombs as weapons of initiation, facilitation, retribution, or elimination of evidence because the crime itself may take on a different form depending on the motivation. For example, if a certain gang uses arson to initiate new members, a pattern may develop, and when patterns develop in criminal activity, it makes it easier for law enforcement, detectives, and criminologists to track and prevent these crimes.

Use of Fire and Bombs by Juvenile Gang Members

According to Johnson, Beckenbach, Killborne, one of the most important law enforcement strategic objectives is to protect citizens by preventing the acquisition and use of any weapon by juvenile gang members, especially fire and explosives (2013). One of the first steps is to identify the weapons of choice, and the behavioral and psychological implications of the adoption and use of specific weapon types by gang involved juveniles. For example, research indicates having been in a gang fight and lifetime polysubstance use were more potent predictors of weapon choice (Vaughn, Howard, Matthew & Harper-Chang 2006). This type of clinical forensic information ultimately serves a desirable public safety outcome by promoting evidence-based interventions.

The use of arson and bombs by juvenile gangs and gang affiliated youth has received even less criminological attention than the use of arson and bombs in adult gangs and organized crime groups. even though media accounts of juvenile gangs' use of arson and bombs have been around for decades. There is periodical documentation in a 1958 Denver, Colorado newspaper that arson was being used as a means to initiate juvenile gang members. Juvenile gang members admitted that "in order to gain gang membership they were told to set a fire (Ludington Daily News, 1958)."

Violent Weapon Use in Juvenile Gangs

It is estimated that two out of five gang members are juveniles and there are currently approximately 782,500 gang members in the United States, therefore it can be deduced that there are about 313,000 juvenile gang members in the United States (Egley & Howell, 2011). Eighty-eight percent of juvenile offenders have reported that they carry a gun on them at all times when they are outside of their home and fifty percent of gang members have reported that they have fired a gun (OJJD, 1999).

The penchant for weapons use by gang-involved youth has serious consequences for both the youth themselves and the public. Gang affiliated juveniles have a strong penchant for using weapons due to the fact that they lead very dangerous lives. Violence is a part of gang culture and the use of arson and bombs have become an integral part of the violent culture promoted by the street gang lifestyle. The risk of being killed is 60 times greater among juvenile gang members than the general population (OJJDP, 2009). Despite considerable law enforcement efforts, deterring juvenile youth gang members from using weapons remains a significant challenge for those working in the criminal justice system, even when working with a small group of repeat offenders (Braga et al., 2001).

The aforementioned issues in recidivism of weapons use with gang involved juveniles is compounded by JFSB specific risk elevations. These youth are usually involved in several fires before they are caught, and frequently do not stop the behavior even after it has been identified. The forensically-relevant risk of reoffending amongst gang involved youth who engage in JFSB further increases due to the fact that they frequently present with inadequate social skills, mental health-related problems (i.e., some combination of ADHD, PTSD, Conduct Disorder or ASD referred to as the DSM-5 Quadrant), family discord, parent psychopathology, and a distorted decision making cognitive schema that reflexively prompts them to use weapons in the commission of various crimes.

Contributing Factors to JFSB in Juvenile Gangs

Because the 2005 National Gang Crime Research Center did include juvenile gang affiliated offenders in their sample, the results may be cautiously interpreted in the context of juvenile gang affiliated offenders. As discussed above, the use of arson and bombs as weapons in gang related crimes seems to be motivated by either one or a combination of the following factors; gang member initiation, facilitation of a crime, the cover up or elimination of evidence, and vengeance based retribution.

In the juvenile arena, two of these motivating factors stand out in media accounts and relevant literature; gang member initiation, and cover up or elimination of evidence (FEMA, 2012; Carolina Fire Journal, 2011; National Gang Crime Research Center, 2005). A juvenile who is gang affiliated may thus have different reasons for engaging in JFSB than a juvenile who is not gang affiliated. There is currently no formal system in place for identifying the gang-affiliation of juvenile fire setters and bomb makers.

Understanding the motivation behind gang-related juvenile fire setting behavior (GR-JFSB) can be helpful to law enforcement and criminologists in the juvenile arena for the same reasons it is helpful in the adult arena, it can help them to identify patterns of GR-JFSB and criminal activity and thus serve to intervene and prevent GR-JFSB in a more efficient and effective manner. Knowing whether or not a juvenile fire setter is gang affiliated can have important implications for the intervention and prevention of arson and bomb related crimes and therefore has implications in the realm of public safety.

Related Research on Juvenile Fire Setting and Bomb Making

Although research regarding the use of arson and bombs as weapons by juvenile gangs is lacking, there is research that separately addresses the problems of juvenile fire setting and bomb making (JFSB). Internationally, JFSB represent a costly, life-threatening problem for youth under the age of 19 (Brett, 2004; Doley, 2003b; Epps & Hollin, 2005). The damages from these fires are estimated to cause the deaths of 420 people and cost 1.3 billion dollar each year. Unfortunately, these numbers seem to be increasing every year (Campbell, 2014). In the United States, 22 percent of school property fires were intentionally set and have estimated damages of over 100 million dollars (Federal Emergency Management Agency, 2004; Flynn, 2007). The law enforcement response is not only costly in terms of resources allocated, but also in increased potential for injury risks to first responders.

Motivations of Juvenile Fire Setting and Bomb Making

Motivational Typologies of JFSB Utilized by the Alpha Research Institute. Include:

- Curious Without Understanding (Age or Cognitive Impairment Related).
- Child/Juvenile Mentally Disordered Offender (Resolved or Unstable).
- Crisis (Chronic or Atypical).
- Delinquent JFSB (Specific or General).
- Fire-starting - Intentional (Social, Academic, Independence-Seeking).
- Fire-starting - Accidental (Direct Flame or Circumstantial).

Frequency of Juvenile Fire Setting and Bomb Making

Although the reported rates of adult perpetrated violent crime incidents in the United States have lowered steadily over the past twenty years, the rate of all crimes perpetrated by juveniles is rising. Most crimes committed by juveniles fall into the arena of property crimes (Miller, 2014). Arson is an offense which straddles both violent crime and property crime in terms of both legal violation and psychological motivation (Hill, 1982). According to the latest available research, the rates of juvenile arson have increased steadily over the last two decades (Stadolnik, 2000).

Approximately 282,600 intentionally set fires are reported to fire departments annually in the United States. Two out of five, or approximately 40 percent of these cases, are set by youth under the age of 18. Therefore, approximately 113,000 intentionally set fires are set by juveniles every year in the United States (Campbell, 2014). It is important to note that it is statistically unclear whether or not the approximately 113,000 intentionally set fires are started by 113,000 different individuals or if a number of fires have been set by the same individual. It is more than likely the latter of the two, as research indicates that many juveniles who set fires have done so multiple times. The numbers reflected here are only based on what is reported to law enforcement and researches, the actual numbers are more than likely much higher than what the statistics reflect as it is clear that many fires go unreported and many youth do not readily report gang-affiliation (Campbell 2014, National Gang Crime Research Center, 2005).

Juvenile Fire Setting and Mental Health Considerations: DSM-5 Quadrant

Despite failure to reach a threshold of diagnostic criterion for a DSM-5 disorder, most juveniles referred for JFSB behaviors exhibit behavioral, emotional, and cognitive correlates fitting on this DSM-5 based quadrant (See figure 1 below). For more detailed descriptions of each disorder listed in the quadrant, please see the glossary of terms.

The skill of differential diagnosis of symptoms through clinical-forensic assessment is critical to obtaining a functional understanding of the motivational typology. The overlap in these four areas is substantial, and treatment to reduce JFSB behavior may require attention for more than one quadrant of symptomology (Johnson, 2014b).

Figure 1.

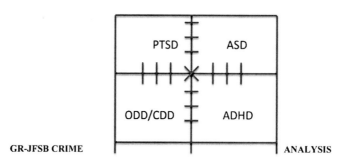

Figure 2.

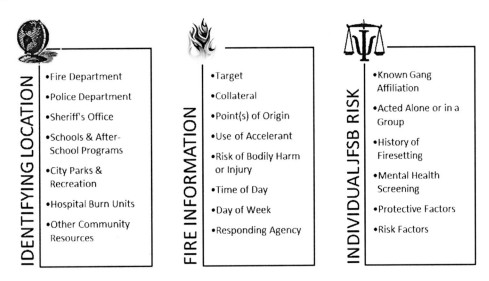

GR-JFSB CRIME ANALYSIS

The crime analysis of GR-JFSB information is conducted in three parts. The location of the fires, information about the fire, and information about the gang affiliated youth participating in high risk JFSB behaviors (figure 2).

Identifying Geographic Locations of Fires

It may seem common sense that identifying the location of arsons in a community would be easy. After all, arson is a serious crime, easily marked by extensive damage and significant paper trails, isn't it? Not necessarily so. Arson is not documented as a crime unless it reaches the threshold of a chargeable offense established by the jurisdiction. This means the incident must be reported, investigated, and identified as arson. It is believed that most juvenile fire setting is never reported (Glancy, Spiers, Pitt, & Dvoskin, 2003; Johnson & Jones, 2014).

Many fire causes are reported as unknown due to a number of factors. Two of the common reasons for "unknown cause" reports were past issues with the National Fire Incident Reporting Software (*U.S. Fire Administration Structure Fire Cause Methodology*, 2014), or insufficient evidence to support arson charges, despite the suspicions of the fire investigators. Fires with limited collateral damage may not be reported for judicial intervention, therefore never receive the label of arson. There is no national or international data base that functions as a repository for JSFB. Although it is important to note that there is an ongoing effort through the International Association of Fire Fighters (IAFF) to develop what is being referred to as a Youth Fire Information Resource and Evaluation (Y-FIRES) (Johnson, 2014 personal communication).

Due to these identification issues it is important to thoroughly investigate and vet all information obtained to create geographic location information about community arson activities. If an accurate profile of GR-JFSB is going to be produced, it is important to identify who is responding to the fires in the community.

Gathering Factual Fire Information from Records: How and Why

Information about the fire itself is generally available from the individuals who responded to the fires. They routinely generate fire or police reports, which may be supplemented by reports generated through ongoing investigations. Examples of some of the questions to ask when developing a list of these responders and sources of information are:

- If a community member calls an emergency number, is the fire department always notified?
- If the fire is already extinguished, is it handled by the police department?
- If there are jurisdictional boundaries, and if so are there policies in place to share information about fire-incidents?
- If the fire occurs in a school, who is the school reporting the fire to? Is the school reporting all fires or only those with substantial damage?
- What information is collected about a fire by a particular community responder group?
- What releases might you need to access the information collected?

Once you know who is responding to the fires, it is much easier to ascertain what information you will be able to gather about the fires themselves. The use of computerized software, maps, and other means of creating analytic reports based on this information is called geo-mapping. Geo-mapping provides a way in which both researchers and law enforcement personnel can examine the relationship between JFSB and juvenile gang activity.

Geo-Mapping

The use of geo-mapping software is useful in discerning where certain and specific phenomena occur and helps lend insight into why certain phenomena may be occurring in certain regions or areas. Geo-mapping is a useful way to present data and provides visuals of where this data is coming from. Geo-mapping also provides information regarding where there is a lack of data indicating a minimal occurrence of certain phenomena or lack of reporting of such phenomena. Geo-mapping can be a particularly helpful tool for law enforcement and the field of criminology as it provides insight into where specific crimes are being committed.

Geo-mapping has been successfully utilized to document specific crimes over time. For example, if there are a higher number of robberies in a certain neighborhood, law enforcement can warn local business owners and better assist them in preparing for and thus possibly preventing a robbery in their own business. Law enforcement can also examine this data and better determine how to utilize their resources, if robberies are being committed often in a particular neighborhood, local law enforcement may consider dispatching extra officers to that particular neighborhood for a six month time frame in order to intervene and hopefully prevent more robberies from occurring. Geo-mapping can thus be immensely helpful in guiding the allocation of law enforcement resources as well as other local resources that could be of help in the intervention and prevention of crimes and in the promotion of public safety.

In instances when geo-mapping data indicates that few or no juvenile fire setting incidents occur, this could be an indication that fires are being underreported. Additional resources may be allocated to this region in order to improve public awareness and encourage reporting. Alternatively, this particular region may provide fire safety education in schools, churches, and at community events or may have community service providers dedicated to educating the public about fire safety and treating juvenile fire setters. This type of community could potentially serve as a model for other communities.

Geo-Profiling

Geo-profiling takes the concept of geo-mapping and integrates it into a particular context. For example, in the field of criminology and criminal justice, geo-profiling is used to research crime. If law enforcement personnel and researchers can pinpoint not only where certain crimes are being committed, but also the motivation for why they are being committed, they may be able to better understand the nature of these crimes. This understanding could lead to more effective intervention and prevention strategies. For example, geo-profiling has been used by law enforcement to document criminal gang activity in urban regions and has helped law enforcement gain a better understanding of where certain gang territories begin and end, thus if a gang related crime is committed in a certain territory, law enforcement can reference geo-profiling data to determine which gang or gangs might be involved based on the gang territory where the crime was committed. Geo-profiling can also be used to predict violence in a certain neighborhood following a previously isolated incident. This information provides law enforcement a place to start when investigating crimes committed in communities with strong gang presences.

The above examples illustrate how geo-profiling can help facilitate the research and handling of juvenile gang related fire setting. In terms of juvenile fire setting, geo-profiling provides data regarding regions where intentionally set fires occur more frequently. Not only does juvenile fire setting geo-profiling data provide information about where fires are occurring, it also provides information about where fires are not occurring, and this is also helpful and relevant forensic information.

Agency Collaboration in Gang Related Juvenile Fire Setting and Bomb-Making

In terms of gang related fire setting behavior, geo-profiling data can provide researchers and law enforcement with data based on geo-mapping that is helpful in understanding whether a juvenile fire setter may or may not be gang affiliated and whether or not the fire setting behavior is related to criminal gang activity. Understanding the motivating force behind a crime is crucial in understanding why it was committed and who may have committed it. Thus, the drawing connections between juvenile fire setting and juvenile gang activity is forensically relevant in investigating arson crimes and understanding whether or not an arson crime was gang related, which could certainly prove essential in solving the crime as well as in maintaining and promoting public safety.

The identification of the juveniles involved in the GR-JFSB requires more agency collaboration, and a higher level of screening expertise. The individual(s) screening these juveniles should have specialized interviewing skills, support from a licensed mental health clinician, and a substantial knowledge of both gang activity and JFSB. These factors are especially important in the identification of gang-affiliated youth at high risk of JFSB behaviors.

Pulling Levers Model

The focused deterrence strategy identified as pulling levers is an example of a successful pairing of crime analysis and policing strategies put into action. At its most elementary, this specific problem-oriented policing technique involves the identification of a specific criminal problem, and the identification of individuals responsible for the majority of the calls related to that problem in a community, followed by structured approach to sanctioning those individuals for those behaviors. This results in a reduction of the rate and impact of that criminal behavior in the community (Braga, 2008; Corsaro, Brunson, & McGarrell, 2013). The reduction of GR-JFSB at the community level may be well served via the use of the pulling levers model by community and regional task force groups.

Below is an example of the application of the Pulling Levers Model to GR-JFSB adapted from the National Institute of Justice Journal's publication entitled, "Pulling Levers: Getting Deterrence Right."

1. Select target category of criminal behavior to be addressed, in this case the target behavior is GR- JFSB.
2. Identify a target audience of agencies that have the capacity to address GR-JFSB in the particular geographic region. In San Diego, California for example, Juvenile Forensic Services, The Department of Juvenile Justice, San Diego Police Department gang units, gang outreach programs, and FEMA.
3. Create a specific and structured deterrence message that will be delivered to the target audience. The target audience is the targeted group of criminal offenders. The response plan should include what kind of criminal behavior warrants a response from the authorities and should describe in detail what the specific response will be. For example, in the context of GR-JFSB a structured deterrence message could include information about the legal consequences of engaging in fire setting and/or bomb-making behavior as a juvenile. The deterrence message can be delivered through the news, social media, or posters and billboards in the area.
4. Follow through with response plan that was put in place. The agencies that are identified to address the particular criminal problem should put in place a formal line of communication with one and other, for example a monthly meeting. In the GR-JFSB example, all above listed agencies could send one representative to a monthly meeting to ensure communication between agencies and to follow up with any ongoing responses.
5. Continue to communicate with the targeted group of criminal offenders as the response strategy unfolds making sure to draw explicit connections between the behavior of the targeted group of criminal offenders and the response of the authorities. In the context of GR-JFSB this would entail sending messages through the news and social media that the response to a GR-JFSB incident was the result of a specific plan put in place by authorities to handle this kind of criminal behavior.

BARRIERS TO EFFECTIVE SERVICES

There are barriers to sharing information including unique departmental approaches to deterrence policies, and disparate (sometimes conflicting) definitions for arson and explosives-use, across multiple federal, state, and community agencies (Johnson & Jones, 2014). Despite these challenges, the shared goal of promoting public safety through decreased GR-JFSB can be realized using modern, evidence-based approaches and techniques. Crime analysis, the gathering of quantitative and qualitative information about a criminal behavior or group of criminal behaviors, paired with policing strategies that have been found to be effective for specific communities, increase the effectiveness of crime prevention and reduction programs (Santos, 2014).

Difficulties Inherent in Working across Disciplines and across System Domains

The complexity of issues presented in gang involved JFSB cases means that a diverse collection of disciplines will interact with these juveniles at some point. To no surprise, there are numerous challenges confronting the work with JFSBs after they have been brought into the various systems (e.g., mental health and criminal justice).

There are three disadvantages associated with cross professional work with gang involved juvenile fire setters and bomb makers. First, it takes time to arrange and conduct these contact sessions whether by phone, Internet protocol, or in person. Second, systems are bureaucracies with their own cultures, forms, rules and regulations. Finally, egos and personalities have to be negotiated around in order to work on these JFSB cases.

There are four advantages that outweigh the disadvantages for working cross professionally. First, it provides the greatest source for complete information on the JFSB that can be used in addressing individual issues. Second, the culturally responsive and individualized approach is best achieved through the coordinated efforts of various disciplines and systems. Third, meeting together can help to coordinate and integrate a collective "we" that promotes growth in the skill sets of providers as they become exposed to the strategies or techniques used in various disciplines. Finally, working with other disciplines builds capacity by extending information gathering, as well as sharing and facilitating innovative interventions (e.g., developing a comprehensive treatment plans). The dynamics between various disciplines (e.g., social and forensic mental health) can be shaped by the influences of the judicial system (i.e., defense versus prosecution).

Lack of Formal Training for First Responders

At the point of first contact, usually fire service or police officers are the first contacts with JFSB. On the scene, there are decisions made to impact all the subsequent work with JFSBs. For example, a fire investigator may decide to not refer a case to mental health because of some gender-based bias that fires set by girls are not as dangerous as those set by boys. As a result, some female offenders may actually receive a stern lecture and be allowed to go free. Younger JFSBs are sometime rewarded with being allowed to wear a fire hat of sit in the cab of the fire truck. Fire investigator reports may contain statements that amount to mental health diagnoses (e.g., I think this child has ADD or some other mental disorder).

In an extensive review of the FEMA model, the authors found a paucity of evidence with regards to the continuum of risk to public safety associated with the differences in fire setting behavior. The clinical, developmental, and/or forensic distinctions between the youth are often disregarded for a one-size-fits-all approach. For example, a juvenile who plays with matches may receive the same educational program as a juvenile who intentionally set fire to an occupied home (Gaynor, 2002; Kolko, 1985; Mastrangelo, 2012). The location of the service delivery is likewise not a significant concern. The educational program may be delivered at a fire station, a juvenile's home, or in juvenile detention facilities (Cole et al., 2006; "Fire Engineering," 2005, "Oshkosh Fire Department," 2014; Kolko et al., 2006). Educational programs vary widely in content as well (Cole et al., 2006). Time commitments range from single contact one hour sessions to 12 week multi-hour programs (Bennett, Gamelli, Duchene, Atkocaitis, & Plunkett, 2004; Gaynor, 2002; Institute of Social Analysis, 1994). These issues indicate a lack of empirically-based structure in the educational regimen.

According to FEMA's directive, juvenile fire setting behavior categorized as other than little risk is to be referred for evaluation by a mental health professional (Gaynor, 2002). A review of the literature reveals minimal training and guidance available for the US fire service in regard to how to determine the appropriateness of a particular case for a mental health referral. To make matters worse, there is also limited knowledge about the related clinical issues and approaches to treatment of fire setting behavior in the mental health profession (Paul Schwartzman et al., 1999). Much of the reviewed literature tailored to US fire service recommends the interviewer rely on subjective judgment and the self-reported responses of the juvenile fire setters and their families to determine the appropriate disposition of the case. This can be problematic in assessment of fire setting risk, even for experienced forensic mental health professionals (Johnson, Fessler, Wilhelm, & Stepensky, 2014).

Lack of Formal Training for Mental Health Professionals

Juvenile firesetting and bomb making is a behavior posing significant risk of great bodily injury to the involved juveniles, bystanders, and emergency responders. The belief that most fire setting is "curious" and therefore "low-risk," espoused by FEMA since 1978, may lead to significant under-reporting of JFSB. This belief may also lead to the treatment of JFSB behaviors by providers without adequate knowledge of the complex behavioral, emotional, and cognitive correlates (Johnson 2014b).

Working with JFSB cases is one of the most challenging clinical forensic tasks for professionals. JFSBs are often referred for help from a mental health professional under the assumption that when accurate assessment and appropriate intervention by a professional is provided, fire setting or bomb making recidivistic and escalation behaviors can be reduced. Unfortunately, clinical, risk assessment, motivational, and capacity for treatment factors of JFSBs is often missed by licensed mental health professionals. Mainly because these professionals lack the experience, training, and supervision required to competently work with JFSBs (Johnson 2014c).

There is a paucity of licensed mental health professionals with the requisite training, supervised experience, and knowledge of evidence based practices associated with JFSB. In addition, it is challenging to distinguish between qualified and unqualified service providers. As a result, far too many JFSB cases are ether missed diagnostically or misdiagnosed (Johnson, 2014). JFSB work has many faces that cannot be entirely explained by one discipline or system. A silo intervention mentality does not result in the clinical forensic and public safety of gang-involved JFSB cases. If nothing else takes place in serving JFSBs there must be an emphasis placed on the importance of collaboration (i.e., cross-professional) during all phases of the work with them. Efforts to gain acknowledgment of the relevance of other disciplines and systems is critical to these cases.

It certainly can be legitimately argued that there is a shortage of mental health services for juvenile offenders and these problems are even worse for gang involved JFSBs. For example, court-involved, non-incarcerated (CINI) juveniles represent about two-thirds of the juvenile justice population (Puzzanchera & Adams, 2009). Moreover, a significant portion (i.e., about a third or half) of this population meets DSM criteria for a psychological disorder (Gavazzi, Yarcheck, & Chesney-Lind, 2006). More troubling, this group is also at increased risk for persistent reoffending and self-reported antisocial activity (Schubert, Mulvey, & Glasheen, 2011).

The aforementioned unwanted juvenile circumstances have contributed to a traditional adjudication shift into exploring common mental health goals for JFSBs that can be shared between defense and prosecuting attorneys as well as judges. As an alternative to incarceration, many licensed and qualified mental health professionals are now practicing in a legal setting as a result of their work with juvenile fire setters and bomb builders.

What role licensed mental health professionals play is circumscribed to offering evidenced based interventions aimed at addressing the public safety risk factors presented by these cases (Johnson, Beckenbach, & Killbourne, 2013). Theoretically, mental health professionals in these gang involved JFSB cases are ostensibly risk assessment and therapeutic extensions of departments of corrections and rehabilitation. The precise role of the mental health professional in this context is in concert with the administration of justice espoused by both defense and prosecuting attorneys.

Reluctance of Reporting in Schools

By default, most fires that occur with JFSBs have school age youth involvement. Many of these fires are set at schools. Yet, some school system personnel are reluctant to refer these youth. Instead, many schools choose to handle these cases internally through various disciplinary channels. Social work can play a central role in case management but oftentimes the clinical issues associated with these cases receive little attention due to the priority placed on the public safety matters.

Defense vs. Prosecution Attorneys in Gang Involved JFSB Cases

It is not unusual for JFSB cases to wind up in juvenile court. The culture and tone of these cases can take on less of an adversarial quality. Our discussion here is limited to the types of JFSB cases that find their way into the juvenile court system where the youth has been assessed as being competent.

One of the main differences (i.e., excluding serious acts) between the juvenile and adult justice systems lies in their overall aim. For the juvenile justice system, the main aim is to rehabilitate and reform the juvenile offender so that they can resume functioning normally in society. Thus, the focus is more on alternative sentences that keep the juvenile out of jail, such as probation, parole, and diversionary programs.

There are four ways that juvenile system is distinct from adult. First, the juveniles are accused of delinquent acts as opposed to actual crimes. When the delinquent acts are very serious, they may be considered crimes and the juvenile may be tried in the adult system. The case is heard and decided by a judge only. Third, the actions (i.e., maturity and culpability factors) of a juvenile are used to craft a plan for rehabilitation. Finally, the juvenile courts are less formal when contrasted with the adult system.

Both the defense and prosecuting attorneys are officers of the court. They are charged with trying to help administer justice in the gang involved JFSB cases. Attorneys on both sides (i.e., defense and prosecutors) are key players in gang involved JFSB cases because of what should be a non- adversarial psychological process. One of the most frequent and important types of evidence that prosecutors and defense attorneys encounter in JFSB cases is psychological evidence that is often contained in a forensic report written by a licensed psychologist. From a defense attorney perspective, a Supreme Court's decision in In re Gault, 387 U.S. 1 (1967) articulated due process protections in delinquency proceedings, including the right to counsel. In addition, the Court equated the role of defense counsel in delinquency proceedings to be the same as those in an adult criminal case. Defense attorneys are trained to balk at mental health experts and reports because of the concern that a juvenile might disclose incriminating information (e.g., charged offense or about other uncharged crimes) that could be contained in the forensic psychological report or disclosed by testimony of a mental health expert witness. For example, in Estelle v. Smith, 451 U.S. 454 (1981), the Court ruled that the Fifth Amendment Privilege Against Self-Incrimination is applicable to information disclosed during the course of a psychological evaluation.

The forensic psychological evaluation process involves the compilation of information and the formulation of evidenced based opinions pertaining to the gang involved JFSBs' public safety risks, motivations, and capacity to appropriately respond to interventions. The psychological report and separate subsequent treatment are a part of a process whereby qualified opinions are disclosed to the court, attorneys and family. Qualified mental health professionals (e.g., knowledge of the legal and professional JFSB practice, laws, and applicable clinical issues) working with these cases must reflexively conduct self-audits for biases, determine perceived losses of fairness, and seek to maintain appropriate professional boundaries in the work with attorneys. Most attorneys and psychologists are on some level cognizant of the complexities involved in JFSB cases. Despite the criticism of the appropriateness of experts, the overlapping of clinical forensic and public safety issues has forced an expansion of the juvenile justice system with respect to the role of cross-disciplinary professionals (e.g., fire service, law enforcement, mental health and social services).

REFERENCES

Akbaş, S., Ahmet, T., Koray, K., Ozan, P., Tülay, K., & Omer, B. (2013). Characteristics of Sexual Abuse in a Sample of Turkish Children With and Without Mental Retardation Referred for Legal Appraisal of the Psychological Repercussions. *Sexuality and Disability, 27*(4), 205–213. doi:10.1007/s11195-009-9139-7

American Psychiatric Association. (2013). *Diagnostic and Statistical Manual of Mental Disorders (DSM-5)*. Arlington, VA: American Psychiatric Association.

Arson Required for Juvenile Gang Initiation. (1958, April 5). *Ludington Daily News*. Retrieved on July 6, 2014 from: http://news.google.com/newspapers

Augimeri, L. K., Enebrink, P., Walsh, M., & Jiang, D. (2000). Gender-specific childhood risk assessment tools: early assessment risk lists for boys (earl-20b) and girls (earl-21g). In Handbook of Violence Risk Assessment. New York: Routledge Taylor & Francis Group.

Bennett, B., Gamelli, R., Duchene, R., Atkocaitis, D., & Plunkett, J. (2004). Burn Education Awareness Recognition And Support (Bears): A Community-Based Juvenile Firesetters Assessment And Treatment Program. *Journal of Burn Care & Research; Official Publication of the American Burn Association, 25*(3), 324–327.

Braga, A. A., Kennedy, D. M., Waring, E. W., & Piehl, A. M. (2001). Problem-oriented policing, deterrence, and youth violence: An evaluation of Boston's Operation Ceasefire. *Journal of Research in Crime and Delinquency, 38*, 195–225.

Brett, A. (2004). 'Kindling theory' in arson: How dangerous are firesetters? *The Australian and New Zealand Journal of Psychiatry, 38*, 419–425. PMID:15209833

Campbell, D. (2014). *Intentional Fires.* National Fire Protection Agency. Retrieved on September 15, 2014 from: http://www.nfpa.org

Cole, R., Crandall, R., Kourofsky, C., Sharp, D., & Blaakman, S. (2006). *Juvenile Firesetting: A Community Guide To Prevention & Intervention.* Elizabeth: Fireproof Children/Prevention.

Corsaro, N., Brunson, R. K., & McGarrell, E. F. (2013). Problem-Oriented Policing and Open-Air Drug Markets: Examining the Rockford Pulling Levers Deterrence Strategy. *Crime and Delinquency, 59*(7), 1085–1107. doi:10.1177/0011128709345955

David, C. F., & Kisner, J. A. (2000). Do Positive Self-Perceptions Have a `Dark Side'? Examination of the Link between Perceptual Bias. *Journal of Abnormal Child Psychology, 28*(4), 327–337. doi:10.1023/A:1005164925300 PMID:10949958

DeMatteo, D. S., Marlowe, D. B., & Festinger, D. S. (2006). Secondary Prevention Services for Clients Who Are Low Risk in Drug Court: *A Conceptual Model. Crime and Delinquency, 52*(1), 114–134. doi:10.1177/0011128705281751

Dickens, G. L., Sugarman, P. A., & Gannon, T. A. (Eds.). (2012). Fire setting and Mental Health Theory, Research and Practice. London: RCPsych Publications.

DiIorio, C., Pluhar, E., & Belcher, L. (2003, December 08). Parent-child communication about sexuality: A review of the literature from 1980–2002. *Journal of HIV/AIDS Prevention & Education for Adolescents & Children, 5*(3-4), 7–32. doi:10.1300/J129v05n03_02

Dishion, T. J., & Patterson, G. R. (1992). Age effects in parent training outcome. *Behavior Therapy, 23*(4), 719–729. doi:10.1016/S0005-7894(05)80231-X

Doley, R. (2003). Pyromania: Fact or fiction? *The British Journal of Criminology, 43*(4), 797–807. doi:10.1093/bjc/43.4.797

Egley, A. J., & Howell, J. C. (2013). *Highlights of the 2011 national gang youth survey. Working for youth justice and safety.* Washington, DC: U.S. Department of Justice.

Enayati, J., Grann, M., Lubbe, S., & Fazel, S. (2008). Psychiatric morbidity in arsonists referred for forensic psychiatric assessment in Sweden. *Journal of Forensic Psychiatry & Psychology, 19*(2), 139–147. doi:10.1080/14789940701789500

Engineering, F. (2005). *National Fire Academy Announces Juvenile Firesetter Intervention Specialist (Jfis) I & Ii Leadership (R628) Course.* Retrieved March 7, 2014, From Http://Www.Fireengineering. Com/Articles/2005/07/National-Fire-Academy-Announces-Juvenile-Firesetter-Intervention-Specialist-Jfis-I-Ii-Leadership-R628-Course.Html

Epps, K., & Hollin, C. R. (2000). Understanding and treating adolescent fire setters. In G. Boswell (Ed.), *Violent children and adolescents: asking the question why?* (pp. 36–55). London: Whurr.

Farrington, D. P. (1989). Early predictors of adolescent aggression and adult violence. *Violence and Victims, 4,* 79–100. PMID:2487131

Federal Bureau of Investigation. (2011). *Arson.* Crime in the United States.

Federal Emergency Management Agency. (2004). *The Fire Risk to Children*. Washington, DC: United States Fire Administration.

Federal Emergency Management Agency. (2005). *School Fires*. Washington, DC: United States Fire Administration.

Federal Emergency Management Agency. (2012). *Understanding Youth Fire setting Behaviors*. FEMA.

Flynn, J. (2007). U.S. Structure Fires in Eating and Drinking Establishments. In Fire Analysis and Research Division. National Fire Protection Association.

Frick, P. J., & Viding, E. (2009). Antisocial behavior from a developmental psychopathology perspective. *Development and Psychopathology, 21*(04), 11111131. doi:10.1017/S0954579409990071 PMID:19825260

Gavazzi, S. M., Yarcheck, C. M., & Chesney-Lind, M. (2006). Global risk indicators and the role of gender in a juvenile detention sample. *Criminal Justice and Behavior, 33*(5), 597–612. doi:10.1177/0093854806288184

Gaynor, J. (2002). *Juvenile Firesetter Intervention Handbook*. Sociotechnical Research Applications, Inc.

Geller, J. L. (1992). Pathological fire setting in adults. *International Journal of Law and Psychiatry, 15*(3), 283–302. doi:10.1016/0160-2527(92)90004-K PMID:1399186

Glancy, G. D., Spiers, E. M., Pitt, S. E., & Dvoskin, J. A. (2003). Commentary: Models and Correlates of Fire setting Behavior. *The Journal of the American Academy of Psychiatry and the Law, 31*, 53–57. PMID:12817843

Gottfredson, S. D., & Moriarty, L. J. (2006). Statistical Risk Assessment: Old Problems and New Applications. *Crime and Delinquency, 52*(1), 178–200. doi:10.1177/0011128705281748

Grant, J. E., & Kim, S. W. (2007). Clinical characteristics and psychiatric comorbidity of pyromania. *The Journal of Clinical Psychiatry, 68*(11), 1717–1722. doi:10.4088/JCP.v68n1111 PMID:18052565

Hanson, M., Mackay, S., Atkinson, L., & Staley, S. (1995). Fire setting during the preschool period: Assessment and intervention issues. *Canadian Journal of Psychiatry, 40*, 299–303. PMID:7585398

Hart, C. H., Newell, L. D., & Olsen, S. F. (2003). *Parenting skills and social-communicative competence in childhood in Handbook of Communication and Social Interaction Skills*. Lawrence Erlbaum Associates, Publishers.

Hawkins, D. J., Herrenkohl, T. I., Farrington, D. P., Brewer, D., Catalano, R. F., Harachi, T. W., & Cothern, L. (2000). *Predictors of youth violence. Juvenile Justice Bulletin (NCJ-179065)*. Washington, DC: U.S. Dept. of Justice, Office of Juvenile Justice & Delinquency Prevention.

Henggeler, S. W. (1989). *Delinquency in adolescence*. Newbury Park, CA: Sage.

Hill, R. W. (1982). Is Arson An Aggressive Act Or A Property Offence? A Controlled Study Of Psychiatric Referrals. *Canadian Journal of Psychiatry, 27*, 648–654. PMID:7159867

Huebner, A. J., & Howell, L. W. (2003). Examining the relationship between adolescent sexual risk-taking and perceptions of monitoring, communication, and parenting styles. *The Journal of Adolescent Health, 33*(2), 71–78. doi:10.1016/S1054-139X(03)00141-1 PMID:12890597

Institute Of Social Analysis. (1994). *National Juvenile Firesetter/Arson Control And Prevention Program.* Author.

Jayaraman, A., & Frazer, J. (2006). Arson: A growing inferno. *Medicine, Science, and the Law, 46*(4), 295–30. doi:10.1258/rsmmsl.46.4.295 PMID:17191632

Johnson, R., Beckenbach, H., & Kilbourne, S. (2013). Forensic psychological public safety risk assessment integrated with culturally responsive treatment for juvenile fire setters: DSM-5 implications. *Journal of Criminal Psychology, 3*(1), 49–64. doi:10.1108/20093821311307767

Johnson, R., Fessler, A., Wilhelm, M., & Stepensky, A. (2014). Towards A Forensic Psychological Evaluation Of Juvenile Fire Setters: Parent Power. *J Forensic Res, 5*(214), 2.

Johnson, R., & Jones, P. (2014a). Identification of Parental Endorsement Patterns: An Example of the Importance of Professional Attunement to the Clinical-Forensic Risk Markers in Juvenile Fire setting and Bomb Making. *The American Journal of Forensic Psychology, 32*(2).

Johnson, R., Jones, P., Ryan, K., & Gafford, O. (2014b). *Juvenile Fire Setters And Bomb Makers: A Forensic Psychological Update Using Biopsychosocialcultural Parent Endorsement Patterns In Juvenile Fire Setters And Bomb Makers To Rethink The Design Of A Third Generation Risk Assessment Instrument.* In Acjs 51st Annual Meeting, Philadelphia, PA.

Kent, R. (2001). *Data construction and data analysis for survey research.* New York, NY: Palgrave Publishers.

Kolko, D. J. (1985). Juvenile Firesetting: A Review And Methodological Critique. *Clinical Psychology Review, 5*(4), 345–376. doi:10.1016/0272-7358(85)90012-1

Kolko, D. J., Herschell, A. D., & Scharf, D. M. (2006). Education And Treatment For Boys Who Set Fires: Specificity, Moderators, And Predictors Of Recidivism. *Journal of Emotional and Behavioral Disorders, 14*(4), 227–239. doi:10.1177/10634266060140040601

Kolko, D. J., & Kazdin, A. E. (1992). The emergence and recurrence of child fire setting: A one-year prospective study. *Journal of Abnormal Child Psychology, 20*(1), 17–37. doi:10.1007/BF00927114 PMID:1548392

Labree, W., Nijman, H., Van Marle, H., & Rassin, E. (2010). Backgrounds and characteristics of arsonists. *International Journal of Law and Psychiatry, 33*(3), 149–153. doi:10.1016/j.ijlp.2010.03.004 PMID:20434774

Mastrangelo, A. (2012). *Identifying Juvenile Firesetters: A Survey Of The Operating Procedures, Risk Assessment Instruments And The Characteristics Of Juvenile Firesetter Intervention Programs In The United States.* (Thesis). City University Of New York, New York, NY.

Metzler, C. W., & Noell, J. (1994). The social context of risky sexual behavior among adolescents. *Journal of Behavioral Medicine, 17,* 419.

Miller, L. (2014). Juvenile Crime And Juvenile Justice: Patterns, Models, And Implications For Clinical And Legal Practice. *Aggression and Violent Behavior, 19*(2), 122–137.http://dx.doi.org/10.1016/j.avb.2014.01.005

Moffitt, T. E. (1993). Adolescence-limited and life-course-persistent antisocial behavior: A developmental taxonomy. *Psychological Review, 100,* 674.

National Gang Crime Research Center. (n.d.). Bomb and arson crimes among American gang members: A behavioral science profile. *Journal of Gang Research, 9*(1), 1-38.

Odgers, C. L., Moffitt, T. E., Broadbent, J. M., Dickson, N., Hancox, R. J., Harrington, H., & Caspi, A. (2008). Female and male antisocial trajectories: From childhood origins to adult outcomes. *Development and Psychopathology, 20*(02), 673–716. doi:10.1017/S0954579408000333 PMID:18423100

Office of Juvenile Justice and Delinquency Prevention (OJJDP). (1997). *Reporting Crimes Against Juveniles.* Washington, DC: U.S. Department of Justice.

Office of Juvenile Justice and Delinquency Prevention (OJJDP). (1999). *Promising strategies to reduce gun violence.* Washington, DC: U.S. Department of Justice.

Oshkosh Fire Department. (2014). Retrieved March 5, 2014, from http://www2.ci.oshkosh.wi.us/fire/dpt_overview.htm

Perrino, T., González-Soldevilla, A., Pantin, H., & Szapocznik, J. (2000). The Role of Families in Adolescent HIV Prevention: A Review. *Clinical Child and Family Psychology Review, 3*(2), 81–96. doi:10.1023/A:1009571518900 PMID:11227063

Puzzanchera, C., & Adams, B. (2009). Juvenile Arrests 2009. Office of Juvenil Justice and Delinquency Prevention (OJJDP). Washington, DC: U.S. Department of Justice. Retrieved from http://www.ojjdp.gov/pubs/236477.pdf

Ritchie, E. C., & Huff, T. G. (1999). Psychiatric aspects of arsonists. *Journal of Forensic Sciences, 44*(4), 733–740. doi:10.1520/JFS14546J PMID:10432607

Santos, R. B. (2014). The Effectiveness of Crime Analysis for Crime Reduction: Cure or Diagnosis? *Journal of Contemporary Criminal Justice, 30*(2), 147–168. doi:10.1177/1043986214525080

Schubert, M., Mulvey, E. P., & Glasheen, C. (2011). Influence of mental health and substance use problems and criminogenic risk on outcomes in serious juvenile offenders. *Journal of the American Academy of Child and Adolescent Psychiatry, 50*(9), 925–937. doi:10.1016/j.jaac.2011.06.006 PMID:21871374

Schwartzman, Fineman, Slavkin, Mieszala, Thomas, Gross, Spurlin, & Baer. (1999). *Juvenile Firesetter Mental Health Intervention: A Comprehensive Discussion Of Treatment.* Service Delivery, And Training Of Providers (Report).

Simpkins, S. D., Bouffard, S. M., Dearing, E., Kreider, H., Wimer, C., Caronongan, P., & Weiss, H. B. (2009). Adolescent adjustment and patterns of parents' behaviors in early and middle adolescence. *Journal of Research on Adolescence, 19*(3), 530–555. doi:10.1111/j.1532-7795.2009.00606.x

Slavkin, M. L. (2000). Juvenile fire setters: A report of the juvenile fire setter intervention project. *Journal of Psychosocial Nursing, 38,* 6–17.

Stadolnik, R. F. (2000). Drawn To The Flame: Assessment And Treatment Of Juvenile Firesetting Behavior. Professional Resource Exchange. Retrieved from.http://www.amazon.com/dp/1568870639

Sullivan, P. M., & Knutson, J. F. (1998). The association between child maltreatment and disabilities in a hospital-based epidemiological study. *Child Abuse & Neglect, 22,* 271–288.

Unnever, J. D., Cullen, F. T., & Agnew, R. (2006). Why is "bad" parenting criminogenic? Implications rival theories. *Youth Violence and Juvenile Justice, 4*(1), 3–33. doi:10.1177/1541204005282310

U.S. Department of Justice. (1998). *Pulling Levers: Getting Deterrence Right.* Washington, DC: U.S. Department of Justice.

U.S. Fire Administration Structure Fire Cause Methodology. (2014). Retrieved from http://www.usfa. fema.gov/fireservice/nfirs/tools/fire_cause_category_matrix.shtm

Vaughn, M. G. (2006). Do prior trauma and victimization predict weapon carrying among delinquent youth? *Youth Violence and Juvenile Justice, 4*(4), 314–327. doi:10.1177/1541204006292665

Vaughn, M. G., Fu, Q., Delisi, M., Wright, J. P., Beaver, K. M., Perron, B. E., & Howard, M. O. L. (2010). Prevalence and correlates of fire-setting in the United States: Results from the National Epidemiological Survey on Alcohol and Related Conditions. *Comprehensive Psychiatry, 51*(3), 217–223. doi:10.1016/j. comppsych.2009.06.002 PMID:20399330

KEY TERMS AND DEFINITIONS

ADD: *Attention Deficit Disorder* is characterized by inattentiveness, difficulty becoming focused or staying focused on a task, hyperactivity, and difficulty controlling impulses.

ASD: *Autism Spectrum Disorder* is a disorder characterized by social deficits, communication difficulties, stereotyped or repetitive behaviors and interests, sensory issues, and in some cases, cognitive delays.

CDD: *Conduct disorder* is a repetitive and persistent pattern of behavior in children and adolescents in which the rights of others or basic social rules are violated.

DSM-V Quadrant: Four psychiatric diagnoses containing behavioral, emotional, and cognitive correlates to juvenile fire setting behavior.

FEMA: Federal Emergency Management Agency, FEMA is a United States government agency whose primary purpose is to coordinate responses to large disasters such as floods, hurricanes, tornadoes, earthquakes, and fires.

GR-JFSB: Gang Related Juvenile Fire Setting Behavior.

JFSB: Juvenile Fire Setting Behavior.

JFSBs: Juvenile Fire Setters and Bomb Makers.

ODD: *Oppositional Defiant Disorder* is defined by the DSM-5 as a pattern of angry/irritable mood, argumentative/defiant behavior, or vindictiveness lasting at least six months and exhibited during interaction with at least one individual who is not a sibling.

PTSD: *Post Traumatic Stress Disorder* is an anxiety disorder characterized by hyperarousal disturbing recurring flashbacks, avoidance or numbing of memories of the event, and these symptoms continue for more than a month after the occurrence of a traumatic event.

Pulling Levers Model: Focused deterrence strategy involving the identification of both a specific criminal problem and the individuals or community agencies responsible for responding to the specific criminal problem as well as a structured and formal approach to sanctioning the responsible individuals and agencies to address the criminal problem.

Chapter 6
Sticks and Stones:
When the Words of Hatred become Weapons – A Social Psychological Perspective

Robin Maria Valeri
St. Bonaventure University, USA

Kevin Borgeson
Salem State University, USA

ABSTRACT

The present chapter takes a social psychological approach to understanding hate groups and how hate groups use hate as a promotional tool and as an implement of aggression. As a promotional tool, hate groups use hate to attract new members to their organizations and to promote their beliefs to the mainstream public. Hate also serves as an incendiary, to fuel the emotions of their members, to incite them into action, and to wield against their targets. In this chapter we will attempt to explain why people hate and how they justify their hatred and resulting actions through a number of social psychological theories including realistic group conflict (Bonacich, 1972; Sherif et al., 1961/1988) relative deprivation (Catalono et al., 1993; Hepworth & West, 1988; Hovland & Sears, 1940), social identity theory (Abrams & Hogg, 1990; Festinger, 1954; Tajfel & Turner, 1986; Thoits & Virshup, 1997) and terror management (Pyszczynski, Solomon, & Greenberg, 1997; 2005; Solomon, Greenberg, & Pyszczynski, 1991; 2004).

BIRDS OF A FEATHER: A WEB OF HATE

In today's high-tech and globally connected world, hate groups are reaching out to like minded individuals and groups to spread their beliefs. While some hate groups are changing their image to look and act more mainstream in an effort to reach the average citizen and even influence politics others hate groups are maintaining or enhancing their fear evoking image and extending their reach by collaborating with like minded groups. Two recent examples of the latter are, in the United States, collaboration between the hate gang Public Enemy Number I with the prison gang the Aryan Brotherhood and, in Germany, neo-Nazis and other hate groups collaborating with Football Hooligans to spread anti-Muslim sentiment.

DOI: 10.4018/978-1-4666-9938-0.ch006

In March 2007 the Union Times (Flaccus 2007) published a story about the white supremacist gang Public Enemy Number 1 (PENI) teaming up with the Aryan Brotherhood, a powerful white supremacist prison gang. According to the article "The alliance (between the two groups) was cemented in 2005 when Donald Reed "Popeye" Mazza, an alleged leader of Public Enemy No. 1, was inducted into the Aryan Brotherhood." The alliance has benefited PENI by raising its prestige. According to the article since the alliance PENI, which is known for dealing in drugs and guns, committing white collar crimes such as computer fraud, credit card fraud, identity theft, and violent crimes including assault and murder (Anti-Defamation League, 2007), has more than doubled its ranks. In the article, Flaccus (2007) reports that "heavy recruiting (by PENI) is taking place throughout California and Arizona, and members have been picked up by police in Nevada and Idaho." This alliance also benefits the Aryan Brotherhood who, because they are recognized by the California Department of Corrections as a prison gang, are segregated from the general prison population in Secure Housing Units. The alliance with PENI allows the Aryan Brotherhood to continue to be influential. Because PENI members are, at least initially, placed in the general population, they can serve as middlemen for the Aryan Brotherhood, conducting criminal business such as drug dealing, both inside and outside of prison on their behalf (Anti-Defamation League, 2007; Flaccus, 2007).

In November 2014 (Germany's New Right) Spiegel International, in a story about an anti- Islamist Salafist rally that occurred at the end of October in Cologne, reported that almost 5000 Hooligans gegen Salafisten (Hooligans against Salafists), a "…loose association of neo-Nazis, nationalists and football rowdies…," after being stirred up by the right wing hate rock group Kategorie C marched through Cologne, spreading hate and destroying property. According to the article "Thousands of hooligans appear to have left their football clubs of choice behind in favor of uniting against a common enemy: the presumed danger of Islam. In addition, they have joined forces with neo-Nazis and other racists." The article suggests that the alliance between the various football hooligan groups can be traced back to 2012 when Borussenfront invited representatives from various hooligan groups to a "cross-club exchange." After much drinking and complaining about left wing Ultra groups who had been trying to combat racism at football stadiums, those present decided to band together to form the Gnu Honnters (New Hunters). As the Gnu Honnters threatened Ultra groups, attended Katergorie C concerts, and participated in football tournaments such as the "Swastika Cup" their membership grew and they began to attract hate group members. "The hooligans' success in the battle against the Ultras resulted in a flood of new right-wing members. Meetings began attracting attendees who had previously been active in the 'Nationalen Widerstand' (National Resistance) or in now-banned groups such as the 'Kameradschaft Aachener Land.' (Germany's New Right, 2014)"

DEFINING HATE

Researchers have offered a variety of definitions of hate (for a more thorough discussion of hate see Sternberg, 2005). Definitions that are relevant to this chapter are ones that suggest that hate can derive from real or perceived inequities, target a group, and drive behavior. Allport (1954) defines hate as an emotion of extreme dislike or aggressive impulses toward a person or group. Key in Allport's conceptualization of hate is its relationship to aggressive impulses and that these impulses may be directed to a group. Hate groups target other groups or the members of other groups based on their group membership rather than individual attributes and use the reasons behind their hatred as the rational for their aggression.

Similarly, Fromm's definitions of hate (1990; 1992), which he divides into rational hate and character-conditioned hate, suggests that the target of hate may be a group. In the case of rational hate, the basis for one group's hatred of another group, the outgroup, is that the outgroup is seen as taking the resources of or threatening your own group, the ingroup. In the case of character-conditioned hate, hate, or the readiness to hate, is viewed as part of the individual's personality, is irrational, unfocused, or targetless. The individual, because he/she finds pleasure in expressing hate, searches for an excuse to hate. If that individual's culture fosters prejudice than the excuse to hate and the target are defined by the culture. Important to this chapter, is Fromm's suggestion that hate may stem from long standing prejudices and/or from the belief that another group has benefited in some way, e.g., economically or socially, at the expense of or to the detriment of one's own group. We will revisit these notions when we discuss realistic group conflict, relative deprivation, and social identity theory.

The definition of hate offered by the FBI (Schafer & Navarro, 2003), while similar to that of Fromm's, adds an important caveat, linking an individual's hatred to his/her own insecurities. Like Fromm, the FBI divides hate into rational hate, inspired by an injustice, and irrational hate, based on a person's race, religion, sexual orientation, ethnicity, or national origin. The FBI's definition also suggests that people use hate to mask their own insecurities and that they can regain a sense of self-worth by relegating the target of their hate to a lower status then themselves.

Finally Sternberg proposed a triangle of hate that is, in some sense, the inverse or opposite of his triangle model of love (Sternberg 1986; 2006). Similar to his triangle model of love, hate is composed of three components, passion, the negation of intimacy (as opposed to intimacy), and commitment. These three components can occur singularly, paired with one of the other components, or occurring, all three together, to produce seven different types of hate (For a more complete discussion of this model see Sternberg, 2003). Sternberg, as part of his model of hate, suggests that individuals' will distance themselves from the target of hate (negation of intimacy) and devalue the target (cognitive component). These two components are key characteristics of hate messages which encourage their members to see themselves as superior to the target by devaluing and dehumanizing the target.

These definitions of hate offer touch stones that we will return to throughout the chapter. The first touch stone is that hate can stem from real or perceived injustices or inequities. The belief that one's group has been treated unfairly or unjustly is at the heart of explanations for prejudice, realistic group conflict, relative deprivation, and social identity theory. The second touchstone is the target of hate. The group that is perceived to have caused the injustice becomes the target of hate. The third is that people who hate use hated to mask their own insecurities or shortcomings. Hate groups offer people who hate a sanctuary in which they can freely express their hate and provide a culture which confirms their beliefs in the injustice of how they have been treated, nurtures their prejudice and hate toward the perceived cause of that injustice, while at the same time increasing the individual's self-worth, both through feelings of belonging and through validation of their beliefs. The fourth is that hate can be the driving force behind aggressive actions. Hate groups frequently encourage their members to act on their hate.

HATE GROUPS/HATE GANGS

Two advocacy groups, The Southern Poverty Law Center, based in Montgomery, Alabama and the Athena Institute, based in Budapest, Hungary, offer similar definitions of hate groups. The Southern Poverty Law Center (Hate Map, 2014) defines a hate group as any group "with beliefs or practices that attack or malign an entire class of people, typically for their immutable characteristics." The Athena Group provides a similar, but more detailed definition, "Domestic extremist or hate groups are organized, formal or informal groups that in the name of an ideology carry out verbal, symbolic, or physical aggression or call for such acts against certain people or a definable community of people based mostly on - real or perceived -characteristics such as national or ethnic origin, race, religion or sexual orientation (Berecz & Dominam 2012, p. 15)." Both of these definitions suggest that (1) hate groups are motivated by ideology; (2) their hatred is directed toward a group or groups of individuals because that group has a characteristic the hate group deems objectionable and counter to their beliefs and (3) that the hate group aggress in some way, symbolically, verbally, or physically, against their target. However, neither of these definitions explicitly states that the aggression is unlawful or that criminal activity is a regular and condoned part of the group's activities. This vagueness or omission regarding criminal activity runs counter to definitions of gangs which definitively state that reoccurring criminal actively is a feature of gang activity, occurs on behalf of the gang, and is condoned by gang members. For example, according to the 2014 Florida's Statute 874.03 Criminal Gang Enforcement and Prevention " 'Criminal gang' means a formal or informal ongoing organization, association, or group that has as one of its primary activities the commission of criminal or delinquent acts, and that consists of three or more persons who have a common name or common identifying signs, colors, or symbols, including, but not limited to, terrorist organizations and hate groups." The question is "Are all hate groups hate gangs? Certainly many hate groups, especially prison based hate groups would meet the definition of a gang. Depending on the extent of a hate group's activities and a nation's laws regarding freedom of speech in regard to hate speech, a hate group who limits its activities to talk or writing may not be engaging in criminal activity and therefore may not meet the definition of a gang. That being said, many hate groups, as discussed in the following sections, do engage in or promote criminal activity.

Prevalence of Hate Groups

The Athena Group (Berecz & Domina, 2012) identified 115 active domestic terrorist groups in thirteen European countries, with the majority (67%) in Western Europe. To be included in this list a group had to score 4 or higher on the FBI's Seven-Stage Hate Model (Schafer & Navarro, 2003). This means that the group had to take some action against the target, ranging from taunting, to attacking, with or without a weapon, to destroying the target. According to the report 33% of these extremist groups had ties, via cooperation or shared membership, to a political party, 34% had no direct links, and for the remaining 33% political ties were unknown. The Athena Group, using a simple classification system in which radial animal rights groups, radical environmentalist groups, anarchists, communists and any group with no tendencies toward racism, xenophobia, homophobia, etc. were classified as far left and all other groups as far right, reported that there were three times as many far right groups as far left groups.

According to the Southern Poverty Law Center (Holthouse, 2009) in 2008 there were 926 hate groups active in the United States, which is a 4% increase from 2007, when there were 888 hate group and a 54% increase from 2000 when there were 602 hate groups.

In the United States, the stereotype of a hate group member is a Neo-Nazi skin head with a shaved head and tattoos. While there is evidence that membership in these organizations has declined since the 1920s, these groups still exist, have reportedly experienced an increase in numbers, and include the Ku Klux Klan, Neo-Nazi Groups, and Racist Skinheads.

Beirich (2014) suggests that the internet has benefitted hate groups because it allows people to readily access information, anonymously if they choose, and to communicate with likeminded people. According to Beirich (2014), membership on Stormfront's website went from 5000 in January 2002, to 286,000 registered users in 2014. Beirich states

A typical murderer drawn to the racist forum Stormfront.org is a frustrated, unemployed, white adult male living with his mother or an estranged spouse or girlfriend....Instead of building his resume, seeking employment...he projects his grievances on society and searches the Internet for an excuse or an explanation unrelated to his behavior or the choices he has made in life...From right-wing antigovernment websites and conspiracy hatcheries, he migrates to militant hate sites that blame society's ills on ethnicity and shifting demographics. He soon learns his race is endangered – a target of "white genocide."

Note that Beirich's description paints a picture of an insecure individual whose self-worth needs bolstering. This is consistent with the FBI's definition of hate, described previously.

Reach of White Supremacist Prison Gangs

In Smashing the Shamrock, an article in the Winter 2012 issue of Intelligence Report, a publication of the Southern Poverty Law Center, the authors suggest that white supremacist prison gangs are strengthening their ties to white supremacist groups outside of prison and expanding their criminal activity to include drug and weapons trafficking as well as violence, robbery, murder, and perhaps even terrorist plots to blow up federal buildings using a variety of incendiary devices and delivery systems.

The report described the pervasiveness of these gangs in federal and state prisons, their efforts to collaborate with outside white supremacist groups, and their involvement with drug and arms trafficking. According to the report, the most notorious and powerful white supremacist prison gang, the Aryan Brotherhood, has chapters in all of the major federal and state prisons. Although their members constitute less than 1/10 of 1 percent of the prison population in the United States, murders committed in their name constitute 18% of prison murders. In the past, the gang's violence was largely confined to prison and targeted black and Hispanics prison gangs. However, some Aryan Brotherhood members, after their release from prison, continue to act on their white supremacist beliefs. Two notorious cases are the 1998 dragging and murder of an African American James Byrd in Jasper, Texas and the post 9-11 (October 2001) murder of a Bangladeschi gas station attendant because he looked Arab.

In 2010 the Orange County (California) Register (Hardesty 2010) reported on a two year multiagency operation composed of County, State, and Federal law enforcement agencies that resulted in the arrest of 34 white supremacist gang members, some of who belonged to the Aryan Brotherhood (the white supremacist prison gang mentioned above), Public Enemy Number One (PEN1, reportedly the largest white supremacist gang in the United States), La Mirada Punks, West Coast Costa Mesa Skins, Nazi Low Riders and the O.C. Skins. Chargers were filed at the State and Federal level and included extortion, conspiracy and solicitation of aggravated assault, murder, parole violations, non violent felonies, and illegal weapons and narcotic sales.

On November 20, 2013 The Spokesman Review (Hill 2013) reported that the Aryan Brotherhood had placed a $10,000 bounty on two African American teenagers who were accused of beating to death 88-year-old Delbert Belton, a World War II veteran.

White Supremacist Makeover

While many hate groups and their members, like the Aryan Brotherhood, overtly proclaim their hate through their dress and tattoos, some of these groups are trying to change their image in an effort to become more mainstream and acceptable to the "average" American (Bello, 2008). This includes changing their dress from the more traditional brown Nazi uniform with a swastika armband to black fatigues. It also includes more sophisticated changes in "branding" and action. For example a Pennsylvania hate group, the Keystone State Skinheads, changed their name to the more banal Keystone United, revamped their image to be "pro white" activists, and shifted their activities away from the violence associated with skinheads to more family friendly events such as meeting in public libraries (Civilrights.org, 2009) and organizing an October "Leif Ericson Day Celebration" that included Celtic Folk Musicians (Holthouse, 2009).

The success of these makeovers is evident by the increased number of broadcasters that interview their members and site them or their research as legitimate and credible sources. For example, Paul Fromm a Canadian white supremacist, with ties to Stormfront.org and a non-white anti-immigration activist founded a seemingly benign organization called Canada First Immigration Reform Committee (Zaitchik, 2010). On August 4, 2008, Fromm was interviewed by Fox News's Steve Brown as a free speech activist. It should be noted that Lou Dobbs has, on a number of occasions, interviewed leaders of anti-immigration groups who have ties to white supremacists groups without mentioning these ties. In contrast, Wolf Blitzer, when he interviews members of such groups makes clear that the Southern Poverty Law Center has identified them as a hate group (Beirich & Potok, 2005).

In Germany men like Felix Menzel (Spiegel 2014) are cognizant of the interplay between image and influence and work to project an intelligent, reasonable, polite image when talking with others because they know that doing so will make it more likely people will listen to them and consider what they are saying. Men like Menzel realize that people who scream, salute, and goose step are often dismissed without being heard.

Research suggests that hate groups, by presenting themselves as more mainstream, make be more effective at getting people to attend to their message and be persuaded by it. Borgeson and Valeri (2004) compared the ability of participants to recognize the intolerance and anti-Semitic nature of hate websites. In the study participants viewed one of three webpages before responding to questions about the content. All of the webpages had the same content but differed in the type of banner head. The three banner heads used were *Jews are Taking Over the World*, *Jew Watch*, or *News Watch*. Participants rated *Jews are Taking Over the World* as significantly more intolerant than either of the other webpages. Participants did not distinguish between the intolerance of *Jew Watch* and *News Watch*. In a follow-up study (Valeri & Borgeson, 2005) these researchers examined the impact of a "Whites Only" content notice on participants' attitudes and thoughts about a webpage. Participants rated *Jews are Taking Over the World* and *Jew Watch* as significantly more anti-Semitic then *News Watch* when the webpage was preceded by the "Whites Only" notice. Individuals' thoughts about a webpage were significantly more negative when the webpage was preceded by that notice. These results suggest that while warning people that a message is from a hate group makes their thoughts more negative it may not be enough to keep them from recognizing the intolerance of a message that looks mainstream, as in the case of *News Watch*. As a result viewers of the latter may be more likely to attend to and be persuaded by the latter type of materials.

Research (Eagly & Chaiken, 1993) in attitude change and persuasion suggests that appearing more mainstream and moderate may be an effective means for changing attitudes and recruiting new members.

This research (Eagly & Chaiken, 1993) suggests that people tend to reject messages that fall outside their latitude of acceptance. So to change attitudes, you must start by expressing an attitude that is within someone's latitude of acceptance and then slowly change that person's attitude to a more extreme position. The tactic of appearing more mainstream is of serious concern because it demonstrates that hate groups are becoming savvy in their influence tactics. Especially in today's world, in which we are inundated with information and thus, unable to carefully analyze every communication, we are often dependent on simple heuristics as the basis for our decisions. For hate groups, messages delivered by mainstream looking individuals in moderate tones are more likely to appear acceptable. This makes it more likely that people will listen to the message and be persuaded by it than if the message espoused took an extremist position and/or was delivered by a fanatic.

Other Hate Groups

In the United States, in addition to these groups there are growing militia movements such as the Sovereign Citizens Movement, border patrol groups such as the Minutemen, anti-immigrant groups, and anti-Lesbian, Gay, Bi-Sexual, Transgender Groups. There has also been a relatively recent revitalization of NeoConfederacy Groups.

Non-White Hate Groups

There are also a growing number of non-white hate groups. There has been an increase in the number of Black Supremacist groups such as the more militant extremist members of Black Hebrew Israelites. These extremists, like members of the White Supremacist movement who are adherents of Christian Identity, believe that Jews are descendants of the devil. But unlike the White Supremacists, the Black Supremacists advocate the death of or enslavement of whites.

Our present discussion of hate groups and hate gangs should make it clear that hate knows no boundaries. Any group can hate just as any group can be the target of hate. Hate also knows no boundaries in that hate can impact attitudes as well as actions. The desired attitude change can be at the individual level or, as demonstrated by the statistic offered by the Athena Group that 33% of European hate groups had some form of political affiliation, at the national political level. Hate based actions can range from taunting to terrorist plots.

WHY PEOPLE HATE

Much of the reasons why groups dislike and even hate each other can be traced back to theories of prejudice and aggression. Blumer (1958) explained the cause of prejudice as being relational. According to Blumer, prejudice arises from the dominant group's belief that it is not only intrinsically different from but also superior to another subordinate group. Blumer suggests that it is these feelings of superiority over and distinctiveness from the subordinate group that lead to prejudice toward the subordinate group as well as provide the basis for the belief that the dominant group has proprietary claims to the available resources. Blumer suggests that the perception among the dominant group, that the subordinate group is trying to take some of these resources, further adds to the antipathy toward that subordinate group and justifies the dominant group's actions toward the subordinate group. Blumer's theory provides a good starting point for our present discussion of why groups come not only to dislike, but to hate, discriminate, and aggress against other groups because it touches on elements key to our discussion. These are the beliefs that the groups are different from each other, that one group is superior to another, and that resources play a role in intergroup animosity. To further explore each of these elements we turn to the theories of realistic group conflict, relative deprivation, and social identity theory.

Both realistic group conflict and relative deprivation discuss the role of resources in the development of intergroup hatred. As will be discussed in the following section, with realistic group conflict, the disagreement between the groups stems from conflict over scarce resources. The conflict is what drives the increased ingroup cohesiveness and increased animosity toward the outgroup. In relative deprivation, the animosity toward the outgroup stems from feeling that one's group is not doing as well as should be expected in relation to either the past, or more often, in relation to some other group. It is the deprivation which leads to the development of negative attitudes toward the outgroup. Whereas with social identity theory, classifying oneself as part of one group and not part of another group is the driving force behind the more positive assessment of one's own group. It is this resulting "we are better than them" which then leads to the inequitable distribution of goods.

Realistic Group Conflict

Realistic group conflict, based on the work of Sherif and colleagues (Sherif, 1966; Sherif, Harvey, White, Hood, & Sherif, 1961/1988; Sherif & Sherif, 1982) suggests that a zero sum game/situation, in which one side's win or gain results in the other side's loss, leads to the development of dislike and conflict between opposing groups.

In what has become a classic study, the Sherifs and colleagues studied boys at a summer camp, at Robbers Cave State Park in rural Oklahoma, during the 1950s. The boys all came from two parent homes and were white, protestant, and middle class. Additionally, the boys were all considered to be well adjusted and of average intelligence. Before going to camp none of the boys knew each other. The boys were divided into two groups and each group attended camp, across the park from each other, and without knowing the existence of the other boy's camp. During the first few days the boys engaged in normal summer camp activities, swimming, hiking, sports, etc. During that time each group of boys established their own norms, leaders, favorite activities, and a group name, the Rattlers and the Eagles. The camp leaders then let the campers know about the existence of the other camp and set up a series of competitions between the two camps. The competitions included baseball, touch football, tug of war, tent pitching, cabin inspection, and treasure hunting. At the end of the tournament the winning team would receive highly desirable prizes, a trophy, individual medals, and camping knives, and the losing team would receive nothing. As the competition progressed attitudes and behaviors between the boys on the opposing team went from friendly and sportsmanlike to unfriendly and unsportsmanlike. Name calling, pranks, and fighting developed between the two groups. Finally, when the winning team, the Eagles, was celebrating their victory, the Rattlers raided their cabins and stole their camping knives. The behavior of the boys highlights key features of realistic group conflict. Because the two groups of boys were competing against each other and only one team could win, as the competitions progressed, each team of boys became more cohesive and their attitudes toward their teammates became more positive. Conversely attitudes toward members of the other team became more negative. Additionally, the team on the losing side of each competition experienced frustration, and, in the end, the team on the losing side in the overall competition, experienced frustration. The frustration further fueled negative attitudes to the boys on the opposing team. This combination of frustration, ingroup favoritism, and animosity toward the opposing team made the situation ripe for escalation to actual physical conflict which is what occurred between the opposing teams of campers.

Research by Struch and Schwarts (1989) provides further insights into realistic group conflict, ingroup bias, and aggression. These researchers measured the religiousness and ingroup bias of Israelis as well as their attitudes and willingness to aggress against an ultraorthodox religious group. Their results suggest that how much a group is willing to aggress against another group is related to how much the ingroup's interests are perceived to conflict with that of the outgroup. Specifically, the larger the perceived conflict of interest between the two groups the more willing they were to aggress against the outgroup.

In sum, realistic group conflict stems from competition between groups for any scarce resource, such as clean water, jobs, or land, or whenever another group is perceived as a threat to the survival of one's own group. At such times, positive feelings and cohesiveness toward members of one's own group increase and negative feelings and prejudice toward the other group increase. Prejudice toward the outgroup is especially likely to spike when one's group is feeling particularly vulnerable (Faulkner et al; 2004). Current real world examples of this can be seen in the increase in anti-immigrant sentiment caused by high unemployment and/or economic downturns that is occurring in many countries around the world including Australia, Greece, Ireland, Spain, and the United States.

One such example of anti-immigrant sentiment appeared in the Irish Times on April 29, 2014, *Ireland, Spain, and Greece see Biggest Change in Attitudes to Immigrants*. In the article (Turner & Cross, 2014), a significant increase among Irish and Greeks in negative attitudes toward immigrants between 2002 and 2010 was reported. According to the article, data from the European Social Survey, a survey of 12 European countries, was used to compare attitudes toward immigrants across these 12 European countries at three different times, in 2004, prior to a large flow of immigrants, in 2006, at the height of the economic cycle, and in 2010, after the financial crash. While attitudes toward immigrants remained relatively unchanged overall, Ireland and Greece saw the largest decrease in positive sentiment and the largest increase in negative sentiment. In 2006, 49% of the Irish population believed immigration was good for the economy. That number fell to 23% in 2010. Conversely, the number of people believing immigration was bad for the Irish economy increased by 10% between 2002 and 2010.

In Greece, anti-ethnic sentiment is clearly demonstrated by the group Golden Dawn. On May 6, 2014, members of this extreme right party Golden Dawn were able to join parliament on a tide of anti-immigration sentiment that allowed them to win 7% of the vote. The anti-immigrant sentiment of Golden Dawn is clearly captured in Helena Smith's June 7, 2014 article *SS Songs and anti-Semitism* for the Guardian, in which she reports an exchange between two Golden Dawn members about leaders of the organization, "These gentlemen (Golden Dawn Leaders) are patriots, proud Greek nationalists, and they know how to deal with the scum, the foreigners who never pay taxes, who steal our jobs, who have taken over our streets." His companion responds "Let's not forget all the faggots and the Jews, the wankers who control the banks, the foreigners who are behind them, who came in and fucked Greece." These comments provide real world examples of each of the components of hate put forward by Sternberg. Certainly the economic and political forces at work in shaping a country's economy, whether it is Greece's or that of another country's are outside the scope of this chapter. Our purpose in providing these examples is to show that discontent especially in the face of scarce resources provides a fertile ground for sowing the seeds of hate as describe by realistic group conflict.

Relative Deprivation

As mentioned in the discussion of realistic group conflict, an economic downturn can result in negative feelings and prejudice toward another group. According to realistic group conflict this would occur because you see your group as competing with another group for scarce economic resources and that your losses must be the result of their gains. Research on relative deprivation suggests that negative feelings can result when you believe that you have less than what you should have or expected to have. Note that you may not necessarily be poor or living in poverty, only that you are less well off than what you had expected.

Relative Deprivation: Temporal

Brown (2005) suggests that there are two possible sources of relative deprivation. The first is temporal. You compare your current state with where you were in the past, the strides you were making, and then project forward to where you should be now. If what you have now is less than what you had projected, you experience relative deprivation. An early, but real world example of temporally produced relative deprivations comes from research on lynchings in the American south. A study first conducted by Hovland and Sears (1940) and then with data reanalysis by Hepworth and West (1988) regarding lynchings in the American South from 1882-1930, revealed a relationship between cotton prices and the number of lynchings. Hovland and Sears reported a negative correlation, that as cotton prices fell the number of lynchings increased. Hepworth and West (1988), using more sophisticated time-analysis statistics were able to refine this conclusion and reported that the number of lynchings was highest when a recession followed an economic upturn. Thus, just as people are starting to feel hopeful and are anticipating that things are improving for them economically their hopes are dashed and they experience feelings of frustration and relative deprivation (Davies, 1962). The resulting aggression derives from feelings of frustration and annoyance (Berkowitz & Harmon-Jones, 2004; Dewall et al., 2007). In the case of the lynchings, white Americans scapegoated African Americans as the cause of the falling cotton prices and the reason why they were worse off. They did this because, at that time, it was by and large safe for whites to aggress against and even kill African Americans and go unpunished by the law.

Relative Deprivation: Fraternalistic

A second type of relative deprivation, referred to as fraternalistic deprivation (Runciman 1966) occurs when you compare your group to another similar or relevant group. In this case, you examine how poorly or well the other group is fairing and from there, project how well your group should be doing in relation to this other group. As with the temporal form of relative deprivation, you feel relatively deprived when your group falls short of where you expect them to be relative to the other group's standing. As shown in Runciman's (1966) survey of class attitudes among the English, a group can feel relatively deprived even when they are doing well. The deprivation comes from not doing as well as expected. Runciman's results suggest that many white-collar workers, who, although objectively better off than their blue-collar counter-parts, felt relatively deprived. The reason for this stemmed from the fact that they perceived the blue collar workers as experiencing a greater gain in prosperity than they were experiencing.

More recent research on fraternalisitc relative deprivation (Vanneman & Pettigrew, 1972) incorporates more subtle differences in attitudes base on comparisons made at both the individual and group level. These researchers describe someone who is doing well both personally and as a group as Doubly gratified, someone who is doing poorly personally but well as a group as Egoistically deprived, someone who is doing well personally but poorly as a group as Fraternally deprived, and someone who is doing poorly at both the individual and group level as Doubly deprived. For their research, Vanneman and Pettigrew surveyed over 1000 White Americans and asked them to assess how they thought they were doing economically in relation to other White Americans and in relation to Black Americans and to determine whether these assessments related to their reported prejudice toward Blacks or their attitudes toward a number of policies including combating poverty and segregation. People who were fraternally deprived or doubly deprived were the most prejudice. Additionally, people who were fraternally deprived also had the most negative attitudes toward policies to reduce segregation and poverty. In general, people who are fraternally deprived tend to express the greatest prejudice or negative attitudes toward other groups (Abeles, 1976; Bobo, 1988).

The research on relative deprivation is important to the current chapter because, as suggested by Valeri and Borgeson (2007), hate groups, in an effort to garner support, are becoming savvy at framing their messages. Rather than being anti-Black, anti-gay, or anti-Jewish, they present themselves as pro-white and suggest that Whites are under attack, that they are being threatened economically, and put at a disadvantage relative to other groups in terms of employment, college admissions, and other economic issues. Thus they refer to affirmative action as anti-White prejudice, quotas, or minority preferences. In their research, Valeri and Borgeson manipulated how affirmative action policies were framed and examined the impact of message framing on the attitudes of over 100 White Americans. Participants read a mock editorial in which the need for affirmative action was framed as having been caused by either passed advantages to Whites or past disadvantages toward Blacks. The effects of affirmative actions were framed as either resulting in disadvantages to Whites or advantages toward Blacks. Relative deprivation would suggest that whenever the message was framed as giving a greater advantage to Blacks over Whites, the White participants should respond negatively. Consistent with this, participants responded significantly more negatively to affirmative action when it was framed as past advantages to Whites being offset by affirmative action policies disadvantaging whites.

In Europe, the growing nationalism in many countries reflects the feeling that the needs of the majority population are being ignored in favor of the growing immigrant population. The following quote exemplifies these feelings, "[Linda Elisson] the 29-year-old Swede is unemployed, says she's been neglected by her government, and, like almost 800,000 of her compatriots, she voted for anti-immigrant Sweden Democrats in last weekend's election... (Donahue & Rolander, 2014)"

Social Identity Theory and Ingroup Identification

In both realistic group conflict and relative deprivation outgroup prejudice is the end result of competition over resources. It is the conflict, in the former theory, or the feelings of relative deprivation, in the latter, that leads to the development of prejudice toward the outgroup. While realistic group conflict or relative deprivation may lead to the development of or heighten ingroup sentiment, the relationship may not be unidirectional. For example, strong ingroup sentiment can help drive the pro us, anti them sentiment behind realistic group conflict. Strong ingroup sentiment, referred to as ingroup bias (Brewer, 1979; Halevey, et al., 2008; Mullen et al., 1992; Sumner, 1906; Tajfel, 1982; Tajfel, et al., 1971) can in, and of itself, produce biased behavior in favor of one's ingroup and against the outgroup. The strength of ingroup favoritism is evident in laboratory research on *minimal groups* (Tajfel, 1982; Tajfel & Billig, 1974; Tajfel, et al., 1971). In this research a minimal group is formed by assigning individuals to a group based on some arbitrary characteristic. Individuals then engage in an activity or perform work as part of these short term artificially created groups. Even in these minimal groups, participants express more positive feelings and attitudes toward their own group members and give more resources to their group then they do to the outgroup. The more highly identified an individual is with their ingroup the more favoritism they will show their own group (Hodson, Dovidio, & Esses, 2003).

According to social identity theory, part of the reason behind ingroup favoritism is that we want to feel good about ourselves. Part of who we are and how we feel about ourselves comes from the groups to which we belong and how we evaluate those groups. Thus, if we want to feel good about ourselves we need to feel good about the groups to which we belong. To do this we compare our group to other groups. If our group compares favorably to another group, outperforms it or is better than the other group on some dimension, than those positive evaluations of our group carry over to how we evaluate and thus feel about ourselves. This is true even for groups where our belonging is more vicarious (Cialdini et al., 1976; Snyder et al., 1986).

The trick to enhancing our self-esteem through our groups is finding appropriate groups to whom we can compare our group and have our group come out as being superior. We do this at the individual level by engaging in social comparison (Festinger, 1954). We can engage either in upward social comparison, comparing ourselves to those who are better or better off, or in downward social comparison, comparing ourselves to those who are worse or worse off. The former, upward social comparison can have negative repercussions for our self-concept. While it might motivate you to work harder in order to attain the level of success achieved by those who are better, stronger, or smarter it could also make you feel quite bad about yourself and your lack of ability, achievement, etc and even give up (Blanton et al., 1999; Collins, 1996; Vrugt & Koenis, 2002) . On the other hand, engaging in the latter type of comparison, downward social comparison can enhance our self image by allowing us to feel superior, smarter, stronger, etc (Gibbons & Gerrard, 1989; Suls, Martin, & Wheeler, 2002; Wood, 1989; Wood, Taylor, & Lichtman, 1985). Just as we can engage in social comparison at the individual level we can do the same for our groups.

At the group level, we compare our group to other groups. Consistent with social comparison at the individual level, comparing your group to a group that is worse off, whether it is in terms of perceive or actual abilities, values, or means, leads to a more positive evaluation of your group and makes you feel better about your group and thus feel better about your own self. You can see your group as better than the other group by enhancing your group's image, associating it with positive stereotypes, and/or you can see your group as better than the other group by derogating the other group or associating them with negative stereotypes (Aberson, Healy, & Romero, 2000; Cialdini & Richardson, 1980; Rubin & Hewstone, 1988). These stereotypes can then be the basis for prejudice which taken together or separately can be used to rationalize discriminatory behavior. After all, if our group is smarter, harder working, has better values and morals, don't we deserve more?

An extreme example of lauding your own group and derogating the outgroup can be found in the beliefs of Aryan Nation members. As discussed by Borgeson and Valeri (2007), Two Seed Line Identity, a denomination of Christian Identity, is followed by most Aryan Nation members. According to Two Seed Line Identity (Walters, 2001), Eve had sex with both Adam and the Devil on the same day which resulted in the birth of two offspring, one from Adam and one from the Devil. The descendants of Eve and Adam are today's white Anglo-Saxons and the descendants of Eve and the Devil are the Jews. The contrast between seeing your own group as the descendants of Adam and Eve and your enemy's group as descendants of the Devil provides the basis for why your group is morally superior to the other group. Certainly by portraying your enemy as descendants of the Devil provides ample reason to dislike them, discriminate against them and to try and eliminate them (Borgeson & Valeri, 2007).

Integrating Why People Hate

Realistic group conflict, relative deprivation, and social identity theory provide somewhat different starting points for the development of negative attitudes or prejudice toward outgroups which can then be used to justify discrimination. But the theories are not incompatible. In fact they share some important similarities, and can work together to present a more complete explanation of the driving forces behind prejudice and discrimination. As mentioned previously, realistic group conflict and relative deprivation are both tied to resources. Realistic group conflict cannot, by itself, explain all prejudice and discrimination, because real conflict over scare resources or threats to survival are not always at the heart of ingroup-outgroup bias. Relative deprivation explains some of the conflict unexplained by realistic group conflict, because it broadens the scope to include expectations as to what one's share of resources should be and what happens when those expectations are not met. Key to both relative deprivation and social identity theory is comparison between one's own group and another group. For social identity theory we start by seeing ourselves as part of a group. That necessarily leads to people thinking their group is better than the outgroup, and as a result dividing resources in a manner that favors their own group. The development of prejudice can develop either in response to our thoughts, that we are better than them, which leads to positive attitudes toward our group and negative attitudes toward their group or as a means of justifying our discriminatory behaviors. Relative deprivation also assumes that we see ourselves as being part of a group, but the negative evaluation of that other group, the development of our prejudices, stems from our feeling relatively deprived in relation to them which can then lead to discrimination or aggression against that group.

THE MESSAGE OF HATE

In the United States the recent rise in hate groups has been attributed to the election of the first African American president, Barack Obama, and to a poor economy. White supremacist blame the down turn in the economy, from job loss to the subprime mortgage on minorities and the rise in immigration. Don Black, a former Grand Wizard of the Klan and founder of the oldest hate group website Stormfront, in a February 2009 interview with CNN (Chen, 2009) reported that on the day after Obama's election more than 2000 people joined his Web site. Similarly, David Duke, also a former Klan leader and now a neo-Nazi, reported a sharp increase in the number of people visiting his website after the election of Obama. Jeff Schoep, head of the National Socialist Movement, suggested that when times are tough people turn to hate groups for answers and that his group provides the needed answers for white people (Civilrights.org State of hate).

Hate is not just on the rise in the United States. It is on the rise globally. On June 4, 2013 Global Voices correspondent Lordes Sada reported, as translated by Anna Williams, that extreme right political parties were on the rise throughout Europe, including Austria, Bulgaria, France, Hungary, and Italy and were gaining political power. For example, the Swiss People's Party captured 29% of the votes in 2007 and Norway's Progress party received 22% of the vote in 2009. According to the article "The mass influx of immigrants during the economic boom, which has worsened current employment figures, has spurred ultra right parties' racism and xenophobia largely directed toward the Muslim community. They have used the emergence of radical Islam in Europe, perceived by many Europeans as a threat to western values- to incite hate and win votes."

As discussed in the above section Why People Hate, animosity toward outgroups often grows out of real or perceived competition for resources.

WHY HATE MESSAGES APPEAL

According to terror management theory (Greenberg, Pyszczynski, & Solomon, 1986; Solomon, Greenberg, & Pyszczynski, 1991) people, like all creatures, want to stay alive. But because we humans have awareness and are the object of our own awareness, we realize that at some point, perhaps soon, we will die. Thoughts of our own, possibly imminent death can cause us terror. To manage this terror we create a cultural world view which gives life, as well as our own specific lives, meaning. Cultural world views offer us the possibility of being able to transcend death, either figuratively or literally, provided that we live up to the standards of our worldview. To do this we create the perception that we are living up to our cultural world views and are thus eligible for immortality.

According to terror management theory, self-esteem derives from our belief that life is meaningful and that we, by fulfilling our cultural world views, are leading a meaningful life. Thus we need culture to give life in general, as well as our own individual lives meaning. Without culture, life and our our own individual lives would be meaningless. While it might seem that as long as each of us has a culture, we can all be content as we strive to achieve our culture's values. Unfortunately this is not the case. The problem arises when we realize that not everyone shares our cultural world views. Once we realize there are different cultures with different values and beliefs, the question, "Whose beliefs are correct?" arises. Can we all be right? Unfortunately, the answer to this is, more often than not, no. Different beliefs and values call in to question the legitimacy of our own cultural beliefs and thus how we have been living our lives and the value of the life we have been living. If we decide our culture's values and beliefs are wrong, then we need to change our views about what gives life meaning and change the way we are living our lives. Alternatively, if there are enough shared values and beliefs between cultures, we might be able to meld our views and practices into one culture and live together peacefully. Finally, if we decide our cultural world views are correct than other cultures must be wrong. We can respond to this by trying to convince the other cultures of our beliefs, by derogating the other group, or at the extreme, eliminating the other group. You might be thinking there is another alternative, "We could just let others believe what they want, even though we know they are wrong." Unfortunately, as both life and research demonstrate this seldom happens. Much of the drive and conviction behind hate stems from the "we're right and they're wrong" and the attitudes and behaviors this leads to. (For an excellent summary of terror management research and how it relates to terrorism, see Pyszczynski, Solomon, and Greenberg, 2003.)

In short, research on terror management theory suggests that thinking about one's own death causes us to bolster and defend our own cultural world views. We do this by rewarding and revering people who uphold our world views and by disparaging or punishing those who oppose or transgress against our world views (Pyszczynski, Wicklund, Floresku, Koch, Gauch, Solomon, & Greenberg,1996; Rosenblatt,

Greenberg, Solomon, Pyszczynski, & Lyon,1989). Especially important to this chapter is the variety of ways we respond to those who oppose our world views. After thinking about our own death, we respond to others with opposing worldviews not only with dislike and prejudice but by physically distancing ourselves from them and by physical aggressing against them (Greenberg, Pyszczynski, Solomon, Rosenblatt, Veeder, Kirkland, & Lyon, 1990; Greenberg, Simon, Porteus, Pyszczynski, & Solomon, 1995). The responses described here are consistent with the components of hate, especially the negation of intimacy, suggested by Sternberg's (2003) model of hate.

Given the previous discussion regarding the increase in hate group membership post the election of Obama a more thorough discussion of research by Schimel et al. (1999), because of its prescient prediction of these very outcomes, is necessary. Schimel and colleagues (1999) in a series of five studies examined the impact of death salience on stereotype activation and reactions to stereotype inconsistent behavior. Of particular interest is Study 3 in which they examined the impact of mortality salience (high vs. low) on liking and personal ratings (intelligent, conceited, nice, arrogant, antisocial, trustworthy, hostile, hardworking, hypocritical, friendly, freeloader, and productive) of an African American who either dressed and reported activities that confirmed or disconfirmed stereotypes. In the high mortality salient condition, the African American who dressed and acted in a manner that disconfirmed stereotypes was rated as less likeable than the African American who dressed and acted in a manner that confirmed stereotypes. Similarly, the African American who disconfirmed stereotypes was rated more negatively on the combined personality dimensions than the African American who confirmed stereotypes. In contrast, in the low mortality salience condition, the African American who disconfirmed stereotypes was rated as significantly more likeably and more positively on the personality dimensions than the African American who confirmed stereotypes. These authors concluded that although, under normal circumstances, white Americans prefer minority members who assimilate and thus disconfirm stereotypes, when mortality salience is high, they prefer minority members who confirm stereotypes.

So, how does this relate to the increase in hate group membership post the election of Barak Obama? Part of the reason for this, is that for hate group members, this is their worst, or at least one of their worst fears. The election of an African American President might be the "final straw" that pushed them to join a hate group. But the results of Schimel and colleagues' research (1999) suggest that for "every day Americans," who are living in a time of global terrorism and war, when death, or reminders of death are everywhere, we are living in the equivalent of a high mortality salient condition. The result is there is an increased preference for minority group members who confirm stereotypes and a decrease in liking for and approval of a minority group member who disconfirms stereotypes. Consequently, liking for and approval of President Obama, because he disconfirms stereotypes, will be low.

COMMUNICATING HATE

As with any group or organization, communication serves multiple functions. Within a group, communication is essential for sharing information, spreading ideas, and strengthening group bonds. Communication with people outside of the group serves to inform and persuade others of the group's views and as a means of recruiting new members.

While Hate Groups have relied upon traditional means of communication, both face-to-face and written communication, posters, pamphlets, leaflets, and books, their use of radio and cable television, evidences their willingness and ability to take advantage of available technology. Today hate groups still rely on the more traditional methods of communication but they have also taken advantage of all that modern technology has to offer. The proliferation of the internet and social media allows hate groups to inexpensively communicate with likeminded individuals around the world and to spread their message and recruit on a global level. Additionally the ability to cheaply and easily produce music delivered by downloading off the internet or via CDs has allowed hate groups to produce and distribute their message to adolescents via music, whether its hate rock, hate folk, or "gansta rap."

In Print

In our current high-tech world of mobile phones, social media, and the internet one might assume that print media and communication is outdated. But just as printed books and newspapers still exist, albeit at a more scaled back level, so too does print propaganda in the form of flyers, leaflets and pamphlets. In a recent NY Times article (29, September 2014) *At Gateway to Hamptons, Ku Klux Klan Advertises for New Members,* reporter Al Baker (2014) discusses the KKK's recruitment of new members in the Hampton Bay area through the distribution of flyers. Baker writes "(The pamphlets) are stuffed into plastic sandwich bags, along with a few Jolly Rancher candies serving as weights, and tossed onto driveways in the dead of night." The distributed material included a recruitment form and a pamphlet describing some of the KKK's views, specifically, anti homosexual and anti illegal aliens. Robert J. Jones, a leader in the Loyal White Knights who was interviewed by Baker, suggests that similar materials were being distributed in other areas around the country.

Face-to-Face or Interpersonal Communication

Borgeson and Valeri (2009) provide a profile of Aryan Nation members which includes a discussion about how the individuals interviewed became members of the Aryan Nation. Thirty nine percent of the people interviewed reported that a friend introduced them to the group and an additional 9% reported that they became involved with the Aryan Nation while in prison. Therefore, just under half of the people interviewed were recruited by an existing member of the group, whether it was a friend or fellow inmate. However, it should be noted that 87.5% of the people interviewed had previously belonged to another hate groups suggesting that for many being part of a hate group was part of their lifestyle or beliefs. Given the high frequency of involvement in previous hate groups, means of recruitment to the Aryan Nation may not be typical of other hate groups. Also, given that 21 of the 24 people interviewed were male, means of recruitment may be different for women.

Research by Blee (1996) on women in white supremacist groups reveals that the majority of women are recruited to these groups through personal interactions with current group members. Blee interviewed 34 women who were members of either the Ku Klux Klan or Neo-Nazi groups. Of these 34 women, 26 were convinced to join by a friend or family member. Only 8 were motivated to seek out these groups based on their own personal convictions.

In addition to these "one-on-one" recruitment methods, there are also speeches and rallies. For example, Matthew Heimback, a graduate of Towson state and founder of the White Student Union, who is considered by many to be the up-and-coming face of white supremacy in the United States, has spoken at a variety of white supremacist events (Potok, 2013).

There are also hate based rallies and marches like the one in Cologne in October 2014 in which an estimated 5000 demonstrators, primarily football (soccer) "hooligans," neo-Nazis, and nationalists, marched against the perceived Islamic threat (Germany's New Right, 2014) or the over 100 anti-Islamic rallies help by Sturzenberger (Right-Wing Extremism, 2014). These events can be catalysts for hate. Rallies and marches increase the cohesiveness of the participants and strengthen their beliefs. They can legitimizing the unspoken fears of observers, provide them with concrete evidence that others share their beliefs, and offer them a safe haven in which they can express their fears with likeminded people. At the same time the demonstrations communicate a clear threat to the group they oppose.

Internet and Social Media

Hate has been online since the early 1980s. In 1999, the Anti Defamation League (ADL) reported that between 300 and 1,000 of the 8 million sites on the World Wide Web were hate sites ("Downloading Hate," 1999). Conlin and Prasso (2002) reported that after the September 11 destruction of the World Trade Center the number of hate sites doubled to about 2000. While hate websites may account for only a small percentage of websites, the internet allows hate groups to create an electronic community of hate in which they can quickly and easily connect with likeminded individuals. In *The Consequences of Right Wing Extremism*, the ADL suggests that Hate Groups have benefited from the internet in three key ways. It allows individuals or groups to access hate propaganda anonymously, instantaneously, and often times freely, to coordinate activities among members or between groups, and to make money in new ways.

A quick visit to any one of the hate sites, whether it is Stormfront's, the National Socialist Movement's, the KKK's, or David Duke's site, will provide the viewer with an idea of the scope of information available easily, anonymously, and freely. Typically the websites include information about joining, as well as information about upcoming events, such as the Stormfront Seminar or NSM's (National Socialist Movement) National Rally, and access to blogs, where you can read and respond to posts. Many of these sites also have radio programs that you can tune into. Some of the sites have information available in several languages, including recruitment flyers, advice on your rights, and recruitment "talking points" related to the economy, gun rights, and illegal aliens. With regard to posting upcoming events, the websites are a key way for these organizations to post upcoming events, including, as discussed below, hate or white power music events. Just as it does for any group, the web provides an inexpensive means to advertise your event to people around the world.

One example of the internet facilitating the meeting of two hate group members is the story of Daniel Cowart and Paul Schlesselmann. On October 22, 2008, just days prior to the election of Barack Obama, these two men were arrested for plotting to assassinate him, shoot 88 African Americans, and behead another 14. These men had met through the internet (Date, 2008).

More recently, the Islamic State has been successful at using the internet and social media for self-promotion and to recruit followers. In a National Public Radio Broadcast (Savvy PR) about the Islamic State it was suggested that because the Islamic State has successfully used social media that they have been able to convince more than 500 people to travel from Britain to Syria and fight on their side in the civil war. The Islamic State has also used social media to encourage their "new members" to commit heinous crimes against non believers in their own countries (Terlato, 2014). On September 24, 2014, just a few days after the Islamic State released a video encouraging followers to kill non believers, an 18 year old man in Australia attacked two counter-terrorism officers, stabbing and wounding them with a knife (Neubauer, 2014). The assailant was fatally shot by the first victim. As mentioned in the discussion of hate groups and the definition of a group, social media has changed the concept of group. In this case, a teenager, who's only known association with the Islamic State is by watching their videos on social media, self-identifies as a group member and acts at their urging. Given that he is unknown to the group, would the assailant be considered a member of the Islamic State? Would the crime be included in statistics on hate group activity?

Another consequence of communication via the internet and social media is that it facilitates extreme actions and/or group polarization, through persuasion, comparison, and differentiation. A phenomenon of group decision making is group polarization (Fraser et al., 1971). Research on this topic suggests that groups make more extreme decisions than the decision that would be made, had the decision of each individual member been averaged. In fact, research on group polarization suggests that the more extreme a group is to begin with the more extreme its decision will be. While the examples mentioned above include both individual actions and small group actions, the dynamics of group polarization are in play and lead to these extreme actions.

The first catalyst of group polarization is persuasion. In this case polarization occurs as group members share their views (Burnstein & Vinokur, 1973; Vinokur & Burnstein, 1974). Initially, each group member has their reasons for believing or supporting their position but, most likely, they don't know or have all of the possible ideas. As ideas are shared, each member is exposed to new ideas or reasons. These new ideas are incorporated into and strengthen their position. Thus, through discussion, members persuade each other about the validity of their position. As a result, not only is each individual's own position and that of the group strengthened but their convictions are also strengthened. For example, if, prior to group discussion, I had two reasons for believing that pigs fly, was fairly certain that my belief was true, and was willing to invest 10 units of time or money in pursuit of my convictions, what will happen when, as a result of group discussion I learn new reasons why I should believe that pigs fly? After group discussion I now have more reasons for believing that pigs fly, and am, as a consequence, even more certain that my convictions are true, and will be willing to invest even more units of time or money in pursuit of achieving my convictions. The internet and social media facilitate the sharing and learning of new ideas among like minded people. Thus, this sharing of ideas facilitates the radicalization of individual members as well as the group through persuasion.

For the sake of the present discussion, elements two and three, comparison and differentiation, will be discussed together (Blaskovich et al., 1975; Codol, 1975; Mackie & Cooper, 1984; Sanders & Baron, 1977). To start, each individual, prior to group discussion probably believes that they are average or better than average group members, and therefore that their beliefs and actions are typical or better than that of the average group member. During discussion, the norms of the group will become apparent. Some members will realize that they and their beliefs fall short of the group's standard. To rectify this situation they will bring their views in line with the group. Additionally, some group members who wish to stand out or to demonstrate the strength of their convictions will be motivated to take a position that is in the direction of, but more extreme than the group norm. With regard to hate groups, as members post their beliefs and actions, the group's norms are made salient. People who fall shy of these norms will increase their beliefs, commitments, and actions to match that of the group. Others will attempt to exceed the norms to gain membership to the group or to demonstrate their commitment to the group.

Beirich (2014a) describes the trajectory of how someone can progresses from reading and lurking on the hate websites to becoming an active member and frequent poster to acting on their beliefs, including murder. Beirich, citing a two-year study by Intelligence Report suggests that Stormfront users "have been disproportionately responsible for some of the most lethal hate crimes and mass killings since the site was put up in 1995….The Report's research shows that Stormfront's bias-related murder rate began to accelerate rapidly in early 2009, after Barack Obama became the nation's first black president."

Music

Music is one of the core elements of skinhead culture, whose origins can be traced back to the late 1960s England. In fact music, both "ska" and "reggae" played a key role in the formation of the skinhead movement and is, still today, a defining feature of skinhead culture. Music not only provided a means of expressing identity it facilitated the grown of the skinhead movement from England to the rest of Europe, American, and eventually around the world. Just as music is central to the culture of traditional skinheads it is also a key element of racist or Neo-Nazi skinhead culture and many other hate groups.

Early British skinheads listened to Jamaican "ska" also known as "skinhead reggae" or "bluebeat" and were influenced by the clean-cut look, dress, language, and values, most notably racial tolerance, associated with the culture (Hebdige 1979; Stolzoff, 2000). As the number of skinhead fans for these groups grew they began to influence the music. The bands began to recognize and respond to their skinhead fan base by including references to them in song lyrics. For example Symarip's (1969a) songs entitled "Skinhead Moonstomp" and "Skinhead Girl'' make obvious reference to skinheads in both their titles and lyrics. In the early 1980s, the skinhead culture, via Punk music imported from Britain, began to grow in the United States. Punk music provided American youth with a means of expressing their individuality and separating themselves from mainstream America (Lamy & Levin, 1985).

The 1980s was also a time of economic unrest and high unemployment in England. It was during this time that the Neo-Nazi skinheads, skinheads who espouse prejudice and discrimination against minorities and Jews emerged in England (Marshall 1994; 1997). These racist skinhead groups were associated with the National Front Political Party in England which also had ties to "white power" rock (Zellner 1995). Also at this same time in the United States, there was growing disillusionment with the government. In the 1980s, America was recovering from Watergate, the Iran-Hostage situation, and gas rationing. Changes were also being made to educational and employment policies resulting from the Civil Rights movement. As a result many people, especially whites, and more specifically white males felt adrift and lost in a world where their place or position had been upended. As was happening in England with the growing Neo-Nazi skinhead population, some of these individuals found solace in White-Supremacist Groups and the lyrics of white power rock.

The ADL (Bigots who Rock) suggests that there are more than 500 hate rock bands worldwide and that most of these formed after 1982 when the band Skrewdriver, founded by Ian Stuart Donaldson and considered to be one of the earliest and most prominent hate rock bands, began playing hate rock. The Skrewdriver website, although obviously not unbiased in its views, states "In 1982 his (Ian Stuart Donaldson's) band, Skrewdriver, sent shockwaves throughout the entire world when it introduced Nationalist and Racial lyrics to it's music, something which at that time was unheard of." The website describes Donaldson's contributions to the Aryan race as "Throughout the ages, certain men have stepped up at the proper times to guide the Aryan race from it's destructive course and lead it down the path of salvation. Adolf Hitler…are all important examples, however, no one has ever been able to open as many youthful eyes as Ian Stuart Donaldson….Skrewdriver became known in every White Country around the globe. From England to Italy, America to Germany, Ian Stuart was at the forefront of the White Power Scene."

In Europe, the fall of the Berlin Wall in 1989 and the end of communism, because they lead to the lifting of import controls on CDs, opened the door to the proliferation of hate music in Europe (Beirich, Essay Racist Music). Beirich suggests that between 1992 and 1997 there was a significant increase in the European hate music industry and that this industry was larger in Europe than in the United States. According to Beirich, white power music can be found in every European country and is especially prevalent in the Czech Republic, Germany, Hungary, Poland, Serbia, and Slovakia. Beirich reported that a 1997 survey conducted in Sweden showed that 12% of 12-19 year olds listened to white power music. Beirich also suggests that in the early 2000s in Poland, approximately 15,000 of the country's 39 million people were involved in the racist skinhead scene. Sales of music by racist groups are comparable to that of successful local pop bands. In Germany the National Democratic Party openly sold white power music to raise money for elections.

There are several genres of white power music, which include hatecore, a white supremacist version of hardcore punk; National Socialist Black Metal Music (NSBM), a white supremacist form of death metal; white power folk music, and even, although much less common, white power hip hop (Lassir, 2012). Hate music is not limited to white supremacists, and includes "gangsta rap" and "Narco Corridos," or drug ballads.

As mentioned previously, the Anti-Defamation League has compiled a list of 541 hateful music groups. Although most of these bands are in Europe, because of available technology much of the music can either be downloaded or shipped to a fan.

The influence between hate music and hate groups is probably a circular one, and similar to that of media violence and aggression. People who hate are probably drawn to hate music because they agree with the views expressed. People who hate also create hate music as a means of expressing their views and sharing those views with others. A major concern of the mainstream public, including parents and law enforcement, is that hate music may persuade naïve listeners, people who are initially attracted to the music or group because of its similarity in name or sound to hard rock or other types of music, through exposure, to agree with the beliefs expressed in the lyrics and become attracted to hate groups. This view is one shared by white supremacists themselves. William Pierce, leader of the neo-Nazi National Alliance, sees hate rock as a means for recruiting youth. As reported by the ADL (Hate Rock Online: New Tool for Racists…), Pierce states "Music speaks to us at a deeper level than books or political rhetoric: music speaks directly to the soul."

Wade Page, the man responsible for fatally shooting 6 people and wounding 4 others at a Sikh temple in Oak Creek, Wisconsin on August 5, 2012, was a white supremacist who became involved in the white power music scene after attending a 2000 white power music festival, Hammerfest (Elias, 2012; Oak Creek, 2012). Page then began playing in several white power bands including Hammerskin and even forming his own band End Empathy in 2005 (Elias, 2012).

In a recent (2014) National Public Radio story *Controversial Mexican Musician Temporarily Retires from Drug Ballads* Alfred Rios, also known as El Komander, says he has been pressured by the Mexican government, in the form of fines, bans, and cancelled concerts, to retire from music. El Komander sings what is referred to as Narco-Corridos or ballades that tell the story of the drug trade. The lyrics of one song are "With machine guns and bazookas on our necks, cutting off the heads of those who cross our paths, we're bloodthirsty and crazy. We love to kill." While El Komander suggests that he is just telling a story about what is happening around him in Mexico. Others such as Dave Gaddis, a retired regional director for the DEA in Mexico, suggest that these songs are "public relations campaigns by these cartels in order to establish a certain level of popularity…and these Corridos actually help them do that."

Hate rock or white power concerts also provide a venue for like minded people to come together and share their views. Often times these concerts are advertised online and people may drive hundreds of miles to attend (Hate with a beat www.cnn.com/2012/08/08opinion/nasatir-white-power-bands). Prior to the 2000 ban on the music organization Blood & Honour, there were approximately 180 white power concerts a year (according to Antifaschistische INFO-BLATT (AIB), as cited in Beirich). In the United

States, most white power concerts are relatively small in size and held in more obscure locations, warehouses, fields, or backyards, rather than music clubs. However, Hammerfest, a racist rock festival, has been a much more popular music event as had Nordic Fest, prior to a successful 2008 lawsuit by the Southern Poverty Law Center.

A final concern regarding hate music is that it is a lucrative business "Each year, extremist companies such as Pierce's Resistance Records sell tens of thousands of hate rock CDs, many, if not most, over the internet, bringing millions of dollars into the hate movement" (ADL Hate Rock Online http://archive. adl.org/extremism/intro.html). In 1999 the European neo-Nazi music industry was worth $3.4 million per year and in the early 2000s, prior to the death of Pierce, Resistance Records was selling 70,000 CDs and making a net profit in the hundreds of thousands of dollars. Those profits were used to fund the neo-Nazi group National Alliance (Beirich, SPL Essay: Racist Music.)

In summary, technology has greatly expanded the reach of hate groups and their propaganda. All of the older methods of transmitting hate, interpersonal and print, are still available. The internet and social media now make it possible for hate groups to reach millions of people inexpensively and instantaneously. Hate groups have developed the savvy to use these resources to recruit new members and retain existing ones.

SHOULD HATE SPEECH BE BANNED?

The United States, because of the First Amendment's protection of free speech, allows for the publication of hate music and hate speech, whether in print, on the internet, or through social media. Thus, in the above discussion of communication via print, a news story regarding the distribution of KKK materials in the Hamptons was presented. As part of the news article, mention was made that, because the materials are considered to be free speech and thus constitutionally protected, no crime was committed (Baker, 2014).

Valeri and Borgeson (2005) discuss four alternatives for dealing with hate. These included legally restricting or censoring hate speech, combating hate speech with information and positive speech, allowing hate speech but rating hate content, or doing nothing. The first alternative is one that is or has been chosen by some countries, is consistent with several International Human Rights Guidelines, and was discussed by Nemes (2002). According to this view, hate speech is discriminatory and inflammatory. Banning hate speech is a way to help curtail the spread of hate and protect minorities from harm. One of the difficulties with this approach is that while bans may help curtail hate speech, achieving an100% ban on hate speech in a world of inexpensive and ever advancing technology is impossible. It is too easy for hate groups to produce their own hate materials, whether in the form of printed materials, CDs, or DVDs, and to maintain a global presence by continually setting up new hate sites when old ones are closed down. A second shortcoming of banning hate speech is that it runs counter to the view that free speech takes precedent over all other rights and freedoms because free speech is essential for democracy (Becker, Byers, & Jipson, 2000). Proponents of free speech promote countering hate speech with your own speech (Goldsborough, 2001; Nemes, 2002). For example the Anti-Defamation League and Southern Poverty Law Center each maintain websites and have extensive information about hate and means for combating hate available on their websites. The third approach is to develop and implement a hate rating system similar to the rating systems used to identify profanity, violence, or nudity in films and music and to implement this hate rating system on all materials including the internet. As we, the chapter authors, consider these alternatives, we shudder at the do nothing approach and find the second alternative to be the most feasible in terms of implementation.

A FINAL CASE

Just recently the American Freedom Defense Initiative sponsored a Muhammad Art Exhibit and Contest in Texas (Stack 2015). Approximately two hours into the exhibit two gunmen opened fire on officers outside the exhibit. Both men were shot and killed. The gunmen were later identified as followers of Islam who prayed at the same mosque. Although the F.B.I. is still investigated their ties to terrorist organizations, one of the gunmen had been identified by the F.B.I. as a jihadist terrorist (Fernandes, Pérez-Peña, & Santos, 2015). Additionally the Islamic State extremist group ISIS has tried to associate itself with the two gunmen (Bilefsky & Hubbard, 2015). While the events are tragic, they highlight important points made in this chapter. The American Freedom Defense Initiative, a seemingly benign sounding group, promoted the event as a celebration of free speech, thus aligning itself with a value dear to Americans. The Southern Poverty Law Center classifies the American Freedom Defense Initiative as a hate group. While many Americans might have known of this classification and agree with it there are others who, because of the benign name, may not have realized that the group is considered to be a hate group. As discussed previously even if people did know of the label, labeling materials as coming from a hate group does not necessarily keep people from attending to the message nor does it necessarily result in people recognizing the intolerance of the message. From an attitude change perspective, given that many Americans will agree with the American Defense Initiative's position on Free Speech at least part of the group's message will fall within their latitude of acceptance and thus open the door for them to consider additional information from this group and to be persuaded by them. The actions of the gunmen will make it more likely that these same Americans, regardless of their previous beliefs about the American Defense Initiative, will defend the organization's actions, thus moving them one step, however small, into the influence of this group.

The American Defense League organized the event as a celebration of free speech. The attack by the gunmen, because the exhibit is viewed as offensive to Mohammed bring to the forefront of American's consciousness the clash between American Culture, specifically freedom of speech, a right guaranteed by the Constitution in the United States, and Islamic culture that views depiction of Mohammed as offensive. Recall that terror management theory suggests that when mortality is salient and there is a class of cultures, we respond by distancing ourselves from, disparaging, and aggressing against those with different cultural world views. Unfortunately, this recent example, because it occurred on American soil will likely raise the ire of many Americans, pushing them to become more nationalistic, more anti-Muslim, and more willing to aggress against Muslims and the threat posed by ISIS and other Islamic Terrorists.

Finally given that these events have occurred at a time when potential presidential candidates are seeking the spotlight, announcing their intentions to run for the Presidency, and unfurling their campaigns, it is likely that these events will greatly impact political debate in the United States. Politicians, in their bid to gain public approval and support will be pushed to take more extreme views in the hopes of distinguishing themselves against their opponents.

CONCLUDING COMMENTS

At the opening of the chapter two examples of hate groups becoming stronger by developing ties to other hate gangs were presented. As part of the chapter we also discussed the efforts of some hate groups to change their image from that of a hate gang to a more mainstream group. Finally we concluded the chapter by discussing the efforts of a more politically motivated hate group to influence American's attitudes and politics. Part of the purpose behind these disparate cases is to show that hate can be used by a variety of groups to draw people to their cause, justify their actions, and inspire people to act.

Hate groups such as the Aryan Brotherhood or Public Enemy Number I, who are very upfront about their hatred, as noted by the FBI (Schafer & Navarro, 2003), tend to appeal to people who are feeling disenfranchised, low in self-esteem, or insecure. These groups, because they are so upfront and adamant in their hatred, can be more readily identified by both the average citizen and by law enforcement. Because the rhetoric of these groups is so blatantly hate-filled and prejudice it is likely to fall into the attitudinal latitude of rejection of many people and therefore be ignored by them. But, as mentioned above, these very same messages often appeal to those who are disenfranchised.

In contrast, some hate groups such as Keystone United have become savvier in their tactics. Their attempts to appear more mainstream and to moderate their speech are helping them to gain credibility, appeal to a wider audience, and even be interviewed and cited by news organizations as credible sources of research. Consequently these hate groups, especially given some of their more innocuous sounding names, can be more difficult to identify. It takes motivation as well as time and effort to research the roots of these groups and to trace news stories or political messages back to them. Especially given our fast paced world in which we are inundated with messages, these groups, unless clearly identified as hate groups by the media, may have a better chance of impacting mainstream politics because they are more difficult to identify and their messages more difficult to trace back to them. And, as we know, even with the label of a hate group, many people may still not recognize the intolerance of the groups.

The diversity of hate groups presented in this chapter from gangs to more savvy political groups, as well as the range of tactics used to gain followers and shape public opinion should make it clear that hate groups are quite heterogeneous. Consistent with the theme of the book we have discussed hate gangs. But we also wished to show that hate is not confined to gangs or that hate groups are static entities. As discussed in this chapter, hate groups including hate gangs, can, have, and do adapt, whether it's by changing their affiliations, image, message, target audience, or modes of communication.

Consequently, the strategies designed to combat hate and hate groups will need to be equally adaptable to counter their efforts. For example, strategies to deal with the more blatant hate groups, their followers, and recruits will need to be different from those used to deal with the more subtle hate groups, their followers, and recruits. Combating the latter type of hate group will be especially difficult because people may not realize they are being targeted and manipulated by them. Efforts to combat these more subtle hate groups and their messages will involve educating the public so that they can more readily identify a hate group and recognizing the influence of their hate messages in the media and on mainstream politics.

As discussed, hate groups have learned to use the internet and social media to their advantage, while at the same time continuing to use more traditional means of spreading their communication. The result is that hate groups are not only reaching more people with their message of hate, but persuading people of their beliefs, and spurring them to act on those beliefs. Discussions as to whether or how hate speech should be regulated are outside the scope of this chapter.

That being said, it is easy to become overwhelmed or discouraged in the face of so much hate and the myriad reasons offered by hate groups to justify their hate. One might be tempted to give up or look the other way. As with the discussion on hate speech, the question arises as to what can be done to combat the message of hate put forward by hate groups? Unfortunately there is no simple answer to this question. If we return to the definitions of hate and the reasons why people hate, we see that hate can stem from or be facilitated by us versus them categorizations, from the perceptions of real or imagined conflict over resources and from cultures that teach hatred.

With regard to the negative attitudes, hate, and discrimination that can result simply from us versus them categorizations, a few solutions involve bring the two group together so that members from the "us" and "them" group can interact. The contact hypothesis dates back to Allport (1954) and includes several conditions that must be met in order to be successful (Miller & Brewer; 1984; Pettigrew & Tropp, 2006). One solution offered by Miller and Brewer (1984) is to bring groups together and promote interaction at the individual or interpersonal level rather than at the group level so that people "decategorize" themselves and the individuals they are interacting with. The idea behind decategorization is that as we get to know people and build relationships at the individual level, positive attitudes and friendships will develop and prejudices will be disconfirmed. An alternative to decategorization is recategorization of us versus them, into a superordinate "we" category (Gaertner, et al, 1993). The ideas behind the recategorization are that by forming a superordinate category "we" all become ingroup members and animosity disappears.

Another driving force behind hate is real or imagined conflict over scarce resources. Issues surrounding the rights to resources and the distribution of them are more difficult to solve and require political as well as psychological changes and are outside the scope of the present chapter.

A final avenue to explore with regard to counteracting hate, especially hate that is learned, is whether the development of prejudice and hate can be curtailed "in the nursery" by teaching children from an early age empathy, compassion, and cooperation.

REFERENCES

Abeles, R. P. (1976). Relative deprivation, rising expectations and black militancy. *The Journal of Social Issues*, 32(2), 119–137. doi:10.1111/j.1540-4560.1976.tb02498.x

Aberson, C. L., Healy, M., & Romero, V. (2000). Ingroup bias and self-esteem: A meta-analysis. *Personality and Social Psychology Review*, 4(2), 157–173. doi:10.1207/S15327957PSPR0402_04

Abrams, D., & Hogg, M. A. (1988). Comments on the motivational status of self-esteem in social identity and intergroup discrimination. *European Journal of Social Psychology*, 18(4), 317–334. doi:10.1002/ejsp.2420180403

Allport, G. W. (1954). *The Nature of Prejudice*. Reading, MA: Addison-Wesley.

Anti-Defamation League. (2007). *PENI Public Enemy Number 1: California's growing racist gang*. Anti-Defamation League. Retrieved on May 1, 2015 from http://archive.adl.org/learn/ext_us/peni_report.pdf

Becker, P. J., Byers, B., & Jipson, A. (March 2000). The contentious American debate: The First Amendment and internet-based hate speech. *International Review of Law, Computers & Technology, 14*.

Beirich, H. (2014a). *White homicide worldwide. Intelligence Report*. Southern Poverty Law Center.

Beirich, H. (n.d.). *Racist music*. Southern Poverty Law Center. Retrieved October 31, 2014 from http://www.splcenter.org/get-informed/intelligence-files/ideology/racist-music/racist-musicon

Beirich, H. & Potok, M. (2005). *CNN's Lou Dobs refuses to cover anti-Latino racism in anti-immigration activist groups and citizen border patrols.* Intelligence Report. Southern Poverty Law Center.

Bello, M. (2008, October 21). White supremacist target middle America. *USA Today*.

Berecz, T., & Domina, K. (2012). *Domestic Extremism in Europe: Threat Landscape*. Athena Institute.

Berkowitz, L., & Harmon-Jones, E. (2004). Toward an understanding of the determinants of anger. *Emotion (Washington, D.C.)*, *4*(2), 107–130. doi:10.1037/1528-3542.4.2.107 PMID:15222847

Bilefsky, D., & Hubbard, B. (2015, May 5). ISIS Claims Link to Shooting at Texas Event Showing Muhammad Cartoons. *New York Times*. Retrieved May 5, 2015 from http://www.nytimes.com/2015/05/06/world/middleeast/isis-texas-muhammad-cartoons.html

Blanton, H., Bunk, B. P., Gibbons, F. X., & Kuyper, H. (1999). When better-than others compare upward: Choice of comparison and comparative evaluation as independent predictors of academic performance. *Journal of Personality and Social Psychology*, *76*(3), 420–430. doi:10.1037/0022-3514.76.3.420

Blaskovich, J., Ginsburg, G. P., & Howe, R. C. (1975). Blackjack and the risky shift. II: Monetary stakes. *Journal of Experimental Social Psychology*, *11*(3), 224–232. doi:10.1016/S0022-1031(75)80024-2

Blee, K. (1996). Becoming a Racist: Women in Contemporary Ku Klux Klan and Neo- Nazi Groups. *Gender & Society*, *10*(6), 680–702. doi:10.1177/089124396010006002

Blumer, H. (1958). Race prejudice as a sense of group position. *Pacific Sociological Review*, *1*(1), 3–7. doi:10.2307/1388607

Bobo, L. (1988). Attitudes toward the black political movement: Trends, meaning, and effects on racial policy preferences. *Social Psychology Quarterly*, *51*(4), 287–302. doi:10.2307/2786757

Bonachich, E. (1972). A theory of ethnic antagonism: The split labor market. *American Sociological Review*, *37*(5), 547–559. doi:10.2307/2093450 PMID:4634743

Borgeson, K., & Valeri, R. (Eds.). (2009). *Terrorism in America*. Boston, MA: Jones & Bartlett.

Borgeson, K., & Valeri, R. M. (2004). Faces of hate. *Journal of Applied Sociology*, *21*(2), 99–111.

Borgeson, K., & Valeri, R. M. (2007). The enemy of my enemy is my friend. *The American Behavioral Scientist*, *51*(2), 182–195. doi:10.1177/0002764207306050

Brewer, M. B. (1979). In-group bias in the minimal intergroup situation: A cognitive-motivational analysis. *Psychological Bulletin*, *86*(2), 307–324. doi:10.1037/0033-2909.86.2.307

Burnstein, E., & Vinokur, A. (1973). Testing two classes of theories about group-induced shifts in individual choice. *Journal of Experimental Social Psychology*, *9*(2), 123–137. doi:10.1016/0022-1031(73)90004-8

Catalano, R., Dooley, D., Novaco, R., Wilson, G., & Hough, R. (1993). Using ECA survey data to examine the effect of job layoffs on violent behavior. *Hospital & Community Psychiatry*, *44*, 874–878. PMID:8225302

Chen, S. (2009, Feb 2). Growing Hate Groups Blame Obama Economy. *CNN.com*.

Cialdini, R. B., Borden, R. J., Thorne, A., Walker, M. R., Freeman, S., & Sloan, L. R. (1976). Basking in reflected glory: Three (football) field studies. *Journal of Personality and Social Psychology*, *34*(3), 366–374. doi:10.1037/0022-3514.34.3.366

Cialdini, R. B., & Richardson, K. D. (1980). Two indirect tactics of image management: Basking and blasting. *Journal of Personality and Social Psychology*, *39*(3), 406–415. doi:10.1037/0022-3514.39.3.406

Codol, J. P. (1975). On the so called 'superior conformity of the self' behavior: Twenty experimental investigations. *European Journal of Social Psychology*, *5*(4), 457–501. doi:10.1002/ejsp.2420050404

Collins, R. L. (1996). For better or for worse: The impact of upward social comparison on self-evaluation. *Psychological Bulletin*, *119*(1), 51–69. doi:10.1037/0033-2909.119.1.51

Conlin, M., & Prasso, S. (2002). A Plague of Hate Sites. *Business Week*, *3770*, 14.

Consequences of Right Wing Extremism. (n.d.). Anti-Defamation League. Retrieved October 31, 2014 from http://www.adl.org/assets/pdf/combating-hate/The-Consequences-of-Right-Wing-Extremism-on-the-Internet.pdfon

Date, J. (2008, Oct 27). Feds Thwart Alleged Obama Assassination Plot. *ABC News*.

Davies, J. C. (1962). Toward a theory of revolution. *American Sociological Review*, *27*(1), 5–19. doi:10.2307/2089714

Dewall, C. N., Baumeister, R. F., Stillman, T. F., & Gailliot, M. T. (2007). Violence restrained: Effects of self-regulation and its depletion on aggression. *Journal of Experimental Social Psychology*, *43*(1), 62–76. doi:10.1016/j.jesp.2005.12.005

Donahue, P., & Rolander, N. (2014, September 15). *Protest Buffets EU Elites as Sweden Votes Anti-Immigrant*. Retrieved 2014 from www.businessweek.com/news/2014-09-15/protest-buffets-ey-elites-as-sweden-votes-anti-immigrant

Eagly, A. H., & Chaiken, S. (1993). Process theories of attitude formation and change: Attribution approaches and social judgment theory. In *The Psychology Of Attitudes*. Harcourt Brace Jovanovich College Publishers.

Elias, M. (2012). *Sikh Temple Killer Wade Michael Page Radicalized in Army*. Intelligence Report 148. Southern Poverty Law Center.

Right-Wing Extremism: Germany's New Islamophobia Boom. (2014). Spiegel Online.

Faulkner, J., Schaller, M., Park, J. H., & Duncan, L. A. (2004). Evolved disease-avoidance mechanisms and contemporary xenophobic attitudes. *Group Processes & Intergroup Relations*, *7*(4), 333–353. doi:10.1177/1368430204046142

Fernandez, M., Pérez-Peña, R., & Santos, F. (2015). *Gunman in Texas shooting was F.B.I. suspect in Jihad inquiry*. Retrieved on May 5, 2015 from http://www.nytimes.com/2015/05/05/us/garland-texas-shooting-muhammad-cartoons.html?_r=0

Festinger, L. (1954). A theory of social comparison processes. *Human Relations, 7*(2), 117–140. doi:10.1177/001872675400700202

Flaccus, G. (2007). Alliance adds to gang's clout: Public Enemy No. 1 more brazen since teaming up with Aryan Brotherhood. *Union Times*. Retrieved on May 1, 2015 from http://www.utsandiego.com/uniontrib/20070304/news_1n4gang.html

Florida Statute 874.03 Criminal Gang Enforcement and Prevention. (n.d.). Retrieved April 29, 2015 from http://www.leg.state.fl.us/statutes/index.cfm?mode=View%20Statutes&SubMenu=1&App_mode=Display_Statute&Search_String=gang&URL=0800-0899/0874/Sections/0874

Fraser, C., Gouge, C., & Billig, M. (1971). Risky shifts, cautious shifts, and group polarization. *European Journal of Social Psychology, 1*(1), 7–30. doi:10.1002/ejsp.2420010103

Fromm, E. (1990). *Man for himself: An inquiry into the psychology of ethics.* New York: First Owl Books. (Original work published 1947)

Fromm, E. (1992). *Anatomy of human destructiveness.* New York: Holt. (Original work published 1973)

Gaertner, S., Dovidio, J. F., Anastasio, P. A., Bachevan, B. A., & Rust, M. C. (1993). The common ingroup identity model: Recategorization and the reduction of intergroup bias. In W. Stroebe & M. Hewstone (Eds.), *European Review of Social Psychology, 4.* Chichester, UK: Wiley. doi:10.1080/14792779343000004

Germany's New Right: The Unholy Alliance of Neo-Nazis and Football Hooligans. (2014). Spiegel Online. Retrieved on January 1, 2015 from http://www.spiegel.de/international/germany/new-right-wing-alliance-of-neo-nazis-and-hooligans-appears-in-germany-a-1000953.html

Gibbons, F. X., & Gerrard, M. (1989). Effects of upward and downward social comparison on mood states. *Journal of Social and Clinical Psychology, 8*(1), 14–31. doi:10.1521/jscp.1989.8.1.14

Goldsborough, R. (2001, October). Dealing with hate on the internet. *Teacher Librarian, 29*, 46.

Greenberg, J., Pyszczynski, T., & Solomon, S. (1986). The causes and consequences of the need for self-esteem: A terror management theory. In R. F. Baumeister (Ed.), *Public self and private self* (pp. 189–212). New York: Springer-Verlag. doi:10.1007/978-1-4613-9564-5_10

Greenberg, J., Pyszczynski, T., Solomon, S., Rosenblatt, A., Veeder, M., Kirkland, S., & Lyon, D. (1990). Evidence for terror management theory: II. The effects of mortality salience reactions to those who threaten or bolster the cultural worldview. *Journal of Personality and Social Psychology, 58*(2), 308–318. doi:10.1037/0022-3514.58.2.308

Greenberg, J., Simon, L., Porteus, J., Pyszczynski, T., & Solomon, S. (1995). Evidence of a terror management function of cultural icons: The effects of mortality salience on the inappropriate use of cherished cultural symbols. *Personality and Social Psychology Bulletin, 21*(11), 1221–1228. doi:10.1177/01461672952111010

Halavy, N., Bornstein, G., & Sagiv, L. (2008). "In-group love" and "out-group hate" as motives for individual participation in intergroup conflict: A new game paradigm. *Psychological Science, 19*(4), 405–411. doi:10.1111/j.1467-9280.2008.02100.x PMID:18399895

Hardesty, G. (2010). D.A.: Arrests Cripple white-supremacist gangs. *Orange County Register*. Retrieved on April 29, 2015 from http://www.ocregister.com/articles/white-280585-county-orange.html

Hate, D. (1999)... *Economist, 353*, 30–31.

Hate Group Maps. (n.d.a). *Intro*. Retrieved January 31, 2015 from: http://www.athenainstitute.eu/en/projects/

Hate Groups Maps. (n.d.b). *Extremist Groups*. Retrieved January 31, 2015 from: http://www.athenainstitute.eu/en/hate_groups/

Hate Map. (n.d.). Retrieved October 29, 2014 from: http://www.splcenter.org/get-informed/hate-map

Hebdidge, D. (1981). *Subculture: The Meaning of Style*. New York: Routledge.

Hepworth, J. T., & West, S. G. (1988). Lynchings and the economy: A time-series reanalysis of Hovland and Sears (1940). *Journal of Personality and Social Psychology, 55*(2), 239–247. doi:10.1037/0022-3514.55.2.239

Hill, K. (2013). Aryan Brotherhood may target teen suspects, police say. *The Spokesman Review*. Retrieved on April 29, 2015 from http://www.spokesman.com/stories/2013/nov/20/aryan-brotherhood-may-target-demetruis-glenn/

Hodson, G., Dovidio, J. F., & Esses, V. M. (2003). Ingroup identification as a moderator of positive-negative asymmetry in social discrimination. *European Journal of Social Psychology, 33*(2), 215–233. doi:10.1002/ejsp.141

Holthouse, D. (2009). *Hate Groups Active in 2008*. Intelligence Report. Southern Poverty Law Center, Issue No. 133.

Hovland, C. I., & Sears, R. (1940). Minor studies in aggression: VI. Correlation of lynchings with economic indices. *The Journal of Psychology, 9*(2), 301–310. doi:10.1080/00223980.1940.9917696

Lassir, N. (2012, August 8). Hate with a beat: White power music. *CNN.com*.

Mackie, D., & Cooper, J. (1984). Attitude polarization: Effects of group membership. *Journal of Personality and Social Psychology, 46*(3), 575–585. doi:10.1037/0022-3514.46.3.575

Marshall, G. (1994). *Spirit of 69: A Skinhead Bible*. S.T. Publishing.

Marshall, G. (1997). *Skinhead Nation*. S.T. Publishing.

Miller, N., & Brewer, M. B. (Eds.). (1984). *Groups in Contact: The Psychology of Desegregation*. New York: Academic Press.

Mullen, B., Brown, R., & Smith, C. (1992). Ingroup bias as a function of salience, relevance, and status: An integration. *European Journal of Social Psychology, 22*(2), 103–122. doi:10.1002/ejsp.2420220202

Myers, D. G., & Lamm, H. (1976). The group polarization phenomenon. *Psychological Bulletin, 83*(4), 602–627. doi:10.1037/0033-2909.83.4.602

Nemes, I. (2002, October). Regulating hate speech in cyberspace: Issues of desirability and efficacy. *Information & Communications Technology Law*, *11*(3), 193–211. doi:10.1080/1360083022000031902

Neubauer, I. L. (2014, September 24). A teenage terrorism suspect is shot dead in Australia after attacking police. *Time World Australia*.

Oak Creek Sikh temple shooter had military background, white supremacist ties. (2012, August 6). *Milwaukee Journal-Sentinel*.

Pettigrew, T. F., & Tropp, L. R. (2006). A meta-analytic test of intergroup contact theory. *Journal of Personality and Social Psychology*, *90*(5), 751–783. doi:10.1037/0022-3514.90.5.751 PMID:16737372

Potok, M. (2013). *The little Fuhrer: Matthew Heimbach goes all the way*. Posted in Hatewatch Blog: Anti-Semetic, Neo-Nazi of the Southern Poverty Law Center.

Pyszczynski, T., Solomon, S., & Greenberg, J. (1997). Why do we need what we need? A terror management perspective on the roots of human social motivation. *Psychological Inquiry*, *8*(1), 1–20. doi:10.1207/s15327965pli0801_1

Pyszczynski, T., Solomon, S., & Greenberg, J. (2005). *In the wake of 9/11: The psychology of terror*. Washington, DC: American Psychological Association.

Pyszczynski, T., Wicklund, R. A., Floresku, S., Koch, H., Gauch, G., Solomon, S., & Greenberg, J. (1996). Whistling in the dark: Exaggerated consensus estimates in response to incidental reminders of mortality. *Psychological Science*, *7*(6), 332–336. doi:10.1111/j.1467-9280.1996.tb00384.x

CivilRights.org. (2009). *The State of Hate: White Supremacist Groups Growing, Confronting the New Faces of Hate: Hate Crimes in America 2009*. Author.

Rosenblatt, A., Greenberg, J., Solomon, S., Pyszczynski, T., & Lyon, D. (1989). Evidence for terror management theory I: The effects of mortality salience on reactions to those who violate or uphold cultural values. *Journal of Personality and Social Psychology*, *57*(4), 681–690. doi:10.1037/0022-3514.57.4.681 PMID:2795438

Rubin, M., & Hewstone, M. (1998). Social identity theory's self-esteem hypothesis: A review and some suggestions for clarification. *Personality and Social Psychology Review*, *2*(1), 40–62. doi:10.1207/s15327957pspr0201_3 PMID:15647150

Runciman, W. G. (1966). *Relative Deprivation and Social Justice*. London: Routledge and Kegan Paul.

Sada, L. (2013, June 4). Extreme anti-immigrant groups spread throughout Europe. *Global Voices*.

Sanders, G. S., & Baron, R. S. (1977). Is social comparison irrelevant for producing choice shifts? *Journal of Experimental Social Psychology*, *13*(4), 303–314. doi:10.1016/0022-1031(77)90001-4

Savvy PR. (2014, August 30). *Savvy PR campaign has lured many to fight in Syria's civil war*. National Public Radio.

Schafer, J. R., & Navarro, J. (2003) The seven stage hate model: The psychopathology of hate groups. *FBI Law Enforcement Bulletin*.

Schimel, J., Simon, L., Greenberg, J., Pyszczynski, T., Solomon, S., Waxmonsky, J., & Arndt, J. (1999). Stereotypes and terror management: Evidence that mortality salience enhances stereotypic thinking and preferences. *Journal of Personality and Social Psychology, 77*(5), 905–936. doi:10.1037/0022-3514.77.5.905 PMID:10573872

Sherif, M. (1966). *In common predicament.* Boston: Houghton Mifflin.

Sherif, M., Harvey, O. J., White, B. J., Hood, W. R., & Sherif, C. W. (1961). *The robbers cave experiment: Intergroup conflict and cooperation.* Middletown, CT: Wesleyan University Press.

Sherif, M., & Sherif, C. W. (1982). Production of intergroup conflict and its resolution – Robbers Cave experiment. In J. W. Reigh (Ed.), *Experimenting in society: Issues and examples in applied social psychology.* Glenview, IL: Scott, Foresman.

Smashing the Shamrock. (2012). Intelligence Report. Southern Poverty Law Center.

Smith, H. (2014, June 7). SS Songs and anti-Semitism. *The Guardian.*

Snyder, C. R., Lassegard, M. A., & El Ford, C. (1986). Distancing after group success and failure: Basking in reflected glory and cutting off reflected failure. *Journal of Personality and Social Psychology, 51*(2), 382–388. doi:10.1037/0022-3514.51.2.382

Solomon, S., Greenberg, J., & Pyszczynski, T. (1991). Article. In M. P. Zanna (Ed.), A terror management theory of social behavior: The psychological functions of self-esteem and cultural worldviews (pp. 91–159). San Diego, CA: Academic Press.

Solomon, S., Greenberg, J., & Pyszczynski, T. (2004). The cultural animal: Twenty years of terror management theory and research. In J. Greenberg, S. L. Koole, & T. Pyszczynski (Eds.), *Handbook of experimental existential psychology* (pp. 13–34). New York: Guilford Press.

Stack, L. (2015, May 3). *Texas police kill gunmen at exhibit featuring cartoons of Muhammad.* Retrieved on May 5, 2015 from http://www.nytimes.com/2015/05/04/us/gunmen-killed-after-firing-on-anti-islam-groups-event.html

Staff, S. (2014). *The end of tolerance? Anti Muslim movement rattles Germany.* Retrieved from http://www.spiegel.de/international/germany/anti-muslim-pegida-movement-rattles-germany-a-1009245.html

Sternberg, R. J. (1986). A triangular theory of love. *Psychological Review, 93*(2), 119–135. doi:10.1037/0033-295X.93.2.119

Sternberg, R. J. (2003). A duplex theory of hate and its development and its application to terrorism, massacres, and genocides. *Review of General Psychology, 7*(3), 299–328. doi:10.1037/1089-2680.7.3.299

Sternberg, R. J. (2005). From Plato to Putnam: Four ways to think about hate. In R. J. Sternberg (Ed.), *The psychology of hate* (pp. 3–35). Washington, DC: American Psychological Association. doi:10.1037/10930-000

Sternberg, R. J. (2006). A duplex theory of love. In R. J. Sternberg & K. Weis (Eds.), *The new psychology of love* (pp. 184–199). New Haven, CT: Yale University Press.

Stolzoff, N. C. (2000). *Wake the town and tell the people: Dancehall culture in Jamaica*. Duke University Press.

Struch, N., & Schwartz, S. H. (1989). Intergroup aggression: Its predictors and distinctness from in-group bias. *Journal of Personality and Social Psychology, 56*(3), 364–373. doi:10.1037/0022-3514.56.3.364 PMID:2926634

Suls, J., Martin, R., & Wheeler, L. (2002). Social comparison: Why, with whom, and with what effect? *Current Directions in Psychological Science, 11*(5), 159–163. doi:10.1111/1467-8721.00191

Sumner, W. G. (1906). *Folkways*. New York: Ginn.

Tajfel, H. (1982). Social psychology of intergroup relations. *Annual Review of Psychology, 33*(1), 1–39. doi:10.1146/annurev.ps.33.020182.000245

Tajfel, H., & Billig, M. (1974). Familiarity and categorization in intergroup behavior. *Journal of Experimental Social Psychology, 10*(2), 159–170. doi:10.1016/0022-1031(74)90064-X

Tajfel, H., Billig, M. G., Bundy, R. P., & Flament, C. (1971). Social categorization and intergroup behavior. *The Journal of Social Psychology, 1*, 149–178.

Tajfel, H., & Turner, J. C. (1986). An integrative theory of social conflict. In Psychology of intergroup relations. Chicago, IL: Nelson Hall.

Terlato, P. (2014, September 23). ISIS Calls For Australian Killings: The Chilling Statement That One Expert Says Is A 'Game-Changer'. *Business Insider Australia*.

Thoits, & Virshup. (1997). Me's and We's: Forms and functions of social identities. In R. D. Ashmore & L. J. Jussim (Eds.), *Self and Identity: Fundamental Issues* (pp. 106-133). Academic Press.

Turner, T., & Cross, C. (2014). *Ireland, Spain, and Greece see biggest change in attitudes to immigrants*. Retrieved November 1, 2014 from http://www.irishtimes.com/news/world/ireland-spain-and-greece-see-biggest-change-in-attitudes-to-immigrants-1.1776615

Valeri, R., & Borgeson. (2005). Identifying the face of hate. *Journal of Applied Sociology, 22*, 91–104.

Valeri, R., & Borgeson. (2007). Reframing affirmative action: Examining the impact on white Americans. *Michigan Sociological Review, 21*, 193–209.

Vanneman, R. D., & Pettigrew, T. F. (1972). Race and relative deprivation in the urban United States. *Race, 13*(4), 431–486. doi:10.1177/030639687201300404

Vinokur, A., & Burnstein, E. (1974). Effects of partially shared persuasive arguments on group-induced shifts: A group problem solving approach. *Journal of Personality and Social Psychology, 29*(3), 305–315. doi:10.1037/h0036010

Vrugt, A., & Koenis, S. (2002). Perceived self-efficacy, personal goals, social comparison, and scientific productivity. *Applied Psychology, 51*(4), 593–607. doi:10.1111/1464-0597.00110

Walters, J. (2001). *One Aryan Nation under God*. Naperville, IL: Sourcebooks.

Wood, J. V. (1989). Theory and research concerning social comparison of personal attributes. *Psychological Bulletin, 106*(2), 231–248. doi:10.1037/0033-2909.106.2.231

Wood, J. V., Taylor, S. E., & Lichtman, R. R. (1985). Social comparison in adjustment to breast cancer. *Journal of Personality and Social Psychology, 49*(5), 1169–1183. doi:10.1037/0022-3514.49.5.1169 PMID:4078672

Zaitchik, A. (2010, August 20). Paul Fromm: The lonely voice of Canadian Hate. *Hate Watch*. Posted in the Southern Poverty Law Center's Anti Immigrant.

Zellner, W. W. (1995). *Countercultures: A Sociological Analysis*. New York: St. Martin's Press.

Chapter 7
Youth Gang Exit:
A Canadian Perspective

Laura Dunbar
University of Ottawa, Canada

ABSTRACT

Youth gangs and their members have been studied in a variety of contexts; however the issue of desistance has received less attention. This chapter seeks to address this gap. In order to situate the material to be covered, the chapter begins with an introduction to the topic of youth gangs. Next, an overview of the concept of desistance and how it is measured is provided. Following that is a review of some prominent criminological perspectives demonstrating that leaving the gang is a complex process involving the interaction of a combination of factors. The process of desistance and methods for leaving the gang are also briefly discussed. Several approaches have been developed to address youth gangs and their members. These approaches are reviewed and different interventions under these headings are discussed with Canadian examples provided. Finally, an argument for the development of a comprehensive strategy for youth gang exit is presented.

INTRODUCTION

In *Nasty, Brutish, and Short: The Lives of Gang Members in Canada*, Totten (2012) draws upon in-depth interviews with 519 gang members over the past 17 years. He explores the process of gang exit, his arguments supplemented by the stories of his participants. Charlie, aged 24 and a long-time gang member, discusses the process of leaving the lifestyle:

I came to a long-sought conclusion that I wanted to exit gang life and my current status in gangs which is high. Regardless, this proved to be difficult due to my lifestyle and reputation, which has always preceded me... Gangs, as you know, are difficult to exit. After years of being involved my life is woven deep in the fabric of the gang... I need help and support. (p. 200)

DOI: 10.4018/978-1-4666-9938-0.ch007

OTTAWA, ON – Canada's capital city is known for politics but now is earning a reputation for gang violence. A record number of gang-related shootings in 2014 have left residents wondering if the normally sleepy city has changed. Marc Clairoux understands the allure of gangs all too well. He joined a neighbourhood gang in west-end Ottawa at 13, then a skinhead gang at 18 – all for the feeling of family and belonging. "Close friends of mine were dying", says Clairoux, who spent 17 years in the gang before leaving almost a decade ago. "It was an ugly way to live and I had to just take a look at myself and my family and think that I need to get away from this." Clairoux notes that he didn't find gang involvement was worth it in the end. "I've had so many restrictions put on my life because of it." It's a feeling Clairoux recalls as he hears of a record increase in gun violence in the nation's capital. The gang is a difficult thing to leave and an exit strategy is required (excerpts from Stone, 2014).

Gangs and gang members have been studied in a variety of contexts; information has been gained about the history, demographics, subcultures, criminal involvement, membership patterns, and group processes. Yet not all stages of gang involvement have received equal attention. Most of the research has focused on the processes of joining or of maintaining membership over time; the question of desistance has received much less attention.

This chapter seeks to address this gap and is laid out as follows. First, in order to situate the material to be covered, the chapter begins with an introduction to the topic of youth gangs. Next, an overview of the concept of desistance and how it is measured is provided. Following that is a review of some prominent criminological perspectives demonstrating that leaving the gang is a complex process involving the interaction of a combination of factors, including: maturation; individual choice; relational, social, and institutional forces and practices; and structural level constraints and opportunities. The process of desistance and methods for leaving the gang is also briefly discussed. Several approaches have been developed to address youth gangs and their members. These approaches are reviewed and different interventions under these headings are discussed with Canadian examples provided. Finally, an argument for the development of a comprehensive strategy for youth gang exit is presented.

BACKGROUND

Defining 'Gang'

While there is little consensus among researchers on the 'true' definition of a gang and who is a gang member (Esbensen, Winfree, He, & Taylor, 2001; Peterson, 2000), some general criteria have been established:

- There is often a generational dimension; gangs are a phenomenon related to youth (Ayling, 2011; Esbensen et al., 2001; Mohammed, 2007).
- They are characterized as a self-formed association of peers bound by mutual interests, and who utilize symbols of belonging and modes of communication that are more or less noticeable to outsiders (Mohammed, 2007).
- Organization is seen as a necessary, though not sufficient, defining feature; the gang is an organized social system governed by a leadership structure that has defined roles (Sánchez-Jankowski, 1991, 2003).

In the above respects, gangs are similar to other social groups. One widely used benchmark for assessing whether a given social group is a 'gang' is the engagement by group members in criminal behaviour, some of which may involve violence, on a regular basis (Esbensen et al., 2001; Mohammed, 2007; Peterson, 2000). For example, several police services across Canada use the following definition developed by the Canadian Association of Chiefs of Police (CACP) Street Gangs Committee in June 2011:

A 'gang' refers to any group of three or more people, formally or informally organized, which may have a common name or identifying sign or symbol, whose members individually or collectively engage in or have engaged primarily in street level criminal behaviour, creating an atmosphere of fear and intimidation within the community.

The Youth Gang Problem

Youth gangs are a ubiquitous problem of contemporary society. Gang members account for a disproportionate amount of criminal behaviour and commit a variety of offences, including property offences, drug trafficking and importation, fraud, robberies, assaults with weapons, and homicides (Boyce & Cotter, 2013; Hemmati, 2006). In Canada, law enforcement officials have reported a rise in gang rivalry characterized by mounting gang violence. Gang activity has changed over the past several years: there is now more violent crime, more inter-gang conflict and more lucrative drug trafficking, resulting in more wars over territory (Kelly & Caputo, 2005). Figure 1 demonstrates that since data on gang-related homicide in Canada became available in 1991, there has been a general increase in the rate until its peak in 2008. With 95 homicides considered by police to be gang-related in 2012, the rate has remained stable for a third year in a row at 0.27 victims per 100,000 population (Boyce & Cotter, 2013).

Youth gangs are characterized as harmful to individuals, communities, and society as a whole (Caudill, 2010). Their activities may result in the direct victimization of others. Sensational media headlines often

Figure 1. Gang-related homicides, Canada, 1992 to 2012
Source: Homicide in Canada, 2012

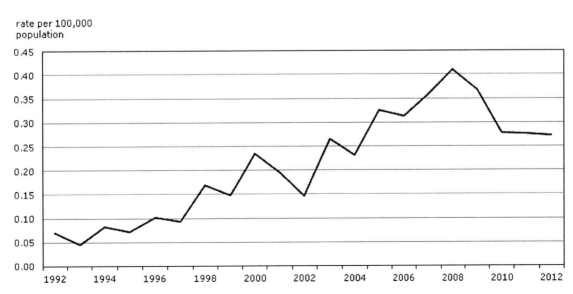

draw attention to the unintended victim of gang-related violence – the innocent bystander. In Canada, recent high-profile incidents include the 2005 Boxing Day shooting in downtown Toronto, Ontario that resulted in the death of 15-year-old bystander Jane Creba. The incident involved a shootout between rival gangs. A more recent example is the June 2012 Eaton Centre shooting in Toronto, Ontario. Promoted as gang related – the result of internal gang strife – the incident left 24-year-old gang-affiliated Ahmed Hassan dead and six other innocent bystanders injured. The impact of gang-related activities on the community, and larger social systems is also enormous, and sometimes not well recognized. For example, members of gang-affected communities must live within a culture of violence and there are social costs in lost potential and fear of crime inhibiting the normal activities of citizens. The financial costs to the justice and health care systems are also considerable (Chatterjee, 2006).

In addition, involvement in the gang lifestyle can lead to problems for its members, including: dropping out of school; lack of employment success; exposure to and involvement with drug and alcohol use; increased risk of victimization; and teenage parenthood. Participation reduces gang members' connections to other mainstream social activities and they may cut ties to social groups and organizations such as family, friends, schools, and religious communities in order to focus more intensively on gang participation and identity. The longer an individual is involved, the more severe the effect is likely to become. Contact with the criminal justice system may lead to community supervision or to placement in a custodial facility resulting in the mark of a criminal record that further limits individual growth and progress in education and/or employment (Pyrooz, Sweeten, & Piquero, 2013; Thornberry, Krohn, Lizotte, Smith, & Tobin, 2003; Young & Gonzalez, 2013).

The extent of the negative implications associated with youth gang involvement demonstrates the necessity of examining the issue of desistance and presenting research that provides, both theoretically and empirically, a greater understanding of the processes surrounding it.

Why Youth Join Gangs

Before undertaking an investigation of desistance, it is important to identify the factors associated with a decision to pursue gang membership. The reasons why young people join a gang in the first place may provide insight into their rationales for leaving. The motivations for joining may include some of the following:

- A gang can be seen as a source of protection; a way to address concerns about personal safety and security, whether as a result of personal experiences of violence or due to a fear or expectation of such violence (Stinchcomb, 2002; Taylor, 2009).
- A gang can provide the means to acquire material possessions and resources that may not be available through legitimate means. In many instances, joining a gang and a turn to illegal activities is a way for individuals to increase income and achieve financial goals (Lurigio, Flexon, & Greenleaf, 2008; Sánchez-Jankowski, 1991; Stinchcomb, 2002).
- A gang can act as a social organization that provides its members with entertainment or the status associated with other groups. In many cases the gang is the primary social institution in the neighbourhood. It also provides members with an opportunity to meet others and can be a source of access to drugs and alcohol (Sánchez-Jankowski, 1991, 2003; Stinchcomb, 2002; Wood & Alleyne, 2010).

- A gang can offer a source of emotional support to its members and provide individuals with a sense of belonging. Membership can offer a source of self-esteem and identity, as well as companionship and support; the gang becomes a surrogate family for its members, through which they can fulfill personal needs (Klein, 1995; Lurigio et al., 2008; Taylor, 2009; Wood & Alleyne, 2010).
- A gang may be attractive to those facing difficult social and economic conditions including poverty, low educational performance, lack of job-related skills, and social disorganization; they may feel that there is no better alternative to a life of crime and gang involvement (Grekul & LaBoucane-Benson, 2007).

It is important to emphasize that individuals join a gang for a variety of reasons, and these are not exclusive of one another. The decision to join is often well thought out and the individual believes that this is best for their interests at the moment (Sánchez-Jankowski, 1991).

WHAT IS DESISTANCE AND HOW IS IT MEASURED?

In the field of criminology, 'desistance' is generally defined as the cessation of offending or other anti-social behaviour. Bushway, Piquero, Broidy, Cauffman and Mazerolle (2001) state that true desistance occurs when an individual's rate of offending is indistinguishable from zero – in other words, when there is no empirical difference from non-offenders. Applied to the topic of youth gangs, desistance is the complete termination of gang involvement. It is characterized as a state achieved by an individual – distinguishing gang member (persister) from non-gang member (desister).

Various authors have pointed out the shortcomings of a dichotomous definition of desistance, and some have suggested instead that a 'process' view of desistance may provide a more accurate picture of the concept. According to Pyrooz and Decker (2011), gang desistance refers to the "declining probability of gang membership – the reduction from peak to trivial levels of gang membership" (p. 419). It is realized as individuals lessen their participation in group activities (e.g., meetings, social events, criminal events) as well as reducing the weight they place on the prominence of the gang and their identification with the gang.

This understanding of desistance includes complementary processes of 'knifing off' (separating oneself from the triggers associated with the behaviour) and 'cognitive transformation' (a change in one's way of thinking). This dynamic approach recognizes that there may be different paths to desistance. It should be noted that these pathways are rarely straightforward; they are better described as dynamic and uncertain, happening over time and in response to a given situation. This perspective assumes that desistance does not occur as an abrupt termination ('break point'), but rather as a gradual reduction in the frequency, severity and versatility of gang-related actions and behaviour (Kazemian, 2007). However, even then, desistance is rarely absolute and so-called 'desisters' may continue to engage in gang-related conduct (Healy, 2010).

CRIMINOLOGICAL PERSPECTIVES ON MOTIVES FOR LEAVING THE GANG

As gang involvement follows similar patterns to involvement in a criminal career (onset, continuity and desistance), criminological perspectives offering explanations for desistance from crime may also be relevant for providing an understanding of desistance from youth gang involvement. In the following section, some of the prominent theories in the general crime desistance literature are presented as a starting point for discussion and are then applied to the topic of leaving youth gangs. Some limitations of the current perspectives are also provided. These theories are categorized by their approach to addressing the issue of desistance.

Individual Focused Approach

Theory of Maturational Reform

One of the most consistently documented findings in criminology is the existence of the 'age-crime curve', which shows that official and self-reported criminal activity decreases during late adolescence and early adulthood. For most individuals, participation in crime generally begins in the early teenage years, peaks in late adolescence or young adulthood, and ends by middle adulthood (Piquero, Farrington, & Blumstein, 2003). Developmental change in late adolescence and early adulthood facilitates the attainment or refinement of competencies and values that make criminal behaviour less attractive and less acceptable. Changes in moral reasoning, future orientation, impulse control, and/or susceptibility to peer influence may help steer individuals away from anti-social behaviour and toward more socially desirable activities (Steinberg & Cauffman, 1996).

Temporary Nature of the Gang Lifestyle

Similar to desistance from crime, theories of maturational reform have been used to explain why youth gang members decide to disengage from the group. Thrasher's (1927) seminal study of gangs in Chicago, and most subsequent studies, proposed that individuals who were in gangs simply matured out of them as they got older. While the gang may serve a variety of functions for youth at particular points in their lives, for most, the situation is temporary. While there are individuals who maintain their gang involvement for extended periods, for most, gang membership is a short-lived status (Carson, Peterson, & Esbensen, 2013). Gang membership among adolescents typically averages two years or less. Former gang members often describe having 'grown out of the gang', or simply having 'gotten too old' for the gang lifestyle (Battin, Hill, Abbott, Catalano, & Hawkins, 1998; Thornberry, Lizotte, Krohn, Farnworth, & Jang, 1994). This acknowledges the temporal dimension of lived experience – the ways in which people and circumstances change over time; youth do not spend all of their lives in the gang doing gang 'stuff' (White, 2008).

Theory of Rational Choice

One of the earliest approaches to address desistance from crime focused on the idea that individuals make a rational decision to stop offending (Farrall, Hunter, Sharpe, & Caverley, 2014). From this perspective, the decision to continue or stop offending may be based on a reappraisal of its costs and benefits. Mulvey and colleagues (2004) suggest that individuals often report some identifiable event that prompted them to re-think the potential costs of anti-social or harmful behaviour. Giordano, Cernovich and Rudolph (2002) identify 'cognitive transformations' (changes in outlook and thinking) that contribute to the reduction of offending. They include a shift in an individual's openness to change and exposure to a 'hook' or sets of hooks for change (e.g., employment, marriage, family). It should be noted, however, that these hooks cannot change a person who does not want to make an effort to change on their own (Meisenhelder, 1977). Substantial and lasting changes in criminal behaviour rarely come about only as a result of passive experience; such changes involve significant participation by the individual acting as their own 'agent of change' (Maruna, 1999).

Reappraising Costs and Benefits of Gang Membership in the Context of Violence

Many individuals believe that at the time of their decision to join, the gang is capable of providing them with a number of advantages that would enhance the quality of their lives (Sánchez-Jankowski, 1991). When this is no longer the case, and gang membership starts to become detrimental, the decision to leave the gang may be made.

As one example of the application of the rational choice theory, previous research has found that gang exit is often associated with violent incidents (Decker & Lauritsen, 2002; Ngo, 2010). Youth who identify being in a gang also report significantly greater levels of victimization than non gang-involved youth (Wortley & Tanner, 2004) and so gang members may have a strong motivation to escape violence. Decker and Lauritsen (2002) found that personal experience of violence was the most commonly reported reason for leaving the gang, suggesting that increased risk for victimization may lead a youth to desire a gang-free life (Pyrooz & Decker, 2011; Wood & Alleyne, 2010). While internal violence (initiation rites or 'beating in') and mythic violence (stories of altercations between gangs) may serve to intensify gang bonds at the outset and during membership, the impact of real violence encourages desistance. There seems to be a limit to the tolerance that the individual gang member has for personal experiences of violence, the threat or fear of personal violence, or having family members be the victims of violence. In this sense, the very activity that serves to keep gangs together can also provide the motivation for leaving the gang (Decker & Lauritsen, 2002).

Limitations

Under the individual focused approach, a main assumption is the primacy of the individual actor and the belief that the explanation for gang involvement may be found in motivational and behavioural systems (Matza, 1964). The theory of maturational reform assumes that individuals engage in criminal behaviour as a result of immaturity – they are characterized as impulsive, insensitive, risk-taking and short sighted. Yet, many gang-related acts require a certain level of maturity to be carried out successfully. For example, gang-based drug dealers are often characterized by their entrepreneurial spirit – their ability to manage contacts, understand the market, organize the division of labour, and control the competition (Sánchez-Jankowski, 1991).

The theory of rational choice suggests that the decision to continue or give up the gang lifestyle is based on a conscious reappraisal of its costs and benefits; promoted by an internal re-orientation concerning the potential harms of continued involvement. However, while individuals may weigh the pros and cons of their behaviour, they are doing so within a particular context. The decision to desist is based on a circumstantial rationality; individuals base their decisions on a calculation of what is best for them at that particular time (Sánchez-Jankowski, 1991) and not on objective indicators of harm. Further while individuals make decisions, their circumstances may limit their capacity to live up to these decisions (Farrall & Bowling, 1999). Where they reside, who their associates are, and their ability to find alternative ways to make money will likely impact their resolve. Considering these circumstances, rational choice theory alone cannot account for decisions to leave the gang lifestyle (Sampson & Laub, 2005).

Relationship Focused Approach

Theory of Social Bonds or 'Informal Social Control'

Under this perspective, a general belief is that individuals are inherently disposed to offend because crime offers short-term gains; the central aim of those with criminal dispositions is to satisfy desires in the quickest and simplest way possible (Gottfredson & Hirschi, 1990). The development of pro-social bonds may redirect a person's life path away from offending. These bonds provide individuals with a stake in conformity, make deviant activity less acceptable and useful, and provide a reason to return to a conventional lifestyle. Conversely, those who lack these bonds are more likely to stay involved in criminal behaviour as they have less to lose from sanctions and ostracism. Increased capacities and expectations to work, engagement in serious romantic relationships, starting a family, and fulfilling community roles may result in reduced exposure to and decreased attractiveness of settings where criminal involvement is prevalent (Cernkovich & Giordano, 2001; Maruna, 2001; Mulvey et al., 2004). Individuals gradually acquire stakes in these social institutions, which serve to add structure to their lives and act as a source of informal monitoring and emotional support (Laub, Nagin, & Sampson, 1998).

However, supporters of this perspective hold that the relationship between pro-social ties and desistance has 'strings attached' (Uggen, 1996). For instance, Sampson and Laub (1995) argue that employment by itself does not affect desistance. Rather, "employment coupled with job stability, commitment to work, and mutual ties binding workers and employers" reduces criminality (p. 146). Desistance depends not only on the existence of pro-social attachments but also on their perceived strength and quality, and on the individual's commitment to these new interactions (Sampson & Laub, 1993). If these new roles and opportunities create valued experiences that are important to the individual, then that individual may reach a point where the new lifestyle becomes a reality that is worth protecting. This investment in new pro-social roles is believed to develop over an extended period, as an individual builds a social base that helps to avoid future opportunities for criminal involvement (Mulvey et al., 2004).

Theory of Differential Association or 'Social Learning'

As an extension of the above perspective, the theory of differential association provides insight into how the process of desistance occurs. It suggests that criminal behaviour is learned and the principal part of learning happens within important social groups (Sutherland & Cressey, 1960). Akers (1997) proposes that crime is learned through the development of beliefs that crime is acceptable in some situations, the positive reinforcement of criminal involvement (e.g., approval of friends, financial gains), and the imitation of the criminal behaviour of others – especially if they are people that the individual values. These variables that explain initiation into crime may also account for cessation from crime; desistance is initiation in reverse. Association with non-criminal friends and significant others, less exposure or opportunities to model or imitate criminal behaviour, developing definitions and attitudes favourable to conformity and abiding by the law, and reinforcement discouraging continued involvement in crime are all part of the process of desistance (Laub & Sampson, 2001).

Increasing Stake in Conformity – Bonds and Attachments to Conventional People and Activities

Just as the development of pro-social ties may help to direct an individual away from involvement in crime and deviant behaviour, youth may diminish their involvement in gangs as they develop increased ties to non-deviant friends, significant others and family members, an increasing commitment to social institutions, and take up opportunities for pro-social integration such as employment or parenthood (Decker & Lauritsen, 2002; Esbensen et al., 2001; Wood & Alleyne, 2010). All of this discourages continued gang involvement. Movement out of gangs and into family and work environments represents a restructuring of routine activities that reduces exposure to situational contexts conducive to gang-related behaviour. Further, the growth of social bonds is like an investment process; as the social bond to legitimacy grows, the incentive to desist from gang involvement increases because more is at stake, and there are more effective systems of obligation and restraint (Laub & Sampson, 2003; Sampson & Laub, 1993). If these newly acquired social attachments and engagements are reinforced (e.g., opportunities to advance in employment), the youth's resolve to exit from the gang may strengthen and desistance will continue. However if, they break down (i.e., employment is lost or a relationship breaks up), then the youth may consider a return to the gang lifestyle (Wood & Alleyne, 2010).

Limitations

Under these perspectives, there is a lack of discussion of the broader community context (Elder, Johnson, & Crosnoe, 2003). For example community characteristics, such as socio-economic status, residential instability, and the heterogeneity of residents may allow for a broader understanding of the conditions in which social bonds are able to develop (Jacob, 2006). When a community is disorganized, it may impede the development of social ties. Without support for individuals or resources provided to families, the ability of other social institutions to foster social bonds with those seeking to desist from the gang lifestyle may be hindered.

Social Structure Focused Approach

Desistance requires a supporting social structure for positive activities, and this can only exist if an individual has access to the necessary building blocks (capacity, skills, and inclination) for its construction (Mulvey et al., 2004). Further, a range of wider social, institutional and societal forces and practices that are beyond the control of the individual (Farrall & Bowling, 1999) may present barriers and obstacles to the process of desistance; they may affect an individual's potential to succeed in making the transition into the 'pro-social world'. Farrall, Bottoms and Shapland (2010) suggest that recent changes in the economy, employment structures, the educational system and the housing market have served to restructure the legitimate routes out of crime and have influenced the availability of and access to such routes for offenders.

Barriers and Obstacles to Leaving the Gang

Part of the process of exiting the gang involves addressing barriers and obstacles to disengagement. Membership may be sustained if individuals believe there are no alternative places to go outside the gang, and if they assume they will be rejected by conventional society. Gang members come from a variety of ethnic, demographic and socio-economic backgrounds. However, the majority of youth involved in gangs tend to come from groups and areas that suffer from the greatest levels of economic inequality, disadvantage and social disorganization (Chettleburgh, 2003; CISC, 2006; Wortley & Tanner, 2004). There are clear indications that both the economic position and sense of exclusion of certain groups have been getting relatively worse; young men, those most likely to be involved in youth gangs, have felt this income inequality most acutely (Bania, 2009; Heisz, 2005). The relative economic position of young men aged 16-29 years has declined over the past twenty years both in terms of their rate of full-time employment and in their earnings (Beaujot & Kerr, 2007).

Long-term gang membership may have limited the individual's ability to acquire education and marketable skills for the workforce, thereby limiting options for employment if he/she decides to leave. The type of employment that assisted many individuals in making the move away from the lifestyle in the past (manual or un-skilled labour) has largely disappeared, to be replaced by jobs that require more formal educational or trade qualifications, or by lower status jobs (Farrall et al., 2010). In turn, these limited opportunities may result in the benefits of staying in the gang being seen as outweighing the consequences of being a gang member.

Further, social barriers, such as the 'gang' label, public perceptions of the individual as a gang member, and stigma of former gang membership, may limit opportunities as well as an individual's ability to leave the gang. Gang identities often remain fixed in the public's perception long after the decision to leave the gang has been made and acted on. Youth may continue to be seen as gang members by their own gang, rival gangs, the police, and the community (Decker & Pyrooz, 2010). Gang insignias, criminal records and other acts committed while a gang member may hinder their ability to integrate into the pro-social world (Decker & Lauritsen, 2002).

These negative labels and stigmatization can leave young people with a sense of exclusion and pessimism about the future (Bania, 2009; Chettleburgh, 2007; Totten, 2000) and may even propel marginalized individuals deeper into the gang subculture. These individuals may give up on traditional means of success and adopt survival strategies that are based in the present, on 'living day to day'. These individuals may be more likely to maintain continued gang membership. For them, initiating the process of desistance may be much more difficult.

Summary

There is a general acknowledgment that no one criminological theory can completely explain the motivation for desistance. Increasingly, theorists have drawn these different perspectives together, arguing that the process of desistance involves the interaction of a combination of factors that push or pull an individual away from the gang (Farrall & Bowling, 1999; Farrall et al., 2014). These include: the temporary nature of membership and the importance of aging and maturation; an accumulation of perceptions that run opposite to the gang's function and a desire to escape violence; the development of bonds and attachments to conventional people and activities; and an absence of structural barriers and obstacles.

THE DESISTANCE PROCESS AND METHODS FOR LEAVING THE GANG

Methods for leaving refer to modes employed in order to exit the gang. In other words, how one is able to exit the gang and whether that exit is met with resistance. First and foremost, it should be acknowledged that although there is a commonly held perception that gang membership is a lifelong commitment, most individuals that join gangs also leave gangs. Despite myths and sensationalized claims, for example that members must be beaten out of the gang or must undertake a series of exceptional and often illegal tasks in order to be permitted to leave, research indicates that not only is it possible to leave, but the process of doing so can be fairly uneventful (Decker & Lauritsen, 2002). However, it is important to be mindful that individuals may still maintain membership with a gang out of a fear of the perceived violence to accompany exit or from old rivals attempting retribution if they do leave (Bolden, 2013; Pyrooz et al., 2013).

In general, desistance can be characterized as a fluid process. The shift in identification from 'gang member' to 'non-gang member' may be expressed in incremental decreases in involvement in gang-related activities and a cognitive shift to a non-gang status (Carson et al., 2013). Maruna and Farrall (2004) propose a useful distinction between two stages in the process of reform: primary desistance, which can be characterized as any break in gang-related activity; and secondary desistance, a more long-term process, which results in the reframing of personal identity into a new conventional self. Secondary desistance is treated as a long-term process during which an individual must gradually develop a new sense of identity as a 'non-gang member'. The process is complete when this new identity is internalized. The consolidation of changes to an individual's perspective of himself/herself is a process that can take considerable time. Pathways to change usually contain relapse experiences, which are a normal part of any reform process (e.g., recovery from addiction). It should be acknowledged that an individual may cycle back to an earlier stage after a failed desistance attempt (Healy, 2010).

As noted above, the process of desistance is seldom instantaneous and it is not always permanent. Most ex-gang members report gradually severing the bonds between themselves and the gang (Decker & Lauritsen, 2002). They usually leave the gang through a process similar to their entry into it – in a series of steps and commitments often involving decreasing commitment to the gang and gang members, and increasing loyalty to conventional individuals and institutions (Decker & Lauritsen, 2002; Spergel, 1995). Further, the process of leaving the gang is often more difficult than joining. Since gangs are perceived to meet the unfulfilled needs of their members, individuals may be reluctant to leave out of a fear of the loss of these benefits. Gang members are unlikely to desist from gang involvement until and unless a suitable alternative to this support system has been found (Bolden, 2013).

The desistance process may also be dependent on additional factors, such as the individual's level of engagement within the gang. The gang literature demonstrates that it is more difficult for core members to leave than it is for peripheral members, and individuals who are weakly embedded in gangs desist at a faster rate than those more deeply embedded (Pyrooz et al., 2013). Ties to the gang are important to understanding the point at which the gang loses its power over individuals and they become open to cutting their connection to the group. The severing of ties provides a transitional phase between active gang membership and former gang membership. However, many ex-gang members continue to engage with the gang lifestyle through varying degrees of attachments and activities with others in the gang. In particular, ex-gang members with close friends and family members in the gang may remain entangled in a series of ties to the group, as involvement in this social network may have been a motive for joining initially (Pyrooz, Decker, & Webb, 2014; Thornberry et al., 2003).

SOLUTIONS AND RECOMMENDATIONS

The theoretical perspectives discussed above help to provide a clearer understanding of why and how youth desist from gang involvement. This allows for the situation of interventions that seek to address the issue. The following section provides an overview of some of the different types of intervention that exist to promote and support desistance among gang-involved youth. Some examples of current Canadian programs based on these approaches are also identified. First, a discussion on defining and measuring success is provided, and a note on program evaluation in the Canadian context is offered at the end of the section.

Defining and Measuring Success

The notion of 'success' in youth gang interventions is debatable; a distinction can be made between 'insertion' and 'integration' as different definitions or measures of success. In the case of insertion, the focus is primarily on the point at which the youth decides to leave a gang, and tries to take up what would be considered a more legitimate path. Usually, the emphasis is on reducing the risk that the youth will return to the gang. Interventions involve attempts to increase the willingness and ability of the youth to exercise greater self-control (such as cognitive skills development or anger management programs) or initiatives that seek to impose greater levels of external control on the youth (involving intensive monitoring and supervision activities, especially on the part of agents of the criminal justice system) (Hastings, Dunbar, & Bania, 2011). Success is measured in terms of outcome; interventions are expected to yield tangible results (Ilan, 2010) – in this case a lack of recidivism.

Since desistance has been conceptualized as a process, success is perhaps better understood in the context of an individual's ongoing journey toward successful integration within the community (Uggen, Manza, & Thompson, 2006). Integration involves a more positive definition of success; shifting the focus to a more inclusive concern with providing a youth gang member with a sense of well-being and of hope, and with the skills and resources needed to improve his/her objective standing in terms of agreed upon measures such as the social determinants of health (e.g., education, employment, health services, housing, income and social inclusion) (Farrall & Calverley, 2006). Positive changes in these indicators are likely to have an impact on the youth's trajectory in the longer term and therefore may provide a better assessment of the performance of interventions (Mears & Butts, 2008). Success is measured in terms of process; interventions should yield gradual perceivable improvements in the lives of youth gang members (Ilan, 2010).

Types of Intervention

Suppression and Control

The traditional approach to address youth gangs is suppression by the criminal justice system (Chettleburgh, 2007). Strategies focus on the criminal behaviour of gang members, and usually employ a coordinated justice response emphasizing arrest, prosecution, and incarceration (Bania, 2009; Jones, Roper, Stys, & Wilson, 2004; Westmacott, Stys, & Brown, 2005). Over the past number of years, many Canadian

144

municipal police departments have developed gang units (including Toronto, Edmonton, Regina, Ottawa, Montreal, Winnipeg, and Abbotsford). The Royal Canadian Mounted Police (RCMP) and various provincial forces have also initiated gang units, often in collaboration with municipal squads (Totten, 2012).

The Combined Forces Special Enforcement Unit of British Columbia is the province's anti-gang police unit[1]. It is an integrated joint forces operation that draws and develops highly specialized officers from federal, provincial and municipal agencies around the province. This integrated approach enhances intelligence sharing, coordination, and strategic deployment against threats of violence posed by organized crime groups and gangs in British Columbia. The Unit's mandate is to target, investigate, prosecute, disrupt, and dismantle the gangs and the members that pose the highest risk to public safety due to their involvement in gang violence.

The Calgary Police Service Organized Crime Operations Centre (OCOC) was established to coordinate the extensive resources required to tackle the city's gang problem. By exchanging intelligence, techniques and proven strategies with other North American cities that have successfully addressed gang crime and violence, a comprehensive plan to suppress gang activity has been developed. The gang strategy has four pillars: education; prevention; disruption; and investigation[2].

Individual Development Approach

The most common of the following approaches to be discussed, the main objective of interventions under this heading is to increase basic capacities, skills and individual propensities to help youth shift their life trajectories from gang-associated behaviours and affiliations to more pro-social lifestyles. Programs and services that help youth to change their attitudes and deal with their problems have been shown to have a positive impact on their willingness to leave their gang. Most interventions are targeted at individual behaviour and offer content focusing on perspective taking, moral reasoning, increasing self-esteem, developing a stronger self-identity, promoting the acquisition of conflict resolution skills, better managing actions and feelings (self-control), and making positive choices (Di Placido, Simon, Witte, Gu, & Wong, 2006; Grekul & LaBoucane-Benson, 2007).

The Gang Prevention Strategy (GPS)[3] implemented by Living Rock Ministries based in Hamilton, Ontario targets youth aged 13 to 25 who are at risk of gang involvement, or are already gang-involved. GPS is based on the Wraparound model[4]. Key elements of the program include being assigned a coach, developing a case management plan, meeting with the coach for at least one hour per month for the first three months, and participating in at least one hour of programming activities each week for a defined three-month period.

Youth At Risk Development (YARD)[5] implemented by the Youth Education and Intervention Unit of the Calgary Police Service (CPS) Community and Youth Services Section (CYSS) based in Calgary, Alberta targets youth between the ages of 10 and 17 who are gang-involved or at risk of engaging in gang-related activity. While YARD was originally proposed as a Wraparound model, its approach evolved into a hybrid of case management with features of the model. It is a citywide program that focuses primarily on prevention and intervention, by aiming to address the roots of gang involvement at the individual level through an emphasis on social development and rehabilitation. The program consists of the following core activities: individual assessment; case management; direct contact with YARD team (police officer and social worker); referrals to a variety of community resources (based on participant need); and support services to parents.

Relationship Development / Community-Based Approach

Interventions under this heading serve to facilitate new sources of support, including working with the family, identifying new peer groups, and establishing a support network for the youth at school, at work, and in the community. When the social structure that the gang provides is no longer present in the youth's life, it is crucial to teach them how to seek out and gain support that can help sustain positive efforts. Research has suggested that for individuals to disengage from the gang, membership, with its heavy reliance on a collective identity, must be replaced by an equally meaningful identity (Kassel, 2003).

Some programs focus on strengthening family bonds – reducing/mediating family conflicts; building positive relationships; family management skills; parenting skills; and providing opportunities for families to spend positive time together. Others focus on the development of healthy positive peer relationships – gaining access to more positive peer groups to meet the need for belonging and socialization (recreational, educational, social, mentoring, and faith-based programs). Finally, peer-mentoring programs allow youth to share similar experiences, validate each other's reality, and gain a greater sense of self-esteem, as individuals feel useful to other group members. Further, it gives gang members the opportunity to learn from those who have chosen to leave the gang lifestyle behind (Young & Gonzalez, 2013).

Helping gang members to improve their education and offering them training opportunities might play an important role in helping them to leave their gang. Some gang exit programs provide gang-involved youth with access to educational, training, and employment programs. Other programs offer remedial education, life skills and job training services, and mentoring opportunities to encourage youth to develop supportive relationships with employers. However, only a few programs go on to provide youth with actual employment opportunities.

Regina Anti-Gang Services (RAGS)[6] implemented by the North Central Community Association (NCCA) based in Regina, Saskatchewan targets gang-involved youth (primarily Aboriginal) and young adults aged 16 to 30 years old as well as their parents, their family, or both. RAGS integrates elements of several evidence-based models, including Wraparound, Multisystemic Therapy (MST)[7], harm reduction, and also cultural and faith-based support. Participants of RAGS take part in intensive daily services. Focusing on the social context in which gang-related behaviours develop while targeting individual change, interventions use the family as the primary area of work to build the youth's and family's strengths. An intensive case management model is used to target problems that predict known risk and protective factors, both for individuals and groups. The program provides four core activities: life skills programming for young men; Circle Keeper program for young women; intensive gang exit counselling; and outreach to schools and institutions.

Breaking the Cycle: Youth Gang Exit and Youth Ambassador Leadership Employment Preparation Project[8] implemented by the Canadian Training Institute based in Toronto, Ontario targets youth between the ages of 15 to 23 who are involved or have been involved in a youth gang and are currently unemployed or not attending school. Breaking the Cycle is a gang exiting initiative designed to provide youth with an opportunity to adopt healthy life skills and employment strategies that enable them to leave youth gangs and be reintegrated into schools and communities. *Phase 1 – Gang Exit Strategy* is an intensive, two-week training program, followed by one week of case management. Youth are provided with educational and job training opportunities, and learn to develop supportive relationships with peers, parents, and employers. *Phase 2 – Youth Ambassador Leadership and Employment Program* recruits, trains and employs youth with leadership potential to become community advocates against youth gang involvement and violence. Youth participate in community awareness presentations which deglamourize the gang image and suggest pro-social alternatives to gang involvement. Case management, leadership skills development, community contact, and outreach are also involved.

Structural Approach

The focus of these interventions is on addressing structural level barriers and on generating opportunities. Emphasis is placed on the importance of addressing issues related to social context especially those with a clear orientation towards community integration, and on the development of opportunity structures that provide youth with a 'sense of hope' – this relates to the level of opportunity provided by society (actual versus perceived) and to the willingness and ability of the representatives of these institutions to include formerly gang-involved youth. Some programs and services seek to increase social determinants of health and to help youth exit gangs safely and live successfully in the larger community. They may provide support in the form of mental health interventions, health care, substance abuse treatment, tattoo removal, assistance with housing referrals, court attendance and criminal justice supports, and addressing food and income support needs (Hastings et al., 2011).

These interventions focus more comprehensively on the issue of youth gang involvement with the goal of designing a strategy to foster community mobilization and organizational change and development. This involves the coordinated action of criminal justice officials, local residents, youth, community groups, civic leaders and a range of agencies to plan, strengthen, or create new opportunities or create linkages to existing organizations for gang-involved youth, and to coordinate programs and services within and across agencies (Fritsch, Caeti, & Taylor, 1999).

The Durham Youth Gang Strategy (DYGS)[9] implemented by the Durham Family Court Clinic (DFCC) and the Murray McKinnon Foundation (MMF), based in Durham region, Ontario targets youth between 12 and 18 years of age, at risk of being involved in gang activity, already involved in gang activity, or attending high-risk schools. The DYGS is based on the Comprehensive Gang Model[10] and the primary program components include community mobilization, social intervention, opportunities provision, support, and organizational change and development. A one-to-one approach is used to implement therapeutic interventions such as cognitive behavioural therapy, solutions-focused therapy and group work. Youth are paired with positive role models to encourage a healthy adult relationship. Another component of the program is to get youth involved in their community in a meaningful way by becoming an educator or mentor for other youth. Upon graduation, certain youth are asked to be role models. The program also aims to strengthen and develop partnerships by inviting social service agents as well as lawyers, judges, police and non-traditional services to community forums. This serves to educate the public on gangs in general, such as the consequences of joining a gang, and to discuss the local gang problem.

Youth Alliance Against Gang Violence (YAAGV)[11] implemented by the Prince Albert Outreach Program Inc. based in Prince Albert, Saskatchewan targets Aboriginal youth, aged 12 to 21, who are gang-involved or at high risk of gang involvement. YAAGV is a community-based program that uses the Circle of Courage[12] approach as its foundation, and incorporates elements of Wraparound and MST into the design. The program involves six components: counselling; a presentation team highlighting the dangers of youth violence, bullying and gang involvement; senior and junior Won Ska Cultural Schools (alternative school program); youth activity centre; van outreach (providing healthy meals, needle exchange services, condom distribution, counselling information and service referrals); and court outreach (courthouse visits offering legal, counselling, information and referral services).

A Note on Evaluation

While rigorous evaluations of gang interventions have been rare in Canada, some programs and services have shown promise in effectively addressing youth gang desistance. Interventions focusing on increasing the psychological capacities of youth gang members through cognitive-behavioural approaches that emphasize perspective taking, moral reasoning or problem-solving skills to resolve interpersonal disputes, as well as programs focusing on human capital development such as education and employment skills have been shown to be effective. There has also been an emphasis placed on the importance of addressing issues related to social context – comprehensive community-based approaches – especially those with a clear orientation towards community integration (Mulvey et al., 2004). These interventions have been shown to be more effective at reducing recidivism than the standard suppression strategies and punitive responses to youth gangs (NCPC, 2012).

FUTURE RESEARCH DIRECTIONS

Enforcement interventions alone have limited effects on reducing gang involvement. This is not surprising given that there is almost no mention in the desistance literature of motives related to law enforcement or the criminal justice system (e.g., fear of arrest or incarceration) as explanations for a decision to exit the gang. This suggests a mismatch between traditional gang-control policies, which seek to deter gang activity through the use of criminal justice sanctions, and the reality of gang membership (Greene & Pranis, 2007). These enforcement practices can even lead to unintended consequences and counter-productive impacts, including: increasing the cohesiveness of a gang and its attractiveness to vulnerable youth; promoting a counter-productive reaction in targeted gang members resulting in increased criminal behaviour and/or the encouragement of such behaviour in others; and creating a damaging cycle of imprisonment and release of youth gang members (Ayling, 2011; Bania, 2009; Chettleburgh, 2007; Decker, 2004). Enforcement practices that serve to exclude youth gang members from mainstream society and to categorize them based on their level of risk to recidivate appear likely to hamper the processes of desistance. A more effective approach recognizes that relapses are common, even within a desisting pathway, and that automatic harsh enforcement may create more problems in the longer term (Farrall et al., 2010; Maruna, LeBel, Mitchell, & Naples, 2004).

It is also important to move beyond individual developmental interventions that focus solely on modifying the characteristics and 'risk factors' of individual gang members. This approach justifies action that seeks to change individuals rather than society itself. It overlooks the ways in which institutions and policy processes themselves contribute to the social problems involving young people, and instead emphasizes the need to change and/or reform individuals (White, 2008).

A comprehensive strategy must address the specific dimensions of the gang problem at the local level (McGloin, 2005). Peer group influences and social forces in the community contribute to gang involvement (Stinchcomb, 2002). These factors also have an effect on the process of gang desistance, and must be included in the future development of responses. What is needed is the development of opportunity structures that provide young people with a 'sense of hope'. It is important that various sectors work together to implement interventions that seek to encourage and help gang members break their ties with the gang and successfully work their way back into society. This involves collaboration between a network of agencies and organizations, including: law enforcement and criminal justice agencies; the school system; youth services and recreation organizations; employers; social services agencies; as well as community and grass-roots organizations.

Finally, new approaches must be devised that are capable of capturing the complex nature of the wider structural circumstances that constrain or facilitate individuals' abilities to change their lives. For example, there is little value in encouraging youth to 'maximize their potential' or prepare them for the workforce through job training programs if they are unlikely to find adequate employment based on current labour market conditions. Failing to acknowledge broader social factors (i.e., issues of poverty, lack of affordable housing, barriers to education, unemployment, mental health issues, racism and discrimination) may encourage and support gang membership (Bania, 2009). These factors are beyond the control of the individual gang member.

CONCLUSION

If we are serious about addressing and supporting youth gang exit in Canada, and want to help individuals such as the one depicted in Figure 2, we need to develop a comprehensive strategy informed by research examining why and how youth desist from gang involvement, and that combines elements of the intervention approaches listed previously. Without a shift to a comprehensive strategy that addresses all aspects of the complex nature of youth gang involvement in the development of youth gang exit policies and interventions, we are setting up youth gang members who wish to desist for failure, and we may be making matters worse in the process.

Figure 2. Leaving the gang is a complex process involving the interaction of a combination of factors, and requiring a range of interventions to promote and support desistance

REFERENCES

Akers, R. L. (1997). *Criminological theories: Introduction and evaluation* (2nd ed.). Los Angeles, CA: Roxbury.

Ayling, J. (2011). Gang change and evolutionary theory. *Crime, Law, and Social Change, 56*(1), 1–26. doi:10.1007/s10611-011-9301-x

Bania, M. (2009). Gang violence among youth and young adults: (Dis)Affiliation and the potential for prevention. *Institute for the Prevention of Crime Review, 3*, 89–116.

Battin, S. R., Hill, K. G., Abbott, R. D., Catalano, R. F., & Hawkins, J. D. (1998). The contribution of gang membership to delinquency beyond delinquent friends. *Criminology, 36*(1), 93–115. doi:10.1111/j.1745-9125.1998.tb01241.x

Beaujot, R., & Kerr, D. (2007). *Emerging youth transition patterns in Canada: Opportunities and risks.* Ottawa, ON: Policy Research Initiative.

Bolden, C. L. (2013). Tales from the hood: An emic perspective on gang joining and gang desistance. *Criminal Justice Review, 38*(4), 473–490. doi:10.1177/0734016813509267

Boyce, J., & Cotter, A. (2013). *Homicide in Canada, 2012. Juristat, 33(1).* Ottawa, ON: Statistics Canada.

Bushway, S. D., Piquero, A., Broidy, L. M., Cauffman, E., & Mazerolle, P. (2001). An empirical framework for studying desistance as a process. *Criminology, 39*(2), 491–515. doi:10.1111/j.1745-9125.2001.tb00931.x

Carson, D. C., Peterson, D., & Esbensen, F.-A. (2013). Youth gang desistance: An examination of the effect of different operational definitions of desistance on the motivations, methods, and consequences associated with leaving the gang. *Criminal Justice Review, 38*(4), 510–534. doi:10.1177/0734016813511634

Caudill, J. W. (2010). Back on the swagger: Institutional release and recidivism timing among gang affiliates. *Youth Violence and Juvenile Justice, 8*(1), 58–70. doi:10.1177/1541204009339872

Cernkovich, S., & Giordano, P. (2001). Stability and change in antisocial behavior: The transition from adolescence to early adulthood. *Criminology, 39*(2), 371–410. doi:10.1111/j.1745-9125.2001.tb00927.x

Chatterjee, J. (2006). *A research report on youth gangs: Problems, perspectives and priorities.* Ottawa, ON: Research and Evaluation Branch, Community, Contract and Aboriginal Policing Services Directorate, Royal Canadian Mounted Police.

Chettleburgh, M. C. (2003). *2002 Canadian police survey on youth gangs.* Ottawa, ON: Astwood Strategy Corporation.

Chettleburgh, M. C. (2007). *Young thugs: Inside the dangerous world of Canadian street gangs.* Toronto, ON: Harper Collins Publishers Ltd.

Criminal Intelligence Service Canada (CISC). (2006). *Project spectrum: 2006 situational overview of street gangs in Canada.* Ottawa, ON: Author.

Decker, S. H. (2004). *From the street to the prison: Understanding and responding to gangs*. Alexandria, VA: American Correctional Association.

Decker, S. H., & Lauritsen, J. L. (2002). Leaving the gang. In C. R. Huff (Ed.), *Gangs in America* (3rd ed., pp. 51–67). Thousand Oaks, CA: Sage Publications. doi:10.4135/9781452232201.n4

Decker, S. H., & Pyrooz, D. C. (2010). Gang violence worldwide: Context, culture and country. In Graduate Institute of International and Development Studies (Ed.), Small arms survey, 2010: Gangs, groups, and guns (pp. 129-155). Cambridge, UK: Cambridge University Press.

Di Placido, C., Simon, T. L., Witte, T. D., Gu, D., & Wong, S. C. P. (2006). Treatment of gang members can reduce recidivism and institutional misconduct. *Law and Human Behavior, 30*(1), 93–114. doi:10.1007/s10979-006-9003-6 PMID:16729210

Elder, G. H. Jr, Johnson, M. K., & Crosnoe, R. (2003). The emergence and development of life course theory. In J. T. Mortemer & M. J. Shanahan (Eds.), *Handbook of the life-course* (pp. 3–19). New York, NY: Springer. doi:10.1007/978-0-306-48247-2_1

Esbensen, F.-A., Winfree, L. T. Jr, He, N., & Taylor, T. J. (2001). Youth gangs and definitional issues: When is a gang a gang and why does it matter? *Crime and Delinquency, 47*(1), 105–130. doi:10.1177/0011128701047001005

Evans, D., & Sawdon, J. (2004). The development of a gang exit strategy: The Youth Ambassador's Leadership and Employment Project. *Corrections Today, October*. Retrieved from www.cantraining.org/BTC/docs/Sawdon%20Evans%20CT%20Article.pdf

Farrall, S., Bottoms, A., & Shapland, J. (2010). Social structures and desistance from crime. *European Journal of Criminology, 7*(6), 546–570. doi:10.1177/1477370810376574

Farrall, S., & Bowling, B. (1999). Structuration, human development and desistance from crime. *The British Journal of Criminology, 39*(2), 252–267. doi:10.1093/bjc/39.2.253

Farrall, S., & Calverley, A. (2006). *Understanding desistance from crime*. London, UK: Open University Press.

Farrall, S., Hunter, B., Sharpe, G., & Calverley, A. (2014). *Criminal careers in transition: The social context of desistance from crime*. Oxford, UK: Oxford University Press. doi:10.1093/acprof:oso/9780199682157.001.0001

Fritsch, E. J., Caeti, T. J., & Taylor, R. W. (1999). Gang suppression through saturation patrol, aggressive curfew, and truancy enforcement: A quasi-experimental test of the Dallas anti-gang initiative. *Crime and Delinquency, 45*(1), 122–139. doi:10.1177/0011128799045001007

Giordano, P. C., Cernovich, S. A., & Rudolph, J. L. (2002). Gender, crime and desistance: Toward a theory of cognitive transformation. *American Journal of Sociology, 107*(4), 990–1064. doi:10.1086/343191

Gottfredson, M. R., & Hirschi, T. (1990). *A general theory of crime*. Stanford, CA: Stanford University Press.

Greene, J., & Pranis, K. (2007). *Gang wars: The failure of enforcement tactics and the need for effective public safety strategies.* Washington, DC: Justice Policy Institute.

Grekul, J., & LaBoucane-Benson, P. (2007). *An investigation into the formation and recruitment process of Aboriginal gangs in Western Canada.* Ottawa, ON: Public Safety Canada.

Hall, S., & Sawdon, J. (2004). *Report to Human Resources and Skills Development Canada on the Breaking the Cycle: Youth Gang Exit and Youth Ambassador Leadership Employment Preparation Project.* Toronto, ON: Canadian Training Institute.

Hastings, R., Dunbar, L., & Bania, M. (2011). *Leaving criminal youth gangs: Exit strategies and programs.* Ottawa, ON: Institute for the Prevention of Crime, University of Ottawa.

Healy, D. (2010). *The dynamics of desistance: Charting pathways through change.* Portland, OR: Willan Publishing.

Heisz, A. (2005). Ten things to know about Canadian metropolitan areas: A synthesis of statistics. Canada's trends and conditions in census metropolitan areas series (Analytical Paper, Catalogue no. 89-613-MIE – No. 009). Ottawa, ON: Statistics Canada.

Hemmati, T. (2006). *The nature of Canadian urban gangs and their use of firearms: A review of the literature and police survey (Research Report rr07-1e).* Ottawa, ON: Department of Justice Canada.

Ilan, J. (2010). 'If you don't let us in, we'll get arrested': Class-cultural dynamics in the provision of, and resistance to, youth justice work. *Youth Justice, 10*(1), 25–39. doi:10.1177/1473225409356760

Jacob, J. C. (2006). Male and female youth crime in Canadian communities: Assessing the applicability of social disorganization theory. *Canadian Journal of Criminology and Criminal Justice, 48*(1), 31–60. doi:10.3138/cjccj.48.1.31

Jones, D., Roper, V., Stys, Y., & Wilson, C. (2004). *Street gangs: A review of theory, interventions, and implications for corrections* (Research Report R-161). Ottawa, ON: Correctional Service of Canada.

Kassel, P. (2003). The crackdown in the prisons of Massachusetts: Arbitrary and harsh treatment can only make matters worse. In L. Kontos, D. Brotherton, & L. Barrios (Eds.), *Gangs and society: Alternative perspectives* (pp. 229–252). New York, NY: Columbia University Press.

Kazemian, L. (2007). Desistance from crime: Theoretical, empirical, methodological, and policy considerations. *Journal of Contemporary Criminal Justice, 23*(1), 5–27. doi:10.1177/1043986206298940

Kelly, K., & Caputo, T. (2005). The linkages between street gangs and organized crime: The Canadian experience. *Journal of Gang Research, 13*, 17–31.

Klein, M. W. (1995). *The American street gang: Its nature, prevalence, and control.* New York, NY: Oxford University Press.

Laub, J. H., Nagin, D., & Sampson, R. J. (1998). Trajectories of change in criminal offending: Good marriages and the desistance process. *American Sociological Review, 63*(2), 225–238. doi:10.2307/2657324

Laub, J. H., & Sampson, R. J. (2001). Understanding desistance from crime. In M. Tonry (Ed.), *Crime and justice: A review of research* (Vol. 28, pp. 1–69). Chicago, IL: University of Chicago Press.

Laub, J. H., & Sampson, R. J. (2003). *Shared beginnings, divergent lives: Delinquent boys to age 70.* Cambridge, MA: Harvard University Press.

Lurigio, A. L., Flexon, J. L., & Greenleaf, R. G. (2008). Antecedents to gang membership: Attachments, beliefs, and street encounters with the police. *Journal of Gang Research, 15,* 15–33.

Maruna, S. (1999). Desistance and development: The psychosocial process of "going straight". In M. Brogden (Ed.), *The British Criminology Conferences: Selected proceedings* (Vol. 2). Belfast, Ireland. Retrieved October 15, 2014, from http://www.britsocrim.org/v2.htm

Maruna, S. (2001). *Making good: How ex-convicts reform and rebuild their lives.* Washington, DC: American Psychological Association Books. doi:10.1037/10430-000

Maruna, S., & Farrall, S. (2004). Desistance from crime: A theoretical reformulation. *Kölner Zeitschrift für Soziologie und Sozialpsychologie, 43,* 171–194.

Maruna, S., LeBel, T. P., Mitchell, N., & Naples, M. (2004). Pygmalion in the reintegration process: Desistance from crime through the looking glass. *Psychology, Crime & Law, 10*(3), 271–281. doi:10.1080/10683160410001662762

Matza, D. (1964). *Delinquency and drift.* New York, NY: John Wiley.

McGloin, J. M. (2005). Policy and intervention considerations of a network analysis of street gangs. *Criminology & Public Policy, 4*(3), 607–635. doi:10.1111/j.1745-9133.2005.00306.x

Mears, P., & Butts, J. (2008). Using performance monitoring to improve the accountability, operations, and effectiveness of juvenile justice. *Criminal Justice Policy Review, 19*(3), 264–284. doi:10.1177/0887403407308233

Meisenhelder, T. (1977). An exploratory study of exiting from criminal careers. *Criminology, 15*(3), 319–334. doi:10.1111/j.1745-9125.1977.tb00069.x

Mohammed, M. (2007). Des « bandes d'ici » aux « gangs d'ailleurs »: comment définir et comparer? In M. Mohammed & L. Mucchielli (Eds.), Les bandes de jeunes: Des « blousons noirs » à nos jours (pp. 265-285). Paris, FR: La découverte.

Mulvey, E. P., Steinberg, L., Fagan, J., Cauffman, E., Piquero, A. R., Chassin, L., & Losoya, S. H. et al. (2004). Theory and research on desistance from antisocial activity among serious adolescent offenders. *Youth Violence and Juvenile Justice, 2*(3), 213–236. doi:10.1177/1541204004265864 PMID:20119505

National Crime Prevention Centre (NCPC). (2012). *Prevention of youth gang violence: Overview of strategies and approaches.* Retrieved October 15, 2014, from http://www.publicsafety.gc.ca/prg/cp/ygpf/ygpf-osa-eng.aspx

Ngo, H. V. (2010). *Unravelling identities and belonging: Criminal gang involvement of youth from immigrant families.* Calgary, AB: Centre for Newcomers.

Peterson, D. (2000). Definitions of a gang and impacts on public policy. *Journal of Criminal Justice, 28*(2), 139–149. doi:10.1016/S0047-2352(99)00036-7

Piquero, A., Farrington, D., & Blumstein, A. (2003). The criminal career paradigm. In M. Tonry (Ed.), *Crime and justice: A review of research* (Vol. 30, pp. 359–506). Chicago, IL: University of Chicago Press.

Pyrooz, D. C., & Decker, S. H. (2011). Motives and methods for leaving the gang: Understanding the process of gang desistance. *Journal of Criminal Justice, 39*(5), 417–425. doi:10.1016/j.jcrimjus.2011.07.001

Pyrooz, D. C., Decker, S. H., & Webb, V. J. (2014). The ties that bind: Desistance from gangs. *Crime and Delinquency, 60*(4), 491–516. doi:10.1177/0011128710372191

Pyrooz, D. C., Sweeten, G., & Piquero, A. R. (2013). Continuity and change in gang membership and gang embeddedness. *Journal of Research in Crime and Delinquency, 50*(2), 272–299. doi:10.1177/0022427811434830

Sampson, R. J., & Laub, J. H. (1993). *Crime in the making: Pathways and turning points through life.* Cambridge, MA: Harvard University Press.

Sampson, R. J., & Laub, J. H. (1995). Understanding variability in lives through time: Contributions of life course criminology. *Studies on Crime and Crime Prevention, 4,* 143–158.

Sampson, R. J., & Laub, J. H. (2005). A general age-graded theory of crime: Lessons learned and the future of life-course criminology. In D. P. Farrington (Ed.), *Advances in criminology: Testing integrated developmental/life-course theories of offending* (Vol. 14, pp. 165–182). New Brunswick, NJ: Transaction.

Sánchez-Jankowski, M. (1991). *Islands in the street. Gangs and American urban society.* Berkeley, CA: University of California Press.

Sánchez-Jankowski, M. (2003). Gangs and social change. *Theoretical Criminology, 7*(2), 191–216. doi:10.1177/1362480603007002413

Spergel, I. A. (1995). *The youth gang problem.* New York, NY: Oxford University Press.

Steinberg, L., & Cauffman, E. (1996). Maturity of judgment in adolescence: Psychosocial factors in adolescent decision making. *Law and Human Behavior, 20*(3), 249–272. doi:10.1007/BF01499023

Stinchcomb, J. B. (2002). Promising (and not so promising) gang prevention and intervention strategies: A comprehensive literature review. *Journal of Gang Research, 10,* 27–45.

Stone, L. (2014, December 31). Ottawa gun violence reaches record 48 shootings: It's heartbreaking. *Global News.* Retrieved from http://globalnews.ca/news/1749129/ottawa-gun-violence-reaches-record-48-shootings-its-heartbreaking/

Sutherland, E. H., & Cressey, D. R. (1960). *A theory of differential association. Principles of criminology* (6th ed.). Chicago, IL: Lippincott.

Taylor, S. S. (2009). How street gangs recruit and socialize members. *Journal of Gang Research, 17,* 1–27.

Thornberry, T. P., Krohn, M. D., Lizotte, A. J., Smith, C. A., & Tobin, K. (2003). *Gangs and delinquency in developmental perspective.* New York, NY: Cambridge University Press.

Thornberry, T. P., Lizotte, A. J., Krohn, M. D., Farnworth, M., & Jang, S. J. (1994). Delinquent peers, beliefs, and delinquent behaviour: A longitudinal test of interactional theory. *Criminology, 32*(1), 47–84. doi:10.1111/j.1745-9125.1994.tb01146.x

Thrasher, F. M. (1927). *The gang: A study of 1,313 gangs in Chicago*. Chicago, IL: University of Chicago Press.

Totten, M. (2000). *Guys, gangs and girlfriend abuse*. Peterborough, ON: Broadview Press.

Totten, M. (2012). *Nasty, brutish, and short: The lives of gang members in Canada*. Toronto, ON: James Lorimer & Company.

Uggen, C. (1996). *Age, employment and the duration structure of recidivism: Estimating the "true effect" of work on crime*. Paper presented at the American Sociology Association Conference, New York, NY.

Uggen, C., Manza, J., & Thompson, M. (2006). Citizenship, democracy, and the civic reintegration of criminal offenders. *Annals AAPSS, 605*(1), 281–310. doi:10.1177/0002716206286898

Westmacott, R., Stys, Y., & Brown, S. L. (2005). *Selected annotated bibliography: Evaluation of gang intervention programs (Research Brief B-36)*. Ottawa, ON: Correctional Service of Canada.

White, R. (2008). Disputed definitions and fluid identities: The limitations of social profiling in relation to ethnic youth gangs. *Youth Justice, 8*(2), 149–161. doi:10.1177/1473225408091375

Wood, J., & Alleyne, E. (2010). Street gang theory and research: Where are we now and where do we go from here? *Aggression and Violent Behavior, 15*(2), 100–111. doi:10.1016/j.avb.2009.08.005

Wortley, S., & Tanner, J. (2004). Social groups or criminal organizations? The extent and nature of youth gang activity in Toronto. In B. Kidd & J. Philips (Eds.), *From enforcement and prevention to civic engagement: Research on community safety* (pp. 59–80). Toronto, ON: Centre of Criminology, University of Toronto.

Young, M. A., & Gonzalez, V. (2013). *Getting out of gangs, staying out of gangs: Gang intervention and desistance strategies*. Retrieved October 15, 2014, from http://www.nationalgangcenter.gov/Content/Documents/Getting-Out-Staying-Out.pdf

ADDITIONAL READING

Decker, S. H., & Pyrooz, D. C. (Eds.). (2015). *The handbook of gangs*. West Sussex, UK: John Wiley & Sons, Inc. doi:10.1002/9781118726822

Maxson, C. L., Egley, A. Jr, Miller, J., & Klein, M. (Eds.). (2013). *The modern gang reader* (4th ed.). New York, NY: Oxford University Press.

Pearce, J. (2009). *Gangs in Canada*. Edmonton, AB: Quagmire Press.

Totten, M. (2012). *Nasty, brutish, and short: The lives of gang members in Canada*. Toronto, ON: James Lorimer & Company.

KEY TERMS AND DEFINITIONS

Community Focused Approach: Examines the settings, such as schools, workplaces and neighbourhoods, in which social relationships occur and seeks to identify the characteristics of these settings that are associated with the gang lifestyle. Strategies at this level are typically designed to impact the climate, processes, and policies in a given system.

Desistance: A decline over time in some behaviour of interest; often conceptualized and viewed as a process. In considering the process of desistance from gang involvement, the question of interest becomes what happens along the way; what are events and influences that encourage a reduction in gang-related activities and promote decreasing affiliation with the gang.

Gang: A phenomenon related to youth and characterized as a gathering of individuals bound by mutual interests, and governed by a leadership structure with (more or less) defined roles. One widely used benchmark for assessing whether a given social group is a gang is the engagement by group members in criminal behaviour, some of which may involve violence, on a regular basis.

Individual Focused Approach: Examines the biological, psychological, behavioural, and mental characteristics of youth gang members. Strategies at this level are often designed to promote pro-social attitudes, beliefs and behavior, and emphasis is placed on the willingness and ability of the individual to exercise greater self-control and on identifying objective versus perceived opportunities and the individual's preparation to take advantage.

Intervention: An instance of external, organized, and intentional involvement in the course of individual lives, carried out with the aim of changing or ensuring a particular outcome. There are several possible targets (individual, relationship, community, and social structure) in which specific risk and protective factors associated with youth gangs are addressed with the goal of reducing involvement.

Relationship Focused Approach: Examines close relationships that may impact the lives of youth gang members including peers, partners, and family members. Strategies at this level are often designed to provide gang-involved youth with opportunities for pro-social supportive relationships.

Social Structure Focused Approach: Examines the broad societal factors that help create a climate in which youth gang activity is encouraged or inhibited. These factors include social and cultural norms, and the health, economic and social policies that help to maintain inequalities between groups in society. These approaches focus on addressing and reducing patterns of stress, inequality and relative deprivation with emphasis placed on providing opportunities to improve the social determinants of health for youth gang members.

Success: There are different definitions and measures of this concept as it relates to youth gang interventions. 'Disassociation' or 'disaffiliation' examines the point at which the youth decides to leave the gang and focuses on recidivism (negative definition, outcome measure). 'Integration' examines perceivable improvements in the youth's life and focuses on social determinants of health (positive definition, process measure).

Youth: Defined in the *Youth Criminal Justice Act* (S.C. 2002, c. 1) as a person between 12 and 17 years of age. In this chapter, 'youth' is more broadly defined in an attempt to better capture the increasingly longer transition to adult roles in Western societies (individuals attend school for more years, delay entry into the workforce, marry later and delay the birth of a first child). In this case, the upper bracket of 'youth' can be extended into the early to mid-twenties.

ENDNOTES

1   For more information on British Columbia's anti-gang police, see http://www.cfseu.bc.ca/en/files/ CFSEU-BC-Report.pdf

2   For more information on the Calgary Police Service's four-point strategy, see http://www.calgary.ca/ cps/Pages/Community-programs-and-resources/Crime-prevention/Gangs-Calgarys-gang-strategy. aspx

3   For more information on this intervention program, see Public Safety Canada's website: http:// www.publicsafety.gc.ca/cnt/rsrcs/pblctns/gng-prvntn-strtgy/index-eng.aspx

4   The Wraparound model is used with adolescents who have serious emotional disturbances and are at risk of out-of-home placement. It refers to a specific set of practices to develop individualized care plans based on the strengths, values, norms and preferences of the child, family and community.

5   For more information on this intervention program, see Public Safety Canada's website: http:// www.publicsafety.gc.ca/cnt/rsrcs/pblctns/yth-rsk-dvlpmnt/index-eng.aspx

6   For more information on this intervention program, see Public Safety Canada's website: http:// www.publicsafety.gc.ca/cnt/rsrcs/pblctns/rgn-nt-gng/index-eng.aspx

7   MST is an intensive family- and community-based treatment program that focuses on addressing all environmental systems that impact chronic and violent youth offenders – their homes and families, schools and teachers, neighbourhoods and friends. MST recognizes that each system plays a critical role in a youth's world and each system requires attention when effective change is needed to improve the quality of life for youth and their families.

8   For more information on this intervention program, see Evans and Sawdon (2004); Hall and Sawdon (2004).

9   For more information on this intervention program, see Public Safety Canada's website: http:// www.publicsafety.gc.ca/cnt/rsrcs/pblctns/drhm-strtgy/index-eng.aspx

10   Also known as the Spergel Model, the Comprehensive Gang Model was originally developed by the Office of Juvenile Justice and Delinquency Prevention (OJJDP) in the United States. The model presumes that gangs become chronic and serious problems in communities where key organizations are inadequately integrated and there are not sufficient resources available to target youth at risk of gang involvement and youth involved in gangs. To address these problems, it calls for community institutions – including law enforcement, social welfare agencies, and grass roots organizations – to work together to achieve a more integrated, team-oriented approach that encompasses prevention, intervention and suppression activities.

11   For more information on this intervention program, see Public Safety Canada's website: http:// www.publicsafety.gc.ca/cnt/rsrcs/pblctns/yth-llnc/index-eng.aspx

12   The Circle of Courage is a traditional indigenous model of youth development. Based on the four parts of the medicine wheel, the approach draws from indigenous philosophies of child rearing and education, and resilience research.

Section 2
Latin America

Chapter 8
Gender Dynamics of Violent Acts among Gang Affiliated Young Adult Mexican American Men

Kathryn M. Nowotny
University of Colorado at Boulder, USA

Charles Kaplan
University of Southern California, USA

Qianwei Zhao
University of Southern California, USA

Alice Cepeda
University of Southern California, USA

Avelardo Valdez
University of Southern California, USA

ABSTRACT

This chapter examines how gender dynamics shape violent acts among Mexican American young adult males with a history of adolescent gang membership. We use the concept of hegemonic masculinity to examine the various ways that gender is performed in acts of violence (Connell, 1995). Masculinity is not a fixed entity or individual personality traits, masculinities are "configurations of practice that are accomplished in social action and, therefore, can differ according to the gender relations in a particular setting" (Connell & Messerschmidt, 2005:836). In other words, "gender identity is never a completed project, but always a developmental process which unfolds within a social context" (Messner, 1990:209). Nevertheless, the tendencies for aggression and violence are central to what it means to be masculine (Messerschmidt, 2000; Crowley, Foley et al., 2008) because "real men" must show others that they are not afraid (Kimmel, 2010). We examine the unfolding of masculine identity among disadvantaged Mexican American men in two different yet related contexts: violent acts with other men and the retelling of these violent acts. Among disadvantaged men, in general, social class is central to masculinity because these men are likely to have limited options in accomplishing their masculinity compared to men with more advantages (Britton, 2011; Messerschmidt, 1993; Stretesky & Pogrebin, 2007). The type of masculinity expressed by Mexican American males, more specifically, varies depending on a constellation of variables related to social class including income, generational status, education, and association with the criminal justice system (Rios, 2011; Valdez, 2007).

DOI: 10.4018/978-1-4666-9938-0.ch008

INTRODUCTION

We assert that the men in this study perform "manhood acts" (Schrock & Schwalbe, 2009) through their engagement in violent behavior and posturing with other men. Others have attributed these types of gendered behaviors among this population as hypermasculinity defined as an exaggerated demonstration of physical strength and aggression (Harris, 2008) and some criminologists have argued that criminal acts, in general, can be interpreted as an endeavor to prove a type of masculinity. For instance, Dekeseredy and Schwatz (2005) argue that "violence is, under certain situations, the only perceived available technique of expressing and validating masculinity" (p. 362). This type of "hard" masculinity based on physical prowess (Spaaij, 2008) is explicitly fashioned through bodily relations in which the human body is turned into a weapon to be used against other bodies (Messner, 1990). Men who prove their manhood by using violence may only call on physical violence in certain situations (threatened by perceived rival) or spaces (the street) and not in others (the home) (Copes & Hochstetler, 2003). Nevertheless, this type of aggressive masculinity located in particular times and spaces has complex interrelationships with other cultural sites such as the family, labor markets, and criminal legal system (Spaaij, 2008). For example, men with few outlets for performing masculinity within the formal labor market may be more likely to engage in criminal and violent behaviors in certain situations as a mechanism for constructing their masculinity. Violence can be just one of many ways of "doing gender" in a culturally specific way (DeKesseredy & Schwartz, 2005).

The men described in this chapter comprise a distinct group of Mexican American young adult males. Considering culture and class variables, masculinity may be more salient among Latinos than other race/ethnic groups (Alvirez, Bean et al., 1981; Galanti, 2003; Rios, 2011) as Mexican American men hold significantly more traditional attitudes toward male roles (Ojeda, Rosales, & Good, 2008). Research also suggests that nonimmigrant street-oriented Latino youth may be more susceptible to cultural values systems that are associated with violence (Umemoto, 2006; Vigil, 1988) and that persons of Mexican origin may be especially vulnerable given their persistent racialized status (Telles & Ortiz, 2008). The Mexican cultural concept of *machismo* signifies male power, aggression, and honor but also fearlessness, self-sufficiency, and courage (Valdez, 2007). Quintero and Estrada (1998) identify a type of *machismo* in the U.S.-Mexico border context (the site of the current study) that operates within the world of drugs and life on the streets as distinguished from the *machismo* of the home. This cultural model of *machismo* is embedded in other meanings that revolve around using violence to gain social status and respect, achieving a degree of protection and self-defense, and promoting drug use and abuse to the detriment of other more positive cultural models of *machismo* and manhood.

Goffman's *theory of the presentation of self* (1959) and Turner and Tajfel's *theory of intergroup conflict* regarding social identity (1979) are integrated together as the theoretical framework for this chapter. In the theory of the presentation of self, Goffman presents a dramaturgical model of human life and uses it as the conceptual model for understanding life-in-society. In this view, people in everyday life are actors on stage, and the audience consists of those who observe what others are doing, the parts are the roles that people play, the dialogue consists of ritualized conversational exchanges, and the costuming consists of whatever clothing happens to be in style. According to the theory, the initial definition of the situation projected by an individual tends to provide a plan for the cooperative activity that follows, and any projected definition of the situation also has a distinctive moral character. Society is organized on the principle that any individual who possesses certain social characteristics has a moral right to expect that others will value and treat them in an appropriate way.

This helps predict certain social interaction on the basis of perceived status differentials and their perceived legitimacy and stability and projected self-image in interaction with significant others. The theory also indicates that when an individual appears before others, they will have many motives for trying to control the impression they receive of the situation. For an individual gang member, the gang is one of the fields for the presentation of self, and he will try to mobilize his activity so that it will convey an impression to others that it is in his interests to convey.

According to Turner and Tajfel's theory of intergroup conflict, a group is conceptualized as a collection of individuals who perceive themselves to be members of the same social category, share some emotional involvement in this common definition of themselves, and achieve some degree of social consensus about the evaluation of their group and of their membership of it. Social groups provide their members with an identification of themselves that is to a very large extent relational and comparative. They define the individual as similar to or different from, as "better" or "worse" than, members of other groups. *Social identity* consists of those aspects of an individual's self-image that derive from the social categories to which an individual perceives themselves as belonging. This description regarding social identity provides a perspective on individual gang member's self-concept derived from perceived membership in the gang as a relevant social group.

STUDY METHODS

This paper examines narratives of violence from interviews conducted with Mexican American young adult former adolescent gang members recruited from highly disadvantaged neighborhoods in San Antonio, Texas located 120 miles from the U.S.-Mexico border. The qualitative data used in this analysis is part of a larger National Institutes of Health, National Institute on Drug Abuse (R01 DA023857) funded study that employs a multi-method longitudinal cohort design using a nested qualitative component to investigate the long term social and health consequences of youth gang membership (n=275). The findings are based on analysis of ethnographic data, qualitative life history interviews, and violent scenario questions described below.

San Antonio's population in 2008 was estimated at 1.3 million with over 50 percent of Mexican descent (U.S. Census Bureau, 2008), primarily 2nd and 3rd generation Mexican Americans. The city's economic base is centered on service and tourism and is sustained by one of the lowest wage structures in the United States (Bauder, 2002). In the neighborhoods where these men live median household income is $25,575 with 29 percent of these families living in poverty and an unemployment rate of 11 percent (U.S. Census Bureau, 2008). Additionally, 58 percent of adults aged 25 and over have less than a high school education. In San Antonio, low income Mexican Americans inhabit a social context and culture with concentrated poverty, a thriving drug market, and high rates of crime and incarceration (Valdez, 2007).

During 1996 and 1997 extensive ethnographic fieldwork was carried out in order to develop rosters of adolescent gangs in Mexican American neighborhoods in the West Side. Once the gangs were identified and the rosters developed, a stratified random sample of gang members was obtained. The fieldworkers then set out to recruit participants and bring them to a field office located in the West Side for interviewing. The fieldworkers were middle-aged men from the West Side who have a good reputation. Importantly, throughout and even after the conclusion of the initial project the field staff remained in contact with many of the participants. The research team worked closely together in the same area conducting several other projects. Some of the participants identified by the fieldworkers were eligible for the study, but others not eligible were still tapped to help recruit eligible participants. Field staff also regularly assisted by giving participants rides to pay their bills, helping to fill out paperwork such as disability, referring them to employment sources, or providing other referrals. Therefore, when it came time to conduct a follow up study some 13 years later the location and recruitment of participants was not as difficult as one might imagine.

The project asked about gang formation and activities, social networks, parental and school involvement, drug use, and violence. The focus of the follow up study (2008-2012) was on the long-term social and health consequences of youth gang membership. The mixed methods interview, which lasted 3 to 4 hours, covered the following topics: (1) socio-demographic information including employment, housing and incarceration histories; (2) prevalence of drug use and involvement in crime, violence, illegal activities and high risk sexual behaviors; (3) standardized self-report measures of mental and general health status; (4) histories and characteristics of partners and peers; and (5) biological blood and urine assessments as well as some physical and physiological measures. The narratives of violence were elicited as part of a qualitative section of the interview by asking, "People are sometimes involved with violence either themselves or with the people that they hang out with, can you tell me about the last violent incident that you were involved with or that you experienced?" Participants are instructed to "tell a story" and the interviewer uses probing questions to generate a "thick description" (Geertz, 1973). The qualitative questions are embedded throughout the interview schedule as a way to gather data from the point of view of the participant and as a way to break up the monotony of standardized questions.

Transcripts are from a subsample of 79 participants and were analyzed by coding and conceptual mapping of emergent dimensions in the qualitative data. Open coding was accomplished by a line-by-line reading. Core coding categories were identified including location, bystanders, weapons, injury, alcohol and drugs, and relationships. Selective coding proceeded after the core categories were identified which led to more specific nuances found within each larger core coding categories. Specific formal patterns emerged that reflect the distinct circumstances and reactions to conflict experienced by the men in this study including self-images, reasons for violence, neutralizations of violence, and impression management.

STUDY SAMPLE

The men in this study reflect the socio-demographics of their community. The average age is 31 years (SD=2.4). All are of Mexican descent with 98.9 percent being U.S.-born and the majority (88%) being native to San Antonio. On average, participants completed 9 (SD=1.4) years of school with 16 percent graduating from high school and 34 percent earning a GED. At the time of the interview, 40 percent were employed full-time, part-time, or working occasionally with 39 percent of participants reporting to be living with a parent or relative. During the month prior to the interview, 26 percent reported a monthly income of $500 or less and about half (49%) reported a monthly income between $500 and $2,000. One in five participants (20%) reported a criminal activity as their major source of income.

When asked about gang membership, 13 percent reported that they are still affiliated in some capacity with their youth street gang and 8 percent reported that they are now affiliated with a prison gang (Valdez, 2005). Despite the minimal gang affiliation, these men report high levels of criminal behaviors within the year prior to the interview. Just over half (55%) reported that they participated in at least one criminal activity other than using drugs. The most common reported were for violent acts: fighting (39%), carrying a weapon (36%), selling drugs (32%), other violent acts (e.g., shooting, rape, assault)

(20%), unarmed robbery (14%), shop lifting ($50 or less) (12%), burglary (7%), selling weapons (7%), and armed robbery (6%). Less than 5 percent reported other offenses such as arson, vandalism, car theft, taking car parts, and pimping.

FINDINGS

The findings are organized analytically along two dimensions that include the gendered violent act and the representation of the violence. These dimensions represented the broadest and most frequent categories that emerged from the coding of our data. The first dimension, the violent act, was examined in terms of its essential properties that included gendered self-images of violence, reasons for engaging in the violence, and performativity of violence. The second dimension, the representation of the violence and the corresponding way men make sense of the conflict, was constructed through the gender dynamics of the interview process situated within the context of the study. This dimension included the essential properties of the neutralization process, drug and alcohol as reasons for the violence, and the participant as the dangerous aggressor.

THE GENDERED VIOLENT ACT

Violent Self-Images

There are three *self-images* described by the men in this study: violent, perceived violent by others, and non-violent. According to Athens (1997), self-image always relates to an individuals' interpretation of the situation and that image directly influences how one decides to act for oneself and towards others. Thus, this analysis attempts to understand how men understand their own violent identities and how these are operationalized in the moments of conflict that are narrated.

In the first self-image, men see themselves as being a violent person and they think that others view them as violent as well. For example, one month before the interview Roger was walking through a park and got jumped by three teenagers described as looking "homeless and messed up [on drugs]." Roger describes the incident:

It just happened out of the blue and I didn't know who this guy was or anything. He just takes a swing at me and he hits me. And the thing about the hit was that he hit me and it didn't hurt but he caught me off guard. So to make a long story short, I stabbed him. I'm mad all the time now, just the way things are. I'm always mad and always ready to fight. So, I pick up the knife and I stab him.

In the second self-image, men see themselves as being non-violent but they think that others perceive them as violent. Joe found out not only that his brother-in-law was abusing his nephew but also that his family was keeping it from him. So he orchestrated a family BBQ as a means to confront his brother-in-law. In his explanation for the secrecy Joe said, "They already knew what I would do if I were to find out. They like tried to blow it off," indicating that his family knew that he would respond with violence. Men who define themselves as non-violent characterize the third self-image. In talking about a violent altercation with an acquaintance that owed him money, John said, "You know, those violent days are kind of past me, but I'm too nice to people. I try to be cool with people and they take my kindness for a weakness, you know what I'm saying? I'm not like that man, you know? I'm not really like that. But he had it coming to him that *puto*." John doesn't see himself as a violent person or someone who goes around beating up others but nonetheless felt it was necessary to use violence to control the behavior of another person.

Even though these men may show any one of the three variants of self-images they all share the characteristic of still having the potential to be dangerous, never vulnerable. Hollander (2001) uses the concepts of *perceived vulnerability* and *perceived dangerousness* to refer to "shared beliefs about the perceived openness of particular social groups to violent victimization on one hand and their perceived potential for perpetrating violence on the other" (p. 87). Women are attributed the self-image of being weak, passive, dominated, and inherently rape-able (Marcus, 1992) while men are portrayed with a general gendered self-image as privileged, dominating, and able to resist exploitation (Schrock & Schwalbe, 2009). These men construct the "other" as vulnerable and thus feminine and themselves as dangerous and thus masculine. Hence, gender is used as an act of violence in and of itself (Das, 2007). Put another way, issues of masculinity are made relevant through the categorization of the characters involved in the violent act (Andersson, 2008). These masculine categories and gendered positions are used in negotiating a masculine identity through violence (and through the retelling of violence). To this end, it is ironic that the men in this study have little perceived vulnerability since they have experienced high rates of victimization. Almost all (95%) reported being shot at with a gun at least once during their lifetime with 38 percent reporting that they have been shot and injured with a gun. A similar amount have been stabbed (39%) and beaten severely (44%). As Messner (1990) notes in their study of violence in sports, "the body-as-weapon ultimately results in violence against one's own body" (p.211).

Reasons for Engaging in Violence

Participants provided several reasons for engaging in violence including being disrespected, mad-dogging, coercion, and defense. Disrespecting and mad-dogging are expressive forms of violence as a response to verbal or behavioral cues such as speaking out of line or giving dirty looks. *Expressive violence* is unplanned and born out of anger, rage, or frustration (Decker, 1993; Fox & Allen, 2014; Miethe & Drass, 1999). Coercive and defensive forms of violence are more instrumental. They typically entail the use of violence to change the behavior of someone else. *Instrumental violence* is characterized as being conducted for explicit future goals (Decker, 1993; Fox & Allen, 2014; Miethe & Drass, 1999). What all four of these reasons for violence have in common is the challenging of masculinity and specifically of challenging male honor (Hossain & Welchman, 2005). This individualized male sense of honor is associated with rank or social status that can be gained through personal action, which is different from other cultural perspectives of sacred honor associated with the traditional extended family and honor killings (Dogan, 2014).

Fights over being disrespected often occur in the presence of others in a public setting and the participant who is disrespected typically initiates the violence. Violent acts over being disrespected occur with close friends or family members. For instance, Ronnie was walking down the street preparing to smoke a joint with a friend and younger cousin:

My cousin pissed me off. So I punched him and I broke part of his face. He tried to show off in front of Loco, my homeboy. I mean dude just did ten years of his life [in prison] and I'm going... you know? The reason why I hit him was because I had already warned him to stop disrespecting me, stop disrespecting me. That was my cousin. That's my blood.

Ronnie felt that his younger cousin was disrespecting him by the way he was acting in front of Loco. It is not only the actions of his cousin but that they were done in the presence of someone Ronnie respected. In a similar situation, Nick was at a party with his friends and his brother showed up drunk. Nick felt that his brother was disrespecting him by acting foolish in front of his friends. This led to an altercation where Nick threatened his brother with a gun and forced him to leave the party saying, "Yeah… just respect, you know? If I was being *necio* (foolish) and shit at his friends' party… I wouldn't even act like that, you know?" As in the previous case, Nick felt that a family member was disrespecting him in front of other people who he considers to be equals.

Fights initiated over "mad-dogging" were similar to fights over being disrespected. They involved participant initiated violence to a perceived verbal assault while in a public place in the presence of bystanders. However, these violent acts differ in that mad-dogging is likely to occur with strangers. For example, one participant stated, "We were at my brother-in-law's house just chilling, smoking, drinking in the front yard and then their neighbors got there that live in front. They started mad-dogging, just looking at us ugly. So we just went over there and started fighting with them." This participant felt threatened in the same way as the previous case except that the challenge was more direct and from a person not known to the participant. Similarly, Richard got into an altercation with his neighbor who he thought was making catcalls at his wife:

Him and his friend were drinking, and his friend was kind of big. So he's out there with his friend and I guess he feels like 'Ok, now I have back-up' or whatever. So he's there looking at me all hard and everything and I tell him, 'What are you looking at?' So they just got up. They were waiting for me to say something and so I said something. And then I noticed that that guy was bigger and that there were two of them, so I went back and got my club from the car.

Coercive forms of violence were more purposive. A small number of men mentioned using violence during the course of robberies but coercive measures also include trying to manipulate the behavior of others, that is, to show power and control over others. For instance, Joe, introduced previously, stated:

I found out that my brother-in-law had been abusive to my nephew so I whooped his ass bad. I uh… fractured his face like I just went off on him and I fractured his face, broke his hand, and fractured his skull. He started crying and I told him, "Now you know how a 4 year old feels when he's helpless, when you got somebody bigger than you beating on you."

Joe used violence as a means of showing power and control over his brother-in-law to stop the abuse. In another instance, Alberto helped his friend retrieve money that was owed to him by one of his customers:

Well my friend got jacked or burned you could say because he was selling some heroin and they didn't give him the right amount of money, you know? Something was worth $600 and they only gave him $400 and they said they would pay him the $200 later. Then already passed a month and this dude was just doing the run around. He was not answering the phone or nothing. So finally we caught him.

Similarly, defensive forms of violence are carried out in the defense of others. Christian was at a party when one of his female friends showed up with bruises on her body:

I have three girls that are three sisters, you know, they're cool with me and I call 'em my sisters. You know they cook for me, whatever. This dude had punched her and made her some bruises. I told him about it and he was like, "Man stay out of my business. Mind your own business." I was like "shiiiit." He said something smart so I said, "What's up bro?" This and that. He said, "Do you wanna go outside?" I said, "Let's go!" And we went out to the street and I hit him first and he kind of stumbled on the ground and my homeboys went at him.

When his friend reveals that another man hit her, Christian confronts him. In a similar situation James describes a shootout that happened one year ago. Six old gang members including the participant were at a party with the youngsters (new gang members):

It just so happens that one of the rival gangs that we used to go head to head with, the younger generation of the gang, I guess they wanted to make a name for themselves or what not. They went to jump a friend of mine, Marcus. They jumped him and he was with his girlfriend and we told them to leave it alone catch it another day because he was with his girlfriend. But they didn't want to listen. So we were trying to get them to leave. They didn't notice that we had surrounded them. They were like "Why should we leave?" We all had guns, so we were like "We don't want to have to get violent. Just leave." They made it like they were gonna leave but instead of leaving they go to the trunk of the car and they pull out their guns. So the next thing you know we have a shootout. We have a shootout right there on the front of the yard.

Like Christian, James engages in a shootout in defense of his friend Marcus.

These reasons for fighting can be considered threats to masculinity and particularly threats to male honor. Hegemonic masculinity is associated with heterosexuality, toughness, power, and competitiveness (Connell, 1995). We see this play out in the way that the participants felt challenged or threatened by others. Participants exerted dominance over other men through the use of physical violence as a response to a perceived slight whether directed at them personally or to others. Moreover, the various self-images analyzed above are also strongly associated with specific reasons for engaging in violence. These self-images shape the way men make sense of and rationalize the conflict and with that their subsequent social action. The expressive forms of violence tend to be associated with violent self-images since participants see themselves as violent and are willing to use violence with little provocation (i.e., verbal or behavior cues) or use more violence than may be necessary (e.g., stabbing as a response to being punched). Conversely, instrumental forms of violence tend to be associated with violent to others or non-violent self-images as participants do not necessarily see themselves as violent but will use violence in a more purposive way when necessary.

The Performativity

Finally, there is a *performativity* to these acts of violence. The performance in these violent acts is carefully managed to create a particular impression with the audience: that of reasserting masculinity and restoring honor by demonstrating that he will not be dominated, that he is more powerful than the other man, and that he is in control. Much like Taylor (1997) in her analysis of public torture in Argentina, "while the aim of [the violence] is to reduce the victim to 'powerlessness' this also holds for the spectator" (p. 130). Moreover, "prior acts of violence extenuate the committal of present and future acts" regardless of the type of self-image he holds (Feldman, 1997). That is, since he has the capacity to be dangerous and has been in the past, especially with his youth gang, he is expected to be violent now otherwise he is not adequately performing masculinity. This is illustrated in the quotes above. In every situation of violence there were multiple actors present to witness the initial provocation and subsequent violent social act.

THE REPRESENTATION OF GENDERED VIOLENCE

The second dimension of analysis emerged from the act of the participants producing their narratives. That is, the participants were found to construct representations of violence in the course of relating their violent acts. The interview itself was a *scene of social interaction* where gendered performances occurred. Therefore, the narratives need to be situated within the context in which they were created; that is, within the context of the study and interview.

Neutralization

Neutralizations are typically offered for violence among those who disapprove of violence as a means of justifying the use of violence in particular situations (Agnew, 1994). Paradoxically, the men in this study seemingly approve of the use of violence and are willing to engage in it with little to no provocation or as a way to alter the behavior of others, yet still provide justifications in their narratives for the violence in order to neutralize negative reactions from the listener; in this case the interviewer. Most of the men justified their violence using discourses about violence and blameworthiness of victims. This was found to be a specific form of impression management constructed in the retelling of the violence to a listener that embodied the status of "scientist". These men were not telling their violent stories to similar peers but to seemingly "non-violent" men (perhaps in the past, but not now in their scientific role) who may not ascribe to the same form of "street" masculinity identified by Quintero and Estrada (1998). In short, the men were well aware that the study was for a university and would be reviewed by "doctors." Therefore, they may have felt the strong need to justify or neutralize their actions.

Drug and Alcohol Justifications for Violence

Drugs and alcohol were found to be a common justification for violence in the study. According to Goldstein's tripartite conceptual framework of the *drug-violence nexus*, drug use alters behavior by reducing inhibitions or instigating aggression (Goldstein, 1985). A consistent finding in the literature is that drug and alcohol use and violent crime are statistically correlated and joint behaviors (Harrison, Erickson, Adlaf & Freeman, 2001) and drug use predict violence and victimization (Weiner, Sussman, Sun & Dent, 2005). For Mexican American young gang members specifically, Valdez, Kaplan and Cepeda's (2006) study indicates that drug use interacts with an individual gang member's risk for violence to affect violent behavior outcomes. The nature of the evidence, however, prohibits the establishment of a causal link (Murdoch & Ross, 1990; Zhang, Wieczorek & Welte, 1997).

For example, Alex was drinking with his two cousins who are brothers. The brothers started fighting and Alex joined in. The older of the two brothers stabbed his younger brother in the head:

Yeah, well Patron I can handle, I can handle the tequila. You know, I can drink a bottle of Jose [Cuervo] by myself. But these dudes, you know, they can't drink. That's why I don't really drink with them no more like that. If I give them a couple of shots tsss that's it. I usually busted out bottles, "Hey come on, we're gonna..." you know, but nah... I got tired of that. I was always the one that everybody was mad at because I was the one that had the liquor: "Hey, well it's your fault." Well, what? I didn't stab him. [laughs] That's them! It's not my fault they can't control [their liquor]!

There are two different forms of impression management in this narrative. First, the violence is neutralized by alcohol. Second, Alex boasts that he can drink an entire bottle of tequila by himself while his cousins can't handle it. Tolerance for large amounts of alcohol has been found to be associated with lower class masculinities and hypermasculinity as a way to compete in dominance games with other men (Campbell, 2000). As another example, Mike minimized his violence saying, "It was just a disagreement and we were all drinking and you know when you are drinking and you drink too much and one thing led to another and somebody had a disagreement so by the time we knew it we were all fighting."

The Dangerous Aggressor

It is important to note that all of the narratives of violence collected in this study were instances where the participant was the dangerous aggressor, never the vulnerable one. The participant was always the "winner" of the fight in that the other man did wrong, was blameworthy, and sustained greater injury. This is emblematic of the victim-perpetrator dichotomy: victims are seen as powerless, weak and passive recipients of violence while perpetrators are portrayed as having all of the power and freedom to act in the situation (Kvist, 2002). Even when he is the victim of a crime in the legal sense he's still the dangerous aggressor. For example, Angel had an attempted burglary on his home the week prior to the interview and in response he shot at the would-be-burglar. Angel notes that he purposely does not kill him because of his perceived young age. However, he is careful to point out that he could have killed him if he wanted to:

I shot at the house next door because I didn't want to hit him. I just wanted him to hear the shot. I could have shot him but I didn't want to hurt him. I mean I could have killed him but I didn't want to shoot him. Yeah, I didn't want to because my mom went through a lot when my brother passed. And this guy was young he was maybe 14, maybe 16.

"Victim" and "masculine" are seen as incompatible due to cultural discourses equating masculinity with dominance and control (Kiesling, 2005) especially within the cultural frame of *machismo* that the men in this study draw on. The type of *machismo* that operates within street life is embedded in meanings about honor, courage, power, and fearlessness with bodies facilitating this masculine agency such that self-worth is dependent upon embodied capacity for power. According to Messerschmidt (1999), "the body intervenes in social interaction as a physical resource that socially symbolizes a boy's masculine identity" (p. 215). Reputation and status for the men in this study rely heavily on their willingness to put themselves in dangerous situations. Therefore, their masculine bodies are not only constructed in terms of fighting ability but also in terms of bodily capacity to consume large amounts of alcohol and drugs.

DISCUSSION

Within the context of racial segregation, community disadvantage, gang membership, and a specific type of masculinity that promotes violence to gain social status and respect, achieving a degree of protection and self-defense, and promoting drug use and abuse (Quintero & Estrada, 1998), we see how different self-images of violence are operationalized and how they are congruent with how men make sense of conflict. Men interpret these situations as challenges to their masculinity and thus act violently. The performance of violence is as much about sending a message to the audience as it is to the person the violence is enacted upon: that men deserve respect, they are in control of others behaviors, and they have the capacity to protect vulnerable others. Additionally, the narratives are situated within the context they were created: within the context of the study and interview. Participants construct a representation of violence in their retelling of violence and these representations constitute or become the violence (Jhally, 1997). During this process, drug, alcohol, and violence-minimizing neutralizations were utilized as ways to justify themselves.

Goffman's theory of the presentation of self sheds light on the interpretation of participants' violent behavior and their perception of their violent behavior. They are actors on the stage and act in a masculine way that is considered to be favorable to others within their social networks. Their multiple projected manhood self-images tend to provide a plan for the cooperative activity that follows, and they had a moral right to expect that others will value and treat him in an appropriate way during social interactions. Thus, when others violated their expectations, they utilized violence to show people their perceived status differentials. In addition to this, impression management efforts were demonstrated during the narrative process, which reflects their desire to convey a specific impression to others. Components of Turner and Tajfel's theory of social identity (1979) are also reflected in the study. The participants social identity consists of those aspects of their self-image that derive from the gangs to which they belong. The gang identity also contributes to their violent behavior and their understanding of the violence dynamic within a specific context.

Due to the long-term relationship between the field staff and participants, there are several issues related to the presentation of the self emerged during the follow-up study. Based on feedback from field staff and interviewers, some returning participants felt like they were indebted or were doing a favor for the field staff by conducting the follow up interview. This may have influenced the data in three unique ways. First, when asked about the last violent incident they experienced, participants seemed to provide a flashy or fantastic story rather than more mundane or everyday violence one may experience. Participants are very much aware that they were recruited specifically because they were in a gang so there may have been some motivation to provide a "typical" gang experience. Second, participants may have wanted to provide a "good" story to help the field staff "look good." Last, since the study was focused mostly on health, participants may have conflated "violence" with "injury," although, it is also possible that participants do not recognize more subtle forms of violence as violence (e.g., racist remarks, slapping, etc.). Moreover, the primary interviewer for the project is matched with the participants in that he is a 30 year old Mexican American male who grew up and currently resides in the West Side. This matching may influence the interview process in terms of the *neutralizations* (Agnew, 1994) and *impression management* (Goffman, 1959) performed by the participants.

This study enhances our understanding of the way that cultural constructions of gender influence violent acts that are important for constructing interventions for violence that are especially intertwined with the Mexican-American family (Valdez et al., 2013). For example, based on the findings in this study an intervention may focus on prosocial ways that Mexican American men can perform masculinity within a context of limited opportunity. This is especially important since many of these Mexican American men come from families with multigenerational involvement in poverty, crime, and residential instability (Moore, 1991) and many of these men have internalized self-concepts that define and devalue them as minorities (Valdez, Cepeda, & Kaplan, 2009). Conceptually, this study demonstrates that when researching violence it is important to examine not only the violence as an event within a specific context but the representation of that violence to scientists within the study context itself. Moreover, it is of importance that individuals' self-identifications are constructed by multiple intertwining factors, such as social group memberships, gender, ethnicity, social class, culture, and context. In addition, the qualitative nature of this study has been effective in promoting in-depth understanding of Hispanic gang violence, while at the same time has limited potential to be generalized. Thus, further research about the interplaying mechanisms among various components that contribute to individuals' self-image building is in urgent need.

REFERENCES

Agnew, R. (1994). The Techniques of Neutralization and Violence. *Criminology, 32*(4), 555–580. doi:10.1111/j.1745-9125.1994.tb01165.x

Alvirez, D., & Bean, F. et al. (Eds.). (1981). *The Mexican American Family. Ethnic Families in America.* New York, NY: Elsevier Press.

Andersson, K. (2008). Constructing young masculinity: A case study of heroic discourse on violence. *Discourse & Society, 19*(2), 139–161. doi:10.1177/0957926507085949

Athens, L. (1997). *Violent Criminal Acts and Actors: Revisited.* Champaign, IL: University of Illinois Press.

Bauder, H. (2002). *Work on the west side: Urban neighborhoods and the cultural exclusion of youth.* Boulder, CO: Lexington Books.

Britton, D. (2011). *The gender of crime.* Lanham, MD: AltaMira Press.

Campbell, H. (2000). The Glass Phallus: Pub(lic) Masculinity and Drinking in Rural New Zealand. *Rural Sociology, 65*(4), 562–581. doi:10.1111/j.1549-0831.2000.tb00044.x

Connell, R. W. (1995). *Masculinities.* Cambridge, UK: Polity Press.

Connell, R. W., & Messerschmidt, J. W. (2005). Hegemonic Masculinity: Rethinking the Concept. *Gender & Society, 19*(6), 829–859. doi:10.1177/0891243205278639

Copes, H., & Hochstetler, A. (2003). Situational Construction of Masculinity among Street Thieves. *Journal of Contemporary Ethnography, 32*(3), 279–304. doi:10.1177/0891241603032003002

Crowley, S. L., & Foley, L. J. (2008). *Gendering Bodies.* Lanham, MD: Rowman and Littlefield.

Das, V. (2007). *Life and Words: Violence and the Descent into the Ordinary.* Berkeley, CA: University of California Press.

DeKeseredy, W. S., & Schwartz, M. D. (2005). Masculinities and Interpersonal Violence. In Handbook of Studies on Men and Masculinities. Sage Publications. doi:10.4135/9781452233833.n20

Dogan, R. (2014). Different Cultural Understandings of Honor That Inspire Killing: An Inquiry Into the Defendant's Perspective. *Homicide Studies*, *18*(4), 363–388. doi:10.1177/1088767914526717

Feldman, A. (1997). Violence and Vision: The Prosthetics and Aesthetics of Terror. *Public Culture*, *10*(1), 24–60. doi:10.1215/08992363-10-1-24

Fox, K. A., & Allen, T. (2014). Examining the Instrumental-Expressive Continuum of Homicides: Incorporating the Effects of Gender, Victim-Offender Relationships, and Weapon Choice. *Homicide Studies*, *18*(3), 298–317. doi:10.1177/1088767913493420

Galanti, G.-A. (2003). The Hispanic Family and Male-Female Relationships: An Overview. *Journal of Transcultural Nursing*, *14*(3), 180–185. doi:10.1177/1043659603014003004 PMID:12861920

Geertz, C. (1973). *The Interpretation of Cultures*. New York, NY: Basic Books Classics.

Goffman, E. (1959). *The Presentation of Self in Everyday Life*. Harpswell, ME: Anchor.

Goldstein, P. (2003). The drugs/violence nexus. *Crime: Critical Concepts in Sociology*, *4*, 96.

Harrison, L. D., Erickson, P. G., Adlaf, E., & Freeman, C. (2001). The drugs-violence nexus among American and Canadian youth. *Substance Use & Misuse*, *36*(14), 2065–2086. doi:10.1081/JA-100108437 PMID:11794584

Hollander, J. A. (2001). Vulnerability and Dangerousness: The Construction of Gender through Conversation about Violence. *Gender & Society*, *15*(1), 83–109. doi:10.1177/089124301015001005

Hossain, S., & Welchman, L. (2005). *Honour: Crimes, Paradigms and Violence Against Women*. London, UK: Zed Books.

Jhally, S. (1997). *Stuart Hall: Representation and the Media*. Media Education Foundation.

Marcus, S. (Ed.). (1992). *Fighting Bodies, Fighting Words: A Theory and Politics of Rape Prevention*. New York, NY: Routeledge.

Messerschmidt, J. W. (1993). *Masculinities and crime: Critique and reconceptualization of theory*. Lanham, MD: Rowman and Littlefield.

Messerschmidt, J. W. (1999). Making Bodies Matter: Adolescent Masculinities, the Body, and Varieties of Violence. *Theoretical Criminology*, *3*(2), 197–220. doi:10.1177/1362480699003002004

Messerschmidt, J. W. (2000). *Nine Lives: Adolescent masculinities, the body, and violence*. Boulder, CO: Westview Press.

Messner, M. A. (1990). When bodies are weapons: Masculinity and violence in Sport. *International Review for the Sociology of Sport*, *25*(3), 203–220. doi:10.1177/101269029002500303

Miethe, T. D., & Kriss, A. (1999). Exploring the Social Context of Instrumental and Expressive Homicides: An Application of Qualitative Comparative Analysis. *Journal of Quantitative Criminology*, *15*(1), 1–21. doi:10.1023/A:1007591025837

Moore, J. W. (1991). *Going down to the barrio: Homeboys and homegirls in change*. Philadelphia: Temple University Press.

Murdoch, D., & Ross, D. (1990). Alcohol and crimes of violence: Present issues. *Substance Use & Misuse, 25*(9), 1065–1081. doi:10.3109/10826089009058873 PMID:2090635

Ojeda, L., Rosales, R., & Good, G. E. (2008). Socioeconomic status and cultural predictors of male role attitudes among Mexican American men: Son más machos? *Psychology of Men & Masculinity, 9*(3), 133–138. doi:10.1037/1524-9220.9.3.133

Quintero, G. A., & Estrada, A. L. (1998). Cultural Models of Masculinity and Drug Use: "Machismo," Heroin, and Street Survival on the U.S. - Mexico Border. *Contemporary Drug Problems, 25*(Spring), 147.

Rios, V. M. (2011). *Punished: Policing the Lives of Black and Latino Boys*. New York, NY: New York University Press.

Schrock, D., & Schwalbe, M. (2009). Men, Masculinity, and Manhood Acts. *Annual Review of Sociology, 35*(1), 277–295. doi:10.1146/annurev-soc-070308-115933

Spaaij, R. (2008). Men Like Us, Boys Like Them: Violence, Masculinity, and Collective Identity in Football Hooliganism. *Journal of Sport and Social Issues, 32*(4), 369–392. doi:10.1177/0193723508324082

Stretesky, P. B., & Pogrebin, M. R. (2007). Gang-Related Gun Violence: Socialization, Identity, and Self. *Journal of Contemporary Ethnography, 36*(1), 85–114. doi:10.1177/0891241606287416

Tajfel, H., & Turner, J. C. (1979). An integrative theory of intergroup conflict. *The Social Psychology of Intergroup Relations, 33*(47), 74.

Taylor, D. (1997). *Disappearing Acts: Spectacles of Gender and Nationalism in Argentina's "Dirty War"*. Durham, NC: Duke University Press.

Telles, E. E., & Ortiz, V. (2008). *Generations of exclusion*. New York: Russell Sage.

Umemoto, K. (2006). *The truce: Lessons from an LA gang war*. Ithaca, NY: Cornell University.

U.S. Census Bureau. (2008). 2006-2008 American Community Survey. Washington, DC: Author.

U.S. Census Bureau. (2009). Census Bureau Estimates Nearly Half of Children Under Age 5 Are Minorities. Washington, DC: Author.

Valdez, A. (2005). Mexican American Youth and Adult Prison Gangs in a Changing Heroin Market. *Journal of Drug Issues, 35*(4), 842–867. doi:10.1177/002204260503500409 PMID:21614143

Valdez, A. (2007). *Mexican American Girls and Gang Violence: Beyond Risk*. New York, NY: Palgrave Macmillan. doi:10.1057/9780230601833

Valdez, A. (2007). Machismo. Encyclopedia of Race and Racism, 2(G-R), 271-274.

Valdez, A., Cepeda, A., & Kaplan, D. (2009). Homicidal Events among Mexican American Street Gangs: A Situational Analysis. *Homicide Studies, 13*(3), 288–306.

Valdez, A., Cepeda, A., Parrish, D., Horowitz, R., & Kaplan, C. D. (2013). An adapted brief strategic family therapy for gang affiliated Mexican American adolescents. *Research on Social Work Practice*, *23*(4), 383–396. doi:10.1177/1049731513481389

Valdez, A., Kaplan, C. D., & Cepeda, A. (2006). The Drugs-Violence Nexus among Mexican-American Gang Members. *Journal of Psychoactive Drugs*, *38*(2), 109–121. doi:10.1080/02791072.2006.103998 35 PMID:16903450

Vigil, J. D. (1988). *Barrio Gangs: Street Life and Identity in Southern California*. Austin, TX: University of Texas Press.

Weiner, M. D., Sussman, S., Sun, P., & Dent, C. (2005). Explaining the link between violence perpetration, victimization and drug use. *Addictive Behaviors*, *30*(6), 1261–1266. doi:10.1016/j.addbeh.2004.12.007 PMID:15925136

Zhang, L., Wieczorek, W. F., & Welte, J. W. (1997). The nexus between alcohol and violent crime. *Alcoholism, Clinical and Experimental Research*, *21*(7), 1264–1271. doi:10.1111/j.1530-0277.1997. tb04447.x PMID:9347088

Chapter 9

In Hand, Out of Hand:
Weapons and Violence Culture in Large Latino Gangs

Ami C. Carpenter
University of San Diego, USA

ABSTRACT

This chapter interrogates the nature and function of weapons in Latino gang culture, and is divided into three parts. It begins by defining Latino gangs in the Americas, and classifying them into Mexican-American gangs, Mexican gangs, and Central American gangs. Despite differences in region, economic situation, generations and cultural characteristics, I draw broad similarities by focusing specifically on large, organized gangs within each of the three classifications. The second section interrogates the logics and motivations driving gangs' use of weapons, along with the psychological and instrumental functions of weapons use for Latino gangs. The chapter's third section is a substantial conclusion which argues for approaches to gang-violence which derive from the field of peace and conflict studies, including short-term approaches to violence reduction (gang ceasefires and truces) and longer term, ecological approaches based on the theoretical framework of community resilience.

ELIZABETH'S STORY

Elizabeth had served in the Air Force and was living comfortably on the East Coast, when she learned her twin sister had been murdered in Los Angeles, California. She and her mom immediately flew out to recover the body, and find out what had happened. Hospital workers provided the details of the death: Elizabeth's sister had been cut open from esophagus to stomach. But after speaking with her sister's friends, Elizabeth learned the rest of the story: her sister had been trafficking drugs across the border for the gang MS-13. A bag of heroin burst inside her, and gang members had cut her open to retrieve the product. A few days later, Elizabeth's mother suffered a massive heart attack and died...In that trau-matized state, having lost her twin sister and her mother, Elizabeth decided to join MS-13 to find the perpetrators. She began hanging out with her sisters' friends, who were affiliated with the same gang. Her sister's friends used drugs, and so she began using the same drugs – crystal meth and heroin. She

DOI: 10.4018/978-1-4666-9938-0.ch009

needed to fit in. And it wasn't long before she began dating a gang member in order to gain entry. But the cost of entry was higher than she could have imagined: she was gang-raped by 13 guys and then given a knife and told to fight for her life. Afterwards, they gave her more drugs, and she took them. She took them to numb the pain. She took them because now she wanted them....Elizabeth became completely absorbed into 'the life'. In a bitter irony, she ended up working for years with MS-13 trafficking other women from Mexico into San Diego, along with drugs, and herself working as a prostitute. This what they call 'the life'.

ALEX'S STORY

Alex is the grandson of a founding member of a large prison gang in the United States. He was "born into the gang" as he described it, becoming a member when he was only 11. It was expected, he explained, because his grandfather and uncle were was such a high-ranking member. "My cousins gave me my first joint at 10", he recalls. "My mother found us and was so pissed off! She didn't want them corrupting me. But there wasn't nothing she could really do." Alex had a rough home life. Like the vast majority of people who end up in a gang, he suffered abuse and neglect at the hands of his parents. When I meet him, I am astounded by his eloquence and intellect. Alex went to private schools and has a degree in Finance from a well-known university. Those skills, however, he put to use running various aspects of business for his prison gang. He was also an assassin for the organization. "If you saw my record, you'd be shocked" he tells me, before sharing a litany of violent acts – some of which prosecutors do not know about. Alex is highly trained in heavy weaponry, including rocket launchers, and reveals that his organization has a significant stockpile (and pipeline) of military weapons. Most surprising for me was the disconnect between the calm, young man in front of me and his revelations that he enjoyed violence, that he loved killing. Alex has been reflecting on this while in prison, and tells me that ultimately he traces it back to a childhood bereft of basic compassion. Alex is married, and is serving 30 years.

INTRODUCTION

This chapter is about the logics of gang life, and how weapons fit into it.

If we want to understand about the relationship between people in gangs and weapons, we have to start by seeing the world in which armed violence makes sense: the intergang environment. It is a highly competitive social space where trust is contracted to small circles, and projection of strength is a required life skill. Gangs often live immediate environments equivalent to that of a warzone, and their mentality reflects a heightened state of conflict escalation[1], which includes the development of hostile attitudes, perceptions, and goals toward 'other' groups. Gangs therefore live by values and beliefs that support the use of violence to settle disputes, achieve group goals, recruit members, and defend identity (Stretesky & Pogrebin, 2007).

Like any social identity group, gang members in their respective trusted circles share an understanding of the world they believe is unique to their particular group. Gangs employ coded languages, customs, beliefs, symbols, and patterns of behavior, which differentiate them from 'others' in the intergang environment. They differ, however, in their use of violence, and weapons. Violence, varying from killing, torturing, beating, extorting, sexual violence, to premeditated emotional abuse – goes hand in hand with gang life.

Yet the majority of Latino gang members are not violent or criminally active. They number among the vast majority of human beings who have a hard time imagining killing other people, raping other people, and taking pleasure in ultra-violent behavior. So we have to ask: where did members of large gangs learn that stuff? How did those behaviors become deemed acceptable? Specific to this chapter, why do people in large Latino gangs emulate or enact violence, and why do they choose the weapons they do? The answer to these questions lies within the intergang environment, and how it encourages weapons *use*.

Size Matters

Since the majority of my experience is with organized armed groups, this chapter focuses on *large, organized* gangs. The distinction between large and small street gangs is important, encapsulated in what some researchers calls "first generation" and "second-generation" gangs. First generation street gangs are concerned with "turf"; they lay claim to an area surrounding their neighborhood and "focus their attention on turf protection to gain petty cash and on gang loyalty within their immediate environs" (Manwaring, 2005, p. 9). Second generation gangs are larger, "organized around illicit economies like drug trafficking...operate across several cities or even internationally, have links to transnational criminal organizations (TCOs) like drug cartels, and feature a more centralized leadership and a more hierarchical structure than first-generation gangs"(Sullivan & Bunker 2012, p. 44).

Second generation Latino gangs[2] also have in common two interlinked objectives: making money and self-preservation. Heavy involvement in drug trafficking meets both of these objectives; the main underground economy bankrolling the activities of Latino gangs is drug trafficking, followed (in some cases) by sex trafficking. Participation in these underground industries however is linked to the propensity for weapons use. For those conducting financial transactions in the highly competitive intergang environment, projecting strength is a requirement for both self-preservation and protecting market share.

Relatedly, large organized street gangs are also more likely to use lethal weapons and deadly violence in pursuit of their objectives. In the United States, guns are the preferred lethal weapons of choice for gangs.[3] In part, this is because guns are available. For example in the United Kingdom where guns are illegal, gangs use knives and increasingly rape (Townsend, 2014); in Zimbabwe, gangs use bricks, knives and strangulation. In part, however, it is because *lethal* violence is a norm in intergang relations. In large, organized gangs that are the focus of this chapter, willingness to kill another human being is what differentiates real members from wannabes, and helps individuals climb the 'corporate ladder'.

I. HISPANIC/LATINO GANGS IN THE AMERICAS

Latino gangs[4] can be classified into Mexican-American gangs, Mexican gangs, and Central American gangs. Each of the three types reflects differences in region, economic situation, generations and cultural characteristics (Starbuck, Howell, & Lindquist, 2001). However all are organized around illicit economies like drug trafficking or human trafficking, and all operate regionally and/or internationally. Throughout this chapter, for the sake of space and clarity, I will refer only to specific gangs in each category (see Table 1).

Table 1. Gangs by category

Latin Kings Mexican Mafia M-18	MS-13 M-18	La Familia Los Zetas

Mexican-American Gangs

The Almighty Latin King Nation (or Latin Kings) based in Chicago is the largest Hispanic gang in the United States with an estimated following of 20,000 to 35,000. Latin Kings is organized into chapters, which operate in 39 US states, 206 cities, and areas in Latin America, Spain and Europe. Although its founding members were Puerto Rican, the majority of its members in the Midwest US are of Mexican heritage. Its leadership structure is highly organized and hierarchical.[5]

However many Mexican-American gangs are found in the southwest border region of the United States. They tend to be multi-generational, family based networks based on discrete territories. Mexican-American gangs are thus deeply embedded in US-Mexico border communities through generations of family members. Second generation Mexican-American street gangs are affiliated with the umbrella organization La Eme, otherwise known as the Mexican Mafia. The Mexican Mafia is a prison gang that was formed in the late 1950's in the California Department of Corrections.

La Eme is not presided over by a single leader. Leadership structure consists of a very small, tight knit group of people who have the authority to order murders. Each individual has a specific crew consisting of "comandadas" (officers) who carry out those orders and oversee criminal activities. La Eme controls all Hispanic Gangs in southern California, which are known collectively as *Surenos*[6] or "southerners". Surenos are not a cohesive unit. The term is a designation that ultimately all Hispanic gangs in Southern California pay taxes and allegiance to La Eme. Surenos consists of different gangs, many of whom are rivals. However in terms of structure, second generation Sureno gangs exhibit a core –periphery structure. The core is made up of older individuals, usually run by a "big homie" who has been released from prison and has direct ties (perhaps is an "associate) of La Eme. They are mistrustful of peripheral members, and contain activity within core group.

Mexican Gangs

Mexican gangs are more complicated to classify. The vast majority of Mexican gangs are small, youth gangs or *pandillas* that are organized by barrio (neighborhood) barrio and contain less than a few dozen members. A police officer in Mexico's Baja state described it this way:

There are lots of "pandillas" in Baja but those are really just groups of kids who are territorial and engage in delinquent behavior (graffiti, some robbery, but nothing really organized). Then there are criminal groups (delinquencia organizadas), which are more like cells of the [drug] cartels. (Confidential Baja Police Officer, Field Interview Mexcali, 2012)

Because this chapter focuses on large, organized street gangs, I focus on the *delinquencia organizadas*, which I call "armed Mexican gangs". Firearms are illegal in Mexico, thus when a gang is armed, a higher level of organization and criminal activity can be inferred. The systematic use of weapons by a gang signifies more organized involvement in illicit industry, for example taking control of a nightclub where women and drugs are trafficked. "Setting up a store" for greater control over product and distribution requires arms for protection, and indicates that the store pays taxes to "the establishment" (Mexican transnational criminal organizations, or MDTOs) for access to their product (LoneWolf, 2004).

Leadership structure is similar to Mexican-American gangs. Just as Surenos are tied to La Eme, armed Mexican gangs are tied to one (or more) of the major drug cartels in Mexico. The cartels contract the gangs to carry out specific activities. Below, a Department of Justice official describes how the relationship was organized between the Tijuana Cartel (also called the Arellano Felix Organization or AFO) and armed Mexican gangs.

In AFO, you have five brothers making all the decisions. Each had 10 lieutenants, and each of them had three sergeants, and each sergeant had six crews, and each crew 10-30 people. Each group was self-sufficient, everything they got they split half – half went to the boss. Whatever they needed to go to pay their overhead: kidnapping, extortion, moving dope, they'd pay their guys with money or dope. They'd get holiday bonuses. Some groups were really good at distribution and not killing, some good at both, some at kidnapping, some at money laundering. (Confidential Department of Justice official, Field Interview San Diego, 2012)

Figure 1 shows what this basic structure looks like. The picture would be even busier if all five brothers, and crews for all three sergeants, were depicted.

Figure 1. Mexican gang-cartel relationship [abbreviated]

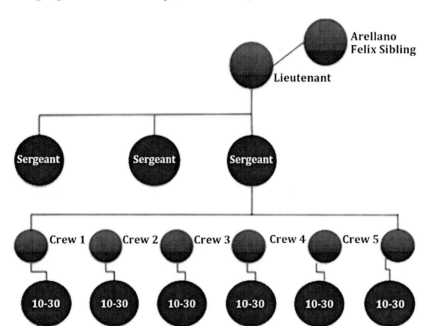

Central American Gangs

The two largest Central American gangs – MS-13 and M-18 (18th Street gang) – also operate transnationally. Both gangs originated in the 1980s as refugees from the civil wars in Central America fled to the United States, landing in Los Angeles. MS-13 formed to protect Salvadoran immigrants from being victimized by other gangs. Its founding members had fought in the civil war and had guerilla warfare training, and MS-13 exercised extreme forms of violence previously unseen in Los Angeles. The 18th Street gang formed in the 1960s by Mexican immigrants who were not allowed to be members of already existing Hispanic gangs. With a multicultural ethos, 18th Street was the first Hispanic gang to allow different ethnicities to be members.

MS-13 and M-18 became bitter rivals. Aggressive recruitment and territorial expansion by each gang led to turf wars with other gangs, and "by the 1990s, federal prosecutors were pushing to deport tens of thousands of immigrants with criminal records" (Johnson, 2014, para 15).

Gang members were targeted by new laws and sent back to their home countries, including Honduras. Back in Central America, the young men trained in gang warfare began to reconstruct the world they knew in Los Angeles and other American cities..."These gangs are part of the cultural fabric of the U.S., not Central America," says John Sullivan, a gang specialist with the Los Angeles County sheriff's department. "We deport them, and they're bigger and badder than any gangs there, and they dominate. And now we have areas [in Central America] that are widely destabilized, with a high degree of violence." (Johnson, 2014, para 9)

MS-13 and M-18 are structured as loosely connected cells or *cliques*. Like their Mexican counterparts, both gangs cooperate with larger TCOs for specific tasks like contract killings, storage and sometimes transportation. The relationship between a particular cell or clique is a contract labor approach, quite like the Mexican crews described above (and depicted in Figure 1). As Steven Dudley has noted, "More often than not, they represent disposable personnel ("desechables") who will never fit into the hierarchical and disciplined structures that the large criminal organizations have created" (2011, para 4).

What Do Latino Gangs Have in Common?

The majority of scholars agree that gangs emerge in specific socioeconomic contexts. Many Latino gangs began in urban areas, parts of cities "experiencing a range of weak enforcement mechanisms, low levels of economic well-being, insufficient government capacity, and significant societal divisions" (Locke, 2012, p. 1). In other words, gangs themselves are demonstrative of wider patterns of inequality, corruption and institutional weakness.

Unsurprisingly, gangs flourish in areas neglected by governments. Research shows that poor governance[7] contributes to the emergence of groups involved in various illicit trades. About half of all illicit transactions take place in areas[8] "experiencing a range of weak enforcement mechanisms, low levels of economic well-being, insufficient government capacity, and significant societal divisions" (Locke, 2012, p.1). Corruption, inequality, exclusion, and lack of job creation are all correlates (Muggah, 2012).

In these spaces, gangs represent cohesive social groups that provide identity and meaning to their members. Positive effects are profoundly psychological and include self-esteem, perceived support, love, acceptance, and – perhaps most importantly – security. In El Salvador, for example, the retreat of the state has institutionalized alternative 'tribes' in urban communities. Identity in certain municipalities revolves around membership in MS-13 and M-18. The members of cliques speak of themselves as families – in some cases, they consist of several extended families with deep kinship bonds. In some US communities, the draw is more pragmatic. A former Latin Counts member recalled the necessity of joining up in Detroit.

From the age of like 11 to 17 I was involved in a little clique out there; you know like I said it's a little more ravaged in Detroit than it is here in San Diego. Out there it's more of a necessity than over here... [because] they have more opportunity here; doesn't get below freezing here. Crime is more, back in Michigan, crime is more like a necessity for people who are poor and ravaged compared to people here who have a lot more. (Former Latin Counts member, Field Interview San Diego, 2013)

In their origin, gangs were formed to provide social networks that were often lacking in many minority communities. Poverty and underdevelopment is a primary factor, manifesting not only in lack of financial resources but also lack of educational opportunities, meaningful employment options, prejudice against the poor, and denial of basic human dignity. In fact, several gangs that I have studied emerged in response to social injustices, but metastasized into different kinds of organizations. Take the Latin Kings for example, the largest Hispanic/Latino street gang in the United States. As already noted, the Latin Kings emerged in 1940s Chicago as a self-defense group made up of Mexican and Puerto Rican men to protect their communities, and address the oppressive racism and prejudice that newly arrived immigrants were experiencing. But over time, the organization lost touch with its founding ideology and became instead one of the largest and most violent gangs in the US. These days their time and energy are expended on criminal activities, not social change.

In Mexico, a similar story explains the emergence and decline of the gang La Familia, which was based in the state of Michoacán. Over 30 years, La Familia grew from a small group of vigilantes sworn to protect the state from drug dealers and criminals, to become an armed wing of the Gulf Cartel, trained with Los Zetas, and split into an independent organization in 2006. From its founding, La Familia's stated purpose was to bring social and public security to Michoacán (Sullivan & Logan, 2009). The organization espoused a religious philosophy of social justice and protection of innocents, criticized violence against civilians, and justified their own assassinations and beheadings as 'acts of protection'. Likened to the Revolutionary Armed Forces of Colombia (FARC), La Familia's brand of social control included curfews, employment, promotion of family values, and enforced adherence to speed limits (Carpenter, 2013). However like all organizations, La Familia continued to grow and adapt to its environment. They split from the Gulf Cartel to form their own trafficking organization, and eventually became the largest supplier of Methamphetamines to the United States.

We must neither romanticize nor underestimate the communal ties of such groups. Children who join gangs *feel* safer, but the truth is that being involved in a gang puts them at a greater risk of victimization (Melde et al, 2009). However research has also shown that Latino Gangs offer levels of emotional support and financial protection that are lacking in many of their households (La Rosa & Rugh, 2005). In Mexican American barrios of Los Angeles youths' self-identity gets thoroughly entangled with the gang. "The gang provides the youth with the basic psychological ingredients for self-identification and becomes an ego ideal. Toughness and other street values are reinforced by characteristic psychological traits such as the lack of empathy" (Flores, 2012, slide 18). Most gang members I have interviewed tell a variation of the story below, recounted by a former enforcer for the Mexican Mafia, who described himself as someone who enjoyed hurting people.

I wasn't raised by a mother, you know what I mean? I'm like a product of the streets…I had an alcoholic violent mom, and I had a gang father who just didn't know how to show [love], had been in prison all of my life.

Summary

The intergang environment involves and encourages weapons use for a variety of reasons discussed in the next section. Weapons are most often defined as things that are designed or used to cause harm to living beings, structures or systems. This simple idea has to be unpacked if we wish to understand the role of weapons in large Latino gangs. Instead of treating weapons as nouns (things) or adjectives[9], I view weapons *use* as a verb (an action). Since human actions have meaning and context, we can inquire about both when it comes to weapons and gangs.

II. WEAPONS USE AND THE INTERGANG ENVIRONMENT

We should begin by dispelling the myth that large gangs are disproportionately prone to use violence. The "drawbacks" associated with intergang violence (Gambetta, 2009, p. 35) includes attracted unwanted attention by law enforcement (increasing possibility of arrest), and associated costs of time and resources. An additional drawback associated with intra-gang violence is the chilling effect on members' faith in a gang to protect them if internal gang violence is a norm. "For all these reasons", James Densley writes, "gangs actually incentivize disciplined use of violence within their organization…[and] require evidence of one's capacity to "discipline" their potential for violence" (2012, p. 304).

Still, all the gangs discussed in this chapter do use weapons, and so we can ask: what functions do weapons use play in the intergang environment? I have sorted my answers into two categories: psychological functions and instrumental functions.

Psychological Functions

Weapons use has four psychological functions in the world of Latino gangs. First, use functions to *reinforce important aspects of gang identity*. Gang identity is highly competitive, and glorifies loyalty, strength, and toughness. People in gangs often live in immediate environments equivalent to that of warzones[10], and their mentality reflects a heightened state of emotional arousal. When people are already aroused by anger, the mere presence of a weapon or a picture of a weapon can lead people to behave more aggressively.[11] Gang members have a cultivated proclivity towards hostile attitudes, including anger and a desire to punish 'other groups'.

'Other' groups can be society at large. Taken as a whole, gang identity is *oppositional* – meaning it is defined against the dominant society's rules and conventions. Gang identity includes a profound distrust of formal authority driven by the belief police are out to get you because of your color or background. Perhaps unsurprisingly (given the marginalized areas where gangs flourish), research has shown the level of harassment and racism encountered by groups of people correlates with the likelihood of stable, oppositional identities. But leaving society aside, there are plenty of competing groups closer to home to 'otherize' and compete against.

Enculturation is a second psychological function. Enculturation refers to the process of socialization into and maintenance of the norms of one's indigenous culture, including its salient ideas, concepts, and values (Herskovits, 1948). It is a broad construct[12] encompassing behavior, values, and knowledge (Kim & Abreu, 2001). As noted, gang behavior is highly competitive, consistent with group psychology in war contexts. In turn, hyper-competitive patterns of behavior are motivated by values of loyalty, strength, toughness, and pride in physical, mental or sexual prowess (Copes & Hochstetler, 2003; Wilkenson, 2001). Two types of knowledge – tactical and ideational – drive weapons use. The former refers to tactical knowledge or familiarity with weapons; Barthalow et al (2005) has proposed that weapons familiarity mediates the likelihood of their use. The latter refers to the belief that violence is an acceptable way of resolving conflict. Cultural acceptance of violence is a risk factor for experiencing all kinds of violence (Champion & Durant, 2001) and is learned in childhood, either through direct exposure to violence (corporal punishment) and/or through witnessing violence in the family and in the community (World Health Organization, 2009).

Initiation is a third psychological function (not to be confused with *recruitment*, an instrumental function discussed below). To fit in, new members must adopt the violence culture, and enacting violence reinforces belongingness – in no small part because enacting violence changes human psychology. As Neil Kressel observed, "Once people commit their first evil act, often without much thought, a new logic pushes them on toward more heinous atrocities'" (2002, p. 171). Seasoned gang members are well aware of this truth, which is why "joining up'" usually involves acts of extreme violence. Gangs differ in the severity of the act required, typically referred to as "putting in time", but assassinations are well known rites of passage for both men and women (although often, women must submit to gang rape and assaults by male gang members to demonstrate their commitment to the group).

Fourth, weapons use and ownership can provide a psychological sense of *'realness'*. The intergang environment creates a competitive ethos where being 'real' or 'legitimate' as opposed to 'fake' or a 'wannabe' gang members is a real and dangerous dynamic. Lauger (2012, p. 97) has argued that, in addition to the pressure faced by street-oriented males in general to demonstrate that they are real men, "male gang member are subjected to a unique need to demonstrate that they are both real men *and* real gang members" (emphasis mine). Unfortunately, the intergang environment is "filled with contradicting evaluations and generalized uncertainty" about the 'realness' of gang members. Like other social groups, members of gangs overestimate the status of their gang relative the assessment of their peers in the intergang environment.

A gang member's need to reconcile any disagreement between his or her gang's collective identity and conflict peer assessments forces the gang members to demonstrate authenticity according to his or her understanding of "real". At best, this need forces gang members to validate their identity by employing harmless signifiers of gang status (symbols or codes)...at worst, this need causes gang members to behave in a manner consistent with their gang's collective identity [of which] violence is a core element (Lauger 2012).

Lauger concludes that this dynamic partially explains why gang members are more heavily involved in criminal activity.

Instrumental Functions

Weapons serves instrumental functions as well, when they are used intentionally in the pursuit of particular ends. *Recruitment* is one of the most primary. In general, weapons use can fulfill three different goals in recruitment: signaling trust, punishing, and enticing. Problems of trust are particularly pronounced for gangs wishing to recruit new members. Successful recruitment requires sousing out who, among wannabes (and potential undercover informants), can be trusted. Requiring recruits to perform a violent act (an assassination or rape) weeds out those unwilling or incapable of doing so, and thus signals trustworthiness (Densley, 2012).

Violence can also be used as a recruitment tactic by threatening desired recruits with consequences for *not* joining. In Honduras and El Salvador, children growing up in gang territories are told that they must join up or die.

[In Honduras] young people are forced to choose sides once they reach adolescence. The cartels need local support from the gangs, and the gangs need foot soldiers. Pressure on families is enormous. "These kids know that once they're in, their life span is short and brutal," says Sheehan. "So they're resisting, and the gangs are looking at this as a threat and wiping them out" (Johnson, 2014, para 27)

On the flip side, weapons can also used to *entice* would-be recruits with the spectacle of extreme violence.

Inflicting extreme and gruesome acts of violence also serves to *terrorize and intimidate* rivals. A variety of weapons may be used to rape, behead, torture, main and kill. Latino gangs differ in their use of this strategy. The armed Mexican gangs working for Los Zetas have no compunctions about using terror tactics. Their methods include gladiator-like fights to the death, beheadings, decapitation, and burning people alive.

However other Latino gangs kill people selectively in an effort to limit 'civilian' casualties. For example, the Mexican Mafia famously has bans on drive-by shootings (punishable by a $1000-$10,000 penalty), prostitution, and domestic violence.[13] Back in Mexico, the Knights Templar (KTM) claims to adhere to codes of behavior that reject killing for pleasure or money, and extols democratic and religious freedom (Leon, 2011). KTM members are advised to consider carefully whether a murder is necessary and to provide service and protection to community members. In March 2012, the group called a truce during Pope Benedict XVI's visit to Mexico announced via banners (*narcomantas*) that read "The Knights Templars are holding off on all violent action, we are not killers, welcome to the Pope" (Martinez, 2012).

Transnational gangs in Mexico and Guatemala also vary based on the type and severity of violence waged, whether patronage strategies are used with local communities, and public image concerns associated with extreme violence and civilian casualties. Due to the highly networked structure of MS-13 and M-18 discussed above, it is more accurate to speak of *cliques* exhibiting degrees of extreme violence. While numerous M-18 cliques numerous cliques are focused narrowly on turf protection or more broadly on maximizing profit through drug trafficking including through territory belonging to rival gangs, the Revolutionary or "R" faction of M-18 played the lead role in negotiating a ceasefire with MS-13 in El Salvador.

The same differences are found in MS-13, an organization that as a whole has cultivated a reputation for extreme violence. Although "any member of MS-13 will explain...that their ultimate goal is to become the most powerful gang in the world" (Leap, 202, p. 36), MS-13 cliques differ in local identities and behaviors. Some cliques, like Normandie Locos in Honduras have targeted civilians in public, politically motivated attacks – most recently a public bus in reprisal for Honduras's crackdown on MS-13 gang members (Craul, 2005). Other cliques claim to be focused primarily on day to day life in particular neighborhoods, as described by "Blue" who is second in command of the clique "running" La Victoria neighborhood in El Salvador.

Blue talks of the MS[-13] as a social organization that protects the "civilians" in the neighborhood. They help get water lines connected. They're refurbishing the community hall. To him, it's normal that residents have to pay rent to the gang for these services… "There are colleagues who don't have a mother or anything, and only the gang helps them — no one else" (Beubian, 2011, para 26).

What Blue refers to as 'rent', we would call extortion. If his account is true, than this instance is closer to functional taxation. In many other instances though, extortion is used as a weapon to sow fear. For example, as of July 2014, 700 people have been killed in Guatemala for failing to pay extortion fees (Gurney, 2014).

Summary

Weapons use serves six main functions in the intergang environment of Latino gangs: reinforcing gang identity, socializing and initiating new members, projecting 'realness' or credibility, recruitment, and intimidation. Reflecting on the depravities adopted by Latino gangs and the culture of violence instilled by repetitive anti-civilian atrocities, reducing violence seems a daunting task. What recourse do communities have in dealing with large gangs that are organized around illicit economies, particularly drug and human trafficking?

III. RESILIENCE TO VIOLENCE

Communities can increase their resilience in areas dominated by gang culture and crime by attending to sources of greatest social vulnerability (Norris et al. 2008), with efforts to build social capital, and challenge anti-social behavior. Resilient communities engage pro-actively with the dynamics of violent conflict. In the context of urban violence,

Positive effects of resilience might thus be observed when legitimate actors and institutions – local government, schools, faith-based organizations or NGOs – offer urban services that strengthen civil solidarity or generate new practices and coalitions capable of managing or reducing violence. (Jutersonke & Kartas, 2012. p. 3)

Resilient communities are characterized by *adaptive capacity* – the ability of the community to adjust its characteristics of behavior and expand its coping range under existing or future conditions (Brooks & Adgers, 2005). Ultimately community resilience to gang violence is a function of how individuals and groups act collectively, and learn and incorporate new knowledge (Holling & Walker 2003).

We can understand community resilience as a set of adaptive capacities, and as a strategy for promoting violence prevention and community health. In the past four decades, resilience has gained considerable traction in studies about how communities cope with war and violence. Of particular interest is positive resilience or the "condition of relative stability and even tranquility in areas recently or intermittently beset by violence (Davis, 2012, p. 9)."

Probably the most dramatic form of resilience is that evidenced by concerted or proactive efforts on the part of communities to actively wrest control of their daily situation in ways that could be considered a form of resistance to the power and influence of armed actors. (ibid).

How have communities accomplished this? By challenging the norms that support violence, and transforming sources of exposure to victimization and violent acts.

Interviews in Guatemala revealed that community members and groups have used negotiation, mediation, dialogue, and restorative justice methods to limit levels of violence and prevent young people from joining MS-13 or Calle-18. In Quichean communities, conflict resolution strategies were oriented towards the application of Mayan law and order, youth discipline and preventing criminality (Carpenter, 2013). Municipal governments in Guatemala have also engaged armed groups to reduce local violence. A recent study concluded that non-corrupt municipal governments, authentically accountable to residents, were able to keep violence and crime at a minimum when they actively negotiated with local criminal networks, mediating between their interests and the needs of the community.

Another example is the recent peace treaty between MS-13 and Calle-18 in El Salvador, brokered in part by the Catholic Church. Commonly referred to as Track II diplomacy by the field of conflict resolution, this unofficial initiative has led to a sixty percent decrease in violence. In May of 2012, the gangs extended their truce to school zones and agreed to end forced recruitment of child soldiers. Under the radar, the Catholic Church has been using similar outreach strategies with armed gangs in Mexico. "The government tells me not to talk to the narcos", a high-ranking official in the Catholic Church told me on a recent visit to Southwestern Mexico, "but of course I do. I have no other choice for protecting my parishes."

Law enforcement agencies in the United States have used a similar approach for almost a decade to reduce gang violence. So called "comprehensive approaches" include engagement with gangs by interventionists, individuals or teams who mediate conflicts between rival gangs and try to prevent tit-for-tat escalation when a violent incident occurs. In the Southern California border region, engagement has produced peace treaties and peace summits between rival gangs, and a halt to drive-by shootings. Engagement strategies are usually backed up with targeted enforcement concentrating on the worst offenders (Kleinman, 2009). So called "smarter policing" is even more effective when coupled with community projects to build social capital between community members and law enforcement (Kennedy, 2011) and by prioritizing high school graduation, providing needed social services, and taking a public health approach to drug use (Waller, 2006). When piloted in US cities, the approach has led to marked declines in violence.

CONCLUDING THOUGHTS

Community resilience to gang violence is not about eradicating gangs themselves; it's about taking proactive and multi-faceted actions to reduce social vulnerability, boost communities' adaptive capacities, and challenge gangs on their culture of violence. Latino gangs are more than a crime problem, and their activities are not purely domestic affairs shaped by discrete neighborhood interests and localized disputes over territory. As economic actors, they are deeply invested in drug trafficking and are embedded in support networks, in both Mexico and Guatemala, that contain high-ranking politicians, members of the military, and other actors with clout. Officeholders in both countries participate in international criminal networks and have exploited official positions to engage in international drug trafficking or more local racketeering. Despite 20 years of 'drug wars' Mexican and Central American gangs have thrived because security forces, politicians, and people in the business community benefit from the profit of drug trafficking.

Mexican-American gangs (and Central American gangs operating in the US) lack these mafia-like connections to the US government. However an important commonality is that Latino gangs in the US are deeply embedded in US-Mexico border communities through generations of family members. As one gang expert put it, "These gangs are so deeply embedded in the community, they *are* the community. They're never going away" (Felix Aguirre, Field Interview San Diego, 2012). Yet herein lies a silver lining, in the words of gang researcher John Hagedorn (2005, p. 163).

As social actors within poor communities with weak mechanisms of formal social control, gangs, militias, factions and cartels have the capacity not only to wage war, but to rein it in.

REFERENCES

Bargent, J. (2013). Murders in Honduras Rising Despite Gang Truce. *Insight Crime*. Retrieved June 8, 2014 from http://www.insightcrime.org/news-briefs/murders-in-honduras-rising-despite-gang-truce

Bartholow, B. D., Anderson, C. A., Carnagey, N. L., & Benjamin, A. R. Jr. (2005). Interactive effects of life experience and situational cues on aggression: The weapons priming effect in hunters and nonhunters. *Journal of Experimental Social Psychology*, *41*(1), 48–60. doi:10.1016/j.jesp.2004.05.005

Beubien, J. (2011). *El Salvador Fears Ties Between Cartels, Street Gangs*. National Public Radio. Retrieved April 24, 2012 from http://www.npr.org/2011/06/01/136829224/el-salvadorfears-ties-between-cartels-street-gangs

Bisin, A., Patacchini, E., Verdier, T., & Zenou, Y. (2011). *Formation and Persistence of Oppositional Identities*. CEPR Discussion Paper No. DP8380. Retrieved July 12, 2014 from http://ssrn.com/abstract=1846262

Brooks, B. (2012). Sao Paulo Could Face Gang War with Truce Collapse. *Associated Press*. Retrieved August 1, 2014 from http://news.yahoo.com/sao-paulo-could-face-gang-war-truce-collapse-082756745.html

Carlson, M., Marcus-Newhall, A., & Miller, N. (1990). Effects of situational aggression cues: A quantitative review. *Journal of Personality and Social Psychology*, *58*(4), 622–633. doi:10.1037/0022-3514.58.4.622 PMID:14570078

Champion, H. L., & Durant, R. H. (2001). Exposure to violence and victimization and the use of violence by adolescents in the United States. *Minerva Pediatrica*, *53*, 189–197. PMID:11455306

Chivis, M. (2012). The Knights Templar Cartel is Calling a Short Truce. *Borderland Beat*. Retrieved April 30, 2014 from http://www.borderlandbeat.com/2012/03/knightstemplars-cartel-is-calling.html

Cotton, P. (1992). Violence Decreases with Gang Truce. *Journal of the American Medical Association*, *268*(4), 443–444. doi:10.1001/jama.1992.03490040011002 PMID:1619732

Decker, S., Bynum, T., & Weisel, D. (1998). A Tale of Two Cities: Gangs as Organized Crime Groups. *Justice Quarterly*, *15*(3), 395–425. doi:10.1080/07418829800093821

Gurney, K. (2014). 700 Extortion-Related Murders in Guatemala through July 2014: NGO. *Insight Crime*. Retrieved August 30, 2014. http://www.insightcrime.org/news-briefs/guatemala-700-homicides-extortion-2014

Johnson, S. (2014). American-Born Gangs Helping Drive Immigrant Crisis at U.S. Border: Central America's spiraling violence has a Los Angeles connection. *National Geographic Magazine*. Retrieved August 30, 2014 from http://news.nationalgeographic.com/news/2014/07/140723-immigration-minors-honduras-gang-violence-central-america/

Jones, N., & Cooper, S. (2011). Tijuana's Uneasy Peace May Endure, Despite Arrests. *Insight Crime*. Retrieved September 2, 2014 from http://www.insightcrime.org/investigations/tijuanas-uneasy-peace-may-endure-despite-arrests

Jutersonke, O., Muggah, R., & Rodgers, D. (2009). 2009 Urban violence and Security Interventions in Central America. *Security Dialogue*, *40*(4-5), 373–397. doi:10.1177/0967010609343298

Katz, C. M., Maguire, E. R., & Choate, D. (2011). A cross-national comparison of gangs in the United States and Trinidad and Tobago. *International Criminal Justice Review*, *21*(3), 243–262. doi:10.1177/1057567711417179

Kennedy, D. (2011). *Don't Shoot: One Man, A Street Fellowship, And The End of Violence in Inner-City America*. New York: Bloomsbury.

Kleiman, M. (2009). *When Brute Force Fails: How to Have Less Crime and Less Punishment*. Princeton University Press.

Klein, M. (1995). Street Gang Cycles. In J. Wilson & J. Petersilia (Eds.), *Crime*. Oakland, CA: ICS Press.

Klein, M., & Maxson, C. (2006). *Street Gang Patterns and Policies*. New York: Oxford University Press. doi:10.1093/acprof:oso/9780195163445.001.0001

Kodluboy, D. W., & Evenrud, L. A. (1993). School-based interventions: Best practice and critical issues. In A. P. Goldstein & C. R. Huff (Eds.), *The Gang Intervention Handbook*. Champaign, IL.: Research Press.

Kraul, C., Lopez, R. J., & Connell, R. (2005). MS-13 Blamed for Massacre on Bus. *The Seattle Times*. Retrieved July 2, 2014 from http://seattletimes.nwsource.com/html/nationworld/2002283961_gangslaying22.html

Kressel, N. (2002). *Mass Hate: The Global Rise of Genocide and Terror*. New York: Plenum Press.

La Rosa, M., & Rugh, D. (2005). Onset of Alcohol and Other Drug Use Among Latino Gang Members. *Alcoholism Treatment Quarterly*, *23*(2), 67–85. doi:10.1300/J020v23n02_05

Lauger, T. (2012). *Real Gangstas: Legitimacy, Reputation, and Violence in the Intergang Environment.* Rutgers University Press.

Leap, J. (2012). Jumped. In *What Gangs Taught Me about Violence, Drugs, Love, and Redemption* (p. 36). Beacon Press.

Leon, L. (2011). When Religion Kills: The Narco-Traffickers of the Borderlands. *Religion Dispatches Magazine.* Retrieved April 2014 from http://www.religiondispatches.org/archive/atheologies/5009/when_religion_kills%3A_the_narco-traffickers_of_the_borderlands

Maguire, E. (2013). *Research, Theory and Speculation on Gang Truces.* Wilson Center, Unpublished Paper. Retrieved April 3, 2014 from http://www.wilsoncenter.org/sites/default/files/Maguire%20%20US%20and%20Trinidad%20-%20Paper.pdf

Maguire, E. R., Katz, C. M., & Wilson, D. B. (2013). *The Effects of a Gang Truce on Gang Violence. Background Paper for Wilson Center.* Washington, DC: American University.

Martinez, O. (2013). *El Naufragio de Una Tregua. Background Paper for the Wilson Center.* Washington, DC: Wilson Center.

McDermott, J. (2012). Money Runs out for Belize Gang Truce. *Insight Crime.* Retrieved December 13, 2013 from http://www.insightcrime.org/news-briefs/money-runs-out-for-belize-gang-truce

McDermott, J. (2013). Medellin Truce Inches Groups Closer to Criminal Hegemony. *Insight Crime.* Retrieved October 4, 2014 from http://www.insightcrime.org/news-analysis/mafia-truce-brokered-in-medellin

Muggah, R. (2011). The Transnational Gang: Challenging the Conventional Narrative. In T. Shaw & A. Grant (Eds.), *Ashgate Research Companion to Regionalism.* London: Ashgate.

Muggah, R., & Reiger, M. (2012). *Negotiating Disarmament and Demobilization in Peace Processes: What is the State of the Evidence?* Norwegian Peacebuilding Research Centre. Retrieved February 12, 2014 from http://www.peacebuilding.no/Themes/Peacebuilding-in-practice/publications/Negotiating-disarmament-and-demobilisation-in-peace-processes-what-is-the-state-of-the-evidence

Muggah, R., & White, N. (2013). *Is There a Preventive Action Renaissance: The Policy and Practice of Preventive Diplomacy and Conflict Prevention.* Norwegian Peacebuilding Research Centre. Retrieved February 12, 2014 from http://www.peacebuilding.no/Themes/Peacebuilding-in-practice/publications/Is-there-a-preventive-action-renaissance-The-policy-and-practice-of-preventive-diplomacy-and-conflict-prevention

National Gang Crime Research Center. (1995). *Gang Prevention and Gang Intervention: Preliminary Results from the 1995 Project GANGPINT.* National Needs Assessment Gang Research Task Force.

Stretesky, P. B., & Pogrebin, M. R. (2007). Gang-Related Gun Violence: Socialization, Identity, and Self. *Journal of Contemporary Ethnography, 36*(1), 85–114. doi:10.1177/0891241606287416

Sullivan, J. P., & Logan, S. (2009). *Mexico's 'Divine Justice'.* International Relations and Security Network. Retrieved June 21, 2012 from http://www.isn.ethz.ch/isn/Current-Affairs/Security-Watch/Detail/?lng=en&id=104677

Townsend, M. (2014). Gangs draw up lists of girls to rape as proxy attacks on rivals: Gangs assault rivals' sisters and girlfriends as a 'low risk' method of asserting dominance. *The Guardian.* Accessed August 30, 2014, from http://www.theguardian.com/society/2014/jul/19/gangs-rape-lists-sex-assault

Waller, I. (2006). *Less Law, More Order: The Truth about Reducing Crime.* Westport, CT: Praeger.

World Health Organization. (2009). *Changing Cultural and Social Norms that Support Violence.* Retrieved August 29, 2014 from http://www.who.int/violence_injury_prevention/violence/norms.pdf

ENDNOTES

[1]   Conflict escalation is defined as increased intensity of a conflict and severity in tactics used to wage it. Conflict escalation is associated with heightened emotions (blame, anger, fear) and hostile perceptions of (and goals towards) 'other' groups.

[2]   From here forward, use of the word *gang* is taken to mean large, Latino second generation street gangs.

[3]   The 2008 National Gang Threat Assessment reports that for the five year period ending in 2007, 94.3% of gang related homicides supposedly involved the use of a firearm and that gang members are increasingly using guns in conjunction with other crimes. For violent gang members, guns are the tools of the trade.

[4]   Latino gangs as used from here on out refers only to large, organized street gangs.

[5]   For details, see Gang Profile: The Latin Kings at the National Gang Research Center: http://www.ngcrc.com/ngcrc/page15.htm

[6]   *Surenos* refers to all Southern California criminal street gangs except the Maravilla gangs of East Los Angeles. Maravilla gangs are so named for the nickname they gave to the housing project of which they were residents: maravillosa or "marvelous". Maravillas were members of the Mexican Mafia prison gang when it began in the 1950s, but became disillusioned with the rules of the organization and decided to un- align themselves. They refused to pay taxes to the Mexican Mafia; as a result, the Mexican Mafia put Maravilla gangs on "green list" meaning kill on sight. It was not until recently that the "kill on sight" order against the Maravilla sets was recalled by the leadership of the Mexican Mafia.

[7]   According to the World Bank, poor governance is "associated with corruption, distortion of government budgets, inequitable growth, social exclusion, and lack of trust in authorities.

[8]   Locke used these characteristics to describe weak countries, but parts of cities and jungles (to name only two other areas) are just as aptly described. They are best described as fragile areas, or alternatively governed spaces. See Anne Clunan Harold A. Trinkunas (2010). *Ungoverned Spaces: Alternatives to State Authority in an Era of Softened Sovereignty.* Stanford University Press.

[9]   The Oxford dictionary supplements its definition of weapon with use of the concept as an adjective – weaponed – and, interestingly enough, it's example is the following: *You've got to be weaponed to live and to survive in the Detroit underground."* This automatically broadens the meaning of a weapon from "a thing designed or used for inflicting bodily harm or physical damage" to include (indirectly) the role of context.

[10]   I wrote earlier that most youth gang members are born into environments of lawlessness, poverty and underdevelopment which manifests as a lack of financial resources, educational opportunities, meaningful employment options, prejudice against the poor, and denial of basic human dignity alongside endemic violence. In this hostile environment, psychological attributes include the development of hostile attitudes, perceptions, and goals toward 'other' groups.

[11]   The so-called 'weapons effect' has been documented inside and outside the lab. Carson and Miller (1990) reviewed 56 published studies which confirmed that simply seeing a weapon increases aggression in both angry and nonangry individuals.

[12]   In psychology, a construct refers to an explanatory variable which is not directly observable.

[13]   According to the details of Oreja's 2011 federal indictment, and inmate interviews by the author.

Section 3
Europe

Chapter 10
"It's a Vicious Game":
Youth Gangs, Street Violence, and Organised Crime in Modern Britain

Dev Rup Maitra
University of Cambridge, UK

ABSTRACT

This chapter explores the activities and characteristics of street gangs and organised crime groups in contemporary British society. Although numerous studies exist which investigate youth delinquency and group violence in Britain, there is less research which specifically investigates contemporary British criminal gangs - carrying out such an exploration is the organising principle of this chapter. Through conducting qualitative research at an adult men's prison in England and its surrounding area, this chapter attempts to articulate the experiences of prisoners and street-offenders on this subject. The results illustrate the entrenched role street gangs and organised crime groups hold in certain areas of England; not only are they seen as viable alternatives to gainful employment, but their activities are often sanctioned by the communities within which they are based. Subsequently, a high level of violence is normalised within such communities, including heightened levels of weapon usage by gang members, both within and outside prison.

CASE STUDIES

1. Rob[1]: A Case Study in Gang Activity

Rob is serving a lengthy custodial sentence at an adult prison in England. Although this is his first conviction for a serious offence, he has been to several prisons and young offenders' institutions in the past. He is in his early twenties but says, "I feel like I'm 45", blaming this exhaustion on his prolonged involvement in criminality. This has ranged from street gang activity to being involved with an organised crime group. Rob grew up on an English council estate which he refers to as being "one of three mad estates" in his area. He goes on to say that rival estates had to do "business" with one another out of necessity, and describes his particular estate in the following terms: "In mine, you'd be shouting your gang

DOI: 10.4018/978-1-4666-9938-0.ch010

name; guys get shot on the estate, run over with cars, even. People got stabbed and died on the estate". Rob started drug-dealing at the age of 14, and his rapidly escalating criminality had a detrimental effect on his family: "Like I said, with [gang name], they'll go for your family. So when I was living with me Dad, his house got shot-up. So I got kicked out".

Because Rob was from a particular area, beginning a criminal 'career' automatically led to his affiliation with that area's organised crime group. By the age of 15, Rob was combining his street-based drug dealing with robberies; his gang would "get tooled up with machetes" to rob businesses – newsagents, off-licences, petrol stations. As well as financial gain, the robberies were done for his 'rep' – street reputation. This notion of street reputation permeated all aspects of criminal behaviour, with gang leaders continually putting pressure on Rob to 'up his game': "I was buying pure cocaine…and then doubling it up… [and soon] I became a middleman, where you're a couple of rungs below the wholesalers. So you're buying from the leaders, and you've got a few levels below you – the runners. I became a middleman quite young, 'cos I could sell. It's a vicious game, all about making money and upping your rep." However, Rob is emphatic in his desire to 'go straight' upon his release:

Drug dealing's not a living: either the police catch you and you're banged-up, or you end up dying. Your money's never your own, you can't prove your income, the police can pull you over whenever they want. I'd rather be a bum on the street or work in McDonalds than go back to dealing; I'd rather have a good night's sleep than go back to that. Then in prison, you got to wake up being a gangster every day. Once I'm sentenced, I'll serve my time, and then I'm done with it. I know what it is – I am it.

2. Dan: "It's All about Family"

Dan is a persistent-offender, having served several prison sentences during his life; he is currently serving a short custodial sentence. Dan originates from a particular community, within which there are elements of organised criminal behaviour, as well as general violence and delinquency similar to that of street gangs. In fact, the specific cultural group Dan hails from is characterised by deep family ties, illustrated by his own introduction to crime by his father:

It starts from a young age: you're listening to your dad when you're about five years old; when you're older, there's questioning and explaining with your dad. And then there are scams: you sell someone a laptop case with bottles of water in it, swapping the laptop for water when they're not looking. We was all about scams…we could buy and sell a lot of the other communities because you've always got family backup.

Dan's opinions around the importance of family show that familial connections are the lynchpin of his community's gang, even though he never uses the term 'gang' to describe his own cultural group. Although Dan states that "a grudge could be held over something silly…like [a household good]", he continues by stating that individuals have to help fellow community members because "it's all about family". This leads to there being a sharp resistance from rival gangs to cause conflict with Dan and his associates:

Put it this way, people think we're silly people; but we're not silly people. If you fuck with us, we'll fuck with you. And we've got a bigger crew than you. If you leave us alone, we'll leave you alone. It's only a phone call to [name of city] or [name of another city] and there're all up here. We'd do the same. You gotta do it...you're family.

These close links within the community extend to within the prison, where Dan states that there is "another one of ours [a member of his community] on my wing...only a timid lad" which is why Dan "keep[s] a closer eye on him...I won't let anyone pick on one of me own". It appears, then, that Dan's operates within a criminal network which functions in very similar ways to street and prison gangs. Similarities include the importance given to values such as loyalty and support, as well as the use of violence to resolve disputes. Dan also states that he has taught his sons to fight from a young age, "so they can handle themselves". Moreover, he states that disputes are often resolved by the community "elders", something else in common with formalised gangs. Although Dan insists that he "wasn't really interested in the gang stuff" during adolescence, his offending is sharply linked to a collective, cultural identity. Furthermore, his crimes are inextricably linked to group-offending from within the community. Dan goes on to state that he will be back in prison soon after the end of his current sentence: he will return to his community, and continue committing crime.

INTRODUCTION

During the 1990s, there was a substantial increase in the rates of gang-related crime and violence in England (Walsh 2003). This continued throughout the following decades, illustrated by increases in the levels of arrest, charge and prosecution of gang members (Home Office 2011). Moreover, the following decades witnessed a growth in the numbers of gang-related murders, especially amongst youths. For example, there were 26 gang-related murders in London, in 2007 (Pitts 2008). Additionally, 20% of those arrested for the 2011 London riots were gang members, with gangs accounting for approximately 22% of serious violence in London, and 50% of shootings in London in that year (Ministry of Justice 2011). However, the problem of gang violence is by no means confined to London; gang activity has been noted in most of England's major cities, with gang members being linked to the August 2011 riots in Birmingham, Manchester and Nottingham (Centre for Social Justice 2012), as well as at the epicenter of London's riots (Thomas 2012).

Recent events such as these have led to street gangs' activities being subjected to increased scrutiny (see, e.g., Morrell *et al.* 2011; Newburn 2011; Centre for Social Justice 2012). Much of this attention has been from the popular press, although there has been some academic focus directed towards this subject matter. Until recently, the majority of academic studies on street gangs were to be found in the United States (e.g. Taylor 1993; Yablonsky 1997; Venkatesh 2008). English research focused more on delinquent peer groupings (e.g. Patrick 1973; Winlow and Hall 2006) and sub-cultures of violence such as football hooliganism (Williams *et al.* 1989; Pearson 2012). However, there is a growing body of scholarly work which examines street gangs and organised crime groups[2] within England (e.g. Pitts 2008; Densley 2012; Hobbs 2013). This has also included studies which investigate the effects of gang activity on the prison environment, including the increased rates of violence linked to prison gangs (Wood & Adler 2001). Furthermore, existing studies have also attempted to explore the personal narratives of gang members' lives: what motivates some youths to join street gangs; what activities they participate in upon affiliation; why certain individuals 'exit' their gangs and desist from crime more generally; and why other gang members choose, instead, to rise through the gang's 'ranks'. However, a lacuna that exists in the current body of literature is regarding the movement of gang members from street-based delinquency to more organised criminality.

EXISTING ACADEMIC RESEARCH

Criminal Gangs and Gang Violence

Much of the existing literature on gang affiliation and gang violence emanates from the United States; this is indicative of the established presence of gangs in many American cities (Kahn 1978). These studies have identified gangs as being central to youth delinquency (Kantor & Bennett 1968; Klein 1971), as a principal component of both inter and intra-racial violence (Dawkins 1989; Chin *et al.* 1992), and as a central facet of organised criminal activity (Fagan 1989; Klein *et al.* 1991). Academic studies of organised crime groups exist alongside biographical accounts of such groupings, both in Britain and the United States (e.g. Borrell & Cashinella 1975; Pritchard 2008). There also exist numerous autobiographies produced by ex-gang members themselves (e.g. Smith 2005; Cummines 2012). Although such first-hand accounts provide personal narratives of gang activity, academic studies subject the topic of gangs to a more penetrating and critical analysis. Indeed, more recent studies on gang organisation (e.g., Bouchard & Spindler 2010; Densley 2014) should be read in conjunction with older research (e.g., Fagin, 1989; Decker *et al.* 1998) to trace how some street gangs have evolved into organised crime groups, and how the 'diving line' between the two has shifted. For example, Thrasher's (1924) text from the early twentieth-century constitutes one of the first attempts at explaining the difference between organised gangs and disorganised crime groups. Indeed, much of the literature makes this distinction between general group delinquency and the activities of organised crime groups: whereas the former involves youths committing anti-social behaviour in the communities they inhabit (Bond-Taylor 2005), the latter is typified by hierarchical structures with a greater degree of formalisation (Gambetta 2009). This is not to say that there is a clear, consistent 'boundary' between street gangs and organised crime groups ('OCGs'). Indeed, the latter are characterised by a number of specific features: a more systematic approach to their activities, more sophistication in the crime committed, and a greater degree of codification. In particular, their activities are often more serious in their nature than offences committed by street gangs (Saviano 2006).

The greater degree of organisation amongst OCGs has prompted state authorities to formulate specific responses to their criminal activities, illustrated by the creation of law enforcement units dedicated to tackling the problem. As well as a high degree of formalisation, OCGs are characterised by their primary purpose being wealth accumulation. This can be contrasted to more general street gang activity, where anti-social behaviour and street-level drug dealing are the principal manifestations of daily gang activity. This is in spite of the limited financial returns most low-level drug dealers receive (Levitt & Dubner 2005; Venkatesh 2008; Pitts 2008). Often, the thrill of engaging in such acts is the primary motivation for participation, characterised by Jack Katz (1988) as being one of the 'seductions' of crime.

The Study of Street Gangs

One of the most comprehensive analyses of street gangs is Frederic Thrasher's (1927) classic *The Gang*, a text that presents a panoramic view of gang membership, and highlights the various entities which have bearing upon street gangs. Although Thrasher's original text dates from the early twentieth-century, many of the characteristics attributed to gangs within the study are still relevant in contemporary society. For example, the reluctance of gang members to divulge information to the police (Thrasher 1927:203) is still a pertinent feature of gang life, meaning that gang conflicts continue to be outside the ambit of the rule of law (Dasgupta 2010; Densely 2012). Equally, the influence of the media on gang members' activities (Thrasher 1927:108) continues to affect gang affiliated youths, possibly even more so than previously (Ro 1996; Kubrin 2005). There are, however, very few references made by Thrasher (1927) to drugs and firearms, which is indicative of the minimal role these played in street gangs of the early twentieth-century. This can be contrasted with the current situation as regards gangs, where drug dealing is pivotal to many modern gangs' activities (Pincomb & Judiscak 1997; Venkatesh 2008). Furthermore, the role of firearms is a central facet of modern gang activity in both the United States and Great Britain (Davidson 1997; Skogan *et al.* 2009). This is indicative of the heightened levels of violence within contemporary gangs, as compared to the lower levels of serious violence within gangs of the early and mid-twentieth century (Thrasher 1927; Short & Strodtbeck 1965). Thrasher's study highlights how particular features of early-twentieth century America had a bearing on the activities of street gangs: taking part in the informal economy through scavenging for scrap metal, for example (Webster *et al.* 1919; Thrasher 1927). There has, then, clearly been a movement away from the misdemeanours and minor delinquency of the mid-twentieth century (Drake & Cayton 1945 in Venkatesh 2001). For a limited number of contemporary gangs, this has been replaced by a violent and 'corporate' framework (Levitt and Venkatesh 2000; Densley 2012).

Gangs and Organised Crime in Wider Society

The activities of gangs and OCGs are usually concentrated in particular geographical areas (Bottoms & Wiles 2003), and police responses which focus on targeting these 'hotspots' of delinquency have a moderate deterrent effect (Sherman & Weisburd 1995; Braga 2001). Nevertheless, these suppression responses alone are not adequate in stemming the gang violence witnessed in urban communities (Jackson 1989; Mays 1997). Consequently, recent gang prevention strategies have focused less on orthodox policing, and more on informal dispute resolution (Skogan *et al.* 2009). While still focusing on violence hotspots, initiatives such as *Ceasefire Chicago* adopt a more holistic approach to counteracting the deleterious effects of street gangs; such programmes use non-state actors to resolve gang disputes, and have led to marked decreases in gang-related murders (Decker 2001; Skogan *et al.* 2009). However, such approaches are only able to counter-act street-level gang activity, and even then, not with uniform success (see Wilson & Chermak 2011). Nevertheless, mediation has been replicated in certain communities within the U.K. Typically, there exist longstanding hostilities towards the police from such communities (Jefferson 1993; Bowling & Phillips 2007). Consequently, it is presumed that non-involvement of the police is often a more effective method of dispute resolution in such communities. However, as has already been noted, such strategies cannot counter more organised criminal activity, which is often further away from the street-level.

A further emerging approach has been to consider gang-related violence as a public health issue, particularly in relation to firearms offences (Prothrow-Stith 1995; Hemenway 2004). Again, this deviates from the orthodox perspective, which views gang-related offences as merely a law and order issue, to be counteracted with pro-active policing alone. In fact, such perspectives are borne out of the belief that gangs are produced within socially isolated communities, typified by the migration of those who would otherwise provide supervision and inhibit violence within those communities (Taylor *et al.* 1984;

Sampson & Groves 1989; Sampson & Wilson 1995). The consequence, then, is the emergence of ghettoes, characterised by particular social values such as the glamorisation of violence and encouragement of hyper-masculinity (Schur 1969; Prothrow-Stith 1991; Anderson 1999). Moreover, studies focused on street gangs have also concluded that an individual's association with delinquent peers is the most significant predictor of subsequent gang membership (Hill *et al.* 1999; Brownfield 2006). This gang affiliation is, in turn, a predictor of violence/delinquency in itself (Thornberry 1998; Battin *et al.* 1998). The ages of those associated with such criminality has also received prolonged academic attention. In particular, the theoretical perspective of life-course criminology supports the view that there is a 'core' age-range during which the most criminal activity is committed (Farrington 1986; Wolfgang *et al.* 1987). It is also during this age range that an individual's involvement with gang activity reaches its peak, including heightened levels of violence (Hagedorn 1988). Additionally, witnessing trauma during childhood has been identified as a predictor of gang membership during adolescence. This is especially the case for children brought-up in conflict zones, whose subsequent gang activity is characterised by extreme violence (Balasunderam 2009; Orjuela 2011). This heightened involvement of youths in gang activity leads to the *youth* street gang being delineated as a specific subset of delinquent activity (Lasley 1992; Shelden 2004/2013 – own emphasis). There is now a growing body of research which focuses on the trajectories taken by youth gang members – in particular, involvement by street gang members in organised criminality (see, e.g., Pitts 2008; Densley 2014). Whereas disorganised gangs are characterised by a lack of permanent membership and expressive violence, organised gangs typically contain members who use violence for instrumental means and focus more on pecuniary gain through activities such as drug dealing (see Decker *et al.* 1998).

Street Gangs in England

There has, however, been reluctance from some British academics to use the term 'gang' in relation to *all* groups engaged in delinquent activity. This is primarily because of the belief that gangs require a level of codification and formalisation – both of which are absent from purely delinquent groups. Further reluctance is borne out of the view that referring to gangs adds a degree of glamorisation to what would otherwise be classed as merely anti-social behaviour (Hallsworth & Brotherton 2011; Criminal Justice Joint Inspection 2010). Such concerns are particularly heightened in relation to youth street gangs. There is a wide academic consensus that youth delinquency in twentieth-century Britain was typified by an absence of coherent, organised groupings (Scott 1956; Patrick 1973/2012). Although such groupings did engage in disruptive behaviour, delinquency and violence (Spencer 1964; Patrick 1973/2012), they were predominantly "loosely knit, amorphous gatherings of boys who joined and left at will" (Farrant 1965 in Patrick 1973/2012:143). Downes (1966), for example, presents one extensive study of youth delinquency in 1960s London. Again, the conclusion reached is that such sub-cultures of violence lacked the necessary structuration, organisation and codification to be described as proper gangs. However, contemporary society has witnessed the emergence of far more criminal groupings which are closer to the model of OCGs. This is particularly apparent with gangs which engage in drug dealing (Silverman 1994; Pearson and Hobbs 2001). Moreover, the fluid nature of organised criminality has resulted in such activities affecting society at various levels (Hobbs 2013). The end result, then, is a wider presence of criminal gangs in daily life.

There also exists a fluid, shifting 'boundary' between street gangs and OCGs. For much of the twentieth century, gangs in the U.K. were viewed as purely being part of the youth sub-culture – in relation to fashion and music, for example. However, there have been substantial developments in this regard. For example, Densely (2013) and Harding (2014) have investigated the topic of gang organisation in England, and their research shows that street gangs in the UK are far more organised than previously thought. This has led to street gangs carrying out activities which were previously the preserve of OCGs, and sometimes entering into 'partnerships' which such groups. Moreover, the average age of gang members has extended, so that there are now both younger and older gang members (Densley 2013; Harding 2014). Such changes mean that current governmental/community intervention practices will need to be developed when tackling future gang violence in Britain.

Gang Structures and the Importance of Trust

In addition to literature surrounding the development of gangs, there has been extensive study into how they are structured. This has included a focus on youth street gangs (e.g. Pitts 2008; Densley 2012), the networks through which organised crime groups function (e.g. Gambetta 2009; Prowse 2012), as well as prolonged study into prison gangs (e.g. Fong *et al.* 1996). Further studies have concluded that many gangs place an acute emphasis on the induction of potential gang members (Densely 2012; Duran 2013), and that great importance is placed upon the containment/ transmission of information surrounding the gang's daily activities (Densely 2012). This includes a concern with how information is gathered and disseminated for the purposes of crime commission, as well as an awareness of how evidence of illegal activities is later disposed. With the exception of purely delinquent groupings, such as networks of drug users, a high level of trust *between* members is central to the sustainability of a typical criminal gang (Gambetta 2009; Deuchar 2009- own emphasis).[3] It is partly because of the importance placed on *intra*-gang relationships that social network analysis (SNA) is particularly relevant to the study of gang structuration (see Papchristos et al. Forthcoming). SNA has regularly been deployed as a methodology to investigate gangs, and is seen as a development from the more individualistic perspective of its preceding social theories (Everton 2012). SNA views groups as being composites of their individual members, allowing research to focus on the meso and macro levels, as well as the micro level (Densley 2012; Everton 2012). An analysis of gangs based on SNA concludes that the role of trust is as central to the street gang as it is to OCGs and terrorist networks (Carrington 2011; Prowse 2012). Just as trust is a central component in developing social capital between individuals in a *pro*-social setting (Dasgupta 2010- own emphasis), trust is also essential for individuals who want to progress in *anti*-social groupings.

In fact, it can be argued that unlike legitimate activities - where trust is predicated on notions of personal integrity and internalised, pro-social norms (Dasgupta 2010) – criminal networks are more likely to attract those who are less trustworthy and reliable (Densley 2012). Accordingly, members of 'dark networks' – such as youth street gangs, terrorist groups, and organised crime groups - eschew the usual methods of enforcing trust for more violent alternatives (Hobbs 1995).[4] Everton (2012) conducts a detailed analysis of how these 'dark networks' have evolved, and underscores the centrality of trust in ensuring an illegal group's survival. This is even more apparent in OCGs, where sustainability is dependent upon the recruitment of individuals who are both loyal *and* capable of engaging in violence (Prowse 2012 – own emphasis). Moreover, a gang's structural framework does not remain static throughout time. In fact, changes are precipitated both from within the network, as well as through influences from outside of the network (Snijders *et al.* 2010; Everton 2012). For example, imprisonment may serve to heightened gang activity in some contexts (Knox 2005). Such gangs are then classified as 'alive networks' (Everton 2012), where arrest/imprisonment does not preclude gang activity.

Gang Leaders and Inter-Gang Connections

Not only are there links between gang members themselves, but there are also links between different gangs. This can range from a temporary truces existing amongst rival gangs, to situations where smaller gangs affiliate themselves with their larger counterparts (Sherman 1970; Aldridge 2010). Moreover, it should also be remembered that delinquent peer groups and OCGs often work in unison, especially regarding the supply of drugs (Pitts 2008). This leads to the manifestation of organised criminality at lower levels than academics and authorities usually envisage (Stelfox 2002). Many existing studies not only analyse how these criminal networks are structured, but investigate how these structures can be disrupted (see, e.g., Sageman 2004). Such literature emphasises that police and other law enforcement ought to shape their responses with the structure of gangs in mind. Although a closed network is especially difficult to *penetrate*, it is the more diffuse network formation which poses the most formidable resistance – a structure which is spread out across a wide geographical area (Granovetter 1973; Borgatti *et al.* 2009). Additionally, a network's members being linked by weak ties leads to new information being more regularly shared (Burt 1992; Borgatti *et al.* 2009). However, a network characterised by strong ties can lead to its members being exposed to the same information multiple times (Gambetta 1996). Therefore, although networks comprised of weak links are less durable, they can simultaneously lead to greater efficacy. Consequently, such networks also lead to greater economic advancement for its members, especially in the short term (Gambetta 1996; Dasgupta 2010).

One of the most relevant dimensions of network analysis, in relation to gangs, is the role played by leaders. Traditional street gangs are characterised by loose leadership and an informal, networked structure (Sullivan & Bunker 2007). This can be contrasted to OCGs, which are typified by a more centralised leadership (Sullivan & Bunker 2007). Moreover, certain U.S. prison gangs are structured so as to have a 'chairman' or 'president' with ultimate control over the gang's activities (Camp & Camp 1985; Buentello 1986; Fong *et al.* 1996).[5] An individual's power within such a network is the inevitable corollary of their centrality to the group (Bavelas 1948). However, somewhat paradoxically, removing such key actors does not necessarily have a disruptive effect on the organisation as a whole (Everton 2012). This is especially the case if high levels of trust exist between all of a gang's members.[6] Accordingly, attempting to prevent some gangs from operating requires a more nuanced approach than merely targeting its central figures. Indeed, a network-analysis of gangs can be linked to wider criminological studies of deprived areas. For example, Cureton (2011: 44) argues that the economic decline of African-American locales led to "more and more street corner *social networks* that tuned into criminogenic opportunities… Hustlers, pimps, drug pushers, common street thugs and petty criminals dominated the neighbourhood streets…and street ethics emerged" (own emphasis).

METHODOLOGICAL NOTE

The data contained within this chapter were gathered through conducting interviews with prisoners and street-offenders in a particular area of England. Through carrying-out research in various locales, the research was conducted within Marcus' (1995) framework of a 'multi-sited' ethnography: where there is more than one research-site, and the results collected from various areas are collated when writing-up the findings. In total, one month was spent at the research-sites. Access was formally gained to enter the prison, with staff and prisoners being made aware of the study's aims. As regards the 'street' component of the research, a member of the community acted as a 'gate-keeper' to gang-affected areas; this facilitated conversations with individuals who were knowledgable about the subject-matter.[7] The results, therefore, were gathered from interviews with both gang members and participants who were not gang-affiliated. As regards the former, many of the problems identified in relation to gang members' reluctance to partake in academic research (Thomas 2012), especially within a prison environment (Camp & Camp 1985; Fong & Buentello 1991), were borne out during this research. This was especially true with regard to gang members who were less senior, and those who were approached within a group-setting. Although loyalty prevented some from taking part in interviews, more junior members were also fearful of being labelled a 'grass' [informant]. All of these methodological challenges had to be overcome through developing trust, allaying fears that the research was connected to the police, or would have an adverse effect on the upcoming trials of gang members on remand. These limitations resulted in the study being more dependent on the involvement of certain participants; this is reflected by the overrepresentation of some individuals in the results. A total of 22 individuals were interviewed, and their responses are contained within this Chapter. A qualitative analytical framework was used to interpret the data, and a thematic analysis conducted via the 'bottom up' approach which is most useful when conducting inductive, sociological research (Morrell 2008).

One beneficial aspect of the research was that pilot studies had been carried-out at the same prison and same area in the past: this led to informal social contacts being developed with prisoners and street-offenders, which assisted the research process. This chapter focuses on analysing this firsthand data, primarily collected through formal interviews. These data were supplemented by informal conversations with street-offenders, prisoners and uniformed staff, as well as observations conducted during an ethnographic study of the prison and its surrounding area. Often, the research methodology had to be adapted, taking into account the daily changes which occurred at the research-sites. Indeed, the gulf between theoretical methodological parameters and research practicalities cannot be overstated. For example, research ethics were often viewed as an unnecessary hindrance by many prisoners and some prison officers; the issue of informed consent had to be proactively raised and adhered to by the researcher. Additionally, interviews had to take place on an 'available and willing' basis – with prisoners in the laundry room or workshop, lingering by a cell-door or pool-table, or accompanying prisoner officers during a cigarette-break or lunch. Fieldwork on the streets was an even more complex process, both in relation to safety and ensuring that participants' suspicions could be allayed. Trust had to be developed, and extensive efforts had to be made in order to gather usable data.

RESULTS AND ANALYSIS

After this initial phase of data-collection, the data were manually transcribed, and then subjected to a thematic analysis; this, in-turn, led to the emergence of four principal themes: Territorialism; Familial Background; Loss/Absence of Social Capital; Violence through Weapons. Furthermore, the links between street gangs and OCGs were made apparent in most participants responses.[8] The clearest findings to emerge were that almost all participants had been attracted to gang activity due to the entrenched nature of such groups in their local neighbourhoods. Gang activity was not only seen as a viable alternative to gainful employment in these areas, but such activity was often sanctioned by these communities: by family members, kinship groups and others, all of whom placed a premium on 'representing the area'. Claiming affiliation to geographical region was just one of the alternative set of social norms in which gang members were socialized. Indeed, gang affiliation led to the normalization of a host of 'deviant' norms which were transferred into prison if gang members entered custody. Whether an individual was a street gang member or an OCG member, a symbiotic relationship existed between the wider community and these criminal groupings. Consequently, involvement in criminality was deep-seated, difficult to combat and, at times, inter-generational.

Territorialism

The majority of participants agreed that there was a strong territorial element to gang affiliation within their local area; moreover, these gang-loyalties did not dissolve within prison. Unlike certain prisons (see Phillips 2008), where gangs are formed on the basis of practicality (creating groups which are large enough to exert a palpable influence on the prison environment), gang identities at the sample-sites appeared to be less fluid, with affiliations based on longstanding animosities:

In here, you're either [name of gang] or [name of gang] or you got your group of mates. End of. In other jails it's different. (Asif; prisoner)

Several respondents identified this characteristic, specific to the geographical region where the research was conducted. However, they were unable to provide reasons as to why this was the case, unable to attribute the more durable and tribal nature of gang affiliation at the research-sites. However, a minority of respondents considered street territorialism to have been superseded by the drug-market: that previous loyalties based on one's area had now been supplanted by the primacy of heroin on the streets:

Bill (non-prisoner): Gangs have always boiled down to drugs. When we were 15/16 [years old] the weed started it, but there wasn't as much rivalry; 'cos weed's not 25 quid a piece.
Interviewer: Unlike heroin, you mean?
B: Exactly. Before, you'd be out on the graft [robbing] with your gang, and you'd share it all out. Now, it's all about 'I'm alright Jack'. Before, you stuck together. Now you'll get robbed by the same lads you slept on the sofa with.

In all such discussions, the name of the area's main OCG eventually arose; this was true for both research conducted at the prison, and on the surrounding streets. However, not a single respondent classified the OCG as being a gang. Rather, several 'off-shoot' street gangs were highlighted: these had branched-off from the main OCG, and allied themselves to the crime group. For all members affiliated to this OCG, territorialism played an especially significant role, with one participant stating at the outset: "I'm not from [name of city] – I'm from [name of OCG area]." This entrenched loyalty to area has been identified in the existing criminological literature on English gangs (see, e.g., Fraser 2014), and was apparent throughout the research process. Race was also a pertinent theme when participants discussed their home-areas, and this affected the cultural compositions of criminal groupings:

My area used to have a white line around it...and it was very racist...but with [name of OCG], it's just white lads now. If there are any black lads in my area, I'm mates with them...it's not about colour. I'm from [name of area] first – that's it. (Rob; prisoner)

Somewhat paradoxically, even this staunch loyalty to an OCG's territory was tempered by fragmentation of past structures. For example, Rob[9] spoke of two neighbouring housing estates, which used to operate as part of the same OCG, but were now rivals: "The estates are splitting up now – different ones operate in different ways, and there's problems between 'em". Many participants placed this significant importance on their housing estates and home areas, presented as crucibles of deprivation and conflict. Moreover, the experience of imprisonment was not far removed from one's pre-prison life, including associating with similar groups of people: "You're guaranteed to know someone in here" (Ben; prisoner). This reflected Carroll's (1974:228-229) view that "life in the…ghetto is functional for survival in the walled ghetto of the prison…The adaptiveness of…ghetto subculture to the prison is…evident in the social organisation of prisoners." Although Carroll was referring to African-American ghettoes in the United States, this study's respondents described a similar relationship existing between prison and the streets.

Respondents' attachments to their housing estates were indicative of the rigid, spatial segregation of contemporary society – the socially disadvantaged being left in particular geographic regions which are subsequently characterised by violence and conflict (Rock 2002). Many gangs were named after the areas or streets from which they originated, with geographical conflict being the foundation to the existence of such gangs. It is this concept of place upon which street gangs operate - notions of territory predicate much gang activity and gang violence (Kintrea *et al.* 2008; Deuchar 2009; Fraser 2014). Respondents underscored the importance given to territory, and its central role in gang activity:

Where I grew up, a gang is a group of people, a number of people together…mates going to the park together, to the shops together; different sides, different areas. Gangs have been like that for years: you're a part of the estate, getting shot at, and I got dragged into it. (Sam; Prisoner)

Territorialism, then, was the most appropriate way in which many respondents could articulate what gangs were. Indeed, many participants, both in prison and on the streets, found it difficult to conceptualise what constituted a 'gang'. It was a question which few had been asked, and many participants took time to express their definition of what they considered to be a gang. For prisoners who were not gang-affiliated, the term 'gang' was more associated with youth street gangs and general delinquency: "Just a group of lads hanging about on the street corner at night (Nick; non-prisoner); "Just lads being together on the streets…cos it's the streets that make you" (Karl; non-prisoner).

However, prisoners who were more seriously involved with gangs were able to operationalise the term 'gang' in a way which emphasised its instrumentality:

A gang is a powerful criminal organisation who can get things sorted and get things done. (Steve; prisoner)

Prisoners who were active gang-members/had been gang-affiliated in the past, were able to provide such responses, which comported with previous studies into English gang activity (e.g. Stelfox 2002). This reflected their greater levels of exposure to gangs, which are normally characterised by their 'closed' nature (Everton 2012), especially within prison (Camp and Camp 1985 cited in Wood and Adler 2001:170). Accordingly, it was only through repeated visits to the research-site that a sufficient level of trust could be developed to facilitate detailed answers. Rob's personal narrative provided the clearest example of street gang members 'maturing' into affiliation with an OCG (see case-study at the start of this chapter).

Familial Background

This research also found there to be varying levels of familial involvement across different gangs. Rather than the family-oriented 'clan' structures of the Mafia (Saviano 2006), there was only a sporadic presence of family ties within the gangs which were studied. Although there were a dwindling number of 'crime families', more general gang activity was often devoid of this familial dimension. Indeed, members of the same family were often affiliated to two rival street gangs[10]:

Andrew (prisoner): I'm [Gang A], but my uncles are [Gang B], my aunties are [Gang B]. One of my aunties is currently inside: she was one of the [Gang B] heads – a godmother.
Interviewer: Is she still a godmother?
A: Yeh. She's in jail for [name of offence]. Laughs.
I: But that's surprising to me…that you're quite high-up in [Gang A], and you've got family members in [Gang B]. Doesn't that cause any problems?
A: Nah, nah… It's weird: jail's mad.

I was at dinner with one guy from [Gang A], his mum, and they said that his cousin from [Gang B] had had a hit put out on him – and that it was the other cousin who'd been contracted to carry out the hit. Now, this was on a Sunday…Sunday roast…I mean, Caribbean meal, mothers, churches and then one cousin gets asked to kill another…just 'cos they're from rival gangs. I mean, what can you say to that? (Angelo; non-prisoner)

However, respondents also spoke of both the benefits and detriments of having senior gang members within the family. On the one hand, their seniority could afford a level of protection to other family members living in violent locales:

I'm an older one…one of the bosses…I don't fear no-one; I don't care. Like, my younger brother's on the outside, but no-one would even touch my brother. (Andrew; prisoner)

Equally, however, the dangers involved in gang-activity could also affect family members, leading to precautionary measures having to be taken:

My mum won't move from the estate; so while I'm in here, I've got my boys [gang members] circling her house everyday like they was CIA. (Patrick; prisoner)

A further significant finding was regarding the role of fathers: that a father's absence played a crucial role in individuals being introduced to delinquent behavior. The father's position within a nuclear family is often described as being 'instrumental', occupying a relatively powerful position as compared to other family members (Parson and Bales 1955; Elmer 2008; Cureton 2011:39). Moreover, an absence of the father from daily life is a feature often identified in delinquency literature, referred to as a 'father deficit' which leads to 'father hunger' (Katz *et al.* 1999; Kruk 2008; Glynn 2011). Participants generally agreed that father absenteeism was seen as leaving a gap with street gangs could subsequently exploit:

If your Dad's a wrong 'un [bad person] and you're a weakling, you're obviously gonna be a target for these gangs. (Bill; non-prisoner)

After mum and dad split-up, the only way I could see Dad was by going to the pub. So I started going to the pub, to borrow money off him. And all the other young lads in the pub, outside the pub, we were all there to visit our dads. So I started hanging round with them, and we influenced each other. If me dad was around, I could have been properly disciplined. (Bradley; non-prisoner)

On the other hand, certain migrant-communities contained far more of a familial element, reflective of the kinship networks which are 'imported' by crime groups from specific countries (Hobbs 2013):

My dad showed me how to work out if a house was good enough to knock [rob]. I'd go out with him, and then we'd share it out; he'd be talking to them at the front door, and I'd creep in through the back. You see, you've always got family backup, but you also hold a grudge for generations. If there wasn't so many grudges, then we'd be one hell of a fucking gang. (Kevin; prisoner)

Kevin's response was a rare example of deep familial gang involvement, mirroring the structuration of Italian crime families (Saviano 2006) and the intergenerational component of some Glaswegian gangs (Deuchar 2009). Generally, however, familial involvement was shown to be not as extensive. For many participants, family was superseded by loyalties to gang areas and other factors which were taken into consideration:

When I was a kid, all the different families fought. Me dad was away all the time, and two of me older brothers were with [a gang], but I didn't join 'em – nah. For me it was more about areas, football teams. You had separate gyms depending on which area you were from. And if anyone caught you wearing a different team's football shirt, you got levelled (attacked). (Bill; non-prisoner)

Each respondent, then, placed a different degree of importance upon the family in relation to gang activity. This divergence in responses reflects Thrasher's (1927) assessment that family influence varies from one gang to another: whereas family bonds were central to the certain American gangs of the early twentieth-century, there was a marked absence of family involvement in other gangland groups. A similar situation was apparent amongst the gangs studied for this research.

Loss/Absence of Social Capital

This study's participants were invariably from areas where there was a lack of social capital, and an absence of pro-social communities. Gang affiliation, then, was identified as providing gang members with a collective identity, something displaced in Western societies during the period of modernity (Jacques 2009). As well as the instrumental role gangs played – through providing financial benefits to members – gangs also served a more expressive, symbolic purpose:

Gangs give you a cause - it's something to be a part of. Even in here you've got loads of weak people, little people. But then you got the gang, with their 'generals' and their 'privates'. There's a pull to it. (Bradley; non-prisoner)

If I went to a local pub I would immediately sense an atmosphere change and sense people trying to be nice towards me and stay on my good side. We was the elite! (James; prisoner)

Street gangs were also viewed as exploiting the lack of purpose felt by many disadvantaged youths. In particular, gang leaders were seen as deceiving younger gang members by not informing them of the realities of gang-life[11]:

To be honest, I blame a lot of it on the rap culture - for glamourising it. It's a power thing. I was just laying out a chessboard, and it's got me thinking: the youngsters are like the pawns – they're completely expendable. (Phil; prisoner)

Because of the environment some participants were brought up in, gangs were able to "pull" them in, as Bradley stated. For example, father absenteeism and the involvement of parents in delinquent activities have been identified as principle features of 'street families' (Anderson 1999). Such families are denoted by their social disorganisation, self-destructive behaviour and an inability to inculcate pro-social values in their children (Wilson 1996; Anderson 1999). Furthermore, gang members' home areas were inevitable socially and economically deprived, reflecting theoretical references to 'the ghetto' in existing academic literature (e.g. Anderson 1999; Wacquant 1998). Prisoners' socio-economic backgrounds, then, were reflective of the class divisions and economic inequalities in contemporary England. Consequently, the absence of social capital left a void which street gangs sought to fill, focusing on establishing one's 'name' and 'rep':

It's about making a profit, and making your name. (Martin; non-prisoner)

You'll have a leader of [name of gang] with 10 kids by 10 different women, in 10 different cities. And he talks about passing his name onto his kids. Cos his baby-mothers' names mean nothin', you know? (Angelo; non-prisoner)

A further point worthy of mention is the role of social capital in relation to gangs. Social capital is one characteristic of economically prosperous areas, whose residents benefit from its presence (Putnam 1997). As a concept, it refers to the benefits individuals can receive through informal social networks, organisations and the accumulation of trust (Putnam 2000; Dasgupta 2005). Crucial to this concept is the pro-social disposition of such networks (Dasgupta 2005). However, respondents in this study felt an acute sense of being far removed from these pro-social parts of society. In effect, gang affiliation was viewed as offering an alternative path to progress through society. Materialism was seen as being an integral part of such progress, and gang activity was held as providing the only means to achieve such material goods. From this perspective, gangs served an instrumental purpose, by allowing members to accumulate money:

I was an entrepreneur. I could sell on that estate, stood at the back. I'd rob the cider trucks, sell clothes, swap things. It was more about the money than the gangs. You start at the bottom. You're living in a shithole, looking up to the bigman who's rolling about in a Mercedes and you think to yourself, 'I want some of that'. (Bill; non-prisoner)

People around me had nice trainers, what I didn't have. The older lads had nice cars, girls, you see it all on Facebook now, don't you? It's the pull of money. (Bradley; non-prisoner)

Delinquent groupings were presented as alternatives to pro-social networks, allowing the individual a means to get "what I didn't have" (Bradley). Gangs were also able to capitalise on the absence of positive social capital in certain areas. In essence, formal state organisations are expected to provide goods and services to the general public (Wacquant 1998). Through the provision of such facilities, trust is built with the mass population, creating 'state social capital' (*ibid*). In the alternative, a lack of services such as adequate education, housing and healthcare can lead to the erosion of trust between the public and government. Wacquant (1998:25) terms this as 'negative social capital', disproportionately affecting society's most marginalised citizens. This study's participants presented myriad examples of the state 'retreating' from their areas, which led to a state of lawlessness:

My area was notorious. The taxis wouldn't go there, the buses wouldn't either. If you got caught in a rival estate, even the police wouldn't go in. So eventually it becomes you against them...you versus the police. Even the local chippy had its counter covered in metal guards, and just a little hatch to get your chips. So that's what I grew up in, you know? (Phil; prisoner)

Where I grew-up, it was such a mad estate that even the police would stay away...they wouldn't come in without back-up, if at all. (Rob; prisoner)

An abandonment by the state leads to feelings of social disenfranchisement, whereby individuals believe they have no stake in collective society (Morell *et al.* 2011); this perception is often heightened in the value-obsessed culture of the contemporary societies (Bauman 2000; Winlow & Hall 2006). In such times, more emphasis is placed upon the end results of activities rather than the means through which these results are pursued (Bauman 2000). For some gangs, the pecuniary gain – and subsequent benefits which result from this – are of the upmost importance (Venkatesh 2008). This was reflected at the research-sites, where benefits ranged from being able to "blow £8,000 on a night out" (Rob; prisoner) and "live a jet-set lifestyle through the drug culture" (Steve; prisoner), to more inconspicuous benefits, such as the ability to pay for private legal representation:

My lawyer's all sorted; I don't got to worry about legal aid...if you got a legal aid lawyer, you're gonna get a legal aid sentence. (Patrick; prisoner)

It was also clear that for many participants, gang activity proved a means of escaping areas which were characterised by negative social capital: "I'm out of the estate now. The only reason I go to the estate is to visit my mum" (Owen; prisoner). The inability to escape economically deprived situations has also been linked to psychological problems (Bhui *et al.* 2014), and participants spoke of the sense of hopeless arising from such areas: "Where I grew up, you were set up to fail" (Sam; prisoner). More-over, accentuated levels of negative social capital were predicted as having the potential to significantly worsen gang activity:

Now they [the government] start cutting benefits: no crisis loans, no budgeting loans, discharge grant's gone down, cutbacks in housing. Soon, gangs won't be stealing to feed drug habits, they'll be stealing food. It'll be us against the police – riots everywhere. It'll go off big time, mate. (Phil; prisoner)

The Use of Weapons

In addition to the financial dimensions of gang activity, violence – and in particular the use of weapons – played a substantial role in 'gang life'. The preponderance of weapon usage by prison gang members was noticeable, reflecting the elevated levels of assaults carried out by such individuals in prison (Wood 2006; Wood & Adler 2001). Andrew was a senior member of 'Gang A' and spoke of his weapon usage as being a normal part of prison life:

When I was in [name of prison], I was shanked-up [carrying a knife] anyway, so if you step-up to me in a cell, I'm ready to go – it's on, you gets me? I'm a big lad, so if wanna take me on, you take me on...I'm shanked-up. Laughs. (Andrew; prisoner)

Similar statements were delivered by other gang/OCG members, especially those who were involved at a more senior level:

I won't take no shit from anyone...if someone's got a problem with me, we'll do it one-on-one, and I'll slash their face open there and then. (James; prisoner)

During my last sentence I was in [name of prison], where you need to make yourself a weapon, and you're walking on egg shells. It's more serious, 'cos you have a lot of gang members, and you'd have magazines like FHM, Loaded all taped onto chest as a stab-proof vest. (Steve; prisoner)

For prison gang members, weapon-usage was part of a wider pattern of violent behaviour. For example, gang-affiliated prisoners spoke more openly about wishing to assault prison staff, and had a higher rate of carrying-out such assaults when compared to non-gang members (fieldnotes). Interviews with prison gang members also revealed their heightened-levels of weapon usage outside of prison; and the continued presence of weapons in their lives, as well as in the lives of their peers:

Like, say if my mate gets shot, then I'm gonna shoot whoever shot him, and it goes on...gettin' shot at was a regular thing. (Ricky; prisoner)

Firearms were also seen as being part of the wider 'gang scene', with many prisoners associating gun-crime with younger gang-members:

Fighting's redundant now, it's all about the guns. And it's the young ones who are mad...cos it's easy to get a gun. And now with all the people trafficking...if I was one of them, I'd just tell my man that I'm smugglin' into the country to put a gun in his pocket. (Patrick; prisoner)

And it's worse now, 'cos the kids have got guns. You've got your gangsters in your cars, and the young ones on their pushbikes, with guns. All the shit's put on the foot soldiers. (Bill; non-prisoner)

In general, gang members were explicit in their recollections of shootings and the role of firearms in their pre-prison lives. For example, one participant recalled that guns played a key role in all of this crimes, since "we was doing high level crime: cash in transit, armed robbery, drug dealer robberies. A [particular] shooting made me realise this was getting progressively worse"; James, prisoner). Such statements corroborated existing research, which highlights the heightened role of firearm usage, in England, in the 1990s/2000s (Bullock & Tilley 2002; Howell 2012; Heale 2008; Walsh 2003). However, some prison gang members disagreed with the prevailing narrative, arguing that "the fear of getting shot at has died down now; it's gone down" (Leon; prisoner). One gang member explained that the reason for this in the following terms:

Patrick (prisoner): *It's not a problem now like it was...10, maybe 15 years ago. You compare the numbers of shootings you used to see 15 years ago to now...and there's a big difference.*
I: *And why is that?*
P: *Cos, first of all, a lot of them [the gang members] are dead. A lot are locked up...on the 15th year of a 28 year sentence. And the police do a lot of surveillance now; it's like Big Brother.*

Overall, however, this study's results showed that weapon-usage was not the sole preserve of gang members. This finding is consistent with previous research on this subject, which identifies the high numbers of weapons in certain deprived communities (see, e.g., Anderson 1999; Taylor 1993; Hobbs 1995; Winlow & Hall 2006: 132-133). Accordingly, the use of weapons was a common occurrence on the streets where much of the fieldwork was conducted for this research. For example, when one participant spoke of attempting to stop an acquaintance from returning to crime, he stated: "I had to confront him as he was bagging up [the drugs], pistol on his table, ready to go" (Paul; non-prisoner). Another participant, who was also not affiliated to any gang, spoke of "holding onto a knife for weeks, hoping to do in [attack] the guy who'd killed my brother" (James; non-prisoner). Such responses illustrated that weapons were merely seen as one component of criminal activity, and were not remarkable in the areas from which participants originated. Moreover, both gang members and non-gang members utilised weapons for self-defense, as well as for settling disputes.

CONCLUSION

This study's data illustrate the prolific criminal 'careers' of the gang and OCG members who were interviewed. For example, the chapter began with Rob's personal narrative, showing a progression from street gang to OCG, with his being 'recruited' to the OCG for being a particularly violent street gang member. Furthermore, whereas some participants saw gang membership in mainly social terms, others viewed it as serving more instrumental purposes. For some respondents, the use of weapons and force was also instrumental, whereas for others, this violence was primarily expressive. In almost all such cases, however, high levels of violence had been normalised within their communities. This included heightened levels of weapon usage by gang members – both within and outside prison. Subsequent gang structures were entrenched in these locales, usually sustained by fictive kinship networks, sometimes by actual family ties. The results obtained also showed that gangs were a strong force within the prison which acted as one of the research sites. Indeed, loose gang structures were readily imported from the streets into the prison. Although the area's OCGs were somewhat more formalised, there was still the lack of rigid, hierarchical groups one might expect when studying this area of crime. However, this did not lead to gang violence being any less serious and severe. Indeed, it is worth noting that such behavioural norms were not limited to gang members, who had often been brought up in similar environments to individuals who eventually pursued criminal 'careers' outside the fold of gang membership. Accordingly, just as the 'boundary' between gangs and OCGs was often unclear, so too were there overlaps between the experiences of prison gang members and other prisoners.

Overall, this study also illustrated that there were many reasons which drove individuals to join gangs. For some participants, there was the hope that gang-affiliation would provide a durable sense of identity. Criminological literature has long identified this importance of collective identity, often facilitated through delinquent sub-cultures such as the street-gang (Cohen 1955). In this research, participants formulated such identities through referring to their 'area' or 'estate', which were often synonymous with their street gang or OCG. However, most gang activity was conducted to acquire financial/material benefits: drugs, wealth, as well as status. Some gang members spoke of pecuniary interests alone, highlighting the pivotal role commerce plays in much of contemporary gang activity (Levitt & Dunbar 2005; Venkatesh 2008; Pitts 2008). However, some gang members also spoke of the 'gaps' in their earlier lives that gangs sought to 'fill': an absence of fathers, for example. For these individuals, there were deeper factors behind gang affiliation, reflecting the personal insecurity individuals often feel in modern society (Giddens 1991; Young 2001): the need to belong to a 'family' of some sort; and using the gang to provide a narrative to an individual's life. It is due to such phenomenological reasons – as well as structural and economic factors – that gang violence continues to be a serious problem within certain parts of British society.

REFERENCES

Anderson, E. (1999). *Code of the Street: Violence and the Moral Life of the Inner City*. W. W. Norton & Co.

Barker, T. (2014). *Outlaw Motorcycle Gangs as Organized Crime Groups*. Springer. doi:10.1007/978-3-319-07431-3

Bauman, Z. (2000). *Liquid Modernity*. Cambridge, MA: Polity Press.

Bhui, K., Warfa, N., & Jones, E. (2014) *Is Violent Radicalisation Associated with Poverty, Migration, Poor Self-Reported Health and Common Mental Disorders?* Retrieved 12 October 2014 from: http://www.plosone.org/article/info%3Adoi%2F10.1371%2Fjournal.pone.0090718

Bouchard, M., & Spindler, A. (2010). Groups, gangs, and delinquency: Does organization matter? *Journal of Criminal Justice*, *38*(5), 921–933. doi:10.1016/j.jcrimjus.2010.06.009

Bullock, K., & Tilley, N. (2002). *Shooting, gangs and violent incidents in Manchester: Developing a crime reduction strategy*. London: Home Office.

Camp, G. M., & Camp, C. G. (1985). *Prison Gangs: Their Extent, Nature and Impact on Prisons. US Dept. of Justice*. Washington, DC: US Govt. Printing Office.

Carrington, P. J. (2011). Crime and Social Network Analysis. In J. Scott & P. J. Carrington (Eds.), *The SAGE Handbook of Network Analysis*. Los Angeles, CA: SAGE Publications Inc. doi:10.4135/9781446294413.n17

Carroll, L. (1974). *Hacks, Blacks and Cons: Race Relations in a Maximum Security Prison*. Waveland Press, Inc.

Centre for Social Justice. (2012). *Time to Wake Up: Tackling gangs one year after the riots*. Retrieved 11 October 2014 from: http://www.centreforsocialjustice.org.uk/UserStorage/pdf/Pdf%20reports/Gangs-Report.pdf

Cohen, A. K. (1955). *Delinquent Boys: The Culture of the Gang*. New York: The Free Press.

Cureton, S. R. (2011). *Black Vanguards to Black Gangsters: From Seeds of Discontent to a Declaration of War*. University Press of America.

Dasgupta, P. (2010). *A Matter of Trust: Social Capital and Economic Development*. SCI Discussion Paper Series. Manchester, UK: Sustainable Consumption Institute; Working Paper No. 1.

Decker, S., Bynum, T., & Weisel, D. (1998). "A Tale of Two Cities": Gangs as Organized Crime Groups. *Justice Quarterly*, *15*(3), 395–425. doi:10.1080/07418829800093821

Densely, J. A. (2014). It's gang life, but not as we know it: The evolution of gang business. *Crime and Delinquency*, *60*(4), 517–546. doi:10.1177/0011128712437912

Densley, J. A. (2012). Street Gang Recruitment: Signalling, Screening, and Selection. *Social Problems*, *59*(3), 301–321. doi:10.1525/sp.2012.59.3.301

Densley, J. A. (2013). *How Gangs Work: An Ethnography of Youth Violence*. Palgrave. doi:10.1057/9781137271518

Deuchar, R. (2009). *Gangs, Marginalised Youth and Social Capital*. Trentham Books.

Duran, R. J. (2013). *Gang Life in Two Cities: An Insider's Journey*. Columbia University Press.

Everton, S. F. (2012). *Disrupting Dark Networks (Structural Analysis in the Social Sciences)*. Cambridge University Press. doi:10.1017/CBO9781139136877

Fagin, J. (1989). The social organization of drug use and drug dealing among urban gangs. *Criminology*, *27*(4), 633–669. doi:10.1111/j.1745-9125.1989.tb01049.x

Fong, R. S., & Buentello, S. (1991). The detection of prison gang development: An empirical assessment. *Federal Probation*, *55*, 66–69.

Fong, R. S., Vogel, R. E., & Buentello, S. (1996). Prison Gang Dynamics: A Research Update. In Gangs: A Criminal Justice Approach. Anderson Publishing Co. and Academy of Criminal Justice Sciences.

Giddens, A. (1991). *Modernity and Self-Identity: Self and Society in the Late Modern Age*. Stanford University Press.

Glynn, M. (2011). *Dad and me - Research into the problems caused by absent fathers*. Retrieved 18 April 2013 from: http://www.addaction.org.uk/news.asp?section=80&itemid=735&search

Harding, S. (2014). *The Street Casino: Survival in Violent Street Gangs*. Policy Press. doi:10.1332/policypress/9781447317173.001.0001

Hememway, D. (2004). *Private Guns, Public Health*. University of Michigan Press.

Hobbs, D. (1995). *Bad Business - Professional Crime in Modern Britain*. Oxford University Press.

Hobbs, D. (2013). *Lush Life: Constructing Organized Crime in the UK*. Clarendon Studies in Criminology. doi:10.1093/acprof:oso/9780199668281.001.0001

Home Office. (2011). *Ending Gang and Youth Violence: A Cross-Government Report, including further evidence and good practice case studies*. London: Home Office.

Howell, J. C. (2012). *Gangs in America's Communities*. SAGE Publications Inc.

Jacques, M. (2009). *When China Rules the World*. Penguin Books.

Kahn, B. (1978). *Prison gangs in the community: a briefing document for the California Board of Corrections*. Academic Press.

Kantor, D., & Bennett, W. I. (1968). Orientation of Street-Corner Workers and Their Effects of Gangs. In S. Wheeler (Ed.), *Controlling Delinquents*. New York: Wiley.

Kintrea, K., Bannister, J., Pickering, J., Suruki, N., & Reid, M. (2008). *Young People and Territoriality in British Cities*. York, UK: Joseph Rowntree Foundation.

Klein, M. W. (1971). *Street gangs and street workers*. Englewood Cliffs, NJ: Prentice Hall.

Klein, M. W., Maxson, C. L., & Cunningham, L. C. (1991). "Crack," street gangs, and violence. *Criminology*, 29(4), 623–650. doi:10.1111/j.1745-9125.1991.tb01082.x

Knox, G. W. (2005). *The Problem of Gangs and Security Threat Groups (STG's) in American Prisons Today: Recent Research Findings from the 2004 Prison Gang Survey. National Gang Crime Research Center Ministry of Justice Research Series 2/11. March 2011. Understanding the psychology of gang violence: Implications for designing effective violence interventions*. London: Ministry of Justice.

Morell, G., Scott, S., McNeish, D., & Webster, S. (2011). *The August Riots in England: Understanding the Involvement of Young People. A Cabinet Commissioned Report*. London: NatCen.

Morrell, E. (2008). Six Summer of YPAR. In J. Cammarota & M. Fine (Eds.), *Revolutionizing Education: Youth Participatory Action Research in Motion*. Routledge.

Newburn, T. (2011). *Reading the Riots: Investigating England's Summer of Disorder*. Retrieved 12 October 2014 from: http://www.guardian.co.uk/uk/2011/dec/05/anger-police-fuelled-riots-study

Papachristos, A. V., Braga, A., & Hureau, D. (Forthcoming). Social Networks and the Risk of Gunshot Injury. *Journal of Urban Health*. PMID:22714704

Patrick, J. (1973/2012). *A Glasgow Gang Observed*. Neil Wilson Publishing.

Pearson, G. (2012). *An ethnography of English football fans: Cans, cops and carnivals*. Manchester University Press. doi:10.7228/manchester/9780719087219.001.0001

Pearson, G., & Hobbs, D. (2001). *Middle Market Drug Distribution. Home Office Research (Study 227), Development and Statistics Directorate.* London: Home Office.

Phillips, C. (2008). Negotiating identities: Ethnicity and social relations in a young offenders' institution. *Theoretical Criminology, 12*(3), 313–331. doi:10.1177/1362480608093309

Pitts, J. (2008). *Reluctant Gangsters - The Changing Face of Youth Crime.* Willan Publishing.

Prowse, C. E. (2012). *Defining Street Gangs in the 21ˢᵗ Century: Fluid, Mobile and Transitional Networks.* Springer.

Putnam, R. D. (1995). *Bowling Alone: The Collapse and Revival of American Community.* Simon and Schuster Ltd.

Rock, P. (2002). Social Theories of Crime. In M. Maguire, R. Morgan, & R. Reiner (Eds.), *The Oxford Handbook of Criminology* (3rd ed.). Oxford University Press.

Saviano, R. (2006). *Gomorrah* (V. Jewiss, Trans.). MacMillan Publishers.

Shelden, R. G., Tracy, S. K., & Brown, W. B. (2013). *Youth Gangs in American Society* (4th ed.). Wadsworth Publishing. (Original work published 2004)

Stelfox, P. (1998). Policing Lower Levels of Crime in England and Wales. *Howard Journal of Criminal Justice, 37*(4), 393–406. doi:10.1111/1468-2311.00108

Taylor, C. S. (1993). *Girls, Gangs and Drugs.* Michigan State University Press.

Thomas, S. (2012). Revisiting Brixton: The War on Babylon 1981. In D. Briggs (Ed.), *The English Riots of 2011: A Summer of Discontent.* Waterside Press.

Thrasher, F. M. (1927). *The Gang.* Chicago: The University of Chicago Press.

Venkatesh, S. A. (2008). *Gang Leader for a Day: A Rogue Sociologist Takes to the Streets.* Penguin Press HC.

Wacquant, L. (1998). Negative social capital: State breakdown and social destitution in America's urban core. *Netherlands Journal of Housing and the Built Environment., 13*(1), 25–40. doi:10.1007/BF02496932

Walsh, P. (2003). *Gang War: The Inside Story of Manchester's Gangs.* Milo Books.

Williams, J., Dunning, E., & Murphy, P. (1989). *Hooligans Abroad* (2nd ed.). Routledge.

Wilson, J. M., & Chermak, S. (2011). Community-driven violence reduction programs: Examining Pittsburgh's One Vision One Life. *Criminology & Public Policy, 10*(4), 993–1027. doi:10.1111/j.1745-9133.2011.00763.x

Wilson, W. J. (1987). *The Truly Disadvantaged: The Inner City, the Underclass and Public Policy.* Chicago: University of Chicago Press.

Wilson, W. J. (1996). *When Work Disappears: The World of the New Urban Poor.* Knopf.

Winlow, S., & Hall, S. (2006). *Violent Night: Urban Leisure and Contemporary Culture.* Berg.

Wood, J. (2006). Gang Activity in English Prisons: The Prisoners' Perspective. *Psychology, Crime & Law*, *12*(6), 605–617. doi:10.1080/10683160500337667

Wood, J., & Alder, J. (2001). Gang activity in English prisons: The staff perspective. *Psychology, Crime & Law*, *7*(1), 167–192. doi:10.1080/10683160108401793

Yablonsky, L. (1997). *Gangsters: Fifty Years of Madness, Drugs and Death on the Streets of America*. New York University Press.

Young, J. (1999). *The Exclusive Society: Social Exclusion, Crime and Difference in Late Modernity*. SAGE Publications.

ENDNOTES

[1]   To preserve the anonymity of participants in this chapter, all individuals are referred to by pseudonyms. Both case studies are composed of testimonies gathered from prisoners serving sentences at the prison which acted as one of the study's research-sites.

[2]   Many studies describe organised criminality as being formed of 'organised crime gangs' or 'organised crime syndicates'. However, for consistency, the term 'organised crime group' (or 'OCG') is used throughout this chapter.

[3]   This trust amongst gang members can be contrasted with the lack of trust many gangs feel towards the wider community, often borne out of social distance from these communities (Putnam 2000; Deuchar 2009).

[4]   Dasgupta (2010:11-12) identifies a range of 'pro-social dispositions' which ensure that individuals in daily society do not renege on promises. Examples include "shunning people who break agreements" so that an individual "feels shame or guilt in violating the norm, and this prevents her from doing so." This can be directly contrasted with criminal networks, where individuals keep to their end of the bargain *not* due to a fear of being shamed or shunned, but due to a fear of violent repercussions (Hobbs 1995; Gambetta 2009).

[5]   Fong *et al.* (1996) identify two American prison gangs (the Texas Syndicate and the Mexican Mafia) as operating along such lines, whereby the gang leader has supreme primacy over its more junior and subordinate members.

[6]   Just as trust in conventional societies can be attributed to a range of structural and cultural factors (Karstedt 2001), its development within criminal gangs is also a nuanced process. In particular, it is affected by concerns around the credibility and motives of individuals professing to be trustworthy (Gambetta 2009).

[7]   See Anderson (1978) and Whyte (1943) for further examples of 'gate-keepers' being successfully used by criminology researchers.

[8]   To distinguish between participants who were prisoners and those who were not in prison, the term 'prisoner' and 'non-prisoner' accompany each pseudonym.

[9]   Rob was a member of the area's main OCG (see case study at the start of this chapter).

[10]   For ease of reference, these two gangs are referred to as 'Gang A' and 'Gang B' in the following section.

[11]   Interestingly, the majority of gang leaders interviewed did not mention this piece of information, most likely because they were the ones doing the exploiting. Indeed, it was non-gang affiliated prisoners who spoke most candidly on this topic. Only one OCG leader mentioned the following: "I would usually select/recruit people I knew and eager youngsters who I deemed as potential [sic]. Then a whole period would commence like a grooming stage…I would take them out a lot, mentor them, impress them…I would like to see them commit a crime so I could see how they coped, executed it, reacted. I'd also use red herrings and spies to see if they was talking about what they had done or heard" (James; prisoner). He went on to state that junior gang members would be used for "leg work, drop offs, pick-ups, [anything involving] unnecessary riskiness" (*ibid*).

Chapter 11
An Exploratory Study of Prison Gangs in Contemporary Society

Dev Rup Maitra
University of Cambridge, UK

ABSTRACT

This chapter investigates the composition of prison gangs, their effects on the prison environment, and their relationships with street gangs. Through conducting an ethnographic study of an adult men's prison in England, the chapter attempts to articulate the experiences of prison gang members, as well as prisoners exposed to high levels of gang activity. The results illustrate the established role gangs play within English prisons, but also the relevance of other groups, collectives and "sets" within the penal environment. Through analysing the gathered data, I aim to show the important - but not defining - role gangs play within an English prison. Moreover, when compared to the American prison system, gangs are far less entrenched in English prisons; this can partly be attributed to the deeper historical roots of American prison gangs, as well as their highly racialized dimensions. The chapter begins with two case-studies, the subjects of which are prisoners from the research site.

CASE STUDIES

1. Zain[1] : "I'm Not in a Gang – I'm a Businessman"

Zain is serving a custodial sentence for a gang-related crime, but does not self-identify as being a gang member. Rather he describes himself as being "a businessman". He does not describe his criminal history in any great length, characterising his 'drift' into criminality in the following terms: "Gangs are all about postcodes – areas; I got dragged into it. Actually, I started off legitimate, doing good things - just chilling out, playing football and stuff. But then I was like hanging around with 32 year olds when I was 24…and then in [name of area] you've got some racist police officers, so that pushes you towards it [crime]." As well as the influence of these older peers, Zain attributes a wider family role to crime commission, stating that "once you're out and about, you end up getting to know who's who [in the criminal world]…your cousins and whatever else". After getting "out and about", Zain became established with

DOI: 10.4018/978-1-4666-9938-0.ch011

the criminal groups who operated in his area, and these bonds continue to strongly exist in prison: "Me and my family moved to [name of area] when I was a teenager…so when I'm on [name of wing], it's chilled out, 'cos it's all the lads are from [name of area] and we're all equal." Whilst Zain is adamant that "there aren't no gangs in here" he conceded that in the prison "there's just three sets of lads", and goes on to identify each of these "sets" by racial group.

Although Zain only briefly mentions the crime he is in prison for, it is clear that his street loyalties applied in prison from the very beginning of his custodial sentence: "When I was on [name of prison wing], our group was made up of about 35/40…lads. But we stuck together. So if any dickhead comes out, we sort it out. Later, us lads got with [name of gang]. Then a couple of racists come onto our wing. They soon got filled in [attacked], and it was sorted out." However, Zain has never self-identified as a gang member, stating that he is "more of a businessman. You see, when you say gang, I think hand signs, red bandanas, dogs. We didn't have none of that". Accordingly, even though his own crime was classed by the Courts as being gang-related, he blames this on the media, who "talk rubbish", and "don't know what goes on…They get it all wrong." He laughs at the offences he has been convicted of and adamantly states, "I'm not in no gang!" Zain also does not appear to be focused on his past or future, instead, directing most of his attention towards his time in custody. His "group of mates" from the streets ensures that he is not victimized by other prison gangs, who "know who's vulnerable" and who "sniff you out" if your enter prison knowing no-one: "They'll be waiting at the gates…that's jail life".

2. Martin: "The Old Gangsters Had Time for You"

Martin is older than most of his fellow prisoners, and has been in prison many times. Although not a gang member himself, he has associated with several 'gangsters' both in prison, as well as on the streets. For example, he grew up on the same council estate as one prominent gang-leader and says: "I grew up with [name of gang leader] and he was a decent fella; went to borstal with him an' all. I've never got no trouble from him. If you're good to him he looks after you". Maintaining informal, social connections with 'old school' criminals have helped Martin during his various sentences. Moreover, he realizes that there are particular ways to behave in order to make one's time in prison easier: "There's an easy way to do prison, and a hard way to do prison; and respect's a two way street – if you want the officers to treat you with respect, you gotta show them respect. The gang members of today don't show that".

Martin has never been gang affiliated, and his offence history illustrates that he has almost exclusively operated as a 'lone offender'. When asked why he never joined a gang, Martin pauses, and replies that he was "too busy playing sports and stuff. Plus, none of my family was ever involved in gangs". In spite of this, he believes that gangs have profoundly changed over the past decades, and explains these changes in the following terms:

In the '80s, you had groups of fellas – the old gangs. They owned their own businesses, but they didn't agree with burglaries and stuff. They was respected as gangs, you know? They got collateral and families got looked after…But in the last 15 or 20 years it's become all about the drugs and guns. Look, the gangs have morphed into different things…a lot of it is to do with drugs. In the '80s, I'd never even heard of heroin and crack cocaine.

Due to his age, Martin may be romanticizing some details about the past. However, the changes he describes are corroborated by other prisoners and prison officers. In particular, Martin emphasizes that "the trouble's never ending" with younger gang members. He further highlights how street problems permeate into the prison, where "it's all about drugs, fights [and] grassing." In particular, he identifies two street gangs that operate in his current prison, and highlights the link between drugs and gang activity:

You can't have [name of gang] and [name of gang] on the same wings – they'll kick off... [the] officers know of it, and they keep 'em separate. Otherwise they'll fight. Now you got dealers in prison...certain groups control the wing – muscles and distribution. Years ago, if you had trouble you sorted it out with your fists. Now, the young ones from [names of gangs] are all about knives, drugs and guns.

In summary, Martin outlines his belief that "people latch onto the gangs now, but it's just kids running around with guns – they've changed how they operate." As regards prison gangs of the past, he simply states the following: "Even though they're all retired now, they're still handy [violent]. They could do you some damage inside here, or get it done to you...the old gangsters had time for you."

INTRODUCTION

Gang members in English prisons have been identified as being responsible for elevated levels of prison disturbances, violence and rule violations (Wood & Adler 2001, Wood 2006); their presence also leads to non-gang-affiliated prisoners being subjected to increased rates of bullying (Wood et al. 2009). Moreover, American prison gang members commit a disproportionate number of in-prison offences (Camp & Camp 1985; Pollock 2005; Trulson & Marquant 2009), although such offences are predominantly not gang related (Trulson & Marquant 2009). These facts notwithstanding, there has seldom been an agreed definition of what constitutes a prison gang. In part, this can be attributed to the contested notion of gangs in wider society (Pitts 2008; Hallsworth and Silverstone 2009), many of which are imported into the penal environment (Jacobs 1977). Such definitional problems are also apparent within prisons themselves, affecting operational responses. For example, prison authorities often struggle to differentiate between collective of prisoners that are friendship groups rather than gangs. This, in turn, affects prisons' operational responses to combating gang activity. More recently, the role of religion has also become a prominent feature of many prison gangs (Hamm 2007; Earle & Phillips 2013); this adds a further dimension to their study, and their effects on the penal environment.

THE CHANGING ROLE OF PRISON GANGS

Accordingly, the changing role of contemporary prison gangs is an area of study that requires investigation. In order to explore some of these issues, this chapter analyses qualitative data which were collected within an adult-male prison in England, and then subjected to thematic analysis. The results illustrate the established role gangs play within English prisons, but also the relevance of other 'cliques', collectives, groups and 'sets' within the penal environment. Through analysing the gathered data, I aim to show the important - but not defining - role gangs play within an English prison. Many of these prisoner groupings are imported from the streets, but racial, religious and cultural identities also affect associations. Accordingly, I also aim to illustrate how the interplay between race and religion has led to some established 'prison hierarchies' of the past being displaced: rather than the previous situation of white, organised criminals invariably securing dominance on prison wings (Hobbs 2013), the situation in English prisons now is more nuanced (Liebling 2011). Such phenomena are particularly apparent within long-term custodial settings (Liebling 2011), where increasing numbers of prisoners are converting to Islam (Liebling 2011) . In such instances, prisoner identity can be seen as being formed through the 'deprivations' of imprisonment, a concept first articulated by Sykes (1958). This process of 'prisonization' exists alongside the important role played by street gangs – whose members are 'imported' from the streets, and continue their gang-related activities behind bars. The results will also underscore the role such 'prison street gangs' (Howell 2012) play within the penal environment.

A REVIEW OF THE LITERATURE

American Prison Gangs

A History of Gang Presence

The prevalence of contemporary American prison gangs can partly be attributed to their prolonged presence within the American prison system. Indeed, the first documented American prison gang can be traced back to the 1950s, in the state prisons of Washington (Fleisher 2006). Although America's first prison gangs comprised of white prisoners, there was soon a proliferation of black prison gangs. This was linked to the growing collective identity of black prisoners, particularly during the 1960s and 1970s (Jacobs 1977). Such gangs were often a continuation of their street equivalents (Carroll 1974), leading to closer links developing between street and prison gangs (Jacobs 1974, 1977; Decker 2001). The number of prison gangs also proliferated because prison officers were able to exert less control due to judicial rulings, and prisoners "organised themselves for self-protection and power dominance" (Buentello *et al* 1991:4).

This solidification of gang identities has continued to the present day. Indeed, many prison gangs are composed of street gang members who directly transplant their outside loyalties into the prison – gangs that consist of the same members, operating along the same lines (Pyrooz *et al.* 2011). There are also examples of racial (Kahn 1978) and religious gangs (Hamm 2007) in the American prison system. Affiliation to these gangs supersedes street gang affiliation, and they are specific to particular prisons. For example, prisons in Texas and California have long experienced *de facto* racial segregation; this led to rival street gangs often merging under expansive, 'race-based' prison gangs for the purposes of protection and self-preservation (Kahn 1978).

This is a trend that has continued, and, in many instances, prisoners have no choice but to affiliate themselves to racial gangs. In inner-cities, however, street gangs have long been 'imported' into the prison environment; this leads to a continuation of their street rivalries once in prison. One of the most authoritative sources on this topic is James Jacob's *Statesville* (1977), where there is a clear description of gangs in Stateville Correctional Center, Illinois. Developing his previous study (1974) on gangs behind bars, Jacobs' ethnographic analysis documents the influence of gangs operating within Stateville Prison. Gang violence is shown to coexist with the political and racial ideologies of Black Nationalism (Jacobs 1977, pp. 155-164), the National of Islam (Jacobs 1977, Chapter 3), and Hispanic separatism (Jacobs 1977). However, central to Jacobs' study is the finding that gangs have been imported into the prison setting. Many such gangs have a long history on the streets, having developed in specific ghettoized communities (Keiser 1968; Cureton 2011). The movement of these gangs comports with Irwin and Cressey's importation thesis, according to which "the 'prison code'…is also part of the *criminal* code, existing outside prisons… [and so] a clear understanding of inmate code cannot be obtained simply by viewing a 'prison culture' or 'inmate code' as an isolated system springing solely from the conditions of imprisonment" (Irwin & Cressey 1962:145). This notwithstanding, prison gang members often 'export' their behaviours and characteristics one their sentences are completed (Pyrooz *et al.* 2011; Decker 2001).

'From the Street to the Prison, from the Prison to the Street'[2]

Accordingly, another area deserving exploration is the post-release activities of gang members. Indeed, the "growth of prison gangs and the…effects of returning inmates can affect local gang activity" (Howell 2012:180). Wacquant (2004) terms the symbiotic relationship between street and prison gangs as a 'deadly symbiosis', whereby 'gangbangers' from the streets are socialized in environments which almost prepare them for the prison environment. Similarly, the prison solidifies the deviant behaviours of gang members, so that if they are released, these characteristics are again exported to the streets. There have been other studies that have examined the relationships between imprisoned gang members and their street counter parts (see, e.g., Jacobs 2001; Valdez 2005). These studies conclude that prison gang members have profoundly affected the streets. This is primarily because prisoners continue to strongly identify with their street gang after-release (Scott 2004 in Howell 2012: 274). Accordingly, it is difficult for authorities to break the links that exist between prison and street gangs (Pyrooz *et al.* 2011). Therefore, law enforcement agencies have to implement strategies that vitiate the 'pull' of street gangs for ex-prisoners, made more complicated in instances where family members are also gang-affiliated (Howell 2012). There has, however, been a limited amount of research in this area, despite the wide body of work on American prison gangs more generally.

It is because prison gangs have existed in the United States for far longer than they have in England that there is a greater amount of American literature on the subject (e.g. Carroll 1974; Marquant & Crouch 1985; Moore 1978; Irwin 1980). Much of this research corroborates the view that American prison gangs are cohesive structures, imported from the streets and operating along rigid lines of demarcation (Ussem & Kimball 1996; Wacquant 2009). Moreover, their compositions have been affected by factors such as the racial history of the United States, organised criminality and mass-migration (Carroll 1974; Jacobs 1974, 1977). The Mexican Mafia is perhaps the most well-known of these gangs, having established itself within the American penal system and the wider public consciousness. Indeed, there is extensive research into the Mexican Mafia, including the gang's origins (see, e.g. Kahn 1978), its militaristic leadership structure (see, e.g., Fong 1990; Blatchford 2009) and the extreme levels of violence its members use to dominate both events within prisons as well as criminal activities on the streets (Skarbeck 2014). Furthermore, prison gang members play a dominant role in racial violence within American prisons (Carroll 1974; Jacobs 1979), a problem that has worsened due to entrenched racial segregation in American prisons (Knox 2005). Such racial violence has partly been attributed to a power vacuum left by administrative changes to the American penal system in the twentieth-century (Perkinson 2010). Additionally, the established presence of African-American and Hispanic gangs led to the *reactive* formation of White prison gangs throughout the twentieth-century (Knox 1994, 2005- own emphasis).

However, this is by no means a recent phenomenon; alignment to expansive gangs/groupings has long been a means of facilitating protection from violence within the prison (Carroll 1974). Such groups are most able to provide a collective sense of security if they have cohesive, formalised structures. The majority of American prison gangs are characterised by this centralised leadership, more organised than street gangs but less codified than international crime syndicates (Sullivan & Bunker 2007). Existing research indicates that prison gangs in the Unites States also vary in their formations: they range from 'paramilitary' structures, hierarchical frameworks, to 'steering committee' structures (Fong *et al.* 1996). The last of these can be classified as being a more decentralised, 'chain' formation (Borgatti *et al.* 2009), similar to committees that oversee legitimate organisations such as businesses or recreational bodies. A steering committee structure ensures that there is greater parity between gang members, giving the appearance of more equality between them (Fong *et al.* 1996). The very presence of such established, codified networks suggests the greater level of professionalism within American prison gangs as compared to their English equivalents.

The Role of Race

Racial identity is also at the forefront of many American criminological studies on gangs (e.g. Valdez 2005; Anderson 1990; Cureton 2011). In particular, a disproportionately high conviction rate for African-Americans (Anderson 1999; Taylor 1993) – and their correspondingly high prison population (Alexander 2000; Cureton 2011:34) - has led to many studies predominantly focusing on the experiences of African-American prisoners (e.g. Carroll 1974; Noble 2006). Moreover, race is a key feature of many prison gangs in the United States, affecting group compositions and behaviour. In particular, there are some prison gangs who consider racial solidarity to be as important as conventional, criminal gang activity (Kahn 1978; Knox 2004). Several use the term 'security threat group' (STGs) to describe such gangs studies (e.g. Wells *et al.* 2002; Knox 2012); STGs are classified as "any group of three or more persons with recurring threatening or disruptive behavior" (Wells *et al.* 2002:6). However, whereas earlier research differentiated between security threat groups and prison gangs (e.g. Fong & Vogel 1995), many recent studies no longer makes this distinction (e.g. Fong *et al.* 1996). The earlier distinction was made due to the lack of internal structures within security threat groups (Fong & Vogel 1995). However, over time it has been concluded that security threat groups have evolved to become near equivalents of the archetypal prison gang (Fong *et al.* 1996).

Although such gangs are expansive within particular prisons (Kahn 1978), the power exerted by a prison gang is not always proportionate to its size (Camp & Camp 1985). For example, the Aryan Brotherhood prison gang comprises of approximately 0.1% of the American federal prison population, but is responsible for approximately 20% of murders within the American penitentiary system (Holthouse 2005). Such race-based gangs are particularly prevalent in specific states, most notably California and Texas. In the Californian prison system, a further development has been growing numbers of African-American gang members who have converting to Islam (e.g. Hamm 2009, 2013). Consequently, religious symbols have become new signifiers of gang identity, along with more conventional 'signs' such as clothes (Anderson 1999) and tattoos.

Prisoner Tattoos

There has also been academic literature produced on prison gang tattoos in the United States (e.g. Struyk 2006; Riley 2006; Phelan & Hunt 2011). The cultural practice of getting tattooed to denote gang affiliation can largely be traced to central and South America (Struyk 2006; Phelan & Hunt 2011). However, there are also tattoos that are particular to white supremacist prison gangs (Riley 2006). Moreover, a differentiation can be drawn between street gang tattoos and prison gang tattoos, with the former using numerical codes more often (Riley 2006). Just as tattoos form a central component to many gangs in the United States, they play an equally important role in many gangs operating within Canada. Again, many of these tattoos are used by gangs from Latin America, as well as gangs from Russia and Ireland (Canada Border Services Agency – Organised Crime Section, 2012). There has been far less research into prisoner tattoos in English prisons. For example, it would be pertinent to investigate whether English prisoners' tattoos are the same as those found in wider society, or whether they also act as 'gang signifiers'. However, until very recently, there was a minimal amount of literature on gangs within English prisons.

PRISON GANGS IN ENGLAND

A New Area of Study

Traditionally, there has been limited academic attention towards English prison gangs. Primarily, this is because there were very few prison gangs operating within England throughout the twentieth century. Indeed, the majority of 'in-prison' groupings consisted of prisoners who had committed their offences collectively, and continued to sustain these criminal friendships once in prison (Morris *et al.* 1963; Hobbs 1995). Moreover, the high-recidivism rate amongst persistent offenders would lead to these individuals being exposed to one another on a regular basis (Hobbs 1995). However, such groupings could not be classified as being prison gangs: they lacked the codification, structure and other identifiers of 'the gang' proper. Rather, they were pre-existing friendship groups that were solidified within prison. It was only with the advent of street gangs, which bore closer similarities to American youth gangs, that there became a palpable presence of gangs within English prisons. In turn, this has led to a greater amount of research into English prison gangs (e.g. Wood & Alder 2001; Wood 2006; Phillips 2008, 2012a; Wood *et al.* 2009).

English and American Gangs: A Comparison

Some prisoners in England are reluctant to subscribe to the notion that they are members of prison gangs (Criminal Justice Joint Inspection 2010). In particular, there has been increased attention directed towards the emergence of Muslim prisoner groupings within England. As a consequence of this, non-Muslim prisoners are often threatened by the solidarity groups of Muslim prisoners show (Phillips 2008; Phillips 2012a; Earle & Phillips 2013). Such sentiments are indicative of the anxieties felt by non-dominant prisoners in several countries, especially as regards larger gangs. In particular, Chicago witnessed the emergence of 'supergangs' between 1956 and 1970, whereby the most dominant street gangs annexed smaller counterparts (Sherman 1970; Short 1974; Klein 1971; Jacobs 1977); the resulting enlarged gangs were eventually imported into Stateville Penitentiary, and functioned as the most dominant prison gangs in that institution (Jacobs 1974; Jacobs 1977). Whilst Jacobs (1974, 1977) concludes that imprisoned Chicago gang members must abide by written codes and rules, existing studies portray contemporary English prison gangs as being far less structured (Phillips 2012; Wood & Adler 2001).

Unlike the deliberate cessation of hostilities between rival Chicago gangs once in prison (Jacobs 1974), young English gang members contend that conflicts often continue to ferment during periods of imprisonment (Phillips 2008, 2012a). This is, perhaps, indicative of the more individualistic culture of the late modern prison (Crewe 2009), as well as the absence of gang 'generals' as existed in American inmate population of the twentieth-century (Jacobs 1977; Fong *et al.* 1996). However, being in prison also leads to the dissolution of some street gang loyalties. Rather than rivalries being predicated on specific 'postcodes' or housing estates, prisoners pledge allegiance to more general areas of origin (Pitts 2008). However, not only does imprisonment alter pre-existing gang formations, but such groupings shift from prison to prison. Therefore, once gang members are distant from their hometown, gangs operate under even wider rubrics of geographical origin. For example, an ex-young offender participating in an ethnographic study (Pitts 2008: 113) contends that "if they transfer you...up north, it's London against Manchester or Liverpool." Prisoners who align themselves to such gangs are motivated less by ideology, and more to ensure that they are part of a group large enough to exert a protective influence throughout the prison. However, there ought to be further examination of whether such sentiments are as applicable in adult prisons.

Academic attention has, however, been directed towards the racial dimensions of prison gangs (Phillips 2012a). Although England's prisons have not witnessed the same levels of racial hostilities as their American equivalents, parts of England witnessed street gangs forming in direct response to the racial hostilities felt by particular communities (Alexander 2000; Kennedy 2004; Thomas 2012). To what extent these gangs have been transposed into English prisons is an area that needs further investigation. Moreover, contemporary society has witnessed the emergence of secret racial groupings in English prisons, including prisoners aligning themselves to extreme nationalist organisations (Wood 2006). This is indicative of the increasingly levels of cultural conflicts within the contemporary prison system, often denoted by the emergence of religious fault lines (Earle & Phillips 2013). Nevertheless, English prisoners who overtly subscribe to white nationalism have often been segregated for their own protection (Phillips 2008:14). Therefore, although there are often racial undertones to the power dynamics within English prisons (Phillips 2008, 2012a, 2012b), there appear to be no documented equivalents to the segregated, race-based gangs of the United States.

Methodology

This study's results were gathered through two weeks of ethnographic study at an adult men's prison in England. The primary means of data-collection was through conducting long interviews with prisoners who were gang-affiliated, or highly knowledgeable of gang activity; this purposive sampling was, most often, conducted by prison officers and members of the prison administration who were aware of the study's objectives and its sampling criteria. Although there were occasional instances of 'snowball' sampling (gang leaders introducing me to more junior gang members), the methodology was predominantly based on purposive sampling. Formal, long-interviews with these prisoners were combined with informal conversations that took place on prison landings, workshops and throughout the prison more generally; such conversations took place with prisoners as well as prison officers and members of the prison administration – i.e. non-uniformed staff. Through spending two week at the prison, components of an ethnographic study were also incorporated into the research design: this included observing prisoner-behaviour in social settings, spending time with prisoners on their wings, in their cells and around the prison more generally. These elements of ethnography allowed for a more holistic, panoramic view of prisoner groupings, "sets" and gangs. Throughout the two weeks at the prison, notes were taken, and these were transcribed at the end of each day.

Upon transcription, the data were subjected to a thematic analysis, and conclusions drawn. It should be noted that it was challenging to collect candid responses on prison gangs throughout the entire research process. This is something that has been highlighted by previous researchers (e.g. Wood 2006; Camp & Camp 1985), with reasons ranging from gang members not wanting to incriminate themselves (Wood 2006) to abiding by the gang 'code of silence' (Fong *et al.* 1992). These were very real problems during the research process, especially in relation to more junior gang members. Such individuals were particularly concerned about being viewed as a 'grass' (informant) by senior gang members, putting themselves at risk: "Once you're labelled a grass, that shit sticks" (Rob; Prisoner). Certain prisoners were also concerned that interview data could be used against them during their trial, or would be used by prison authorities to detrimentally affect their time in prison (fieldnotes). Accordingly, it is important to note that relationships of trust had to be built with prisoners, something assisted by my having conducted prior research at the prison.

Results and Analysis

The data gathered from long interviews were fully, manually transcribed. Thereafter, they were coded, and a grounded-theory approach was used to analyse the data. This is an inductive, 'bottom up' approach to data analysis, "whereby analytical themes emerge from the data collected. The emphasis is on the researcher avoiding going into the field with preconceived ideas and a thematic focus but allowing such themes to emerge from the fieldwork" (Noaks & Wincup 2004: 122-123). This led to the emergence of the following, final 'core' categories: Pre-Prison/In-Prison Identity; Gangs vs. Organised Crime; and Penal Power. For ease of reference, the category of 'Penal Power' is further sub-divided in the analysis below. In essence, a theme which pervaded all of the categories was that prison gangs were not primarily shaped by the experiences prisoners endured behind bars. Although some gangs did form in prison for the first time, the overwhelming majority were transposed from the streets into prison. Moreover, this did not just include formalised street gangs with defined memberships, gang names and hierarchical structures of leadership. Indeed, more informal markers of association – being from the same area, of a same cultural or religious background – also deeply affected 'in prison' associations. Such prisoner groupings operated in similar ways to the prison's more established gangs, and acted as *de facto* gangs themselves. Similarly, OCGs were a distinct presence at the research-sites, imported from the streets, yet distinct from street gangs. OCG members, too, negotiated their identities in particular ways.

Pre-Prison/ 'In-Prison' Identity

This was the most substantial category to emerge, encompassing an extensive portion of prisoners' life experiences. Prisoners generally placed an acute focus on their pre-prison identities, where gangs often played a central role. Accordingly, prisoners who were affiliated to street gangs, or who had close associations with known gang members, were granted a degree of protection within prison. Understandably, a prisoner's 'social standing' in the criminal world, offence history and personal characteristics all affected his 'in-prison' identity, something which should be clear from the analysis below. It should also be noted that even prisoners who were not gang affiliated were relatively protected so long as they had pre-existing social connections with gang members, 'gangsters' or organised criminals:

Martin: Like I was sayin', gangs can also be like businessmen...those were the fellas I grew up with. Interviewer: And were you in any of their gangs? M: Nah, nah, not me. But like I said, I knew [name of gangster] for a long time, so when we was in here together, he looked out for me - kept an eye out for me. I: In this prison? M: Yeh. I don't get no hassle from the other lads. I just keep me-self to me-self.

If you're asking me if I've been affected by bullying, I'd say nah. I do my own thing. And like I said, I've got my group of mates and [name of OCG], so...you know? (Zain)

These social connections - developed on the streets, and often involving gang members – ensured that non-gang-affiliated prisoners were protected from the predatory behaviour which prison gangs were said to exhibit. Existing literature links the presence of prison gangs to higher incidences of bullying and victimisation amongst prisoners (Fong *et al.* 1996), and research has also identified that prison gang members are *themselves* at a higher risk of being attacked (Ireland & Power 2012 – own emphasis) [3]. Prisoners in this study also stated that lone prisoners faced difficulties, enduring threats from established prisoner-collectives and prison gangs. 'Lone prisoners' were typically individuals who were not from the criminal-world and consequently had few social connections within prison. Such individuals were not part of existing groups, and were therefore exploited, but not recruited, by the prison's gangs:

They [the gangs] know who's vulnerable - who can be bullied, intimidated. If you're coming in here on your own, they'll be waiting at the gates. They sniff you out. (Zain)

In spite of *prisoners* being aware of which individuals were gang affiliated, *prison authorities* often had to identify gangs through prison records and police intelligence, as well the types of offences for which their members were convicted. Often, gang members would be incredulous at being identified in public:

When it comes to gangs, there's always more hype. Like, my Co-D's [Co-Defendants] don't even know each other, but they [the media] say my Co-D's are in a gang – they say it's gang-related. (Rob)

Many prisoners who were convicted of gang-related offences spoke of their "Co-D's", indicative of the role gangs played in their offending behaviour. However, the same prisoners simultaneously disassociated themselves from gangs during the interview process (fieldnotes). These prisoners also identified two particular gangs (referred to as 'Gang A' and 'Gang B' in this chapter) as having the greatest rivalry within the prison. Whilst not as expansive and powerful as Jacobs' (1977) classification of prison 'supergangs', there was a clear continuation of street conflicts within the prison – something that Jacobs identified as being a central characteristic of gang 'importation' into prisons. This was also clearly illustrated by prisoners' responses on the subject-matter:

There's loads of gang members in here. Alarm bells always going off, the wings getting locked down 'cos of the gang members fighting. Visits are a clash point as well. The older ones are calmer, but...they [Gangs A and B] just don't get on at all. So there's wing segregation, and [Gang A] are kept in one part of the jail, [Gang B] in another part. (Zain)

Prisoners from [Gangs A and B] are kept apart – the wings don't mix. You're in a confined space and the young lads are cheeky, so it's going to blow up. But it's not just about gangs – it's about personal problems, too. Lads who've got issues from the outside need to be kept separate, and it's difficult to keep personal problems apart. (Bradley)

Bradley's response indicated that the role of gangs within English prisons is a more nuanced than in the American prison system. Whereas American research identifies gang activity as being the defining feature of the prison existence (Fong & Buentello 1991; Skarbek 2014), gang affiliation was more of an undercurrent at research-site. Whilst prisoners gave some examples of serious gang conflict in the prison, the lives of most prisoners were not defined by gang membership. James, a senior gang member, corroborated this by stating: "In all the prisons I've been in, there's never been one where people are like, 'yeh, this prison's run by this gang'. And I've been in prisons all over the country". However, once imported into the prison, gangs served to provide networks of protection for their members. Both Gangs 'A' and 'B' were equally dominant outside of prison as they were inside, with their 'in-prison' identity being an accurate reflection of their dominance on the streets:

Martin: 'Course I know about [Gang A] and [Gang B]. Outside, it's all to do with profit and making your name. The trouble's never ending. These young kids do stuff for the gangs, and you've got 14 year olds, 15 year olds looking up to the older gang members. In the last 15 or 20 years it's become all about the drugs and guns. Interviewer: And what about inside prison? M: With [Gangs A and B] it's all about drugs, fights, grassing. You don't grass on your own – not on your own doorstep.

Pre-Prison/ 'In-Prison' Rivalries

Similarly, 'in-prison' relationships between these two gangs were reflective of the situation on the streets of the local area. This conformity between street/prison gang affiliations has long been identified in American research, where the imprisonment of gang members is "almost a homecoming" whereby "the gang member from the street has no trouble whatsoever in adjusting to the new environment" (Jacobs 1974:399). Prisoners spoke of a similar convergence in the pre-prison/prison identities of gang members. However, unlike American prisons, there was interplay between formal gangs and informal groupings. Zain referred to this by simply stating: "We're mates – we stick together".

Additionally, there was some continuation of street rivalries within prison walls, mirroring previous studies in England (e.g. Joint Justice Commission 2010; Phillips 2008). This fragmentation of convict solidarity is also reflected in the contemporary American prison system. In the past, prison gang leaders would enforce a strict cessation of hostilities amongst imprisoned gang members (Jacobs 1974). However, the 1980s and 1990s witnessed the emergence of a 'Pepsi generation': a cohort of prisoners who no longer deferred to older gang members in prison, and who perpetuated street rivalries during imprisonment (Hunt *et al.* 1993). The result was a changed prison landscape in the United States, whereby racial solidarity alone no longer led to harmonious relations. This was illustrated most clearly by an increase in the number of prison assaults between the Bloods and the Crips, both African-American street gangs (*ibid*). Developing the terminology used by Hunt *et al.* (1993), this study's respondents referred to prisoners who were part of a 'post-Pepsi generation': holding even less loyalty to vertical gang leadership than before. This state of affairs was shown by street-based disputes ("beefs") continuing to ferment within this prison:

It's all about issues from the outside coming in here – revenge. They [rival gang members] don't mix. Like, say there's one of [Gang A] and ten of [Gang B], that one won't go into that wing. (Zain)

Sometimes issues come in [to prison] from outside; with gang issues, when it's on, it's on. Even if you move me to another prison it's gonna follow me: the beef's inescapable. (Dylan)

When it comes to gangs, violence is daily: it's about money, drugs, firearms, Robberies, shootings…And they [gang members] don't plan as much nowadays, and they use guns more; the only way to hold onto money is with the gun. And they'll tax the dealers; and the same ones [gang members] give problems in here – drugs, mobile phones. Everyday people get done in [attacked]. I: What sort of reasons do they get done in for? P: Not paying for drugs, street troubles, informing on someone; and there's a family side of gangs as well. Because in here, it's easy to call a gang member on the out[side]. (Liam)

Although gang disputes often continued in the prison, both the 'pre-prison' and 'in-prison' identities of certain individuals were clearly more powerful than others. On the one hand, seniority was illustrated by gang members' interactions with one another: being able to order someone out of a room, or stopping an argument between two gang members indicated a level of seniority (fieldnotes). On the other hand, there were 'lone gangsters' who were not affiliated to any gangs, but were shown deference and respect by other prisoners:

And then you've got [name of gangster] and his associates who run [name of area]. When he was in here, all the other prisoners kept well away from him – that's because they know his history – what he can do to you. (Prison Officer)

However, hierarchical power structures were more apparent within the prison's organised crime groups ('OCGs') than within its smaller street gangs. This was indicative of the most entrenched nature of OCGs in the prison and its surrounding area: of the more methodical approach such groups used when committing crimes, of the more severe consequences for transgressions in behaviour, and of a greater number of prisoners who were affiliated to OCGs as compared to smaller prison gangs. Again, such reputations existed due to the street activities of OCGs. Their members were typically older, convicted of more serious offences, and their 'in-prison' identities were merely continuations of their 'pre-prison' reputations, which had often been created over several decades:

I'm willing to fight, I'm not gonna take any shit. When I first come on this wing, I already had a reputation. It's 'cos I'm respected; it's about being well-known, gettin' kudos. I: So people give you a bit space? P: Yeh, they tread carefully. And the sort of stuff I've done, the number of years I've been inside, even tho' I'm not that old, it all adds up…It's like when we were outside, most would be very wary around us, and I suppose intimidated – scared. If a rival OCG or any person came with the intention of looking for any of us, it would be maximum immediate violence which eradicated this problem for us straight away. (James)

Gangs vs. Organised Crimes

Whether prisoners were gang members, or affiliated to OCGs, there was almost a unanimous opinion that a difference existed between 'gangs' and 'organised crime'. Indeed, this was separation was supported by prison officers and members of the prison administration. Although much of the American literature refers to these two categories synonymously (e.g. Skarbek 2014), this study's respondents made a clear distinction between the two entities:

During my case...they [the media] said it was a gang. But I've never viewed myself as being a gang member or as being part of a gang. I'm part of organised crime. Gangs and OCGs and different and differ very much from each other as do numbers. OCGs are usually a more intelligent group, making them dangerous to a different level so they don't need the numbers; it's not a high number involved in them. (James)

The difference between gangs and OCGs is that the latter are more money orientated – not so much turf based... it's organised criminals, who've got the money and noose to organise high level jobs...But with gangs, they're younger, a group of lads who've got together. They're dealing drugs, but they're more street dealers. (Prison Officer)

Older prisoners, in particular, spoke of the dissolution of previous behavioural norms ("The gangs have changed how they operate. It's now a case of: "I want it, I'll take it. But the old gangsters were folk heroes." – Martin), although prison officers cautioned against reading too much into such romanticized accounts. However, most respondents agreed that members of OCGs operated within a different set of norms to 'street gangsters'.[4] Indeed, gang-affiliated prisoners displayed behaviour that comported more with the street-based norms of the African-American 'gangsta': this includes clothing, appearance, language and behaviour (Anderson 1999; Cureton 2002; Klein 2002: 246; Noble, 2006).

Central to this identity was expressing a defiance and rebellion towards authority; this was, at times, apparent during the interviews conducted as part of this study (fieldnotes). However, members of OCGs were mostly conciliatory during the research process, as they had "nothing to prove" (John). It was clear, then, that there were broad differences between OCGs and street gangs, both in their operations and behaviours. For example, the more disciplined nature of OCGs was transplanted into the prison: their members were less boisterous, kept their distance from other prisoners, and were disdainful of street gang members. Many of their principles were based around 'old school' notions such as fighting 'one-on-one' and accumulating respect:

On this wing, they [gang members] are all vultures. They're all out to spot whoever's weak, and if you let them do it once, they'll do it again. So I'll fight – I'll do some damage... batter someone if they deserve it. I've had occasions where someone's tried something, and I go into their cell, and do them in right there – one-on-one. And if I've got two of my lads causing grief with each other, I'm there to sort it. It's 'cos I'm respected; it's about being well-known, gettin' kudos. (James)

Such responses were consistent with the findings of previous studies on the sociology of English prisons (e.g. Morris *et al.* 1963) and English organised crime (e.g. Hobbs 1995, 2013). Namely, that organised crime continues to attract 'real men' who 'play it cool' (Sykes 1958), adhering to certain behavioural norms. However, other prisoners argued that OCGs no longer held the positons of absolute power. For example, the drugs-market was seen as creating divisions within OCGs: this led to fragmentation and an erosion of the steadfast group solidarity which characterised OCGs in the past:

Before, if you hit one lad from [name of OCG] all of [name of OCG] would jump on you. Now, the gang thing's going out; there's no loyalty in it anymore. Heroin killed it – the loyalty. (Phil)

Prisoners involved in organised crime also spoke of these newer divisions arising: intra-group rivalries that were not apparent in the past. Nevertheless, OCGs continued to exert an influence on many wings of the prison. However, this was usually characterised by a discrete presence rather than the more brash displays of power by the prison gangs.

Penal Power

Although the prison was not 'run' by any particular gang, refraining from conflict with the prison's gangs was seen as crucial to survival in prison: "The gangs can do whatever they want" (Arif). Established gangs were described as having 'strength in numbers', exerting substantial power, and instigating attacks within prison. Such gangs were in the overwhelming majority, and only one prisoner also spoke of gangs being formed within prison to provide defensive support networks:

Interviewer: What can you tell me about gangs in prison? Mark: When it comes to gangs, problems stem from on the road and gangs on the street; and also, non-gang members team up for protection. There's gang members all over this prison; you can contact people on the other wings. I: And where are there the most gang members? M: You see them at Chapel, at Mosque. You either form your own gang in prison or you join your gang [from the outside] to protect yourself.

This statement is significant because it highlights that it was not solely 'imported' street gangs which existed at the site. As regards its validity, several prison officers also spoke of such groups existing, although none of their members were identified. This differentiation between established prison gangs – imported from the streets – and *ad hoc* groups that formed for the first time in prison, for the purposes of protection, is an important one. This latter category could be classified as 'defensive friendship groups', viz. small numbers of prisoners who group together for their own protection, and loosely know each other from outside of prison (Criminal Justice Joint Inspection 2010). However, gang members who participated in this research were part of more structured, entrenched gangs, reflective of their street gangs. Yet members of established gangs were not always vocal about the penal power they exerted. Indeed, this reflected the more developed nature of gang identity within an adult prison as compared to a young offenders' institution, and the more mature mindset of prisoners (Phillips 2008; Criminal Joint Justice Inspection 2010):

When it comes to gangs, there's a big different between juveniles and adult jails. In juvenile, they're tryin' to prove a point. In adult jail you've proved your point, so people just get on, you know? If they're immature, they'll try and fight with you. (Bradley)

If you want to do gang research, it's better you go to the YOIs [Young Offenders' Institutions]...youngsters will be singing like canaries there. (Daniel)

Such responses indicated that young offenders are more vocal about their gang allegiances, reflecting the central role gangs play in the lives of such adolescents (Phillips 2008). This is, then, transferred into young offenders' institutions, where there is a more consistent pattern of rival gangs being segregated:

In [name of Young Offenders' Institution] you had the lads from [name of area] on one end, and us on the other end....in YOIs they keep us apart...they think you're gonna be a gang and misbehave together. But in here it's different. You soon grow up in here. (Stuart)

Although there were similar examples of gangs being 'kept apart' at the research-site, segregating gang members was not a policy that was consistently applied. Accordingly, there were times when gang members would fight due to being in close proximity to one another: "I'll be on [name of wing] and see a member of [name of rival gang] and think to myself, 'Why've they put me in here with him? Obviously we're gonna fight" (Zac). Equally, the brute strength and violence that characterised much of the prison's gang activity would sometimes be directed towards 'undesirable' prisoners. For example, Zain stated: "Nonces [child abusers] and racists get filled in [attacked] ASAP. We don't like child killers, racists, men who've hurt women." Penal power was, therefore, deployed to demonstrate which prisoners were 'undesirables' and which prisoners' offences were morally unacceptable. As regards the latter, the issue of 'respect' was a significant component in the power-relations between prison gang members. In particular, older prisoners were critical of the new generation of gang members:

A lot of these young gang members don't have no respect. Like when you're working in the kitchen, they'll kiss their teeth at you if there's lumps in the gravy. So I'll confront them and ask, "You got a problem?" And then they'll say, "Nah, nah, it's not you – it's the kitchen chefs". You gotta remind these little shitbags who you are. (Zain)

Interviewer: Are today's prison gangs different to those of the past? Martin: Yeh. The youngsters of [Gang A and Gang B] have no respect for human life. Like I said, the old gangs had a lot of respect. They had a different way of working, they had time for you - know what I mean? Even in here, they looked after their own. So the old cons in here still have a lot of respect if they're ever in here.

Penal Power and Race

As regards the racial component to penal power, this was a complex theme. It should be noted that there was limited segregation based along racial lines, something reflected in the general dynamics of the prison, and supported by the responses given during interviews. Most participants in this study originated from racially diverse areas, identified as being one reason why there was this lack of race-based segregation (prison officer, pers. comm.). This is fundamentally different to the composition of American prison gangs, where there is a rigid enforcement of - and rigid adherence to - racial segregation within prisons (Knox 2005; Jacobs 1977; Fleisher & Decker 2001). In particular, Carroll (1974: 156-171) documents how American prisoners' experiences began to be shaped by nascent racial hostilities and a climate of mutual suspicion in the mid/late-twentieth century. Nevertheless, cultural solidarity was an important part of how certain gangs deployed their penal power. This was particularly apparent with gangs of foreign prisoners (non-British nationals):

When the [name of foreign gang] come in, it's usually in waves – when they've all been convicted of a large-scale offence. And they keep themselves to themselves – on the same wing, talking in their own language. To be honest, they're model prisoners; you get no trouble from them. But they're more like businessmen, so the English lads leave them alone...everyone knows how dangerous [name of foreign gang] are. (Prison Officer)

Language barriers (Phillips 2008) and cultural differences (Bhui 2009) often result in some foreign prisoners leading separate 'lives' in prison. This was apparent within the research site, where foreign gang members would congregate and socialise separately (fieldnotes). Moreover, many such gangs maintained cohesive structures, something that resulted from shared ethnic and cultural backgrounds. This is a feature that has long been noted amongst 'immigrant gangs' (Thrasher 1927; Montero 1979; Chin 1990), and aids in strengthening their identities in prison. Despite the collective identities of the prison's foreign gangs, - often engendered through familial ties - there was a general absence of *racial* schisms at the prison: "When it comes to the gangs, it's not a racial thing" (Bradley). Prisoners' experiences of multiculturalism in wider society often affect their acceptance of other races within prison (Phillips 2008). Moreover, prisoners and prison officers identified the large number of mixed-race prisoners as being one reason why there were relatively low levels of racial conflicts. This did not, however, totally discount a racial subtext to prison gangs:

Most of the gangs are black lads kissing their teeth, wearing their pants down low. I don't like it. Then you get the occasional white lad in their gang, trying to talk black. It just sounds stupid. (Zain)

You see, when you say gangs, I think of black lads, really. (Bradley)

However, views expressed on race are often linked to participants' own ethnicities (Phillips 2012a, 2012b; Glynn 2014). Accordingly, whilst many white prisoners did not view race as being a particularly salient feature of prison life, black prisoners were more vocal on the issue of racial identity. Most notably, black prisoners who were ex-gang members spoke of the perceptions that arose around black men associating together:

Geoff: What would you say a gang is? If me and him [points to another black prisoner] and a few other black lads is standing together, would you think that's a gang? Eddie: Cos you see, sometimes when me and my brotha over there are stood with another six or seven Afro-Caribbean males, they [the officers] will look at us as if we was a gang...laughs. (Original Emphasis)

This notion of 'blackness' has been extensively developed by Gilroy (1995) and is now identified as not only constituting a positive label of identity, but also as something that facilitates the conceptualisation of a ghetto-based, threatening 'other' (Alexander 2008: 13 cited in Phillips 2012: 55). Such pre-conceptions often germinate within a prison environment, where a group of black prisoners socialising together may immediately be thought of as being gang members (Brookes *et al.* 2012: 21). More generally, race was a complex and often contradictory topic. For example, Zain spoke of three "sets" of prisoners, divided along racial lines, but also referred to "white and Asian" prisoners acting together to attack "racists".

Penal Power and Religion

The issue of Islam within prison was often mentioned by prisoners and prison officers. Although there was a noticeable number of British Pakistani prisoners at the sample site, when referring to the role of Islam among prisoners, particular focus was direct towards Category A Prisons. A crucial distinction was made between the cultural divisions which arose in lower security prisons, and the presence of religious extremism in the Category A 'dispersal system'. Ali, who had spent time in a Category A Prison, referred to extremism causing tensions between 'extreme' Muslims, and 'non-extreme' Muslims such as himself:

Ali: The Muslim guys in [name of prison] are good people, yeh? But they're extreme people. They're older people, and they'd take my TV, take my PlayStation. Interviewer: And what did you do when they took your stuff? A: What can you do? They're proper big people. They're in their cells all day, doing bench-presses, sit-ups, that sort of thing. If you're Muslim they'll make you pray at this exact time. They'll tell you to stop playing pool when they're about to pray. And they're very exact...they'll only eat by sitting on the floor. They'll say, "Brother, you must eat sitting down. You must drink sitting down. Don't drink stood up, Brother".

This presence of Islamic fundamentalism led to tensions arising *within* groups of Muslim prisoners, as well as causing conflicts with the non-Muslim prison population ("Radicalization's a problem, I tell you. They'll try and get you to convert, but I ain't converting. It's a serious issue – no joke". Eddie, Prisoner). However, the emergence of faith identities could also lead to there being lower levels of racial and gang-based divisions among those prisoners who did convert to Islam. This materialised through prisoners of various ethnicities (and indeed rival gang factions) being united under the overarching framework of Islam:

A lot of them [prisoners] become Muslim, and if a rival gang member's in the same prison as him, and he's also become Muslim, he won't fight no more – he's changed his ways. Asian lads, black lads, white lads, it don't matter...all go Muslim prayers together. (Ali)

A prisoner's faith identity, then, was identified as a rapidly developing aspect of penal power. In particular, the interaction between faith and gang affiliation indicated a gradual redistribution of power within some prisons. This was facilitated by coercive measures as well as more subtle acts: "When you first come in, the Muslim lads will have left you £40 or £45 worth of canteen (food) in your cell. And you can't give it back. So, you feel like you owe them something" (Ali). However, at the sample-sites, the vast majority of respondents agreed that religion was more of a 'background issue': that although there were divisions and hostilities, much of this was more cultural. Moreover, only a few prisoners such as Ali had been in a Category A Prison. Therefore, the 'trick down' of such issues from Category A Prisons to the wider penal system was limited, and, at the time of writing, religious extremism was not a significant presence at the sample site. Rather, penal power was held by more 'conventional' gangs, OCGs and established criminals.

At a base-level, this penal power was significantly affected by hyper-masculinity and its projection. Such notions of physical prowess and strength are central to the 'criminal world' (Cohen 1955; Hobbs 1995; Jefferson & Carlen 1996), and are particularly acute for gang members (Levi 1994; Levi & Maguire 2003). This notion of hyper-masculinity was reflected in the daily interactions at the prison – how prisoners walked, communicated with one another, and how prisoners communicated with prison officers (fieldwork notes). This importance of physicality has often been ignored in sociology (Shilling 1991). However, the human body conveys its own form of social capital, with social status and achievement both being conveyed through physical appearance (Chang 2006). This 'body capital' (Wacquant 2005, 2007) played an important role in shaping prison life at the research-site, especially amongst gang members; it fundamentally affected prisoners' abilities to physically challenge those with whom they had disputes. This, in turn, had a profound effect on the power-dynamics within the prison. Accordingly, being a member of a dominant prison gang meant a prisoner was granted a degree of protection, even if he was not a particularly large or strong individual: "In here, gangs are about protection. That's our mentality. Gangs are different types of people" (Zain).

CONCLUSION

This study's results showed the clear links between prison gangs, which operated within the research site, and street gangs in surrounding area. It should be noted that data were gathered from a specific prison, and therefore cannot be generalized for the whole of England.[5] Nevertheless, prisoners' responses consistently identified that there was a high level of gang 'importation' into the prison from the streets; this included conventional street gangs as well as OCGs. However, many of these prison gangs were amorphous groupings, with only slightly more organisation than delinquent peer groups. In this regard, prison gangs in England appear to be far less developed and expansive that gangs within American prisons. Inevitably, there were conflicts that arose within prison, often emanating from street-based "beefs" permeating into the prison. However, attempts were also made to prevent such disputes from arising. One way this was done was through the prison's informal policy of keeping rival gangs separate. Moreover, prisoners usually associated with their known peer-groups, attempting to ensure that they were not victimized or 'sniffed out' by the gangs as being vulnerable.

In addition to this, prisoners were often unsure of what constituted a 'gang', and whether they were part of one. Prison officers and members of the prison administration were able to provide more operationalised definitions of gangs, indicative of their greater knowledge of such theoretical discussions. Furthermore, certain prisoners did not self-identity as being gang members, even though their activities and criminal histories bore strong similarities to the academic parameters around 'gangs'. There were also sharply contrasting views on what constituted a gang, and the differences between gangs, OCGs and friendship groups. Although gangs clearly exerted power within the prison, the lines of demarcation between these groupings were not always clear. Accordingly, further research is needed to clarify these issues. In particular, attention should be drawn towards the experiences of prison gang members in England, their effects upon fellow prisoners and the wider penal system. Distinctions should also be made between street gangs in prison and OCGs, as well as groups of foreign prisoners, religious groupings and lone 'gangsters'. The interactions within and between such groups is a subject-area worthy of much further exploration.

REFERENCES

Alexander, C. (2000). *The Asian Gang: Ethnicity, Identity, Masculinity*. Berg 3PL.

Alexander, M. (2008). *The New Jim Crow: Mass Incarceration in the Age of Colorblindness*. The New Press.

Anderson, E. (1990). *Streetwise: Race, Class, and Change in an Urban Community*. University of Chicago Press.

Anderson, E. (1999). *Code of the Street: Violence and the Moral Life of the Inner City*. W. W. Norton & Co.

Bhui, H. S. (2009). Foreign national prisoners: Issues and debates. In H. S. Bhui (Ed.), *Race & Criminal Justice*. Sage. doi:10.4135/9781446215951.n9

Blatchford, C. (2009). *The Black Hand: The Story of Rene "Boxer" Enriquez and His Life in the Mexican Mafia*. Harper Collins.

Brookes, M., Glynn, M., & Wilson, D. (2012). Black men, therapeutic communities and HMP Grendon. *Therapeutic Communities: The International Journal of Therapeutic Communities*, *33*(1), 16–26. doi:10.1108/09641861211286294

Camp, G. M., & Camp, C. G. (1985). *Prison Gangs: Their Extent, Nature and Impact on Prisons*. Washington, DC: US Govt. Printing Office.

Carroll, L. (1974). *Hacks, Blacks and Cons: Race Relations in a Maximum Security Prison*. Waveland Press, Inc.

Chang, V. W. (2006). *Body Capital and Socioeconomic Mobility*. PARC Research Report. Retrieved 23 September 2014 from: http://gcc.pop.upenn.edu/pilot-award/body-capital-and-socioeconomic-mobility

Chin, K. (1990). *Chinese Subculture and Criminology: Non Traditional Crime Groups in America*. Westport, CT: Greenwood Press.

Cohen, A. K. (1955). *Delinquent Boys: The Culture of the Gang*. New York: The Free Press.

Crewe, B. (2009). *The Prisoner Society – Power, Adaptation and Social Life in an English Prison*. Oxford University Press. doi:10.1093/acprof:oso/9780199577965.001.0001

Criminal Justice Joint Inspection. (2010). *The management of gang issues among children and young people in prison custody and the community: a joint thematic review*. London: HM Chief Inspector of Prisons.

Cureton, S. (2011). *Black Vanguards and Black Gangsters – From Seeds of Discontent to a Declaration of War*. University of America Press.

Decker, S. H. (2001). *From the Street to the Prison: Understanding and Responding to Gangs*. Impact Publications.

Earle, R., & Phillips, C. (2013). Muslim is the New Black: New Ethnicities and New Essentialisms in the Prison. *Race and Justice*, *3*(2), 114–129. doi:10.1177/2153368713483322

Fleisher, M. S. (2006). *Societal and correctional context of prison gangs*. Cleveland, OH: Case Western Reserve University, Mandel School of Applied Social Sciences.

Fleisher, M. S., & Decker, S. H. (2001). An Overview of the Challenge of Prison Gangs. *Corrections Management Quarterly*, *5*(1), 1–9.

Fong, R. (1990). The Organizational Structure of Prison Gangs: A Texas Case Study. *Federal Probation*, *1*(54), 36.

Fong, R. S., & Buentello, S. (1991). The detection of prison gang development: An empirical assessment. *Federal Probation*, *55*, 66–69.

Fong, R. S., & Vogel, R. E. (1994). A Comparative Analysis of Prison Gang Members, Security Threat Group Inmates, and General Population Prisoners in Texas Dept. of Corrections. *Journal of Gang Research*, *2*(2), 1–12.

Fong, R. S., Vogel, R. E., & Buentello, S. 1996. Prison Gang Dynamics: A Research Update. In Gangs: A Criminal Justice Approach. Anderson Publishing Co. and Academy of Criminal Justice Sciences.

Gilroy, P. (1995). *The Black Atlantic: Modernity and Double-Consciousness*. Harvard University Press.

Glynn, M. (2014). *Black Men, Invisibility, and Desistance from crime: Towards a Critical Race Theory from Crime*. London: Routledge.

Hallsworth, S., & Silverstone, D. (2009). "That's life innit": A British perspective on guns, crime and social order. *Criminology & Criminal Justice*, *9*(3), 359–377. doi:10.1177/1748895809336386

Hamm, M. (2007). *Terrorist Recruitment in American Correctional Institutions: An Exploratory Study of Non-Traditional Faith Groups*. National Criminal Justice Reference Services.

Hamm, M. (2009). Prison Islam in the Age of Sacred Terror. *The British Journal of Criminology*, *49*(1), 667–685. doi:10.1093/bjc/azp035

Hobbs, D. (1995). *Bad Business - Professional Crime in Modern Britain*. Oxford University Press.

Hobbs, D. (2013). *Lush Life: Constructing Organized Crime in the UK*. Clarendon Studies in Criminology. doi:10.1093/acprof:oso/9780199668281.001.0001

Howell, J. C. (2012). *Gangs in America's Communities*. SAGE Publications Inc.

Hunt, G., Riegel, S., Morales, T., & Waldorf, D. (1993). Changes in Prison Culture: Prison Gangs and the Case of the 'Pepsi Generation'. *Social Problems*, *40*(3), 398–409. doi:10.2307/3096887

Ireland, J. L., & Power, C. (2012). Prison Gangs Seen as a Source of Friendship. *The British Psychological Society*. *Annual Conference*, London.

Irwin, J. (1980). *Prisons in Turmoil*. Boston: Little Brown.

Irwin, J., & Cressey, D. (1962). Thieves, convicts and the inmate culture. *Social Problems*, *10*(2), 145–155. doi:10.2307/799047

Jacobs, J. (1974). Street Gangs Behind Bars. *Social Problems*, *21*(3), 395–409. doi:10.2307/799907

Jacobs, J. (1977). *Stateville - The Penitentiary in Mass Society*. The University of Chicago Press.

Jacobs, J. (1979). Race Relations and the Prisoner Subculture. In N. Morris & M. Tonry (Eds.), *Crime and Justice*. Chicago, IL: The University of Chicago Press. doi:10.1086/449057

Kahn, B. (1978). *Prison gangs in the community: a briefing document for the Board of Corrections*. California Board of Corrections.

Kennedy, H. (2004). *Just Law: The Changing Face of Justice, and Why it Matters to Us All*. Chatto & Windus.

Klein, M. W. (1971). *Street gangs and street workers*. Englewood Cliffs, NJ: Prentice Hall.

Klein, M. W. (2002). Street gangs: A cross-national perspective. In C. R. Huff (Ed.), *Gangs in America III*. Thousand Oaks, CA: Sage. doi:10.4135/9781452232201.n15

Knox, G. W. (1994). *An Introduction to Gangs* (3rd ed.). Bristol: Wyndham Hall Press.

Knox, G. W. (2005). *The Problem of Gangs and Security Threat Groups (STG's) in American Prisons Today: Recent Research Findings from the 2004 Prison Gang Survey*. National Gang Crime Research Center.

Levi, M. (1994). Masculinities and white-collar crime. In T. In Newburn & B. Stanko (Eds.), *Just Boys Doing Business*. London: Routledge.

Levi, M., & Maguire, M. (2003). Violent Crime. In M. Maguire, R. Morgan, & R. Reiner (Eds.), *The Oxford Handbook of Criminology* (3rd ed.). Oxford University Press.

Matthews, R. (2002). *Armed Robbery*. Willan Publishing.

Montero, I. (1979). *Vietnamese Americans: Patterns of Resettlement and Socioeconomic Adaptation in the United States*. Boulder, CO: Westview Press.

Morris, P., Barer, B., & Morris, T. (1963). *Pentonville: A Sociological Study of An English Prison*. Routledge and Kegan Paul.

Phillips, C. (2008). Negotiating identities: Ethnicity and social relations in a young offenders' institution. *Theoretical Criminology*, *12*(3), 313–331. doi:10.1177/1362480608093309

Phillips, C. (2012a). It Ain't Nothing Like America with the Bloods and the Crips: Gang Narratives Inside Two English Prisons. *Punishment and Society*, *14*(1), 51–68. doi:10.1177/1462474511424683

Phillips, C. (2012b). *The Multicultural Prison: Ethnicity, Masculity and Social Relations among Prisoners*. Clarendon Studies in Criminology. doi:10.1093/acprof:oso/9780199697229.001.0001

Pitts, J. (2008). *Reluctant Gangsters - The Changing Face of Youth Crime*. Willan Publishing.

Pollock, J. M. (2005). *Prisons: Today and Tomorrow* (2nd ed.). Jones and Bartlett Publishers.

Scott, G. (2004). "It's a sucker's outfit": How urban gangs enable and impede the integration of ex-convicts. *Ethnography, 5*(1), 107–140. doi:10.1177/1466138104041590

Sherman, L. W. (1970). *Youth Workers, Police and the Gangs: Chicago 1956-1970.* (Master's Thesis). Division of Social Sciences, University of Chicago.

Shilling, C. (1991). Educating the Body: Physical Capital and the Production of Social Inequalities. *Sociology, 25*(4), 653–672. doi:10.1177/0038038591025004006

Short, J. F. (1974). Youth, Gangs and Society: Micro and Macrosociological Processes. *The Sociological Quarterly, 15*(1), 3–19. doi:10.1111/j.1533-8525.1974.tb02122.x

Skarbeck, D. (2014). *The Social Order of the Underworld: How Prison Gangs Govern the American Penal System.* Oxford University Press. doi:10.1093/acprof:oso/9780199328499.001.0001

Sykes, G. M. (1958). *The Society of Captives: A Study of a Maximum Security Prison.* Princeton University Press.

Taylor, C. S. (1993). *Girls, Gangs and Drugs.* Michigan State University Press.

Thomas, S. (2012). Revisiting Brixton: The War on Babylon 1981. In D. Briggs (Ed.), *The English Riots of 2011: A Summer of Discontent.* Waterside Press.

Thrasher, F. M. (1927). *The Gang.* Chicago: The University of Chicago Press.

Trulson, C. R., & Marquant, J. W. (2009). *First Available Cell: Desegregation of the Texas Prison System.* Austin, TX: University of Texas Press.

Valdez, A. (2005). Mexican American youth and adult prison gangs in a changing heroin market. *Journal of Drug Issues, 35*(4), 843–867. doi:10.1177/002204260503500409 PMID:21614143

Wacquant, L. (2004). *Deadly Symbiosis.* Cambridge, MA: Polity Press.

Wacquant, L. (2005). Carnal Connections: On Embodiment, Apprenticeship, and Membership. *Qualitative Sociology, 28*(4), 445–474. doi:10.1007/s11133-005-8367-0

Wacquant, L. (2007). *Body & Soul: Notebooks of an Apprentice Boxer.* OUP USA.

Wood, J. (2006). Gang Activity in English Prisons: The Prisoners' Perspective. *Psychology, Crime & Law, 12*(6), 605–617. doi:10.1080/10683160500337667

Wood, J., & Alder, J. (2001). Gang activity in English prisons: The staff perspective. *Psychology, Crime & Law, 7*(1), 167–192. doi:10.1080/10683160108401793

Wood, J., Moir, A., & James, M. (2009). Prisoners' gang-related activity: The importance of bullying and moral disengagement. *Psychology, Crime & Law, 15*(6), 569–581. doi:10.1080/10683160802427786

ENDNOTES

[1]   To preserve the anonymity of participants in this chapter, all individuals are referred to by pseudonyms.

[2]   Pyrooz *et al.* (2011)

[3]   This higher incidence of harm encountered by prison gang members stems from the fact that rival gang members are often seeking to attack them, based on feuds stemming from the streets (this is something which was supported by accounts prison gang members gave during fieldwork). However, one should distinguish such incidents from the risk of victimization faced by lone-prisoners, which occurs for wholly different reasons (see above).

[4]   Most prisoners did not elaborate on what links, if any, existed between street gangs and OCGs. Certain prisoners (e.g. Rob) clearly spoke of their progression from street gang activity to affiliation with OCGs. However, this is an area of study that requires further research.

[5]   The generalizability of the data is also affected by the fact that only a limited number of prisoners were willing to participate in the research; certain prisoners were also more willing to fully engage with the research process, as is illustrated by the overrepresentation of these individuals in the results. However, these problems are almost inevitable when researching prison gangs (Camp and Camp 1985).

Chapter 12
Surviving the Streets of Makeevka:
A Study of Subculture of Street Children in Ukraine

Andrej Naterer
University of Maribor, Slovenia

ABSTRACT

The chapter explores the subculture of street children in Makeevka, Ukraine. Drawing upon qualitative and quantitative data gathered during longitudinal anthropological field research their surviving strategies along with social structures, economic activities and substance abuse are presented. In addition, extra-, intra- and inter-group violence is analyzed with an emphasis on the child's situational interpretation and adoption of the code of the street through subsequent code/identity switching and subcultural reactions.

INTRODUCTION

"I was chatting with Sveta while we were sitting in the dust on a sidewalk. She told me that she was pregnant with Vinik [at the time the leader of the group of street children living in the center of the city]. I was shocked – she was only 13 years old and had already been living on the street for more than two years. She told me that she didn't want to go back home, because all of her friends were living on the street.

"How about your country? It's probably very nice over there?" she asked.

I didn't know how to answer. Is it really that nice where I come from? I started babbling something about our beautiful scenery and kind people..."

"Do you have guys like us?" she asked so directly that it was good that I was sitting down, for I otherwise I would surely have fallen on my backside.

DOI: 10.4018/978-1-4666-9938-0.ch012

"What do you mean?" I asked, trying to escape giving a direct answer.

"Well, Bomzhi..." she strived to clarify.

"What?"

"Bomzhi... well, homeless guys, living on the street..."

It was... awkward. How could I tell her that yes, we do have homeless people, but it's completely different. In my hometown of Maribor there are not even 10 of them, they're adults and in some respects, they have it easy... We have no children living in sewers, engaging in prostitution and shooting dope into their veins... (diary fragment, Naterer, 2007, p. 1)

The aim of this chapter is to present a picture of the daily life of street children in Makeevka, Ukraine and to describe the strategies that enable them to survive outside the traditional frames of socialization. Apart from the data gathered during my direct fieldwork among the street children, this account is based on my earlier work published in the anthropological monograph *Bomzhi, street children Makeevka* (Naterer, 2007) and two articles, "Bomzhi and their subculture: an anthropological study of the street children subculture in Makeevka, eastern Ukraine" (Naterer & Godina, 2011) and "Violence and street subculture: a study of social dynamics among street children in Makeevka, East Ukraine" (Naterer, 2014).

The street children who are presented in this chapter are runaways who have banded together for survival in the harsh environment of the Ukraine. Unlike street gangs, they don't create or acquire an identity through membership in an organization. They look to each other for support to replace their absent traditional family. However, like gang members they participate in crime, such as theft, deviant behaviour, such as prostitution and substance abuse, such as consumption of intravenous narcotics, which all together present a way of coping with their harsh daily reality.

Method

The information presented here was collected during fieldwork among street children in Makeevka between 2000 and 2012, with 16 months of direct, in-field participation. A non-random sample of 68 street children was chosen and researched (52 boys, 16 girls, average age 13.6 years). The participants were living in four groups at four different locations in the city: Group 1 in the centre of Makeevka; Group 2 in the suburban part of the city (10 km from the centre) - Ziljoni quarter; Group 3 approximately 8 km from the centre of the city - Pushka quarter; and Group 4 near the centre of the city. In order to protect their identities when presenting qualitative data, pseudonyms have been used. Data collection was performed at locations occupied by street children such as the main bus station, the Marshrutka station, the Pasazh shopping-mall, the Univermag shopping-mall, the central market, restaurants and surrounding buildings.

The study was designed as an integration of qualitative and quantitative approaches. The three main methods employed were as follows:

- **Participant Observation:** Participant observation of the day-to-day life of street children in four groups. Data was gathered in the form of field notes written as a diary, field reports and conversation records;

- **Interview:** A questionnaire with flexible, open-ended questions inquired about each participant's current personal situation, family background, interpersonal relationships within the group, living conditions on the street and their future aspirations; transcripts were coded (the first stage through open-ended coding, the second stage through axial/focused coding), and on the topic of violence: three major categories of violence together with relevant functions were identified; multi-stage, semi-standardized interviews were conducted on the topic of violence;
- **Visual Notes:** Photo and video equipment were used to create a series of video records of the children's everyday life – between 2005 and 2008 photo cameras were distributed among the participants in order to analyze photo material created by the street children themselves.

The following additional methods were employed:

- **A Questionnaire with Pre-Coded Questions:** With the main aim of gathering socio-graphic and quantitative data;
- **Observation without Participation:** Employed with the main aim of triangulation (noting the differences between data gathered using participant observation and interviews);
- **Thematic Drawings:** The children were given paper and pencil and were asked to draw a thematic picture (i.e., "Please draw the worst situation on the street.", "Please draw a happy moment on the street."), in order to sample their pictorial perception of life on the street. After creating the pictures, the children were asked to interpret the content in an interview (triangulation with focused-coded data). All the data was later triangulated mostly as a combination of participant observation – visual notes – interview.

DEFINING STREET CHILDREN IN MAKEEVKA, UKRAINE

When Ukraine declared its independence in 1991, the long awaited modernization and democratization, to the great amazement of the Ukrainian people, resulted in the collapse of the national economy and a severe decline in living standards, particularly in urban areas of Eastern Ukraine. A 47% decline in GDP, 25% increase in the adult mortality rate (WHO 2010) and an 85% rise in unemployment from 1995 to 2000 (UNECE 2010) are just some examples of the social devastation Ukrainians experienced. Makeevka, an industrial city in the Donetsk region, was one of the Ukrainian cities where the impact of the crisis was the greatest. In 2004, a local newspaper in the region reported that the minimum survival income was in fact 40% higher than the officially guaranteed income provided by minimum wages and pensions (Naterer & Godina, 2011). In this respect the state of transition for many Ukrainians appeared as a constant struggle for survival, forcing them to invent all sorts of additional survival mechanisms, from producing their own food in urban areas, to pawning goods or even adopting semi-legal and illegal economic activities. The children who subsequently started appearing on the streets throughout the region within this period were a direct result and one of the saddest manifestations of the crisis:

The collapse of the Soviet Union led to a mass migration to cities and an economic crisis that left many families below the poverty level with inefficient and insufficient social assistance for those who needed it. This resulted in the return of a long-forgotten phenomenon in modern Russia – neglected and homeless children. (ILO, 2000, p. 9)

Street children are known throughout the region of the former Soviet Union as *besprizorniki* (Bose-witz, 1988) or *Bomzhi* (Naterer & Godina, 2011), meaning "without a defined place of living." In Ma-keevka, Ukraine, these are mainly boys between 10 and 16 years old, most of whom have been on the streets for more than 5 years. Since street children were not counted by the census, the exact number of children living on the streets of the city is not known; some NGOs estimate the number to range from 1000 to 2000 (Naterer, 2010; Naterer & Godina, 2011). Most of them are not orphaned and come from matrifocal familial environments, with high exposure to unemployment, criminality, addiction to inhal-ants, pharmaceuticals, and opiates, neglect and domestic violence. With regard to domestic violence, the children reported regular strong verbal and psychological aggression and mild to moderate forms of physical violence, including slapping and hand-beating, with the perpetrators being predominantly the male members of the family. Despite the relatively insignificant physical injuries, these forms of violence have a serious impact on children. The victims perceived them as violations of their rights and reported great suffering and feelings of victimization. These findings identify their social background as high risk and are in accordance with studies confirming that substance abuse, criminal activity and violence are more likely to become part of a child's behavior if it has been experienced in their family relationships (Tyler, 2006; Naterer, 2014). However, their transition from home to the street appear to be in most cases a gradual process:

Informant 10, 12 years old, commenting on his transition to the street:

I came [to Makeevka] after I was bomzheval [living occasionally on the street] with my friends for several months in Zhdanovka and Makeevka... Then, all of a sudden, I just stayed in Makeevka...

How did you manage to survive? (A. N.)

Easily! All of my friends are here... Some of them I already knew, from the times when we were guliali [strolling, slang expression for a kind of subcultural activity and a powerful social code of solidarity among street children in Makeevka] together... Other guys I got to know later.

Why did you stay? (A. N.)

Why? I don't know... but then again, what would I do in Zhdanovka? It's a small pasiolak [small town]... There is nothing there! And everybody knows you.

Why didn't you stay at home? (A. N.)

There is genuine shit happening where I'm coming from. I'm telling you, my family - genuine shit... my dad is drinking, my mom is drinking, my grandma' was taking care of us [siblings]... If you ask me, here [on the street] it's way better..."What do you mean? (A. N.)

Friends are here, food is better, you do whatever you want to do...

Survival on the street is based on a combination of resilience and adaptability. A major source of in-come for street children in Makeevka is begging, which is often combined with other forms of economic activity, mostly collecting scrap materials and performing odd-jobs like guarding stands in the market-place. Criminal activities were relatively rare and comprised mostly petty crimes like pick-pocketing.

Informant 1, (10 years old – commenting on economic activities, interview fragment, 2000):

I am not good at it [begging]... I am ashamed of it. My sister, on the other hand, has no problems with it – she sits at the entrance of the marketplace, puts on her full-of-pity-face and stretches out her hand. In several hours she can get a whole salary... If me or one of my friends would do this in the same way, people would torment us to go to work!

What do you usually do? How do you get your money? (A. N.)

Usually we collect scrap metal and empty bottles... sometimes we sneak into the factory [the scrap-recycling plant, Cheryomushki district, Makeevka]... there you can find chushky [slang expression for cut-off pieces of scrap metal] of 25 kilos or more... and you can go and take as much as you can carry, you just have to watch out for the guards.

And then? (A. N.)

Then? We take it to another priomka [slang expression for re-selling point] and sell it.

Most of the money is spent on alcohol, cigarettes and inhalants, the most common combination of abused substances (Naterer & Godina, 2011; Naterer 2014). Many street children also engage in relatively frequent intravenous consumption of the psychotropic substance *Baltushka*.

Another key to survival on the street is integration. While living on the streets, children in Makeevka develop elaborate social networks that enable them to survive in the harsh environment. The children are not nomads; they organize themselves into social formations that resemble subcultures. These groups are territorial, and of particular importance are social relations within their territory, which is comprised of public space, collective private space and semi-private space (Naterer & Godina, 2011).

Public space is a space of great fluidity for the city's population, of numerous transitory and imper-sonal relationships, and of anonymity. Street children perceive public space as tied to the social control of police, social institutions, and adults, all of which could be, since they are not part of their subculture, sources of income. Within this space, children assume the stereotypical role of victimized individuals who are in need of help and pity, and adopt strategies that are either deviant, such as begging, or delin-quent (pick-pocketing and shop-lifting) or both.

Collective private space is known as *teplukha,* a slang expression for the underground heating system that street children use as shelter. Collective private space represents for them the concept of safety, group collectivity and independence, and offers escape from formal social control. Since it is well hidden, it also gives them a chance to escape from their public role of victim. The children keep the *teplukha* well camouflaged, physically inaccessible, and highly mobile (figure 1).

Informant 7 (explaining the importance of teplukha)

Our liuk [Russian word for hatch door, and a slang word for teplukha, underground shelter]... well, like an apartment to other people...

Figure 1. Teplukha

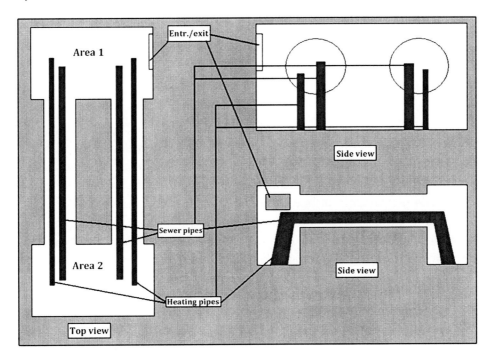

Yep... eating, shitting and sleeping, all in one place! Ha, ha, ha... (Informant 12)

Semi private space is the most important space for the social and economic activities of the street children. It includes local marketplaces, bus stops, shopping malls and other often-frequented locations within the micro-region of the city where they engage in different sorts of work, as porters, cleaners or attendants. To insure their survival, the children maintain good, direct and lasting social and personal relations with other people. There is considerable evidence of cooperation and solidarity between street children and other visitors, including vendors and customers in the marketplace (Naterer & Godina, 2011, p. 27):

Informant 4, 17 years, (commenting on relationships outside the group- interview fragment, 2004):

I leave all my valuables with auntie Masha [the lady selling bread at the local marketplace]... I have all my documents there, photographs you took last year, a small radio...

Is your stuff safe there? (A.N.)

Sure! We [group members and vendors] are friends. We all know each other by name... We help them, they help us.

Because of its great importance, semi private space can be a place of conflict, particularly when it is entered by outsiders such as other street children, local drug addicts, or anybody who could endanger their good image or social relationships.

This marketplace is ours... we have to protect it. If I came to visit you and stole something, would you invite me again? You would throw me out and never invite another bomzh again... (Informant 4, 17 years, interview fragment, 2004).

STREET CHILDREN AND THEIR SUBCULTURE

The definition of sub-culture as developed by Milton M. Gordon (1947) presents a basis for modern understanding of the concept of subculture, for it is not merely a group within a group, but *a world within itself* (Gordon, 1947, p.41). The key feature of Gordon's understanding of subculture can be found in two opposite characteristics of this social phenomena: particularities of a subculture that are a basis for differentiation, and the production of distinction and inseparable connections of this social formation to a broader social, cultural and historical context within which it is embedded. Classical sociological studies and concepts of subculture evolved within the traditions of the Chicago school and Centre for Contemporary Cultural Studies (Gelder & Thornton, 1997). In the early period of the tradition of the Chicago school, the term *social world* was used to describe complex intergroup patterns of social interaction (Lutters & Ackerman, 1996, p. 4), and classical studies like Cressey's *Taxi-Dance Halls* (Cressey, 1932 in Lutters & Ackerman, 1996) were based upon the concept. Later the concept of subculture evolved and was mostly applied in research on social deviance and youth delinquency in urban areas. One of the first systematic modern studies of a deviant subculture is Cohen's *Delinquent Boys* (Cohen, 1955), where the subculture is understood as a specific, collective way of coping with common problems of social adjustment, mostly problems of social status (Cohen, 1955, p. 28-73). Two other opposing forces remain active throughout the process of formation of the subculture:

...the delinquent subculture takes its norms from the larger culture but turns them upside down. The delinquent's conduct is right, by the standards of his subculture, precisely because it is wrong by the norms of the larger culture.

In this respect, by rearranging social criteria the subculture offers a new system of norms and values which enables the participants to escape previously experienced frustrations (Cohen, 1955, p. 28-65).

The classical concept of subculture as a delinquent social formation was later shown to be insufficient by several post-subcultural researchers, including Bennett (1999) and Bourdieu (1993). The need for a redefinition of the concept of subculture was motivated by modern global social trends, such as the emergence of *mainstream* and *substream,* and led researchers to the development of new concepts such as those of *clubculture, taste* and the *neo-tribe* (Muggleton & Weinzierl, 2003, p. 3-4).

When referring to street children as social groups, many authors describe them as subcultures (Chitradub, 1998; Beazley, 2003a; 2003b; Davies, 2008). However, closer analysis of both the street children and classical subcultures shows that they are not fully compatible in the strict meaning of the term. Classical concepts, Cohen's for instance (Cohen, 1955) tie the subculture to a class, and see its emergence in collective perception of and reaction to a perceived problem. Although manifesting many subcultural properties such as a specific image, language, behaviour, and social organization on the street that functions as a common solution for individual survival in harsh urban environments (Naterer & Godina, 2011), they cannot be regarded as a class. Concepts offered by other authors, like that of *a social world* by Shibutani (1955), or that of the neo-tribe by Maffesoli (Weinzierl & Muggleton, 2003), also fail to explain the subcultural nature of street children. These terms are too loose and fluid to fully depict the world of street children. At the same time they are also too exclusively focused on individual perceptions of participation in a social phenomenon and cannot therefore explain the participation of street children, which is driven by a different set of factors (Naterer & Godina, 2011; Aptekar & Stoecklin, 2014) and in their eyes totally involuntary.

When street children in Makeevka form into groups, these groups cannot be perceived as a subculture in a classical meaning of the term, but a subculture of a particular kind (Naterer, 2010; Naterer & Godina, 2011; Naterer, 2014). Groups comprise anywhere from 5 to 15 members. The number of members is not fixed and varies according to many factors, from season and weather to the political situation in the country or pressure from the police. Membership in a group is of vital importance for survival on the street:

We stick together during the winter because it is cold outside. Last winter it was -28 [ºC] and down here [in the teplukha] it is + 30 [ºC]. (Informant 5, 14 years, group no. 3, interview fragment, 2006).

And:

...when the police chase us, it is better to split. The group is easier to catch than individuals... (Informant 4, 12 years, group no. 1, interview fragment 2002).

Street children in Makeevka exhibit the following core characteristics of a classical subculture: image, language, and behaviour specific (internal, *subcultural*) culture. However, since they are not class determined and are individually motivated to run to the street, and since their social formation is not a mechanism for social adjustment or a way of coping with status frustrations, they fundamentally differ from Cohen's *Delinquent boys* (Cohen, 1955). At the same time, street children in Makeevka also exhibit many of the characteristics described in post-subcultural studies, and can also be regarded as a form of neo-tribe. Their collective identity (including street image, language and attitude) is not based on traditional structures such as gender or class, and they have a strong material motivation for their participation in the group on the street. However, they cannot be understood fully as a neo-tribe, for that concept focuses exclusively on patterns of consumption and state of mind, *expressed in form* (Muggleton & Weinzierl, 2003, p. 12). Street children in Makeevka also exhibit a relatively high level of rigidity in systems of inclusion and exclusion, which according to Maffesoli is absent in neo-tribes.

Therefore, we proposed an alternative concept of the subculture of street children in Makeevka (Naterer & Godina, 2011), where it must be understood as an entity on a continuum, with the classical subculture (Cohen, 1955) on one end and neo-tribes (Muggleton in Weinzierl, 2003) on the other (Table 1):

Street children subculture exists on two levels. The surface level is observable by other people, and consists of image (clothes, shoes, and hair), language (the language of the street) and behaviour. The hidden level is not directly observable, because it is comprised of attitudes, beliefs, and worldviews that are specific to the lived experiences of these children.

In classic subcultures, skinheads and surfers for instance, the image appears in the form of a prescription (Stratton, 1981, p. 182), which must be fulfilled in order to enter the subculture. In the case of street children in Makeevka, it seems that the image emerges as a product of necessity, and is characteristic of their way of life. However, this is not necessarily so. First, street children in Makeevka have enough money to buy themselves new, even fashionable clothes. The data we gathered shows that street children in Makeevka have, on average, from 40 to 150 grivna (app. 6 to 25 EUR) at their disposal daily, yet they

Table 1. Subculture of street children in Makeevka on a neo-tribe continuum (Naterer & Godina, 2011, p. 35)

Classic Subculture (Cohen, 1950)	Street Children in Makeevka	Neo-Tribe (Maffesoli, 1960 in Muggleton and Weinzierl, 2003)
Collective rbesponse to problems of social adjustment, motivated by common perception of situation	Collective response to individual problems and motivation	Collective identity not based on social structures (class and gender)
Determined by social norms	Only partly determined by social structures (gender and class)	Patterns and practices of consumption, which form new forms of temporary socialities
Inverted system of social norms	Partly Inverted system of social norms	Non-inverted system of social norms
Short-term hedonism	Short-term hedonism	Short-term hedonism
Delinquent behaviour	Rarely delinquent behaviour	Rarely delinquent behaviour
Specific language	Specific language	Specific language
Rigid social structure	Rigid and flexible social structure	Flexible social structure

do not spend it on new clothes. The reason is that dirty old clothes have a subcultural value. If someone is not dressed in dirty old clothes, he or she cannot be a full member of the street subculture. Also, in their groups one must satisfy image criteria in order to enter the subculture (Naterer and Godina, 2011, p. 29).

... I found Informant 7, who I hadn't seen for at least a year. I was shocked – he was all dirty, dressed in old clothes, oversized boots and a repulsive bonnet. A genuine Bomzh! I had known him for several years, he was so clean and tidy, almost spiffy... I asked him what happened. He told me that since he tried Baltushka for the first time, he does not go home anymore... And I've also noticed that he is more accepted by the group... they [group peers] don't see him as Pisun [slang expression referring to male genitals] anymore... (A. N. diary fragment, January 2005).

In contrast to subcultures that adhere to prescribed elements of distinct, usually market-dictated styles, street children belong to a deviant subculture, for it is not possible to go to the local shop and buy a set of "street-children-style" clothes. Therefore, the requirements for entering the subculture must be regarded as inverted. First, one has to adopt the latent level of this subculture by becoming homeless and by living with a group in order to produce the manifest level of their image.

Much the same can be said about both subculture-directed attitude and language. A distinct attitude is a part of the subcultural system of norms and mores that are translated into a set of idiosyncratic actions and perceptions (Naterer & Godina, 2011). Subcultural attitudes take many forms but are at the same time a part of the survival mechanism. These attitudes are the result of a child's acquired street identity and his interpretation of the current situation. Therefore, to outsiders these children may appear to be helpless victims, to the researcher as manipulative, deceptive and evasive respondents, and to other street children as either friends or foes. Street language, as another manifestation of the street children subculture, functions as a cohesive factor for the group and an instrument of isolation from the public (Naterer and Godina, 2011, p. 29). It is based on words created by street children that are taken from Russian vocabulary, truncated, modified in composition and pronunciation, and concatenated into new, subcultural words (Table 2):

Table 2. Examples of the transformation of Russian into subcultural words

Russian Word	Subcultural Word
domek (small house)	*do-ko-me-kek*
krysha (roof)	*kry-ky-sha-ka*
tepla trasa (heating system)	*te(i)plukha*
bayan (music instrument, form of accordion)	*bayan* (injection)
gharazh (garage)	*gharazh* (plastic needle compartment)
Musar (garbage)	*Musar* (police officer)

Substance Abuse

Substance abuse is an extremely widespread hazard threatening street children on a global scale (Naterer, 2010; Naterer & Godina, 2011; Aptekar & Stoecklin, 2014). Among the most often abused substances are alcohol, tobacco and inhalants (Aptekar 1988; Lalor 1999; Chitradub 1998; Morakinyo in Odejide 2002), while hard drugs appear to be rarely if ever used by street children (Lalor 1999, p. 766). Substance abuse in one form or another is common among the street children in Makeevka and is inseparably tied to life in the street subculture. All of the children who participated in the study presented here used tobacco, which is the most popular substance every child who participated used tobacco. Inhalants are also very popular (used by 61 children, 89.7%) and alcohol (used by 54 children, 79.4%). The most common combination of substance abuse was the combination of alcohol, cigarettes and inhalants, used by 55% of the children. Intravenous consumption of the psychotropic drug Baltushka was also very common; in combination with cigarettes and alcohol, it was used by up to 25% of the study participants. Since 86.5% of children reported that they consumed these substances on a daily basis, the frequency of abuse is clearly very high.

The data gathered on motivation for substance abuse points to the great impact of peer influence. Participants started smoking even before coming to the street and most reported a daily consumption of 10 to 15 cigarettes as completely common. Consumption of inhalants, on the other hand, is by self-report introduced to the child after his or her entrance into the street subculture. On average, an individual child consumes from 5 to 8 tubes of glue, which is usually bought at a local marketplace. Occasionally, glue is replaced by cheaper substitutes such as paint or paint thinner, but as soon as funds permit, they switch back to glue as soon as possible:

Informant 8 (commenting on the consumption of glue)

... glue is more expensive, so if you don't have enough money, you have to take the paint. There are guys who like paint more, but we don't... it's more heavy and it gives you headaches and makes you nauseous.

Inhalants are popular because of their hallucinogenic effect.

Informant 4 (commenting on the effects of inhalants)

... some guys say that they feel better when they sniff paint, 'cause it makes them fell less hungry and warmer. That's all true but I think we all do it 'cause once you start sniffin', you see things... you know, hallucinations.

What do you mean? (A. N.)

It's different for everybody… some people see strange birds, some see energy, we even have a pacan [slang expression for a group member], who dances, you know, like that kung-fu shit… for instance, I see a rabbit every time I'm sniffin'… all of a sudden he [the rabbit] appears and at the same time - vanishes! So I'm constantly on guard for him… I'm gonna catch that little fucker one day, he, he… Well… Yes, I know it's only a hallucination, I'm not stupid, you know, but it's one hell of a lot of fun!

By self report, beer, vodka and *samagon* [homemade brandy] are the most common forms of alcohol consumed by street children in Makeevka. Alcohol is consumed relatively rarely and almost never individually. For subculture participants, drinking is a social event:

Informant 5 (commenting on alcohol consumption)

… it doesn't make any sense, drinking by yourself. It's for alcoholics. It's different with us [street children]. I'd rather buy somebody [group peer] a bottle of samagon so we can get drunk together!

The word *Baltushka* or *Boltushka* is a slang expression for a substance that street children consume intravenously. The expression comes from the Russian word *baltatj* [to mix, to stir, to shuffle and also to prattle or to babble]. Baltushka is a mixture of a flu medication called Efect, *Marganjec* [Potassium permanganate KMnO4], vinegar and water.

Informant 13, 17 years old:

…who showed me how to make baltushka? Hmm… it was Pasha. He was on that stuff for quite some time. But he was using baltushka when he didn't have the money for Fen [Fen is a slang expression for Ephedrine]. He showed me and my cousin Vadjim everything, where to buy all the ingredients, how to make the brew, how to prepare the needles, everything…

The main ingredient, flu medicine, is first acquired from a local pharmacy. Capsules are emptied onto a piece of newspaper, and the contents, small red and blue beads, are ground with an empty beer bottle into a fine powder. This powder is poured into a plastic cup and water is added. The quantity of water depends on the quantity of flu medicine and on the number of consumers.

Kolja, 16 years old (explaining while preparing Baltushka):

Then you have to stir… and you add Marganjec… one krishka [Russian for a small roof, plug or cork; slang expression for the measure for adding KMnO4 to Baltushka] or more, it depends on the quantity of Efect. If you put in too much Marganjec, the brew will be too strong, gets hot enough to melt the cup in your hand… and you cannot put this in your vein. If you put too little Marganjec, it won't work… it reacts… You have to stir until you get a brown color… look, now this is pink. That means I have to stir some more, ha, ha, ha…

When all the ingredients have been mixed, the mixture is filtered and distributed among group members. It is important to note that the children are very capable and are able to calculate the amount that is to be distributed per person to a tenth of a ml.

Informant 13, 17 years old:

I liked it at once. Then [the time, when Pasha introduced the substance] we [he and Vadjim] were using this stuff for... hmm, I think two or three months. Then we [he and Vadjim] showed everything to Sashka and Ruslan [their group peers], and after one month everybody in our group was using it.

Informant 14, 16 years old:

At first I didn't like it that my friends were using Baltushka. I told them it was dangerous... I know people, addicts, crazy ones... but then they talked me into it - just try... and now you see [pointing to his underarm], ha, ha, ha... but I can quit any time.

Although Baltushka is identified by law as a psychotropic drug, and it is illegal for an individual to possess the mixture, the components are easily accessible and can be bought in most pharmacies across the city. Children who use the mixture consume from 4 to 10 ml, at rates of 4 to 8 times a day.

Informant 13, 17 years old:

I use 8 kub of [1 kub is a slang expression for 1 ml in a hypodermic needle] several times a day. I cannot say how many times... 3, 4 or 5 times. The more the better, ha, ha, ha... Many times, if there is a lot of money. Once time we had something like 50 grivna. Can you imagine that! That was a lot of Efekt! That day I had... I don't know, something like 20 shots. Imagine that... but not only me, there were 5 of us and everybody stabbed himself something like 20 times.

Research has shown that Baltushka itself does not result in any direct physical addiction, even though consumption might be very frequent. Street children who have been using the substance on a regular basis report that they can quit at any time without having any withdrawal crisis or other side effects.

Informant 15, 16 years old:

I can be without this [Baltushka] for as long as I want to. For instance - some time ago I was in juvenile prison... the police took me from the street and they locked me up for one month. Then, when I came home, I didn't go on the street for another month. All this time without sniffing glue, shooting Efekt and drinking... I was just smoking. And nothing happened, no pain, no shaking, like those guys that shoot Fen (Ephedrine), absolutely nothing... But the first time I came to ljuk [slang expression for the underground system of heating pipes, similar to teplukha], to the guys, I just couldn't resist it. I had to do it.

The consumption of Baltushka is a highly ritualized event (Naterer, 2010; Naterer & Godina, 2011), which is evident from the special tools for preparation, the elaborate and complex vocabulary concerning preparation and consumption of the substance, and the system of roles and relations involved. It is a social event in the sense that it is never confined to an individual but always includes a group.

The consequences of Baltushka consumption are severe. According to observations made from 2005 until 2009, children who frequently used Baltushka developed symptoms similar to epilepsy, reduced mobility, speech obstruction and several forms of mental disturbance. In the middle of 2006 the first two cases of permanent disability appeared, when two children were hospitalized. The first case of indirect death as a result of Baltushka use appeared in June 2006 when informant 13 was found dead under some bushes and by 2012, most of the Baltushka users from group 3 were dead.

Representative of local NGO specializing in helping drug addicts, interview fragment, 2011:

Children who use Baltushka are in great danger, even greater than older addicts. They are not only smaller and younger, but are also using other drugs. Baltushka is very dangerous because of the Marganjec that they mix into the brew. The substance is used for a wide variety of products, even in the production of rocket engines and explosives. It was also very popular for medical purposes in the former Soviet Union and now in Ukraine. People use it mainly for stomach aches and skin diseases, but in very small amounts. Addicts also use this stuff as a reagent, but in other mixtures you don't need as much as in Baltushka. It has terrible side effects... once introduced it does not leave your body; it goes straight to your knuckles and joints (figure 2). But it also produces a psycho-physical state that is similar to epilepsy. In the beginning this state is short and relatively unnoticeable but it gets longer and stronger through repeated consumption. Eventually children start to avoid this nasty feeling by using more of the stuff.

Evidence suggests that street children consuming Baltushka are aware of the hazard. They all witnessed the devastating effect of the drug and most of them even questioned their own actions tied to the consumption of the drug. Since the subcultural cognitive model recognizes Baltushka as dangerous or even lethal, children developed idiosyncratic mental models that incorporated the appropriate solution. To them, as well as to everybody else, it was evident that Baltushka consumers often get sick or die. Every one of them elaborated his or her own version of reality in which he or she as consumer could avoid the danger. When asked during interviews if they knew what had happened to a recent victim of Baltushka, they often replied: "Yes, but he was already sick," or "yes, but he was *shooting* [injecting] more than anybody else" or "yes, but he was smaller and younger than me." In one case, God was involved:

Figure 2. Consuption of Baltushka

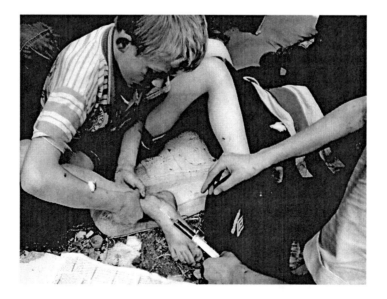

Informant 13 (arguing with a peer about his religious beliefs)

What!!! You fucker... you are saying that I don't believe in God... Ok, I don`t go to church, but look (showing his forearm full of needle scars)... Do you see what I do? Well, what do you think? I would be long dead if God wasn't taking care of me!

This kind of idiosyncratic mental model is common; it enables children to cope with stressful situations and at the same time to continue consuming the drug.

Violence, Social Structure, and the *Code of the Street*

Violence is one of the most important factors influencing street life, particularly when those living on the street are children. Violence is one of the most frequently cited reasons for children to flee their families (Aptekar, 1994; Tyler, 2006; Naterer, 2014), and widespread violence is among the most frequently occurring events in a street subculture (Magazine, 2003; Davies, 2008; Naterer & Godina, 2011). Street children are not merely victims, however, but are in fact active participants in street violence. The propensity for violence among these children is heavily influenced by a history of caretaker abuse (Talyer, 2006), substance abuse (Crawford, Whitbeck, & Hoyt, 2011) and by the "code of the street" (Naterer, 2014).

Evidence suggests that violent behaviour is learned through early negative interactions in coercive families (Patterson, DeBaryshe, & Ramsey, 1990). These negative experiences subsequently influence interactions in other social settings and tend to propel violent adolescents toward aggressive situations (Caspi, Elder, & Bam, 1989). The perpetuation of violence has been explained with the concepts of *interactional* and *cumulative continuity*, within which an individual's style, hostility for instance, "/.../ evokes reciprocal, sustaining responses from others in ongoing social interaction, thereby reinstating the behavior pattern across the individual's life course whenever the relevant interactive situation is replicated" (interactional continuity) (Caspi, Elder, & Bam, 1989, p. 375), while keeping behavioral patterns sustained through progressive accumulation of their own consequences (cumulative continuity) (Caspi, Elder, & Bam, 1989, p. 377). Studies of homeless youth that support this idea are numerous (Aptekar, 1994; Chitradub, 1998; Magazine, 2003; Tyler, 2006; Davies, 2008; Naterer & Godina, 2011; Naterer, 2014).

However, to fully understand violence among street children, their micro social context, particularly participation in a street subculture, must also be considered. One of the basic characteristics of street children is collectivity, for it is nearly impossible to find a child living on the street by him or herself (Aptekar, 1988, 1994; Magazine, 2003; Davies, 2008). For protection and material, social, psychological and emotional support, street children form into groups that can be described as subcultures with a relatively stable and distinct social structure (Chitradub, 1998; Magazine, 2003). Through integration in a street subculture, children also acquire new identities that ensure survival outside traditional frames of socialization (Beazley, 2003; Naterer & Godina, 2011). These identities are incorporated in an existing idiosyncratic psycho-social frame and do not re-personalize a child. Nevertheless, they heavily influence behaviors and profoundly shape the children's individual trajectories and street careers. Within this context, violence often results in the repulsion and disempowerment of children but can at the same time attract them and can be seen as a form of capital and a source of control (Parkes, 2007).

Anderson's *Code of the Street* (1999) is one of the best analyses of violence in street subculture. One of Anderson's core arguments is that the persistent threat of violence and the status insecurity of children result in the development of the belief that survival on the street depends on their adoption of aggressive behavior (Anderson, 1999). This belief is not dependent on an individual's actual inclination to violence:

Most people identify themselves as "decent," but in the interest of deterrence, especially when danger and uncertainty loom, it often becomes important for individuals "to know what time it is," and to be perceived as more "street" than "decent" and to act accordingly; a premium is placed on being able to read public situations and then to "code switch" when appropriate. (Anderson 2002, p. 1534)

In other words, when faced with a coercive situation, in order to avoid interpersonal transgression, one must show no weakness and become aggressive, for by adopting a "decent"[1], non-aggressive resolution, one risks becoming a victim.

Street children in general are not entirely congruent with Anderson's (1999) ghettoized gangs – they are seldom delinquent or aggressive per se and tend to blend into their micro social environments (Aptekar, 1994; Chitradub, 1998; Magazine, 2003; Davies, 2008; Naterer & Godina, 2011). Nevertheless, the *code of the street*, though based on cooperation and integration, includes violence as an essential element of their life on the street.

Among street children in Makeevka, three distinctive categories of violence can be observed (Naterer, 2014):

- Violence coming from the general social environment, directed toward a particular group of street children or an individual street child (extra-group);
- Violence between two groups of street children (inter-group); and
- Violence coming from the group and directed inwards (toward a peer or peers, intra-group).

Extra-Group Violence: "Scars as a Sign of Victimization"

Extra-group violence, originating from the general social environment and directed toward the group or an individual street child, is by self-report the most common form of violence experienced by street children in Makeevka. It includes all sorts of psychic violence (intimidation), verbal violence (harsh language, yelling) and physical violence (slapping, beating). In the interviews and thematic drawings, the children described most instances of abuse as coming from local landlords, local gang members, drug addicts, car owners and the police.

Landlords yell at us and beat us if they catch us... and the police, the uniformed guys... they come and beat us, because their bosses force them to fulfill their daily work quota... if they catch you sniffing glue, they spill it on your head and rub it in your hair...they forced Sasha to swallow a whole fistful of Analgin [version of Aspirin] on the spot, because they thought he had narcotics.

And:

... drug addicts came and started harassing Wem [nickname] ... after a heavy beating they stabbed him with a broken bottle... in the liver. We found him bleeding, half dead ... (Informant 8, 15 years, 2008)

Cases of sexual violence within this context are rare, but when they do occur, they have a greater impact on street children than other forms of violence:

... one day, this djadka [elderly gentleman] approached me and my friend, as we were sitting on a sidewalk... He asked us what we were doing, if we were hungry... he was very sweet and friendly and invited us to his apartment, saying that his wife would cook something for us. We went with him... when we entered the vestibule of a building, he dropped his shopping bags and jumped on us. I managed to escape but he raped my friend... she is bit younger and smaller than me and couldn't resist. It was devastating for her... and for me too.

Did you go to the police? (AN)

Hell no! Some girls that went to the police [after a similar situation] were locked up at the police station and abused by the policeman as well..." (Informant 3, 13 years, 2002)

Street children in Makeevka perceive extra-group violence as a direct assault and report a high level of individual suffering. The involvement of non-street participants (police officers, for instance) in these acts prevents activation of the *code of the street,* and the children have no option but to remain "decent" and accept the outcome. Their coping strategies in such confrontations are based on avoidance or escape. This form of violence has a strong negative impact on the street children, for they suffer and are victimized and marginalized. However, important social functions for their subculture are to be found in the creation and maintenance of distinctiveness and consequently the consolidation of subcultural identity: "They [police] see us as sub-humans. Well, they look the same to us... that's why we call them *musara* [rus. garbage]." (Informant 8, 17 years, 2010).

However, their social and cultural capital combined with their street identity enables them to exploit the situation. Street children in Makeevka have based their economy on begging and other charitable actions by the general public (Naterer & Godina 2011), and the *identity of a victim* is one foundation of their success. Therefore, when violent encounters occur, the children inevitably strive to exploit them: excessive yelling during the incident, and obvious, exaggerated limping and moaning after a violent encounter are often part of the show in order for them to be perceived as victims. They often go around showing off their wounds in order to obtain sympathy: "... they [the general public] have to see you as poor and ill-fated. Otherwise they will not give you any money" (Informant 3, 13 years, 2002).

Inter-Group Violence: "Scars as War Medals"

Inter-group violence emerges between two different groups of street children. The origin of this form of violence is to be found in the distinct relationship between street children subculture and their local social environment and other groups of street children. Street children in Makeevka are not nomads; they are predominantly localized and well integrated into the social networks within a particular micro-region of the city. Each group lives within a separate territory centered on the local marketplace. Most of their activities are defined by social relationships in the marketplace; they work, eat and sleep there and generally spend most of their time either in or in the vicinity of the marketplace. Most of their social network is based on good relationships in the marketplace; such relationships form the basis for survival on the street, and children take good care of them. They regard this territory as their semi-private space.

Elsewhere I (Naterer & Godina, 2011) have shown that street children do not engage in delinquent acts within their own territory. That does not mean that they cannot be delinquent; delinquent acts by individuals or the group are performed in public spaces, outside their private and semi-private spaces. However, the spaces that one group perceives as public are usually occupied by other groups of street children and are fiercely defended. These kinds of intrusions commonly result in verbal and mild to moderate physical violence between the two groups. Although rare, cases of severe violence occasionally occur and sometimes lead to serious injuries or even death.

… Natasha told me about E. …few years back, he went to the Krasny rinok [Red Marketplace]. He roamed there all day long, sniffing glue, picking pockets… having fun. Of course, he knew it was dangerous because of the group living in the center of Makeevka, but since nothing happened, he decided to stay there overnight. Then they [group in the center] caught him. They each beat him up and demanded money. He didn't have anything, so they beat him up some more, poured gasoline all over him and set him on fire. I was shocked! Not only because of his physical scars, but also because of the psychological scars he must have suffered. Eventually, I forced myself to approach E. and ask about the event. To my surprise, he was more than happy to tell me all about it and even suggested that I photograph the scars. He was almost showing them off, as if they were medals from the war – look what I have, he bragged I survived and came back to tell the tale… the group peers almost ogled… (AN, diary fragment, 2000).

This form of violence has a strong impact that is mostly limited to the direct physical suffering of the individual child. By occurring deep within a subcultural context, these acts offer a whole range of both conventional and street codes to be adopted by an individual. Yet it is evident that children tend to adopt street codes with respect to the support that can be expected from their peers – the more peers involved in a coercive situation, the more likely it is that violence will occur:

… if you're alone in a situation like that it's not good to be too brave… it's not wise.

What is… wise I mean (A.N.)

Well… try reasoning with them [intruders]… or just shut-up.

Running away? (A.N.)

No, no… no. That would be even worse… they would catch you and you'll get it. If you don't have a buddy in that group with whom you've been guljal [rus. stroll, important code of solidarity among street children], just don't go near them. (Interview fragment, 2009)

This form of violence also acts as a strong element in the self-regulation of the social system on the street. Firstly, it limits the level of delinquent acts performed by the street children population within the city. It functions as a system of social control for street children by street children; it maintains an established social order and discourages or hinders different groups of street children from engaging in delinquent acts: "… I've been here all my life. All my friends are here… we are the guardians of our *rinok* [Marketplace]!" (Informant 4, 18 years, 2006). Secondly, it has a strong impact within the subcultural context. Groups engage in violent acts toward other groups for the primary purpose of reaffirming the symbolic boundary of their own semi-private (the marketplace for instance) and private spaces (*teplukha*). It is not just about the preservation/protection of their space, but also about manifesting the group's power and ability to control their own environment. The results of violence, particularly if an individual has the opportunity to display them (scars, loot or trophies, for instance) enable the accumulation and demonstration of prestige, which can be directly linked to the acquisition of subcultural capital and promotion within the social structure of the group. Thirdly, these violent acts also enable an individual child to experience the sense of belonging to a social group and his or her own power of control over the situation: "I need the group and the group needs me!" (Informant 4, 2006). Street children perceive this category of violence as part of the game - a set of rules pertaining to street life, and they make no connection to any violation of their personal rights, victimization or obvious suffering. Within this context they function as active participants, although not always as direct perpetrators: "That's life on the street – bite and get bitten!" (Informant 5, 15 years, 2010).

Intra-Group Violence: "What Can I Do… This Is the Street"

Intra-group violence originates within the group and is directed inwards, toward group peers, usually from the top downwards. Most violent acts of this kind are limited to verbal and mild to moderate physical violence, and scuffles and tussles are a part of day-to-day life within the group. However, severe physical and sexual violence occasionally appear as an extension of the common level of violence:

… again I've noticed how the rest of the guys were picking on M. They were pushing and kicking him and S. told me that this was pretty common. He also told me that group peers abused him sexually. Through a series of interviews I've managed to piece together M.'s story: M. is a bit younger and weaker than the rest of the guys. They started picking on him, and since he [M.] rebelled and didn't want to knuckle under, the violence only increased. After a while group peers, mainly D. [the group leader] and S., proposed that the others focus their kicks on the left side of M.'s torso. Even that didn't convince M. to conform. The situation escalated on one occasion when, after a severe beating, guys dragged him into the teplukha and raped him in turns (A.N. diary fragment, 2000).

This kind of violence is strictly limited to the interior life of the group and its social structure. Children perceive violent acts of this kind as a part of social normality in life within the subculture and rarely connect it to any violation of rights or victimization. This context presents ultimate subcultural reality: it enforces the code of the street while rendering alternatives, particularly individual interpretations of "decent," almost impossible. Together with the ability to accumulate economic benefits (looted belongings) and social advantages (gaining alliance through collective attack), the main function of these acts remains the sanctioning and social positioning of individuals and the maintenance of the group's social/ hierarchical structure:

Why is he [M.] allowing himself to be treated like that [referring to rape]? (AN)

What do you mean? Like he has a choice… yeah, he has a choice – go live by himself! Who would wanna to do that? Nobody!

Socialization, Street Identity and Group Dynamics

Socialization of children into a street subculture usually starts even before the children leave their homes (Naterer & Godina, 2011; Naterer, 2014). It proceeds through a simple process that the children themselves describe as "hangin' out" with peers on the street. During this period children acquire new social and cultural capital and position themselves on the periphery of street subculture as part-time members. Once a part-time member perceives the group on the street as a stable alternative to life at home, he or she tends to interpret the home situation as abusive and unbearable, and the probability of running away rises dramatically. "When you spend more time on the street than at home... you are officially *bomzh* [acronym for a homeless person and slang expression for a street child]" (Informant 6, 17 years, 2006).

Acquisition of a street identity also begins with socialization into a street group; however, it can be activated only when the child actually starts living on the street. Activation/accumulation of new social, cultural and subcultural capital can only be performed in the context of the street, outside traditional frames of socialization, although these frames can never be fully bypassed or omitted. Street children regularly reported experiencing an inner conflict about values when facing awkward situations: "I know that beating other people or stealing is bad, but what can I do... this is the street" (Informant 7, 14 years, 2002).

Data shows that there two important sets of forces involved in the formation of these value conflicts – a centripetal force (*me, acting as a member of the group*), pulling a member towards the center of the group, and a centrifugal force (*me, acting as an individual*), pulling him away from the group. By entering a street group, children abandon neither conventional identities nor norms and values. They merely add new elements to the already existing frame of their psychosocial structure. Using Anderson's (2002) terminology, they do not regard themselves exclusively as "street" or "decent" but as both at the same time, which works fine in solving average problems in daily life on the street. However, in situations that are either exceptionally important, such as financial opportunity, or genuinely threatening, such as external attack, the subculture as a social system kicks into action and boosts cohesion and responsiveness by subordinating participants. The primary instrument for this intervention is the hierarchical social structure of the group.

Data show that all participating groups of street children in Makeevka have a hierarchical social structure. The main function of the hierarchy in the group is to ensure the survival of individuals in challenging situations by boosting the group's collective responsiveness. Although different in appearance and function, the social structures of these groups follow the same general rule: the more challenging or dangerous the situation facing the group or a peer, the more hierarchical the formation must be in order to solve the problem. Among groups of street children in Makeevka, it is evident that groups living in challenging environments, the city center, for instance, develop a higher level of group hierarchy and employ a greater level of violence in maintaining the structure (see Figure 3: Social structure of Group 1). During challenging situations, the frequency of violent acts within all groups stays relatively the same, while the severity increases dramatically (see Figure 4: Changing social structure of Group 4). In these situations, the group structure demands greater subordination of peers, which enables the leader to spearhead the (counter) attack or solve the problem collectively and the group as a whole to prevail: "When these things happen [attack] you don't think with your own head... you usually just go and follow D. [group leader]. He is like our general, ha, ha" (Informant 7, 14 years, 2002).

Adoption of the code of the street, particularly the elements that lead to participation in violent acts, has a profound impact on the trajectories and street careers of these children. During their street careers, most

Figure 3. Social structure of Group 1

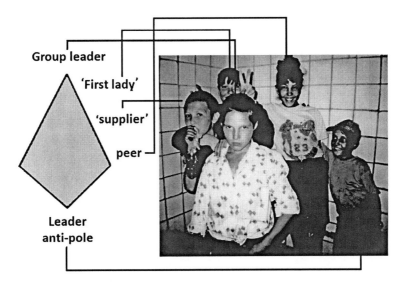

Figure 4. Changing social structure of Group 4

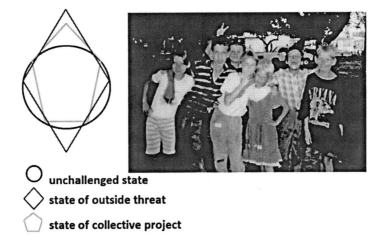

of children (n=47) had already been detained at least once and by 2012 six of them were imprisoned (on charges of either possession or active use of weapons), while five had died a violent death on the street.

The codes and violence emerging among street children are clearly different from those presented by Andreson. Andreson's *code* (1999) implies that low-status young men experience status insecurity, which hinders their social advancement and culminates in their belief "that their self-worth is dependent on the ability to command respect in public" (Brezina et al. 2004, p. 305). This is one of the main reasons for their cultivation of a tough image and a violent attitude. The *Code of the street* of street children, on the other hand, is based not on status insecurity but on the direct need to survive outside traditional frames of socialization (Naterer, 2014), which is the main element governing their attitudes, perceptions, norms and values, relationships, social formations and other aspects of their lives. At the core of this code are the values of cooperation and solidarity (Aptekar, 1988, 1994; Chitradub, 1998;

Davies, 2008 and others), while the values of respect or masculinity remain on the periphery. Violence must therefore be approached from a different angle, not as an expression of an individual acting for himself, but as an expression of individuals as participants in a street children subculture and therefore of the collective. Anderson's code of the street provides a good explanation for the violence occurring within groups of street children as an instrument of identification, interaction, inner social mobility and structural maintenance. For street children, adopting the *street code* literally means cooperating and surviving (Naterer, 2014).

REFERENCES

Anderson, E. (1999). *Code of the Street: Decency, violence, and the moral life of the inner city*. New York: Norton.

Anderson, E. (2002). Ideologically Driven Critique. *American Journal of Sociology, 6*(6), 1533–1550. doi:10.1086/342772

Aptekar, L. (1988). *Street Children of Cali*. Durham, NC: Duke University Press.

Aptekar, L. (1994). Street Children in the Developing World: A Review of Their Condition. *Cross-Cultural Research, 28*(3), 195–224. doi:10.1177/106939719402800301

Barfield, T. (Ed.). (1997). *The Dictionary of Anthropology*. Malden, MA: Blackwell Publishers Inc.

Barnard, A., & Spencer, J. (Eds.). (2002). *Encyclopaedia of Social and Cultural Anthropology*. London, New York: Routledge.

Beazley, H. (2003). The construction and protection of individual and collective identities by street children and youth in Indonesia. *Children, Youth and Environments, 13*. Retrieved from colorado.edu/journals/cye

Bemak, F. (1996). Street researcher – A new paradigm redefining future research with street children. *Childhood, 3*(2), 147–156. doi:10.1177/0907568296003002002

Bourdieu, P. (1993). *The Field of Cultural Production*. New York: Columbia University Press.

Brezina, T., Agnew, R., Cullen, F. T., & Wright, J. P. (2004). The Code of the Street: A Qualitative Assessment of Elijah Anderson's Subculture of Violence Thesis and Its Contribution to Youth Violence Research. *Youth Violence and Juvenile Justice, 2*, 303-328.

Caspi, A., Bem, D. J., & Elder, G. H. Jr. (1989). Continuities and consequences of interactional styles across the life course. *Journal of Personality, 57*(2), 375–406. doi:10.1111/j.1467-6494.1989.tb00487.x PMID:2769561

Chitradub, S. (1998). *The Culture of Street Children in Thai Society*. Development Consultancy Services.

Cohen, A. K. (1955). *Delinquent Boys: The Culture of the Gang*. New York: The Free Press.

Crawford, M. D., Whitbeck, L. B., & Hoyt, D. R. (2011). Propensity for Violence Among Homeless and Runaway Adolescents: An Event History Analysis. *Crime and Delinquency, 57*(6), 950–968. doi:10.1177/0011128709335100 PMID:22865932

Davies, M. (2008). A Childish Culture?: Shared understandings, agency and intervention: an anthropological study of street children in northwest Kenya. *Childhood, 15*(3), 309–330. doi:10.1177/0907568208091666

Ember, C. R., & Ember, M. (2003). *Encyclopaedia of Sex and Gender: Men and Women in the World's Cultures.* Springer.

ILO/IPEC Working Paper. (2000). *In-depth Analysys of the Situation of Working Street Children in Saint Petersburg. Report.* St Petersburg: ILO/IPEC.

Lalor, K. (1999). Street children: A comparative perspective. *Child Abuse & Neglect, 23*(8), 759–780. doi:10.1016/S0145-2134(99)00047-2 PMID:10477236

Letícia, M. K., Forster, M. K. L., Tannhauser, M., & Barros, H. M. T. (1996). Drug use among street children in southern Brazil. *Drug and Alcohol Dependence, 43*(1-2), 57–62. doi:10.1016/S0376-8716(96)01288-4 PMID:8957143

Luttens, W. G., & Ackerman, M. S. (1996). An Introduction to the Chicago School of Sociology. *Interval Research, Proprietary.* Retrieved from: http://userpages.umbc.edu/~lutters/pubs/1996_SWL-Note96-1_Lutters,Ackerman.pdf

Magazine, R. (2003). Action, personhood and the gift economy among so-called street children in Mexico City. *Social Anthropology, 11*(3), 303–318. doi:10.1017/S0964028203000223

Morakinyo, J., & Odejide, A. O. (2003). A community based study of patterns of psychoactive substance use among street children in a local government area of Nigeria. *Drug and Alcohol Dependence, 71*(2), 109–116. doi:10.1016/S0376-8716(03)00093-0 PMID:12927648

Naterer, A. (2007). Bomzhi-street children in Makeevka. Subkulturni azil: Maribor.

Naterer, A. (2010). *An anthropological analysis of the street children subculture* (Dissertation). Ljubljana: FDV.

Naterer, A. (2014, June 26). Violence and the Code of the Street: a study of social dynamics among street children in Makeevka, East Ukraine. *Journal of Interpersonal Violence,* 1-16.

Naterer, A., & Godina, V. V. (2011). Bomzhi and their subculture – an anthropological study of the street children subculture in Makeevka, East Ukraine. *Childhood, 18*(1), 20–38. doi:10.1177/0907568210379924

Parkes, J. (2007). The Multiple Meanings of Violence – Children's talk about life in a South African neighbourhood. *Childhood, 14*(4), 401–414. doi:10.1177/0907568207081848

Patterson, G. R., DeBaryshe, B., & Ramsey, E. (1990). A Developmental Perspective on Antisocial Behavior. *The American Psychologist, 44*(2), 329–335. doi:10.1037/0003-066X.44.2.329 PMID:2653143

Scheper-Hughes, N., & Bourgois, P. (Eds.). (2004). *Violence in War and Peace: An Anthology.* Oxford, UK: Blackwell.

Thornton, S. (1995). The social logic of subcultural capital. In *The Subcultures Reader*. London: Routledge.

Tyler, K. A. (2006). A Qualitative Study of Early Family Histories and Transitions of Homeless Youth. *Journal of Interpersonal Violence, 21*(10), 1385–1393. doi:10.1177/0886260506291650 PMID:16940403

UNECE. (2010). Retrieved 18 February 2010 from: www.unece.org

WHO. (2010). Retrieved 18 February 2010 from: www.who.int

ENDNOTE

[1] "Decent" in Anderson's conception depicts the set of value orientations of conventional society, while "street" remains associated with "the troublesome aspects of the ghetto life" (Anderson, 2002: 1533).

Section 4
Africa

Chapter 13
Cape Town Gangs:
The Other Side of Paradise

Don Pinnock
University of Cape Town, South Africa

ABSTRACT

Almost all gang studies throughout the 20th century and most in the 21st locate the reasons for both gang membership and a tendency to violence in the environments within which young people are raised: family, neighbourhood, school, poverty, access to drugs and general deprivation. In Cape Town all these were present under apartheid and still persist 20 years after the country became a democracy. The reasons for this persistence have to do with global and local economics, skills shortages, corruption, political mismanagement and neglect of certain neighbourhoods and are beyond the scope of this chapter. Rather, acknowledging these influences, this study looks at how gangs are defined and examines them from a more finely grained perspective.

INTRODUCTION

Woven deeply into the urban tapestry of Cape Town is a shadow city, its threads firmly anchored in the capitalist economy, knotted into local control and governance systems and extending far beyond the borders of the country. Its activities are hidden to all but those who know where to look and – when you do – it suddenly seems to be everywhere. Its influence is considerable and maintained through covert connections, graft, coercion, illegal trade and, not infrequently, murder. It has a history. (Pinnock 2016)[1]

Until the early-1990s South Africa was a country encircled by fences and surveillance systems with soldiers on the alert for ANC guerillas and the threat of communism. Its borders were protected against penetration by anyone other than official travellers and wide-eyed holidaymakers. On the Cape Flats, the job of the police was to control the political volatility and hunt down spies and saboteurs. Illicit activities were low on the apartheid government's perceived list problems and, accordingly, these flourished. For citizens already victims of harsh racism and aware of police complicity in applying it, state designations of legality were considered largely irrelevant or merely a challenge to overcome or undermine.

DOI: 10.4018/978-1-4666-9938-0.ch013

An example of this in Cape Town is the subversion of bottle stores, a seemingly small matter with large implications. In line with the perception that Coloured (mixed race) people abused alcohol, throughout the 1970s and 1980s the government owned, managed and limited to about 20 the number of bottle stores in Coloured areas. These did not allow credit to 'non-whites' and were generally bleak places with nowhere to sit, eat, dance or listen to music. This attempt at control backfired when individuals fitted their houses as shebeens where illegal liquor could be bought and consumed in congenial surroundings. Shebeening spread rapidly across the Cape Flats, supported covertly by large alcohol producers that found these watering holes a convenient way to offload low-grade wine and spirits. (Standing 2006)[2]

Trouble easily follows alcohol consumption, however, and shebeen owners could not expect police to respond to calls from illegal establishments. In most areas the local gang was amenable to a protection arrangement against alcoholic excesses by patrons. They had the added value of being lookouts against police raids and for collecting outstanding debts from customers on payday. Gangs could, unasked, also insist on protection payments from shebeens in return for not wrecking them, a practice that was to extend to all business in some areas. A gang member from Manenberg put it planely (Lambrechts 2013)[3]:

See, sometimes the HL"s (Hard Livings) can come in and rob you...They can take the stuff anytime if they want to, but if you want protection you've got to pay us for the protection so that you don't get robbed and if you don't want to die, you also have to pay for protection.

Certain police officers, alert to useful additions to their own pay and pleasure extracted favours from shebeen owners in the form of cash, liquor and meat. In the 1980s, while in a Hanover Park shebeen interviewing the owner, I was startled when two uniformed officers walked in and, after a brief conversation with the shebeener, left with four bottles of brandy. None of the customers batted an eyelid. Shebeens were technically illegal but, in practical terms, largely ignored.

A similar situation resulted from the prohibition of mandrax tablets, which were developed as a cheap legal sedative. In the 1970s mandrax became popular as a recreational drug when mixed with alcohol, then exploded across the Cape Flats when smoked in a 'white pipe' mixed with cannabis. Banned in the late 1970s, its import and eventually local manufacture became one of the most lucrative illegal industries in Cape Town. It was sourced by merchants and sold on the streets by gang members. From minor skirmishes, deadly gang wars soon erupted over control of sales turf. In this way gangs grew in wealth and power.

After 1994 a door opened and the world entered. Through it poured political goodwill, investment, tourists and the criminal underworld. From top government officials and businessmen to kids on the ghetto street corner, the boom in illegal goods and services changed everything.

In the slipstream of globalization throughout the 1980s, transnational criminal activity had spread throughout the world, operating across national boundaries and outpacing the ability of enforcement agencies to contain it (Gastrow 1998).[4] This change fed on the expanding information and communication revolution, the increasing interconnection of banking systems and the opening up of opportunities following the end of the Cold War. Particularly, however, it fed off transitional political confusion and targeted weakening of control systems in Russia, Central Europe, South America and Africa (Gastrow 1998).[5] After 1994 a globally reenergized city like Cape Town – conveniently positioned between east and west and historically a colonial conduit for import and export – could hardly escape the attention of worldly savvy criminal networks.

As road transport links to the north opened up into Zimbabwe, Zambia and the Congos, in the secret containers on trucks, trains and ships went poached ivory, rhino horn, abalone, rare metals, and precious stones. Return journeys brought drugs, cheap imitation clothing, cigarettes and other useful international items. Often these imports were paid for in stolen motor vehicles. Crime, particularly indigenous and transnational crime, flourished. Mark Shaw notes that weakening border controls in South Africa,

occurred at a time when transnational criminal operations were expanding; just like 'legitimate' multinational businesses, East Asian, Nigerian and East European groups bought into local South African criminal operations and expanded them, or contracted subsidiary organisations to conduct their work for them. (Shaw 1997)[6]

By 2001, the Minister for Safety and Security at the time, Steve Tshwete, was to claim that organised crime had 'extended its tentacles into South Africa after the country's return to the global arena (Tshwete 2001). 'Since it opened to the world, he said, [South Africa] had felt the effects of transnational organised crime syndicates attempting to extend their tentacles to 'new markets':

Given South Africa's relatively well-developed infrastructure, modern telecommunication systems, technology and business practices, it would appear that the scope of organised crime has evolved from generally small-scale local operations to international syndicates.[7]

The growth in criminal activity following the end of the Cold War and the globalization of economies occurred so fast that police and policymakers were slow to catch up. Urban hubs like Nairobi, Johannesburg, Lagos, Dakar, Kinshasa and Addis Ababa and Cape Town have become the epicentres for the spread of organised crime across the sub-continent (Shaw 2013).[8] Estimating its scale has become difficult because extensive corruption at government level in many countries has reduced official crime reporting and warped statistics. For this reason the volume of seized drugs, for example, is no longer a useful indicator of total illicit drug flows.

Criminal groups entering South Africa's porous borders in the 1990s were found by Andre Standing to include the Russian Mafia, Chinese Triads, Nigerian networks, Italian Mafia, Colombians, Peruvians, Pakastanis, Bulgarians, Portuguese and Congolese. To these were added weapons-trained, demobbed SADF and umKhonto we Sizwe soldiers and local Special Defence Unit members. The effect of these changes on some Cape Flats gangs was increasing 'corporatisation' and Standing quotes estimates by some authorities that these were responsible for as much as 70% of all crime on the Flats (Standing 2006).[9]

In economically depressed areas of the city, with the transitional police force in disarray and seismic shifts in the balance of political authority, the power of the law was severely limited by a widespread feeling that it was not legitimate. This reduced resistance to other, more immediate centres of power and less legal forms of income. Waning legal agency was not confined to Cape Town but was and still is a worldwide problem. The United Nations Research Institute for Social Development, reporting on transnational crime, noted perceptively that,

At a time of narrowing economic opportunity across wide areas of the world, participation in the illegal economy ... constitutes one of the few realistic options available to many families who simply need to ensure a basic level of subsistence. Illegality makes certain commodities or services unusually profitable (Cited in Standing 2006).[10]

Criminal power is partly the ability to claim ownership of a territory through the provision of certain goods and services, raising income and protection for some and the use of threat or outright violence. In this way it accrues status for its leaders who become both respected and feared. According to Standing, the rise of criminal power is 'a rational, rather than deviant response to economic hardship – what some sociologists call an adaptive mechanism to poverty. Cheap stolen goods 'dull the ache of deprivation'.

Crime bosses, whether they're gang leaders or independent drug merchants able to buy gang power, are essentially the result of inadequate state authority and its inability to provide a monopoly of force and basic social and economic security (Standing 2006). [11] They're self-appointed providers of arbitrary and illicit forms of justice.

We turn now to the gangs themselves, but with an essential caveat. A general impression in government and local media is that gangs are the cause of crime in Cape Town. While they do engage in crime, deal drugs, act violently at times and have been implicated in many murders, they are not the main perpetrators of contact crime (SA Police Crime Stats 2014).[12] Areas of the city with the highest levels of reported crime are mostly those with low gang presence and large populations of recent migrants. Gangs are simply a more organised and observable aspect of a city which has high levels of very generalised violence within families, towards peers and partners, in drunken shebeen brawls, out of bravado and during robbery. So while I'll be focussing on gangs and particularly their younger members, we need to keep in mind that the problem of disaffected youth is much wider than the gang turfs under discussion and exists for similar reasons. Cape Town doesn't have a gang problem so much as a youth problem of which gangs are one of the outcomes.

That this problem will continue to grow unless major economic and social transformation occurs is assured by a frightening demographic. Africa is experiencing rapid population growth and urbanization. At the present rate, by 2050 it will be home to twice as many people – 2,1 billion – equaling a quarter of the world's population. It's an exponential growth rate with no equivalent in human history (Shaw & Reitano 2013).[13] If present urban income disparities continue, rising social unrest and violence throughout the continent are inevitable.

ORGANISED CRIME: MEN IN THE SHADOWS

What is common to all gang involvement by whatever model we assess them, is best understood as entanglement. The term is useful in its ambiguity, implying both ensnarement and a barrier, generally of barbed wire, used to impede access by an enemy. It also implies disorder and confusion while at the same time tight coils of engagement. More than two decades after South Africa's first democratic election, the situation for an ever-growing number of under-trained, unemployed young people on the dusty streets of the Cape Flats is an increasing entanglement in activities that are at times illegal, not infrequently violent and moated by lack of social agency.

But there are others, better organised and networked, who have agendas beyond survival, clan affiliation, a cellphone and the next hit and are generally considered as being involved in organised crime. As we have seen, descriptions of organised crime overlap those of street gangs, making theoretical disentanglement difficult. In a study of organised crime, researcher Klaus von Lampe lists over 180 definitions.[14]

On the ground, however, the differences are less indistinct and the gap between a corner street hustler and an organisation such as The Firm or a drug importer is, to quote Peter Gastrow (1998), similar to the one which would exist between a street hawker and a successful international import/export and wholesale business.[15]

An appropriate term for people who associate around a common purpose is French-derived word 'syndicate'. According to the South African police, a crime syndicate is defined broadly as 'a well organised and structured group with a clear leadership corps, which is involved in different criminal activities such as drug trafficking, vehicle theft or money laundering. Such syndicates have well established contacts with national and international criminal organisations, cartels or mafia groupings' (see Shaw 1998, p1).[16] Other terms that have been used are warlords and violent entrepreneurs (Shaw & Reitano 2013).[17]

By 1999 police intelligence claimed that over 800 syndicates were then operating in the country, with a collective membership of 12 000 'primary suspects'. Of these groups, 300 were believed to also operate either elsewhere in Africa or internationally (Shaw 1999).[18] An indication of transnational criminal activity can be seen from a report by the Washington-based Global Financial Integrity (GFI), which estimated that from 2003 to 2012 illicit financial flows from Sub-Saharan Africa were US$528.5 billion. From South Africa in 2012 alone these amounted to US$29.13 billion (Kar & Spanjers 2012).[19] Just under 80% of this flow was due to deliberate mis-invoicing and 'leakages' in the balance of payments – basically money laundering:

Usually, through export under-invoicing and import over-invoicing, corrupt government officials, criminals, and commercial tax evaders are able to easily move assets out of countries and into tax havens, anonymous companies, and secret bank accounts. [20]

According to GFI, illicit financial outflows from sub-Saharan Africa outpaced official development assistance going into the region at a ratio of at least two to one. Sustained illicit outflows have turned the continent into a net creditor to the rest of the world (Global Financial Integrity, quoted in Shaw & Reitano 2010).[21] Of the 145 developing countries assessed in terms of illicit flows, South Africa was ranked, alarmingly, at 12th.

These transactions go far beyond what is generally considered foreign and local crime syndicates and into the boardrooms of national and international corporations. Groups within these respected entities fit almost every definition of organized crime. We need to keep this in mind when considering the relationship between gangs and structured criminal associations. Crime syndicates in low-income areas dealing in illicit substances and transactions are a major problem in their areas of operation, but minor players in much larger and extremely damaging levels of corporate crime.

Most studies of organized crime exhibit a worrying amnesia about what used to be called white-collar, financial crime but which is simply corporate racketeering, preferring to focus on the 'with weapons' variety. This seemingly unconscious distinction between 'our crime' and 'their crime' further complicates a clear understanding of organized crime. However this chapter is about the impact of gangs on young people at risk and, at this level, organized crime is definitely the 'with weapons' variety.

To understand this layer of organized crime in Cape Town we need to see where it fits into the context of general gang activity. It's difficult to estimate how many people are, in terms of the SAPS depiction, 'a well organised and structured group with a clear leadership corps' in contact with 'national and international criminal organisations, cartels or mafia groupings'. But the numbers are probably very low. They constitute a criminal elite and most are in the drug business, with other interests being in smuggling, prostitution, car theft, protection rackets, nightclubs and possibly weapons procurement. They own substantial capital, legitimate business or properties and are relatively conspicuous in their

Table 1.

Violent		
Type	**Reasons/Actions**	**Who are they?**
Warrior	Honor	amaVuro, AmaVatos, etc.
Tik soldiers	Money for drugs	Street flies
Prison	Safety/sex/trade	26, 27, 28
Merchants	Drug sales/turf defense	Most minority race gangs
Corporates 1	Market control, money laundering	Hard Livings etc.
Franchise	Market Control	Americans etc.

communities if they're locals. They include individual drug merchants, the upper levels of larger gangs such as the Hard Livings, Americans, Sexy Boys and Mongrels and Chinese Triads, Russian, Italian and East European mafias, Moroccans and Nigerians (Tables 1 and 2).

The presence of foreign 'high flyers' hit the headlines in 2011 when nightclub security boss Cyril Beeka was killed in a drive-by shooting. He and his staff were accused by a presedential task force as being 'soldiers' for the Italian Mafia and its alleged 'banker', Vito Palazzolo. A year later Serbian fugitive Dobrosav Gavric, Russian Igor Russol and Moroccan Houssain Ait Taleb appeared in the Cape Town Magistrate's Court for activities related to organised crime. Russol was accused of extorting R600 000 and a Porsche Cayenne from businesses in and around Cape Town, Gavric (who was facing extradition to Serbia to serve a 35-year jail sentence for three murders) for fraudulently entering South Africa. Taleb was Beeka's assistant. The following year, Western Province MEC for community safety, Dan Plato, claimed that the emergence of international fugitives and an internationally linked underworld was a danger to the province and that Cape Town's nightclubs were connected to both Cape Flats gangs and syndicates in Eastern Europe, the Balkans, North America and elsewhere (quoted in Davids 2012).

I am worried about the fact that so many high-profile underworld figures are involved in Cape Town. I am worried about the number of foreign nationals involved in organised crime in Cape Town. My question is: why are all these foreign people heading for Cape Town, doing their business in Cape Town and finding Cape Town so cosy and appropriate?[22]

Table 2.

Non-Violent		
Type	**Reasons/Actions**	**Who are they?**
Corporates 2	Market edge, money laundering	Legal companies
Local syndicates	Illicit markets	Individuals, gang bosses
Foreign syndicates	Illicit markets	Chinese, Nigerians, Russians, Zimbabweans, etc.
Tenderpreneurs	Contracts	Hard Livings, new elite
Political mafias	Skimming, contracts	Government officials
Government agents	Money laundering, theft	Government administrations and top polititcians

He said the city was dealing with high profile, professional and sophisticated gang and drug bosses. 'We need people to outplay them. I do not believe the SAPS in its current format is in that position.'

Is the city underworld in the thrall of foreign racketeers? The truth is much more complex and interesting. A 2005 United Nations report on Crime and Development in Africa concluded that '...Africa may have become the continent most targeted by organised crime'. It noted that indications from drug seizures were that Africa was increasingly being used to route drugs destined for other markets (quoted in Hübschle 2013).[23] In 2010 researcher Annette Hübschle concluded that in Southern Africa criminal groups appeared to have created a 'free-trade zone' for illicit commerce through various trans-national networks, with drug smuggling being the greatest concern (Hübschle 2103).[24] In a special report on organized crime in Southern Africa, she found that:

- **Cannabis:** Grown throughout Southern Africa is being marketed in Europe and North America. Its routes are also serving as a conduit for illegal diamonds, stolen vehicles, rhino horn and ivory;
- **Cocaine:** From countries such as Bolivia, Colombia and Venezuela is entering the sub-region, via Brazil, through Nigeria and Mozambique, the routes being run by loosely-associated networks. West Africa has emerged as a major transit and repackaging hub for cocaine flowing from Latin America to European markets. About 13 per cent of cocaine trafficked to Europe is being transited via Guinea-Bissau, which amounts to at least 25 tons per year with a minimum market value of $4,29 billion;
- **Methaqualone:** The main ingredient of mandrax, is being manufactured in China and India and entering the sub-region via Mozambique, Swaziland, Zimbabwe and Zambia. In the Western Cape 'tik factories' are obtaining the ingredients in exchanges of abalone through hinese Triad gangs. Nigerians have been implicated in street-level distribution of tik (methamphetamine), but its sale is mainly controlled by local merchants and gangs;
- **Heroin:** Comes from poppy fields in India, Pakistan, Afghanistan and China and enters Southern Africa by air or sea, mainly through Zanzibar or Dar es Salaam where West African distributers disseminate it into the continent. In South Africa, Nigerian and Tanzanian syndicates appear to control delivery to merchants;
- **Stolen Motor Vehicles:** Are a major currency in drug deals, a system which bypasses more easily traced money transactions. Hijacked luxury or off-road vehicles and taxis form the bulk of this trade;
- **Gold and Natural Resources:** Illicit trafficking in gold and natural resources out of Central Africa, particularly the Democratic Republic of Congo, is facilitating sustained insecurity caused by armed groups and is feeding to illicit flows estimated at over $1,2 billion a year.
- **Cybercrime:** Three West African countries – Nigeria, Ghana and Cameroon – are ranked among the top countries in the world where cybercrime is most prevalent, contributing to a global flow of some $600 million a year. Improved communication technology has drawn Africa deeper into the global economy, making it more susceptible to crime;
- **Money Laundering:** A report by the United States (US) State Department on money laundering claims that Kenya's financial system may be laundering more than $100 million each year;
- **ATM Bombings:** Involve Mozambican and South African groups, often with connections to mines (for explosives) or former apartheid police officers unable to find employment elsewhere. Other organized groups target specialized goods such as electronic goods, clothing and jewellery in house robberies. Pakistani dealers are said to specialize in stolen cellphones destined for Nigeria.

Most drug routes into the city fly well below the radar, but occasionally an error or a police bust raises them into view. In December 2010 a small fishing vessel returning from the high seas to Knysna was searched and 1.7 tonnes of cocaine were found onboard. Two years later four 25-kilogram waterproof bags washed up on the Southern Cape shores. They contained 99% pure cocaine and were identified from a logo stamp as having originated in Bolivia or Peru. They may have been part of a floating consignment dropped into the Mozambique Current further north with signal transmitters attached for recovery off the KwaZulu-Natal or Cape coasts. In April 2014 the Australian Navy intercepted a vessel off the Kenyan coast carrying livestock. A search turned up more than 1000 kilogrammes of heroin concealed as cement.

These are a few visible pointers to an illegal drug supply chain into and through Southern Africa estimated by the 2013 National Drug Master Plan to be worth around R136 billion a year or 6.4% of the region's GDP. While many of the drug shipments conduit through South Africa, a number remain behind for local consumption. This has led to a dramatic increase in drug use, presently double the global average. The country is also the biggest user of cannabis and mandrax and has one of the highest prevalence of substance use disorders in the world.[25]

During the apartheid years South Africa's relative exclusion from the world economy tended to isolated it from hard drugs such as cocaine and heroin. After 1994 the country was regarded as an untapped drug market. New markets or existing ones were consolidated and gang activity increased to take advantage of the change. According to research buy Charles Goredema and Khalil Goga (2014) of the Institute for Security Studies:

the patterns of the trade have become well established .... with cocaine originating from the Andean region in South America and heroin emanating from Asia – predominantly Afghanistan and surrounding countries. Traffic routes that directly connect South Africa to these regions carry significant quantities of drugs to Cape Town, but it is evident that supplies are supplemented by imports entering by land through Angola and Namibia (cocaine) and Mozambique and Madagascar (heroin).[26]

Together with the illegal export of rhino horn, ivory and exotic species, drug dealing has earned South Africa the reputation of being the hub of organized crime in the sub-region with an estimated 953 active syndicates in 2014, many being foreigners from Nigeria, Pakistan, India, China and Europe (Goredema & Goga 2014).[27] The high drug flow levels are partly because of South Africa's geographical location, but also because of a good banking system, poor border controls and a police force able to occasionally disrupt but ultimately not stem the traffic. Added to this, writes Gareth Newham from the Institute of Security Studies, is the low risk of being brought before the courts, the ease with which a false passport can be used to enter the country and leave it, and the possibility of corrupting the police to get out of trouble (quoted in Owen 2014).[28] More than six in ten crimes in the country are drug related with the Western Cape being the highest.[29]

All these activities require levels of sophistication that would classify as organized crime. But who's in control? After 1994 when trans-national crime began taking off, local Cape gangs were confronted by sophisticated operators attempting to muscle in on their traditional turfs. The days of parochial, neighbourhood-based operations were clearly numbered. These threats, compounded by the formation of PAGAD (People Against Guns and Drugs) targeting drug merchants, was to totally transform the structure and relationships of gangs on the Cape Flats. It was to be a battle for survival and dominance on an utterly altered terrain. According to Standing (2005):

The result of this tumultuous period for gangs was an increase in their power and financial base and a rapid sophistication in, and increased brutality of, their business practices, partly learnt from the foreign syndicates with whom they now came into contact.[30]

Criminologist Irvin Kinnes found that what distinguished international syndicates from local gangs was the former's ability to supply drugs in large quantities. But though Nigerians and Chinese syndicates dominated the importation routes, they were blocked by local gangs from entering the retail market. Where they tried they were attacked (Kinnes 2000).[31] Moroccans who started a parking and protection scheme for city nightclubs ended up in gunfights with local shooters. Big-time drug dealers like Colin Stansfield and Jackie Lonte could marshal local soldiers in defense of their turf, as could gang leaders such as brothers Rashied and Rashaad Staggie. Lonte's gang, the Americans, had been covertly supplied with drugs by the previous government's Civil Cooperation Bureau in return for quelling political unrest against apartheid and dominated the mandrax market (Kinnes 2000).[32] When Stansfield was arrested in 1996, he was estimated to be worth R30-million. The combined membership of the Hard Livings and Americans in 1994 was between 3 000 and 10 000 fighters. The 'Big Men' were purchasing valuable real estate and exploiting gaps in state provision to buy community loyalty through their support for sport, welfare and cultural activities.

In the early 1990s local drug merchants and gang bosses – possibly coordinated by Stansfield – banded together to found The Firm in order to rationalize and consolidate control over the market. Markets and turf were agreed upon and gang fights subsided, being considered bad for business. As not all gangs were members of the cartel, the peace did not last long, particularly following the attacks on gang leaders and the gruesome murder of Rashaad Staggie by PAGAD in 1996. By then, however, the upper ranks of big gangs such as the Hard Livings, Americans, Mongrels and Sexy Boys had effectively fought off any takeovers by foreign syndicates (Kinnes 2000).[33] According to Kinnes (2000), 'Considering the fact that these gangs had access to all parts of the Western Cape through their distribution networks, their transformation into criminal organisations was a natural outcome.'[34]

One of the reasons for the success local gangs had in holding their ground, according to the SAPS head of Operation Combat, General Jeremy Veary (2014), was their randomness, violence and incorporation of prison gang discipline. Foreign gangs like the Chinese Triads had traditional ways of doing business but were scared by the unpredictability of local gangs.

You're sitting here and speaking normally but you don't know when the people are deciding to kill you. Gangs have this mystique, you know, you cannot tie them down. You come to make a deal and with 500 grand and the guys rob you. Simple as that. The Triads started saying no, we're not going to pay you with money any more. We're going to pay you in methaqualone and ephedrine in exchange for abalone. Then things went stable. So what you're talking about now is not control by foreign syndicates but supply lines.[35]

By 2003, Western Cape Minister of Community Safety, Leonard Ramatlkane (quoted in Standing 2005), was able to link the leadership of larger local gangs to organized crime:

The nature of gangsterism in the Western Cape today has become increasingly ruthless and business orientated. Participation in gang activity is still substantially driven by such elements as group identity, self-protection, pride, boredom and turf. However, the bottom line is money, where highly organised and well-connected gang bosses preside over vast business empires.[36]

As we will see below, however, the base of these 'empires' is less stable and organized than Ramatlkane suggests, with systems open to costly disruption and armed young men always alert for violent takeover and, when trouble happens, needing to bribe or shoot their way back into the driving seat.

PRISON GANGS: OLD AND MEAN

Prisons are containment systems designed to keep criminals off the streets. At this, and only this, they are successful. There are about 10-million prisoners in the world – one person in every 700. According to the World Prison Brief, South Africa has the largest prison population in Africa and the ninth biggest in the world. However, according to the South African Minister of Correctional Services, Sibusiso Ndebele (2014), retribution through imprisonment has not deterred crime.[37] 'Since retribution is narrowly focussed on moral reprobation or outrage against criminal conduct,' he said, 'it fails to adequately reform offending behaviour and to repair harm experienced by victims of crime.'

The cost of what the Minister is essentially calling a failed institution is staggering. According to the inmate support programme NICRO, in 2014 South Africa had 162 162 people in custody, 49 695 of them awaiting trial. It cost taxpayers, according to the Minister, R329.2 a day to house each inmate and prevent them from escaping. That amounts to around R19.4 billion a year. Between the years 1995 and 2014, prisoners serving life sentences jumped by an astonishing 2197% – at the time of writing there were around 21 000 inmates serving from 20 years to life. The true madness of the situation is that recidivism – re-imprisonment – is between 55 and 95%. At huge cost, people are being recycled through the prison system with no positive value to themselves or the country (Jules-Macquet 2014).[38] In all aspects other than containment – apart perhaps from a public requirement for revenge – prisons are intolerable and a complete failure. They simply cannot work because their very nature is paradoxical.

The Department of Correctional Services is essentially being asked to look after people nobody wants to care for and is supposed to solve damage that's been done to them, sometimes, since birth.[39] It is required to 'correct' antisocial behaviour, to make people 'better'. But the worst conceivable place to attempt that is in jail. Behind prison walls, what relationships young people had with parents, partners and friends are terminated and they join others who are equally stressed, distressed and alienated. There they are further depersonalized, violated and victimized and return to society angry, unambitious, vengeful and schooled in brutal gang practices.

If one was to trace the beginnings of the process that steers young people to prison, it would find failed or destructive relationships – father, mother, sibling, teacher, peers, society or all of these. If prisons were to be truly corrective, they would assist young people to gain insights into this relationship failure. They would provide opportunities for them to restore self respect, reliance on their own integrity and to change. This is precisely what prisons throughout the world do not do. And in South Africa the need for relationships, self respect and protection against cruelty is feeding fierce, hierarchical and violent prison Numbers gangs. Another impossible paradox is that demands by the public and politicians to lower the crime rate is prodding the criminal justice system to be increasingly vengeful. But revenge labels, ostracizes, alienates and breeds antisocial, criminal behaviour, recidivism and an escalating prison population. It's a system destined to dysfunction and is increasingly out of control.

Yet despite these conditions, as poverty increases in marginalized communities, a chilling corollary is emerging. According to the Institute of Race Relations, 'living conditions might be better in prison than on the outside … and some gang members preferred to be in prison so they could remain in their gangs.'[40] The number of years spent in prison, said SAIRR researcher Kerwin Lebone (2012), is therefore no longer a deterrent.[41]

There's another anomaly about incarceration that needs consideration. From the early 19th Century in Europe, imprisonment changed from being pre-punishment detention to punishment itself.[42] It has since become, according to the philosopher Michael Foucault (1977), 'a detestable solution which one seems unable to do without … one cannot see how to replace it.'[43] Deprivation of liberty makes it possible to precisely quantify the penalty by varying the time of detention rather than varying the conditions under which detention takes place. Given the increasing scale of incarceration, this is a bureaucratic and logistical necessity, keeping the same form whether the prisoner is sentenced for a month or a lifetime. Walls and not conditions are the punishment for the crime. Previous life is annihilated and imprisonment becomes a coercive theatre in which the only audience are the actors themselves. In his study of an American maximum-security prison, Gresham Sykes (1958) argues that:

[the] frustrations [of captivity] … carry a more profound hurt as a set of threats or attacks which are directed against the very foundations of the prisoner's being. The individual's picture of himself as a person of value – as a morally acceptable, adult male who can present some claim to merit in his material achievements and his inner strength – begins to waver and grow dim.[44]

Being created, in the words of Foucault (1977), 'is another class and another human species. A zoology of social sub-species and an ethnology of the civilizations of malefactors, with their own rites and language.'[45] In these conditions, he says, 'prison fabricates delinquents ... it brings back, almost inevitably, before the courts those who have been sent there.' In this sense, delinquency is the vengeance of prison on the justice system.

It's a central tenet of law that you're innocent until proved guilty. If detention within a prison is in itself punishment for wrongdoing, in 2013 more than 53 000 legally innocent people were being wrongfully punished as awaiting trial prisoners. Many of them were children (as an indication, between April 2010 to March 2011, 75 435 were charged by the police, though of course many of them were diverted from detention centres)(Muntingh & Ballard 2012).[46] Awaiting trial prisoners are, in this way, being forced to attend schools of delinquency. Their constitutional rights are clearly being violated but, given the grinding slowness of the judicial system – the gathering of evidence, finding witnesses, securing court dates and the ineptness of much detection and documentation – what's the alternative? In the present system there is none. But the paradox remains: prisons create that which they wish to destroy.

This chapter is not about prison gangs *in* prison, but about their effect on those who are not. But a brief look behind the locked gates is instructive. Much has been written about these brutal gangs, the most notable being *The small matter of a horse: life of Nongoloza Mathebula 1876–1948* by Charles van Onselen (1985), *The Number* by Johnny Steinberg (2004) and *Gods Gangsters* by Heather Parker Lewis (2010).[47]

In the hands of Van Onselen (1985), one of South Africa's foremost investigative historians, the story is about a band of robbers in late 19th century Transvaal and Natal who preyed on black migrant miners returning home from the Transvaal mines with their pay packets. It's also about a Zulu youngster named Mzuzepi Mathebula who allowed a farmer's horse to stray and was required to work off the debt of its absence. Mzuzepi escaped to Johannesburg, worked as a groom for some highway robbers, learned the trade and changed his name to Jan Note and later to Nongoloza. The erstwhile groom formed his own band of robbers who named themselves Umkosi Wezintaba (Regiment of the Hills) which was organized as a para-military unit.

Nongoloza imbued his bandit army with a political purpose. 'I reorganised my gang of robbers,' he reported to his captors in 1912. 'I laid them under what has since become known as Nineveh law. I read in the Bible about the great state Nineveh which rebelled against the Lord and I selected that name for my gang as rebels against the Government's laws' (quoted in Department of Justice Annual Report 1912).[48]

According to Steinberg (2004), it was said that Nongoloza was imbued with magic, that the bullets of white policemen and soldiers bounced off his skin. 'In early proletarian lore, he was something of a Janus-faced monster: horrible because he was undiscerningly brutal, enticing because he showed that "even the poor can be terrible"'.[49]

During the Anglo-Boer War, Nongoloza and many Ninevites were incarcerated at Cinderella Prison in Boksberg. On release, he shifted his group to caves near Johannesburg, undertaking housebreaking and farm holdups, which included shooting dead a policeman. By 1912 the robbers were being described by police as Nongoloza'a Army. Its leader was arrested and given a life sentence, along with many of his generals, and began organizing his 'army' within prison walls along strict military lines. By the early 1930s, gang derivatives of the Ninevites had a presence in almost every prison across the country. Out of this developed the Numbers gangs – 26, 27 and 28s – which operate with extreme and often casual brutality and the ready taking of blood (Vearey, n.d.).[50]

In the hands of prison inmates, this story has blossomed into a durable mythology, a code of conduct, a dress code echoing that of late 19th century Boer and British armies, a secret language and an unwritten 'book' that needs to be memorized. In the absence of written records, the system of identifying gang members and their rank is ingenious. Any new prisoner who claims to be a member is required to recite the gang history and to 'dress' himself equal to his rank. This must be '*sabelad*' in the language of the gangs – *shalombom* for the 26s and 27s, and *ndyaza* for the 28s.[51] He is asked: 'Who are you? Where do you come from? How will I recognize you?' Whereupon he must identify his rank, gang and imaginary uniform.[52] The mythology includes an arch-criminal Pomabaza or Po (a shamanistic figure) who initiated Nongoloza and one Kilikijan into a life of plunder, the death of a bull called Rooiland (upon which the 'book' of the 28s is written), a white stone upon which Pomabaza's 'story' was written in blood (and later broken) and a parting of ways between Nongoloza and Kilikijan over same-sex intercourse (hence the division between 26's who forbid it and 28s who practice it).

The numbers gangs were formed on strict military lines, echoing the uniforms and structures of Anglo-Boer War soldiers as well as police and prison warders with whom they are in constant contact. They have their own parliament, legal system, punishments territories and economy. The 26s, for example, have a Makwezi (president), generals, captains, sergeant majors, lawyers, doctors, inspectors, teachers and soldiers. In a detailed report on prison gangs, General Jeremy Vearey lists the six laws of the 26s as:

1. You will not do what you want;
2. You will not lie to your brother or argue with him;
3. You will respect the honest work of police and wardens;
4. You will not sleep under the same blanket with your brother (no sex);
5. You will not physically harm a non-prison-gang member the first time he offends you and first give him two warnings before harming him;
6. You will die with your brother under the flag of the 26s.[53]

The 28s have similar systems, except that they add rules of conduct between the soldier or golden line (males) and the private or silver line ('females'). The Numbers gangs are forbidden to fight each other and their spheres of influence and action are divided. The 26s are permitted robbery and theft by subterfuge (but not violence) and must distribute the gains evenly, the 28s fight on behalf of all three camps for better prison conditions and can engage in sodomy and the 27s guarantee gang law and keep the peace between all three camps. If blood is spilled, they spill it in return. Prisons being what they are, however, conflict between gangs does take place, but it's strictly regulated and attempts are made by senior gang members to quell it as quickly as possible. Non members of the Numbers, however, are fair game and often victims of extreme violence.

The memory of Nongoloza is a myth built from scraps of fact, but is greater than merely a myth. It is, as Steinberg points out, not a story one tells but a set of practices one enacts. Its twists and turns are memorized in the long days of doing time and punched into the skin of inmates as crude tattoos depicting shields of the bull Rooiyard, bayonets of the Boer War, sunrise (26s), sunset (28s), guns, comments and personal pain. But the form that the myth took was in response to the conditions that prisoners faced. As Veary (n.d.) has pointed out in a detailed analysis of prison gangs, 'criminals militarise in response to you. The Nongoloza banding together as an army took its form in response to the army during the Boer War. That was what they knew. You take the shape of what you face.'[54]

On the streets throughout most of the 20th century, prison gangs were known about but considered to be prison business. Until the late 1980s it was understood that the walls between prison and street were total, but they suddenly began to crumble. One of first cracks may have begun in Cape Town with the imprisonment of the druglord Jackie Lonte. This coincided with the clamour beyond prison walls for apartheid to end and a sense of impending democracy. Lonte was, by any standards, immensely rich and had access to supplies of mandrax which he could smuggle into prison. There was no way a man like that would stand for the requirements and physical torments of Numbers gang membership and he had the means to buy himself clear. But the mythology and structure of the Numbers intrigued him.

Whether or not he was a catalyst, at about the same time Number gangs in the Western Cape closed their 'bloodlines', ending stabbing as a requirement for membership. Until then, to be a part of a prison Number was a lengthy and rigorous process, in which one could only climb the ranks after serving many brutal years in prison, a process which almost always required shedding blood (Teheri-Keramati 2014).[55] Closing the bloodlines was, according to Steinberg (2004), a cataclysmic decision:

To stab, and to be subjected to violence and deprivation in the wake of stabbing, was the centrepiece in the initiation process. It animated the world behind bars, providing it with its fundamental meaning. Why did it happen? I don't know. Some of it may have had to do with the changing relationship between prison gangs and street gangs. Whatever the reasons, the closing of the blood lines caused havoc.[56]

Shortly afterwards, conflict erupted between the gold and silver lines of the 28s in Victor Verster Prison and spread throughout the Western Cape. This rumbled on towards 1994 when the country experienced the worst outbreak of prison violence on record. Over the period of four months there was unrest in 53 prisons and in most cases inmates attempted to burn down the institutions – 37 inmates were killed and hundreds of prisoners and warders were injured. One of the reasons was said to be the failure of the new ANC government to offer expected widespread amnesty (Steinberg 2014).[57]

Whatever the reasons for the riots or the closing of bloodlines, the outcome was to weaken the Numbers gangs within the prison system. But on the streets of the city something strange was happening.

Prisoners began arriving claiming to be *ndotas*, able to *sablea* and, after a fashion, answer correctly to their rank – but had never before been in jail. When asked who'd initiated them they'd answer: The Americans or The Scorpions. What the prison old-timers discovered was that druglords like Jackie Lonte, Colin Stansfield and Ernie Lastig had 'stolen' the Numbers traditions to build armies on the streets.[58] The sacrilege was compounded when Lonte returned to prison in 1996 as a 26 and declared war on the 28s. The reason had to do with turf wars between gangs on the streets that now embraced Numbers allegiances, but bringing street rivalries to prison and declaring war without being an initiated fighting general carried a death penalty. But nobody would touch him. An informant told Steinberg (2014):

He was Jackie, and Jackie meant more than anything else. So we raised our American flags in our cells and we went to war with the 28s. Something like that had never happened before. After that, the Number was never the same again. [59]

By the late 1990s, two of the major Cape gangs – the Americans and The Firm (a cartel formed by Colin Stansfield to regulate drug sales on the Cape Flats) – were using Number rituals. The Americans considered themselves 26s and The Firm 28s and their leaders designated themselves generals and appointed captains, sergeants, judges, inspectors and soldiers. The Mongrels, being 26s, had a natural alliance to the Americans and Born Free Kids while the Cape Town Scorpions and Mafias aligned themselves with the 28s, bringing about congruency between prison gang stratification and street gang rivalry. According to Steinberg. 'The street gangs took the world of the prison – its metaphors, its nomenclature, its logic – and imprinted it on the ghettos.'[60] The power of Numbers mythology is described by Vearey (2014):

You speak a new language. You have new symbols through which you look at reality. You do not walk around fearfully anymore. It is the brand, the power that comes with that myth is what he represents. It's the type of power that comes with being a gang member. The Number makes a philosophy out of it, makes a belief system out of it. You get told all these myths about the great fight between the Numbers and the eight stars falling form the sky and the seven stars falling into the green grass....[61]

The sudden proliferation of Numbers traditions and mythologies on the streets in the early 1990s was not mere caprice, but in response to an external threat. The Cape gangs had always been regional affairs, defending a specific township turf in order to sell, dagga, liquor or mandrax. With the opening of borders to the world after 1994, as we have seen, foreign syndicates arrived and began to muscle in on the various illegal markets. In response, the bigger gangs like the Americans, Scorpions and Hard Livings had to strengthen their organisations, expand their markets, control their customers and to both compete and cooperate with foreign syndicates. There were also huge profits to be made with the introduction of heroin, cocaine and tik.

The new drug millionaires needed to create and maintain province-wide networks and ensure unwavering allegiances from buyers and sellers while keeping foreign syndicates at bay. The fierce, highly structured traditions and practices of the Numbers gangs were made for the task, requiring chains of command, strict adherence, the use of a secret language and easy linkages across turf boundaries. The mythology of the Numbers was also immensely appealing to young gang members in need of a 'story' to live by. According to an 'elder' in both prison and street gangs in Hanover Park (Peterson 2015):

The Numbers have discipline. This is their biggest influence on the gangs. The Numbers made them more organized. Gang members look up to the Numbers. They look to the Numbers for guidance. You won't find a leader of a gang that's not a Number.[62]

Initially, high-ranking street gang bosses entered prison and bought their way into the upper ranks of the Number and, on discharge, possessed new powers and networks. Increasingly, lower ranks are seeing spells of imprisonment as a way to bolster their credibility once back on the streets. During his work on the low-income neighbourhood of Overcome, Yashar Taheri-Keramati (2014) found that prison gangsters, wanting to cash in on the street gangsters' financial successes, were willing to 'sell' their names, affiliations and Number to those strong enough to buy them. Continually challenged by street gangs, they were forced to 'fast track' and offer protection to street gangsters in return for their patronage on release.[63] In return, on emerging from prison, Numbers members had a fraternity, a support system and a level of credibility on the streets. Sira, a member of the Vuros gang in Khayelitsha, said at first his gang had nothing to do with the Numbers.

But the more guys were getting arrested and taking a number inside the more it also played a role in outside gangs. After a time the guys wanted to be arrested, though they were afraid. But when we got arrested we met old friends who already had prison number. We needed to choose which number we wanted to become. I am 26 in this group, then you have guys who 28 in the same group. These days prison is not something we are afraid of because when we and our friends and older brothers with Numbers inside come out we're respected and have a place on the corner.[64]

By 2000, intelligence officials estimated that local gangs were in control about 90% of the mandrax, cocaine and dagga markets in the Western Cape, with Nigerians, Moroccans, Chinese and other syndicates controlling the rest.[65] Within a few years since the country's democratic elections, the Cape gangs had relegated the foreign syndicates to bulk providers. 'There's no foreign influence in the Cape Flats,' according to a gang leader interviewed in Hanover Park. 'The guys who mostly support the gangs are the Bongos (Nigerians) mainly with *unga* and *tik*. But they have no influence among the guys. Their only connection is supply.'[66]

By the second decade after the end of apartheid, the 'robber baron' interpretation of Nongoloza had been absorbed into most street gangs, giving them a sophisticated ideology through which to view the world and a language. According to researcher Luke Lee Skywalker, this gave street thugs with no previous code of honour a coherent history and philosophy, elevating them above their former status.[67] Having a secret language, according to a member of the Mongrels, is a very powerful thing:

It's a communication system across gangs. Very useful. If I negotiate with gangs I give them the power to say hello and to know who I am. Then I ask them the same with sabela and they must tell me. I make myself known to them and they make themselves known to me then we will know we are ndotas, you see? Now we know each other. If I go to a leader of a gang and can't sabela how can he talk to me? But he throws me a Number and I throw a Number back in a certain way, old school. Then they know.[68]

In this way Cape Flats gangs have wholly absorbed the Numbers ethos. According to Jonathan Jansen of Fusion Manenberg (2014), which attempts to rehabilitate gang youths,

The prison number gangs tie everything together. In the last 10 or 15 years there was a deliberate attempt to get it to open its secrets, to spill onto the streets and get every gang to buy into the network. In a sense there are now no gangs, except for very small ones, that are not also prison gangs. Nobody can negotiate peace if there are no number gang people involved. The ndotas need to talk. They can cross boundaries, walk in any territories, protected by their Number status.[69]

In the migration to the streets, however, the hard distinctions between the Numbers have become less defined, the codes of honour have shifted. 'Gangs aren't just single Numbers anymore, a Manenberg gang member told me, 'and in a war a Number will fight a Number. Not inside, but outside it's different:'

Outside the numbers don't count the way they do inside. You come out of prison and ask me what I'm doing and I'll remind you I was out here taking blood and where were you? To work yourself up outside is not to work yourself up as a Number. You spend 10 or 15 years in prison and come out, you can't tell the lighties what's what. They'll sommer shoot you.

In the face of these changes, most lifers behind bars have no purchase. Prison gangs will continue to flourish because they're a response to the system of incarceration. But in fact their members are the cooped-up custodians of a usable tradition for purposes beyond their reach. Instead of an association to create tough men annealed in the flames of violence, their closely guarded traditions are now increasingly badges of honour for new recruits passing through the prison system on the way to higher things. For jailed druglords, prison is free board and lodging from where they conduct external business deals on smuggled cellphones.

MERCHANT GANGS, BROTHERHOODS AND STREET SOLDIERS

'Over here you have the Big Man,' said Trappies (2015) explaining a certain merchant-gang's structure by moving objects on the table, 'and beside him here are two or three captains. This is where the money lives. Then over there are the inspectors, the gatekeepers, they check who can come in. Often those are the only ones people see. And then there are the core members – shooters, dealers, robbers – who do the business. And then, far down the line, are the tik soldiers; young guys, druggies, people who can be issued a gun and told to fight in return for drugs or money or for the hell of it.'[70]

Joey tells it slightly differently about another big merchant gang. 'There's the main man, Staal [not his real name], and then there's *Die Draad* and *Die Glas*. These guys are the fighting generals. But they must obey the code of rules. Even Staal can be punished for disobeying them. We can all talk equal under the rules – nobody is above them. Staal became leader because when he came out of jail the gang was leaderless so he got the guys together and he helped them, paid bail, looked after them. He's the leader because he's organised and respected. Then there are the soldiers – here in where we sit not so many, but over in Lavender Hill around 4 000.

'The gang isn't about housebreaking or robbery, it's about drugs and smuggling. In the gang only certain people smuggle drugs, you see. It won't be the leader. Guys get paid to sell. They're employed. If a member robs or breaks into a house it isn't really a gang thing. That's true of all the big gangs. If you see there's somewhere you can break in or someone you can rob and you're not a smuggler you can do that on your own. You can be independent.'[71]

General Peter Jacobs (2014), head of Police Intelligence in the Western Cape, corroborated this structure: 'Say you have 20 guys standing outside Etosha Court in Hanover Park. Four of them are shooters, maybe four are *posmanne*, spotters, four more are controllers of drugs. The rest are nothings who can't be trusted with drugs and can't shoot because only the hitmen can. They're just standing there on the corner 'filling' the gang numbers, but they don't get gang money because they do nothing. They're the housebreakers, the street robbers and they must bring money to the gang that way.[72]

'These filler guys are a problem for gangs because they disrupt the order. Maybe he robs someone from an opposing gang and you end up with a big street fight. This happened a while back when an Americans guy robbed the sister of a Hard Livings leader. The HLs killed him and that led to a hell of a battle that lasted over two years with about 35 deaths.

'Or maybe he gets good at stealing flat-screen TVs or copper and he sells to a syndicate and makes good money. Then the gang wants control of the syndicate and there's a struggle. Gangs don't like wars in their territories, it's bad for business, but there's this element in the gang structure that's a pathway to violence and trouble. Another cause is that if there's too much peace the shooters don't have any work so they generate it by provoking retaliation.'

As we have seen, organized criminal syndicates in Cape Town can be found in parts of capitalist corporations, as transnational foreign smuggling operations, as the market networks of drug merchants and among leadership of the most powerful gangs. At times they overlap, network, cooperate or are in conflict with each other. In terms of organizational structure, merchant gangs, the type described above, are a form of 'middle management' – organized at the top, semi-structured in their lower ranks – fluid and volatile. They're the public face of Cape Town's gangland – buying, selling, shooting and robbing their way to notoriety, fortune and cult status.

Some have been around for a long time with up to three generations of family membership, corporate histories going back decades, prison mythology and province-wide areas of operation. Their structures are complex, involving hierarchies, networks and markets. For young members they're clans or brotherhoods – support systems and rites of passage where warriors are tested on the path to adulthood.

Nobody on the Cape Flats is unaware of the overbearing presence of gangs like the Hard Livings, Americans, Jesters, Clever Kids, Mongrels, Sexy Boys and Ghetto Kids. Below them in the hierarchy is a plethora of smaller, turf-based gangs that may start out independently, but at a certain stage are forced into an alliance with the merchant gangs through supply chains or threats. Their followers make up perhaps hundreds of thousands of young people who see themselves as gang members.

Back in the late 1980s the Staggie brothers, leaders of the Hard Livings, realised they had to grow beyond their Manenberg base and offered security to druglords in other areas not aligned to gangs. They ran protection for Colin Stansfield in Elsies River, then offered to same services in Delft. They cornered the prostitution trade in Sea Point and along Voortrekker Road and moved into legitimate construction businesses. A leader was sent to university to study law.

The Americans used their drug money to start a long-haul trucking outfit (Jansen 2014).[73] Both gangs moved into the taxi business and also levied 'protection' fees on businesses and shebeens in areas under their control. In order to pay for drugs from Chinese suppliers, they gained control of abalone poaching operations from Hawston up the east coast to Port Elizabeth. Younger gangs that could have posed an opposition were coopted and corner kids coaxed into the fold. According to Fusion Manenberg director Jonathan Jansen (2014):

There was a big teenage gang, the Stoepa Boys, which became a rival to the other gangs. But the HLs were quick to pull them in. They became Junior HLs. The HLs actually created teenage gangs. They had the Westsider Kids, the Vatos Locos. They became mentors. The gang would keep its name, but when a fight broke out the HLs provided the weaponry. The HLs would park their new cars at their base in Aletta Court for the kids to see and admire. There were cool guys there and pretty girls coming and going. The teenage boys would see that and they'd want it.[74]

School gangs like the Stoepas, Bocca Boys, State Boys and Toy Boys were encouraged with money and favours by the Hard Livings, Americans and Jesters. Long-time Shawco organizer, Cyril Pelston (2014), noted that

Staggie would say: 'We invest in young kids. They're the future of our business.' The kids are very aware of being chosen. There's a 19-year-old who sits in the HL's inner kring (circle). The smart ones can get up in the hierarchy. But most just stay down on the street.[75]

The Staggie brothers worked hard to create a Robin Hood image on the Flats, providing almost the only possibility of employment for young men in their area, buying food for mothers when they ran out, occasionally paying bills and arrears rent and sponsoring a football team. Rashaad ran mobile shops selling essentials in areas where shops were not accessible. When he was killed by PAGAD vigilantes, gangs linked to the HLs formed a front organisation called the Community Outreach Forum (CORE). It organized a large crowd to march on Parliament, ostensibly to bring peace to the Cape Flats. Rashaad's teenage daughters carried a placard that read: 'They killed the world's best father.' But, as Pelston (2014) noted, there was generally a catch:

Because of high unemployment there was no money and they would assist you with rent and stuff. But there was always something behind it. Maybe you had a nice daughter and they would want her. That way many families became quite vulnerable. Kids dropped out of school and they'd be recruited.[76]

Even under POCA (Prevention of Organized Crime Act) legislation it's difficult for police to arrest gang leaders. They rule by word and not deed, avoid using drugs, keep organizationally clean and enforce these rules on men in their upper hierarchy. Excess money is laundered through legitimate businesses. According to gang researcher Irvin Kinnes (2000), in rural areas on the West Coast such as Saldanha, Piketberg, Arniston and Paternoster and South Coast villages like Hermanus, Bredasdorp and Genadendal larger merchant gangs developed a strategy of 'buying the town'.

The action involves gangsters initially buying property in these towns. They would then proceed to buy property that involves common use by the community such as petrol stations, shops and game arcades, to provide the means to recruit local youth to sell their commodities.[77]

Expansion, however, can generate tension and drug sales are often the cause. In a neighbourhood like Manenberg, which is around 10 square kilometres, there are six big gangs selling drugs. So when tension rises it's not so much about territory but control of users. If a user spending thousands of rands a month changes allegiance to another supplier, that's huge provocation. He may change because of bad drugs, better prices elsewhere, the product cut with other stuff or simply low quality. The user may be protected (they have been killed for defection) but the dealers will fight over him because he's a steady income. The dealer has a quota he needs to sell to pay the supplier and now he can't make it. So the new supplier becomes a target.

Despite seeming conflict over markets, however, gang leaders will work to regulate it. When a gang war broke out in Manenberg in 2005, the leaders of the two opposing gangs were seen to have a regular Tuesday date in a city coffee bar (Jansen 2014).[78] The formation of The Firm by gangs in the mid-1990s served to keep down conflict and regulate the drug trade. In general, the upper echelons of the merchant gangs send their children to private schools, frequent expensive clubs and live lives externally indistinguishable from corporate executives which, in a sense, they are. According to Standing (2005):

Many successful gang members move away from the Cape Flats and live in wealthier areas. They are also rumoured to collaborate with leading members of other gangs on business deals, even those who are popularly thought to be their enemies.[79]

For those in lower ranks of merchant gangs, however, life is entirely different. Vulnerable young men, particularly those with family problems, are cynically targeted and lured with promises of cool clothes, drugs, money and status. 'The HLs would drive past in a car and throw out money to us,' a member of the Americans in Manenberg remembered (2014). 'We didn't ask where they got that money. House robbery probably.'[80]

Initiation into the gang is often through rape or the murder of a rival gangster, marking them for unabated revenge requiring protection, which their gang offers. Many are born into families with several generations of street and prison gang tradition and most never get into the top tiers of the gang, content merely to serve the Big Guy. They remain relatively poor. Their situation is highlighted by a poingnant question in the book *Freakonomics* (Levitt & Dubner 2005): why do drug dealers still live with their moms? The answer being that they can't afford to live anywhere else.[81] But they dream big and talk about those who made it. Jansen (2014) asked a youngster why he was hanging around the Fusion Manenberg offices doing nothing. 'He said he could easily get work when he needed it because he's a gunman and can get R20 000 to shoot a guy in the head. Another 22-year-old was, for a while, making R80 000 a month selling abalone to drug suppliers. No programme gives you than much.'[82]

These stories are more likely to be gang hyperbole than true, but they have resonance among youngsters on the street. 'Ordinary gang members are poorly paid,' according to Vearey (2014), 'but they receive protection, food, shelter and legal help when needed. They're looked after as part of a crime family.' But on the occasions when they hit it big, 'no legitimate means would give them such a lifestyle.'

You're not going to be a drug courier if you haven't first proved yourself – that you can keep your mouth shut. You are tested by smaller things. Drugs are the fast cash crop but you can't build your gang around drugs. If one shipment gets hit you're bankrupt. Housebreaking and robbery don't have those problems. They are safer. Not even the police pay attention to it these days because they know all victims are interested in is a number for insurance. So the gangs consider this very low risk but it brings in a lot of money. [83]

Working with Hispanic gangs in the United States, criminologist Mike Carlie identified six levels of membership within big merchant gangs (Figure 1).

Surrounding the powerful leader or leaders he identified a group of older, hard-core members who are deeply enmeshed in gang activities. Beyond them are associates who have a commitment to the gang

Figure 1.

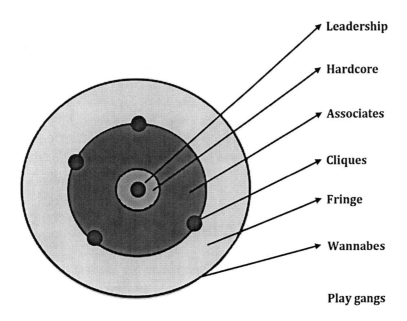

but are not part of leadership structures and, further out still, fringe members who drift in and out of strict gang membership.

Wannabes are not actually gang members, though they may declare themselves to be. They're youths who view the gang as an exciting place to be where they could become 'somebody'. They emulate gang dress, graffiti, hand signs and other gang cultural symbols and may seek to associate with known gang members. Another peripheral grouping Carlie (2002) describes as cliques. These can be called on in times of conflict to bring the gang up to strength. They may be a group around a hard-core member – a sort of gang within a gang – or an associate gang.[84]

The parallels between Hispanic and local gangs – and they are considerable – is the result of similar neighbourhood, family and economic pressures on young people. Carlie's typology also alerts us to the fragmented, even transitory nature of merchant gangs. The further down members are in the hierarchy, the more gangs become, for their young members, entanglements rather than structures, webs of fear and excitement, possibility and disillusionment, status and social isolation and rituals about being a somebody in a harsh world. Vearey, a member of a gang in his youth, remembers the process;

I basically looked at who drove the best cars, who wore the best clothes, who had access the best and they were labelled a gang. So being part of it became part of that particular process. If I needed to protect myself because I'm going to traverse the territory, being a Sicilian is better – because nobody touches the Sicilian because we are not like a structured gang, we're school kids from Elswood, Ravensmead, Elsies River High and Lavis. And we're unpredictable, we're not governed by the Numbers and we don't care who you are, we'll deal with you.[85]

On the Cape Flats, wannabes start young. 'These days it's not unheard of to find a youngster of 14/15 in the gang,' says Pelston (2014), 'and at that age they're almost fearless and have something to prove. The lure of an expensive pair of *tackies* (sneakers) is huge. Kids will perform what's required by the gang to get them. And a cellphone is gold. You can't live without it.'[86] At the lower end of the gangs nothing much has changed for years: 'Kids are still hanging out doing nothing, others selling drugs,' says Jansen. 'They're getting just enough to eat and becoming addicted to the leadership of the gang. And the drugs catch them so easily.'[87] A young gang member named Michael traced his entanglement (2014):

Here there's only smokkle [dealing]. I open my door and every day there's a guy with tik and unga. Every day. And he calls me and says: 'Hey Michael, you must help me here.' First time you try tik you get excited. It's a good feeling. Second time ... then you want it every time. You won't want to do anything else. You have no appetite for eating. You have to have money and you steal for tik. You steal money to buy more tik. And then you're in.[88]

SISTERHOODS: TOUGH SUPPORT CREW

Aala is a delicate-looking girl in her 20s, pretty if you ignore her haunted look and the pallour of too much tik. She's a member of the Bad Girls who, she says, are 'everywhere' – Heideveld, Mitchel's Plain Hanover Park, Bongteheuwel. She's part of a trend that began emerging from around 2010 of girls forming identifiable and named adjuncts to merchant gangs on the Cape Flats. Their male counterparts, Bad Boys, were started by her brothers and other young men when she was in primary school. They'd have 'little wars' with the Young Hard Livings and Westsiders and the girls would support them as an admiring group (Aala 2015).

There's Jester Girls, American Girls, Hard Livings Girls. So when the Bad Boys fight with the Americans and I find an American Girl on my turf bullets will fly and there will be trouble. Some of the girls fight with their own strength but I'm not scary.[89]

According to Barbara Williams (2015) of Rape Crisis, girls join gangs out of a need to belong, to have a voice and to intimidate other girls. They also think they'll have more fun and that they're safer in a gang. Increasingly, though, they join to get access to drugs:

They hang out in 'safe' houses run by powerful older men where people smoke. This makes them more vulnerable. Joining a gang may seem like a way to reduce sexual harassment but in fact it increases it. Once they're in and on drugs, the demand for sex and favours follow and they're hooked.[90]

However, girls in gangs are not necessarily victims and can also derive benefit from their involvement. Andiswa, who lives in Gugulethu, told journalist Pharie Sefali (2014) she enjoyed being in a gang and it was her choice. She liked the clothes they wear and the style of language they used. She also felt protected and said other girls didn't mess with her. 'Other girls want to be like you. When we fight, it's hard. I even have two scars on my back. I was stabbed during a fight with other girls. But it's one of the thrills I had to experience. Now I'm respected.'[91]

This is not the case with many girl-gang members. By becoming 'property' of one gang they become vulnerable to attacks by rival gangs when male members of their gang are not around. They can be beaten, robbed, emotionally abused or raped out of revenge or to provoke a gang fight. This is a problem wherever gangs form. A girl gang member named Melody told a London researcher (Combe 2013):

Rape is used for everything. It's used in initiation. It's used for fun if people are bored. It's used if you refuse to do something. If you fuck something up. Anything. I'm not even going to tell you what happens if you snitch. But it's used for revenge. If someone wants to get to a rival in another gang, they might gang rape a sister or their girlfriend. I know a girl who got gang raped by 12 men.[92]

Ntombi, a Vura Babe in Khayelitsha, was gang raped by the Vato gang because her brother stabbed one of them.

I was very involved in the gang. My brother used to ask me to hide weapons. I also used to fight with other girls on his behalf and other gang members. That life was the best, because he used to steal things and give them to me. I used to shoplift clothes for the gang. In return, they gave me gadgets they got from robbing ... [That was] until I was gang raped and got pregnant. Now I am HIV positive and have left the gang.[93]

For male gang members, female gangsters are often referred to as 'poison' for the trouble they can cause. There's a saying on the Cape Flats that a woman is more dangerous than a loaded gun and battles involving multiple deaths have been started over advances to or unfaithfulness of a gangster's girlfriend. Female members are also used as 'honeytraps', luring opposing gang members into ambush situations with promises of sex. In this way, or simply out of jealousy, gang wars can start which rip through a neighbourhood for years.

Girls join gangs for many of the same reasons that boys do: dysfunctional family life, criminal influence in the household, desire for status, protection, to access signifiers of adolescent success like cool clothes and cellphones and to be understood. They generally play less violent support roles in gang life – stashing drugs and guns or looking good on the arm of a gang member – but their more passive role is changing. 'Social media is telling girls how to stand up for their rights', said Williams. 'They are becoming more outspoken, able to act out their emotions, feel strong. They want to make their voices heard. They feel they can do it through gang membership and in a way they get what they want, but in a very unhealthy way.'[94]

In 2012 a spate of robberies in which stabbing was involved were carried out by both Vura and Vatos Babes in Khayelitsha. Gang researcher Irvin Kinnes saw this as a shift in the activities of female gangs. 'Whereas they previously played roles supportive of men, they were now increasingly becoming part of the teams carrying out violent robberies and shootings.'[95]

For young women, gang life offers few long-term prospects and many perils. Reflecting on her time in a gang, a woman names Margaret commented: ' Street time isn't like real time. [In a gang] you wake up one day and four years have passed. You were 14 a minute ago and now you are 18. You might have a criminal record, a drug habit, a baby. You've probably been knocked around, raped. You have no qualifications. Where do you go from there? Your childhood has vanished.'[96] In Manenberg Aala (2015) saw no escape:

For me it's better to keep to myself, keep inside the house or if I get a job to keep busy. But I'll never dare to say I'm not a Bad Girl because I will always be looked at as a Bad Girl. They will always expect me to do the things I always did. If you're in it to win it you're in it. You can't separate.[97]

For many years, girl gangs have been in the shadows of the city's gang phenomenon, seen (if they are regarded at all) as mere hangers-on or girlfriends. They are, however, a much more complex social phenomenon. They're young women with family, social and educational problems and few chances in search of protection, self development and a broader meaning to their lives. They are also prone to multiple pregnancies and HIV infection and their drug use poses parenting problems as well as epigenetic dangers to their unborn and postnatal children. A deeper and sympathetic understanding of their situation is urgently needed, as is the development of meaningful pathways out of their gang orbit.

WARRIORS IN BLAZERS: EMPTY BATTLES

Warrior gangs operate mainly in high-migrancy areas where poverty and overcrowding are endemic. Because of the nature of the city's in-migration patterns, they are almost exclusively Xhosa-speaking and the largest numbers are in the dormitory suburb of Khayelitsha. In the bleak streets children fight deadly battles for reasons even they find hard to define. Most are school-going age though many have dropped out and hang around together looking for tik or trouble. A large percentage were born in the rural areas of the Eastern Cape and are recent migrants.

Khayelitsha was developed as an urban satellite under apartheid dependent on large-scale commuters into Cape Town. Many working parents leave home around 4.30am to get to work on time and return only late in the evening, travelling under extremely difficult conditions. It's population was estimated by informants to the Khayelitsha Commission at between 400 000 and 450 000 people living in low-cost or squatter accommodation.[98] More than half the residents do not have a Grade 12 school pass and only one in 20 has a tertiary qualification. Four out of every 10 young men under 26 are unemployed and nearly half of all householders live in severe poverty. Khayelitsha has very high rates of contact crime, which means that people feel unsafe much of the time.

These are not easy conditions within which to grow up. Gangs like the amaVuros and amaVatos are mainly children of recent migrants who came to the city seeking a better life but who have not found it. They have lost their rural roots but not found fertile ground in the city. They are, essentially, rootless, desperate and know they have little hope of entering mainstream society. They see parents working for a pittance and peers with matric passes sitting around with no hope of employment. 'The most important question for these young people who prowl the streets with knives and pangas,' wrote researcher Pharie Sefali (2014), 'is how, in that situation, does a boy become a man? If the only possibility is through violence, he will take that route.'[99] The pressure to join a gang is intense, as 16-year-old Ayabulela explains:

If you're a guy in that school, you either smoke drugs, rob people or be part of a gang. If you're a nerdy boy or you don't do what the other guys do, they regard you as gay and you are bullied. So I joined the Vato gang. At first I didn't understand how gangsters live, but now I do and I like the thrill. It keeps me on my toes.[100]

Unlike Coloured gangs who usually battle with guns over drug turf, the Vuras and Vatos seem to be influenced by traditional stick fighting in rural areas from where they or their parents often originate. A gang member pointed out that using pangas, sticks and knives was more 'manly' than using guns. 'We want to feel an achievement when we beat our enemy,' he said. 'Guns have power but give no satisfaction.' The violence has deadly consequences. An average of one person a day is murdered in Khayelitsha, most of the deaths at the hands of these gangs.

Possibly linked to the proximity of rural traditions is a belief in magic. 'I went to to a *sangoma*,' a gang member told Sefali. 'I had to bring a bottle of vodka, money, a small amount of a fresh human blood in a bottle and a small belt that would fit round my arm. Some people bring beads, others small bottles, it all depends on a person and the sangoma. Then a mixture was done for me and was smeared all over the belt, which we call *umkhemi*. Now, when I fight, no one can touch me because power from nowhere overwhelms me. I become invisible and can dodge any weapons that come my way. But when I touch you I can kill you.'[101]

The conventional reasons given for inter-gang violence in places like Khayelitsha have their roots in peer pressure, boredom and displays of masculinity and a search for respect. 'We're not going to stop these fights until all the Vuras don't exist,' a member told Sefali. 'I'm not sure how the fights started. All I know is that we want respect and those Vuras from Makhaza should stop thinking they rule the area and should leave our girls alone.'[102]

A less obvious reason for the violence in such areas is the absence of a fear of consequence. The reason for the Khayelitsha Commission was to address a failure of policing and an extremely low arrest and conviction rate. Testimony after testimony to the commissioners was about seeming indifference by police to the community's needs for a safe environment and callous treatment of victims of crime. The police, in turn, pointed to low station morale, staff and equipment shortages, poor community cooperation, the impossibility of policing warren-like, insufficiently lit streets and calls to houses with no street address or numbers where they were likely to be pelted with stones or shot at. The result was simply ineffective policing.

In the absence of consequences for violence and legal transgression, it became increasingly attractive and, as norm-breaking became more common, the resilience of young men against doing wrong was reduced. Anthony Altbeker (2007) has suggested that norm breaking is determined, in part, by what everyone else is doing. As more people engage in violence without consequence, so more people are tempted to use it (With so many people doing it, what are the chances that *I'll* get caught?).[103] In what Altbeker calls this 'half-made land', young Xhosa men in the city's 'migrant' suburbs – cut adrift from the rural moral bearings of their parents and grandparents and shorn of the consequences of their violent urban actions – are left to chart the limits of their own behaviour by compasses oriented to the opinions of teenage peers with similar moral confusions.[104] Mayhem is inevitable.

For some, such as prison numbers gangs and drug merchants, this turbulence is useful. A Vatos gang member (Kossie 2014) tells it this way:

At first we had nothing to do with prison gangs, but more guys got arrested and took the number inside so the Number played a role in outside gangs. Through the stuff we are doing outside, we'd get arrested, then we meet old friends inside who are already have prison number. You need to choose which number you want to become. I am 26 in this group, then you have guys who 28 in the same group. We are outside but we are also numbers.[105]

The protection from numbers membership inside prison and the orderliness and enhanced illegal supply chain offered afterwards make incarceration a rite of passage into gang seniority. A young gang member told a researcher: We want to be arrested but we are also afraid.'[106]

In time, through contact with prison numbers gangs and an increasing market for drugs like tik, it is likely that warrior gangs will metamorphose into merchant gangs, with all the freight that this implies. Unless prevented from doing so, Khayelitsha and other areas like it will fall under criminal governance and state officials will become mere visitors in territories beyond their control.

CORNER KIDS: WHO'S YOUR DADDY?

Any day of the week the most noticeable social feature of the Cape Flats is the many young people on the streets. Under the flapping washing strung between blocks of flats are toddlers in the sand, youngsters chasing each other about, youths of 10 and older clustered together on the corners and small groups of young men in their late teens and twenties talking earnestly to each other or on cellphones or playing dice. Except on really hot summer days there is always a sense of busyness. If anything, this is a tribute to human inventiveness: the action generally fills a vacuum of boredom and limited choices. It also hides much heartbreak. Almost every family on the Cape Flats has a family history of relocation (through decree or necessity) from the inner-city areas, from squatter camps or from the countryside. In the process, many of the extended families were broken up, most of the houses and flats are overcrowded and the schools are packed to bursting-point. Street life is the spill from families, schools, jobs and overcrowding.

In squatter settlements or blocks of flats, youths are exposed to a harsh choice: either to stay inside, shut off, cramped, with no private space from family; or to move outside, into the shared courtyards, lanes or streets. There's no private or semi-private space on either side of the door. Every action except eating and defecating is a public action and street life becomes the only life possible. It's also a relief from the physical and emotional pressures which youngsters face, and moreover it's where their friends are.

One result is a constant forming and re-forming of playgroups. These are intensely important to youngsters and they're tightly area-bound. Playgroups tend to be formed by the youths who live in a certain block of flats, around a particular open court or a nearby street corner. Like their older brothers, they usually give their group a name – the Como Kids (of Como Court) or Third Street Kids. Generally these playgroups are boys' business; girls are seldom included. And their heroes are the older youths who often use them to run errands. In return they may be offered a cigarette or even a puff of 'zol' (marijuana). They also emulate what they see. A five-year-old in Khayelitsha told journalist Pharie Sephali (2014): 'I like the guys when they fight. I watch. I am not scared of them. When we play with my friends we like to take sticks and also pretend we are fighting.[107]

Of course young peer-group formation is not universal. Some parents go so far as to lock their young children in a flat all day, unsupervised, to prevent contact with the street 'skollies'. But it's the most pervasive pattern in the poorer areas of this city, as in many others. Playgroups, in these areas are substitute families. They're also sites of entertainment and a source of protection from the dangers of being alone. They are also schools for street survival and, very often, the beginnings of gang entanglement. Cyril Pelston (2014), a community worker for Shawco, which runs camps for Cape Flats youths, expressed concern about increasing gang awareness of very young children:

The games the kids play are gang games. You ask them to draw and they draw a gang sign – even younger that seven or eight and they know the signs. These images are important to them. Brothers and fathers are gangsters and they are already sensitized to violence. On a holiday programme a five-year-old had a tiff with a kid and he ran home and got half a cissor that his older brother gave him to stab with. Some really young kids carry firearms because their brothers think they won't be searched. They say 'you keep this for me'. At camps we have to disarm them. You have generations of socialization into gang stuff. It's their normal.[108]

That predisposition to ready violence, according to General Vearey (2015), doesn't begin with the gang, however, but in the home.

Where do kids learn to resolve conflict with violence? They don't learn it from the HLs or the Americans, they learn it in their home. The learn it from seeing a drunk uncle having an argument with the drunk uncle next door and they end up fighting. And if a woman is getting beaten up nobody reports it. It's just 'natural'. If a kid is witnessing domestic day after day, by the time he's 14 he's ready and ripe to be a gang hitman. What is the community doing about that? And now you ask the police to solve the problem. The thing causing a culture of violence in the ghettos where the gangs are strong is the one the community is most silent about.[109]

Of course, most urban adolescents survive in their fashion. The lucky ones have parents who act on an intuition that adolescents need both physical and emotional engagement. Some young people find mentors in their teachers or neighbours or grandparents. Others find adult mentoring in sport or academic achievement. But many find only each other and put together an emotional and symbolic life as best they can: music, dress, fads and fashions, drugs, romances and sexual encounters.

At the outer edge are those who don't have any support systems, who go too far, join gangs which carry them beyond the boundaries of social and legal acceptance. It's these we define as young people at risk, but any transformation of their lives requires that we look at what society provides for and requires of all adolescents. Between the insiders and the outsiders is not a boundary, but a continuum along which teenagers are able to move with surprising ease and speed. Unless South Africa reassesses its commitment to the support, education and parenting of all children – unless families, communities and the collective wisdom of our many cultures are seen as central to this support – then all young people are at risk.

REFERENCES

Altbeker, A. (2007). A country at war with itself: South Africa's crisis of crime. Johannesburg: Jonathan Ball.

Carlie, M. (2002). *Into The Abyss: A Personal Journey into the World of Street Gangs.* Retrieved from http://people.missouristate.edu/MichaelCarlie/site_map.htm

Combi, C. (2013, August 6). Real bad girls, extraordinary insight into London's female gang culture. *The Independent.*

Davids, N. (2012, February 14). South Africa's capital of organized crime. *Times Live.*

Department of Justice. (1912). *Annual Report for the Year 1912.* Author.

Foucault, M. (1977). *Discipline and Punish.* Academic Press.

Gastrow, P. (1988). *Organised Crime in South Africa: an assessment of its nature and origins.* Gauteng: Institute for Security Studies.

Goredema, C., Goga, K. (2014). *Crime networks and governance in Cape Town.* Pretoria: Institute for Security Studies.

Gresham, M. S. (1958). *The Society of Captives: A Study of a Maximum Security Prison.* Princeton, NJ: Princeton University Press.

Hbschle, A. (2010). *Organised crime in Southern Africa: First annual review.* Pretoria: Institute for Security Studies Special Report.

Jules-Macquet, R. (2014). *The state of South African prisons.* Cape Town: NICRO Public Education Series.

Kar, D., & Spanjers, J. (2014). *Illicit Financial Flows from Developing Countries: 2003-2012.* Washington, DC: Global Financial Integrity.

Khayelitsha Commission Report. (2012). Khayelitsha Commission.

Kinnes, I. (2000). Structural changes and growth in gang activities. In *From urban street gangs to criminal empires: The changing face of gangs in the Western Cape.* Pretoria: Institute for Security Studies.

Lambrechts, D. (2013). *The impact of organised crime on social control by the state: a study of Manenberg in Cape Town, South Africa* (PhD Thesis). Stellenbosch.

Levitt, S., & Dubner, S. (2005). *Freakonomics: a rogue economist explores the hidden side of everything.* New York: Harper Collins.

Muntingh, L., & Ballard, C. (2012). *Report on Children in Prison in South Africa.* Community Law Centre.

National Drug Master Plan 2013 – 2017. (2012). South African Government Publication.

Owen, R. (2014, January 17). *Financial Mail.*

Parker-Lewis, H. (2010). *Gods gangsters: The numbers, gangs and South African tattoo prison culture.* Cape Town: Ihilihili Press.

Pinnock, D. (2016). *Gang Town.* Cape Town: Tafelberg.

Ramatlakane, L. (2003). Unpublished document distributed by the Department of Community Safety.

Sefali, P. (2014a). *Gang violence in Khayelitsha.* Cape Town: University of Cape Town Safety and Violence Initiative and Cape Town.

Sefali, P. (2014b). *Khayelitsha ruled by teenage gangsters.* Cape Town: GroundUp June.

Sefali, P. (2014c, September 18). The rise of female township gangs. *GroundUp.*

Shaw, M. (1997) State Responses to Organized Crime in South Africa. *Transnational Organized Crime, 3*(2).

Shaw, M. (1999). The development and control of organized crime in post-apartheid South Africa. In *Organized crime: Uncertainties and dilemmas.* University of Illinois Press.

Shaw, M., & Reitano, T. (2013). *The evolution of organised crime in Africa: Towards a new response.* Pretoria: Institute for Security Studies.

Skywalker, L. L. (2014). *Politics of the Number: an account of predominant South African Prison gang influences* (MA Thesis). University of Cape Town.

Standing, A. (2005). *The threat of gangs and anti-gangs policy.* Pretoria: Institute for Conflict Studies.

Standing, A. (2006). *Organised crime: A study from the Cape Flats.* Pretoria: Institute of Security Studies.

Stein, D., Ellis, G., Meintjies, E., & Thomas, K. (2012). Introduction: substance use and abuse in South Africa. In *Substance use and abuse in South Africa.* Cape Town: University of Cape Town Press.

Steinberg, J. (2004). *Nongoloza's Children: Western Cape prison gangs during and after apartheid.* Johannesburg: Centre for the Study of Violence and Reconciliation.

Steinberg, J. (2004). *The Number.* Cape Town: Jonathan Ball.

Taheri-Keramati, Y. (2014). *Drugs, police inefficiencies, and gangsterism in violently impoverished communities like Overcome* (MA Thesis). Cape Town: University of Cape Town.

Tshwete, S. (2001). Legislative responses to organised crime in the SADC region. In C. Goredema (Ed.), *Organised crime in South Africa: Assessing legislation.* Pretoria: Institute for Security Studies.

Vearey, J. (2015). *Civilian Secretariat for police workshop: The development of a framework for inter-departmental anti-gang strategy in South Africa.* Cape Town Workshop.

Vearey, J. (n.d.). Nongoloza's legacy – prison and street gangs in the Western Cape. *Confidential South African Police Service Report.*

Von Lampe, K. (n.d.). *Definitions of Organized Crime.* Retrieved from www.organized-crime.de/organizedcrimedefinitions.htm

ENDNOTES

[1] This chapter is derived from extensive research for *Gang Town* (Tafelberg, Cape Town 2016). Some passages in this chapter coincide with those in that book, with permission from its publisher.

[2] Standing (2006), A: *Organised crime A study from the Cape Flats* (Institute of Security Studies, Pretoria,) p9.

[3] Lambrechts, Dercia (2013): *The impact of organised crime on social control by the state: a study of Manenberg in Cape Town, South Africa* (PhD thesis, Stellenbosch,) p166.

[4] Gastrow, Peter (1988): *Organised Crime in South Africa: an assessment of its nature and origins* (ISS Monograph 28,).

[5] Ibid.

[6] Shaw, Mark: *State Responses to Organized Crime in South Africa, Transnational Organized Crime,* 3(2), Summer, p. 3

7   Tshwete, Steve: Legislative responses to organised crime in the SADC region, in C. Goredema (ed), *Organised crime in South Africa: Assessing legislation*, Institute for Security Studies, Pretoria, 2001, p 3.

8   Shaw, Mark & Reitano, Tuesday (2013): *The evolution of organised crime in Africa: Towards a new response* (Paper 224, April) pp 2 & 14.

9   Standing, Op cit, p ix.

10 Cited in Standing, 2006, p206

11 Standing, ibid, p204 and 231.

12 SAPS crime statistics, September 2014.

13 Shaw, Mark & Reitano, Tuesday (2013): op cit p14.

14 Klaus von Lampe, *Definitions of Organized Crime*, www.organized-crime.de/organizedcrimedefinitions.htm.

15 Gastrow (1998), p39.

16 SAPS Organised Crime Unit, Anti Organised Crime Measures, August 1997. Quoted in Shaw 1998 p1.

17 Shaw, Mark & Reitano, Tuesday (2013): op cit p2.

18 Shaw, M (1999): The development and control of organized crime in post-apartheid South Africa, in Einstein, S & Amir, M, *Organized crime: Uncertainties and dilemmas* (University of Illinois Press, Illinois,), p65.

19 Dev Kar and Joseph Spanjers (2014): *Illicit Financial Flows from Developing Countries: 2003-2012* (Global Financial Integrity:, Washington, December). The figure for the same year in Russia was US $937.9 billion and China US$249.4 billion.

20 Ibid, p2.

21 Global Financial Integrity (March 2010): *Illicit financial flows from Africa: hidden resources for development* (Washington, DC: GFI) quoted in Shaw & Reitano (2013), op cit, p7.

22 Davids, Nashira (2012): South Africa's capital of organized crime (*Times Live*, 14 February).

23 Quoted in Hübschle, Annette (2010): *Organised crime in Southern Africa: First annual review* (Institute for Security Studies Special Report, Pretoria) p3, supplemented by Shaw, Mark & Reitano, Tuesday (2013) p6.

24 Hübschle, (2010) op cit. p3.

25 *National Drug Master Plan 2013 – 2017* (2012). Presentations by the Financial Intelligence Centre, May 2014. The percentage of estimated use is 32.1% for cannabis and 12.9% for mandrax. Also Dan Stein, George Ellis, Ernesta Meintjies and Kevin Thomas: Introduction: substance use and abuse in South Africa. In Substance use and abuse in South Africa by Dan Stein, George Ellis, Ernesta Meintjies and Kevin Thomas (eds). UCT Press Cape Town, 2012.

26 Goredema, C and Goga, K (2014): *Crime networks and governance in Cape Town* (Institute for Security Studies paper 262).

27 Ibid.

28 Owen, Rebecca, *Financial Mail*, January 17, 2014.

29 Ibid. Between 2001 and 2013 there were 27 097 drug-related arrests in KwaZulu-Natal, 16 854 in Gauteng and 9 118 in the Eastern Cape and 51 512 in the Western Cape.

30 Standing (2005) p1.

[31] Kinnes, Irvin (2000): Structural changes and growth in gang activities, Published in Monograph No 48, *From urban street gangs to criminal empires: The changing face of gangs in the Western Cape.*

[32] Ibid.

[33] Ibid.

[34] Ibid

[35] Interview with Jeremy Vearey, 2014.

[36] Opening address given by Leonard Ramatlakane at the Provincial Gang Strategy, April 2003. Unpublished document distributed by the Department of Community Safety. In Standing (2005) p9.

[37] *Cape Times* 4 April 2014, p6.

[38] Jules-Macquet, Regan (2014): *The state of South African prisons, edition one* (NICRO public education series).

[39] This is a similar problem experienced by the police, as will be explored in the chapter on policing below.

[40] SAIRR study reported in the *Cape Times*, March 6, 2012, p1.

[41] SAIRR study reported in the *Cape Times*, March 6, 2012, p5.

[42] Foucault, M (1977): Discipline and Punish (Kindle edition).

[43] Ibid.

[44] Gresham M. Sykes1958): *The Society of Captives: A Study of a Maximum Security Prison* (Princeton: Princeton University Press, 1958), 79, quoted in Steinberg, Ibid.

[45] Ibid.

[46] Muntingh, L & Ballard, C (2012): *Report on Children in Prison in South Africa*, Community Law Centre.

[47] Steinberg, J (2004): *The Number* (Jonathan Ball, Cape Town). See also Heather Parker Lewis (2010): *Gods gangsters: The numbers, gangs and South African tattoo prison culture* (Ihilihili Press, Cape Town).

[48] Department of Justice, *Annual Report for the Year 1912*, 37

[49] Steinberg: Jonny (2004): *Nongoloza's Children: Western Cape prison gangs during and after apartheid* (Centre for the Study of Violence and Reconciliation).

[50] Vearey, Major General Jeremy: *Nongoloza's legacy – prison and street gangs in the Western Cape.* (Confidential SAPS report, n.d.). As an ANC freedom fighter, Veary was incarcerated at Pollsmoor in 1987.

[51] Ibid.

[52] Ibid.

[53] Vearey, op cit.

[54] Vearey SAPS report, op cit.

[55] Taheri-Keramati, Yashar (2014): *Drugs, police inefficiencies, and gangsterism in violently impoverished communities like Overcome* (UCT Criminology MA thesis)

[56] Steinberg, J (2004): *Nongoloza's Children: Western Cape prison gangs during and after apartheid.* (Centre for the Study of Violence and Reconciliation).

[57] Ibid.

[58] Ibid.

[59] Ibid.

[60] Steinberg (2004) op cit.

61 Interview with Major Jeremy Vearey, Amandla!, 2014.

62 Interview with Nealon Peterson, Hanover Park, January 2015.

63 Taheri-Keramati (2014) Op cit.

64 Interview with Sira, Vuras member, Khayelitsha June 2014.

65 Kinnes: Irvin (2000): *From urban street gangs to criminal empires: The changing face of gangs in the Western Cape* (Institute for Security studies Monograph 48, June).

66 Interview with gang leader, Hanover Park, February 2015.

67 Skywalker, Luke Lee (2014): Politics of the Number: an account of predominant South African Prison gang influences (UCT Masters thesis) p45.

68 Interview with Nealon Peterson, January 2015.

69 Interview with Jonathan Jansen, Manenberg, September 2014.

70 Interview with Trappies, January 2015.

71 Interview with Joey, February 2015.

72 Interview with Major General Peter Jacobs, November 2014.

73 Jonathan Jansen interview, Manenberg, 2014.

74 Jansen Ibid.

75 Interview with Cyril Pelston, Cape Town, 2014.

76 Ibid.

77 Kinnes, Irvin (2000): *From urban street gangs to criminal empires: The changing face of gangs in the Western Cape* (ISS Monograph No 48) p15.

78 Jansen op. cit.

79 Standing, A (2005): *The threat of gangs and anti-gangs policy* (ICS Occasional Paper 116).

80 Interview with Dice, 2014.

81 Levitt, Steven & Dubner, Stephen (2005): *Freakonomics: a rogue economist explores the hidden side of everything* (Harper Collins, New York) p114.

82 Jansen, op cit.

83 Quoted in *Amandla!* interview, Issue 32, on www.amandla.org.za.

84 Carlie, Mike (2002): *Into The Abyss:A Personal Journey into the World of Street Gangs* (http://people.missouristate.edu/MichaelCarlie/site_map.htm).

85 Interview with *Amandla!*, op cit.

86 Pelston, op cit.

87 Jansen, op cit.

88 Interview with Machael, Manenberg, 2014.

89 Interview with Aala (not her real name), Manenberg, January 2015.

90 Interview with Barbara Williams, Rape Crisis, March 2015

91 Sefali, Pharie (2014): The rise of female township gangs (*GroundUp* 18 September).

92 Combi, Chloe (2013): Real bad girls, extraordinary insight into London's female gang culture (*The Independent*, 6 August).

93 Sefali (2014), op cit..

94 Williams (2015) op cit.

95 Quoted by Ilham Rawoot in *Mail & Guardian*, 17 May 2012.

96 Combi (2013), op cit.

97 Aala interview (2015), op cit.

98 *Khayelitsha Commission Report* (2012) p35.

99   Pharie Sefali (2014): Gang violence in Khayelitsha. Safety and Violence Initiative (University of Cape Town and *GroundUp*) 26 November.

100 Ibid.

101 Ibid.

102 Ibid.

103 Altbeker, Anthony (2007): *A country at war with itself: South Africa's crisis of crime* (Jonathan Ball, Johannesburg, p114.

104 Ibid, p 118.

105 Interview with Sira, Khayelitsha, by Lerato Kossie, July 2014.

106 Ibid.

107 Pharie Sefali (2014): Khayelitsha ruled by teenage gangsters, *GroundUp* June.

108 Pelston interview (2014). Op. cit.

109 Vearey, General Jeremy (2015): Civilian Secretariat for police workshop: The development of a framework for interdepartmental anti-gang strategy in South Africa, Cape Town 3-5 March.

Section 5
Asia

Chapter 14

From "Little Flowers of the Motherland" into "Carnivorous Plants":
The Changing Face of Youth Gang Crime in Contemporary China

Simon Harding
Middlesex University, UK

ABSTRACT

This chapter considers youth offending and youth justice in contemporary China noting significant changes due to the rapid economic transformation. Once famous for its low crime rates, the apparent rapid rise in Chinese juvenile delinquency has left the media 'wondering what transformed these little "flowers of the motherland" into "carnivorous plants". The chapter charts changes from the yanda (hard strikes) crackdown in 1983 to the highly publicised anti-crime crackdown in Chongqing. Despite limited data, a picture is emerging of changing influence of triads and altered relationships between organised crime and street gangs, noting street gangs are increasing due to an influx of rural migrants to the mega-cities. The chapter touches upon the risk factors and emergent arguments of this contemporary phenomenon, noting that Zhang et al (1997:299) has suggested that 'China is in an early stage of gang development' possibly equivalent to the USA from 1930s to the 1960s.

INTRODUCTION

This chapter considers aspects of youth offending and youth justice in contemporary China which has been changing over the past two decades. In many ways youth offending is similar to that in the West, however recent rapid economic transformation has initiated rapid changes in the nature and presentation of youth offending. Once famous for its low rates of crime and juvenile delinquency, the apparent rapid rise in Chinese juvenile delinquency has left the media 'wondering what transformed these little "*flowers of the motherland*" into "*carnivorous plants*" in a country striving for a harmonious society',

DOI: 10.4018/978-1-4666-9938-0.ch014

Box 1. From 'little flowers of the motherland' into 'carnivorous plants': the changing face of youth gang crime in contemporary China: Case study

It's 11 pm and it's plain, something is going on down that 50-meter-long alley in Shek Wu Hui. A dozen kids, maybe 14-16, shifting around in an agitated manner, can be going nowhere. The orange light from the street lamp above catches odd highlights revealing the dye jobs on some of the kids' hair. Some have their arms tattooed and black T-shirts can be seen on more than a few. There is an air of nervous apprehension as if something is going to happen. Loud music blares from the game arcades across the street, where inside, young guys are focused on games like Warcraft and King of Fighters.

A couple of older kids, maybe 17-or-19-year-old, seem to be watching for something, standing like sentinels at the entrance to the alley that leads to the back of the games arcade. About 10 meters away is the entrance to still another alley - this one narrower and much, much darker. A few 20-somethings are hanging out there. They smoke. Some stand. Some squat. Some are on cell phones. A couple of cars are cruising around the streets, windows rolled down. Between the two they carry ten young adults. The conventional wisdom down here is that if they have to "get away", they can do it faster with the air conditioner turned off.

There's going to be a fight, says an insider, who knows the scene. The scenario has become pretty common over the last few months. Two branches of the local Wo Shing Wo triad are having a feud. The battles play out in Shek Wu Hui, the district hub surrounded by scores of public housing estates in Sheung Shui. The stage seems set for a bloody battle. Only the timely arrival of the Police Department's Emergency Unit is able to defuse the situation and prevent violence.

Source: Deng (2011) Bloody-minded youth, China Daily HK Edition 23rd June 2011

(China Daily 23rd February 2013). The chapter charts changes over the past thirty years from the *yanda* (hard strikes) crackdown in 1983 to the contemporary and highly publicised anti-crime crackdowns in Chongqing. Despite some obscure Chinese data a picture is now emerging of changing influence of triads and altering relationships between organised crime and street gangs. After reviewing a typology of Asian gangs the chapter considers how street gangs appear to be on the rise in China largely due to the large influx of migrants from rural China to the rapidly urbanised mega cities. These issues are currently the centre of public debate in China and the chapter touches upon the risk factors and emergent arguments in relation to this contemporary phenomenon. Zhang et al (1997:299) has suggested that *'China is in an early stage of gang development'* possibly equivalent to the USA from 1930s to the 1960s.

Youth Offending and Youth Justice in China

The above scenario in Hong Kong has become a noticeable and regular feature, particularly on many of the large public housing projects surrounding the city, notably the New Towns like Sheung Shui, Fanling, Tuen Mun, Tai Po, and Tseung Kwan O. Whilst generating much press and publicity they are indicators of changes taking place in the level, type and activity of youth street gangs in China. Lam Kin-keung, a retired detective station sergeant who spent eight years with the Organized Crime and Triad Bureau has noted that youth street gangs appear to flourish in such public housing neighbourhoods. Many affiliates of these groups are said to be instantly recognisable from their speech, their dress and their posture. Whilst some have direct, definitive links with triads, for others such links are obscured or more ambiguous. Regardless of this the consequence is often the same, young people coming together to fight with steak knives, clubs, and bottles or iron pipes.

Increasingly the participants are getting younger:

They are lost, suffer low self-esteem, come from poverty and abusive backgrounds. They are youngsters who can't find respect - with nowhere else to turn but to the triad societies who give them a sense of belonging they've never known before. Experts note a disturbing trend that recruits entering the triads are increasingly becoming younger. (Deng, 2011)

Retired detective Kin-Keung suggests, "This is because the gang leaders of different factors (branches) - whether they belong to the same triad tong or not - are having more and more direct control over their followers than the dragon heads do. In order to augment their power, the gang leaders have to recruit lots of deviant kids," Continuing his observations he noted that "The phenomena of the triad committing crimes in recent years shows not only more active moves among lower level of triad members, but that they are younger. The expansion of a triad branch can happen very quickly. And the way they commit crimes is getting more ferocious", (Deng 2011-06-23).

Youth crime in China has been changing for the past two decades; however indications are that these changes are now faster and more profound, leading some public debates to question what has happened to Chinese youth? The headline for the China Daily in 25th June 2015 declared '*String of youth violence cases shocks nation*'. The article quoted a survey by the China Youth and Children Research Centre stated that juvenile delinquents were getting younger with more crime linked to drugs and internet use: of China's 279 million juveniles, more than 70 per cent of crimes in 2014 were committed by young people aged between 10 and 25 yrs. The report also emphasises aspects of a 'moral deficit in parenting', (China Daily 25th June 2015).

Migration from rural to urban China is also a causal factor for increased delinquency. The sociology professor at Central China Normal University, Mei Zhigang, says that increasingly juvenile delinquent behaviour in China is being conducted in groups and that this often involves violence, drugs or sexual abuse. He noted that young offenders are often children of the 'left behind' migrant children population, now nearing 100 million, (China Daily 23rd Sept 2013).

Once famous for its low rates of crime and juvenile delinquency, the apparent rapid rise in Chinese juvenile delinquency has left the media 'wondering what transformed these little "*flowers of the motherland*" into "*carnivorous plants*" in a country striving for a harmonious society', (China Daily 23rd February 2013).

In many ways youth offending in China echoes that of the Western industrialised countries, according to Shen and Hall (2015). Their study explores the philosophical bases, policy and practice of Chinese youth justice and contextualises the pattern and nature of youth offending in contemporary China. Whilst they note that Chinese youth justice does not differ formally from that of the Western nations, they recommend the suspension of assumptions when considering the situation in China.

Data on juvenile offending and youth crime can be difficult to locate and that which is available appears to indicate rising levels of youth offending. China's courts sentenced 322,061 juvenile's in 2008, 88,891 of whom were minors under 16, a 1.58 per cent increase year-on-year and making up 32 per cent of overall convictions nationwide. Numbers of juvenile crimes nationwide were 41,763 in 2000, rising to 58,870 in 2003 and 71,472 in 2005. In terms of crime types, robbery accounts for 35 per cent of all juvenile crimes and theft for 38 per cent. Fighting and quarrels were listed as 8 per cent and gang brawls for 4 per cent. In Shenzhen, 98.55 per cent of juvenile crimes were committed by youngsters without a local government household registration, (i.e. migrant), (China Daily - People's Court Review 7th May 2009).

The issue of rising crime levels in China is once more high on the public, government and media agenda. In 2009 one headline in the China Daily announced that '*Crime is a risk to stability: Official*'. It claimed that 'China faces an uphill battle to maintain social stability this year as crime figures continue to rise, according to the country's top judicial leaders', (China Daily, 16th Feb 2009). This led to calls to improve the system of prosecution, notably at district and county level and also to calls to guard against corruption. Similar headlines continue to appear driving national debates and influencing the public mood, often constructing crime as a threat to national security and social harmony. In 2015 the China Daily headline noted '*Gang activity in Guangdong poses 'serious threat*' - Lin Weixiong, Director of Criminal Investigations Bureaus under the Guangdong Dept. of Public Security, stated that task forces were needed to fight gangs involved in drugs, counterfeiting and vote-buying in local elections. This was considered to be a 'serious threat to grassroots governments and organisations' this often interfered with township and village elections', (China Daily, 10th July 2015).

However this is not the first time that crime rises hare garnered news headlines prompting policy outcomes. In fact, periodic crime upswings have been a topic of public debate for the past 30 years. After the commencement of Communist rule China often pro-claimed its success as an almost crime-free society. Against this backdrop, and a baseline of close to zero, any increase in offending might seem not only notable, but potentially alarming. As such, increased crime and rates of crime has become one of many factors arising from rapid urbanisation and significant social change occurring in China. For many, it is a consequence of the speed of change; for others, it is more a symptom of the type of changes occurring and the inequalities arising from these changes. The reaction to these periodic upswings in crime has on occasion been for the central government to initiate a 'crackdown' on crime which for many observers is an opportunity for tighter social control. For example, one such crackdown was announced by Vice-minister of Public Security, Zhang Xinfeng, in the run up to National Day. His announcement instigated a five month nationwide campaign to improve public security in the run up to the 60th anniversary of the found of the People's Republic. The campaigns which involved a crackdown on both gangs and organised crime had the stated aim of 'harmonious social environment',('Crackdown on crime in run-up to National Day', China Daily 28th April 2009).

Not all academics are in agreement that crime rises have in the past been real statistical events. Bakken (2004) in his analysis of China's criminal justice system argues that a critical examination of China's crime rate does not, for example, support the belief that a crime surge took place in the 1980s. During the early 1980s as economic policies became increasingly liberalised and progressive, China underwent what he describes as a 'moral panic about juvenile crime'. Arguing against any evidence pointing towards a 'surge' in crime, he argues that any rise would be a natural occurrence given the rapid urbanisation and population growth, including the maturing of the Chinese Baby boomer population into adolescence, e.g. the population of 14-25 yr olds in China rose dramatically from under 120 million to 272 million in 1987, (Bakken, 2004). He contends that the various anti-crime campaigns which are subsequently undertaken are linked instead to the legitimacy requirements of the communist party regime and its stated defence of the social and moral order of a society undergoing rapid social change.

One such anti-crime campaign undertaken in 1983 was the *yanda* (hard strikes) anticrime campaign. Bakken (2004) claims this was caused largely by a moral panic about youth crime, particularly targeted youth gang leaders (*touzi*) rather than corrupt officials or illicit entrepreneurs. Bakken claims the regime needed to demonstrate authority and control in society and boost its legitimacy whilst undertaking market reforms.

Under the hard strikes campaign the harshest punishments, including capital punishment, were often conducted in public. This included the execution of gang leaders in an attempt to dissolve gangs and eliminate gang recruitment. Summary trials were held of gang leaders aged 16 and over and this became a conspicuous feature of the campaign (Bakken 2004). In 2009, The Yangjiang Municipal Intermediate People's court passed death sentences on five people for the murders of four others by a 43 strong criminal gang. Two were also fined 310 million yuan (US$45.4 million) and 325 million yuan. The gang had admitted involvement in tax evasion, illegal gambling dens, extortion and lynchings, issuing false invoices and using guns for enforcement, (China Daily 4th Dec 2009).

The true picture here is sadly somewhat obscured as Chinese data is unreliable and often politically and socially constructed, including manipulation and 'creative accounting' of crime figures. Bakken is critical of this form of 'penal populism' directed by Deng Xiaoping, but accepts that penal populism 'has a strong foothold in China, (Bakken 2004, p80). Setting the data aside, such policy responses set the template for government reaction to rising crime rates and creating the timely space for political opportunism.

Despite the anti-crime campaigns of the early 1980s the effect on crime itself was clearly limited as more often than nought such criminal gangs and networks survived and thrived. In 1989 a three volume report on crime by the Chinese government identified an increase in gang crime and linked the rises to modernisation and the relaxation of state control. The report identified 36,000 gangs and 138,000 gang members, active in China (Dutton 1997). This compares with analysis in the USA (Egley & Howell 2011 as cited in Pyrooz & Decker 2013, p254) which suggests that there are 28,100 gangs and 731,000 gang members operating in the USA.

By the 1990s the evidence of increased juvenile delinquency in China was all pointing in one direction. By 1999, Wong (1999), and other academics as Zhang (1997; 1998), were in agreement that the improvement and growth in the Chinese economy has led to a genuine statistical increase in delinquency. The increase in juvenile delinquency has also impacted upon the criminal justice and youth justice provision. The Juvenile Protection law (1991) and the Preventing Juvenile Delinquency law (1999) were established to set out and define the duties, responsibilities and authorities of parents and guardians regarding child welfare, education and juvenile justice. Wong also notes that with these new laws there is a noticeable shift from the traditional Chinese model of informal intervention to a more formal structured intervention of delinquency control which might lead to increased custodial sentences for young offenders, (Wong 2004). In China both informal grassroots networks and formal correctional institutions both have a role to play in controlling delinquency. Wong (1999) however contends that the development of fair and independent juvenile justice systems is hampered by low levels of skilled manpower and frequent volunteers staff turnover compounded by the relationship between the control systems and the Communist party machine.

Zhang (1997) advises that research on juvenile justice and delinquency remain largely descriptive with scant trend analysis. In 2001 the China Daily was already reporting the need for improved and increased probation services to curb the rising tide of juvenile delinquency, (China Daily 17th Feb 2001).

Coupled with debates about increased delinquency amongst juveniles have been high profile drives against corruption and diminishing trust in the Chinese police, particularly in urban areas, (Wu, Sun, Hu, 2015). Trust varies considerably across the key urban cities and some observers and academics consider China to have a 'crisis of legitimacy' regarding its police service, (Sun, Hu, Wu, 2012).

Fast forward to 2014/15 and Chinese societies have witnessed a dramatic growth, not only in social and economic terms but in terms of youth crime and delinquency (Xi, 2001; Ngai 2004; Zhang et al, 1993). In China researchers report that the growth of crime and delinquency is largely down to the rise in gang involvement of delinquent youth and that much crime in China involves delinquent youth (Xi 2001).

Public debates, press and media coverage and academic research now centres on the following contributory issues and outcomes: changes in the activities of organised crime networks and the loosening power of the triads; the emergence and expansion of drug trafficking and new drug markets; the role of rural-urban migration and deprived migrant youth; the emergence of youth street gangs; the expansion of youth street gangs in urbanised areas of china and issues of parenting and social control. All of which has taken place as a consequence of rapidly changing socio-economic conditions arising from market liberalisation. This chapter will examine each of these above points in more detail.

Before we focus on China, it is important to consider how Asian gangs are researched and studied and to clarify what is known about different types of youth gang and organised crime group operating in Asia.

Studying Gangs and Organized Crime in Asia and China

Criminology in China, and other parts of Asia, remains a fairly nascent discipline. Academic and institutional research however remains many years behind that of the West. Despite this fact, an emerging body of Chinese criminological studies (Chin 1990; Chin, Huang 2007, Kelly & Fagan 1993; Liu 2004; Song & Dombrink 1994; Song 1996; Wang et al 2002, Wang 2013, Zhang 2014, Zhang et al 1997, Zhang et al 2008, Zhou et al 2004) is expanding the knowledge base and opening up the debates on the applicability of Western theory to occidental social and geo-political conditions. Research into Chinese gangs is similarly engaged and is beginning to present insights into rising delinquency, risk factors for gang affiliation, youth gang involvement, links to organised crime and gambling syndicates, government crackdowns and punitive responses. The Challenges of conducting such research in China are exacerbated by numerous methodological barriers which in many ways need ways of thinking to overcome them. One key issue in China is differentiating between normative youth behaviour, youth criminal activity, youth street gangs and organised crime linked to, or not linked to, national, or even international, crime syndicates. This confusing picture is central to an understanding of crime in China.

Whilst gang research in the US benefits from a long and informed academic tradition, US gang research into Asian gangs and organised crime operating in the US, lags somewhat behind. This is partially explained by various methodological challenges facing those studying Asian gang active in the US, (Song, 1996). Some of these issues identified by Song, (and listed below), will doubtless be pertinent in gang research in Asia and specifically China, namely:

- The unique cultural characteristics and modus operandii of the various criminal groups operating in Asia differs hugely – e.g. drug trafficking groups, Japanese Yakuza, Vietnamese gangs; Tongs, Triads; Taiwanese immigrant gangs; Korean gangs, etc. Thus an understanding of domestic and also international cultural interactions and geo-politics is required.
- The various groups such as organised criminal gangs, triads or underground societies, tongs, gangs, etc, all require accurate classification before research can effectively be undertaken.
- There is a need to re-examine the boundaries of these groups, especially the interfaces between youth gangs and organised crime when talking of Asian crime groups
- Language and cultural barriers are frequently exhibited in Asian gang research with China for example having four major dialects. (In the USA, Asian communities have 34 distinct ethnic groups and even term Asian is unhelpful).
- In the absence of data and reports from NGOs, secondary analysis is often over-reliant on media and public documents
- There are no systematic efforts to evaluate the effectiveness of enforcement measures against gangs or organised crime.

- There is a lack of availability of public documents regarding key data and statistics for example, migration patterns, policing operations, recorded ethnicity, levels of crime reporting and crime recording, etc.
- The exclusive nature of migrant communities and the hidden and secretive nature of organised crime remain a further barrier to research on gangs and organised crime.

It is important to address such methodological deficits for research into Asian groups and organised to move forwards.

Typology of Gangs in Asia

The study of Asian gangs requires clarity regarding the boundaries of the various different criminally active groups. Whilst issues of definition continue to consume Western academics and defy consensus, some similar challenges occupy academic study of Asian criminal enterprises. Most academics focus specifically on one type of criminal enterprise and few have sought to classify Asian gangs or to arrange them on a spectrum which might help clarify for the lay-person the activities, and the networked connections, if any, operating between them. Hua-Lun Huang's (2007) work is one exception to this as he has tried to offer a typological analysis of Delinquent Asian gangs.

Huang argues that differences in gangs are relative and not absolute. He offers a typology of Asian gangs based on three factors – political belief, organisation level and structure and political connection. Thus he identifies 8 different types which operate or have operated in Asia. Delinquent gangs here refer to 'three dissimilar but comparable associations, namely delinquent groups, street gangs, and organized crime 'enterprise', (Huang 2007, p129). He then takes the three categories of political belief, organisational structure and political connection and sub-divides them into two different levels: 'salient/inconspicuous ideology for political belief; tiered/egalitarian organizational arrangements for organisational structure, and patron-client/ no patron-client relationship for political connection', (Huang 2007, p130). Based on these different combinations he offers a classification system for the different types of Asian gangs. This helps differentiate quasi-political or ideological groups from street based groups.

Huang suggests that those groups with a salient ideology should be considered as expressive groups or 'dreamseekers' attempting to realise a stated long-term goal. Those with an inconspicuous ideology however are instrumental groups interested in pursuing economic goals. He claims this classification allows for all historical or contemporary groups to be accounted for, (Huang 2007).

Huang adopts a typological approach to gang classification arguing that gang appearance and growth is linked to territorial expansionism, nationalism, religious extremism of other similar ideology. He suggests that this typology approach is more comprehensive, and therefore more suited to Asia, than typologies based on the Chicago School ecological paradigm. Table 1, below, illustrates the various groupings identified by Huang.

For those seeking to understand the key differences between the active criminal groups in Asia and to familiarise themselves with the range of activity, this is useful starting point. However as a conceptual tool it is useful in elucidating distinctions between various groupings. Certainly the focus on ideology is helpful in explaining why certain gangs have an extenuated lifecycle but it is also helpful in understanding how gangs operate, recruit and conduct business. This chapter shall now focus or the issues of organised crime in China, starting with the role of the 'dark societies' or triads before considering the links between triads and street gangs.

Table 1. Typology of Asian Gangs

Type	Example
Salient ideology + tiered structure + patron-client relationship in politics	The Black Dragon Society. An ultra-nationalist organisation formed in Japan in 1901
Salient ideology + egalitarian structure + patron-client relationships in politics	Chinese triads. Loosely structured groups of ultra-rightist nationalists.
Salient ideology + tiered structure + No patron-client relationship in politics	Abu Sayyaf guerrilla/pirates active as Islamic insurrectionists in the southern Philippines engaged in banditry, kidnapping and piracy.
Salient ideology + egalitarian structure + No patron-client relationship in politics	The Seven Princesses (female) gang in Korea. Those who operate as 'social bandits', peasant robbers or 'virtuous Robin Hoods'.
Inconspicuous Ideology + tiered structure + patron-client relationship in politics	Yamaguchi Gumi of Japan. Partially hidden hierarchical crime syndicate.
Inconspicuous ideology + egalitarian structure + patron-client relationship in politics	Sun Yee On – the largest and most powerful Triad society of Hong Kong. Operates with less bureaucracy than the organised criminal enterprise of the Yamaguchi Gumi.
Inconspicuous ideology + tiered structure + No patron-client relationship in politics	Organised pauper gangs or *gai bang*. These organised beggar rings act a street families and are often headed up by a senior male beggar or 'grandpa' who ensures the group finds food, shelter and work.
Inconspicuous ideology + egalitarian structure + no patron-client relationship in politics	Chinese, Chinese/Vietnamese or Southeast Asian gangs operating in the US and Canada. No associated to tongs, these are profit oriented street gangs raising in income from drugs, vice fraud and gambling.

Source: Huang (2007) From the Asian Boys to the Zhu Lian Bang (the Bamboo Union Gang): A Typological analysis of Delinquent Asian Gangs. *Asian Criminology* 2: 127-143.

Street Gangs vs. Organised Crime

Distinctions between street gangs and organised crime groups was first identified by Thrasher in 1927, followed by others such as Cloward and Ohlin (1960), Spergel (1961), Potter (1994), Klein (1995), and Varese (2006). Assessing and clarifying the differences became important for academics and also for the criminal justice system in terms of enforcement and sanctions. Research into US gangs by Jankowski (1991) noted key differences between street gangs and organised crime at the upper level whilst there was also differences between street gangs and 'crews' or groups of youth operating at the lower level. Curry, Decker and Pyrooz (2014) argue that criminal activity operates on a spectrum from disorganised street gangs up to organised crime and gangs both vary and evolve overtime. In this way Western theory and research echoes the views of Huang and his conceptualisation of the Asian typology and context. As in Western gang research it is still important, if not critical, to distinguish between street level criminal groups and organised crime.

Varese (2010) describes organised crime as specialised networks that rely upon expertise, rather than hierarchy, to undertake criminal activity for financial gain. Recent changes in society have possibly added a further level of distinction between street gangs and organised crime for example, international or transnational organised crime groups increasingly utilise information technology and now often operate, as Dishman (2005, p237) describes them, as a 'leaderless nexus'.

The high-level organised crime syndicates in China differ considerably from youth street gangs, operating secretly and managing huge financial deals; it is in their interests to maintain a low profile. The principal criminal activity of these groups is gambling and its associated activities including vice and money laundering. In 2009 during a money laundering trial 22 organised crime members, including a local policeman were charged and sentenced for using threats of violence to compel trade, extortion, assaults, actual bodily harm, prostitution, false accounting and gambling since 2003, (China Daily, 16th Dec 2009).

Since 2006 Beijing courts have convicted 12,796 people in connection with 1,171 cases of organized crime according to the Supreme People's Court. Of these 4 per cent were sentenced to more than five years in prison. These figures relate to the nationwide crackdown on organized crime instigated early in 2006 to July 2009. Police had investigated 1,267 organised crime cases and disrupted 13,000 gangland organisations. Of these more than 400 were involved in construction, mining and wholesale sectors with the proceeds of these exceeding 4 billion yuan (US$588million). The investigations also included 108,000 other cases including 419 homicides and more than 10,000 assaults. Authorities claimed these results had led to a decrease in violent crime such that by 2008 violent crime was down 11 per cent compared to 2005 (the year prior to the campaign) with 2,700 firearms also seized, (China Daily & Xinhua 1st Sept. 2009).

The Deputy Director of the Criminal Investigation Bureau of the Ministry of Public Security (MPS) said *'gangdom is still active in China'*, noting that gangsters often operated under the 'protective umbrella' of government departments and judiciary departments. From February 2006 and July 2009 Chinese prosecutors authorised the arrests of 44,319 people involved in 9,000 gang crime cases. Of these 42,000 were successfully prosecuted with more than 1,300 sent to labour re-education camps, (China Daily & Xinhua 1st Sept. 2009).

Re-education camps are strictly controlled by tight legal procedures and offenders are designated to the camps following an initial proposal from the police. This proposal is then approved by the labour camp management committee which consists of officials from the judiciary, labour, personnel and public security departments alongside representatives from workers, youth and women's organisations. Detention is supervised by prosecuting agencies. Gang members who are detained in prisons by the Ministry of Justice are purposefully located in prisons outside their home region to reduce opportunities for contact with previous accomplices and to disrupt their networks. Upon release they are subject to stricter parole and probation conditions, (China Daily & Xinhua 1st Sept. 2009).

Gambling

All gambling in mainland China was outlawed until the first welfare lottery was established in 1987. Despite this gambling socially has long been a Chinese social pastime.

In 1978 China's 'open door' policy and subsequent economic reforms made profitable economic development and entrepreneurship a national goal, (Liu 2008) and this came a massive expansion of illegal gambling. However the race for profits, now nationally sanctioned, opened the door for numerous 'get rich quick' schemes. Numerous opportunities now presented for illicit enterprise. To understand this complex picture more clearly it is useful to consider in more detail how gambling works and how it offers illicit business opportunities for the triads.

Three types of gambling schemes operating in China by organised crime syndicates have since been identified (Wang and Antonopoulos (2015): - local gambling dens; trans-regional gambling rings and online gambling networks. Each of these enterprises strategises to optimise the most favourable financial returns in the face of police surveillance and suppression.

Wang and Antonopoulos (2015) note that 'in a country such as China where the legal system is weak and the working of the government is opaque, personal connections (*guanxi*) have become extremely important in various aspects of Chinese business and personal life, including illegal activities, (see also Broadhurst 2012). *Gaunxi* helps to identify customers, partners, and players and also helps to recover debts. It may also help secure financing, resolve disputes and obtain police protection, (Wang & Antonopoulos 2015). *Guanxi* is the key resource for running these connections and acts as both social glue for personal and professional connections but also social lubricant for all transactions.

In the traditional off-shore gambling haven of Macau four major crime syndicates are involved in rolling or exchanging chips. They have all set up sub-branches or agencies in mainland China or they link up with mainland Chinese gangs in order to recover debts (Varese 2011). Debt collection is undertaken by criminal gangs and may involve abduction, assault, torture blackmail and murder. Many businesses try to keep face or *(mianzi)* and so will pay up through the *guanxi* networks, (Wang & Antonopoulos 2015).

The Chinese government are aware of such criminal syndicates and have recently acted to disrupt and destroy them.

Periodic 'Crackdowns'

To address the issues of organised crime and the rise in youth offending about gangs, periodic 'crackdowns' are initiated by local and by central government.

In 2006 China instigated a 'crackdown' on criminal activity leading to the prosecution of upwards of 70,000 gang-related crimes between 2006 and December 2008. This 'crackdown' led to a reduction in murder, robbery and physical assaults of approximately 4per cent for two years. Data from the Supreme People's Court indicated that 337 gang crimes were processed in 2007 which was up 161 per cent year on year. In 2006 and 2007 more than 6,000 criminals received sentences for gang-related offences. Professor of Criminal Law at China University of Political Science, Liang Huaren echoed the comments from the Director commenting that the upsurge in gang-related crime was related to the changing economic and social landscape of China which exacerbated growing inequalities and which were most noticeable between unemployed workers and migrants and others. Whilst gangs and organised crime were clearly linked together and in places indistinguishable, it was suggested that the traditional gang activities of prostitution, gambling, drug production and trafficking were being supplemented by new criminal activity in the construction industry, transport and mining sectors. Money disputes often provided opportunities for gang involvement which then led to racketeering. Gangs were also thought to seek protection by establishing close business links with government officials and corrupt police officials, (Zhu Zie, China Daily, 22nd Dec 2008).

By 2008 China was planning a 'special unit to tackle gangs' – identified as organised criminal groups. Speaking via the China Daily a senior official of the Ministry of Public Security (MPS) said, 'A new division is being planned to combat growing mafia style gangs in the country'. The director of the ministry stated that the fight against gang crime would be a 'lasting task' and sought new legislation to address the issue. Continuing, he said, '*gangs will remain active as the country undergoes dramatic social and economic changes'*. He went further by saying, *'Gang related crimes have become a threat to our social stability and the economy'*, (Zhu Zie, China Daily, 22nd Dec 2008).

In June 2009 authorities in Chongqing instigated a high profile crackdown on organised crime in the city involving 3,000 police, the aim being to dismantle gangs in the city. By August 2009 police had detained 1,544 suspected gangsters from 14 organised gangs with a further 469 suspects still at large. During this crackdown multiple firearms, ammunition and assets were retrieved. Liu Guanglei, Team leader of the city's campaign against organised crime was quoted as saying, *'Chongqing will struggle to stay safe if we don't crack down on the organised gangs'*. Xinhua News Agency was quoted as reporting that 'scores of police officers also accused of protecting criminal gangs have been detained'. It was also reported that local citizens helped in this crackdown by providing useful tip offs, (China Daily 18th August 2009).

Similarly from August to September 2009 police in Guangdong province, Hong Kong and Macao worked in partnership to break up more than 1,340 gangs and address cross-border crime. This operation included 1,872 cases connected to triads and targeted phone and online scams as well as drug manufacturing and trafficking. A total of 8,139 suspects were detained alongside 185 unlicensed firearms and 7.15Million yuan (US$1.05million),(China Daily 25th Sept 2009).

A further notable 'crackdown' was in Chongqing where multiple premises were closed following a high profile intervention organised by the Chongqing government from June 2009 – Nov 2011, (Broadhurst 2013; Wang 2013). The Chongqing crackdown became the most high profile 'anti-mafia campaign' in China and was reported worldwide. It was aimed at putting local criminal organisations out of business whilst offering opportunities to crusade against key influential business and senior government officials under whose auspices the syndicates flourished, (Broadhurst 2013; Broadhurst & Wang 2014).

Triads

One element of organised crime instantly recognisable as associated with China is that of the triads. The Term triad (which is actually English) describes 'dark societies' but overtime has become synonymous with organised crime in China. However, there is considerable imprecision when trying to describe or define both organised crime in China or triads, (Broadhurst & Wa, 2009).

China has a long tradition of triads or semi-secret societies. These were originally formed several hundred years ago as underground political agit-prop groups and have evolved into large societal organisations in most Chinese societies, in China and overseas. Traditionally these organisations of adult men operated as nationalistic or quasi-political societies before transferring into quasi-governmental groups exacting strong-arm functions for various regional administrators across China. After a higher profile involvement in the Boxer Rebellion they retreated into more secretive criminal underworlds from the mid 20th Century. They also have a long history relating to repeated waves of Chinese immigration entering Hong Kong and this has permitted them to maintain recruitment, power and influence.

In communities such as Hong Kong, which are overwhelmingly established and composed of immigrants, the social networks afforded by triad societies was invaluable and the triads offered migrants protection to those vulnerable to unemployment or social exclusion.

Essentially triads now operate as hierarchical organisations offering entrepreneurial opportunities for organised criminal ventures in China, but also in the SE Asia where significant Chinese populations are domiciled, (Chin 1990a; Chin 1986). Famously triads also operate in the USA.

Triads in the US

Importantly similar methods of extortion operate in the United States Chinese community largely operated via the triad societies, (Kelly, Chin, Fagan, 1993). In comparing Chinese gangs in New York City, Chin (1990) identifies several distinctive factors which differentiate Chinese gangs from those of Black, Hispanic or Italian decent. Namely they have their origins in the social and cultural life of the immigrant communities rather than youth fads, fashion or drugs. This facet leads to gangs becoming deeply enmeshed in local business – both legitimate and illegitimate – offering opportunities for financial, social and cultural advancement. This is quite separate from how gangs operate in other communities. The influence of triad society within wider communities is another key difference.

The Asian gangs operating in the US do not necessarily operate in the deprived urban communities typical of black or Hispanic gangs, but instead thrive in Chinese communities which present multiple and varied business opportunities. Chin (1990) notes they are embedded in the triad subculture which is constructed and maintained by secret Chinese societies. Chinese gangs in the US are therefore able to copy or adopt similar practices as operated by triads in China and then claim hereditary rights and links to triad societies. In this way triad norms can be adopted and offer a form of internationalised triad activity including adopting rituals and initiation rites. This tactic permits them to be viewed by the Chinese community as something more than simple street gangs offering certain legitimacy and even romantic historical provenance, (Chin 1990). This in turn creates a shroud of mystery and cultural significance which often generates high levels of fear and intimidation amongst local Chinese populations. This generates an influence which is based on more than violence and thus again it differs from other ethnic gangs. Chin (1990) also suggests that in some places these triad connections are loosening and may change in the future, with the possibility of Chinese gangs adopting and more international street gang flavour. Vietnamese gangs and Fujianese gangs now operate outside of the triad sub-culture and their involvement in street robbery and burglary again distance them from the traditional triads.

Triads in Southern China and Hong Kong

Triad activity includes racketeering and protection in all its forms with local small business including taxis, restaurants, street hawkers and local shops suffering either extortion or enforced price fixing. Alongside extortion often sits money lending, loan-sharking and then debt collection. Drug sales 'patches' or turfs are sometimes sold to street gangs as part of the drug distribution network. Commercial vice operations such as prostitution, sex shops, brothels, gaming halls are targeted alongside more legit operations such as karaoke bars and nightclubs. Hong Kong triads are actively involved in the operation of night-time economy outlets such as saunas, nightclubs, bars, and lounges often operating with an affluent clientele. Hong Kong merchants often report difficulties in conducting business expansion and may find their business investment put at risk due to triad gangs seeking to engage in coercion or extortion for rival companies or groups.

Construction sites, waste disposal and transport groups can be subject to monopoly control and intimidation even takes place within the film industry in Hong Kong. In addition loan-sharking, debt collection, drug trafficking and gambling in various forms are considered natural criminal turf for the triads. Counterfeit production of perfumes, cigarettes and fuel smuggling are relatively new additions and now sit alongside prostitution and pornography as opportunities for generating profits. Opportunities for profiteering and illicit activity are often enhanced by the fact many triads retain profitable links with corrupt police and government officials.

Triads often operate as franchise-type organisations and as long as members pay their dues they can act independently. Triads were partially financed by franchising street violence to linked street gangs who then assisted in intimidation and violence targeted toward both legitimate and illegitimate businesses in Hong Kong. Contract enforcement, debt collection and the elimination of competition were key and highly publicised violence helped build reputations whilst maintaining compliance and discipline. The long term success of triads was also based upon long-established and sub-cultural aspects of loyalty, secrecy and brotherhood and this forms the basis of internal discipline which, according to Paoli (2002), is the foundational discipline of such societies. The use of rituals is notably for initiation, but is still believed to take place in triads though it is often a mystery, (Covey, 2010). Similar codes of honour adopted by triads are sometimes found in street gangs (Lee et al 1996).

It is really only when the triads become involved in violent crime do we get an insight into their links with organised crime. Paoli notes that triad societies are 'not exclusively criminal organisations but are multi-faceted brotherhoods in the form of loose cartels bound by social as well as economic ties' (Paoli 2010, p2). Not all criminal groups or criminal network in Hong Kong are triad related. Triads can be compared in some ways to the Sicilian mafia according to Broadhurst and Wa (2010, p3).

Expansion and Displacement

It is widely reported by academics and the media (China Daily - 29th Dec 2012) that Hong Kong triads are now pushing north into mainland China largely due to a Hong Kong police crackdown and also the opening of new and potentially unexploited, lucrative opportunities. Hong Kong is also believed to be at saturation point with high commercial rents and greater competition for making money. This has led Hong Kong triads to start using Guangdong province as the back-office location for storing drugs, manufacture and storage of counterfeit goods such as fake credit cards.

Local triad meetings and rituals are still conducted in Hong Kong and the regular commercial and public traffic between Hong Kong and Guangdong makes it all but impossible to detect these activities. Hong Kong police estimate approx 3,000 active Hong Kong triad members are operating on the mainland and mostly in Guangdong province. Triad operations in Hong Kong have also not really declined despite the police crackdown. Groups such as Sun Yee On, 14K and Wo Shing Wo are all said to be active in Shenzhen, Huizhou and Dongguan, (China Daily - 29th Dec 2012).

In Guangdong, recent triad operations are noticeable through a range of incidents, e.g. a notorious gangland execution in 2007 which took place in the famous Luk Yu teahouse in Hong Kong; a senior triad boss shot in Dongguan; an assassination plot in Shenzhen to kill the founding chairman of the Hong Kong Democratic party. Other Hong Kong triads spread out to Macao for lucrative gambling receipts and opportunities including managing the VIP rooms at casinos in the city. For example, the Wo triad with its factions of Wo Shing Yee, Wo On Lok and Wo Shing Wo are the longest established triad in Hong Kong boasting an estimated 20,000 members. Criminal activities such as junket operations for high rollers, and loan sharking make up their main income, (China Daily - 29th Dec 2012). Network links between Macao and Zhuhai also permit members to lie low in mainland China if police activity in Macao becomes too problematic. In the pre-handover months in Macao some 14 people were killed by wars between triads and the leader of the notorious 14K group, ('Broken tooth') Wan Kwok-koi, served

15 years for gang related activities. The Chinese control of Macao is now thought to be considerably stronger than in the pre-handover days.

One former Hong Kong police officer with 30 years experience of working with triads states that *'triads can only be operated against. They can never be eliminated. It's like a poisonous fungus. After you've plucked it, it grows back again'*. Moreover the triads operate with lucrative business returns. This means that if one triad folds then others will step in to take over the business and start it up again, (China Daily - 29th Dec 2012).

Triads and Street Youth Gangs

Through cultural representations and more recently via films, Triads have been romanticised by the Chinese as noble cultural societies operating to the Chinese code of Confusion philosophy, (Covey 2010). From this elevated vantage point they can offer a template to younger, more loosely affiliated street gangs who in turn can act as fertile ground for recruitment into triads. The relationships here are not fully explored and often remain contested.

Main (1991) views triads as operating on a spectrum from loosely based street gangs to highly organised criminal networks. Chu (1994, 2000) however suggests triads operate as a pool of potential associates who come together for criminal activities. He identifies the street gang as the lowest tier of this hierarchy, reporting via their gang leaders to area bosses, who in turn were controlled by chairmen. In this interpretation, Chu viewed the street gang as operating with a high degree of organisation compared to the loose social networks of acquaintances operating at the higher levels.

As a result the degrees of 'control' exerted by triads on street gangs may vary by context and by situation, though it seems commonly agreed that street gangs operate as contractors for the triads in some business arrangements (Covey 2010). In this way we may view the relationship between the street gang and the triad in much the same way as Western academics have viewed the relationship between the urban street gang and organised crime, (Thornberry, Densley, Shelden et al 2001).

The triad is headed by adults however it enlists younger recruits to help sustain its criminal interests. Youths may find it offers powerful protection to them with valuable social contacts and often youths then seek to enlist. Whilst enlisting may involve some form of ritual, even those who do not formally enlist often claim to be acting in or for a triad and can name their gang as a form of triad franchise or branch of the society. Street gangs can at times imply connections or links to triads to impress or ward off other rivals. Police often have difficulty in determining real triad societies from bogus or falsely claimed ones, (Ngai, Cheung & Ngai 2007).

Broadhurst and Wa (2009) agree that triads will hire street based youth groups to help protect illegal enterprises; a view supported by both Chin and Zhang 2003. Triads can also be linked with businessmen involved in racketeering, but often these are loosely connected. It is however street gangs that are responsible for street level violence. In this way young men from poor and deprived neighbourhoods provide the lowest tier of the triad society with triad adults recruiting from such neighbourhoods. These adults often act as a successful role model for new recruits or Wannabees recruits, although the age of recent arrestees for violence associated with triads does however suggest that triads might be losing attraction for younger Hong Kong youth.

The links between triad societies, crime networks and youth street gangs have been researched by Lee (2005) and described by Broadhurst and Wa as 'a dynamic form of symbiosis between triad groups, criminal entrepreneurs and delinquent businesses, officials and professionals…associated with triad-related violence', (2010, p20). Central to this is the 'mutual aid orientation' commonly expressed amongst triad societies and their role as 'protector' in the overall command structure of illegal and criminal enterprises. Although some have become niche operators in the protection business whilst others are more favoured as negotiators or financiers. At times this role would expand to include extortion and even generate its own criminal outputs.

Broadhurst and Wa (2010) contend that to expand their shared interests, exploit business opportunities and see-off rivals, these triad societies developed a simple command structure. This usually involved a specialist leader holding strategic governance over the society but linked to underworld criminal networks. Such men are highly skilled operators networked through *Guanxi*. Their ability to quickly muster multiple thugs to act as the 'strong arm' for the enforcement of protection rackets became a regular feature of the presence of triads.

Competition between triads leads occasionally to sporadic violence and ability to organise quick mobilisation is a reputational benefit. Reputational enhancement of triad groups forms a version of 'street capital' (Harding 2015) and defence of earned reputations can also trigger violence. Other disputes occur over territory.

Lethal violence is reportedly declining. According to Broadhurst and Wa (2009) in 1997 approximately 25 per cent of all homicides were linked to triads but by 2001 this has dropped to 5 per cent, and no definable links were evidence by 2004. Fortunately triad linked homicides are infrequent thanks in part to the strict control of firearms. Broadhurst and Wa (2009) report that 50 per cent of the homicides that occurred in the period 1989- 1998 were related to lower-rank street-level confrontations over honour or territory; 21 per cent of homicides were related to business rivalries between competing illicit entrepreneurs; enforcement of 'discipline' of customers (for example unpaid debts) accounted for 17 per cent of homicides; internal sanctions or punishment accounted for 14 per cent and occurred at both street-level ranks and syndicate level ranks.

Changes in Secret Societies

Changes in the political economy in Hong Kong (moving from a manufacturing economy to a financial services economy) and the end of colonial rule have led to changes in the roles and functions of the triads. Essentially triads have adapted to these socio-economic changes and have had to both modernise and transform. Broadhurst and Wa claim the aims of the triads '*have become corporatized and boundaries moved beyond traditional predatory street crime, extortion and drug dealing predicated on brand violence to diverse 'grey' business activities that also include trafficking (anything profitable), vice, copyright, Internet and financial service crimes such as money laundering and fraud'.* (Broadhurst & Wa, 2010, p2).

Part of this functional adaptation includes some previous triads activities, such as vice and drug manufacture, moving from Hong Kong to mainland China where triads are likely to experience considerably reduced surveillance and investigation by the police, largely due to high levels of corruption. According to Broadhurst and Wa (2010, p2) this 'shift in the relative visibility and apparent scope of the triads may thus be a form of organisational transformation and displacement stimulated by the absence of capable guardianship in adjacent cities such as Shenzhen Special Economic Zone (SEZ) and elsewhere in Guangdong and China'.

Chin (1990b) found that being associated to a triad in locations such as Taiwan, Macau or HK both grants and improves social capital. As a result 'a degree of overlap and ambiguity between triad society, illicit business and 'organised crime' is inherent', (Broadhurst & Wa, 2010, p3).

Both Chin and Zhang argue that amongst the Chinese diaspora triads have been in decline and they cast doubt over the existence of global triad networks, (Chin & Zhang 2003). Hong Kong retains its place as a major international hub for transport, finance and business though no evidence has been found of any transnational triad organisation. The triads however do control the drug trade at street level. The wholesale trafficking of drugs appears to still be organised by small groups of entrepreneurs. They note that in Hong Kong the involvement of triads in crime has not increased for the past 20 years. In 2006 only 3 per cent of recorded crime was designated as triad related. At present Broadhurst and Wa (2009) suggest around 50 groups are active according to sources in the Hong Kong Police. The Hong Kong police Organised Crime and Triad Bureau undertake routine patrols and surveillance operations sometimes leading to raids against suspect groups. They also undertake community youth diversion projects in Hong Kong.

Operational Adaptations

Prior to the return of Hong Kong to the People's Republic of China, (PRC), the Hong Kong government established the Organised and Serious Crimes Ordinance (OSCO) in 1994 which created new powers and authority to recoup the proceeds of crime. It was thus aimed at addressing both street-level groups and strategic leaders. Through this route the Hong Kong police targeted money laundering and Boiler Room Fraud cases issuing restraint orders and confiscation orders. The ultimate goal of such activity has been to create a risky environment for triads to operate illegally and to force them to engage in legitimate businesses and business practices. The China Daily has headlined the rise in fraud and warned of the economic impact upon businesses, (The China Daily 20th Feb 2009).

The transformation of Hong Kong's economy into a financial services hub for East Asia has been coupled with a reduced tolerance of triad violence. The old romantic notions of triad societies appears to have a looser grip on the public imagination. The overall effect of the OSCO and other related legislation in the 1990s was to begin a shift from the traditional policing relationships between Hong Kong police and the triads, which partially tolerated them, to one which demonstrates a focussed hostility towards organised crime and attempts to suppress triad subculture. This has had the effect of moving the triads from violence, vice and visibility to reduced visibility and more flexible forms of business enterprise. (Broadhurst & Wa 2009).

In addition to these internal changes in Hong Kong, specifically how it is policed and the broader business environment, there are wider changes in southern China which have led to new developments and expanded opportunities for triads whilst their influence in Hong Kong has been decreasing.

Triads now appear to operate a more flexible and elastic form of business enterprise with greater emphasis on business and a more open door policy to those wishing to join. This is partially recognised as a business response to the fact HK is now fast becoming a service industry society with fewer local shops and businesses to exhort. Human trafficking between HK and China has also now ended with the handover of HK to China, (Parry, 2013).

The opening of the Chinese economy from the 1980s onwards and the return of Hong Kong to the PRC has helped propel the triads through the growth of illicit trade in goods and services to more competitive markets in southern China. The liberalisation of cross-border traffic from Hong Kong to China helped establish the Shenzhen Special Economic Zone and precipitated the extraordinarily rapid urbanisation of Shenzhen and Gaungdong province. Shenzhen itself rose in population from a few thousand in 1980 to almost 15 million by 2014, (Whitwell, 2014).

These emerging Chinese mainland markets outstripped the ability of regional legislators and authorities to regulate and enforce the newly developing markets and thus created opportunities for corruption and protection rackets. Access to justice and dispute resolution was limited and for some unobtainable. Crime in Shenzhen soared with 100,000 offences recorded in 2003 and significant rises in homicide, assault and kidnapping, (South China Morning Post, 2004). By 2006 Shenzhen became the gateway city for drugs for southern China, (South China Morning Post, 2006).

Drugs

Increased urbanisation was spurred on by huge levels of migration from rural areas to the urban cities opening up new markets for drugs, notably heroin, ketamine and methamphetamine. As well as a business opportunity, drug use itself in China remains a national problem.

Drug trafficking and new entrepreneurial drug syndicates have expanded from Hong Kong to Shenzhen and Guangdong province. Though data remains sketchy it is likely that the commercial vice trade which once thrived in Hong Kong has similarly been displaced to Guangdong province. Broadhurst and Wa (2009), note that triads are now actively attempting to enter new markets for criminal activities such as internet gambling, copyright theft, international animal smuggling, counterfeit drugs.

By the end of 2014 China had 2.95 million registered drug users but the actual number is estimated to be more than 14 million, according the China National Narcotics Control Commission (NNCC). The number of synthetic drug users (approx 1.46 Million) overtook the number of registered heroin users in 2014. A total 880,000 drug users were arrested in 2014 with 264,000 entering compulsory detox centres and 197,000 receiving community drug rehabilitation, (China Daily 5th November 2015).

Police have discovered triad gangs were involved in well organised, cross border syndicates. Operation Thunderbolt, jointly operated between Hong Kong, Macao and Guangdong police netted 1,191 people in a month long crackdown on cross -border triads. Gambling dens and vice venues were shut, 40 kilos of ketamine were seized and contraband and counterfeit cigarettes. Kowloon East in Hong Kong had actually noticed a decrease in gang activity since recent court sentences for money extortion such as imposing a monopoly on the purchase of construction worker lunch boxes. In the northern territories of Hong Kong, the main income for gangs comes from illegal gambling. Police noted that some young people were hiring boats for boat trips with friends where they took drugs. Officers from the Crime Prevention Bureau in Hong Kong were seeking to stop triads from recruiting young people, (China Daily 17th Aug 2012).

Cocaine remains expensive and thus less popular in Hong Kong. Nevertheless police smashed a high level and cross-country cocaine tracking syndicate during Operation Vanquisher. Lee (2009) notes that 'over 75 per cent of drug offences by juveniles under the age of 21 yrs typically use Ketamine, whilst cocaine only accounts for approximately 55 of offences'.

Zhang Jun, Vice President of the Supreme People's Court commented that 'a majority of drug crimes are now linked to gangs', (Chuanjiao 2009b). The announcement noted that courts dealt with nearly 44,000 drug cases in 2008 which was up by 12 per cent on the previous year. Drug-related crime was commonly now associated with gangs and violence including a shift in trends from importing ketamine to making it domestically. Raw materials were now often smuggled in and new drugs such as methamphetamine were starting to replace opium and heroin. In 2008 there were 12,243 Methamphetamine related crimes (up 61 per cent) and a further 5,251 from January to May in 2009. This has led to the production of methamphetamine in local apartment blocks and the greater use of gang affiliated youth to deliver and manufacture such drugs. Criminal law in China for smuggling, trading, transporting, manufacturing or trafficking drugs or even possessing drugs 1kg or more of drugs is liable to a minimum of seven years imprisonment. The death penalty is instigated or larger amounts. This type of criminal activity is most commonly located in the provinces of Guangdong, Gaunxi, Yunnan, Sichuan and Guizhou. The Supreme People court has recently toughened its sanctions for those involved in drug offences with new unified capital punishment sanctions for those involved in trafficking using force, international drug trafficking, instigating minors to deal drugs, or those providing premises for drug manufacture, (Chuanjiao 2009b).

E-Crime

Other operational adaptations include the move into Internet crime with some 'e-crime' gangs now targeting older women and approximately 70 per cent of victims are elderly and female. Often they are tricked into releasing bank account details. A crackdown found gangs operating out of six counties in mainlined China using connections to Taiwan and southeast Asia to avoid detection. More than 1,400 suspects were recently detained due to suspected involvement. According to news reports, 'The gangs act like corporations with departments in charge of technology and others in charge of transferring the money', (China Daily 31th Aug 2009).

More Talk, Less Fighting

One noticeable outcome in Hong Kong has been a recent change in how triads operate. This is noticeable in terms of visibility, levels of violence, influence and ways of operating. Some leading triad members have shifted their focus from illegal business into quasi-legal business.

Deng, (2012), writing in the China Daily, reports that 'the city's triad menace related to youth gangs is abating, thanks in large part to the efforts of the police to crack down on the violence, and social workers 'to encourage many young gang members to give up the criminal lifestyle and go straight'. Deng notes that rival gang groups of up to 100 youth would congregate for fighting whilst others became involved in taking ketamine and then playing gaming machines.

To address such issues, the Hong Kong Federation of Youth Groups has been working with 200 'at risk' teenagers. Their activities have reduced the impact and threat of violence from such groups compared to a year ago according to NGOs. The social work outreach team have worked with young kids trying to get them to desist from gang membership. As one youth worker noted back in 2011,

Three nights out of seven we could see triad fights or looting in the neighbourhood. Not all incidents were reported to the police. Sometimes you could see a gang of 40 kids dressed in black hanging out in the basketball court. You could see them in the shopping arcades. (Ken Yeung, a youth worker from Won Tai Sin Outreaching Social Work Team).

In 2010, 30 young people under 20 were arrested and charged with wounding and a further 82 with assault. At Easter 2011 police and social workers were struggling to keep up with referrals and fights mostly between those 14- 19. In 2011, 30 were charged with wounding and 63 with serious assault according to the Police Public Relations Branch in Hong Kong, (Deng, 2012).

Local police operate with informers but resolving issues via the police is not common as many triads settle conflict via cash payments. It is apparently not uncommon for a gang member suffering grievous injury to withdraw his accusation saying he can no longer recognize who inflicted the wounds, (Deng 2012).

The reduction in violence or the reduced inclination to violence has also been noticed by Sociologist Lee King Wa from Chinese University in Hong Kong. He believes the move away from violence is partly due to policing tactics and partially due to a desire to invest in local businesses and cross-border schemes such as the trade in milk powder. He believes that the move into legit businesses has interrupted the triad chain of command as lower-ranks sometimes now act independently without the counsel of the Big Brothers, (Parry, 2013).

This view is supported by other academics who note it has become more difficult to recruit foot soldiers: *'In terms of structure they (the gangs) are not as organised as in the past. They used to be more concerned about the Brotherhood...that made it easier for them to recruit foot soldiers to commit crimes for them - but now it is getting more difficult'*, (Sharon Kwok of City University, Hong Kong, (Parry, 2013).

Whilst younger triad members will often do work for the Brotherhood (triad elders) without pay, Parry (2013) reports that now on occasion youngsters will be paid by triad members just to show up in a show of strength against rivals.

There are some indications that violence, although less frequent, is perhaps now sporadic and uncontrolled. Parry, (2013), reports that lower level triads, which often recruited from schools in large quantities to keep the triad societies thriving over the past 20 years, now sometimes operate outside the control of their bosses. This in turn leads younger members to get involved in violence because they are now less controlled by the older Brothers than in the past. Previously they would seek permission to fight however now they may just fight if they wish to. Also there are reports that they are less picky in choosing members and have different members in different areas. As the juniors recruit their own members the seniors are often cut off from this new network. This view has been supported by other authors such as Lee Kwing-wa, sociologist at the Chinese University of Hong Kong. As he mentioned, Triads now *'talk more and they fight less. They are more calculating, more rational, and it is less about sub-culture and Brotherhood. They talk more about benefits. Different triad groups work together to get business done'*,(Parry, 2013).

Characteristics of Youth Gangs in China

Chinese studies have begun to decipher the different emerging characteristics of youth gangs in China which permits us to summarise the knowledge as follows:

Prevalence

During the 1950s and 1960s youth gangs in China were not considered a problem. Their presence was reported at being as low as 6 cases per 100,000. However by 2005 this had risen to 356 per 100,000, (Zhang, Messner & Liu, 2008). Urban street gangs have in fact been developing and emerging in China since the 1970s and 1980s (Zhang 2002 & Zhang et al 1997) suggesting socio-economic reforms created the climate for street gangs to emerge. However as in the West, statistics are clouded by definitional difficulties, interpretation and collation reluctance, denial and central authorities reluctance to honestly reflect the situation in some cities least they be assessed by central government as under-performing (Covey 2010).

Despite this, it appears that the huge economic developments occurring in China over the last 30 years have been mirrored by cultural changes and sifting patterns of crime, notably juvenile delinquency and increased patterns of offending (Zu-Yuan 1998). Although formal and official data remains elusive, Xiang (1999) identified that approximately 7 per cent of youth delinquency was in fact gang-related. More recently in 2008 Zhao (2008) reported increased gang activity in China.

Cao and Dai (2001) have noted that economic changes have led to increased *anomie* in China alongside considerable inequality between rural and urban areas and also specifically within urban areas. These social changes allow the expression of individualism and personal freedoms with ideological expectations now diminishing alongside the ideological control that was so associated with China's communist rule.

The prevalence of gang involvement in China and gang participation in the West was recently examined by Webb et al (2011) by undertaking a self-reporting study amongst school groups. Results indicated that the US sample displayed a higher prevalence of self-nominated gang membership than in China. The Chinese sample was also lower in 'last year' and 'life time' participation in various criminal activities than in the US sample. As might be expected due to the different cultural and social contexts, there were also definitional challenges re the term gang.

Delinquent Behaviour and Gang Involvement

A recent study by Pyrooz and Decker considers the relationships between delinquent behaviour and gang involvement in China and involved gathering self-reported data from 2,245 school youth in Changzhi in northern China. They found over half the respondents engaged in some form of delinquency in the previous year with 11 per cent reporting gang involvement. Current or former gang members had higher likelihood of overall delinquency and specialisation in violence. Pyrooz and Decker (2012) found that the relationship between gangs and violence, delinquency and offending were similar to those found in the West.

There is no history of self-reported gang studies in China as there is in the US and any use is limited, (Zhang 2008). Webb et al (2011) however did undertake a study of school youth using self-reported questionnaires using the International Self-Report Delinquency (ISRD-2) questionnaire to undertake a comparative analysis between China and the US. Here Pyrooz and Decker (2012) found Chinese youth had lower levels of self-reported delinquent behaviour and lower levels of self-reported gang membership than US youth. However those that did self-report as gang-affiliated reported greater levels of offending and victimisation.

Pyrooz and Decker (2012) argue that results from their self-reported study of Chinese school youth indicate that established criminological theory to explain delinquency can be applied to Chinese youth. They also maintain that parental monitoring, parent and school attachment, peer association and low self-control were correlated with likelihood to offend and specialise in violence.

Organisation

In China youth crime gangs (*qing shao mian fan zui taun huo*) are considered to be loosely connected groups of males aged between 14-25 yr involved in criminal offending, (Zhang (2014). Youth street gangs are thought to differ from organised crime due to their fluid membership, limited cohesion, limited level of organisation and varying definitions of co-offending and group offending particular to China.

Chinese studies have recently come to view contemporary youth gangs in China as more organised and more violent, more technology oriented and engaged in wider types of criminal activity than in the past (Zhang 2014); as a result youth gangs are now an issue of public concern for many Chinese.

To determine levels of organisation within street gangs, Zhang L. (1997) compared both China and US using data from an inmate survey in Tainjin, comparing youth gang characteristics, types of offences and criminal justice responses. Findings show that the level of organisation in a Chinese gang is low compared to the US and that most activity is from mid-teens to early twenties before levelling off – this is consistent with US research. The study of inmates in Tianjin prisons and reform camps identified four key characteristics of gangs in China. Firstly the level of gang organisation is said to be low. Secondly membership is age-graded and often transitory. Thirdly gangs were territorial and associated with clearly defined spatial neighbourhoods. Lastly offending was what Malcolm Klein (1995) would call, 'cafeteria-style' and often low level.

In a further study by Lee et al (1996) of 36 Hong Kong street gangs, the authors found both core and fringe members and that the gangs were not cohesive. They operated autonomously only referring to triad links when in dispute with rival gangs. As in much gang research there was no mention of the role played by girls.

Chu (2000) remains sceptical of the organised nature of such affiliated noting that street gangs often over-claim allegiance – similar to gang 'wannabe's' in the West.

The Hong Kong Federation of Youth Groups believes that the use of *Whatsapp* has also changed the ways youth gangs and triads link up and organise. The App brings multiple young people into a fight instantly whereas otherwise they may simply sit at home and play computer games or take drugs in stairways. Triad clashes are mostly internal rivalries within the triad, (Deng 2012).

Membership

Some differences between western gangs and those in China are more are evident. In China 'Fellow workers' and 'provincials' are a 'relatively common' source of gang membership. This interesting difference reflects the unique social structure of China particularly regarding employment and migration. As found in Russian street gangs and youth groups in China, the workplace often acts as the centre of association and occasionally gang formation (Zhang (2002) and Zhang et al 1997).

Also gang membership does not appear to be correlated to the seriousness of the offense or reason for incarceration – this differs from the USA. Lastly gang related crime does increase the severity of punishment. This is in line with current official policy of cracking down on gangs, (Zhang 1997). Matheron (1988) also noted that street gangs can act as a 'probationary period' for some young gang members before permission to full tiered membership.

Other observations by Zhang (1997) about Chinese street gangs reflect similar gang structures and hierarchies and membership as found in the West; i.e. gangs are largely male, aged between 15-25 with core and peripheral membership and links to local city or neighbourhood territories. Whilst free gang association is always an option many Chinese youth prefer to join gangs associated with triads (Che 1992; Wong 1999).

Loyalty

Chinese studies have identified that youth bond together for common support, common interests, protection, and engage in anti-social behaviour, (Zhou et al 2004; Liu, 2004, Zhang 2014). They also group together for joint criminal enterprise and act together out of bonds of loyalty to friends, which is generally considered to be a 'primary moral standard' (Zhang 2014) and expected social requirement in China. Indeed the research study of inmates in Tianjin stated that 60 per cent of the respondents cited loyalty to friends as the main reason for gang affiliation.

Zhang (1997) and (Covey 2010) both rightly identify that Chinese moral codes of loyalty to family and friends often underpin affiliation and associations at work as well as in the formation of criminal networks.

Recidivism

High levels of recidivism were also identified by researchers Zhang and Huang (1984) who undertook research into 100 youth gangs in Guangzhou. They identified that 49 per cent of gang members were recidivists. This is considered important as recidivists were central in overseeing gang recruitment, training, and organising of activity alongside maintaining discipline and solidarity, (Zhang 2014). As the China Daily news reported, 'From 2002 to 2011, the rate of recidivism of China's juvenile offenders remained at 1 per cent to 2 per cent, according to a white paper on judicial reform published in October of 2012', (China Daily 23rd Sept 2013).

Ken Yeung, a youth worker from Won Tai Sin Outreaching Social Work Team, notes that repeat offending within the triad often helps to embed the youngster within the triad subculture. After a while these youngsters find it difficult to go back into normal society. Yeung acknowledges that those who are more embedded will find it difficult to withdraw and desist and those with chaotic or difficult home lives often stay embedded, (Deng 2012).

Summary

Wang (2006), Zhang (2001) and Zhou et al (2004) have summarised some key characteristic of Chinese gangs thus: Some gangs have defined leadership however mostly the level of group organisations is low; Membership status is generally changeable and impermanent; membership is based on neighbourhood territory, age and occupation (e.g. co-workers, neighbours, school mates); lastly, criminal activity largely involves crime against property and interpersonal violence, (though some specialise in property or vice, most engage in multiple criminal activity), (Zhang 2014).

Risk Factors for Youth Gang Affiliation

Chinese research into youth delinquency and gangs suggests that the common risk factors or predictors for delinquency include levels of attachment to school, moral adherence to Chinese culture, harmony between the generations and integration within society, (Wong 1999; Wong 2001; Zhang & Messner, 1996).

In addition, as identified above, both triads and youth street gangs have been sustained over the years through migration and immigration.

The Role of Rural: Urban Migration

The *Hukou* urban registration system established by the Communist regime effectively initiated a dual system of citizenship separating rural from urban citizens. It prevented rural citizens from becoming urban citizens and was designed to limit migration from rural to urban areas in an attempt to address increasing urbanisation. The economic reforms initiated from the 1980s onwards immediately drew attention to the large surplus of rural labour and the deficit of labour in the expanding urbanised cities. The response was to slacken the restrictions resulting in large migrant movements to the cities. One result, aside from rapid urbanisation, has been a concentration of poor rural migrants in poor and under-serviced neighbourhoods, (Zhang 2014). If lucky they will eventually move to cramped multi-occupancy high-rise developments on the periphery of cities.

Citing Adamson (1998) Ngai, Cheung and Ngai (2007) note that the multiplicity of high-rise housing often tends to diminish community integration in neighbourhoods and may thus act as a future catalyst for gang involvement in China.

One example is the influx of migrants into new towns such as Tseung Kwan O in Hong Kong. This new town had a population of around 100,000 in 1999 and it now stands at nearly 400,000 with 17.5 per cent of the population aged between 10 – 24 yrs. A recent survey in the new town by Caritas Youth and Community Service found that half of the 140 teenagers interviewed claim at least one friend who is connected to triads or is a member of a triad; 30 per cent of the young respondents said they had been harassed by triads themselves. Many triads had local influence before the new towns were built as they operated from local villages. The new towns simply provided opportunities for them to expand their power and to recruit new members. However, younger members are often 'fractious and easily provoked'. In Tseung Kwan O, approximately 90 per cent of the triad members are affiliated to Sun Yee On triad, (Deng 2012).

Children from migrant families are not allowed to attend public high schools in cities. In addition to being separated from their parents they often have to undertake their own schooling at home. Whilst some attend primary or middle educational schools, resources and opportunities are limited. Citing a recent Education report from the 21st Century Education Research Institute realised in April 2015, Wangshu (2015) notes that 20 per cent of the 278.9 million children in China were not able to enter public school in 2013. This is despite an order from central government for local government authorities to ensure migrants can enter local high schools, but city authorities who are attempting to control population increases have often tightened their polices and restricted access. The report which sought to analyse China's educational reforms in 2014 noted that around 36.7 per cent of juvenile criminals attend neither school nor work. Around 27 per cent of juvenile criminals are children whose parents leave them at home whilst the parents seek migrant work in cities and a further 27 per cent of juvenile offenders are children who travel with their parents as migrants to work in cities. According to the national census of 2010, around 35.8 million children in China under the age of 18 travel with their migrant worker parents whilst a further 61 million children are left in rural areas when their parents work in the cities, (Wangshu 21st April 2015).

One response of rural migrants has been for young migrants to group together in street gangs. These gangs are largely comprised of youth from the same province, village or town. These regional ties and the *Guanxi*, or social capital, acquired by family and neighbour ties, act as binding agents for those coming together for criminal activity.

One high profile article in the China Daily reflected the public debates on migrants suggesting that second generation migrants are not as 'hardworking' as the first and become more involved in crime. Often they realise they have a skills deficit and resort to criminal activity. The Statistics from the People's Supreme Court indicate that in 2007, approximately 316,000 juvenile offenders were sentenced, which accounted for one third of China's convicted prisoners: of these some 87,500 were minors, (China Daily 30th Dec 2008).

In line with the argument of migration leading to increased offending, areas with a high rate of migrant influx, such as Guandong have noticed an increase in juvenile offending. For example in Guangdong, (which has 2 million juvenile offenders accounting for almost a quarter of its total population, from 2003 – 2007), the Nanfang Daily newspaper reported juvenile criminal offences increased by 18 per cent year on year. The No1 Criminal Law Court of Jiangsu High People's Court recorded that migrant teenagers were responsible for 87 per cent and 80 per cent of juvenile offences in the cities of Suzhou and Wuxi, respectively. In Zhejiang province in Haishu district, the People's court of Ningbo, (the regional capital) migrant juveniles accounted for 95 per cent of criminal prosecutions. The chief of the Court's Juvenile Tribunal Service was quoted as saying criminals are becoming younger and often have lower educational backgrounds. Approximately three-quarters of juvenile crimes were property related with violence, often including theft and robbery. He further noted that 'crime committed by girls are also becoming crueller and differ less from those of the boys', (China Daily 30th Dec 2008).

In 2009, under the China Daily headline – *'Raising the issue of China's Troubled teens'*, the investigative reporter Xie Chuanjiao, reported on research conducted by the Beijing Municipal Higher People's court, identified that the majority of juvenile offenders came from migrant families whose children experience poor parental care, neglect and limited educational input. Their study indicated that between 40- 80 per cent of delinquency in the city over the previous three years was by migrant youth with no household registration. Those from single parent homes and those leaving school early were particularly at risk of offending. Of 100 studied cases of young people aged 16-18 years, only 16 per cent of juveniles were attending school at the time of the offence. Property crime, theft and robbery were most prevalent followed by assaults and rapes. Interestingly the report noted bias in schools against migrant students with some being charged extra fees. Guangdong province, (which has by 2009 upwards of 30 million migrant workers) had recently revised its rules to permit migrants who had lived in the province for more than seven years to apply for permanent residence permits. Such permits then allow their children to free schooling for nine years and thus save their parents thousands of yuan. In Shanghai, whilst the rates of delinquency of local youth have remained stable (until 2009), crimes committed by migrant youth has risen by almost 70 per cent from 2004- 2007. The city's Municipal Higher People's Court reported that 800 minors were convicted in 1998, rising to 2,682 in 2007. Of these, 1,833 did not have a local household registration and 86 per cent has no education beyond primary school. Zhang Haitang, the Vice President of the Shanghai Higher People's Court allocated this rise to the increase in migrant population of the Shanghai region which has recently increased by 6.6 million including 604,000 adolescents. It was suggested that traditional community or village groups or organisations assisted in addressing youth delinquency but this proved difficult in peri-urban areas dealing with large numbers of migrants, (Chuanjiao 2009a).

Social Control

Wang et al (2002) found that Chinese children whose parents exert strong parental control are less likely to engage in delinquent behaviour, whilst those associating with delinquent peers are more likely to offend. Alongside social control mechanisms and social bond theory, cognitive development, notably academic achievement has been identified as reducing the risks of youth offending in gangs, (Wang et al 2002).

The cognitive and social influences which determine gang involvement have recently been studied by Ngai, Cheung and Ngai (2007) who undertook qualitative interviews with almost 1000 delinquent youth in three cities: Hong Kong, Guangzhou and Shanghai in 1999. All youth were accessed via youth service units, e.g. correctional schools, outreach and social work recruitment. The average age of respondents was 15.8 yrs and mostly male. They identified significant differences between the three cities of Hong Kong, Guangzhou and Shanghai. These differences arise largely due to the different social context of westernized and individualist systems operating in Hong Kong as opposed to socialist and collectivist traditions in mainland China. The results show that the role of parents and the influence of parental control are weaker in mainland China than in Hong Kong however the influence and social control of teachers and the tradition of authoritative control evident in mainland China helps to demonstrate the converse to this finding.

The Ngai, Cheung and Ngai (2007) study found that expected and prior gang involvement of respondents was highest in Hong Kong. Conversely Hong Kong youth demonstrated the lowest scores on youth and friends moral beliefs, parental controls and teacher attachment. Hong Kong youth had higher engagement with social workers. Interestingly the effects of prior gang involvement were noticeably strong in Guangzhou and demonstrated a high predicator of gang activity, (Ngai, Cheung & Ngai, 2007). The authors claim the findings are supportive of the generality of social control functions, pro-social learning, educational attainment and problem solving abilities on Chinese delinquent youth and their involvement with gangs. The socio-cultural differences highlighted were that teachers and social workers are more authoritative in mainland China and in Hong Kong individual and parental influences are key; even though parents often exerted less control there than in mainland Chinese cites.

The study also found that Hong Kong had the highest level of educational attainment and Guangzhou the lowest. Many respondents in Guangzhou were recent arrivals. In line with reports on migrant families struggling to adapt to newly urbanised conditions, Guangzhou youth tended to be boys with a lower socioeconomic background and had only been resident in Guangzhou for a short time. In this context teachers become the prime authoritative influence and control over migrant youth and possibly one of the few inhibitors for gang involvement. The Cultural hub of Shanghai was noted to have the highest level of further education amongst the youth surveyed, and in this context operated as an inhibitor for gang affiliation (Ngai, Cheung & Ngai 2007). Xi (2001) argues that in socialist collectivist mainland China, cognitive development plays a lesser role in youth gang desistence than might be expected.

In Hong Kong, maternal education and length of residence in the city were both positive predictors of youth gang affiliation. Parental controls were more effective in gang desistence in Hong Kong and 'attachment to authoritative professionals is more significant in a socialist collectivist country', (Ngai, Cheung & Ngai 2007, p10). In terms of policy development to address gang affiliation then the authors claim 'bolstering social integration and cohesion in the neighbourhood would be an effective way to deter gang involvement in a collectivist society', (Ngai, Cheung & Ngai 2007).

Parenting Practice

There has been considerable discussion and debate in the Chinese media about parenting styles in China and in particular the unexpected outcomes of the one-child policy. Some believe that China's one-child policy has had a profound effect on parenting practice which in turn has impacted upon youth behaviour and delinquency (Zhang 2014). Zhang argues that Chinese parents develop 'extraordinarily high expectations' of their child, expectations which are often unrealistic and go unmet. For those falling short of this high threshold, or who suffer the stress of fierce peer-group competition, behavioural problems can quickly surface, i.e. this can lead to drug addiction, for others, gang affiliation. Zhang (2014) claims many Chinese parents are more controlling of their children than Western parents and this brings added stress. Chinese parents, he claims, view their children as 'little emperors' within the family and often become spoiled. He suggests this creates a mix of permissive and controlling parenting which generates selfish and impulsive behaviours. Such issues have now become the focus of public debates in China. Indeed some Chinese studies suggest a clear link between such parenting practice and gang related crime and gang affiliation, (Liu 2004; Wang 2005). The All China Women's Federation report that 'left behind migrant children experience lack of security, family closeness, protection and reduced educational opportunities'. This has also led to debates about the influence of social media and TV and also an absence of moral education in favour of academic education, (China Daily 23rd Sept 2013). This however is a topic of little research. What is perhaps clearer is that those who become socially marginalised may drift into gang affiliation.

Recent Changes in Gangs

Importantly however the link between youth street gangs and organised crime remains rather elusive and further research is required to fully explain this. Despite crackdown, (e.g. Chongqing) there have been no evaluations as to the effectiveness of such policies.

The China Daily reported (27th Feb 2009) that organized crime increased sharply in 2008 despite a government crackdown on gangs according to the People's Supreme Court.

The government is largely unreflexive in regards to youth gang crime and have yet to establish suitable and responsive mechanisms to address them. As a result punishment is based on the pre-established codes for addressing organised crime which tend to be more severe than what might be expected for such collective offending. Despite this, according to recent media coverage, these measures retain high levels of public support.

The general view is that youth gangs have emerged as a social problem in China though their full extent and activities remains somewhat unclear and under-researched, leading Zhang (2014) to call for more research and more theoretical engagement in this research. Pyrooz and Decker (2012) support this call for more research into group based violence and specialisation in violence recommending greater use of different methodologies to explore delinquency and gang studies.

REFERENCES

Adamson, C. (1998). Tribute, Turf, honor and the American street gang: Patterns of continuity and change since 1820. *Theoretical Criminology*, 2(1), 57–84. doi:10.1177/1362480698002001003

Bakken, B. (2004). Moral Panics, Crime Rates and Harsh Punishment in China. *Australian and New Zealand Journal of Criminology*, *37*(1 suppl), 37–89. doi:10.1177/00048658040370S105

Broadhurst, R. (2012). Chinese 'Black Societies' and triad-like organised crime in China. In F. Alum & S. Gilmour (Eds.), *Routledge Handbook of Transnational Organised Crime* (pp. 157–171). London: Routledge. doi:10.4324/9780203698341.ch10

Broadhurst, R. (2013). The suppression of black societies in China. *Trends in Organized Crime*, *16*(1), 95–113. doi:10.1007/s12117-012-9174-0

Broadhurst, R., & Wa, L. K. (2009). The Transformation of Triad 'Dark Societies' in Hong Kong: The Impact of Law Enforcement, Socio –Economic and Political Change. *Security Challenges*, *5*(4), 1–38.

Cao, L., & Dai, Y. (2001). Inequality in Crime and China. In J. Liu, L. Zhang, & S. Messner (Eds.), *Crime and Social Control in a Changing China* (pp. 73–88). Westport, Conn.: Greenwood Press.

Che, W. (1992). *Problems of juvenile delinquency in Hong Kong*. Hong Kong: China Book.

Chin, K. (1986). *Chinese triad societies, tongs organised crime and the street gangs in Asia and the United States*. (Unpublished Doctoral Dissertation). University of Pennsylvania.

Chin, K. (1990a). Chinese Gangs and Extortion. In Gangs in America. Sage Publications.

Chin, K. (1990b). *Chinese subculture and criminality: Non-traditional crime groups in America*. New York: Greenwood Press.

Chin, K. (2009). Hejiin: Organised Crime, Business and Politics in Taiwan. In T. W. Lo (Ed.), *Beyond Social Capital: A Case of Triad Financial Crime in Hong Kong and China*. City University of Hong Kong.

Chin, K., Kelly, R., & Fagan, J. (1993). Methodological issues in studying Chinese gang extortion. *The Gang Journal*, *1*(2), 25–36.

Chin, K., & Zhang, S. (2003). The declining significance of Triad Societies in Transnational Illegal Activities: A Structural Deficiency Perspective. *The British Journal of Criminology*, *43*(3), 469–488. doi:10.1093/bjc/43.3.469

China Daily. (2001, February 17). Curbing youth crime. *China Daily*.

China Daily. (2008, December 30). Juvenile crime up among migrants. *China Daily*.

China Daily. (2009a, February 16). Crime is a risk to stability: Official. *China Daily*.

China Daily. (2009b, February 20). Economic crime on rise, firms warned. *China Daily*.

China Daily. (2009c, February 27). Organized crime increases in 2008. *China Daily*.

China Daily. (2009d, April 28). Crackdown on crime in run-up to National Day. *China Daily*.

China Daily. (2009e, August 28). Gangs nabbed in Chongqing: 469 still at large. *China Daily*.

China Daily. (2009f, September 25). Anti-crime sweep smashes 1,300 gangs in south China. *China Daily*.

China Daily. (2009g, August 31). China's 'e-crime' gangs target older women. *China Daily*.

China Daily. (2009h, September 1). Courts convict nearly 13,000 on organised crime charges. *China Daily*.

China Daily. (2009i, December 16). Money-laundering gang trial opens in SW China. *China Daily*.

China Daily. (2012, August 17). Nearly 1,200 snared in month long crackdown. *China Daily*.

China Daily. (2013a, September 23). Teen killers spur discussion on youth crime. *China Daily*.

China Daily. (2013b, September 23). Teen killers spur discussion on youth crime. *China Daily*.

China Daily. (2015a, May 11). Drug users exceed 14 million in China. *China Daily*.

China Daily. (2015b, June 25). String of youth violence cases shocks nation. *China Daily*.

China Daily. (2015c, July 10). Gang activity in Guangdong poses 'serious threat'. *China Daily*.

Chu, Y. K. (2000). *The Triads as Business*. London: Routledge.

Chuanjiao, X. (2009a, May 7). Raising the issue of China's Troubled teens. *China Daily*.

Chuanjiao, X. (2009b, June 26). Gangsters muscling their way into drugs. *China Daily*.

Cloward, R. A., & Ohlin, L. (1960). *Delinquency and Opportunity*. Glencoe: Free Press.

Deng, A. (2011, June 23). Bloody-minded youth. *China Daily*.

Deng, A. (2012, September 6). Just one of the gang. *China Daily*.

Dishman, C. (2005). The Leaderless Nexus: When Crime and Terror Converge. *Studies in Conflict and Terrorism, 28*(3), 237–252. doi:10.1080/10576100590928124

Dutton, M. (1997). The basic character of crime in contemporary China, (Translation). *The China Quarterly, 149*, 160–177. doi:10.1017/S030574100004368X

Egely, A., & Howell, J. C. (2011). *Highlights of the 2009 National Youth Gang Survey*. Washington, DC: Office of the Juvenile Justice and Delinquency Prevention. doi:10.1037/e580942011-001

Harding, S. (2014). *The Street Casino: survival in violent street gangs*. Bristol: The Policy Press. doi:10.1332/policypress/9781447317173.001.0001

Huang, H. (2007). From the Asian Boys to the Zhu Lian Bang (the Bamboo Union Gang): A Typological analysis of Delinquent Asian Gangs. *Asian Criminology, 2*(2), 127–143. doi:10.1007/s11417-007-9033-0

Kelly, R., Chin, K., & Fagan, J. (1993, August). The Structure, Activity, and Control of Chinese Gangs: Law Enforcement Perspectives. *Journal of Contemporary Criminal Justice, 9*(3), 221–239. doi:10.1177/104398629300900304

Klein, M. (1995). *The American street gang: its nature, prevalence, and control*. New York: Oxford University Press.

Lee, C. (2009, February 19). Police make largest cocaine seizure in yrs. *China Daily*.

Lee, F. W., Loi, T. W., & Wong, D. S. W. (1996). Intervention in the decision-making of youth gangs. *Groupwork, 9*(3), 292–302.

Lee, K. W. (2005). *Triad-related homicide 1989-1998.* (PhD thesis). University of Hong Kong.

Liu, C. (2004). The Characteristics and Causes of Youth Gang crime. *Journal of ChangQiu Vocational and Technological College, 11,* 55–56.

Liu, J. (2008). Data sources in Chinese crime and criminal Justice research. *Crime, Law, and Social Change, 50*(3), 131–147. doi:10.1007/s10611-008-9135-3

Luo, S. (2012, December 29). Living on the mean streets. *China Daily.*

Main, J. (1991). The Truth about triads. *Policing: An International Journal of Police Strategies & Management, 7*(2), 144–163.

Matheron, M. S., (1988). China: Chinese triads, the Oriental Mafia. *CJ International, 4*(3), 26-27.

Ngai, N., Cheung, C., & Ngai, S. (2007, Summer). Cognitive and social influences on Gang involvement among delinquents in three Chinese cities. *Adolescence, 42*(166), 381–403. PMID:17849942

Paoli, L. (2002). The Paradoxes of Organised Crime. *Crime, Law, and Social Change, 37*(1), 51–97. doi:10.1023/A:1013355122531

Parry, S. (2013, November 8). Twilight of the triads. *China Daily.*

Pyrooz, D., & Decker, S. (2012). Delinquent Behaviour, Violence and Gang Involvement in China. *Journal of Quantitative Criminology, 29*(2), 251-272.

Shen, A., & Hall, S. (2015). The same the whole world over? A review essay on youth offending from the 1980s and youth justice in contemporary China. *International Journal of Law, Crime and Justice.*

Song, J., & Dombrink, J. (1994). Asian emerging crime groups: Examining the definition of organised crime. *Criminal Justice Review, 19*(2), 228–243. doi:10.1177/073401689401900204

Song, J. H. L. (1996). The Asian Factor: Methodological barriers to the study of Asian Gangs and Organised crime. *American Journal of Criminal Justice, 21*(1), 1996.

South China Morning Post. (2004, January 17). Soaring Crime Rate Dims Shenzhen's Luster. *South China Morning Post.*

South China Morning Post. (2006, May 10). Shenzhen is Key Gateway for illegal Drugs trade. *South China Morning Post.*

Spergel, I. (1961, March). An exploratory research in delinquent subcultures. *The Social Service Review, 35*(1), 33–47. doi:10.1086/640985

Sun, I., Hu, R., & Wu, Y. (2012). Social Capital, political participation, and trust in the police in urban China. *Australian and New Zealand Journal of Criminology, 45*(1), 87–105. doi:10.1177/0004865811431329

Thrasher, F. M. (1927). *The Gang: A study of 1,313 gangs in Chicago.* Chicago: University of Chicago Press.

Varese, F. (2006). How Mafias Migrate. *Law & Society Review, 40*(2), 411–444. doi:10.1111/j.1540-5893.2006.00260.x

Wang, G. T., Qiao, H., Wei, S., & Zhang, J. (2002). Adolescent social bond, self-control and deviant behaviour in China. *International Journal of Contemporary Sociology, 39*(1), 52–68.

Wang, P. (2013). The increasing threat of Chinese organised crime: National, regional and international perspective. *The RUSI Journal, 158*(4), 6–18. doi:10.1080/03071847.2013.826492

Wang, P., & Antonopoulos, G. (2015). Organised Crime and illegal gambling: How do illegal gambling enterprises respond to the challenges posed by their illegality in china? *Australian and New Zealand Journal of Criminology, 0*(0), 1–23.

Wangshu, L. (2015, April 21). Migrant life may lead to youth crime. *China Daily.*

Webb, V. J., Ren, L., Zhao, J., He, N., & Marshall, I. H. (2011). A comparative study of youth gangs in China and the United States: Definition, offending and victimisation. *International Criminal Justice Review, 21*(3), 225–242. doi:10.1177/1057567711418825

(2010). What is Organized Crime? In Varese, F. (Ed.), *Organized Crime.* Routledge.

Whitwell, T. (2014, June 13). Inside Shenzhen: China's Silicon Valley. *The Guardian.*

Wong, D. S. (1999, April). Delinquency Control and Juvenile Justice in China. *Australian and New Zealand Journal of Criminology, 32*(1), 27–41. doi:10.1177/000486589903200104

Wong, D. S. (2004, December). Juvenile Protection and Delinquency Prevention Policies in China. *Australian and New Zealand Journal of Criminology, 37*(1), 52–66. doi:10.1177/00048658040370S104

Wong, S. K. (1999). Delinquency of Chinese-Canadian youth: A test of opportunity, control and inter-generational conflict theories. *Youth & Society, 29*(1), 112–133. doi:10.1177/0044118X97029001005

Wong, S. S. W. (2001). Pathways to delinquency in Hong Kong and Guangzhou (south China). *International Journal of Adolescence and Youth, 10*(1/2), 91–115. doi:10.1080/02673843.2001.9747893

Wu, Y., Sun, I., & Hu, R. (2015). Public Trust in the Chinese police: The impact of ethnicity, class and Hukou. *Australian and New Zealand Journal of Criminology,* (Jan), 21.

Xi, J. (2001). *Research reports on China's Youth.* Beijing, China: China Youth.

Xiang, G. (1999). Delinquency and its prevention in China. *International Journal of Offender Therapy and Comparative Criminology, 43*(1), 61–70. doi:10.1177/0306624X99431006

Yoder, K. A., Whitbeck, K. B., & Hoyt, O. R. (2003). Gang involvement and membership among homeless and runaway youth. *Youth & Society, 34*(4), 441–467. doi:10.1177/0044118X03034004003

Zhang, B. (2001). The Characteristics of Youth Gangs. *Journal of Fu Jain Police College, 62,* 40–95.

Zhang, L. (2008). Juvenile delinquency and justice in contemporary China: A critical review of the literature over 15 years. *Crime, Law, and Social Change, 50*(3), 149–160. doi:10.1007/s10611-008-9137-1

Zhang, L. (2014). Of Marginality and 'Little Emperors': The changing Reality of Chinese Youth Gangs. In *Global Gangs: Street Violence across the world.* Minneapolis, MN: University of Minnesota Press. doi:10.5749/minnesota/9780816691470.003.0005

Zhang, L., & Messner, S. F. (1996). School attachment and official delinquency status in the People's Republic of China. *Sociological Forum*, *11*(2), 285–303. doi:10.1007/BF02408368

Zhang, L., Messner, S. F., & Liu, J. (2008). A Critical Review of Recent Literature on Crime and Criminal Justice in China: Research Findings, Challenges and Prospects (Introduction). *Crime, Law and Social Change: An Interdisciplinary Journal, 50*, 125-130.

Zhang, L., Messner, S. F., Lu, Z., & Deng, X. (1997). Gang crime and its punishment in china. *Journal of Criminal Justice*, *25*(4), 289–302. doi:10.1016/S0047-2352(97)00014-7

Zhang, L., Messner, S. F., Lu, Z., & Deng, X. (1997). Gang crime and its punishment in China. *Journal of Criminal Justice*, *25*(4), 289–302. doi:10.1016/S0047-2352(97)00014-7

Zhang, L., Zhang, L., & Lei, X. (1993). *China's Juvenile Delinquency and Justice*. Beijing, China: World Knowledge.

Zhang, S. X. (2002). Chinese Gangs: Familial and cultural dynamics. In C. R. Huff (Ed.), *Gangs in America III*. Newbury Park, CA: Sage. doi:10.4135/9781452232201.n14

Zhang, Z., & Huang, W. (1984). The role of recidivists in Delinquent Gangs. In Yearbook on Chinese Juvenile Delinquency Studies. Association of Chinese Juvenile Delinquency Study.

Zhou, L., Liu, W., & Wang, Z. (2004). *Contemporary Positivist Criminology: A Study of Crime Patterns*. Beijing: Publishing House of People's Courts.

Zie, Z. (2008, December 22). China planning special unit to tackle gangs. *China Daily*.

Zu-Yuan, H. (1988). China: Juvenile delinquency and its prevention. *CJ International*, *4*(5), 5–10.

Section 6
Pacifica

Chapter 15
Youth Gangs and Youth Violence in Australia

Rob White
University of Tasmania, Australia

ABSTRACT

This chapter provides an introduction and overview of issues pertaining to youth gangs and youth violence in Australia. The first part features the voices of young people from around Australia describing their experiences of youth gang violence. The second part provides a broad overview of biological, psychological and social factors that together shape the propensities for young people, and young men in particular, to join gangs and to engage in youth violence. The final part of the chapter provides more detailed exposition of two gang members, 'Mohammad' and 'Tan', and the everyday complexities of their lives. The chapter concludes by noting that the gang does not have to be seen as an overwhelming influence in the lives of young people, and that their activities and behaviours are more diverse, and include positive elements, than generally given credit in mainstream youth gangs research and analysis.

INTRODUCTION

Gangs connote predatory and violent action, usually by groups of young men. The concept encapsulates notions of aggression, viciousness, chains of brotherhood forged in combat, and codes of obedience and behaviour that discipline individuals to the group's norms and values. Gangs 'do bad', and violence is the clearest expression of this.

Gang members engage in violence on a regular basis. In this respect, each gang member can be seen to 'be bad' insofar as they partake in what are generally viewed as anti-social behaviour and activities. The implication is that there are basic character flaws and moral fissures that allow particular individuals to do things that many of their peers do not.

This chapter explores the lived realities of gang violence in an Australian context and the theoretical explanations for 'doing bad' and 'being bad'. In doing so, it draws largely upon a recent book, *Youth Gangs, Violence and Social Respect*, which is the first book dedicated to the systematic study of Australian youth gangs (White, 2013). It begins with stories by gang members about engaging in violent acts, and

DOI: 10.4018/978-1-4666-9938-0.ch015

the feelings and dynamics accompanying such acts. The chapter then examines biological, psychological and social explanations as to why some young people engage in such violence. At the conclusion of this, the chapter changes tack – away from generalisations about groups and members of groups, to the personal stories of two gang members in Sydney.

The heart of the chapter's discussions revolve around how best to categorise people and experiences in ways that provide accurate and sensitive portrayals of social life, something that is part of an ongoing conundrum for youth gangs research. The third part of the chapter highlights how 'stories' are crucial to interpreting what is going on in regards to specific gangs and gang members. To do this, it uses two brief vignettes to examine the life experiences of gang members 'Tan' and 'Mohammad' (not their real names) to illustrate the importance of biographical portraits to the social analysis of gangs. Social identity has a series of interconnected objective and subjective features that taken together combine to create multiple and varied identities. The fluidity of this has important implications for understanding gang members and for gang interventions.

Methodology and Approach

The research upon which this chapter is based was undertaken over a decade and a half, and involved a series of diverse and discrete projects. The present work thus incorporates insights from a specific study of youth gangs in Melbourne in the late 1990s (see White et al., 1999), findings derived from a national study of youth gangs in Australia in the mid-2000s (White, 2006), and the results of a high school questionnaire administered to over 700 students in Perth schools in the early 2000s (White & Mason, 2006).

The first two initiatives involved face-to-face interviews with young people; one targeting street present young people from various ethnic backgrounds (Vietnamese, Turkish, Pacific Islander, Somalian, Latin American, and Anglo-Australian); the other involving up to 50 interviews in each capital city with young people who self-identified as being gang members. The interview schedule and research process was devised by the chief investigator (for elaboration on the doing of this kind of national and collaborative research see White, 2011). Most of the interviews were carried out by youth and community workers specially chosen for the task because of their knowledge of the local area and their pre-existing relationships with local young people. The Perth survey questionnaire was constructed by the lead researcher in collaboration with Western Australian crime prevention and education officials, and administered via local schools in that city (see White & Mason, 2006). The national study included interviews with Indigenous young people, although Indigenous young people were not pre-selected as such. The focus across the studies was on discerning which individuals and groups are associated with gangs, the nature and extent of their engagement in gang-related behaviour, and the day-today experiences of those young people who identify with youth gang membership in the Australian context.

The observations contained herein reflect these various research endeavours undertaken at different times and in different places around the country with different groups of young people. In the light of this background, the chapter argues that when it comes to youth gangs, there is no set conceptual recipe or trait analysis that can adequately capture the flow and dynamics of everyday life. In social studies of this kind, we tend to find what we look for, 'youth gangs' and 'violent young men', as if these exist in themselves outside of other aspects of young people's lives. However, as this chapter demonstrates, a different cut of the data, a different methodological emphasis – from the group to the individual, from the gang-related activity to the totality of mundane day-to-day activities – reveals far more complicated pictures of how these young people actually live their lives.

Doing Bad: Boys Behaving Badly

Youth gangs are notorious for doing bad things. Indeed, built into the core definitions of 'gang' is the idea of transgression and deviance. It is criminality that defines the group as being a gang or not.

The hallmark of gangs is violence. Gangs are in some ways best defined as groups of young men who regularly engage in acts of violence that range from the more trivial to the lethal. While much dispute exists over gang definitions, there is no disputing the fact that male violence and violence amongst males is ubiquitous – it is everywhere and anywhere where groups of boys and young men gather and hang out. There is also evidence that, especially in American research, girls and young women occasionally engage in violent behaviour, are active members within some gangs, and occasionally form their own gangs (Miller, 2001; Batchelor, 2011). However, the degree, seriousness and prevalence of these activities and associations are much less than in the case of their male counterparts, certainly if the Australian experience is anything to go by (White, 2013).

A key feature of gang violence is that it is group violence. As with much street violence and domestic violence, there is frequently a close association between fighting and alcohol and drug use. Drinking to excess and/or using other drugs are often a prelude to a night of fighting, on all sides. But getting drunk is only part of the picture. Many of the young males involved in gangs are angry young men, and alcohol only fuels the aggression that is already there.

We went out into the city pissed. It's mainly when we were out in the city pissed 'cause if we're round the city pissed, we're out to cause trouble. We're out to fucking – we're angry – someone's fucked us around or someone's ripped us off and we're angry. We don't want to sit and chill anymore. We just wanna get pissed and fucking start a fight. Walk past someone and take his hat and see if he wants to start something [21-year-old male, Sydney]

When asked why they fight, the usual replies make reference to things such as *'the four or five people in my group because they just love fighting'* and to situational triggers such as *'say if we're doing something and someone death stares us, we'll get up and pat 'em'*. One Hobart respondent simply said that is was *'pretty much testosterone'* mixed in with a combination of badmouthing and 'being boys' types of things:

Yeah, just usually some – like a dirty look or someone's trying to chat up the wrong girl and stuff like that, or a common one is they owe money and they haven't paid for it. [21-year-old male, Hobart]

The reasons for fighting vary however, depending upon location and circumstance. Most gang fights involve some kind of rivalry. Typically this involves territory. Other reasons for fighting include competition in relation to graffiti, street racing and drug dealing, and conflicts over girls in the neighbourhood and for girlfriends. A big part of fighting relates to group identity and group perceptions.

For many gang members the fighting is experienced as random, yet constant. Fighting can be planned and groups can arrange to meet at pre-arranged venues and times. However, one gang member pointed out that increasingly the fights are more spontaneous and automatic in nature.

I remember back when I was growing up groups would meet places and have a fight. Today no group would meet nowhere. It's just if you see the other person on the street you give 'em a kicking. You know what I mean? You don't actually go with your group and they come with their group and you have a fight. It's not like that no more. No one comes to fights like that. If you see him on the street you've got him. If he sees you he's got you. So that's how it's changed [19-year-old male, Melbourne]

For gang members there are huge group obligations to fight.

The old saying is "you scratch my back, I'll scratch yours." It all works like that. You know your group of people and they see what they can do. If you're ever in trouble, they're always there. They'll just back you up 100% no matter what. We're like a big family – but yeah, basically we all just stick together. [17-year-old male, Canberra]

You've gotta have trust amongst your friends. There's usually not that much in a gang. There's not a lot of trust, but if you have trust and if you have a bit of power and if you're popular – that makes a gang. [17-year-old male, Melbourne]

The 'rules of engagement' for gang fights also appears to be changing, not only in regards to an apparent increase in the use of weapons. Traditionally there were unwritten rules that guided how young men fought each other. For example, this is captured in the expression 'don't hit a man when he is down'. Issues of fairness and violence that is proportionate to the situation have been undermined by increasing weapons use.

Like people used to fight mostly with their fist. Now they fight with – like "I don't need my muscle like 'cause I've got weapons" – and they're much more easier to get hold of so. [14-year-old female, Perth]

I think a lot of people are now carrying knives and a lot of people probably think it's okay, and a lot of people are more focussed on, umm, not fighting honourably but more just staying alive. So yeah, I reckon it's changed. I think it's gone from, umm, people just, you know, getting a bit involved to people taking out knives and weapons for the sake of fighting [16-year-old male, Perth]

It is not only weapons use, however, that is changing the dynamics of group conflict. An escalation in numbers of combatants can also change the nature of the fighting. The rules of engagement are to some degree situational in nature. That is, they depend upon location (such as school or the street), who is involved in conflict (known protagonists, such as at school or strangers from another neighbourhood), and variables such as age and access to weapons.

How you fight (with fists or with other weapons) is also connected to conceptions of manliness. More generally, the interpretation of violence is defined in terms of specific rules of engagement that help those engaged in it to make sense of it (Decker, 1996, 2007; Howell, 2007; Huff, 1998). These rules refer to violence within the gang such as initiation and fights between gang members, as well as external violence. For example, gang-related violence is often guided by rituals of restraint when a gang member fights another member of the same gang, whereas 'outsiders' are more likely to suffer from a no holds barred approach. Gang responses to and engagement in violence are thus typically defined by the situation, not by the characteristics of the perpetrators as such.

Ambiguities or lack of explicit or implicit rules of engagement can in itself lead to extreme violence insofar as 'anything goes', at considerable cost to everyone involved.

They wanna tell me to jump on someone's head, I was the first one to jump up and fucking stomp on that c***'s head. That's why I got out of that life. I'm not like that anymore. I had all that anger. I got rid of it all. It's gone now man. I just wanted to chill, but now it's all starting to come back. [21-year-old male, Canberra]

Fucking every week there's a fucking big blue and fucking half of us are still in hospital 'cause of cuts and shit, and it's like it's ridiculous, we always end up fucking in hospital – broken legs and shit. [21-year-old male, Canberra]

The nature of the youth violence described here is very much influenced by the fact that all of these young people were all self-identified members of youth gangs.

Being Bad: Getting to the Essentials

If youth gangs are notorious for doing bad things, then what does that tell us about the individual gang members who do these bad things? Does this mean that gang members are bad people because they are being bad? And if most youth gangs are comprised of young men and boys doing bad things, is the problem one of biology rather than social background?

The descriptions of male behavioural traits identified in the literature on men's criminality (and other areas) often reinforce the idea that somehow men, by virtue of being men, are innately more prone to such things as violence and aggression (Collier, 1998).

Biology and Psychology

On the one hand, male behaviour is sometimes reduced to hormones and testosterone levels; on the other, biology is often ignored when it comes to devising responses to youth gang behaviour. It is by no means clear that all aspects of women's and men's behaviour can be neatly separated from biological processes (e.g., the capacity to have children does have meaningful social consequences which are, to some degree, linked to female biology). Further to this, there may well be certain features of being male and being female which are not cross-transferable in the sense that fundamental differences may exist between the two sexes which, in the end, cannot be ignored at a social and cultural level (e.g., average physical size).

Yet, we also know that what is deemed to be a desirable or undesirable quality (in the case of both 'masculinity' and 'femininity') is subject to diverse interpretation (e.g., depending upon class, gender and ethnic background). It is also highly variable in terms of the meaning and consequences of specific social practices under particular social circumstances (e.g., the definition of what an appropriate quality is partly depends upon immediate needs and desires at any given moment). Nevertheless, doubts can be raised about whether or not it is possible to analytically construct a non-essentialist model of masculinity (i.e., one which posits there are no core or innate biological/cultural differences between men and women), and thus whether it is possible to frame an explanation of contemporary social behaviour that can bypass the biological.

The idea that there is a link between the (male) body and certain types of behaviour is certainly not new to criminology. From the days of Lombroso onwards, the presumption that bodies matter forms a key part of biological explanations for criminality (White et al., 2012). The 'science' of phrenology was popular in criminology, for example, for a number of years around the beginning of the twentieth century. For instance, a study undertaken in 1912 by the University of Melbourne was conducted on 355 male inmates at Pentridge prison. The skulls of the (living) prisoners were examined and estimates of the cubic capacity of their brains were made in an attempt to correlate the size of skull to intelligence. It was concluded that cattle stealers had the lowest brain capacity, and that forgers and embezzlers had the highest (Brown & Hogg, 1992).

Sheldon (1940) proposed a theory based on body build (somotype). He wished to establish a link between different body types and criminality. According to Sheldon, human body types can be classed into three broad categories: endomorphic (soft and round), mesomorphic (muscular and strong), and ectomorphic (thin and fragile). Each body type was associated with a particular temperament: endomorphic (relaxed, sociable, and fond of eating), mesomorphic (energetic, courageous, and assertive) and ectomorphic (brainy, artistic, and introverted). It was further argued that mesomorphs were most likely to become criminals. In other words, there was a positive correlation between body type and criminal activity.

Biological explanations of this kind imply that crime is the result of something essential to the nature of the individual. Thus, we are born with certain biological attributes that we cannot change, but that may lock some of us into a life of crime and antisocial behaviour. Certain groups are seen to be more predisposed to crime than others because of biological and social environmental factors.

There remains a continuing tendency among some researchers to reduce the reasons for criminal behaviour to a single cause, either biological or psychological (White et al., 2012). Such work assumes that adult behaviour and personality are overwhelmingly determined by and reducible to single over-arching factors (e.g., body shape, a violence gene). Where offending is linked to biology, the logical extension of the line of reasoning can lead to attempts to correlate certain people (e.g., poor people) with certain 'biologically determined' traits (e.g., intelligence as measured by IQ) and so to criminal offending. Without adequate discussion of the assumptions underlying research of this sort, the search for the causes of criminal behaviour leads inexorably to grossly unwarranted conclusions.

For example, a recent biological reductionist explanation relates to the so called 'warrior gene' allegedly found among Maori men in New Zealand. Media reports explained that the monoamine oxidase (MAO) gene was dubbed the warrior gene by US researchers due to its links to aggressive behaviour. Speaking at the International Congress of Human Genetics in Brisbane, Australia in August 2006, genetic epidemiologist Rod Lea of the Institute of Environmental Science and Research, based at Wellington in New Zealand, went one step further (Daily Telegraph, 2006; Lea & Chambers, 2007). He observed that his research showed that 60 per cent of Maori men have the MAO gene, compared to only 30 per cent of men of European descent. Aggression linked to genetic make-up thus provides fertile ground for explanations that conveniently blame the biology rather than the social environment.

Talk of a 'violence gene' attributes violence solely or mainly to biological factors (for which there is no easy solution or cure). More than this, given the over-representation of minority groups in official crime statistics (especially African-Americans in the USA, Maori in New Zealand, Aborigines in Australia), the genetic explanation clearly has racist applications. The problem is seen as intractable and as originating in the people themselves. Yet, depending upon the group in question, there is nonetheless a link between the biological and the social as these interact to foster certain types of desires, wants and emotions at the level of the body. While not reducing behaviour to the body, the body still constitutes a crucial medium through which the social is actively constructed. What we do with our bodies, what we must do with our bodies and what we like to do with our bodies are intertwined, and are matters of cultural significance and practical socialisation.

And so we cannot ignore the body in social explanations for certain types of behaviour either. Body size and shape do matter, in conjunction with how one is socialised in the use of one's body, and in the type of activity in which people engage. For instance, Australian gangs research finds a close correlation between engagement in physical contact sports and later participation in gangs and gang fights by certain groups of young men (White, 2013).

Explanations at the individual and relationship level look to biological and psychological factors to explain engagement in violence and antisocial behaviour. Yet, not all men are violent, and some men are more violent than others. Some women are violent, while many are not. This implies that while there is a general socio-cultural context that means that some societies are generally more violent than others, and that some groups within society more violent than others, there are nevertheless individual factors that contribute to who, specifically, engages in which kinds of violence.

Psychological factors include such things as temperament, learned social responses, social and communication skills, and perceptions of rewards or penalties for engaging in violence (Roth, 1994). These are influenced by family upbringing and neighbourhood context, as well as being mediated by things such as alcohol and drug use, arousal levels (related to stimulation) and emotional state. There are also biological factors that have an influence on general propensities toward violence. Testosterone in young men, for example, does impact upon potential behaviours. While not reducing behaviour to a simple matter of biology, one's biological and physiological make-up does have a bearing on specific frequencies and types of engagement in violence. Certain neurobehaviour traits, that is, capacities determined by status at birth, trauma and ageing processes such as puberty, may be associated with certain kinds of behaviour. Likewise, transient neurobehavioural states, that describe temporary conditions associated with emotions and external stressors, can influence violent behaviour (Giancola et al., 2006; Roth, 1994). For example, the concept of 'appetitive violence' refers to sensation-seeking behaviour associated with a state of emotional arousal. Thrill-seeking may be activated by group dynamics and beliefs about the appropriateness of violence as a means of mood enhancement (Ching, Daffern & Thomas, 2013).

As mentioned, recent scientific research on genetics and antisocial behaviour has shown an association between certain types of genes (for example, the monoamine oxidase A gene) and a propensity toward physical violence (Beaver et al., 2009). Generally speaking, however, while there is evidence that both genetic and environmental factors contribute to antisocial behaviour, violence per se cannot be reduced to a single genetic factor (Morley & Hall, 2003). Certain genetic and neurobehavioural traits may also provide the grounding for why alcohol affects some people more dramatically than others vis-à-vis intoxication and propensity toward violence (Morley & Hall, 2003; Tikkanen et al., 2009). The relationship of violence and alcohol is both simple and complex. Roth (1994: 4) summarises it well:

Alcohol is the only psychoactive drug that in many individuals tends to increase aggressive behavior temporarily while it is taking effect. However, factors at other levels – behavior patterns when people are not drinking, the setting in which people drink, and local drinking customs, for example – influence the strength of this relationship.

In effect, researchers have suggested both a biological predisposition to violence (based upon genetic and hormonal factors) and to alcohol use (related to blood sugar levels), but these, in turn, are influenced by cultural norms and social settings. Biological drivers (genetics, biochemistry) and social determinants (situational triggers, cultural contexts) are each, in their own right, grounded in the body.

What people do to their bodies also includes drugs other than alcohol. For example, in research on youth gangs at schools in Perth, Western Australia, it was found that gang members were more likely than non-gang members to be engaged in poly-drug use (White & Mason, 2006). The type of drug would most probably include methamphetamine (crystal meth, 'ice') since research tells us that gang members partake in a wider variety of drugs than their non-gang counterparts. This drug has been associated with violent behaviour, although it is not necessarily a direct causal reason for increased violence as such (McKetin et al., 2006). Gang violence has been related to drug dealing, as part of the dangers and processes associated with criminal transactions. It has also been linked to individual use of drugs. In the latter case, interviews as part of a national gangs study (White, 2013) indicated that sometimes particular members of gangs 'got off their heads' and would get 'aggro' as a result of drug use. Occasionally where one person did go 'loopy' and pick a fight with strangers, the rest of the gang would intervene on their mate's behalf to either stop the fight or to provide group back-up for their comrade.

Social Relations and Contexts

The place of violence in society generally, and in the lives of young men in particular, also shapes the propensity for specific violent incidents to occur. In contemporary Australian society, there appears to be a certain 'naturalisation' of violence as an everyday phenomenon, and as a significant form of anger management and conflict resolution. This is especially so for boys and men. We know, for example, that teenage males have a much higher rate of fighting than females. Studies also show that early engagement in anti-social behaviour tends to lead to ongoing, long-term involvement in such behaviour among teenage males (Smart et al., 2004). The majority of boys are familiar with violence – as perpetrators, as victims, as observers. Violence is not new or particularly disturbing for many boys. For others, however, exposure to violence can have socially toxic effects – for themselves, their families and their communities – in regards to self-esteem, fear, performance at school and building trust relationships.

A social structural explanation for street violence tends to view the phenomenon in terms of marginalisation of specific population groups (White & Cunneen, 2006; White, 2008). This marginalisation may have a number of interrelated dimensions, including economic (e.g., poverty), social (e.g., exclusion from mainstream institutions), political (e.g., little or no representation) and cultural (e.g., minority religious or language group). The level of social disorganisation and extent of social capital are also seen as vital ingredients in the criminality or otherwise of specific neighbourhoods (Weatherburn & Lind, 2002). In effect, brutal social conditions provide the groundwork for angry and aggressive people, whose main resource is their body rather than capital or wages.

A related explanation focuses on social identity as a key variable in explaining group formation and street violence (see for example, Collins et al., 2000; White et al., 1999). For example, groups of young people band together for social, cultural and familial reasons. They also do so for protection. Racism directed at ethnic minority populations and the challenges of dealing with the colonial legacy on the part of Indigenous people are also structural factors that have implications for public violence.

Heterosexism is about the ideological, material and symbolic boundaries placed on behaviour and ways of being. Built into heterosexism is the privileging of certain forms of femininity and masculinity over others. A crucial element in the maintenance of heterosexism is the prevalence of a particular form of hegemonic masculinity (Connell, 1995, 2000). For instance, there is a dominant social conception in Australian society regarding what it is to be 'a man'. That is, there is a normative definition that is promulgated through the mainstream social institutions such as schools and the media. The dominant cultural ideals surrounding masculinity are thus supported by existing institutional arrangements. The main elements of this hegemonic masculinity pertain not only to apparent differences between men and women, but to relations of power between men and women, and within the male population itself (Connell, 1995, 2000; Segal, 1990). They include an emphasis on *male domination* (and women's subordination); the *sexual division of labour* (in both the private and public spheres); and *heterosexuality* as the dominant and exclusive, categorisation of male sexuality (and the imposition of selective conventions in regard to acceptable sexual practices). The hegemonic masculine ideal has consequences for men's conceptions of themselves, for their health, and for how they relate to others (White, 2002) and its consequences are especially evident in the area of interpersonal violence.

Work undertaken on violence and masculinity, for example, demonstrates a strong cultural component to violence, especially for males (see Polk, 1994; Messerschmidt, 1997; Tomsen, 2008). Particularly for working class young men, physical prowess or toughness is a form of social capital. In most social milieu, a young man's reputation depends in part upon the credible threat of violence (Polk, 1994). Quick resort to physical combat – as a measure of daring, or courage, or defence of status – appears to be a standard cultural expectation, especially for working class boys and young men. This perhaps explains the widespread nature of violence among school-age male populations. That is, in a context in which 'manhood' is yet to be proven by attainment of paid work, marriage, leaving home or beginning a family of their own, physicality itself, relying upon the body, is one way in which to 'prove oneself' (Connell, 2000; Messerschmidt, 1997; Polk, 1994; Tomsen, 1997, 2008). This would therefore help to explain the prevalence of male violence across the schoolyard, if not the intensity and differences in manifestation.

Opportunity, choice and group affinity all have an impact on how individuals construct or attempt to construct a masculine identity for themselves. The specific social context of the individual is crucial to understanding how different groups of men attempt to negotiate, reconcile or oppose the masculine ideal, in the light of the actual resources at their disposal (see White, 2002). A lack of institutional power and accredited social status often leaves little alternative than physicality itself as the main form of self definition - whether this manifests itself as self-destructive behaviour or as violence directed at the other. Much of the violence is in fact directed at other young men, many of whom are likewise in vulnerable social positions. Much of this occurs in the social context of collective drinking (Tomsen, 1997).

Access to communication technologies (e.g., mobile phones, social networking sites such as Facebook and MySpace), and exposure to modelling of risky fighting behaviours through entertainment technologies and the media (e.g., 'cage fighting'), also have an impact on group decisions and fighting patterns. To respond adequately to street violence we need to appreciate that violence comes in many different forms and that it is shaped by many different factors. It is situation-specific. A typology of violence would need to consider violence from the point of view of Offenders, Victims, Passive observers, Active audience, Authority figures, Venues, Events, and Situations. A wide range of factors need to be taken into account in explaining specific kinds of violence, and in responding to each type of violent episode.

Violence is not only made natural by its very prevalence in the lives of boys and men, but in many cases it is an important source of pleasure. It is the occasions when 'exceptional' violence occurs that provide the excitement and the break from the ordinary routines of everyday life. From the perspective of cultural criminology, physical violence and other types of anti-social behaviour can be interpreted as meaningful attempts to 'transgress' the ordinary (Hayward, 2002). In a world of standardised diversity and global conformities, it is exciting and pleasurable to break the rules, to push the boundaries, to engage in risky and risk-taking activities. To transgress is to deviate. It is to go beyond the ordinary, to seek that adrenaline rush that pushes the boundaries of emotion and convention.

Related to this, we also have to account for the inherent attractions of violence, as violence, in its own right: 'many people feel drawn towards violence because it can give pleasure' (Schinkel, 2004). From one point of view, force or violence may be viewed as rational behaviour to the extent that it is designed to effect change in the target of violence. For example, many young people fight not because of an absence of values, but because of values that hold such behaviour to be a justifiable, common-sense way to achieve certain goals (Lockwood, 1997). This is especially understandable in the context of concerns about masculine identity, and violence that relates to defence of 'male honour'. But the rationale behind the violence need not be simply due to cues or triggers imposed externally. For there is increasing evidence, including recent gang research, that violence also stems from the efforts of young people themselves to engineer situations and events with the intended aim of increasing the likelihood of violence occurring (Jackson-Jacobs, 2004). From this perspective, the gang provides a forum or ready-made structure within which to engage in what is felt to be exhilarating activity. Gangs provide an avenue to increase the thrill factor beyond the norm.

The 'will to violence', as Schinkel (2004) describes it, provides its own reward. However, this 'will' may be overlooked in social scientific research that looks to external causes (such as unemployment, masculinity and/or social inequality). Or, it may be subject to varying forms of 'denial' at the level of personal engagement. For example, interviews with gang members in Melbourne revealed that in some instances individuals from ethnic minority backgrounds did not just fight in order to defend themselves or to confirm their group identity. The research found that periodically some of these young people used the notion of racism as a convenient cover for their own aggression. That is, in some cases the violence was motivated by a desire to engage in the violence itself, rather than in responding to racism as such (White & Perrone, 2001). This phenomenon is not specific to ethnic minority young men as such – rather, it is an attribute that finds general purchase across the diversity of ethnic backgrounds, including mainstream Anglo-Celtic. Violence is thus its own attractor, regardless of the techniques of neutralisation that may be invoked to deny responsibility or wrongdoing.

Gang violence thus may be experienced as 'fun' by participants, in the sense that it provides an adrenaline rush and is associated with 'typical' working class masculine pursuits that define a 'top night out' such as drug taking, drinking and fighting. Fighting can be linked to risk, excitement and thrills as opposed to the boredom and routines of the mundane. It can also be linked to social humiliation and perceived majority attacks on communal identity (and manifest as a 'chip on the shoulder' on part of members of a minority group). Violence can be linked to insecurity and as a source of pre-emptive protection. It can be associated with group dynamics that emphasise masculinity that is informed by certain notions of self-respect and social respect. For many young men, violence exists as the 'normal' form of anger management and conflict resolution – a resort of the first kind.

Exploring Personal Experiences: The Importance of Biography

Gang violence and individual engagement in gang violence warrant explanations that take into account biological, psychological and social factors, and the interaction between these. In addition to these global explanations, however, it is also vital to consider the personal experiences of gang members. The personal search for meaning and the struggle to attain respect are difficult and alienating for many young people precisely because of the systemic limits and pressures on who they are and what they can become. Yet, as demonstrated below, we also need to go beyond the master status of 'gang member' to consider the varied aspects of each person's biography. Biographical accounts, in conjunction with social analysis of communities, demonstrate that people relate and interrelate in complex ways that confound the simplistic stereotype. Life is full of contradictions and paradoxes, and the future is far less predictable than much youth gangs literature suggests.

To put it differently, the richness and complexity of life experience tends to get lost in research that focuses solely or primarily upon one particular group and particular (and usually spectacular) group activities. By exploring more deeply into individual experiences, it is possible as well to view these young people quite differently than the image of angry, aggressive young men blindly engaging in offensive behaviour because that is the group thing to do. More personalised case study reveals complexity and ambiguity, not the one-dimensional 'thug' or 'gangster' of popular imagination.

Social identity has a series of interconnected objective and subjective features that taken together combine to create multiple and varied identities. We are never just who we say we are. We are always a creative project, a self-in-the-making. We are singular, and collective; agents of our own fate and subject to external pressures. Like a chameleon, we change and morph into different people depending upon social context and empirical circumstance. We are local and global at the same time. We are one, we are many – but all of this takes place within our one singular being.

People make sense of their lives in complicated ways. We are all part of wider families and communities than simply those of our friends and colleagues. There are connections between the social circumstances that give rise to gangs and the community relations that sustain them. Just as these connections are situational and depend upon historical as well as contemporary factors, so too the life of each individual within a gang is multi-dimensional. To illustrate this, we can briefly consider the stories of 'Mohammed' and of 'Tan'.

Mohammad's Story

At the time of interview, Mohammad was 17 years old, a Muslim and Lebanese-background young man. He was very conscious of family and cultural ties.

The best thing about my area is that everyone there is just like me. We came from the same place, our parents have the same background and we all speak the same language, we're into the same things and we can -- like we just know -- we just know, you know, how we all feel and that. It's just like one big family over there. We all grew up together and like people from – it's just like a small part of Lebanon in Australia.

Mohammad was subjected to racism at school by one of his teachers, and generally felt that the 'Arabs' and the 'Islanders' were picked on and consciously excluded from student representative bodies. He also felt that the police were racist, especially since most of the time they intervened when nothing wrong was happening.

Most of the time it's because they see a big group of Lebo's hanging out and they just walk up "What are you doing here? Why? Go home. Shouldn't you be at home? Shouldn't you be at school?" And they check up your details and like I remember one time a police officer asked me if I had a record and I never had it -- me I didn't know I had a record. I just thought -- I got into a fight a few weeks before and I thought it was just a caution and I said "No." And usually when you say "No" they walk off, but this guy checked up and after that, you know, started "Fuck you. Lying to the police and you fucking this and fucking that" and pushed me against a wall and that and one of my friends came from behind him, you know, as soon as he put his hand on the police officer another cop came and started elbowing him in the back and then, you know, after that it ended up in a sort of a scuffle between us and them.

Anger at his own immediate situation was compounded by the hurt felt about his family's country of origin in the context of life in Australia. Mohammad commented on the treatment he received compared with other members of the community:

No one calling them "Wog". No one telling them to go back to their country. You know like, you know, you look around and you see all these Aussie kids and they're happy on their skateboards and shit and with their mums and their dads and stuff giving them money and stuff and it's because they're in their country. You can't say nothing to them. But us we should -- no matter how long -- not matter how long we're going to be here and no matter how much the government give us money we're always going to feel like we're outcasts ...I reckon no matter how much money we have, we're never going to be happy, we're never going to feel accepted.

The sense of outrage and injustice translated into aggressive, violent behaviour. Yelling at people on the streets, picking fights with other young people in the district, stirring people up, these were all part of 'normal' group activities. The sense of differentness and alienation was heightened whenever the group went into other suburbs, especially beach suburbs such as Manly.

Being different heavily impacted upon the process of social belonging. It certainly pulled people together into extremely close bonds.

You've always got someone -- someone's always got your back all the time -- all the time. You're never in danger. Like I never feel afraid. Like I can come to Bankstown any time of the day, any time of the year, by myself and I've lived in Bankstown all my life and I've never ever been robbed or harassed or, you know, in Bankstown because of the people I hang out with. You've always got someone to turn to. There's always someone to listen. You can say it's more like a family because we all look after each other. You know a few months ago one of us got ran over and every single one of us went to the hospital every day. Every single one of us went to the hospital every single day until he got out. When he got out at his house we visited him there. So it's like that.

The moral basis of the group's behaviour was partially revealed in answer to a question about the difference between bullying and gang activity. It is here, as well, that we see fluidity in terms of who can or cannot be included within the 'gang'.

Bullying is for people that feel low and the only time they feel good is when they find someone weaker than them. Like we don't bully. We don't sit there and see someone looking at us and say "Oh lets go jump him 'cause he's looking at us." We don't fuck -- there is a few of us that go round jumping people for money and that, but I don't know, but we don't make it as like a hobby to just sit there at the station and look at people and just start bullying 'em and pushing 'em around. Actually we're more like a gangster -- like there's a kid whose twenty-one. He's got Downs Syndrome. He hangs out with us even though he's not Lebanese. He's not Arab. I think he's an Aussie or something, yeah, but he hangs around with us and like we usually protect him from like if anyone ever makes fun of him like we're the ones that will stick up for him.

It is not only protecting the weak and vulnerable, as well as one's mates, that make Mohammad feel good. Other things do too.

Going to the Mosque a lot makes me feel good. I like to help out around the neighbourhood like if my mum needs something or my friends' mums need something or if their dads need help or anything. Like for example the bloke with me out there his dad is building a house down near Bankstown College and I always go down to help him out there for nothing. Yeah that makes me feel good.

Mohammad's story is one of loss and pain, pride and generosity. It is his story, but it is also the story of his country, his neighbourhood, his friends. It is depressing, yet strangely exhilarating and hopeful. It shows the goodness interspersed with the harshness, and how the senseless can make sense at the level of the everyday.

Tan's Story

Tan was 18 years old at the time of interview. He was born in Australia but has a Vietnamese background and speaks Vietnamese at home with his parents. He is a Roman Catholic.

Several years ago, Tan was involved in a criminal gang. Unusually for this specific type of gang, the gang was not comprised of just one ethnic background.

When I was younger I kind of went off and did my stuff. Kind of got recruited into a gang pretty much… and it was funny because they were a different nationality to me. It's actually called the Hong Kong Gang, so a Chinese gang and I was pretty much the only Vietnamese person in that group at that time I think in a level that is pretty high. I was asked to learn a bit of Chinese and stuff, so we could relate sometimes and when there's problems you would know what's going on.

The gang made money by selling drugs, and by stealing and then re-selling items. Tan was recruited to help sell Play Stations that had been stolen from a warehouse. One of his roles in the gang was to facilitate the street-level distribution of stolen goods by finding people to buy the products that they sold, and to find places that were good for an illegal job. In his mid-teenage years, Tan joined the group because he wanted friends, he wanted money and he wanted power. The group he was associated with was based in the city, rather than in the local neighbourhood.

At the local level, however, he created his own group, which likewise had mixed racial and ethnic backgrounds.

Two of them were Chinese and the other one was Australian. That was pretty funny. The reason why I wanted an Australian was because he was big and I thought size counted, so I recruited him. I think the rest were all Vietnamese.

The group was formed consciously and intentionally as a criminal gang. The membership thus reflected the connections and activities of that kind of group formation. Gang activities included group fighting. They also included extortion:

....you've got an area to look after. You walk down, you've got shops you can make money out of. It's just respect money they call it, so we don't destroy, you know, your shop or something. So you walk in and you tell the guy, look you know, you have to pay so much a month.

This was organised violence, at the local level, with ties across the city. Their activities also included robberies, credit card fraud, procuring of passports and drug dealing. They even sold university degrees to overseas students.

In school, Tan experienced what he describes as a subtle form of racism from some of his teachers. For example, they would allow 'Australian' kids to eat freely in class, but tell Tan and his fellow 'Asian' students off if they did it. He also commented on both how unfairly the Lebanese people were treated, and yet how racist one Lebanese student was.

....it was funny because he's the one going around the school bullying everyone else and he's Lebanese. Just because people didn't treat him the way he wanted doesn't mean he had to go around treating everyone else like shit....It was pretty interesting to see that. He was pretty racist for a while. I think now he's grown out of it and it's died down a bit, but yeah it was pretty bad at the time.

Tan has been involved in many violent incidents, including gang fights and single assaults on other youth. He was charged at one stage with 'assault with a deadly weapon' and other charges, but these were dismissed. His early attitude was that nothing really mattered, and that he could not care less about things since there was nothing to lose and nothing to gain. His life started to change around due to the influence of his (now, ex-) girlfriend.

She got afraid of me getting hurt most of the time, so and I didn't want to see her being hurt. I kind of cared for her a lot. I think at that time that was the only thing that I cared for – really, really cared for – so I listened to a lot of things she said.

She convinced me it's not worth dying over. You could die for your country, but not over that.

According to Tan, learning personal responsibility ultimately stemmed from his personal relationship and his desire to respect the wishes of his girlfriend.

After leaving the gang Tan became involved in various youth volunteer activities in the local area. This was motivated by a desire to repair some of the harm he'd done as a gang member.

I think after I left the gang I thought 'I've hurt too many people. It's time for me to give back to the community'. I also do a Church Youth Group. I'm with them as well, so yeah it's something to give back for something I've taken out. I think it helps me feel better, sleep better I think during the night.

Redemption for Tan means taking personal responsibility to change one's life. It also means restoring the balance as much as possible.

Biography and Being In-Between

A more in-depth and less gang-focussed examination of the lives of Mohammad and Tan reveals young people going through extraordinary experiences and finding varying ways of coping with their particular social circumstances. All young people today are growing up in a world that is commonly influenced by things such as globalisation, neo-liberal political economy, war and consumerism. The specificity of personal being, however, is shaped not only by epochal features but the mundane experiences of family, friends, neighbourhood, school and community (see White & Wyn, 2013).

Listening to the stories of Mohammad and Tan allows us to better appreciate the temporal dimension of lived experience – the ways in which people and circumstances change over time. This is important, for as much as anything it precludes locking any individual into a preordained pathway based upon where they are in the here and now. The future is open and mutable, although the parameters of what is possible are structurally bounded by the weight of the past and the institutional opportunities of the present. The determinism of populist gang discourse falls far short in anticipating or explaining the zigzags of real life experiences amongst individuals.

The limitations of conventional approaches to the problem of youth gangs, which tend to define people primarily and solely in terms of gang membership, are also apparent. Each of the young men in our case studies was a gang member, and yet much more than this. They were part of ethnic communities, of families, of school groups and of street scenes. Not all of their lives was spent 'in the gang'. Not all of their time was spent 'doing gang stuff'. Each young man, during the course of their interview, mentioned how scared they were of the violence, of the possibility of not having their close mates around them. They are strong and vulnerable at the same time.

Each of these young men likewise demonstrated the importance of generosity and 'giving' in their lives. Barry (2006) talks about the importance of the expenditure of various kinds of capital, and well as its accumulation, in the lives of young people. By this, she means that people want to expend – to give something to someone else – as part of feeling good about oneself and one's place in the wider community. Far from being always the taker (as implied in gang activities), there is impetus to also be the giver. Both Mohammad and Tan found contentment in giving up their time and energy as a volunteer for their mosque and church respectively. They didn't have to do this – it was freely chosen and pleasurable activity for both of them. Good and bad rarely resides in the individual; it is constructed around practices, not people.

The pragmatic way in which groups are formed and desist is also an important theme. While ethnicity is the key marker of group formation (including youth gangs), this does not preclude interesting exceptions to this general rule. Mohammad spoke about the inclusion of a white Downs Syndrome young man in his group. Tan talked about his criminal gang being led by Chinese and of his own personal group that included Chinese and Australian youth as well as Vietnamese. Racism in general (against Lebanese, against Vietnamese) does not always end in segregation and social division. Personal contacts and personal friendships, built up at school or on the street, for the purposes of the social or the criminal, provide a counterfoil to the tendency to see identity and activity as exclusively exercised through the lens of ethnicity. Moreover, a dislike of 'Australians' (i.e., established, white Anglo-background) in general because of institutional and cultural privileging, and direct experiences of racism, is mediated by personal interactions of a more positive kind.

The common strengths in specific diversities are alluded to in other work that has examined the in-between status of ethnic minority youth.

341

While some young people very consciously claim their ethnic identity, they also link a more tolerant and open-minded attitude in their association with diverse friendship networks. In this way, culturally diverse groups can give young people the ability to associate less problematically with a wider range of 'others', making cross-cultural connections and affiliations. While many of the young people who took part in our research have a sense of exclusion and rejection from mainstream society, for the most part they are not cynical about a commitment to values of tolerance, equality and diversity (Butcher & Thomas, 2003: 32).

Examination of personal biography also provides some indication of the shifting nature of relationships, of how people from diverse ethnic and social backgrounds come into and out of the lives of each individual. A sense of justice, fairness and generosity permeates the accounts of Mohammad and Tan, even in the midst of oppression, racism and social exclusion. These positive qualities are also intrinsically cross-cultural in nature. We understand and empathise with those who 'do good' by protecting the weak and vulnerable, and who volunteer their time to help others. This, too, is a platform upon which to build community solidarity and inter-communal peace.

CONCLUSION

'Doing bad' and 'being bad' are entirely contingent upon societal circumstance, situational factors and personal characteristics. These phenomena require sensitivity to and appreciation of multiple dimensions and many different influences that shape and determine the contours of the lives of young people involved with gangs. Gang violence happens and individuals may engage in such violence – but systematic analysis of the issues reveals that this is neither preordained nor unchangeable.

The gang does not have to be an overwhelming influence in the lives of young people, dominating all relationships and all emotions. Nor does gang-related aggression have to take centre stage everywhere and at all times. There is peace, and giving, and solidarity, and love, and affection, too. If we look for the positives, of gangs and of those who join them, then these, as well, can be found. It all depends upon where and how we turn our analytical gaze.

The kind of approach adopted in this chapter allows for insights that show the dynamics of social relationships as they are constructed in the crucible of everyday choices, negotiations and actions. Who we are is, and always has been, a continuous process. The contours of this process are structurally influenced by matters pertaining to class, gender and ethnicity – but the process itself is marked by ambiguity and paradox as much as by broad propensities and continuities. Herein lies the possibility for positive social transformation, individually and collectively, in dealing with issues of systemic marginalisation and social inequality.

REFERENCES

Bachelor, S. (2011). Beyond dichotomy: Towards an explanation of young women's involvement in violent street gangs. In B. Goldson (Ed.), *Youth in Crisis? 'Gangs', territoriality and violence*. London: Routledge.

Barry, M. (2006). *Youth Offending in Transition: The Search for Social Recognition*. London: Routledge.

Brown, D., & Hogg, R. (1992). Essentialism, Radical Criminology and Left Realism. *Australian and New Zealand Journal of Criminology, 25*(2), 195–230. doi:10.1177/000486658920250302

Butcher, M., & Thomas, M. (2003). Being in-between. In M. Butcher & M. Thomas (Eds.), *Ingenious: Emerging Youth Cultures in Urban Australia*. Sydney: Pluto Press.

Ching, H., Daffern, M., & Thomas, S. (2012). Appetitive Violence: A New Phenomenon? *Psychiatry, Psychology and Law, 19*(5), 745–763. doi:10.1080/13218719.2011.623338

Collier, R. (1998). *Masculinities, Crime and Criminology*. London: Sage.

Collins, J., Noble, G., Poynting, S., & Tabar, P. (2000). *Kebabs, Kids, Cops & Crime: Youth, Ethnicity & Crime*. Sydney: Pluto Press.

Connell, R. (1995). *Masculinities*. Cambridge: Polity.

Connell, R. (2000). *The Men and the Boys*. Sydney: Allen & Unwin.

Cunneen, C., & White, R. (2006). Australia: Control, Containment or Empowerment? In J. Muncie & B. Goldson (Eds.), *Comparative Youth Justice*. London: Sage. doi:10.4135/9781446212608.n8

Daily Telegraph. (n.d., August 8). MAOA Gene and Maori Violence. *Daily Telegraph.*

Decker, S. H. (1996). Collective and normative features of gang violence. *Justice Quarterly, 13*(2), 243–264. doi:10.1080/07418829600092931

Decker, S. H. (2007). Youth gangs and violent behavior. In D. J. Flannery, A. T. Vazsonyi, & I. D. Waldman (Eds.), *The Cambridge Handbook of Violent Behavior and Aggression* (pp. 388–402). Cambridge, MA: Cambridge University Press. doi:10.1017/CBO9780511816840.019

Giancola, P. R., Parrott, D. J., & Roth, R. M. (2006). The influence of difficult temperament on alcohol-related aggression: Better accounted for by executive functioning? *Addictive Behaviors, 31*(12), 2169–2187. doi:10.1016/j.addbeh.2006.02.019 PMID:16563644

Hayward, K. (2002). The Vilification and Pleasures of Youthful Transgression. In J. Muncie, G. Hughes, & E. McLaughlin (Eds.), *Youth Justice: Critical Readings*. London: Sage.

Howell, J. (2007). Menacing or Mimicking? Realities of Youth Gangs. *Juvenile & Family Court Journal, 58*(2), 39–50. doi:10.1111/j.1755-6988.2007.tb00137.x

Huff, R. (1998). '*Comparing the Criminal Behavior of Youth Gangs and At-Risk Youths', Research in Brief, October*. Washington, DC: US Office of Justice, National Institute of Justice.

Jackson-Jacobs, C. (2004). Taking a Beating: The Narrative Gratifications of Fighting as an Underdog. In J. Ferrell, K. Hayward, W. Morrison, & M. Presdee (Eds.), *Cultural Criminology Unleashed*. London: Glasshouse Press.

Lea, R., & Chambers, G. (2007). 'Monoamine oxidase, addiction, and the 'warrior' gene hypothesis. *The New Zealand Medical Journal, 120*(1250), 2. PMID:17339897

Lockwood, D. (1997). *Violence Among Middle School and high School Students: Analysis and Implications for Prevention. National Institute of Justice, Research in Brief.* Washington, DC: Office of Justice Programs, US Department of Justice.

McKetin, R., McLaren, J., Ridell, S., & Robins, L. (2006). *The Relationship between Methamphetamine Use and Violent Behaviour, Contemporary Issues in Crime and Justice, No.97.* Sydney: New South Wales Bureau of Crime Statistics and Research, Crime and Justice Bulletin.

Messerschmidt, J. (1997). *Crime as Structured Action: Gender, Race, Class, and Crime in the Making.* London: Sage. doi:10.4135/9781452232294

Miller, J. (2001). *One of the Guys: Girls, Gangs and Gender.* New York: Oxford University Press.

Morley, K., & Hall, W. (2003). Is There a Genetic Susceptibility to Engage in Criminal Acts? *Trends & Issues in Crime and Criminal Justice, 263,* 1–6.

Polk, K. (1994). *When Men Kill: Scenarios of Masculine Violence.* Melbourne: Cambridge University Press.

Roth, J. (1994). *Understanding and Preventing Violence. Research in Brief.* Washington, DC: National Institute of Justice, US Department of Justice.

Schinkel, W. (2004). The Will to Violence. *Theoretical Criminology, 8*(1), 5–32. doi:10.1177/1362480604039739

Segal, L. (1995). *Slow Motion: Changing Masculinities, Changing Men.* New Brunswick, NJ: Rutgers University Press.

Sheldon, W. (1940). *Varieties of Human Physique.* New York: Harper & Row.

Smart, D., Vassallo, S., Sanson, A., & Dussuyer, I. (2004). *Patterns of Antisocial Behaviour from Early to Late Adolescence. Trends and Issues in Crime and Criminal Justice, No.290.* Canberra: Australian Institute of Criminology.

Tikkanen, R., Sjöberg, R. L., Ducci, F., Goldman, D., Holi, M., Tiihonen, J., & Virkkunen, M. (2009). Effects of MAOA-Genotype, Alcohol Consumption, and Aging on Violent Behavior. *Alcoholism, Clinical and Experimental Research, 33*(3), 428–434. doi:10.1111/j.1530-0277.2008.00853.x PMID:19120058

Tomsen, S. (1997). A Top Night: Social Protest, Masculinity and the Culture of Drinking Violence. *The British Journal of Criminology, 37*(1), 90–102. doi:10.1093/oxfordjournals.bjc.a014152

Tomsen, S. (2008). Masculinities, Crime and Criminalisation. In T. Anthony & C. Cunneen (Eds.), *The Critical Criminology Companion.* Sydney: Hawkins Press.

White, R. (2002). 'Social and Political Aspects of Men's Health'. *Health, 6*(3), 267–285. doi:10.1177/1363459302006003001

White, R. (2006). In J. Short & L. Hughes (Eds.), *Youth Gang Research in Australia* (pp. 161–179). Studying Youth Gangs, New York: AltaMira Press.

White, R. (2008). Australian Youth Gangs and the Social Dynamics of Ethnicity. In F. van Gemert, D. Peterson, & I.-L. Lien (Eds.), *Youth Gangs, Migration, and Ethnicity*. Devon: Willan.

White, R. (2011). The Challenges of Doing Collaborative Research. In L. Bartels & K. Richards (Eds.), *Qualitative Criminology: Stories from the Field*. Sydney: Federation Press.

White, R. (2013). *Youth Gangs, Violence and Social Respect: Exploring the Nature of Provocations and Punch-Ups*. Basingstoke: Palgrave Macmillan. doi:10.1057/9781137333858

White, R., Haines, F., & Asquith, N. (2012). *Crime & Criminology*. Melbourne: Oxford University Press.

White, R., & Mason, R. (2006). Youth Gangs and Youth Violence: Charting the Key Dimensions. *Australian and New Zealand Journal of Criminology*, *39*(1), 54–70. doi:10.1375/acri.39.1.54

White, R., & Perrone, S. (2001). Racism, Ethnicity and Hate Crime. *Communal/Plural*, *9*(2), 161–181. doi:10.1080/13207870120081479

White, R., Perrone, S., Guerra, C., & Lampugnani, R. (1999). *Ethnic Youth Gangs in Australia: Do They Exist?*. Melbourne: Australian Multicultural Foundation.

White, R., & Wyn, J. (2013). *Youth and Society: Exploring the Social Dynamics of Youth Experience*. Melbourne: Oxford University Press.

Chapter 16
The Reorganisation of Gangs in New Zealand

Jarrod Gilbert
University of Canterbury, New Zealand

ABSTRACT

The first decade of the new century has seen significant changes among the gangs of New Zealand. Facing a changing cultural climate in which rebellious young people see membership in traditional 'patch'-wearing gangs as less desirable, New Zealand's established gangs have become starved for recruits. Rather than precipitating a straightforward decline in the country's gang scene, however, what we are seeing is a reorganisation of the gangs. This chapter examines the problems facing the outlaw motorcycle clubs and the patched street gangs, and the numerous and complex nature of the issues facing these groups. It also explores the rise of LA-style street gangs and the similarities and difference that exist between them and New Zealand's traditional gangs.

INTRODUCTION

In the late 1950s, a group teenaged motorcycle riders, part of a wider youth movement known as 'milk bar cowboys', began to mill around outside the Majestic Theatre on Auckland's central hub, Queen Street. They had met outside dances, at milk bars, and on the side of the road when their motorcycles broke down. At a certain point, one of the young bikers, a builder with some artistic abilities, painted an eagle on the backs of his friends' leather jackets. The inspiration came directly from the lyrics of the 1955 hit by the band Cheers, 'Black Denim Trousers and Motorcycle Boots'. The chorus went:

He wore black denim trousers and motorcycle boots
And a leather jacket with an eagle on the back
He had a hopped-up 'cicle that took off like a gun
That fool was the terror of Highway 101.

Far from being a symbol of exclusive membership, the eagle was really a fashion accessory, and if someone wanted one, they could have one. About ten bikers took up the offer.

DOI: 10.4018/978-1-4666-9938-0.ch016

Sometime later, someone suggested that the group of youths should identify themselves as the 'Auckland Outcasts', but the name – full of youthful rebellion – was used infrequently. One of those young bikers, recalls: 'The guy that painted the eagle came up with the name the "Auckland Outcasts", but it wasn't really an adopted name. You didn't go around saying, "I'm an Auckland Outcast." It was just – we must have thought it was cool or something.'

Like the other milk bar cowboys lining Queen Street, the Auckland Outcasts took great pride in their bikes. Motorcycles were more than just a useful means of getting around; they were used to forge an identity within an image-conscious youth movement. Most of the Outcasts rode high-powered British motorcycles with the more stylish having crash bars, twin mirrors, extra chrome, and large mud flaps that would cover the muffler to increase engine noise. The bikers wore leather jackets with lamb's-wool lining, old flying boots and American jeans purchased from seamen docking at Auckland's port. A white scarf was a popular accessory. Surplus from the armed forces offered up New Zealand Air Force and Army greatcoats which the Outcasts draped over their legs while riding, providing the 'in' look as well as all-important warmth.

The Outcasts roared down Upper Queen Street at high speed at night, racing one another, giving pillion rides to girls, and often letting their steel-capped hobnail boots drag along the road to create a shower of sparks.

In the late 1950s, there was little to differentiate the Auckland Outcasts from any number of similar clusters of bikers peppered throughout New Zealand. This soon changed. On one Queen Street night in 1960, while hanging outside the Majestic, the Outcasts met a young American named Jim Carrico. The young man, with an accent familiar from US films, spoke with enthusiasm about a group he rode with in California. That seemingly innocuous meeting proved transformative of the entire New Zealand gang scene. The group he spoke of was the Hells Angels.

INTRODUCTION

In recent years there has been significant changes among the gangs of New Zealand. Facing a cultural climate in which rebellious young people see membership in traditional gangs - those that wear 'back patches' and were inspired by the Hells Angels – as less desirable and are therefore starving them of recruits. The average age of the older-style groups has increased steadily, leaving them further disconnected from youth who were drawn to the violence and active rebellion that fuelled their past popularity.

A number gangs with long histories have collapsed, while many others are facing problems rejuvenating their numbers with young members, particularly given the arrival of a new form of 'LA-style' street gangs (like the Bloods and Crips). Rather than precipitating a straightforward decline in New Zealand's gang scene, then, what we are seeing is a reorganisation of the gangs.

Based on ten years of ethnographic research of numerous New Zealand gangs over a six year period and formal interviews with more than 50 gang members and those associated with them, this chapter examines the weakening existence of traditional gangs in New Zealand and explore the reasons for this decline, including, changes in laws, the increase in pure methamphetamine use, and the weakening of important internal groups bonds. It with also highlight the rise of LA style street gangs and what the internal culture of these new groups will mean for the gang scene and New Zealand society generally.

THE NEW ZEALAND GANG SCENE

In 1960 the world's fourth chapter of the Hells Angels formed in Auckland, New Zealand.[1] It was the first chapter to exist outside of California. This one incident, a fluke of migratory history, transformed New Zealand's gang landscape. Fledgling motorcycle-riding 'milk bar cowboy' groups mimicked the Angels' style and formal hierarchical leadership structure and these helped the groups achieve longevity and became mainstays on New Zealand's gang scene (Gilbert, 2013).

These 'outlaw motorcycle clubs' were primarily distinctive due to the wearing of large back patches, sewn onto a cut-off jacket or vest, displaying the name, location and emblem of their club. According to police, by the early 2000s, there were 21 outlaw clubs in 60 different chapters (each gang may have multiple chapters) and a total membership of around 600.

In a situation seemingly unique to New Zealand, 'street gangs' – groups who do not ride motorcycles – began to also wear back patches and adopted the leadership structure template provided by the Hells Angels. Readily identifiable by these patches and quickly becoming notorious for their violence, two major groups, the Mongrel Mob and the Black Power[2], swiftly became the largest gangs in the country, with several hundreds of members each and chapters in cities and towns throughout New Zealand, including a significant population in prison. Membership in these groups is primarily drawn from poorer areas and as such is predominantly comprised of indigenous Maori people. In the early 2000s, police estimated that there were 140 chapters of what they call 'ethnic gangs' with a total membership of over two thousand.

With a membership initially comprised of teenagers and young men, New Zealand's patched gangs were impulsive, violent and primarily antisocial. The heyday of these gangs, in the 1970s and 80s, was punctuated by public incidents of extreme violence and protracted gang wars that earned both the outlaw motorcycle clubs and the patched street gangs a dangerous reputation. In the intervening years, however, this membership has aged considerably, and the violence for which they were once known has ebbed. The New Zealand gang scene is in a dramatic state of flux.

THE OUTLAW MOTORCYCLE CLUBS

In the first decade of the new millennium the New Zealand's outlaw motorcycle clubs failed to refresh their membership with new recruits or maintain existing members, and subsequently many faltered or folded. Although this was evident throughout the country, nowhere was it more obvious than in Christchurch, a city that had previously been highly populated with such clubs.

Conflicts between Highway 61, a large nationwide outlaw club, and the local chapter of the Black Power street gang in Christchurch had occurred sporadically throughout much of the 1990s due to the close proximity of their clubhouses in the central city. Following one clash between the groups in 1997, Black Power member Max Shannon had walked from the Christchurch District Court laughing, after witnesses refused to testify against him. Shannon's high spirits were soon ended, however. In the early hours of Sunday 6 August 2000, a relatively insignificant incident outside the Revelations nightclub in the central city between Shannon and Highway 61 member Murray Simms reignited hostilities.

Highway 61 took exception to the fact that Shannon chose to fight Simms, who had previously lost partial use of one arm as a result of a motorcycle accident. Later on the morning of the fight, Highway

61 members were summoned to their clubhouse on Maces Road in Bromley where they decided that retribution was required. The club's president, Mathew 'Bomber' Grant suggested that someone had to die (*R v Grant*, Unreported, High Court, Christchurch, Chisholm J, 2001). Detailed retaliatory plans were made and it was decided that Max Shannon would be shot while at his rugby league training. For the remainder of Sunday, Monday, and much of Tuesday, several of the club's 19-strong membership made preparations; gathering up a shotgun, a .38 pistol and ammunition, and stealing a car to use in the shooting.

Just after 7.45pm on Tuesday 8 August 2000, Max Shannon, having finished training at a sports field in Woolston, got into his car. As he did so, the stolen car carrying at least three members of Highway 61 drove past him and numerous shots were fired at Shannon as he prepared to drive away, inflicting injuries that resulted in his death the following day.

Despite members preparing the clubhouse for Black Power retaliation or 'back up', it was from within the club that the biggest threat to Highway 61 existed. At the clubhouse after the shooting, Bomber Grant told his members that, "*If everybody keeps their mouths shut no one will do a big lag*" (italics in original) (*R v Grant*, Unreported, High Court, Christchurch, Chisholm J, August 2001). Unfortunately for Grant, one of the members, fearing prosecution, broke ranks and agreed to testify against those involved. Five members of the club were subsequently charged with murder. Simms, whose initial fight had led to the attack, decided to plead guilty to the murder, and three others, including Grant, were found guilty by a jury, while another was found not guilty. All of the guilty men received mandatory life sentences with minimum parole conditions ranging between eleven and 14 years (*R v Grant*, Unreported, High Court, Christchurch, Chisholm J, 2001).

The convictions were a significant blow to Highway 61 in Christchurch. In the mid-1990s, the club had had three chapters in the city, but these were already in decline by the time of the Shannon murder. One chapter had been decimated by police following convictions for drug dealing from the clubhouse, which was subsequently confiscated under the Proceeds of Crime Act (1991), and the other two chapters had dwindling numbers. The remaining members from these chapters had consolidated under Grant's leadership. With Grant and four others in prison (one, not charged with murder, was jailed for firearms offences in relation to the attack on Shannon) and another having left the gang in order to testify against his comrades, the club was in tatters and eventually the clubhouse was sold.

Although the fall of Highway 61 in Christchurch was punctuated by dramatic events, other outlaw clubs in the city found themselves arriving at the same end point. Along with the three chapters of Highway 61, in the 1990s Christchurch had been home to chapters of the Epitaph Riders, Devil's Henchmen, Templars and Road Knights. By 2010, with the exception of the Epitaph Riders – which had fewer than six members and no clubhouse – none of those clubs remained. The situation in Christchurch, however, was representative of the decline in the outlaw motorcycle scene around the country, with many clubs suffering similar fates.

By 2010, both chapters of the Tyrants (Pahiatua and Levin), the Hastings chapter of the Hells Angels, the Sinn Fein (Upper Hutt), and at least one other chapter of Highway 61 (Auckland), the Lost Legion (Blenheim), the 'Gold Coast' (Kapati Coast) chapter of the Satan's Slaves had either closed or were in a moribund state. Moreover, in 2010, clubs comprising six or so members are considered by many outlaw club members and associates to be in reasonable shape, a number that would have been considered small just a decade earlier.

A Complex Decline

The factors that give rise to gangs are well known to be numerous and complex (Klein, 1995: p.158), and this was certainly the case in New Zealand (Gilbert, 2013). Similarly there were numerous factors contributing toward their decline in the new millennium. The individual importance of each factor is difficult to assess, but together they have proven damaging to the scene generally, and ruinous to many outlaw clubs.

One of the most significant and obvious signs of the problems facing the clubs is the advancing age of most members. Since the early 1980s, the outlaw clubs had benefited from the stability and loyalty of a longer-term membership base. However, by the end of the 1990s and into the new millennium, the clubs were struggling to recruit new and younger members. With unemployment among Pakeha (New Zealanders of European descent) at record low levels, the pool of rebellious and disaffected young Pakeha, from which many outlaw clubs tended to draw members, was shrinking. It is perhaps significant, then, that the Hells Angels[3], the Tribesmen and the Filthy Few, three multi-ethnic outlaw motorcycle clubs, appear to have survived best during the new millennium. Although, reflecting the complex nature of the overall decline, the same cannot be said for Highway 61, a similar group that has gone into a noticeable nationwide decline, although it still maintains a number of chapters and a presence in Australia.

But this economically determinist argument requires caution. The outlaw motorcycle clubs first emerged in New Zealand during prosperous times of the 1960s, and therefore the strengthening labour market offers only a partial explanation for the scene's problems.

A further and more significant explanation for the lack of youthful rejuvenation stems from broad societal changes in social pursuits and fashion. It seems that for many rebellious youth, European and American motorcycles no longer held the appeal that they once did, and instead modified Japanese cars have become increasingly *de rigueur*. Termed 'boy racers', and inspired by overseas media – particularly such American movies as the *Fast and the Furious* film franchise[4] – these motor vehicle thrill seekers and/or enthusiasts drive through streets *en masse*, congregating together, drinking, and often racing one another.

To what degree boy racers have siphoned off potential recruits for outlaw clubs is moot, but what is quite clear is that young people are not being attracted to join the clubs and that this lack of youthful rejuvenation had a significant impact on the outlaw club scene. As the average age of members slowly increased, a generation gap was created between existing members and wider groups of rebellious young men who might have considered joining. In the past, there had been a seemingly limitless of supply of young men wanting to join such groups, and because of this, outlaw clubs were not accustomed to having to actively seek members. Their failure to respond to the changing conditions meant that the issues of aging membership went unchecked. Moreover, the existing members had undergone rigorous prospecting periods – in times of greater competition for patches – and few were willing to simply let new members join in an 'easy' way and so they failed to adequately nurture a dwindling number of prospective members.

Perpetual changes in bellwether factors that help define generations, such as in music, fashion, and social activities, as well as a natural affiliation that exists between men of similar ages, also created something of an age-related 'generational barrier' to membership.

By the 2000s, rebellious young males who showed an interest in the clubs often found themselves surrounded by older men who shared few of their tastes, full of wild stories of the past but no longer engaging in the behaviour that created those stories. Due to the natural maturity that tends to come with age, men of 40 or 50 are not as likely to fight as men of 20, something supported by age related data of violent offenders (Harpham, 2004) and recidivism rates (Nadesu, 2009). Indeed, older members tend to put a handbrake on youthful members or associates of the clubs because they are wary of youthful bravado leading to police attention or sparking inter-gang confrontation. Although in certain clubs older members may not want to draw police attention because it may interfere with illegal money-making ventures, more often than not it is because they simply cannot be bothered with conflict and, often with families of their own, they are more wary of the effects of a long jail sentence. Young men looking toward the clubs then, see something akin to group of their parents and not a vehicle for great rebellion.

Somewhat ironically, given the devastating effects of violent actions undertaken by Highway 61 members in Christchurch, the lack of physical confrontations between gangs may have contributed to their overall decline. The importance of conflict in aiding gang cohesion has been established by early gang studies (Thrasher, 1927; Tannenbaum, 1938), and many examples are evident in New Zealand gang history. It stands to reason, then, that when these conflicts are removed, so too is a key driver that helps to forge important elements of a gang's internal dynamics. Without an enemy for a sustained period of time – without the mirror upon which to reflect – a gang begins to lose some of its sense of self. When an enemy threat is present, there is sharpness to the group; weaker members may leave the gang during times of conflict but those who remain have an increased commitment to the gang, which is therefore strengthened. As the enemy threat diminishes, so too does the gang.

A further factor that negatively impacted on the outlaw motorcycle club scene relates to the liberalisation of liquor licensing laws that occurred with changes to the Sale of Liquor Act (1989). Amongst other things, changes to the law allowed for extended opening hours for drinking establishments, including provisions sanctioning 24 hour licences. As more pubs and bars were open for a greater number of hours, particularly late at night, gang clubhouses were no longer the only place open for people to drink late at night or on Sundays and the competition decreased their role as a social hub. This severely impacted on their support base and their profitability. Like any social institution, people often beget people, so as numbers began to fall away from clubhouses, this precipitated an even steeper decline as the social function that the clubhouse provided to many in the community was reduced. This had two related effects; one was that fewer people were being introduced to the club, and therefore an important recruitment avenue was diminished; the other was that for people who might have sought membership, the general lack of atmosphere lessened their enthusiasm to join the gang. The important community function of a social hub that clubhouses had provided in the past was all but gone.

But perhaps the most significant development to negatively impact on the outlaw clubs – and, the gang scene generally – was the rising popularity of a smokable form of methamphetamine, commonly referred to in New Zealand as 'P', which is an abbreviation of 'pure'.

The Emergence of Pure Methamphetamine or 'P'

Methamphetamine had been evident within the New Zealand outlaw club scene since the 1980s and had traditionally been ingested by nasal insufflation. When intended for 'snorting', methamphetamine is often mixed or 'cut', typically with glucose, which lessens its strength and increases the profit margin for dealers. Pure methamphetamine, however, is uncut to ensure that it is clean to vaporise when heated, and there are significantly greater health problems associated with its use in this form (Topp, Degenhardt, Kaye, & Darke, 2002).

Moderate (defined as monthly) use of pure methamphetamine only slightly increases a person's chance of suffering some psychotic symptoms[5] (Rebecca McKetin, Hickey, Devlin, & Lawrence, 2010). Habitual use, however, not only increases these health risks but can also lead to addiction; and those who withdraw from the drug incur moderate depressive and psychotic symptoms for around a week and a 'craving' that can persist for more than a month (Zorick et al., 2010). Furthermore, the purity of P means that the cost of the drug is high. Priced at more than $100 for a 'point' (one tenth of a gram), habitual P users can quickly be faced with significant financial costs.

Although it can be liquefied and delivered intravenously, the use of needles in the patched gang scene was universally banned by the early 1980s. P, therefore, is usually smoked using a glass pipe and, to a lesser degree, snorted. Although smoking P may be associated with less severe dependence than injecting it, both means of taking the drug result in similar levels of other harms (Rebecca McKetin et al., 2008). This may be in part be due to the fact that those who smoke the drug tend to use more of it than those preferring other forms of delivery (Kinner & Degenhardt, 2008; Rebecca McKetin et al., 2008). Anecdotally, at least, this appears to be the case in the gang scene and members who 'burn' P are typically heavier users than those who snort it. The sociable nature of passing around a pipe and the inoffensive vapour produced by P makes it easy and enjoyable for members to consume together; and over time this meant that the means of taking the drug became as important as the ends (the drug's effect). For example, instead of using a line of two of speed to gain the energy to make it through a long night's activities, smoking P often becomes the focus of an evening, and therefore consumption of the drug is increased.

Certainly, habitual use became widespread within the scene and consequently problems, both social/psychological and financial, became common. Numerous outlaw clubs become concerned by the behaviour and reliability of members who had become 'fried' through P usage, and a number of clubs banned smoking P – although many still allowed snorting it; evincing a common belief, based on the results of collective experimentation and observation, that smoking the drug is at the root of the problem rather than the drug itself.

While the organisational structure adopted by New Zealand gangs has meant that they are able to identify risks and mitigate them, P was largely not identified as great concern nor rapidly addressed by most. There are at least two reasons for this. The first reason is that the drug itself was not new and ingested via the nose it had not caused significant problems. Adding to this, the fact that P was smoked – like marijuana – added a familiar element to the drug, and passing around a pipe became a sociable group activity. The second reason P took hold in many groups is that it was only identified as a problem after a period in which the drug was widely used, by which time many members were habitual users, and psychologically or physically addicted to it. In many gangs, this meant that there was insufficient support amongst members for a ban. Certainly it appears that banning it quickly was the key. Without exception, the groups that did not ban the smoking of P have been the ones to suffer the most significant declines.

The experiences of one South Island outlaw club the effect of P was dramatic and typical. The substantial financial cost involved in using P habitually forced members into debt – to both the club and to outsiders. Although certain members were dealing the drug, the trade only supported its use, and before long it failed to do even that. One member could not afford the payments on his motorcycle and it was repossessed, two others sold their bikes to pay for their habit. Another member suffered a mental breakdown and was committed to a psychiatric hospital for several months. All four were expelled from the gang due to outcomes associated with the use of P, but the drug was still tolerated because key members among the dwindling group still used it and were unwilling to give it up.

In the ever-shrinking outlaw motorcycle club chapter, the loss of four members was significant, and the situation was compounded when the remaining members, becoming demoralised, began to forego their rostered nights on duty at the clubhouse, which meant that associates were unable to access the clubhouse or the bar. Therefore support for the club – offered by an already meagre group of core associates – waned further, almost becoming non-existent. The formal weekly club meetings began to start later and later as members were not turning up on time, if at all. Eventually the meetings stopped altogether. Soon after, the club was failing to pay its power, telephone and pay-television bills.

Within a five-year period the club, which had more than a 30 year history, had transformed from a strong and committed group, to a disparate, unmotivated one. During that time, membership dropped from around a dozen to finally just three members, and eventually it collapsed and dissolved. Given numerous other factors described above, P cannot be totally blamed for the fall of the club, but in this case, without a doubt, it played a primary role.

The problems facing outlaw clubs in New Zealand, then, are many. Indeed, the complexities involved in the decline of the scene appear as many and varied as those involved in their rise. In fact, the outlaw club scene in New Zealand at the end of the first decade of the new millennium was weaker than it has been at any time since the formation of such groups in the late 1960s and early 1970s. But despite the rapid and obvious contractions of outlaw clubs and outlaw club members, it is unlikely that such groups will vanish altogether; at least not in the foreseeable future.

Signs of Life

Although P may yet claim more clubs, many of the remaining groups have banned smoking the drug and thus have nullified a significant threat. Indeed, many of the traditional clubs that have banned smoking P remain in relatively strong positions. For example, The Devil's Henchmen in Timaru, the Mothers in Palmerston North, the Hells Angels in Wanganui and Auckland, and the Head Hunters 'East' Auckland chapter[6] are showing no signs of collapse. Moreover, many clubs are beginning to recognise the difficulties they are facing, and some may begin to take measures to proactively recruit new members. Exactly what form this will take is difficult to predict, particularly given that many of the factors negatively affecting them are beyond their control.

Through the fall of numerous outlaw clubs, however, a natural equilibrium may be achieved; in effect, balancing supply and demand with fewer clubs servicing a smaller pool of prospective members. In this way, the outlaw club scene appears to be consolidating around the surviving clubs – largely those with international connections.

In April 2009 The Hells Angels gave the scene a potentially significant green shoot by forming a new club in the city of Nelson called the Red Devils, which in 2014 became a prospect chapter of the Hells Angels. The Red Devils is an alliance of motorcycle clubs around the world that support the Hells Angels. But whether or not this new club evinces new life within the scene or proves to be a false dawn, may be dependent on the ability of the outlaw clubs generally to engage a younger membership.

Another recent move by the Hells Angels, the launching of a Nomads chapter on Auckland's North Shore, also signals efforts to revive the scene. Formed in February 2011, the Hells Angel Nomads chapter, originally made up of existing members from Wanganui and Auckland, kicked off with a frenzy of activity and promotion. It has been quick to produce and sell support merchandise, establish and internet site, run raffles, and in January 2012 maintained a prominent stall at the Kumeu Classic Car and Hot Rod Festival. Their first pubic event, a 'dice run', was open to riders of all brands of motorcycle – an unprecedented break from New Zealand outlaw club tradition. At the time of writing, the chapter's zeal is paying dividends and it has half a dozen prospects and a number of 'hangarounds': a pipeline equivalent to the outlaw club heyday. The Angels may again be providing a template for the future outlaw scene.

A further development is the formation of the Rebels in New Zealand in early 2011. Australia's largest outlaw club and one with a reputation of rapid expansion, the Rebels entered the country in a dramatic swoop, patching-over numerous Tribesmen members and establishing a number of new chapters by patching-up people without a prospecting period. Within a number of weeks, their total membership was enough to make them among the biggest in the country.

In any event, unless the pendulum of fashion swings back – and the popular television series *Sons of Anarchy* may signal this – the heyday of the outlaw clubs in New Zealand may be long over or at least be fundamentally changing.

THE PATCHED STREET GANGS

Many of the problems faced by the outlaw clubs in the 2000s were also being experienced by the patched street gangs, and consequently many of the arguments in the section above also apply here. Once again, it is an incident in the city of Christchurch that helps illuminate issues relating to the scene.

Early in the first decade of the new millennium, a Mongrel Mob 'Aotearoa' chapter was established in the Christchurch suburb of Phillipstown. The chapter members transformed an old villa into the gang's clubhouse. Typical of all gang clubhouses, the property became the hub for the Mongrel Mob members and their associates to meet and party, but atypical of clubhouses in the 2000s, the gang pad also became a 'tinnie house',[7] a place where one can buy small amounts of marijuana wrapped in tinfoil.

Police attention became focused on the gang when an internal feud erupted after one member of the Aotearoa chapter was expelled from the gang, but was then re-patched as a member of the 'Notorious' chapter, a largely North Island-based chapter of the of the same gang, and subsequently attempted to get members from his old chapter to join the new one. During investigations into violence between the established and new chapters of the Mob, police became alerted to the tell-tale sign of numerous short-term visitors to the Aotearoa Mongrel Mob's address on Wilsons Road and launched Operation Crusade – the name taken from the region's 'Canterbury Crusaders' rugby team, whose home stadium was situated a short distance from the clubhouse. The gang's drug dealing was brash, perhaps best highlighted by the note pinned inside the gate to advertise the price of one tinnie, "$25 or Fuck Off".

During the Operation Crusade, police officers purchased drugs, installed wire taps and bugs, and took surveillance photographs in order to gather sufficient evidence to charge all of the members of the gang and numerous associates with various offences. The resulting trial is believed to be New Zealand's largest criminal case, in terms of the number of defendants; 18 were tried at one time.

The trial lasted four weeks, and 15 of the defendants – including all of the chapter's 13 members – were found guilty of conspiracy to sell cannabis, along with a range of other crimes that came to light during the police investigation, notably firearms and violent offences. The guilty parties were sentenced to between eight months and four-and-a-half years imprisonment, depending on the degree of involvement (*R v Beattie*, Unreported, High Court, Christchurch, Panckhurst J, 2004).

There are three issues relating to this case that demonstrate and reflect issues facing by the patched gang scene generally. The first of these issues is the loss of the gang's clubhouse, the second is the age of those members convicted following Operation Crusade, and the final issue to consider is the effect this bust had on the Mongrel Mob.

Following the arrests of the Aotearoa Mob chapter in Christchurch, the rented villa in Philipstown became a pad without a gang to occupy it and it was subsequently pulled down by the owner, becoming a vacant lot. Similarly around the country, formal clubhouses were disappearing from the patched gang scene. In the first decade of the 2000s throughout New Zealand the Mongrel Mob had left, or been evicted from, properties that had served as gang pads (three of them, following eviction, were burnt out by the gang). Similarly, three chapters of the Black Power chapter (in Christchurch, Wellington, and Hawkes Bay), were all without formal clubhouses. These changes were also evident to police, as reflected by the New Zealand Police Association which in 2009 said that "to a very large extent" the traditional clubhouse "is very much a phenomenon of the past" particularly in urban centres (New Zealand Police Association, 2009: p.7). Although the Police Association attributed this regressive development to gangs pursuing a lower profile due to moves into organised criminal activity, in reality the situation is less deliberate and more complex. As with outlaw clubs, and outlined above, the niche social function performed by the street gang clubhouse was reduced, in part, by Liquor Licensing Act of 1989 (with a greater array of competing drinking establishments available in the cities). Moreover, greater demands from families as members matured meant many clubhouses lost their centrality. In many instances, leases expired on rental properties and another venue was never sourced, or the gangs simply failed to make payments and they were evicted. Other times, as happened with the Mongrel Mob in Christchurch, an event impacted the group to such a degree that the clubhouse was no longer viable. The loss of clubhouses evinces a wider weakness and decline within the setting generally, and one that may in fact exacerbate this decline by removing, what has hitherto been, a key component of the patched gang existence.

This is particularly relevant given that the Black Power and the Mongrel Mob were also facing recruitment issues. Of those convicted following Operation Crusade, the youngest was 26 years old, and most were over 40. Like the outlaw clubs, the patched street gangs were creating generational barriers to new members and a greater maturity is evident in many of these gangs, which, as was the case with the outlaw clubs, resulted in fewer violent incidents. Following the Highway 61 killing of Black Power member, Max Shannon, outlined above, senior Black Power member Shane 'Baldy' Turner appealed for calm, saying that anyone seeking vengeance should think of their families: "My concern is the women and children. Your kids come first, so if a leader wants to drag their families or kids through a war… it's not good for them" (*The Press* 2000). Turner said recently, it was not like it was in the "old days" and there is greater effort to avoid war, whereas in the past "we looked for any excuse [to engage in violence]"[8]. Notwithstanding this, the large patched street gangs – particularly the Mongrel Mob – remain prone to violence, the lack of large scale wars between the groups is further testimony to the influence of the maturing membership.

A combination of this increasing restraint, or age-related inertia, and a drive toward more family-orientated among numerous chapters of the patched street gangs, has helped fortify generational barriers to these traditional gangs and, unintentionally, created a niche market for a youthful new form of 'LA-style' gang. This development is potentially so critical to the street gang scene it will be examined in a discrete section below.

But while youthful recruitment appears to be a significant issue, and many chapters of the large patched street gangs have contracted, overall they seem to have maintained their existing membership far better than their motorcycle equivalents; and there are a number of reasons for this.

The incarceration of the Mongrel Mob chapter in Christchurch would have likely been enough to destroy a smaller gang or most outlaw motorcycle clubs, but the size of the Mongrel Mob meant that it had no discernable impact on the nationwide group. The large street gangs have been able to survive in part due to their sheer weight of numbers, and as such, negative influences on them have been less obvious than on the smaller outlaw clubs. If a group falls away in one place, members from other regions can bolster it, or remaining members can move to join another chapter. Moreover, large contingents of members of these gangs in prison means that attachments and associations remain strong – and are indeed beneficial given the realities of 'might makes right' that exist in prison life – during periods of incarceration.

Furthermore, although the economy strengthened throughout the 1990s, the economic benefits did not impact to the same extent on Maori and Pacific communities, from which the patched street gangs have tended to attract members, meaning these gangs were not as threatened by reducing recruits or the loss of members to mainstream society. A survey of Mongrel Mob members from the mid-1990s (Mob Advisory Panel, 1996) showed how significantly they had become divorced from the legitimate work-force, and while no similar survey has been undertaken since, one can reasonably assert, from anecdotal evidence alone, that this separation has only increased in the new century, making integration back into mainstream life near impossible.

But while macro economic factors have certainly played a part in this social isolation, its entrenchment has been solidified by member commitment to gang life. And it is within that we may find a further explanation as to why patched street gangs have better maintained member numbers. As variously outlined throughout this work, member allegiance to gangs is strong across the board, but within the patched street gangs commitment has often been made patently, and permanently, obvious via facial tattoos of gang or gang-related insignia. The origins of gang related facial tattoos are in the country's prisons in the early 1980s, and this development had obvious implications for members who might consider leaving the gang; acting as such tattoos do as a powerful means of social control.

One policy used in New Zealand prisons to inhibit the threat of gang violence during the influx of gang prison numbers during the 1970s and 1980s was the banning of wearing or displaying gang related insignia (Meek, 1992: p.270). Although prison guards could confiscate gang drawings and the like, tattoos were impossible to regulate.

The genesis of these facial tattoos came from a jailhouse subculture, and they were not initially gang related nor were they related to traditional Maori moko[9], although elements of the latter tradition are now sometimes used in gang tattoos. In what can be seen as secondary deviation (Lemert, 1951) and, quite literally, an exercise in self labelling, some incarcerated men began to imprint dots or stars below the outside edges of their eyes to represent their time in jail; something that criminologist Greg Newbold (2010 pers. comm.) believes has occurred since as early as the 1960s. As gang members began became a significant part of the prison muster a decade later, many followed suit. By early 1980s these tattoos became larger, more obvious, and gang specific. One such inmate to mark his face in this way was Mongrel Mob member, Dennis Makalio. Makalio was sent to prison in the early 1980s after attacking two police officers in the gang's Porirua clubhouse.

Ahhhh, they came in waving their fuckin' batons like Starski and fuckin' Hutch. I thought, fuck that! [So] the gates were closed and I switched off the lights. Well, I fucked them, punched and kicked them, burnt them with cigarettes and all that. The cunts were…bleeding like fuckin' pigs.

The crime was such that Makalio was sent to Auckland's maximum security prison, Paremoremo, where he was among long-term inmates. While there, Makalio marked his face with prison tattoos,

But they [the small facial tattoos] represented jail, eh? I thought what the fuck am I representing jail for when I represent the Mongrel Mob? So I fuckin' did that (pointing to the word 'Mobster' tattooed on his forehead).

It was an extraordinary way to express commitment to the gang, and one that quickly became common among the Mongrel Mob's membership. Facial tattooing, with words like 'Mongrel', 'Mobster', or 'Mob' and/or incorporating the gang's bulldog motif, in many instances grew to cover the face in what the gang calls 'masks'. Many members of Black Power too began to mark their faces with motifs representing their gang.

Makalio says he knows when a prospect is ready to be a full-patched member. With an explicit understanding of the power of facial tattoos, he replied, "Give me his face" (2006, pers. Comm.). But such tattoos do not just exemplify a tremendous degree of loyalty to the gang; they also work as a powerful form of social control. Once a member is marked in such a visible and permanent manner, his ties to the gang become that much harder to break and, as such, the tattoos work to place limits on a member's thoughts of leaving the gang. Even if membership is severed, a man with such tattoos is always going to be perceived as a gang member by the public, and by opposition groups, yet he will lack the social and physical support offered by membership. In this way, these tattoos may have helped to maintain numbers in Black Power and the Mongrel Mob during the first decade of the 2000s.

The Ongoing Impact of 'P'

Like the outlaw clubs, however, the patched street gangs are struggling with the effects of members smoking P. Reflecting the growing popularity of methamphetamine use by the end of the 1990s, an updated version of Black Power's national rules taken from a meeting held in Auckland in January 1999, states that the outlawing of "Hard drugs" is "Deleted", undoubtedly reflecting the popularity, and potential profitability, of methamphetamine. By the mid-2000s, however, many Black Power chapters were beginning to rethink the decision. For example, chapters in Auckland and Hawkes Bay have since banned members from smoking P. One Black Power leader from Hawkes Bay, Mane Adams, said in 2003 that because its use is so widespread amongst members, it is difficult to ban it at the national level. He said that the general feeling is that it's "not desirable, but that if you are using it you are still my brother, but don't do it in my area [where it's banned] or in my face" (pers. comm.). Christchurch Black Power president, Shane 'Baldy' Turner, said in 2005 that his chapter has banned it, though the ban seems to operate on the principle of 'out of sight, out of mind': "Well, it's banned in my club, anyway. If you want to do it and you're in my group then good luck, that's all we say, good luck but we don't want to see you around as long as you're doing it" (pers. comm.).

The Mongrel Mob appears similarly conflicted. The Notorious chapter has publicly scorned P, and in association with the Salvation Army is attempting to get its members off the drug (*NZ Herald* 1010). The Notorious president, Roy Dunne believes that up to 80 percent of the gang was addicted to the drug, and he links the deaths of 12 of his members to its use (NZ Herald 2010).

But banning the drug is not easy and how strictly any ban is enforced is difficult to gauge. Within many chapters of the large street gangs, the drug's use has become so prevalent that to ban it would mean splitting the gangs into two groups, users and non-users. At this stage, at least, its use is tolerated to keep the gangs together; an ironic situation given that in many instances, such as those outlined above in relation to certain outlaw clubs, P is doing significant damage to gangs; making members who habitually use the substance unreliable and more committed to the drug than to the gang.

The problems that P is creating within the gang scene are not going unnoticed by the police. Gang intelligence officer, Senior Constable Mike Watkins said in 2006, "If I could take credit for introducing P into the gang scene, I would. It's done more damage to the gangs than we ever have" (pers. comm.). Despite the gangs being linked to the drug's production and distribution, with few exceptions it appears certain that overall gangs and gang members are victims of the drug rather than benefactors of it.

Since the mid-2000s, social worker and life member of Black Power, Denis O'Reilly has taken up the anti-P cause and runs a national project called Mokai Whanau Ora, which seeks to engage both Mongrel Mob and Black Power leadership in an effort to educate them away from the drug's use and trade (O'Reilly, 2005). O'Reilly has said that it is a "struggle" and that within the large street gangs, "We wax and wane a bit according to availability and the addiction level of leaders but the trend is, I think, downward and away from P" (2008, pers. comm.). Gangs have previously banned the use of heroin, and it is likely that such a ban around the smoking of P will eventuate due to the increasing awareness of its detrimental effects, but this will only occur if – perhaps when – the drug fades from popularity and the ratio of users versus non-users shifts so that the non-users are able to enforce prohibition.

Small Gains

As noted earlier, the problems facing the patched street gangs have not had as devastating an impact as they have had on the outlaw clubs, and in certain instances, Black Power and the Mongrel Mob have benefited from the decline in the outlaw motorcycle club scene. One town where this has been particularly evident is in the small city of Timaru, formerly a stronghold of two outlaw motorcycle clubs. After the establishment of the Devil's Henchmen and Road Knights chapters in Timaru in the late 1970s, no other patched gangs attempted to move into the territory for 30 years. However, by the mid-2000s, both Black Power and the Mongrel Mob had chapters there; the shrinking size and changing internal dynamics of the Devil's Henchmen and Road Knights chapters has meant that neither chapter is willing to engage in a territorial war to protect their turf from new arrivals. Similarly, the Mongrel Mob now has a presence in Blenheim – a town that used to be the exclusive territory of the Lone Legion, and which they had successfully defended against other groups until their apparent collapse in recent times. In Invercargill during June 2006, a fire lit by members of a new Mongrel Mob chapter, who also stole and destroyed at least two of the Road Knights' motorcycles, gutted the Road Knights' clubhouse (*Southland Times* 2008). Retribution, at least publically, by the Road Knights does not appear to have been forthcoming.

But despite these small gains, overall the patched street gang scene is far from flourishing, and while the struggling economy of recent times may offer them support, perhaps their greatest challenge comes from youthful competition via the emergence of LA-style street gangs, which are a surging and potentially critical new development in New Zealand's gang scene.

LA-STYLE STREET GANGS: A LOOK AT THE FUTURE?

Since their inception in the early 1970s, patched gangs have almost exclusively dominated the New Zealand street gang domain. But during the 1990s, another form of gang was quietly emerging as a threat to patched dominance, one which will arguably shape the future of gangs in this country. In 1990, a small article in *The New Zealand Herald* (1990), reported concerns about a group of youths in South Auckland who were wearing "colours" (bandanas) and dressing like "violent American street gangs", and calling themselves the 'Tongan Crip Gang' or 'TCG'. This form of gang was so unfamiliar to New Zealand that the media source incorrectly spelt 'Crip' as 'Crypt'. Using knowledge that reflected the rather homogenous – that being patch wearing – nature of New Zealand's gang scene, police told the *Herald* that they were not a "gang" and were "nothing more than five teenage thugs" (*The New Zealand Herald*). While that may have been true at the time, within a decade of so, by the mid-2000s, these groups had grown in size and in number and may represent the future of New Zealand's gang scene.

Crip gangs are one half of a predominately African-American gang phenomenon. With their counterpart rivals, the Bloods, these two groups were initially formed in the city of Los Angeles in the 1970s, but, driven significantly by popular cultural influences, soon spread throughout America and much of the world; (Covey, 2003; Germet, 2001; Gruter & Versteegh, 2001; Hagedorn, 1999, 2005b). Increasingly throughout the 1990s, these influences became obvious in New Zealand, and these LA-style street gangs became increasingly prominent (Eggleston, 2000).

The trends becoming obvious among youth in New Zealand in the 1990s and 2000s were a reflection of a modern vogue coming out of America, based on hip-hop and rap music. As Covey states, "One only needs to walk through any major city to hear the pervasive influence of 'gangster rap' and hip hop music that promotes the street gang lifestyle" (Covey, 2003: p.30). Hip-hop is seen as a wider cultural trend within the context of poor African-American communities and includes distinct speech patterns, 'MCing', 'DJing', graffiti, dance, ideals and music (Richardson & Scott, 2002). Rap music is a part of hip-hop culture and this type of music is supported by an enormous multi-million dollar industry. In 2000, for example, rap music is believed to have generated U.S.$1.8b in sales (Rose, 2001: p.22).

'Gangsta rap', one particular type of rap music, consistently contains violent lyrics, as well as misogynous themes and hypermaterialism (Ro, 1996). The behaviour of some of its artists has attracted significant publicity. Numerous celebrated rap artists have participated in gang violence and some have been killed, most famously Tupak Shakur and Christopher 'Biggie Smalls' Wallace in 1996 and 1997 respectively (Scott, 2000).

That rap music often equates violence to masculinity and problem solving (Ro, 1996) is significant. Glamorised violence and an emphasis on ostentatious wealth – typically, achieved via crime – is a potential driver of New Zealand's developing youth gang culture; and something that sets apart these gangs from the early formation of the traditional patched street gangs; a point to which I will return.

Notwithstanding the importance of music and music videos, a further influence came about from Hollywood interpretations of gangs including the film *Colors* released in America in 1988 and followed three years later by *Boyz n the Hood*. Eggleston (Eggleston, 2000: p.160) reported that early members of these new gangs in New Zealand linked the rise of Crips and Bloods in this country to the film *Colors*.

Referring to this type of emerging youth gang in New Zealand in the late 1990s, Eggleston believes that the Americanisation of New Zealand has been increasingly influential on this country's youth. He sees the new "gangsta" style being mimicked by these groups as a feature that demarcates them from the existing "more established" New Zealand gangs (Eggleston, 2000: pp.149 & 160). Be this as it may, New Zealand's traditional gangs also had their genesis in American culture, both via the youth movements of the 1950s and later, and more significantly, through the Hells Angels in the 1960s.

Despite these incipient gangs attracting some media concern during the 1990s and the first half of the 2000s, it was in 2006 that they became seen as a significant and pressing problem. Following one killing in October 2005, there were a further nine deaths related to or associated with LA-style street gang violence in wider Auckland in 2006 (The *New Zealand Herald* 2007). Street violence was an ongoing problem in many areas of Auckland, and while the close timing of the killings seemed to suggest otherwise, the killings did not necessarily reflect a dramatic rise in overall youth gang activity. Just two of the deaths were the result of a premeditated intent to kill, with the others being, as one South Auckland police officer said in 2009, "the consequence of booze and bad luck" (pers. comm.). Be this as it may, the fact that the victims or perpetrators were all LA-style gang members drew focus on these new gangs.

As will become clear, the spate of deaths sharpened media and public focus on this new type of gang, particularly in South Auckland where eight of the ten killings took place. The media drew public attention to gangs hitherto unknown to most New Zealanders with names like the 'Juvanyle Crip Boys' or 'JCBs', the 'Motherfucker Ruthless Cunts' or MRCs, and the 'Penion Drive Boys' or 'PDBs'. In the same way as the youth gangs of the 1950s and 1960s, and the skinhead groups of the 1980s, the vast majority of these new formations appear to have little or no organisational structure and they form and dissolve rather quickly.

It is clear that some of these groups have connections to established patched gangs (Ministry of Social Development, 2008b) and their colours reflect this; Those groups associated – through familial ties, social contacts, or simply because they share the same neighbourhood – with Black Power wear blue, and those with connections to the Mongrel Mob wear red. These are, interestingly, the same colours used by the American Crips and Bloods respectively.

Perhaps the most evolved LA-style gang is the Killer Beez. The Killer Beez were founded in Otara, South Auckland, around 2003, under the leadership of Josh Marsters, a member of the predominately Maori and Pacific Island outlaw motorcycle club, the Tribesmen (New Zealand Police, 2006: p.14). The direct and active involvement of a well established adult gang member – Masters turned 30 in 2008 – meant that the group was formed under adult supervision and was not, to use Thrasher (1927), a typical unsupervised 'play group' that often typifies earlier gang formation. Furthermore, Marsters was an impressive figure, and combined with his hard man reputation, earned on the street and in the kickboxing ring[10], his appeal for many wannabe youths is rather obvious.

The gang, with their yellow colours[11] reflecting those of the Tribesmen, flourished and grew quickly, becoming the most widely known LA-style street gang in the country. Their growing profile was aided by media that focused heavily on such groups in the wake of the 2006 spate of killings, and such groups sprung up around the country, similar to the way that the Mongrel Mob spread in the early 1970s. As Inspector Jason Hewett, of the South Auckland police, said in 2009, "If you wanted to join a gang at that time which would you join? The Killer Beez – they were everywhere [in the media] at the time" (pers. comm.).

But, with a remarkable – and atypical – degree of organisational ability, the gang in South Auckland was also creating its own media. Mirroring the links seen in the U.S. between street gangs and the rap music scene, in 2007 the Killer Beez established a recording studio and formed a record label, Colourway Records. The following year they released an album 'Skull Fingers Up'. Like the title, the music videos are clearly linked to the gang – one song *Put Your Colours On*, upholds the theme of gang representation and numerous gang members appear in it. By early 2009, the video had nearly 400,000 hits on the internet video networking site *YouTube* (www.youtube.com). As a further salute to U.S. developments, that being the East Coast-West Coast record label feud[12], at least one the albums songs featured a 'diss' track, which attacked pioneer New Zealand hip-hop label Dawn Raid. Unlike the traditional patched gangs, the likes of the Killer Beez were attuned to, and reflected, current trends and were therefore more relevant and appealing to youth.

In the poor areas of South Auckland, the Killer Beez offered a distinct function for members to fulfil the dream of mimicking the gangster life styles portrayed by their U.S. counterparts. In February 2008, Marsters told the daily current affairs programme, *Campbell Live* (2008), that, "As Killer Beez, we're standing up and saying, if you're not going to give us the options, we're going to create options for ourselves". The opportunities available to many youth in South Auckland were limited, but music was not the only available option to obtain the desired 'ghetto bling' lifestyle. Despite Marsters' explicit denial during the *Campbell Live* interview that he or his gang were involved in the illicit trade, it was to be drug offending that would bring the Killer Beez to nationwide attention just three months after that interview took place.

In May of 2008, numerous members and associates of the Killer Beez, including leader Josh Marsters, were arrested on drugs charges, and police raids on several properties in the South Auckland suburbs of Otara and Papatoetoe uncovered $200,000 in cash and an estimated $500,000 worth of P (*The New Zealand Herald* 6.5.2008). Detective Sergeant Ross Ellwood of the Counties Manukau police said the arrests had "taken the core out of the gang. All the Killer Beez leaders are gone. Some are in custody, some are out on bail but are on very strict bail conditions," (*Herald on Sunday* 2008). Nevertheless prison sometimes has the effect of solidifying gang membership rather than breaking it down. Certainly, by 2014 the Killer Beez have shown no signs of folding and, in fact, there are numerous groups also calling themselves Killer Beez, either as formal associates or as copycat gangs, in the increasingly crowded LA-style street gang scene throughout the country.

While some of these young gangs appear to be acting as feeder groups to the patched gangs, the lack of youthful rejuvenation in New Zealand's traditional gangs suggests that some of these young groups are achieving longevity and becoming permanent entities in their own right, and in the future will continue to provide greater and more direct competition to the established gangs. There is evidence to support this growing permanency: it appears as though the membership base of many of these incipient gangs is getting older, although they are still called 'youth gangs' by the police, a minority of members are now in their 30s (Jason Hewett 2009 pers. comm.).

Looking into the Future

There appears to be an obvious fork in the road for street gangs in this country. The first possible path relies on changes to popular culture and a diminished influence of hip-hop/gangsta culture that may see these young gangs fall away and those members who want to stay involved being absorbed into the traditional patched gangs. The second path will see these current incipient gangs maintain a distinct identity and mature into more organised entities and mark a distinct transformation in New Zealand's gang scene.

It is likely, however, the future will not prove so clear cut and that a middle ground is likely to occur. It seems likely that some of these LA style gangs will survive, and recognising the threat to their dominance, the patched gangs will respond by more actively seeking to recruit young members into their ranks. But whether they are absorbed or continue to exist as separate entities, these future adult gang members are likely to have a significant impact on wider gang activities moving forward. This potential to re-shape the gang scene is tied to a fundamental difference between the formational attitudes of LA-style street gangs and their patch wearing counterparts. To use Merton's (1938) terminology, we can see a very clear shift from 'retreatism' to 'innovation'.

In the early formation of the patched gangs in the 1960s and 1970s, members rejected the ideals of the mainstream and demonstrated their desire to drop out of society through purposely cultivated 'ridgie'[13] dress that was not in keeping with accepted social norms; importantly, this response did not require financial resources. In contrast, this new generation of gang members seeks the accoutrements of success, including designer clothes and jewellery (known as 'bling') that is highlighted in the images in many U.S. rap music videos. As Gruter and Versteegh (2001 p.141) said of the LA-style gangsters emerging in the Netherlands, they "wish to look like the boys in the daily MTV clips". However, this hypermaterialism requires significant financial resources, something that most of these young people are unlikely to be able to access though legitimate means. One inevitable response, therefore, will be a greater degree of profit driven crime within the New Zealand gangs.

CONCLUSION

From their inception in the 1960s and 1970s, the NZ gang scene had been dominated by both outlaw motorcycle clubs and patched street gangs. But in the first decade of the new millennium a reorganisation of the patched gang scene was clearly underway.

Like many businesses that have enjoyed a monopoly, the gangs, faced with changing trends and emerging competition, have struggled to adjust to the challenges of a new era.

While it is much too early to ring the death knell on patched gangs, the challenges faced by these gangs are not insignificant. Nevertheless, these groups have proven resilient in the face of past adversity and their revival cannot be discounted. However, changing fashions among young people mean that such gangs no longer hold the appeal that they once did for rebellious youth looking for a means to express themselves.

More significant to the future of gangs in New Zealand, then, is the rise of LA-style street gangs, which are most prominent in South Auckland, but exist all around the country. Not only are some of these groups perhaps set to challenge the dominant position enjoyed by the patched street gangs for decades, but they may prove to be more troublesome and criminally orientated than New Zealand's traditional gangs.

REFERENCES

Covey, H. C. (2003). *Street Gangs Throughout the World*. Springfield: Charles C Thomas Publisher.

Eggleston, E. J. (2000). New Zealand Youth Gangs: Key Findings and Recommendations from an Urban Ethnography. *Social Policy Journal of New Zealand*, (14), 148-163.

Germet, F. v. (2001). Crips in Orange: Gangs and Groups in The Netherlands. In M. W. Klein, H. J. Kerner, C. Maxson, & G. M. Weitekamp (Eds.), *The Eurogang Paradox: Street Gangs and Youth Groups in the U.S. and Europe*. Dordrecht: Kluwer Academic Publishers.

Gilbert, J. (2013). *Patched: the History of Gangs in New Zealand*. Auckland: Auckland University Press.

Gruter, P., & Versteegh, P. (2001). Towards a Problem-Oriented Approach to Youth Groups in The Hague. In M. W. Klein, H. J. Kerner, C. Maxson, & G. M. Weitekamp (Eds.), *The Eurogang Paradox: Street Gangs and Youth Groups in the U.S. and Europe.* Dordrecht: Kluwer Academic Publishers. doi:10.1007/978-94-010-0882-2_8

Hagedorn, J. M. (2005b). The Global Impact of Gangs. *Journal of Contemporary Criminal Justice, 21*(2), 153–169. doi:10.1177/1043986204273390

Hagedorn, J. M., Hazlehurst, K., & Hazlehurst, C. (1999). Gangs in a Global Perspective. *Contemporary Sociology, 28*(5), 609–611. doi:10.2307/2655049

Harpham, D. (2004). *Census of Prison Inmates and Home Detainees.* Wellington: Department of Corrections.

Kinner, S. A., & Degenhardt, L. (2008). Crystal Methamphetamine Smoking Among Regular Ecstasy Users in Australia: Increases in Use and Associations with Harm. *Drug and Alcohol Review, 27*(3), 292–300. doi:10.1080/09595230801919452 PMID:18368611

Klein, M. W. (1995). *The American Street Gang: Its Nature Prevalence and Control.* New York: Oxford University Press.

Lemert, E. M. (1951). *Social Pathology: A Systematic Approach to the Study of Sociopathic Behaviour.* New York: McGraw-Hill.

McKetin, R., Hickey, K., Devlin, K., & Lawrence, K. (2010). The Risk of Psychotic Symptoms Associated with Recreational Methamphetamine Use. *Drug and Alcohol Review, 29*(4), 358–363. doi:10.1111/j.1465-3362.2009.00160.x PMID:20636650

McKetin, R., Ross, J., Kelly, E., Baker, A., Lee, N., Lubman, D. I., & Mattick, R. (2008). Characteristics and Harms Associated with Injecting Versus Smoking Methamphetamine Among Methamphetamine Treatment Entrants. *Drug and Alcohol Review, 27*(3), 277–285. doi:10.1080/09595230801919486 PMID:18368609

Meek, J. (1992). Gangs in New Zealand Prisons. *Australian and New Zealand Journal of Criminology, 25*(3), 255–277. doi:10.1177/000486589202500304

Merton, R. K. (1938). Social Structure and Anomie. *American Sociological Review, 3*(October), 672–682. doi:10.2307/2084686

Ministry of Social Development. (2008b). *Youth Gangs in Counties Manukau.* Ministry of Social Development.

Mob Advisory Panel. (c1996). *Lower North Island Regions High Mortality Rate 1994-1995 Discussion Paper.* Dunedin: Unpublished.

Nadesu, A. (2009). *Reconviction patterns of released prison: A 60-month follow-up analysis.* Department of Corrections. Retrieved from http://www.corrections.govt.nz/__data/assets/pdf_file/0005/672764/Complete-Recidivism-Report-2009-DOC.pdf

New Zealand Police. (2006). *Tactical Problem Profile: Youth Gangs Counties Manukau East*. Intelligence Section, East Area.

New Zealand Police Association (2009). *Gangs and Organised Crime Bill: Submission of the New Zealand Police Association*. Author.

O'Reilly, D. (2005). *The Things that Bind Us*. Retrieved from http://www.nzedge.com/the-things-that-bind-us/

Richardson, J. W., & Scott, K. A. (2002). Rap Music and Its Violent Progeny: America's Culture of Violence in Context. *The Journal of Negro Education, 71*(3), 175–192. doi:10.2307/3211235

Ro, R. (1996). *Gangsta: Merchandising the Rhymes of Violence*. New York: St. Martin's Press.

Rose, T. (2001). Keepin' it Real. *The New Crisis, 108*(5), 22–25.

Scott, K. (1993). *Monster: The Autobiography of an L.A. Gang Member Sanyika Shakur A.K.A Monster Kody Scott*. New York: The Atlantic Monthly Press.

Tannenbaum, F. (1938). *Crime and the Community*. New York: University of Columbia Press.

Thrasher, F. M. (1927). *The Gang: A Study of 1,313 Gangs in Chicago*. Chicago: University of Chicago Press.

Topp, L., Degenhardt, L., Kaye, S., & Darke, S. (2002). The Emergence of Potent forms of Methamphetamine in Sydney Australia: A Case Study of the IDRS as a Strategic Early Warning. *Drug and Alcohol Review, 21*(4), 341–348. doi:10.1080/0959523021000023199 PMID:12537703

Zorick, T., Nestor, L., Miotto, K., Sugar, C., Hellemann, G., Scanlon, G., & London, E. D. et al. (2010). Withdrawal Symptoms in Abstinent Methamphetamine-Dependent Subjects. *Addiction (Abingdon, England), 105*(10), 1809–1818. doi:10.1111/j.1360-0443.2010.03066.x PMID:20840201

ENDNOTES

[1]   Officially, the Hells Angels record the date as 1961, but the club was in existence and recognized in 1960.

[2]   Although this name was inspired by the American 'Black Power' movement, the Black Power gang bears no relation to it and has no specific social, racial or revolutionary goals.

[3]   Despite losing the Hastings chapter the Auckland and Wanganui chapters remain strong.

[4]   The *Fast and the Furious* film series began with a film of the same title, which was released by Universal Studios in 2001. The film proved to be a box office hit and spawned six further films, the latest of which is due for release in 2015.

[5]   Such as delusional moods, grandiose delusions, delusions of control, delusions of persecution, or hallucinations

[6]   The Head Hunters are something of a crossover between an outlaw club and a patched street gang.

[7]   A 'tinnie' is a small amount of marijuana wrapped in tinfoil.

8   Clearly Turner's attitudes have changed over time as he was actually the instigator of a dramatic gang battle in Christchurch's Cathedral Square in 1980, which resulted in a Black Power member being hit on the back of the head with a small axe; an incident caught on film. A series of stills were reproduced in a book by Ray Comfort (1980).

9   Ta moko is traditional tattooing of the body and face.

10   Marsters has held the WKBF heavyweight title.

11   Initially the group designed a back patch but they have since taken up the usual form of LA-style street gang identification of bandanas, and hand signals.

12   In the mid-1990s, Death Row Records and Bad Boy Records were locked in a public hip-hop/gang war. The two most prominent casualties – one from each side – of this conflict were Tupak Shakur and Biggie Smalls, mentioned earlier.

13   'Ridgies' (derived from 'originals') is the set of original clothing a member was wearing when he was initiated into the gang and given his colours. These clothes were seen as sacred and were never washed, and thus they soon became dirty and tatty.

Compilation of References

(2010). What is Organized Crime? InVarese, F. (Ed.), *Organized Crime*. Routledge.

Aaronson, J. U. (1999). Recruiting, supporting, and retaining new teachers: A retrospective look at programs in the District of Columbia public schools. *The Journal of Negro Education, 68*(3), 335–342. doi:10.2307/2668105

Abeles, R. P. (1976). Relative deprivation, rising expectations and black militancy. *The Journal of Social Issues, 32*(2), 119–137. doi:10.1111/j.1540-4560.1976.tb02498.x

Aberson, C. L., Healy, M., & Romero, V. (2000). Ingroup bias and self-esteem: A meta-analysis. *Personality and Social Psychology Review, 4*(2), 157–173. doi:10.1207/S15327957PSPR0402_04

Abrams, D., & Hogg, M. A. (1988). Comments on the motivational status of self-esteem in social identity and intergroup discrimination. *European Journal of Social Psychology, 18*(4), 317–334. doi:10.1002/ejsp.2420180403

Adamson, C. (1998). Tribute, Turf, honor and the American street gang: Patterns of continuity and change since 1820. *Theoretical Criminology, 2*(1), 57–84. doi:10.1177/1362480698002001003

Addington, L. A. (2009). Cops and cameras: Public school security as a policy response in Columbine. *The American Behavioral Scientist, 52*(10), 1426–1446. doi:10.1177/0002764209332556

Addington, L. A., & Yablon, Y. (2011). How safe do students feel at school and while traveling to school?: A comparative look at Israel and the United States. *Journal of American Education, 117*(4), 465–493. doi:10.1086/660755

Agnew, R. (1994). The Techniques of Neutralization and Violence. *Criminology, 32*(4), 555–580. doi:10.1111/j.1745-9125.1994.tb01165.x

Agnew, R., & Brezina, T. (2010). Strain theories. In E. McLaughlin & T. Newburn (Eds.), *Sage handbook of criminological theory*. London: Sage Publications. doi:10.4135/9781446200926.n6

Akbaş, S., Ahmet, T., Koray, K., Ozan, P., Tülay, K., & Omer, B. (2013). Characteristics of Sexual Abuse in a Sample of Turkish Children With and Without Mental Retardation Referred for Legal Appraisal of the Psychological Repercussions. *Sexuality and Disability, 27*(4), 205–213. doi:10.1007/s11195-009-9139-7

Akers, R. L. (1997). *Criminological theories: Introduction and evaluation* (2nd ed.). Los Angeles, CA: Roxbury.

Alexander, C. (2000). *The Asian Gang: Ethnicity, Identity, Masculinity*. Berg 3PL.

Alexander, M. (2008). *The New Jim Crow: Mass Incarceration in the Age of Colorblindness*. The New Press.

Allen, K. P. (2010). Classroom management, bullying, and teacher practices. *Professional Educator, 34*(1), 1–16.

Allen, K., Cornell, D., Lorek, E., & Sheras, P. (2008). Response of school personnel to student threat assessment training. *School Effectiveness and School Improvement, 19*(3), 319–332. doi:10.1080/09243450802332184

Allport, G. W. (1954). *The Nature of Prejudice*. Reading, MA: Addison-Wesley.

Altbeker, A. (2007). A country at war with itself: South Africa's crisis of crime. Johannesburg: Jonathan Ball.

Alvarez, A., & Bachman, R. (1997). Predicting fear of assault at school and while going to and from school in an adolescent population. *Violence and Victims, 12*(1), 69–86. PMID:9360289

Alvirez, D., & Bean, F. et al. (Eds.). (1981). *The Mexican American Family. Ethnic Families in America*. New York, NY: Elsevier Press.

American Psychiatric Association. (2013). *Diagnostic and Statistical Manual of Mental Disorders (DSM-5)*. Arlington, VA: American Psychiatric Association.

American Psychological Association. (2008). Are zero tolerance policies effective in the schools? An evidentiary review and recommendations. *The American Psychologist, 63*(9), 852–862. doi:10.1037/0003-066X.63.9.852 PMID:19086747

Anderson, E. (1990). *Streetwise: Race, class, and change in an urban community*. Chicago: University of Chicago Press.

Anderson, E. (1990). *Streetwise: Race, Class, and Change in an Urban Community*. University of Chicago Press.

Anderson, E. (1999). *Code of the Street: Decency, violence, and the moral life of the inner city*. New York: Norton.

Anderson, E. (1999). *Code of the street: Decency, violence, and the moral life of the inner city*. New York: W.W. Norton & Company.

Anderson, E. (1999). *Code of the Street: Violence and the Moral Life of the Inner City*. W. W. Norton & Co.

Anderson, E. (2002). Ideologically Driven Critique. *American Journal of Sociology, 6*(6), 1533–1550. doi:10.1086/342772

Andersson, K. (2008). Constructing young masculinity: A case study of heroic discourse on violence. *Discourse & Society, 19*(2), 139–161. doi:10.1177/0957926507085949

Ang, R. P., Huan, V. S., Chua, S. H., & Lim, S. H. (2012). Gang affiliation, aggression, and violent offending in a sample of youth offenders. *Psychology, Crime & Law, 18*(8), 703–711. doi:10.1080/1068316X.2010.534480

Anti-Defamation League. (2007). *PENI Public Enemy Number 1: California's growing racist gang*. Anti-Defamation League. Retrieved on May 1, 2015 from http://archive.adl.org/learn/ext_us/peni_report.pdf

Aptekar, L. (1988). *Street Children of Cali*. Durham, NC: Duke University Press.

Aptekar, L. (1994). Street Children in the Developing World: A Review of Their Condition. *Cross-Cultural Research, 28*(3), 195–224. doi:10.1177/106939719402800301

Arson Required for Juvenile Gang Initiation. (1958, April 5). *Ludington Daily News*. Retrieved on July 6, 2014 from: http://news.google.com/newspapers

Athens, L. (1994). The self as soliloquy. *The Sociological Quarterly, 35*(3), 521–532. doi:10.1111/j.1533-8525.1994.tb01743.x

Athens, L. (1997). *Violent Criminal Acts and Actors: Revisited*. Champaign, IL: University of Illinois Press.

Augimeri, L. K., Enebrink, P., Walsh, M., & Jiang, D. (2000). Gender-specific childhood risk assessment tools: early assessment risk lists for boys (earl-20b) and girls (earl- 21g). In Handbook of Violence Risk Assessment. New York: Routledge Taylor & Francis Group.

Ayling, J. (2011). Gang change and evolutionary theory. *Crime, Law, and Social Change, 56*(1), 1–26. doi:10.1007/s10611-011-9301-x

Bacevich, A. J. (2005). The real World War IV. *The Wilson Quarterly, 29*(1), 36–61.

Bachelor, S. (2011). Beyond dichotomy: Towards an explanation of young women's involvement in violent street gangs. In B. Goldson (Ed.), *Youth in Crisis? 'Gangs', territoriality and violence*. London: Routledge.

Bachman, R., Randolph, A., & Brown, B. L. (2011). Predicting perceptions of fear at school and going to and from school for African American and White students: The effects of school security measures. *Youth & Society, 43*(2), 705–726. doi:10.1177/0044118X10366674

Bakken, B. (2004). Moral Panics, Crime Rates and Harsh Punishment in China. *Australian and New Zealand Journal of Criminology, 37*(1 suppl), 37–89. doi:10.1177/00048658040370S105

Bania, M. (2009). Gang violence among youth and young adults: (Dis)Affiliation and the potential for prevention. *Institute for the Prevention of Crime Review, 3*, 89–116.

Barfield, T. (Ed.). (1997). *The Dictionary of Anthropology*. Malden, MA: Blackwell Publishers Inc.

Bargent, J. (2013). Murders in Honduras Rising Despite Gang Truce. *Insight Crime*. Retrieved June 8, 2014 from http://www.insightcrime.org/news-briefs/murders-in-honduras-rising-despite-gang-truce

Barker, T. (2014). *Outlaw Motorcycle Gangs as Organized Crime Groups*. Springer. doi:10.1007/978-3-319-07431-3

Barnard, A., & Spencer, J. (Eds.). (2002). *Encyclopaedia of Social and Cultural Anthropology*. London, New York: Routledge.

Barry, M. (2006). *Youth Offending in Transition: The Search for Social Recognition*. London: Routledge.

Bartholow, B. D., Anderson, C. A., Carnagey, N. L., & Benjamin, A. R. Jr. (2005). Interactive effects of life experience and situational cues on aggression: The weapons priming effect in hunters and nonhunters. *Journal of Experimental Social Psychology, 41*(1), 48–60. doi:10.1016/j.jesp.2004.05.005

Battin, S. R., Hill, K. G., Abbott, R. D., Catalano, R. F., & Hawkins, J. D. (1998). The contribution of gang membership to delinquency beyond delinquent friends. *Criminology, 36*(1), 93–115. doi:10.1111/j.1745-9125.1998.tb01241.x

Bauder, H. (2002). *Work on the west side: Urban neighborhoods and the cultural exclusion of youth*. Boulder, CO: Lexington Books.

Bauman, Z. (2000). *Liquid Modernity*. Cambridge, MA: Polity Press.

Beaujot, R., & Kerr, D. (2007). *Emerging youth transition patterns in Canada: Opportunities and risks*. Ottawa, ON: Policy Research Initiative.

Beazley, H. (2003). The construction and protection of individual and collective identities by street children and youth in Indonesia. *Children, Youth and Environments, 13*. Retrieved from colorado.edu/journals/cye

Becker, P. J., Byers, B., & Jipson, A. (March 2000). The contentious American debate: The First Amendment and internet-based hate speech. *International Review of Law, Computers & Technology, 14*.

Becker, H. S. (1997). *Outsiders: Studies in the sociology of deviance.* New York: Free Press.

Beher, W. J., Aston, R. A., & Meyer, H. A. (2001). Elementary- and middle-school teachers' reasoning about intervening in school violence: An examination of violence-prone school subcontexts. *Journal of Moral Education, 30*(2), 131–153. doi:10.1080/03057240120061388

Beirich, H. & Potok, M. (2005). *CNN's Lou Dobs refuses to cover anti-Latino racism in anti-immigration activist groups and citizen border patrols.* Intelligence Report. Southern Poverty Law Center.

Beirich, H. (n.d.). *Racist music.* Southern Poverty Law Center. Retrieved October 31, 2014 from http://www.splcenter. org/get-informed/intelligence-files/ideology/racist-music/racist-musicon

Beirich, H. (2014a). *White homicide worldwide. Intelligence Report.* Southern Poverty Law Center.

Bello, M. (2008, October 21). White supremacist target middle America. *USA Today.*

Bemak, F. (1996). Street researcher – A new paradigm redefining future research with street children. *Childhood, 3*(2), 147–156. doi:10.1177/0907568296003002002

Bennett, B., Gamelli, R., Duchene, R., Atkocaitis, D., & Plunkett, J. (2004). Burn Education Awareness Recognition And Support (Bears): A Community-Based Juvenile Firesetters Assessment And Treatment Program. *Journal of Burn Care & Research; Official Publication of the American Burn Association, 25*(3), 324–327.

Bennett, T., & Holloway, K. (2004). Gang membership, drugs and crime in the UK. *The British Journal of Criminology, 44*(3), 305–323. doi:10.1093/bjc/azh025

Berecz, T., & Domina, K. (2012). *Domestic Extremism in Europe: Threat Landscape.* Athena Institute.

Berkowitz, L., & Harmon-Jones, E. (2004). Toward an understanding of the determinants of anger. *Emotion (Washington, D.C.), 4*(2), 107–130. doi:10.1037/1528-3542.4.2.107 PMID:15222847

Best, J., & Hutchinson, M. M. (1996). The gang initiation rite as a motif in crime discourse. *Justice Quarterly, 13*(3), 383–404. doi:10.1080/07418829600093021

Beubien, J. (2011). *El Salvador Fears Ties Between Cartels, Street Gangs.* National Public Radio. Retrieved April 24, 2012 from http://www.npr.org/2011/06/01/136829224/el-salvadorfears-ties-between-cartels-street-gangs

Bhui, K., Warfa, N., & Jones, E. (2014) *Is Violent Radicalisation Associated with Poverty, Migration, Poor Self-Reported Health and Common Mental Disorders?* Retrieved 12 October 2014 from: http://www.plosone.org/article/info%3Adoi%2F10.1371%2Fjournal.pone.0090718

Bhui, H. S. (2009). Foreign national prisoners: Issues and debates. In H. S. Bhui (Ed.), *Race & Criminal Justice.* Sage. doi:10.4135/9781446215951.n9

Bilefsky, D., & Hubbard, B. (2015, May 5). ISIS Claims Link to Shooting at Texas Event Showing Muhammad Cartoons. *New York Times.* Retrieved May 5, 2015 from http://www.nytimes.com/2015/05/06/world/middleeast/isis-texas-muhammad-cartoons.html

Bisin, A., Patacchini, E., Verdier, T., & Zenou, Y. (2011). *Formation and Persistence of Oppositional Identities.* CEPR Discussion Paper No. DP8380. Retrieved July 12, 2014 from http://ssrn.com/abstract=1846262

Bjerregaard, B., & Lizotte, A. J. (1995). Gun ownership and gang membership. *The Journal of Criminal Law & Criminology, 86*(1), 37–58. doi:10.2307/1143999

Blanton, H., Bunk, B. P., Gibbons, F. X., & Kuyper, H. (1999). When better-than others compare upward: Choice of comparison and comparative evaluation as independent predictors of academic performance. *Journal of Personality and Social Psychology*, *76*(3), 420–430. doi:10.1037/0022-3514.76.3.420

Blaskovich, J., Ginsburg, G. P., & Howe, R. C. (1975). Blackjack and the risky shift. II: Monetary stakes. *Journal of Experimental Social Psychology*, *11*(3), 224–232. doi:10.1016/S0022-1031(75)80024-2

Blatchford, C. (2009). *The Black Hand: The Story of Rene "Boxer" Enriquez and His Life in the Mexican Mafia*. Harper Collins.

Blee, K. (1996). Becoming a Racist: Women in Contemporary Ku Klux Klan and Neo- Nazi Groups. *Gender & Society*, *10*(6), 680–702. doi:10.1177/089124396010006002

Blosnich, J., & Bossarte, R. (2011). Low-level violence in schools: Is there an association between school safety measures and peer victimization? *The Journal of School Health*, *81*(2), 107–113. doi:10.1111/j.1746-1561.2010.00567.x PMID:21223278

Blumer, H. (1958). Race prejudice as a sense of group position. *Pacific Sociological Review*, *1*(1), 3–7. doi:10.2307/1388607

Bobo, L. (1988). Attitudes toward the black political movement: Trends, meaning, and effects on racial policy preferences. *Social Psychology Quarterly*, *51*(4), 287–302. doi:10.2307/2786757

Bolden, C. (2013). Tales From the hood: An emic perspective on gang Joining and gang desistance. *Criminal Justice Review*, *38*(4), 473–490. doi:10.1177/0734016813509267

Bolden, C. L. (2012). Liquid soldiers: Fluidity and gang membership. *Deviant Behavior*, *33*(3), 207–222. doi:10.1080/01639625.2010.548655

Bonachich, E. (1972). A theory of ethnic antagonism: The split labor market. *American Sociological Review*, *37*(5), 547–559. doi:10.2307/2093450 PMID:4634743

Borgeson, K., & Valeri, R. (Eds.). (2009). *Terrorism in America*. Boston, MA: Jones & Bartlett.

Borgeson, K., & Valeri, R. M. (2004). Faces of hate. *Journal of Applied Sociology*, *21*(2), 99–111.

Borgeson, K., & Valeri, R. M. (2007). The enemy of my enemy is my friend. *The American Behavioral Scientist*, *51*(2), 182–195. doi:10.1177/0002764207306050

Bosworth, K., Ford, L., & Hernandaz, D. (2011). School climate factors contributing to student and faulty perceptions of safety in select Arizona schools. *The Journal of School Health*, *81*(4), 194–201. doi:10.1111/j.1746-1561.2010.00579.x PMID:21392011

Bouchard, M., & Spindler, A. (2010). Groups, gangs, and delinquency: Does organization matter? *Journal of Criminal Justice*, *38*(5), 921–933. doi:10.1016/j.jcrimjus.2010.06.009

Bourdieu, P. (1993). *The Field of Cultural Production*. New York: Columbia University Press.

Boyce, J., & Cotter, A. (2013). *Homicide in Canada, 2012. Juristat, 33(1)*. Ottawa, ON: Statistics Canada.

Bracy, N. L. (2011). Student perceptions of high-security school environments. *Youth & Society*, *43*(1), 365–305. doi:10.1177/0044118X10365082

Bradshaw, C. P., Waasdorp, T. E., Goldweber, A., & Johnson, S. L. (2013). Bullies, gangs, drugs, and school: Understanding the overlap and the role of ethnicity and urbanicity. *Journal of Youth and Adolescence*, *42*(2), 220–234. doi:10.1007/s10964-012-9863-7 PMID:23180070

Braga, A. A., Kennedy, D. M., Waring, E. W., & Piehl, A. M. (2001). Problem-oriented policing, deterrence, and youth violence: An evaluation of Boston's Operation Ceasefire. *Journal of Research in Crime and Delinquency, 38*, 195–225.

Braga, A. A., Pierce, G. L., McDevitt, J., Bond, B., & Cronin, S. (2008). The strategic prevention of gun violence among gang-involved offenders. *Justice Quarterly, 25*(1), 132–162. doi:10.1080/07418820801954613

Brantingham, P. J., Tita, G. E., Short, M. B., & Reid, S. E. (2012). The ecology of gang territorial boundaries. *Criminology, 50*(3), 851–885. doi:10.1111/j.1745-9125.2012.00281.x

Brett, A. (2004). 'Kindling theory' in arson: How dangerous are firesetters? *The Australian and New Zealand Journal of Psychiatry, 38*, 419–425. PMID:15209833

Brewer, M. B. (1979). In-group bias in the minimal intergroup situation: A cognitive-motivational analysis. *Psychological Bulletin, 86*(2), 307–324. doi:10.1037/0033-2909.86.2.307

Brezina, T., Agnew, R., Cullen, F. T., & Wright, J. P. (2004). The Code of the Street: A Qualitative Assessment of Elijah Anderson's Subculture of Violence Thesis and Its Contribution to Youth Violence Research. *Youth Violence and Juvenile Justice, 2*, 303-328.

Britton, D. (2011). *The gender of crime.* Lanham, MD: AltaMira Press.

Broadhurst, R. (2012). Chinese 'Black Societies' and triad-like organised crime in China. In F. Alum & S. Gilmour (Eds.), *Routledge Handbook of Transnational Organised Crime* (pp. 157–171). London: Routledge. doi:10.4324/9780203698341.ch10

Broadhurst, R. (2013). The suppression of black societies in China. *Trends in Organized Crime, 16*(1), 95–113. doi:10.1007/s12117-012-9174-0

Broadhurst, R., & Wa, L. K. (2009). The Transformation of Triad 'Dark Societies' in Hong Kong: The Impact of Law Enforcement, Socio –Economic and Political Change. *Security Challenges, 5*(4), 1–38.

Brookes, M., Glynn, M., & Wilson, D. (2012). Black men, therapeutic communities and HMP Grendon. *Therapeutic Communities: The International Journal of Therapeutic Communities, 33*(1), 16–26. doi:10.1108/09641861211286294

Brookman, F., Copes, H., & Hochstetler, A. (2011). Street codes as formula stories: How inmates recount violence. *Journal of Contemporary Ethnography, 40*(4), 397–424. doi:10.1177/0891241611408307

Brooks, B. (2012). Sao Paulo Could Face Gang War with Truce Collapse. *Associated Press.* Retrieved August 1, 2014 from http://news.yahoo.com/sao-paulo-could-face-gang-war-truce-collapse-082756745.html

Brown, D. H. (2003). *Santería enthroned: art, ritual, and innovation in an Afro-Cuban religion.* Chicago: University of Chicago Press.

Brown, D., & Hogg, R. (1992). Essentialism, Radical Criminology and Left Realism. *Australian and New Zealand Journal of Criminology, 25*(2), 195–230. doi:10.1177/000486589202500302

Brown, E. (2010). Race, urban governance, and crime control: Creating model cities. *Law & Society Review, 44*(3/4), 769–804. doi:10.1111/j.1540-5893.2010.00422.x PMID:21132958

Brown, J. K. (1963). A Cross-cultural study of female initiation rites. *American Anthropologist, 65*(4), 837–853. doi:10.1525/aa.1963.65.4.02a00040

Bullock, K., & Tilley, N. (2002). *Shooting, gangs and violent incidents in Manchester: Developing a crime reduction strategy.* London: Home Office.

Burnett, G. (1999). *Gangs in Schools*. ERIC Digest [Online]. Retrieved from: http://eric-web.tc.columbia.edu/digests/dig99.html

Burnstein, E., & Vinokur, A. (1973). Testing two classes of theories about group-induced shifts in individual choice. *Journal of Experimental Social Psychology, 9*(2), 123–137. doi:10.1016/0022-1031(73)90004-8

Bushway, S. D., Piquero, A., Broidy, L. M., Cauffman, E., & Mazerolle, P. (2001). An empirical framework for studying desistance as a process. *Criminology, 39*(2), 491–515. doi:10.1111/j.1745-9125.2001.tb00931.x

Butcher, M., & Thomas, M. (2003). Being in-between. In M. Butcher & M. Thomas (Eds.), *Ingenious: Emerging Youth Cultures in Urban Australia*. Sydney: Pluto Press.

Campbell, D. (2014). *Intentional Fires*. National Fire Protection Agency. Retrieved on September 15, 2014 from: http://www.nfpa.org

Campbell, A. (1987). Self definition by rejection: The case of gang girls. *Social Problems, 34*(5), 451–466. doi:10.2307/800541

Campbell, H. (2000). The Glass Phallus: Pub(lic) Masculinity and Drinking in Rural New Zealand. *Rural Sociology, 65*(4), 562–581. doi:10.1111/j.1549-0831.2000.tb00044.x

Camp, G. M., & Camp, C. G. (1985). *Prison Gangs: Their Extent, Nature and Impact on Prisons*. US Dept. of Justice. Washington, DC: US Govt. Printing Office.

Camp, G. M., & Camp, C. G. (1985). *Prison Gangs: Their Extent, Nature and Impact on Prisons*. Washington, DC: US Govt. Printing Office.

Cao, L., & Dai, Y. (2001). Inequality in Crime and China. In J. Liu, L. Zhang, & S. Messner (Eds.), *Crime and Social Control in a Changing China* (pp. 73–88). Westport, Conn.: Greenwood Press.

Carlie, M. (2002). *Into The Abyss: A Personal Journey into the World of Street Gangs*. Retrieved from http://people.missouristate.edu/MichaelCarlie/site_map.htm

Carlson, M., Marcus-Newhall, A., & Miller, N. (1990). Effects of situational aggression cues: A quantitative review. *Journal of Personality and Social Psychology, 58*(4), 622–633. doi:10.1037/0022-3514.58.4.622 PMID:14570078

Carrington, P. J. (2011). Crime and Social Network Analysis. In J. Scott & P. J. Carrington (Eds.), *The SAGE Handbook of Network Analysis*. Los Angeles, CA: SAGE Publications Inc. doi:10.4135/9781446294413.n17

Carroll, L. (1974). *Hacks, Blacks and Cons: Race Relations in a Maximum Security Prison*. Waveland Press, Inc.

Carson, D. C., Peterson, D., & Esbensen, F.-A. (2013). Youth gang desistance: An examination of the effect of different operational definitions of desistance on the motivations, methods, and consequences associated with leaving the gang. *Criminal Justice Review, 38*(4), 510–534. doi:10.1177/0734016813511634

Caruso, P. (1996). Individuality vs. conformity: The issue behind school uniforms. *National Association of Secondary School Principals (NASSP) Bulletin, 80*, 83–88.

Caspi, A., Bem, D. J., & Elder, G. H. Jr. (1989). Continuities and consequences of interactional styles across the life course. *Journal of Personality, 57*(2), 375–406. doi:10.1111/j.1467-6494.1989.tb00487.x PMID:2769561

Catalano, R., Dooley, D., Novaco, R., Wilson, G., & Hough, R. (1993). Using ECA survey data to examine the effect of job layoffs on violent behavior. *Hospital & Community Psychiatry, 44*, 874–878. PMID:8225302

Caudill, J. W. (2010). Back on the swagger: Institutional release and recidivism timing among gang affiliates. *Youth Violence and Juvenile Justice, 8*(1), 58–70. doi:10.1177/1541204009339872

Center for Research on Education Outcomes. (2013). *National charter school study, executive summary.* Stanford University. Retrieved from: http://credo.stanford.edu/documents/NCSS%202013%20Executive%20Summary.pdf

Centre for Social Justice. (2012). *Time to Wake Up: Tackling gangs one year after the riots.* Retrieved 11 October 2014 from: http://www.centreforsocialjustice.org.uk/UserStorage/pdf/Pdf%20reports/Gangs-Report.pdf

Cernkovich, S., & Giordano, P. (2001). Stability and change in antisocial behavior: The transition from adolescence to early adulthood. *Criminology, 39*(2), 371–410. doi:10.1111/j.1745-9125.2001.tb00927.x

Champion, H. L., & Durant, R. H. (2001). Exposure to violence and victimization and the use of violence by adolescents in the United States. *Minerva Pediatrica, 53*, 189–197. PMID:11455306

Chang, V. W. (2006). *Body Capital and Socioeconomic Mobility.* PARC Research Report. Retrieved 23 September 2014 from: http://gcc.pop.upenn.edu/pilot-award/body-capital-and-socioeconomic-mobility

Chatterjee, J. (2006). *A research report on youth gangs: Problems, perspectives and priorities.* Ottawa, ON: Research and Evaluation Branch, Community, Contract and Aboriginal Policing Services Directorate, Royal Canadian Mounted Police.

Chen, S. (2009, Feb 2). Growing Hate Groups Blame Obama Economy. *CNN.com.*

Chen, G. (2008). Communities, students, schools and school crime: A confirmatory study of crime in U.S. high schools. *Urban Education, 43*(3), 301–318. doi:10.1177/0042085907311791

Chettleburgh, M. C. (2003). *2002 Canadian police survey on youth gangs.* Ottawa, ON: Astwood Strategy Corporation.

Chettleburgh, M. C. (2007). *Young thugs: Inside the dangerous world of Canadian street gangs.* Toronto, ON: Harper Collins Publishers Ltd.

Cheurprakobkit, S., & Bartsch, R. A. (2005). Security measures on school crime in Texas middle and high schools. *Educational Research, 47*(2), 235–250. doi:10.1080/00131880500104366

Che, W. (1992). *Problems of juvenile delinquency in Hong Kong.* Hong Kong: China Book.

Chin, K. (1986). *Chinese triad societies, tongs organised crime and the street gangs in Asia and the United States.* (Unpublished Doctoral Dissertation). University of Pennsylvania.

Chin, K. (1990a). Chinese Gangs and Extortion. In Gangs in America. Sage Publications.

Chin, K. (2009). Hejiin: Organised Crime, Business and Politics in Taiwan. In T. W. Lo (Ed.), *Beyond Social Capital: A Case of Triad Financial Crime in Hong Kong and China.* City University of Hong Kong.

China Daily. (2001, February 17). Curbing youth crime. *China Daily.*

China Daily. (2008, December 30). Juvenile crime up among migrants. *China Daily.*

China Daily. (2009a, February 16). Crime is a risk to stability: Official. *China Daily.*

China Daily. (2009b, February 20). Economic crime on rise, firms warned. *China Daily.*

China Daily. (2009c, February 27). Organized crime increases in 2008. *China Daily.*

China Daily. (2009d, April 28). Crackdown on crime in run-up to National Day. *China Daily.*

China Daily. (2009e, August 28). Gangs nabbed in Chongqing: 469 still at large. *China Daily*.

China Daily. (2009f, September 25). Anti-crime sweep smashes 1,300 gangs in south China. *China Daily*.

China Daily. (2009g, August 31). China's 'e-crime' gangs target older women. *China Daily*.

China Daily. (2009h, September 1). Courts convict nearly 13,000 on organised crime charges. *China Daily*.

China Daily. (2009i, December 16). Money-laundering gang trial opens in SW China. *China Daily*.

China Daily. (2012, August 17). Nearly 1,200 snared in month long crackdown. *China Daily*.

China Daily. (2013a, September 23). Teen killers spur discussion on youth crime. *China Daily*.

China Daily. (2013b, September 23). Teen killers spur discussion on youth crime. *China Daily*.

China Daily. (2015a, May 11). Drug users exceed 14 million in China. *China Daily*.

China Daily. (2015b, June 25). String of youth violence cases shocks nation. *China Daily*.

China Daily. (2015c, July 10). Gang activity in Guangdong poses 'serious threat'. *China Daily*.

Ching, H., Daffern, M., & Thomas, S. (2012). Appetitive Violence: A New Phenomenon? *Psychiatry, Psychology and Law*, *19*(5), 745–763. doi:10.1080/13218719.2011.623338

Chin, K. (1990). *Chinese Subculture and Criminology: Non Traditional Crime Groups in America*. Westport, CT: Greenwood Press.

Chin, K. (1990b). *Chinese subculture and criminality: Non-traditional crime groups in America*. New York: Greenwood Press.

Chin, K., Kelly, R., & Fagan, J. (1993). Methodological issues in studying Chinese gang extortion. *The Gang Journal*, *1*(2), 25–36.

Chin, K., & Zhang, S. (2003). The declining significance of Triad Societies in Transnational Illegal Activities: A Structural Deficiency Perspective. *The British Journal of Criminology*, *43*(3), 469–488. doi:10.1093/bjc/43.3.469

Chitradub, S. (1998). *The Culture of Street Children in Thai Society*. Development Consultancy Services.

Chivis, M. (2012). The Knights Templar Cartel is Calling a Short Truce. *Borderland Beat*. Retrieved April 30, 2014 from http://www.borderlandbeat.com/2012/03/knightstemplars-cartel-is-calling.html

Chuanjiao, X. (2009a, May 7). Raising the issue of China's Troubled teens. *China Daily*.

Chuanjiao, X. (2009b, June 26). Gangsters muscling their way into drugs. *China Daily*.

Chu, C. M., Daffern, M., Thomas, S., & Lim, J. Y. (2012). Violence risk and gang affiliation in youth offenders: A recidivism study. *Psychology, Crime & Law*, *18*(3), 299–315. doi:10.1080/1068316X.2010.481626

Chu, Y. K. (2000). *The Triads as Business*. London: Routledge.

Cialdini, R. B., Borden, R. J., Thorne, A., Walker, M. R., Freeman, S., & Sloan, L. R. (1976). Basking in reflected glory: Three (football) field studies. *Journal of Personality and Social Psychology*, *34*(3), 366–374. doi:10.1037/0022-3514.34.3.366

Cialdini, R. B., & Richardson, K. D. (1980). Two indirect tactics of image management: Basking and blasting. *Journal of Personality and Social Psychology*, *39*(3), 406–415. doi:10.1037/0022-3514.39.3.406

CivilRights.org. (2009). *The State of Hate: White Supremacist Groups Growing, Confronting the New Faces of Hate: Hate Crimes in America 2009*. Author.

Cloward, R. A., & Ohlin, L. (1960). *Delinquency and Opportunity*. Glencoe: Free Press.

Codol, J. P. (1975). On the so called 'superior conformity of the self' behavior: Twenty experimental investigations. *European Journal of Social Psychology*, *5*(4), 457–501. doi:10.1002/ejsp.2420050404

Coenen, I. (2013) Blood out: Nihilism in gang culture. In Confronting Death: College Students on the Community of Mortals. Bloomington, IN: iUniverse LLC.

Cohen, A. K. (1955). *Delinquent boys: The culture of the gang*. New York: Free Press.

Cohen, A. K. (1955). *Delinquent Boys: The Culture of the Gang*. New York: The Free Press.

Cole, R., Crandall, R., Kourofsky, C., Sharp, D., & Blaakman, S. (2006). *Juvenile Firesetting: A Community Guide To Prevention & Intervention*. Elizabeth: Fireproof Children/Prevention.

Collier, R. (1998). *Masculinities, Crime and Criminology*. London: Sage.

Collins, J., Noble, G., Poynting, S., & Tabar, P. (2000). *Kebabs, Kids, Cops & Crime: Youth, Ethnicity & Crime*. Sydney: Pluto Press.

Collins, R. (1979). *The credentialed society: A historical sociology of education and stratification*. Waltham, MA: Academic Press.

Collins, R. (1981). On microfoundations of macrosociology. *American Journal of Sociology*, *86*(5), 984–1014. doi:10.1086/227351

Collins, R. (2005). *Interaction ritual chains*. Princeton University Press.

Collins, R. (2009). *Violence: a Micro-sociological Theory*. Princeton, NJ: Princeton University Press.

Collins, R. L. (1996). For better or for worse: The impact of upward social comparison on self-evaluation. *Psychological Bulletin*, *119*(1), 51–69. doi:10.1037/0033-2909.119.1.51

Combi, C. (2013, August 6). Real bad girls, extraordinary insight into London's female gang culture. *The Independent*.

Conlin, M., & Prasso, S. (2002). A Plague of Hate Sites. *Business Week, 3770*, 14.

Connell, R. (2000). *The Men and the Boys*. Sydney: Allen & Unwin.

Connell, R. W. (1995). *Masculinities*. Cambridge, UK: Polity Press.

Connell, R. W., & Messerschmidt, J. W. (2005). Hegemonic masculinity rethinking the concept. *Gender & Society*, *19*(6), 829–859. doi:10.1177/0891243205278639

Conners-Burrow, N., Johnson, D., Whiteside-Mansell, L., McKelvey, L., & Gargus, R. A. (2009). Adults matter: Protecting children from the negative impacts of bullying. *Psychology in the Schools*, *46*(7), 593–604. doi:10.1002/pits.20400

Consequences of Right Wing Extremism. (n.d.). Anti-Defamation League. Retrieved October 31, 2014 from http://www.adl.org/assets/pdf/combating-hate/The-Consequences-of-Right-Wing-Extremism-on-the-Internet.pdfon

Copes, H., & Hochstetler, A. (2003). Situational Construction of Masculinity among Street Thieves. *Journal of Contemporary Ethnography*, *32*(3), 279–304. doi:10.1177/0891241603032003002

Copes, H., Hochstetler, A., & Forsyth, C. J. (2013). Peaceful warriors: Codes for violence among adult male bar fighters. *Criminology*, *51*(3), 761–794. doi:10.1111/1745-9125.12019

Corsaro, N., Brunson, R. K., & McGarrell, E. F. (2013). Problem-Oriented Policing and Open-Air Drug Markets: Examining the Rockford Pulling Levers Deterrence Strategy. *Crime and Delinquency*, *59*(7), 1085–1107. doi:10.1177/0011128709345955

Corsaro, W. A. (1983). Script recognition, articulation and expansion in children's role play. *Discourse Processes*, *6*(1), 1–19. doi:10.1080/01638538309544551

Corsaro, W. A. (1992). Interpretive reproduction in children's peer cultures. *Social Psychology Quarterly*, *55*(2), 160–177. doi:10.2307/2786944

Cotton, P. (1992). Violence Decreases with Gang Truce. *Journal of the American Medical Association*, *268*(4), 443–444. doi:10.1001/jama.1992.03490040011002 PMID:1619732

Covey, H. C. (2003). *Street Gangs Throughout the World*. Springfield: Charles C Thomas Publisher.

Crawford, M. D., Whitbeck, L. B., & Hoyt, D. R. (2011). Propensity for Violence Among Homeless and Runaway Adolescents: An Event History Analysis. *Crime and Delinquency*, *57*(6), 950–968. doi:10.1177/0011128709335100 PMID:22865932

Crewe, B. (2009). *The Prisoner Society – Power, Adaptation and Social Life in an English Prison*. Oxford University Press. doi:10.1093/acprof:oso/9780199577965.001.0001

Criminal Intelligence Service Canada (CISC). (2006). *Project spectrum: 2006 situational overview of street gangs in Canada*. Ottawa, ON: Author.

Criminal Justice Joint Inspection. (2010). *The management of gang issues among children and young people in prison custody and the community: a joint thematic review*. London: HM Chief Inspector of Prisons.

Crowley, S. L., & Foley, L. J. (2008). *Gendering Bodies*. Lanham, MD: Rowman and Littlefield.

Cunneen, C., & White, R. (2006). Australia: Control, Containment or Empowerment? In J. Muncie & B. Goldson (Eds.), *Comparative Youth Justice*. London: Sage. doi:10.4135/9781446212608.n8

Cureton, S. (2011). *Black Vanguards and Black Gangsters – From Seeds of Discontent to a Declaration of War*. University of America Press.

Cureton, S. R. (2011). *Black Vanguards to Black Gangsters: From Seeds of Discontent to a Declaration of War*. University Press of America.

Daily Telegraph. (n.d., August 8). MAOA Gene and Maori Violence. *Daily Telegraph*.

Dasgupta, P. (2010). *A Matter of Trust: Social Capital and Economic Development*. SCI Discussion Paper Series. Manchester, UK: Sustainable Consumption Institute; Working Paper No. 1.

Das, V. (2007). *Life and Words: Violence and the Descent into the Ordinary*. Berkeley, CA: University of California Press.

Date, J. (2008, Oct 27). Feds Thwart Alleged Obama Assassination Plot. *ABC News*.

David, C. F., & Kisner, J. A. (2000). Do Positive Self-Perceptions Have a `Dark Side'? Examination of the Link between Perceptual Bias. *Journal of Abnormal Child Psychology*, *28*(4), 327–337. doi:10.1023/A:1005164925300 PMID:10949958

Davids, N. (2012, February 14). South Africa's capital of organized crime. *Times Live.*

Davies, J. C. (1962). Toward a theory of revolution. *American Sociological Review, 27*(1), 5–19. doi:10.2307/2089714

Davies, M. (2008). A Childish Culture?: Shared understandings, agency and intervention: an anthropological study of street children in northwest Kenya. *Childhood, 15*(3), 309–330. doi:10.1177/0907568208091666

Davis, M. (1999). *Ecology of fear: Los Angeles and the imagination of disaster.* New York: Vintage Books.

De La Rue, L., & Espelage. (2014, July). Family and abuse characteristics of gang-involved, pressured-to-join, and non-gang involved girls. *Psychology of Violence,* 253-65.

Decker, S. H., & Pyrooz, D. C. (2010). Gang violence worldwide: Context, culture and country. In Graduate Institute of International and Development Studies (Ed.), Small arms survey, 2010: Gangs, groups, and guns (pp. 129-155). Cambridge, UK: Cambridge University Press.

Decker, S. H. (1996). Collective and normative features of gang violence. *Justice Quarterly, 13*(2), 243–264. doi:10.1080/07418829600092931

Decker, S. H. (2001). *From the Street to the Prison: Understanding and Responding to Gangs.* Impact Publications.

Decker, S. H. (2004). *From the street to the prison: Understanding and responding to gangs.* Alexandria, VA: American Correctional Association.

Decker, S. H. (2007). Youth gangs and violent behavior. In D. J. Flannery, A. T. Vazsonyi, & I. D. Waldman (Eds.), *The Cambridge Handbook of Violent Behavior and Aggression* (pp. 388–402). Cambridge, MA: Cambridge University Press. doi:10.1017/CBO9780511816840.019

Decker, S. H., & Kempf-Leonard, K. (1991). Constructing gangs: The social definition of youth activities. *Criminal Justice Policy Review, 5*(4), 271–291. doi:10.1177/088740349100500401

Decker, S. H., & Lauritsen, J. L. (2002). Leaving the gang. In C. R. Huff (Ed.), *Gangs in America* (3rd ed., pp. 51–67). Thousand Oaks, CA: Sage Publications. doi:10.4135/9781452232201.n4

Decker, S. H., & Pyrooz, D. C. (2010). On the validity and reliability of gang homicide: A comparison of disparate sources. *Homicide Studies, 14*(4), 359–376. doi:10.1177/1088767910385400

Decker, S. H., Pyrooz, D. C., Sweeten, G., & Moule, R. K. Jr. (2014). Validating self-nomination in gang research: Assessing difference in gang embeddedness across non-current, and former gang members.[online first]. *Journal of Quantitative Criminology, 30*(4), 577–598. doi:10.1007/s10940-014-9215-8

Decker, S. H., & Van Winkle, B. (1996). *Life in the gang.* Cambridge, England: Cambridge University Press. doi:10.1017/CBO9781139174732

Decker, S., Bynum, T., & Weisel, D. (1998). A Tale of Two Cities: Gangs as Organized Crime Groups. *Justice Quarterly, 15*(3), 395–425. doi:10.1080/07418829800093821

DeKeseredy, W. S., & Schwartz, M. D. (2005). Masculinities and Interpersonal Violence. In Handbook of Studies on Men and Masculinities. Sage Publications. doi:10.4135/9781452233833.n20

Del Barco, M. (2011, January 6). L.A.'s homicide rate lowest in four decades. *National Public Radio.*

DeMatteo, D. S., Marlowe, D. B., & Festinger, D. S. (2006). Secondary Prevention Services for Clients Who Are Low Risk in Drug Court: A Conceptual Model. *Crime and Delinquency, 52*(1), 114–134. doi:10.1177/0011128705281751

DeMitchell, T. A., & Cobb, C. D. (2003). Policy responses to violence in our schools: An exploration of security as a fundamental value. *B.Y.U. Education and Law Journal*, 459-484.

Deng, A. (2011, June 23). Bloody-minded youth. *China Daily*.

Deng, A. (2012, September 6). Just one of the gang. *China Daily*.

Densely, J. A. (2013). *How gangs work: An ethnography of youth violence*. Oxford: Palgrave MacMillan. doi:10.1057/9781137271518

Densely, J. A. (2014). It's gang life, but not as we know it: The evolution of gang business. *Crime and Delinquency*, *60*(4), 517–546. doi:10.1177/0011128712437912

Densley, J. A. (2012). Street Gang Recruitment: Signalling, Screening, and Selection. *Social Problems*, *59*(3), 301–321. doi:10.1525/sp.2012.59.3.301

Department of Justice. (1912). *Annual Report for the Year1912*. Author.

Deuchar, R. (2009). *Gangs, Marginalised Youth and Social Capital*. Trentham Books.

Devine, J. (1996). *Maximum security: The culture of violence in inner-city schools*. Chicago: University of Chicago Press.

DeVoe, J., & Kaffenberger, S. (2005). *Student reports of bullying: Results from the 2001 School Crime Supplement to the National Crime Victimization Survey* (NCES 2005-310). U.S. Department of Education, National Center for Education Statistics.

DeVoe, J., Bauer, L., & Hill, M. (2011). *Student victimization in U.S. schools: Results from the 2009 School Crime Supplement from the National Crime Victimization Survey. U.S. Deparment of Education, National Center for Education Statistics*. Washington, D.C.: U.S. Government Printing Office.

Dewall, C. N., Baumeister, R. F., Stillman, T. F., & Gailliot, M. T. (2007). Violence restrained: Effects of self-regulation and its depletion on aggression. *Journal of Experimental Social Psychology*, *43*(1), 62–76. doi:10.1016/j.jesp.2005.12.005

Di Placido, C., Simon, T. L., Witte, T. D., Gu, D., & Wong, S. C. P. (2006). Treatment of gang members can reduce recidivism and institutional misconduct. *Law and Human Behavior*, *30*(1), 93–114. doi:10.1007/s10979-006-9003-6 PMID:16729210

Dickens, G. L., Sugarman, P. A., & Gannon, T. A. (Eds.). (2012). Fire setting and Mental Health Theory, Research and Practice. London: RCPsych Publications.

DiIorio, C., Pluhar, E., & Belcher, L. (2003, December08). Parent-child communication about sexuality: A review of the literature from 1980–2002. *Journal of HIV/AIDS Prevention & Education for Adolescents & Children*, *5*(3-4), 7–32. doi:10.1300/J129v05n03_02

Dills, I. (2012, August 16). Napa schools installing security cameras. *Napa Valley Register*. Retrieved from: http://napa-valleyregister.com/news/local/napa-schools-installing-security-cameras/article_f7a30be2-e823-11e1-8c5c-001a4bcf887a.html

Dishion, T. J., Nelson, S. E., & Yasui, M. (2005). Predicting early adolescent gang involvement from middle school adaptation. *Journal of Clinical Child and Adolescent Psychology*, *34*(1), 62–73. doi:10.1207/s15374424jccp3401_6 PMID:15677281

Dishion, T. J., & Patterson, G. R. (1992). Age effects in parent training outcome. *Behavior Therapy*, *23*(4), 719–729. doi:10.1016/S0005-7894(05)80231-X

Dishman, C. (2005). The Leaderless Nexus: When Crime and Terror Converge. *Studies in Conflict and Terrorism, 28*(3), 237–252. doi:10.1080/10576100590928124

Dogan, R. (2014). Different Cultural Understandings of Honor That Inspire Killing: An Inquiry Into the Defendant's Perspective. *Homicide Studies, 18*(4), 363–388. doi:10.1177/1088767914526717

Doley, R. (2003). Pyromania: Fact or fiction? *The British Journal of Criminology, 43*(4), 797–807. doi:10.1093/bjc/43.4.797

Donahue, P., & Rolander, N. (2014, September 15). *Protest Buffets EU Elites as Sweden Votes Anti-Immigrant.* Retrieved 2014 from www.businessweek.com/news/2014-09-15/protest-buffets-ey-elites-as-sweden-votes-anti-immigrant

Dunbar, E., & Blanco, A. (2014). *Psychological perspectives on culture, violence, and intergroup animus: Evolving traditions in the bonds that tie and hate. APA Handbooks in Psychology* (pp. 377–399). Washington, DC: American Psychological Association.

Duran, B., Duran, E., & Yellow Horse Brave Heart, M. (1998). The trauma of history. In R. Thornton (Ed.), *Studying Native America: Problems and perspectives* (pp. 60–78). Madison, WI: University of Wisconsin Press.

Duran, R. J. (2013). *Gang Life in Two Cities.* NY: Columbia University Press.

Duran, R. J. (2013). *Gang Life in Two Cities: An Insider's Journey.* Columbia University Press.

Dutton, M. (1997). The basic character of crime in contemporary China, (Translation). *The China Quarterly, 149,* 160–177. doi:10.1017/S030574100004368X

Eades, C., Brimshaw, R., Silvestri, A., & Solomon, E. (2011). *'Knife Crime:' A review of evidence and policy* (2nd ed.). London: Center for Crime and Justice Studies.

Eagly, A. H., & Chaiken, S. (1993). Process theories of attitude formation and change: Attribution approaches and social judgment theory. In *The Psychology Of Attitudes.* Harcourt Brace Jovanovich College Publishers.

Earle, R., & Phillips, C. (2013). Muslim is the New Black: New Ethnicities and New Essentialisms in the Prison. *Race and Justice, 3*(2), 114–129. doi:10.1177/2153368713483322

Egely, A., & Howell, J. C. (2011). *Highlights of the 2009 National Youth Gang Survey.* Washington, DC: Office of the Juvenile Justice and Delinquency Prevention. doi:10.1037/e580942011-001

Eggleston, E. J. (2000). New Zealand Youth Gangs: Key Findings and Recommendations from an Urban Ethnography. *Social Policy Journal of New Zealand,* (14), 148-163.

Egley, A. J., & Howell, J. C. (2013). *Highlights of the 2011 national gang youth survey. Working for youth justice and safety.* Washington, DC: U.S. Department of Justice.

Ehrenreich, B. (1998). *Blood rites: Origins and history of the passions of war.* New York: Holt and Company.

Eisenberg, A. (2012, 25 April). *Bullying stories: Dealing with bullying from an adult perspective.* [Web log entry.] Retrieved from: bullyinglte.wordpress.com

Elder, G. H. Jr, Johnson, M. K., & Crosnoe, R. (2003). The emergence and development of life course theory. In J. T. Mortemer & M. J. Shanahan (Eds.), *Handbook of the life-course* (pp. 3–19). New York, NY: Springer. doi:10.1007/978-0-306-48247-2_1

Elias, M. (2012). *Sikh Temple Killer Wade Michael Page Radicalized in Army.* Intelligence Report 148. Southern Poverty Law Center.

Elsinger, P. S., & Smith, C. (2000). Globalization and metropolitan well-being in the U.S. *Social Science Quarterly*, (June), 634–644.

Ember, C. R., & Ember, M. (2003). *Encyclopaedia of Sex and Gender: Men and Women in the World's Cultures*. Springer.

Enayati, J., Grann, M., Lubbe, S., & Fazel, S. (2008). Psychiatric morbidity in arsonists referred for forensic psychiatric assessment in Sweden. *Journal of Forensic Psychiatry & Psychology*, *19*(2), 139–147. doi:10.1080/14789940701789500

Engelhardt, C. R., Bartholow, B. D., Kerr, G. T., & Bushman, B. J. (2011). This is your brain on violent video games: Neural desensitization to violence predicts increased aggression following violent video game exposure. *Journal of Experimental Social Psychology*, *47*(5), 1033–1036. doi:10.1016/j.jesp.2011.03.027

Engineering, F. (2005). *National Fire Academy Announces Juvenile Firesetter Intervention Specialist (Jfis) I & Ii Leadership (R628) Course*. Retrieved March 7, 2014, From Http://Www.Fireengineering.Com/Articles/2005/07/National-Fire-Academy-Announces-Juvenile-Firesetter-Intervention-Specialist-Jfis-I-Ii-Leadership-R628-Course.Html

Epps, K., & Hollin, C. R. (2000). Understanding and treating adolescent fire setters. In G. Boswell (Ed.), *Violent children and adolescents: asking the question why?* (pp. 36–55). London: Whurr.

Esbensen, F., Osgood, Peterson, Taylor, & Carson. (2013). Short- and long-term outcome results from a multisite evaluation of the G.R.E.A.T. Program. *Criminology and Public Policy*, *12*(3), 375-411.

Esbensen, F.-A., & Lynskey, D. P. (2001). Youth gang members in a school survey. In M.W. Klein, H.-J. Kerner, C.L. Maxson & E.G.M. Weitekamp (Eds.), The European paradox: Street gangs and youth groups in the U.S. and Europe, (pp. 93-114). Dordecht: Kluwer Academic Publishers.

Esbensen, F.-A., & Weerman, F. M. (2005). Youth gangs and troublesome youth groups in the United States and the Netherlands: A cross-national comparison. *European Journal of Criminology*, *2*(1), 1477–3708. doi:10.1177/1477370805048626

Esbensen, F.-A., Winfree, L. T. Jr, Ne, H., & Taylor, T. J. (2001). Youth gangs and definitional issues: When is a gang a gang, and why does it matter? *Crime and Delinquency*, *47*(1), 105–130. doi:10.1177/0011128701047001005

Esbensen, F., Peterson, D., Taylor, T. J., & Freng, A. (2010). *Youth violence: Sex and race differences in offending, victimization, and gang membership*. Philadelphia: Temple University Press.

Estrada, J. N., Gilbreath, T. D., Astor, R. A., & Benbenishty, R. (2013). Gang membership of California middle school students: Behaviors and attitudes as mediator of school violence. *Health Education Research*, *28*(4), 626–639. doi:10.1093/her/cyt037 PMID:23525778

Evans, D., & Sawdon, J. (2004). The development of a gang exit strategy: The Youth Ambassador's Leadership and Employment Project. *Corrections Today, October*. Retrieved from www.cantraining.org/BTC/docs/Sawdon%20Evans%20CT%20Article.pdf

Everton, S. F. (2012). *Disrupting Dark Networks (Structural Analysis in the Social Sciences)*. Cambridge University Press. doi:10.1017/CBO9781139136877

Ewick, P., & Silbey, S. S. (1995). Subversive stories and hegemonic tales: Toward a sociology of narrative. *Law & Society Review*, *29*(2), 197–226. doi:10.2307/3054010

Fagin, J. (1989). The social organization of drug use and drug dealing among urban gangs. *Criminology*, *27*(4), 633–669. doi:10.1111/j.1745-9125.1989.tb01049.x

Farrall, S., Bottoms, A., & Shapland, J. (2010). Social structures and desistance from crime. *European Journal of Criminology*, *7*(6), 546–570. doi:10.1177/1477370810376574

Farrall, S., & Bowling, B. (1999). Structuration, human development and desistance from crime. *The British Journal of Criminology, 39*(2), 252–267. doi:10.1093/bjc/39.2.253

Farrall, S., & Calverley, A. (2006). *Understanding desistance from crime.* London, UK: Open University Press.

Farrall, S., Hunter, B., Sharpe, G., & Calverley, A. (2014). *Criminal careers in transition: The social context of desistance from crime.* Oxford, UK: Oxford University Press. doi:10.1093/acprof:oso/9780199682157.001.0001

Farrington, D. P. (1989). Early predictors of adolescent aggression and adult violence. *Violence and Victims, 4*, 79–100. PMID:2487131

Faulkner, J., Schaller, M., Park, J. H., & Duncan, L. A. (2004). Evolved disease-avoidance mechanisms and contemporary xenophobic attitudes. *Group Processes & Intergroup Relations, 7*(4), 333–353. doi:10.1177/1368430204046142

Federal Bureau of Investigation. (2011). *Arson.* Crime in the United States.

Federal Emergency Management Agency. (2004). *The Fire Risk to Children.* Washington, DC: United States Fire Administration.

Federal Emergency Management Agency. (2005). *School Fires.* Washington, DC: United States Fire Administration.

Federal Emergency Management Agency. (2012). *Understanding Youth Fire setting Behaviors.* FEMA.

Feldman, A. (1997). Violence and Vision: The Prosthetics and Aesthetics of Terror. *Public Culture, 10*(1), 24–60. doi:10.1215/08992363-10-1-24

Felson, R. B., Liska, A. E., South, S. J., & McNulty, T. L. (1994). The subculture of violence and delinquency: Individuals vs. school context factors. *Social Forces, 73*(1), 155–173. doi:10.1093/sf/73.1.155

Fernandez, M., Pérez-Peña, R., & Santos, F. (2015). *Gunman in Texas shooting was F.B.I. suspect in Jihad inquiry.* Retrieved on May 5, 2015 from http://www.nytimes.com/2015/05/05/us/garland-texas-shooting-muhammad-cartoons. html?_r=0

Festinger, L. (1954). A theory of social comparison processes. *Human Relations, 7*(2), 117–140. doi:10.1177/001872675400700202

Fine, G. A. (1986). The social organization of adolescent gossip: The rhetoric of moral evaluation. In J. Cook-Gumperz, W. A. Corsaro, & J. Streeck (Eds.), *Children's worlds and children's language* (pp. 405–423). Berlin: Mouton. doi:10.1515/9783110864212.405

Fine, G. A., & Kleinman, S. (1979). Rethinking subculture: An interactionist analysis. *American Journal of Sociology, 85*(1), 1–20. doi:10.1086/226971

Finkel, M. A. (2002). Traumatic injuries caused by hazing practices. *The American Journal of Emergency Medicine, 20*(3), 228–233. doi:10.1053/ajem.2002.32649 PMID:11992345

Flaccus, G. (2007). Alliance adds to gang's clout: Public Enemy No. 1 more brazen since teaming up with Aryan Brotherhood. *Union Times.* Retrieved on May 1, 2015 from http://www.utsandiego.com/uniontrib/20070304/news_1n4gang.html

Flaspohler, P. D., Elfstrom, J. L., Vanderzee, K. L., Sink, H. E., & Birchmeier, Z. (2009). Stand by me: The effects of peer and teacher support in mitigating the impact of bullying on quality of life. *Psychology in the Schools, 46*(7), 636–649. doi:10.1002/pits.20404

Fleisher, M. S. (2006). *Societal and correctional context of prison gangs*. Cleveland, OH: Case Western Reserve University, Mandel School of Applied Social Sciences.

Fleisher, M. S., & Decker, S. H. (2001). An Overview of the Challenge of Prison Gangs. *Corrections Management Quarterly, 5*(1), 1–9.

Fletcher, S. (2012, February 29). *35 security cameras debut in high school*. Retrieved from: http://www.gloucestertimes.com/local/x952196953/36-security-cameras-debut-in-high-school

Florida Statute 874.03 Criminal Gang Enforcement and Prevention. (n.d.). Retrieved April 29, 2015 from http://www.leg.state.fl.us/statutes/index.cfm?mode=View%20Statutes&SubMenu=1&App_mode=Display_Statute&Search_String=gang&URL=0800-0899/0874/Sections/0874

Flynn, J. (2007). U.S. Structure Fires in Eating and Drinking Establishments. In Fire Analysis and Research Division. National Fire Protection Association.

Fong, R. S., Vogel, R. E., & Buentello, S. (1996). Prison Gang Dynamics: A Research Update. In Gangs: A Criminal Justice Approach. Anderson Publishing Co. and Academy of Criminal Justice Sciences.

Fong, R. S., Vogel, R. E., & Buentello, S. 1996. Prison Gang Dynamics: A Research Update. In Gangs: A Criminal Justice Approach. Anderson Publishing Co. and Academy of Criminal Justice Sciences.

Fong, R. (1990). The Organizational Structure of Prison Gangs: A Texas Case Study. *Federal Probation, 1*(54), 36.

Fong, R. S., & Buentello, S. (1991). The detection of prison gang development: An empirical assessment. *Federal Probation, 55*, 66–69.

Fong, R. S., & Vogel, R. E. (1994). A Comparative Analysis of Prison Gang Members, Security Threat Group Inmates, and General Population Prisoners in Texas Dept. of Corrections. *Journal of Gang Research, 2*(2), 1–12.

Forber-Pratt, A., Aragon, S. R., & Espelage, D. L. (2014). The influence of gang presence on victimization in one middle school environment. *Psychology of Violence, 4*(1), 8–20. doi:10.1037/a0031835

Foucault, M. (1977). *Discipline and Punish*. Academic Press.

Foucault, M. (1995). *Discipline and punish: The birth of the prison*. New York: Vintage Books.

Fox, K. A., & Allen, T. (2014). Examining the Instrumental-Expressive Continuum of Homicides: Incorporating the Effects of Gender, Victim-Offender Relationships, and Weapon Choice. *Homicide Studies, 18*(3), 298–317. doi:10.1177/1088767913493420

Fraser, A., & Atkinson, C. (2014). Making up gangs: Looping, labeling and the new politics of intelligence-led policing. *Youth Justice, 14*(2), 154–170. doi:10.1177/1473225414529047

Fraser, C., Gouge, C., & Billig, M. (1971). Risky shifts, cautious shifts, and group polarization. *European Journal of Social Psychology, 1*(1), 7–30. doi:10.1002/ejsp.2420010103

Frick, P. J., & Viding, E. (2009). Antisocial behavior from a developmental psychopathology perspective. *Development and Psychopathology, 21*(04), 11111131. doi:10.1017/S0954579409990071 PMID:19825260

Friedrichs, M. (1999). *Poverty and prejudice: Gang intervention and rehabilitation*. Edge: Ethics of Development in a Global Environment. Available at https://web.stanford.edu/class/e297c/poverty_prejudice/ganginterv/gangsproblems.htm

Fritsch, E. J., Caeti, T. J., & Taylor, R. W. (1999). Gang suppression through saturation patrol, aggressive curfew, and truancy enforcement: A quasi-experimental test of the Dallas anti-gang initiative. *Crime and Delinquency, 45*(1), 122–139. doi:10.1177/0011128799045001007

Fromm, E. (1990). *Man for himself: An inquiry into the psychology of ethics.* New York: First Owl Books. (Original work published 1947)

Fromm, E. (1992). *Anatomy of human destructiveness.* New York: Holt. (Original work published 1973)

Gaertner, S., Dovidio, J. F., Anastasio, P. A., Bachevan, B. A., & Rust, M. C. (1993). The common ingroup identity model: Recategorization and the reduction of intergroup bias. In W. Stroebe & M. Hewstone (Eds.), *European Review of Social Psychology, 4.* Chichester, UK: Wiley. doi:10.1080/14792779343000004

Gagnon, J. C., & Leone, P. E. (2001). Alternative strategies for school violence prevention. *New Directions for Youth Development, 92*(92), 101–125. doi:10.1002/yd.23320019207 PMID:12170826

Galand, B., Lecocq, C., & Philippot, P. (2007). School violence and teacher professional disengagement. *The British Journal of Educational Psychology, 77*(2), 465–477. doi:10.1348/000709906X114571 PMID:17504557

Galanti, G.-A. (2003). The Hispanic Family and Male-Female Relationships: An Overview. *Journal of Transcultural Nursing, 14*(3), 180–185. doi:10.1177/1043659603014003004 PMID:12861920

Garcia, C. (2003). School safety technology in America: Currect use and perceived effectiveness. *Criminal Justice Policy Review, 14*(1), 30–54. doi:10.1177/0887403402250716

Garot, R. (2007). "Where you from?": Gang identity as performance. *Journal of Contemporary Ethnography, 36*(1), 50–84. doi:10.1177/0891241606287364

Garot, R. (2009). Reconsidering retaliation: Structural inhibitions, emotive dissonance, and the acceptance of ambivalence among inner-city young men. *Ethnography, 10*(1), 63–90. doi:10.1177/1466138108099587

Garot, R. (2010). *Who you claim: Performing identity in school and on the streets.* New York: New York University Press.

Gastrow, P. (1988). *Organised Crime in South Africa: an assessment of its nature and origins.* Gauteng: Institute for Security Studies.

Gavazzi, S. M., Yarcheck, C. M., & Chesney-Lind, M. (2006). Global risk indicators and the role of gender in a juvenile detention sample. *Criminal Justice and Behavior, 33*(5), 597–612. doi:10.1177/0093854806288184

Gaynor, J. (2002). *Juvenile Firesetter Intervention Handbook.* Sociotechnical Research Applications, Inc.

Gebo, E., & Sullivan. (2014). A statewide comparison of gang and non-gang youth in public high schools. *Youth Violence and Criminal Justice, 12*(3), 191-208.

Geertz, C. (1973). *The Interpretation of Cultures.* New York, NY: Basic Books Classics.

Geller, J. L. (1992). Pathological fire setting in adults. *International Journal of Law and Psychiatry, 15*(3), 283–302. doi:10.1016/0160-2527(92)90004-K PMID:1399186

Germany's New Right: The Unholy Alliance of Neo-Nazis and Football Hooligans. (2014). Spiegel Online. Retrieved on January 1, 2015 from http://www.spiegel.de/international/germany/new-right-wing-alliance-of-neo-nazis-and-hooligans-appears-in-germany-a-1000953.html

Germet, F. v. (2001). Crips in Orange: Gangs and Groups in The Netherlands. In M. W. Klein, H. J. Kerner, C. Maxson, & G. M. Weitekamp (Eds.), *The Eurogang Paradox: Street Gangs and Youth Groups in the U.S. and Europe*. Dordrecht: Kluwer Academic Publishers.

Giancola, P. R., Parrott, D. J., & Roth, R. M. (2006). The influence of difficult temperament on alcohol-related aggression: Better accounted for by executive functioning? *Addictive Behaviors, 31*(12), 2169–2187. doi:10.1016/j.addbeh.2006.02.019 PMID:16563644

Gibbons, F. X., & Gerrard, M. (1989). Effects of upward and downward social comparison on mood states. *Journal of Social and Clinical Psychology, 8*(1), 14–31. doi:10.1521/jscp.1989.8.1.14

Giddens, A. (1991). *Modernity and Self-Identity: Self and Society in the Late Modern Age*. Stanford University Press.

Gilbert, J. (2013). *Patched: the History of Gangs in New Zealand*. Auckland: Auckland University Press.

Gilroy, P. (1995). *The Black Atlantic: Modernity and Double-Consciousness*. Harvard University Press.

Ginsberg, C., & Loffredo, L. (1993). Violence-related attitudes and behaviors of high school students--New York City. *Journal of Student Health, 63*(10), 438–439. PMID:8133649

Giordano, P. C., Cernovich, S. A., & Rudolph, J. L. (2002). Gender, crime and desistance: Toward a theory of cognitive transformation. *American Journal of Sociology, 107*(4), 990–1064. doi:10.1086/343191

Glancy, G. D., Spiers, E. M., Pitt, S. E., & Dvoskin, J. A. (2003). Commentary: Models and Correlates of Fire setting Behavior. *The Journal of the American Academy of Psychiatry and the Law, 31*, 53–57. PMID:12817843

Glynn, M. (2011). *Dad and me - Research into the problems caused by absent fathers*. Retrieved 18 April 2013 from: http://www.addaction.org.uk/news.asp?section=80&itemid=735&search

Glynn, M. (2014). *Black Men, Invisibility, and Desistance from crime: Towards a Critical Race Theory from Crime*. London: Routledge.

Goffman, E. (1959). *The Presentation of Self in Everyday Life*. Harpswell, ME: Anchor.

Goffman, E. (1986). *Stigma: Notes on the management of spoiled identity*. New York: Simon and Schuster, Touchstone.

Golding, B., McClory, J., & Lockhart, B. (2008). *Going ballistic: Dealing with guns, gangs, and knives*. London: The Policy Exchange.

Goldman, L., Giles, H., & Hogg, M. A. (2014). Going to extremes: Social identity and communication processes associated with gang membership.[forthcoming – online first]. *Group Processes & Intergroup Relations, 17*(6), 813–832. doi:10.1177/1368430214524289

Goldsborough, R. (2001, October). Dealing with hate on the internet. *Teacher Librarian, 29*, 46.

Goldstein, P. (2003). The drugs/violence nexus. *Crime: Critical Concepts in Sociology, 4*, 96.

Goodwin, M. H. (1980). He-said-she-said: Formal cultural procedures for the construction of a gossip dispute activity. *American Ethnologist, 7*(4), 674–695. doi:10.1525/ae.1980.7.4.02a00050

Goredema, C., Goga, K. (2014). *Crime networks and governance in Cape Town*. Pretoria: Institute for Security Studies.

Gottfredson, D. C., & DiPietro, S. M. (2011). School size, social capital, adn student victimization. *Sociology of Education, 84*(1), 69–89. doi:10.1177/0038040710392718

Gottfredson, G. D., Gottfredson, D. C., Payne, A. A., & Gottfredson, N. C. (2005, November01). (2050). School climate predictors of school disorder: Results from a national study of delinquency prevention in schools. *Journal of Research in Crime and Delinquency, 42*(4), 412–444. doi:10.1177/0022427804271931

Gottfredson, M. R., & Hirschi, T. (1990). *A general theory of crime.* Stanford, CA: Stanford University Press.

Gottfredson, S. D., & Moriarty, L. J. (2006). Statistical Risk Assessment: Old Problems and New Applications. *Crime and Delinquency, 52*(1), 178–200. doi:10.1177/0011128705281748

Grant, J. E., & Kim, S. W. (2007). Clinical characteristics and psychiatric comorbidity of pyromania. *The Journal of Clinical Psychiatry, 68*(11), 1717–1722. doi:10.4088/JCP.v68n1111 PMID:18052565

Greenberg, J., Pyszczynski, T., & Solomon, S. (1986). The causes and consequences of the need for self-esteem: A terror management theory. In R. F. Baumeister (Ed.), *Public self and private self* (pp. 189–212). New York: Springer-Verlag. doi:10.1007/978-1-4613-9564-5_10

Greenberg, J., Pyszczynski, T., Solomon, S., Rosenblatt, A., Veeder, M., Kirkland, S., & Lyon, D. (1990). Evidence for terror management theory: II. The effects of mortality salience reactions to those who threaten or bolster the cultural worldview. *Journal of Personality and Social Psychology, 58*(2), 308–318. doi:10.1037/0022-3514.58.2.308

Greenberg, J., Simon, L., Porteus, J., Pyszczynski, T., & Solomon, S. (1995). Evidence of a terror management function of cultural icons: The effects of mortality salience on the inappropriate use of cherished cultural symbols. *Personality and Social Psychology Bulletin, 21*(11), 1221–1228. doi:10.1177/01461672952111010

Greene, J., & Pranis, K. (2007). *Gang wars: The failure of enforcement tactics and the need for effective public safety strategies.* Washington, DC: Justice Policy Institute.

Grekul, J., & LaBoucane-Benson. (2008). Aboriginal gangs and their (dis)placement: Contextualizing recruitment, membership, and status. *Canadian Journal of Criminology and Criminal Justice, 5,* 59-82.

Grekul, J., & LaBoucane-Benson, P. (2007). *An investigation into the formation and recruitment process of Aboriginal gangs in Western Canada.* Ottawa, ON: Public Safety Canada.

Grover, A. R., Jennings, W. G., & Tewksbury, R. (2009). Adolescent male and female gang members' experiences with violent victimization, dating violence, and sexual assault. *American Journal of Criminal Justice, 34*(1-2), 103–115. doi:10.1007/s12103-008-9053-z

Gruter, P., & Versteegh, P. (2001). Towards a Problem-Oriented Approach to Youth Groups in The Hague. In M. W. Klein, H. J. Kerner, C. Maxson, & G. M. Weitekamp (Eds.), *The Eurogang Paradox: Street Gangs and Youth Groups in the U.S. and Europe.* Dordrecht: Kluwer Academic Publishers. doi:10.1007/978-94-010-0882-2_8

Gurney, K. (2014). 700 Extortion-Related Murders in Guatemala through July 2014: NGO. *Insight Crime.* Retrieved August 30, 2014. http://www.insightcrime.org/news-briefs/guatemala-700-homicides-extortion-2014

Hacking, I. (1999). *The social construction of what?* Cambridge, MA: Harvard University Press.

Hagedorn, J. M. (2005b). The Global Impact of Gangs. *Journal of Contemporary Criminal Justice, 21*(2), 153–169. doi:10.1177/1043986204273390

Hagedorn, J. M., Hazlehurst, K., & Hazlehurst, C. (1999). Gangs in a Global Perspective. *Contemporary Sociology, 28*(5), 609–611. doi:10.2307/2655049

Halavy, N., Bornstein, G., & Sagiv, L. (2008). "In-group love" and "out-group hate" as motives for individual participation in intergroup conflict: A new game paradigm. *Psychological Science*, *19*(4), 405–411. doi:10.1111/j.1467-9280.2008.02100.x PMID:18399895

Hall, S., & Sawdon, J. (2004). *Report to Human Resources and Skills Development Canada on the Breaking the Cycle: Youth Gang Exit and Youth Ambassador Leadership Employment Preparation Project*. Toronto, ON: Canadian Training Institute.

Hallsworth, S. (2013). *The Gang & Beyond: Interpreting violent street worlds*. Oxford: Palgrave Macmillian. doi:10.1057/9781137358103

Hallsworth, S., & Silverstone, D. (2009). "That's life innit": A British perspective on guns, crime and social order. *Criminology & Criminal Justice*, *9*(3), 359–377. doi:10.1177/1748895809336386

Hallsworth, S., & Young, T. (2008). Gang talk and gang talkers: A critique. *Crime, Media, Culture*, *4*(2), 175–195. doi:10.1177/1741659008092327

Hamm, M. (2007). *Terrorist Recruitment in American Correctional Institutions: An Exploratory Study of Non-Traditional Faith Groups*. National Criminal Justice Reference Services.

Hamm, M. (2009). Prison Islam in the Age of Sacred Terror. *The British Journal of Criminology*, *49*(1), 667–685. doi:10.1093/bjc/azp035

Hankin, A., Hertz, M., & Simon, T. (2011). Impacts of metal detector use in schools: Insights from 15 years of research. *The Journal of School Health*, *81*(2), 100–106. doi:10.1111/j.1746-1561.2010.00566.x PMID:21223277

Hansen, L. L. (2011a, June 11). *Recognizing the signs of gang recruitment*. Workshop, Western New England College.

Hansen, L. L. (2011b). *"Baby Steps": Educating educators on the risks of gang recruitment*. Annual Conference, American Society of Criminology, Chicago, IL.

Hansen, L. L., & Movahedi, S. (2010) Wall Street scandals: The myth of individual greed. *Sociological Forum*, *25*(2), 367-374.

Hansen, L., & Morin. (2012). *Survey report, first wave*. South Holyoke Safe Neighborhood Initiative.

Hansen, L., Simpson, & Morin. (2013). *Survey report, Residents and Agencies*. South Holyoke Safe Neighborhood Initiative.

Hansen, L. L. (2005). Girl "crew members doing gender, boy "crew" members doing violence: An ethnographic and network analysis of Maria Hinojosa's New York gangs. *Western Criminology Review*, *6*(1), 134–144.

Hansen, L. L. (2005). Research Note: Girl "crew" members doing gender, boy "crew" members doing violence: An ethnographic and network analysis of Maria Hinojosa's New York gangs. *Western Criminology Review*, *6*(1), 134–144.

Hanson, M., Mackay, S., Atkinson, L., & Staley, S. (1995). Fire setting during the preschool period: Assessment and intervention issues. *Canadian Journal of Psychiatry*, *40*, 299–303. PMID:7585398

Hardesty, G. (2010). D.A.: Arrests Cripple white-supremacist gangs. *Orange County Register*. Retrieved on April 29, 2015 from http://www.ocregister.com/articles/white-280585-county-orange.html

Harding, D. J. (2010). *Living the drama: Community, conflict, and culture among inner city boys*. Chicago: University of Chicago Press. doi:10.7208/chicago/9780226316666.001.0001

Harding, S. (2014). *The street casino: Survival in violent street gangs*. Bristol, UK: Policy Press. doi:10.1332/policy-press/9781447317173.001.0001

Harpham, D. (2004). *Census of Prison Inmates and Home Detainees*. Wellington: Department of Corrections.

Harrell, E. (2005). Violence by gang members, 1993-2003. U.S. Department of Justice. Office of Justice programs.

Harrison, L. D., Erickson, P. G., Adlaf, E., & Freeman, C. (2001). The drugs-violence nexus among American and Canadian youth. *Substance Use & Misuse*, *36*(14), 2065–2086. doi:10.1081/JA-100108437 PMID:11794584

Hart, C. H., Newell, L. D., & Olsen, S. F. (2003). *Parenting skills and social-communicative competence in childhood in Handbook of Communication and Social Interaction Skills*. Lawrence Erlbaum Associates, Publishers.

Hart, C. O., & Mueller, C. E. (2013). School delinquency and social bond factors: Exploring gendered differences among a national sample of 10th graders. *Psychology in the Schools*, *50*(2), 116–133. doi:10.1002/pits.21662

Hastings, R., Dunbar, L., & Bania, M. (2011). *Leaving criminal youth gangs: Exit strategies and programs*. Ottawa, ON: Institute for the Prevention of Crime, University of Ottawa.

Hate Group Maps. (n.d.a). *Intro*. Retrieved January 31, 2015 from: http://www.athenainstitute.eu/en/projects/

Hate Groups Maps. (n.d.b). *Extremist Groups*. Retrieved January 31, 2015 from: http://www.athenainstitute.eu/en/hate_groups/

Hate Map. (n.d.). Retrieved October 29, 2014 from: http://www.splcenter.org/get-informed/hate-map

Hate, D. (1999).. . *Economist*, *353*, 30–31.

Hawkins, D. J., Herrenkohl, T. I., Farrington, D. P., Brewer, D., Catalano, R. F., Harachi, T. W., & Cothern, L. (2000). *Predictors of youth violence. Juvenile Justice Bulletin (NCJ-179065)*. Washington, DC: U.S. Dept. of Justice, Office of Juvenile Justice & Delinquency Prevention.

Hayward, K. (2002). The Vilification and Pleasures of Youthful Transgression. In J. Muncie, G. Hughes, & E. McLaughlin (Eds.), *Youth Justice: Critical Readings*. London: Sage.

Hazlehurst, K. M., & Hazlehurst, C. (1998). Gangs and youth subcultures: International explorations. Transaction Publishers.

Hbschle, A. (2010). *Organised crime in Southern Africa: First annual review*. Pretoria: Institute for Security Studies Special Report.

Healy, D. (2010). *The dynamics of desistance: Charting pathways through change*. Portland, OR: Willan Publishing.

Hebdidge, D. (1981). *Subculture: The Meaning of Style*. New York: Routledge.

Heisz, A. (2005). Ten things to know about Canadian metropolitan areas: A synthesis of statistics. Canada's trends and conditions in census metropolitan areas series (Analytical Paper, Catalogue no. 89-613-MIE – No. 009). Ottawa, ON: Statistics Canada.

Hememway, D. (2004). *Private Guns, Public Health*. University of Michigan Press.

Hemmati, T. (2006). *The nature of Canadian urban gangs and their use of firearms: A review of the literature and police survey (Research Report rr07-1e)*. Ottawa, ON: Department of Justice Canada.

Henggeler, S. W. (1989). *Delinquency in adolescence*. Newbury Park, CA: Sage.

Hennigan, K., & Spanovic, M. (2012). Gang dynamics through the lens of social identity theory. In F. A. Esbensen & C. L. Maxson (Eds.), *Youth Gangs in international perspective: Results from the eurogang program of research* (pp. 127–149). New York: Springer. doi:10.1007/978-1-4614-1659-3_8

Hepworth, J. T., & West, S. G. (1988). Lynchings and the economy: A time-series reanalysis of Hovland and Sears (1940). *Journal of Personality and Social Psychology, 55*(2), 239–247. doi:10.1037/0022-3514.55.2.239

Hernandez, A. (1998). *Peace in the streets: Breaking the cycle of gang violence.* Washington, DC: Child Welfare League of America.

Higgins, G. E., Vito, G. F., & Walsh, W. F. (2008). Searches: An understudied area of racial profiling. *Journal of Ethnicity in Criminal Justice, 6*(1), 23–39. doi:10.1300/J222v06n01_03

Hill, K. (2013). Aryan Brotherhood may target teen suspects, police say. *The Spokesman Review*. Retrieved on April 29, 2015 from http://www.spokesman.com/stories/2013/nov/20/aryan-brotherhood-may-target-demetruis-glenn/

Hill, K. G., Howell, Hawkins, & Battin-Pearson. (1999). Childhood risk factors for adolescent gang membership: Results from the Seattle Social Development Project. *Journal of Research in Crime and Delinquency, 36*(3), 300-322.

Hill, K. G., Lui, & Hawkins. (2001, December). Early precursors of gang membership: A study of Seattle youth. *Office of Juvenile Justice and Delinquency Prevention (OJJDP) Bulletin,* 1-5.

Hill, R. W. (1982). Is Arson An Aggressive Act Or A Property Offence? A Controlled Study Of Psychiatric Referrals. *Canadian Journal of Psychiatry, 27,* 648–654. PMID:7159867

Hobbs, D. (1995). *Bad Business - Professional Crime in Modern Britain.* Oxford University Press.

Hobbs, D. (2013). *Lush Life: Constructing Organized Crime in the UK.* Clarendon Studies in Criminology. doi:10.1093/acprof:oso/9780199668281.001.0001

Hodson, G., Dovidio, J. F., & Esses, V. M. (2003). Ingroup identification as a moderator of positive-negative asymmetry in social discrimination. *European Journal of Social Psychology, 33*(2), 215–233. doi:10.1002/ejsp.141

Hogg, M. A., Terry, D. J., & White, K. M. (1995). A tale of two theories: A critical comparison of identity theory with social identity theory. *Social Psychology Quarterly, 58*(4), 255–269. doi:10.2307/2787127

Hollander, J. A. (2001). Vulnerability and Dangerousness: The Construction of Gender through Conversation about Violence. *Gender & Society, 15*(1), 83–109. doi:10.1177/089124301015001005

Hollander, J. A., & Gordon, H. R. (2006). The process of social construction in talk. *Symbolic Interaction, 29*(2), 183–212. doi:10.1525/si.2006.29.2.183

Holmes, S. R., & Brandenburg-Ayres, S. J. (1998). Bullying behavior in school: A predictor of later gang involvement. *Journal of Gang Research, 5*(2), 1–6.

Holthouse, D. (2009). *Hate Groups Active in 2008.* Intelligence Report. Southern Poverty Law Center, Issue No. 133.

Home Office. (2011). *Ending Gang and Youth Violence: A Cross-Government Report, including further evidence and good practice case studies.* London: Home Office.

Hope, A. (2009). CCTV, school surveillance and social control. *British Educational Research Journal, 35*(6), 891–907. doi:10.1080/01411920902834233

Hossain, S., & Welchman, L. (2005). *Honour: Crimes, Paradigms and Violence Against Women.* London, UK: Zed Books.

Hovland, C. I., & Sears, R. (1940). Minor studies in aggression: VI. Correlation of lynchings with economic indices. *The Journal of Psychology*, *9*(2), 301–310. doi:10.1080/00223980.1940.9917696

Howell, J. C. (1998). Youth gangs: An overview. *Juvenile Justice Bulletin*. Retrieved from: https://www.ncjrs.gov/pdf-files/167249.pdf

Howell, J. C., & Lynch, J. P. (2000). Youth gangs in schools. *Juvenile Justice Bulletin*. Retrieved from: https://www.ncjrs.gov/pdffiles1/ojjdp/183015.pdf

Howell, J. C. (2007). Menacing or mimicking? Realities of youth gangs. *Juvenile & Family Court Journal*, *58*(2), 39–50. doi:10.1111/j.1755-6988.2007.tb00137.x

Howell, J. C. (2012). *Gangs in America's Communities*. SAGE Publications Inc.

Howell, J. C. (2012). *Gangs in America's communities*. Thousand Oaks, CA: Sage Publications, Inc.

Howell, J. C. (2015). *The history of gangs in the United States: Their origins and transformations*. Lanham, MD: Lexington Books.

Huang, H. (2007). From the Asian Boys to the Zhu Lian Bang (the Bamboo Union Gang): A Typological analysis of Delinquent Asian Gangs. *Asian Criminology*, *2*(2), 127–143. doi:10.1007/s11417-007-9033-0

Huebner, A. J., & Howell, L. W. (2003). Examining the relationship between adolescent sexual risk-taking and perceptions of monitoring, communication, and parenting styles. *The Journal of Adolescent Health*, *33*(2), 71–78. doi:10.1016/S1054-139X(03)00141-1 PMID:12890597

Huff, R. C. (1998). Comparing the criminal behavior of youth gangs and at-risk youth. Research brief. Washington, DC: Department of Justice. doi:10.1037/e507882006-001

Huff, R. (1998). *'Comparing the Criminal Behavior of Youth Gangs and At-Risk Youths', Research in Brief, October*. Washington, DC: US Office of Justice, National Institute of Justice.

Huizinga, D., & Schumann, K. F. (2001). Gang membership in Bremen and Denver: Comparative longitudinal data. In M. W. Klein, H.-J. Kerner, C. L. Maxson, & E. G. M. Weitekamp (Eds.), *The Eurogang paradox: Street gangs and youth groups in the U.S. and Europe, 231–46*. Dordrecht: Kluwer Academic Publishers. doi:10.1007/978-94-010-0882-2_18

Hunt, G., Riegel, S., Morales, T., & Waldorf, D. (1993). Changes in Prison Culture: Prison Gangs and the Case of the 'Pepsi Generation'. *Social Problems*, *40*(3), 398–409. doi:10.2307/3096887

Ilan, J. (2010). 'If you don't let us in, we'll get arrested': Class-cultural dynamics in the provision of, and resistance to, youth justice work. *Youth Justice*, *10*(1), 25–39. doi:10.1177/1473225409356760

ILO/IPEC Working Paper. (2000). *In-depth Analysys of the Situation of Working Street Children in Saint Petersburg. Report*. St Petersburg: ILO/IPEC.

Institute Of Social Analysis. (1994). *National Juvenile Firesetter/Arson Control And Prevention Program*. Author.

Ireland, J. L., & Power, C. (2012). Prison Gangs Seen as a Source of Friendship.*The British Psychological Society. Annual Conference*, London.

Irwin, J. (1980). *Prisons in Turmoil*. Boston: Little Brown.

Irwin, J., & Cressey, D. (1962). Thieves, convicts and the inmate culture. *Social Problems*, *10*(2), 145–155. doi:10.2307/799047

Jackson-Jacobs, C. (2004). Taking a Beating: The Narrative Gratifications of Fighting as an Underdog. In J. Ferrell, K. Hayward, W. Morrison, & M. Presdee (Eds.), *Cultural Criminology Unleashed*. London: Glasshouse Press.

Jacob, J. C. (2006). Male and female youth crime in Canadian communities: Assessing the applicability of social disorganization theory. *Canadian Journal of Criminology and Criminal Justice, 48*(1), 31–60. doi:10.3138/cjccj.48.1.31

Jacobs, J. (1974). Street Gangs Behind Bars. *Social Problems, 21*(3), 395–409. doi:10.2307/799907

Jacobs, J. (1977). *Stateville - The Penitentiary in Mass Society*. The University of Chicago Press.

Jacobs, J. (1979). Race Relations and the Prisoner Subculture. In N. Morris & M. Tonry (Eds.), *Crime and Justice*. Chicago, IL: The University of Chicago Press. doi:10.1086/449057

Jacques, M. (2009). *When China Rules the World*. Penguin Books.

Jayaraman, A., & Frazer, J. (2006). Arson: A growing inferno. *Medicine, Science, and the Law, 46*(4), 295–30. doi:10.1258/rsmmsl.46.4.295 PMID:17191632

Jennings, W. G., Khey, D. N., Maskaly, J., & Donner, C. N. (2011). Evaluating the relationship between law enforcement and school security measures and violent crime in schools. *Journal of Police Crisis Negotiations, 11*(2), 109–124. doi:10.1080/15332586.2011.581511

Jhally, S. (1997). *Stuart Hall: Representation and the Media*. Media Education Foundation.

Johnson, R., Jones, P., Ryan, K., & Gafford, O. (2014b). *Juvenile Fire Setters And Bomb Makers: A Forensic Psychological Update Using Biopsychosocialcultural Parent Endorsement Patterns In Juvenile Fire Setters And Bomb Makers To Rethink The Design Of A Third Generation Risk Assessment Instru- ment*. In Acjs 51st Annual Meeting, Philadelphia, PA.

Johnson, S. (2014). American-Born Gangs Helping Drive Immigrant Crisis at U.S. Border: Central America's spiraling violence has a Los Angeles connection. *National Geographic Magazine*. Retrieved August 30, 2014 from http://news.nationalgeographic.com/news/2014/07/140723-immigration-minors-honduras-gang-violence-central-america/

Johnson, R., Beckenbach, H., & Kilbourne, S. (2013). Forensic psychological public safety risk assessment integrated with culturally responsive treatment for juvenile fire setters: DSM-5 implications. *Journal of Criminal Psychology, 3*(1), 49–64. doi:10.1108/20093821311307767

Johnson, R., Fessler, A., Wilhelm, M., & Stepensky, A. (2014). Towards A Forensic Psychological Evaluation Of Juvenile Fire Setters: Parent Power. *J Forensic Res, 5*(214), 2.

Johnson, R., & Jones, P. (2014a). Identification of Parental Endorsement Patterns: An Example of the Importance of Professional Attunement to the Clinical-Forensic Risk Markers in Juvenile Fire setting and Bomb Making. *The American Journal of Forensic Psychology, 32*(2).

Johnson, S. L. (2009). Improving the school environment to reduce school violence: A review of the literature. *The Journal of School Health, 79*(10), 451–465. doi:10.1111/j.1746-1561.2009.00435.x PMID:19751307

Johnson, S. L., Burke, J. G., & Gielen, A. C. (2011). Prioritizing the school environment in school violence prevention efforts. *The Journal of School Health, 81*(6), 311–340. doi:10.1111/j.1746-1561.2011.00598.x PMID:21592128

Jones, D., Roper, V., Stys, Y., & Wilson, C. (2004). *Street gangs: A review of theory, interventions, and implications for corrections* (Research Report R-161). Ottawa, ON: Correctional Service of Canada.

Jones, N., & Cooper, S. (2011). Tijuana's Uneasy Peace May Endure, Despite Arrests. *Insight Crime*. Retrieved September 2, 2014 from http://www.insightcrime.org/investigations/tijuanas-uneasy-peace-may-endure-despite-arrests

Jones, N. (2010). *Between good and ghetto: African American girls and inner-city violence*. New Brunswick, NJ: Rutgers University Press.

Jones, S., & Lynam, D. R. (2009). In the eye of the impulsive beholder: The interaction between impulsivity and perceived informal social control on offending. *Criminal Justice and Behavior, 36*(3), 307–321. doi:10.1177/0093854808328653

Jules-Macquet, R. (2014). *The state of South African prisons*. Cape Town: NICRO Public Education Series.

Jutersonke, O., Muggah, R., & Rodgers, D. (2009). 2009 Urban violence and Security Interventions in Central America. *Security Dialogue, 40*(4-5), 373–397. doi:10.1177/0967010609343298

Juvonen, J., Nishina, A., & Graham, S. (2000). Peer harassment, psychological wellbeing, and school adjustment in early adolescence. *Journal of Educational Psychology, 92*, 349–359. doi:10.1037/0022-0663.92.2.349

Kahn, B. (1978). *Prison gangs in the community: a briefing document for the California Board of Corrections*. Academic Press.

Kahn, B. (1978). *Prison gangs in the community: a briefing document for the Board of Corrections*. California Board of Corrections.

Kantor, D., & Bennett, W. I. (1968). Orientation of Street-Corner Workers and Their Effects of Gangs. In S. Wheeler (Ed.), *Controlling Delinquents*. New York: Wiley.

Kar, D., & Spanjers, J. (2014). *Illicit Financial Flows from Developing Countries: 2003-2012*. Washington, DC: Global Financial Integrity.

Kärnä, A., Voeten, M., Poskiparta, E., & Salmivalli, C. (2010). Vulnerable children in varying classroom contexts: Bystanders' behaviors moderate the effects of risk factors on victimization. *Merrill-Palmer Quarterly, 56*(3), 261–282. doi:10.1353/mpq.0.0052

Kassel, P. (2003). The crackdown in the prisons of Massachusetts: Arbitrary and harsh treatment can only make matters worse. In L. Kontos, D. Brotherton, & L. Barrios (Eds.), *Gangs and society: Alternative perspectives* (pp. 229–252). New York, NY: Columbia University Press.

Katz, C. M. (2001). The establishment of a police gang unit: An examination of organizational and environmental factors. *Criminology, 39*(1), 37–74. doi:10.1111/j.1745-9125.2001.tb00916.x

Katz, C. M., Maguire, E. R., & Choate, D. (2011). A cross-national comparison of gangs in the United States and Trinidad and Tobago. *International Criminal Justice Review, 21*(3), 243–262. doi:10.1177/1057567711417179

Katz, C. M., Webb, V. J., Fox, K., & Shaffer, J. N. (2011). Understanding the relationship between violent victimization and gang membership. *Journal of Criminal Justice, 39*(Jan-Feb), 48–59. doi:10.1016/j.jcrimjus.2010.10.004

Katz, C. M., Web, V. J., & Shaeffer, D. R. (2000). Gang intelligence lists: Examining differences in delinquency between documented gang members and nondocumented delinquent youth. *Police Quarterly, 3*, 413–437.

Katz, J., & Jackson-Jacobs, C. (2004). The Criminologists' Gang. In C. Sumner (Ed.), *Blackwell Companion to Criminology*. Malden, MA: Blackwell Publishers.

Katz, M. B. (2007). Why aren't U.S. cities burning? *Dissent, 54*(3), 23–29. doi:10.1353/dss.2007.0069

Kazemian, L. (2007). Desistance from crime: Theoretical, empirical, methodological, and policy considerations. *Journal of Contemporary Criminal Justice, 23*(1), 5–27. doi:10.1177/1043986206298940

Kelly, K., & Caputo, T. (2005). The linkages between street gangs and organized crime: The Canadian experience. *Journal of Gang Research, 13*, 17–31.

Kelly, R., Chin, K., & Fagan, J. (1993, August). The Structure, Activity, and Control of Chinese Gangs: Law Enforcement Perspectives. *Journal of Contemporary Criminal Justice, 9*(3), 221–239. doi:10.1177/104398629300900304

Kennedy, D. (2011). *Don't Shoot: One Man, A Street Fellowship, And The End of Violence in Inner-City America*. New York: Bloomsbury.

Kennedy, H. (2004). *Just Law: The Changing Face of Justice, and Why it Matters to Us All*. Chatto & Windus.

Kent, R. (2001). *Data construction and data analysis for survey research*. New York, NY: Palgrave Publishers.

Khayelitsha Commission Report . (2012). Khayelitsha Commission.

Kinner, S. A., & Degenhardt, L. (2008). Crystal Methamphetamine Smoking Among Regular Ecstasy Users in Australia: Increases in Use and Associations with Harm. *Drug and Alcohol Review, 27*(3), 292–300. doi:10.1080/09595230801919452 PMID:18368611

Kinnes, I. (2000). Structural changes and growth in gang activities. In *From urban street gangs to criminal empires: The changing face of gangs in the Western Cape*. Pretoria: Institute for Security Studies.

Kintrea, K., Bannister, J., Pickering, J., Suruki, N., & Reid, M. (2008). *Young People and Territoriality in British Cities*. York, UK: Joseph Rowntree Foundation.

Kleiman, M. (2009). *When Brute Force Fails: How to Have Less Crime and Less Punishment*. Princeton University Press.

Klein, M. (1995). Street Gang Cycles. In J. Wilson & J. Petersilia (Eds.), *Crime*. Oakland, CA: ICS Press.

Klein, M. (1995). *The American street gang: its nature, prevalence, and control*. New York: Oxford University Press.

Klein, M. W. (1971). *Street gangs and street workers*. Englewood Cliffs, NJ: Prentice Hall, Inc.

Klein, M. W. (1995). *The American Street Gang: Its Nature Prevalence and Control*. New York: Oxford University Press.

Klein, M. W. (1995). *The American street gang: Its nature prevalence and control*. Oxford: Oxford University Press.

Klein, M. W. (1995). *The American street gang: Its nature, prevalence, and control*. New York, NY: Oxford University Press.

Klein, M. W. (2002). Street gangs: A cross-national perspective. In C. R. Huff (Ed.), *Gangs in America III*. Thousand Oaks, CA: Sage. doi:10.4135/9781452232201.n15

Klein, M. W. (2005). The value of comparisons in street gang research. *Journal of Contemporary Criminal Justice, 21*(2), 135–152. doi:10.1177/1043986204272911

Klein, M. W., & Maxson, C. (2006). *Street Gang Patterns and Policies*. New York: Oxford University Press, Inc. doi:10.1093/acprof:oso/9780195163445.001.0001

Klein, M. W., Maxson, C. L., & Cunningham, L. C. (1991). "Crack," street gangs, and violence. *Criminology, 29*(4), 623–650. doi:10.1111/j.1745-9125.1991.tb01082.x

Klein, M. W., Weerman, F. M., & Thornberry, T. P. (2006). Street gang violence in Europe. *European Journal of Criminology, 3*(4), 413–437. doi:10.1177/1477370806067911

Knox, G. W. (1994). *An Introduction to Gangs* (3rd ed.). Bristol: Wyndham Hall Press.

Knox, G. W. (2005). *The Problem of Gangs and Security Threat Groups (STG's) in American Prisons Today: Recent Research Findings from the 2004 Prison Gang Survey. National Gang Crime Research Center Ministry of Justice Research Series 2/11. March 2011. Understanding the psychology of gang violence: Implications for designing effective violence interventions.* London: Ministry of Justice.

Knox, G. W. (2005). *The Problem of Gangs and Security Threat Groups (STG's) in American Prisons Today: Recent Research Findings from the 2004 Prison Gang Survey.* National Gang Crime Research Center.

Kodluboy, D. W., & Evenrud, L. A. (1993). School-based interventions: Best practice and critical issues. In A. P. Goldstein & C. R. Huff (Eds.), *The Gang Intervention Handbook.* Champaign, IL.: Research Press.

Kolko, D. J. (1985). Juvenile Firesetting: A Review And Methodological Critique. *Clinical Psychology Review, 5*(4), 345–376. doi:10.1016/0272-7358(85)90012-1

Kolko, D. J., Herschell, A. D., & Scharf, D. M. (2006). Education And Treatment For Boys Who Set Fires: Specificity, Moderators, And Predictors Of Recidivism. *Journal of Emotional and Behavioral Disorders, 14*(4), 227–239. doi:10.1 177/10634266060140040601

Kolko, D. J., & Kazdin, A. E. (1992). The emergence and recurrence of child fire setting: A one-year prospective study. *Journal of Abnormal Child Psychology, 20*(1), 17–37. doi:10.1007/BF00927114 PMID:1548392

Kraul, C., Lopez, R. J., & Connell, R. (2005). MS-13 Blamed for Massacre on Bus. *The Seattle Times.* Retrieved July 2, 2014 from http://seattletimes.nwsource.com/html/nationworld/2002283961_gangslaying22.html

Kressel, N. (2002). *Mass Hate: The Global Rise of Genocide and Terror.* New York: Plenum Press.

Kubrin, C. E. (2005). Gangstas, thugs, and hustlas: Identity and the code of the street in rap music. *Social Problems, 52*(3), 360–378. doi:10.1525/sp.2005.52.3.360

Kupchik, A., & Ellis, N. (2008). School discipline and security: Fair for all students. *Youth & Society, 39*(4), 549–574. doi:10.1177/0044118X07301956

Kuperschmidt, J. B., & Coie, J. D. (1990). Preadolescent peer. *Child Development, 61*, 1350–1362. PMID:2245729

Kyratzis, A. (2004). Talk and interaction among children and the co-construction of Peer groups and peer culture. *Annual Review of Anthropology, 33*(1), 625–649. doi:10.1146/annurev.anthro.33.070203.144008

La Rosa, M., & Rugh, D. (2005). Onset of Alcohol and Other Drug Use Among Latino Gang Members. *Alcoholism Treatment Quarterly, 23*(2), 67–85. doi:10.1300/J020v23n02_05

Labree, W., Nijman, H., Van Marle, H., & Rassin, E. (2010). Backgrounds and characteristics of arsonists. *International Journal of Law and Psychiatry, 33*(3), 149–153. doi:10.1016/j.ijlp.2010.03.004 PMID:20434774

Lalor, K. (1999). Street children: A comparative perspective. *Child Abuse & Neglect, 23*(8), 759–780. doi:10.1016/S0145-2134(99)00047-2 PMID:10477236

Lambrechts, D. (2013). *The impact of organised crime on social control by the state: a study of Manenberg in Cape Town, South Africa* (PhD Thesis). Stellenbosch.

Lassir, N. (2012, August 8). Hate with a beat: White power music. *CNN.com.*

Laub, J. H., Nagin, D., & Sampson, R. J. (1998). Trajectories of change in criminal offending: Good marriages and the desistance process. *American Sociological Review, 63*(2), 225–238. doi:10.2307/2657324

Laub, J. H., & Sampson, R. J. (2001). Understanding desistance from crime. In M. Tonry (Ed.), *Crime and justice: A review of research* (Vol. 28, pp. 1–69). Chicago, IL: University of Chicago Press.

Laub, J. H., & Sampson, R. J. (2003). *Shared beginnings, divergent lives: Delinquent boys to age 70*. Cambridge, MA: Harvard University Press.

Lauger, T. (2012). *Real Gangstas: Legitimacy, Reputation, and Violence in the Intergang Environment*. Rutgers University Press.

Lauger, T. R. (2012). *Real gangstas: Legitimacy, reputation, and violence in the intergang environment*. New Brunswick, NJ: Rutgers University Press.

Lauger, T. R. (2014). Violent stories: Personal narratives, street socialization, and the negotiation of street culture among street-oriented youth. *Criminal Justice Review, 39*(2), 182–200. doi:10.1177/0734016814529966

Leap, J. (2012). Jumped. In *What Gangs Taught Me about Violence, Drugs, Love, and Redemption* (p. 36). Beacon Press.

Lea, R., & Chambers, G. (2007). 'Monoamine oxidase, addiction, and the 'warrior' gene hypothesis. *The New Zealand Medical Journal, 120*(1250), 2. PMID:17339897

Lee, C. (2009, February 19). Police make largest cocaine seizure in yrs. *China Daily*.

Lee, K. W. (2005). *Triad-related homicide 1989-1998*. (PhD thesis). University of Hong Kong.

Lee, F. W., Loi, T. W., & Wong, D. S. W. (1996). Intervention in the decision-making of youth gangs. *Groupwork, 9*(3), 292–302.

Lemert, E. M. (1951). *Social Pathology: A Systematic Approach to the Study of Sociopathic Behaviour*. New York: McGraw-Hill.

Lenzi, M., Sharkey, Vieno, Mayworm, Doughety, & Nylund-Gibson. (n.d.). Adolescent gang involvement: The role of individual, peer, and school factors in a multilevel perspective. *Aggressive Behavior, 41*(4), 386-397.

Leon, L. (2011). When Religion Kills: The Narco-Traffickers of the Borderlands. *Religion Dispatches Magazine*. Retrieved April 2014 from http://www.religiondispatches.org/archive/atheologies/5009/when_religion_kills%3A_the_narco-traffickers_of_the_borderlands

Letícia, M. K., Forster, M. K. L., Tannhauser, M., & Barros, H. M. T. (1996). Drug use among street children in southern Brazil. *Drug and Alcohol Dependence, 43*(1-2), 57–62. doi:10.1016/S0376-8716(96)01288-4 PMID:8957143

Levi, M. (1994). Masculinities and white-collar crime. In T. In Newburn & B. Stanko (Eds.), *Just Boys Doing Business*. London: Routledge.

Levi, M., & Maguire, M. (2003). Violent Crime. In M. Maguire, R. Morgan, & R. Reiner (Eds.), *The Oxford Handbook of Criminology* (3rd ed.). Oxford University Press.

Levitt, S., & Dubner, S. (2005). *Freakonomics: a rogue economist explores the hidden side of everything*. New York: Harper Collins.

Liu, C. (2004). The Characteristics and Causes of Youth Gang crime. *Journal of ChangQiu Vocational and Technological College, 11*, 55–56.

Liu, J. (2008). Data sources in Chinese crime and criminal Justice research. *Crime, Law, and Social Change, 50*(3), 131–147. doi:10.1007/s10611-008-9135-3

Lockhart, B. (2012, November 17). Cameras watch over Bridgeport chools. *CTPost.com*. Retrieved from: http://www.ctpost.com/local/article/Cameras-watch-over-Bridgeport-schools-4047135.php

Lockwood, D. (1997). *Violence Among Middle School and high School Students: Analysis and Implications for Prevention. National Institute of Justice, Research in Brief*. Washington, DC: Office of Justice Programs, US Department of Justice.

Lopez, C., & DuBois, D. L. (2005). Peer victimization and rejection: Investigation of an integrative model of effects on emotional, behavioral, and academic adjustment in early adolescence. *Journal of Clinical Child and Adolescent Psychology, 34*(1), 25–36. doi:10.1207/s15374424jccp3401_3 PMID:15677278

Luckman, T. (2008). On social interaction and the communicative construction of personal identity, knowledge and reality. *Organization Studies, 29*(2), 277–290. doi:10.1177/0170840607087260

Luo, S. (2012, December 29). Living on the mean streets. *China Daily*.

Lurigio, A. L., Flexon, J. L., & Greenleaf, R. G. (2008). Antecedents to gang membership: Attachments, beliefs, and street encounters with the police. *Journal of Gang Research, 15*, 15–33.

Lutkehaus, N., & Roscoe, P. (Eds.). (2013). *Gender rituals: Female initiation in Melanesia*. Routledge.

Luttens, W. G., & Ackerman, M. S. (1996). An Introduction to the Chicago School of Sociology. *Interval Research, Proprietary*. Retrieved from: http://userpages.umbc.edu/~lutters/pubs/1996_SWLNote96-1_Lutters,Ackerman.pdf

Mackie, D., & Cooper, J. (1984). Attitude polarization: Effects of group membership. *Journal of Personality and Social Psychology, 46*(3), 575–585. doi:10.1037/0022-3514.46.3.575

Magazine, R. (2003). Action, personhood and the gift economy among so-called street children in Mexico City. *Social Anthropology, 11*(3), 303–318. doi:10.1017/S0964028203000223

Maguire, E. (2013). *Research, Theory and Speculation on Gang Truces*. Wilson Center, Unpublished Paper. Retrieved April 3, 2014 from http://www.wilsoncenter.org/sites/default/files/Maguire%20%20US%20and%20Trinidad%20-%20Paper.pdf

Maguire, E. R., Katz, C. M., & Wilson, D. B. (2013). *The Effects of a Gang Truce on Gang Violence. Background Paper for Wilson Center*. Washington, DC: American University.

Main, J. (1991). The Truth about triads. *Policing: An International Journal of Police Strategies & Management, 7*(2), 144–163.

Mallia, R. (2014, October 24). Drones, SWAT surround Summerville game after gang threats. *ABC News 4*. Retrieved from: http://www.abcnews4.com/story/26888495/drones-swat-surround-summerville-game-after-gang-threats

Marcus, S. (Ed.). (1992). *Fighting Bodies, Fighting Words: A Theory and Politics of Rape Prevention*. New York, NY: Routeledge.

Marshall, G. (1994). *Spirit of 69: A Skinhead Bible*. S.T. Publishing.

Marshall, G. (1997). *Skinhead Nation*. S.T. Publishing.

Martinez, O. (2013). *El Naufragio de Una Tregua. Background Paper for the Wilson Center*. Washington, DC: Wilson Center.

Martinez, S. (2009). A system gone bezerk: How are zero-tolerance policies really affecting schools? *Preventing School Failure, 53*(3), 153–157. doi:10.3200/PSFL.53.3.153-158

Maruna, S. (1999). Desistance and development: The psychosocial process of "going straight". In M. Brogden (Ed.), *The British Criminology Conferences: Selected proceedings* (Vol. 2). Belfast, Ireland. Retrieved October 15, 2014, from http://www.britsocrim.org/v2.htm

Maruna, S. (2001). *Making good: How ex-convicts reform and rebuild their lives.* Washington, DC: American Psychological Association Books. doi:10.1037/10430-000

Maruna, S., & Farrall, S. (2004). Desistance from crime: A theoretical reformulation. *Kölner Zeitschrift für Soziologie und Sozialpsychologie, 43*, 171–194.

Maruna, S., LeBel, T. P., Mitchell, N., & Naples, M. (2004). Pygmalion in the reintegration process: Desistance from crime through the looking glass. *Psychology, Crime & Law, 10*(3), 271–281. doi:10.1080/10683160410001662762

Mastrangelo, A. (2012). *Identifying Juvenile Firesetters: A Survey Of The Operating Procedures, Risk Assessment Instruments And The Characteristics Of Juvenile Firesetter Intervention Programs In The United States.* (Thesis). City University Of New York, New York, NY.

Mateu-Galabert, P., & Lune, H. (2003). School violence: The bidirectional conflict flow between neighborhood and school. *City & Community, 2*(4), 353–368. doi:10.1046/j.1535-6841.2003.00060.x

Matheron, M. S., (1988). China: Chinese triads, the Oriental Mafia. *CJ International, 4*(3), 26-27.

Matsueda, K. N., Melde, C., Taylor, T. J., Freng, A., & Esbensen, F.-A. (2013). Gang membership and adherence to the "code of the street.". *Justice Quarterly, 30*(3), 440–468. doi:10.1080/07418825.2012.684432

Matthews, R. (2002). *Armed Robbery.* Willan Publishing.

Matza, D. (1964). *Delinquency and drift.* New York, NY: John Wiley.

Maxson, C. L., & Klein, M. W. (1990). Street gang violence: Twice as great, or half as great? In C. R. Huff (Ed.), *Gangs in America* (pp. 71–100). Newbury Park, CA: Sage.

May, D., & Dunaway, G. (2000). Predictors of fear of criminal victimization at school among adolescents. *Sociological Spectrum, 20*(2), 149–168. doi:10.1080/027321700279938

Mayer, M. J., & Leone, P. E. (1999). A structural analysis of school violence and disruption: Implications for creating safer schools. *Education & Treatment of Children, 22*(3), 333–365.

McCorkle, R. C., & Meithe, T. D. (1998). The political and organizational response to gangs: An examination of a "moral panic" in Nevada. *Justice Quarterly, 15*(1), 41–64. doi:10.1080/07418829800093631

McDaniel, D., Egley, A. Jr, & Logan, J. (2014). Gang homicides in five U.S. cities, 2003-2008. *Morbidity and Mortality Weekly Report, 61*, 46–51. PMID:22278158

McDermott, J. (2012). Money Runs out for Belize Gang Truce. *Insight Crime.* Retrieved December 13, 2013 from http://www.insightcrime.org/news-briefs/money-runs-out-for-belize-gang-truce

McDermott, J. (2013). Medellin Truce Inches Groups Closer to Criminal Hegemony. *Insight Crime.* Retrieved October 4, 2014 from http://www.insightcrime.org/news-analysis/mafia-truce-brokered-in-medellin

McGloin, J. M. (2005). Policy and intervention considerations of a network analysis of street gangs. *Criminology & Public Policy*, *4*(3), 607–635. doi:10.1111/j.1745-9133.2005.00306.x

McKetin, R., Hickey, K., Devlin, K., & Lawrence, K. (2010). The Risk of Psychotic Symptoms Associated with Recreational Methamphetamine Use. *Drug and Alcohol Review*, *29*(4), 358–363. doi:10.1111/j.1465-3362.2009.00160.x PMID:20636650

McKetin, R., McLaren, J., Ridell, S., & Robins, L. (2006). *The Relationship between Methamphetamine Use and Violent Behaviour, Contemporary Issues in Crime and Justice, No.97*. Sydney: New South Wales Bureau of Crime Statistics and Research, Crime and Justice Bulletin.

McKetin, R., Ross, J., Kelly, E., Baker, A., Lee, N., Lubman, D. I., & Mattick, R. (2008). Characteristics and Harms Associated with Injecting Versus Smoking Methamphetamine Among Methamphetamine Treatment Entrants. *Drug and Alcohol Review*, *27*(3), 277–285. doi:10.1080/09595230801919486 PMID:18368609

McNamara, R. H. (2012). *Problem children: Special populations in delinquency*. Durham, NC: Carolina Academic Press.

McVie, S. (2010). *Gang membership and knife carrying: Findings from the Edinburgh study of youth transitions and crime*. The Scottish Centre for Crime and Justice Research.

Mears, P., & Butts, J. (2008). Using performance monitoring to improve the accountability, operations, and effectiveness of juvenile justice. *Criminal Justice Policy Review*, *19*(3), 264–284. doi:10.1177/0887403407308233

Meehan, A. J. (2000). The organizational career of gang statistics: The politics of policing gangs. *The Sociological Quarterly*, *41*(3), 337–370. doi:10.1111/j.1533-8525.2000.tb00082.x

Meek, J. (1992). Gangs in New Zealand Prisons. *Australian and New Zealand Journal of Criminology*, *25*(3), 255–277. doi:10.1177/000486589202500304

Meisenhelder, T. (1977). An exploratory study of exiting from criminal careers. *Criminology*, *15*(3), 319–334. doi:10.1111/j.1745-9125.1977.tb00069.x

Merton, R. K. (1938). Social Structure and Anomie. *American Sociological Review*, *3*(October), 672–682. doi:10.2307/2084686

Merton, R. K. (1957). *Social Theory and Social Structure*. New York: Free Press.

Messerschmidt, J. (1997). *Crime as Structured Action: Gender, Race, Class, and Crime in the Making*. London: Sage. doi:10.4135/9781452232294

Messerschmidt, J. W. (1993). *Masculinities and crime: Critique and reconceptualization of theory*. Lanham, MD: Rowman and Littlefield.

Messerschmidt, J. W. (1999). Making Bodies Matter: Adolescent Masculinities, the Body, and Varieties of Violence. *Theoretical Criminology*, *3*(2), 197–220. doi:10.1177/1362480699003002004

Messerschmidt, J. W. (2000). *Nine Lives: Adolescent masculinities, the body, and violence*. Boulder, CO: Westview Press.

Messner, M. A. (1990). When bodies are weapons: Masculinity and violence in Sport. *International Review for the Sociology of Sport*, *25*(3), 203–220. doi:10.1177/101269029002500303

Metzler, C. W., & Noell, J. (1994). The social context of risky sexual behavior among adolescents. *Journal of Behavioral Medicine*, *17*, 419.

Miethe, T. D., & Kriss, A. (1999). Exploring the Social Context of Instrumental and Expressive Homicides: An Application of Qualitative Comparative Analysis. *Journal of Quantitative Criminology, 15*(1), 1–21. doi:10.1023/A:1007591025837

Miller, J. (2000). *Getting into gangs. In One of the Guys: Girls, Gangs, and Gender* (pp. 35–63). New York: Oxford University Press.

Miller, J. (2001). *One of the Guys: Girls, Gangs and Gender*. New York: Oxford University Press.

Miller, L. (2014). Juvenile Crime And Juvenile Justice: Patterns, Models, And Implications For Clinical And Legal Practice. *Aggression and Violent Behavior, 19*(2), 122–137.http://dx.doi.org/10.1016/j.avb.2014.01.005

Miller, N., & Brewer, M. B. (Eds.). (1984). *Groups in Contact: The Psychology of Desegregation*. New York: Academic Press.

Ministry of Social Development. (2008b). *Youth Gangs in Counties Manukau*. Ministry of Social Development.

Mob Advisory Panel. (c1996). *Lower North Island Regions High Mortality Rate 1994-1995 Discussion Paper*. Dunedin: Unpublished.

Moffitt, T. E. (1993). Adolescence-limited and life-course-persistent antisocial behavior: A developmental taxonomy. *Psychological Review, 100*, 674.

Mohammed, M. (2007). Des « bandes d'ici » aux « gangs d'ailleurs »: comment définir et comparer? In M. Mohammed & L. Mucchielli (Eds.), Les bandes de jeunes: Des « blousons noirs » à nos jours (pp. 265-285). Paris, FR: La découverte.

Montero, I. (1979). *Vietnamese Americans: Patterns of Resettlement and Socioeconomic Adaptation in the United States*. Boulder, CO: Westview Press.

Moore, J. W. (1991). *Going down to the barrio: Homeboys and homegirls in change*. Philadelphia: Temple University Press.

Morakinyo, J., & Odejide, A. O. (2003). A community based study of patterns of psychoactive substance use among street children in a local government area of Nigeria. *Drug and Alcohol Dependence, 71*(2), 109–116. doi:10.1016/S0376-8716(03)00093-0 PMID:12927648

Morell, G., Scott, S., McNeish, D., & Webster, S. (2011). *The August Riots in England: Understanding the Involvement of Young People. A Cabinet Commissioned Report*. London: NatCen.

Morley, K., & Hall, W. (2003). Is There a Genetic Susceptibility to Engage in Criminal Acts? *Trends & Issues in Crime and Criminal Justice, 263*, 1–6.

Morrell, E. (2008). Six Summer of YPAR. In J. Cammarota & M. Fine (Eds.), *Revolutionizing Education: Youth Participatory Action Research in Motion*. Routledge.

Morris, P., Barer, B., & Morris, T. (1963). *Pentonville: A Sociological Study of An English Prison*. Routledge and Kegan Paul.

Moser, C., & Winton, A. (2002). *Violence in the Central American region: towards an integrated framework for violence reduction*. ODI Working Paper No. 171. ODI.

Moser, C. (2004). Urban violence and insecurity: An introductory roadmap. *Environment and Urbanization, 16*(3), 3–16. doi:10.1177/095624780401600220

Moser, C., & McIlwaine, C. (2004). *Encounters with Violence in Latin America: Urban Poor Perceptions from Colombia and Guatemala*. London: Routledge.

Muggah, R., & Reiger, M. (2012). *Negotiating Disarmament and Demobilization in Peace Processes: What is the State of the Evidence?* Norwegian Peacebuilding Research Centre. Retrieved February 12, 2014 from http://www.peacebuilding. no/Themes/Peacebuilding-in-practice/publications/Negotiating-disarmament-and-demobilisation-in-peace-processes-what-is-the-state-of-the-evidence

Muggah, R., & White, N. (2013). *Is There a Preventive Action Renaissance: The Policy and Practice of Preventive Diplomacy and Conflict Prevention*. Norwegian Peacebuilding Research Centre. Retrieved February 12, 2014 from http://www.peacebuilding.no/Themes/Peacebuilding-in-practice/publications/Is-there-a-preventive-action-renaissance-The-policy-and-practice-of-preventive-diplomacy-and-conflict-prevention

Muggah, R. (2011). The Transnational Gang: Challenging the Conventional Narrative. In T. Shaw & A. Grant (Eds.), *Ashgate Research Companion to Regionalism*. London: Ashgate.

Mullen, B., Brown, R., & Smith, C. (1992). Ingroup bias as a function of salience, relevance, and status: An integration. *European Journal of Social Psychology, 22*(2), 103–122. doi:10.1002/ejsp.2420220202

Mulvey, E. P., Steinberg, L., Fagan, J., Cauffman, E., Piquero, A. R., Chassin, L., & Losoya, S. H. et al. (2004). Theory and research on desistance from antisocial activity among serious adolescent offenders. *Youth Violence and Juvenile Justice, 2*(3), 213–236. doi:10.1177/1541204004265864 PMID:20119505

Muntingh, L., & Ballard, C. (2012). *Report on Children in Prison in South Africa*. Community Law Centre.

Murdoch, D., & Ross, D. (1990). Alcohol and crimes of violence: Present issues. *Substance Use & Misuse, 25*(9), 1065–1081. doi:10.3109/10826089009058873 PMID:2090635

Myers, D. G., & Lamm, H. (1976). The group polarization phenomenon. *Psychological Bulletin, 83*(4), 602–627. doi:10.1037/0033-2909.83.4.602

Nadesu, A. (2009). *Reconviction patterns of released prison: A 60-month follow-up analysis*. Department of Corrections. Retrieved from http://www.corrections.govt.nz/__data/assets/pdf_file/0005/672764/Complete-Recidivism-Report-2009-DOC.pdf

Nagendra, S. P. (1971). *The concept of ritual in modern sociological theory*. New Delhi: The Academic Journals of India.

Naterer, A. (2007). Bomzhi-street children in Makeevka. Subkulturni azil: Maribor.

Naterer, A. (2010). *An anthropological analysis of the street children subculture* (Dissertation). Ljubljana: FDV.

Naterer, A. (2014, June 26). Violence and the Code of the Street: a study of social dynamics among street children in Makeevka, East Ukraine. *Journal of Interpersonal Violence*, 1-16.

Naterer, A., & Godina, V. V. (2011). Bomzhi and their subculture – an anthropological study of the street children subculture in Makeevka, East Ukraine. *Childhood, 18*(1), 20–38. doi:10.1177/0907568210379924

National Crime Prevention Centre (NCPC). (2012). *Prevention of youth gang violence: Overview of strategies and approaches*. Retrieved October 15, 2014, from http://www.publicsafety.gc.ca/prg/cp/ygpf/ygpf-osa-eng.aspx

National Drug Master Plan 2013 – 2017. (2012). South African Government Publication.

National Gang Crime Research Center. (1995). *Gang Prevention and Gang Intervention: Preliminary Results from the 1995 Project GANGPINT*. National Needs Assessment Gang Research Task Force.

National Gang Crime Research Center. (n.d.). Bomb and arson crimes among American gang members: A behavioral science profile. *Journal of Gang Research, 9*(1), 1-38.

National Institute of Justice. (1999). *The appropriate use of security technology in U.S. schools: A guide for schools and law enforcement agencies.* Washington, DC: National Institude of Justice.

Nemes, I. (2002, October). Regulating hate speech in cyberspace: Issues of desirability and efficacy. *Information & Communications Technology Law, 11*(3), 193–211. doi:10.1080/1360083022000031902

Neubauer, I. L. (2014, September 24). A teenage terrorism suspect is shot dead in Australia after attacking police. *Time World Australia.*

New Zealand Police Association (2009). *Gangs and Organised Crime Bill: Submission of the New Zealand Police Association.* Author.

New Zealand Police. (2006). *Tactical Problem Profile: Youth Gangs Counties Manukau East.* Intelligence Section, East Area.

Newburn, T. (2011). *Reading the Riots: Investigating England's Summer of Disorder.* Retrieved 12 October 2014 from: http://www.guardian.co.uk/uk/2011/dec/05/anger-police-fuelled-riots-study

Ngai, N., Cheung, C., & Ngai, S. (2007, Summer). Cognitive and social influences on Gang involvement among delinquents in three Chinese cities. *Adolescence, 42*(166), 381–403. PMID:17849942

Ngo, H. V. (2010). *Unravelling identities and belonging: Criminal gang involvement of youth from immigrant families.* Calgary, AB: Centre for Newcomers.

Nuwer, H. (2001). *Wrongs of passage: Fraternities, sororities, hazing, and binge drinking.* Bloomington, IN: Indiana University Press.

Oak Creek Sikh temple shooter had military background, white supremacist ties. (2012, August 6). *Milwaukee Journal-Sentinel.*

Ochs, E., & Capps, L. (1996). Narrating the self. *Annual Review of Anthropology, 25*(1), 19–43. doi:10.1146/annurev.anthro.25.1.19

Odgers, C. L., Moffitt, T. E., Broadbent, J. M., Dickson, N., Hancox, R. J., Harrington, H., & Caspi, A. (2008). Female and male antisocial trajectories: From childhood origins to adult outcomes. *Development and Psychopathology, 20*(02), 673–716. doi:10.1017/S0954579408000333 PMID:18423100

Office of Juvenile Justice and Delinquency Prevention (OJJDP). (1997). *Reporting Crimes Against Juveniles.* Washington, DC: U.S. Department of Justice.

Office of Juvenile Justice and Delinquency Prevention (OJJDP). (1999). *Promising strategies to reduce gun violence.* Washington, DC: U.S. Department of Justice.

Ojeda, L., Rosales, R., & Good, G. E. (2008). Socioeconomic status and cultural predictors of male role attitudes among Mexican American men: Son más machos? *Psychology of Men & Masculinity, 9*(3), 133–138. doi:10.1037/1524-9220.9.3.133

Olweus, D. (1993). *Bullying at school: What we know and what we can do.* Malden, MA: Blackwell Publishing.

Ordog, G. J., Shoemaker, W., Wasserberger, J., & Bishop, M. (1995). Gunshot wounds seen at a county hospital before and after a riot and gang truce: Part two. *The Journal of Trauma Injury Infection and Critical Care, 38*(3), 417–419. doi:10.1097/00005373-199503000-00024 PMID:7897730

O'Reilly, D. (2005). *The Things that Bind Us.* Retrieved from http://www.nzedge.com/the-things-that-bind-us/

Oshkosh Fire Department. (2014). Retrieved March 5, 2014, from http://www2.ci.oshkosh.wi.us/fire/dpt_overview.htm

Owen, R. (2014, January 17). *Financial Mail.*

Palansinski, M. (2013). Security, respect and culture in British teenagers' discourses of knife-carrying. *Safer Communities, 12*(2), 71–78. doi:10.1108/17578041311315049

Palansinski, M., & Riggs, D. W. (2012). Young white British men and knife-carrying in public: Discourses of masculinity, protection and vulnerability. *Critical Criminology, 20*(4), 463–476. doi:10.1007/s10612-012-9161-4

Paoli, L. (2002). The Paradoxes of Organised Crime. *Crime, Law, and Social Change, 37*(1), 51–97. doi:10.1023/A:1013355122531

Papachristos, A. V., Braga, A., & Hureau, D. (Forthcoming). Social Networks and the Risk of Gunshot Injury. *Journal of Urban Health.* PMID:22714704

Parker-Lewis, H. (2010). *Gods gangsters: The numbers, gangs and South African tattoo prison culture.* Cape Town: Ihilihili Press.

Parkes, J. (2007). The Multiple Meanings of Violence – Children's talk about life in a South African neighbourhood. *Childhood, 14*(4), 401–414. doi:10.1177/0907568207081848

Parry, S. (2013, November 8). Twilight of the triads. *China Daily.*

Patrick, J. (1973/2012). *A Glasgow Gang Observed.* Neil Wilson Publishing.

Patterson, G. R., DeBaryshe, B., & Ramsey, E. (1990). A Developmental Perspective on Antisocial Behavior. *The American Psychologist, 44*(2), 329–335. doi:10.1037/0003-066X.44.2.329 PMID:2653143

Pearson, G. (2012). *An ethnography of English football fans: Cans, cops and carnivals.* Manchester University Press. doi:10.7228/manchester/9780719087219.001.0001

Pearson, G., & Hobbs, D. (2001). *Middle Market Drug Distribution. Home Office Research (Study 227), Development and Statistics Directorate.* London: Home Office.

Perrino, T., González-Soldevilla, A., Pantin, H., & Szapocznik, J. (2000). The Role of Families in Adolescent HIV Prevention: A Review. *Clinical Child and Family Psychology Review, 3*(2), 81–96. doi:10.1023/A:1009571518900 PMID:11227063

Perrone, P. A., & Chesney-Lind, M. (1997). Representations of gangs and delinquency: Wild in the streets? *Social Justice (San Francisco, Calif.), 24,* 96–116.

Peterson, D. (2000). Definitions of a gang and impacts on public policy. *Journal of Criminal Justice, 28*(2), 139–149. doi:10.1016/S0047-2352(99)00036-7

Peterson, D. (2012). Girlfriends, gun-holders, and ghetto-rats? Moving beyond narrow views of girls in gangs. In S. Miller, L. D. Leve, & P. K. Kerig (Eds.), *Delinquent girls: Contexts, relationships, and adaption.* Switzerland: Springer International Publishing. doi:10.1007/978-1-4614-0415-6_5

Peterson, D., Taylor, T. J., & Esbensen, F. (2004). Gang membership and violent victimization. *Justice Quarterly, 21*(4), 793–815. doi:10.1080/07418820400095991

Pettigrew, T. F., & Tropp, L. R. (2006). A meta-analytic test of intergroup contact theory. *Journal of Personality and Social Psychology, 90*(5), 751–783. doi:10.1037/0022-3514.90.5.751 PMID:16737372

Phillips, C. (2008). Negotiating identities: Ethnicity and social relations in a young offenders' institution. *Theoretical Criminology, 12*(3), 313–331. doi:10.1177/1362480608093309

Phillips, C. (2012a). It Ain't Nothing Like America with the Bloods and the Crips: Gang Narratives Inside Two English Prisons. *Punishment and Society, 14*(1), 51–68. doi:10.1177/1462474511424683

Phillips, C. (2012b). *The Multicultural Prison: Ethnicity, Masculity and Social Relations among Prisoners.* Clarendon Studies in Criminology. doi:10.1093/acprof:oso/9780199697229.001.0001

Pinnock, D. (2016). *Gang Town.* Cape Town: Tafelberg.

Piquero, A., Farrington, D., & Blumstein, A. (2003). The criminal career paradigm. In M. Tonry (Ed.), *Crime and justice: A review of research* (Vol. 30, pp. 359–506). Chicago, IL: University of Chicago Press.

Pitts, J. (2008). *Reluctant Gangsters - The Changing Face of Youth Crime.* Willan Publishing.

Pitts, J. (2012). Reluctant criminologists: Criminology, ideology and the violent youth gang. *Youth & Policy, 109,* 27–45.

Polk, K. (1994). *When Men Kill: Scenarios of Masculine Violence.* Melbourne: Cambridge University Press.

Pollock, J. M. (2005). *Prisons: Today and Tomorrow* (2nd ed.). Jones and Bartlett Publishers.

Potok, M. (2013). *The little Fuhrer: Matthew Heimbach goes all the way.* Posted in Hatewatch Blog: Anti-Semetic, Neo-Nazi of the Southern Poverty Law Center.

Price, P. (2009). When is a police officer an officer of the law? The status of police officers in schools. *Journal of Criminal Law and Criminology, 99*(2), 541-70.

Prowse, C. E. (2012). *Defining Street Gangs in the 21ˢᵗ Century: Fluid, Mobile and Transitional Networks.* Springer.

Putnam, R. D. (1995). *Bowling Alone: The Collapse and Revival of American Community.* Simon and Schuster Ltd.

Puzzanchera, C., & Adams, B. (2009). Juvenile Arrests 2009. Office of Juvenil Justice and Delinquency Prevention (OJJDP). Washington, DC: U.S. Department of Justice. Retrieved from http://www.ojjdp.gov/pubs/236477.pdf

Pyrooz, D., & Decker, S. (2012). Delinquent Behaviour, Violence and Gang Involvement in China. *Journal of Quantitative Criminology, 29*(2), 251-272.

Pyrooz, D. C., & Decker, S. H. (2011). Motives and methods for leaving the gang: Understanding the process of gang desistance. *Journal of Criminal Justice, 39*(5), 417–425. doi:10.1016/j.jcrimjus.2011.07.001

Pyrooz, D. C., & Decker, S. H. (2013). Delinquent behavior, violence, and gang involvement in China. *Journal of Quantitative Criminology, 29*(2), 251–272. doi:10.1007/s10940-012-9178-6

Pyrooz, D. C., Decker, S. H., & Webb, V. J. (2014). The ties that bind: Desistance from gangs. *Crime and Delinquency, 60*(4), 491–516. doi:10.1177/0011128710372191

Pyrooz, D. C., Sweeten, G., & Piquero, A. R. (2013). Continuity and change in gang membership and gang embeddedness. *Journal of Research in Crime and Delinquency, 50*(2), 272–299. doi:10.1177/0022427811434830

Pyszczynski, T., Solomon, S., & Greenberg, J. (1997). Why do we need what we need? A terror management perspective on the roots of human social motivation. *Psychological Inquiry*, *8*(1), 1–20. doi:10.1207/s15327965pli0801_1

Pyszczynski, T., Solomon, S., & Greenberg, J. (2005). *In the wake of 9/11: The psychology of terror*. Washington, DC: American Psychological Association.

Pyszczynski, T., Wicklund, R. A., Floresku, S., Koch, H., Gauch, G., Solomon, S., & Greenberg, J. (1996). Whistling in the dark: Exaggerated consensus estimates in response to incidental reminders of mortality. *Psychological Science*, *7*(6), 332–336. doi:10.1111/j.1467-9280.1996.tb00384.x

Quintero, G. A., & Estrada, A. L. (1998). Cultural Models of Masculinity and Drug Use: "Machismo," Heroin, and Street Survival on the U.S. - Mexico Border. *Contemporary Drug Problems*, *25*(Spring), 147.

Ramatlakane, L. (2003). Unpublished document distributed by the Department of Community Safety.

Rice, S. (2009). Education for toleration in an era of zero tolerance school policies: A Deweyan analysis. *Educational Studies*, *45*(6), 556–571. doi:10.1080/00131940903338308

Richardson, J. W., & Scott, K. A. (2002). Rap Music and Its Violent Progeny: America's Culture of Violence in Context. *The Journal of Negro Education*, *71*(3), 175–192. doi:10.2307/3211235

Right-Wing Extremism : Germany's New Islamophobia Boom. (2014). Spiegel Online.

Rios, V. M. (2011). *Punished: Policing the Lives of Black and Latino Boys*. New York, NY: New York University Press.

Ritchie, E. C., & Huff, T. G. (1999). Psychiatric aspects of arsonists. *Journal of Forensic Sciences*, *44*(4), 733–740. doi:10.1520/JFS14546J PMID:10432607

Robers, S., Kemp, J., Rathbun, A., & Morgan, R. E. (2014). *Indicators of School Crime and Safety: 2013. (NCES 2014-042/NCJ 243299)*. Washington, DC: U.S. Department of Justice.

Robers, S., Zhang, J., Truman, J., & Snyder, T. D. (2011). *Indicators of school crime and safety: 2011 (NCES 2011-002/NCJ 230812)*. Washington, DC: U.S. Department of Justice.

Roberts, S., Kemp, J., Rathburn, A., Morgan, R. E., & Snyder, T. D. (2013). Indicators of School Crime and Safety: 2013. Bureau of Justice Statistics (BJS) and Institute of Education Sciences, National Center for Education Statistics.

Robinson, P. L., Boscardin, W. J., George, S. M., Teklehaimanot, S., Heslin, K. C., & Bluthenthal, R. N. (2009). The effect of urban street gang densities on small area homicide incidences in a large metropolitan county, 1994-2002. *Journal of Urban Health Bulletin of the New York Academy of Medicine*, *86*(4), 511–523.

Rock, P. (2002). Social Theories of Crime. In M. Maguire, R. Morgan, & R. Reiner (Eds.), *The Oxford Handbook of Criminology* (3rd ed.). Oxford University Press.

Rodriquez, L. J. (2005). *La vida loca: Gang Days in L.A., always running*. New York: Simon & Schuster.

Romer, D. (2009). Adolescent risk taking, impulsivity, and brain development: Implications for prevention. *Developmental Psychobiology*, *52*(3), 263–276. PMID:20175097

Ro, R. (1996). *Gangsta: Merchandising the Rhymes of Violence*. New York: St. Martin's Press.

Rosenblatt, A., Greenberg, J., Solomon, S., Pyszczynski, T., & Lyon, D. (1989). Evidence for terror management theory I: The effects of mortality salience on reactions to those who violate or uphold cultural values. *Journal of Personality and Social Psychology*, *57*(4), 681–690. doi:10.1037/0022-3514.57.4.681 PMID:2795438

Rose, T. (2001). Keepin' it Real. *The New Crisis, 108*(5), 22–25.

Roth, J. (1994). *Understanding and Preventing Violence. Research in Brief.* Washington, DC: National Institute of Justice, US Department of Justice.

Rubin, M., & Hewstone, M. (1998). Social identity theory's self-esteem hypothesis: A review and some suggestions for clarification. *Personality and Social Psychology Review, 2*(1), 40–62. doi:10.1207/s15327957pspr0201_3 PMID:15647150

Runciman, W. G. (1966). *Relative Deprivation and Social Justice.* London: Routledge and Kegan Paul.

Russell, S. L., Gordon, S., Lukacs, J. R., & Kaste, L. M. (2013). Sex/gender differences in tooth loss and edentulism: Historical perspectives, biological factors, and sociologic reasons. *Dental Clinics of North America, 57*(2), 317–337. doi:10.1016/j.cden.2013.02.006 PMID:23570808

Sada, L. (2013, June 4). Extreme anti-immigrant groups spread throughout Europe. *Global Voices.*

Salmivalli, C., Kaukiainen, A., & Voeten, M. (2005). Anti-bullying intervention: Implementation and outcome. *The British Journal of Educational Psychology, 75*(3), 465–487. doi:10.1348/000709905X26011 PMID:16238877

Sampson, R. J., & Laub, J. H. (1993). *Crime in the making: Pathways and turning points through life.* Cambridge, MA: Harvard University Press.

Sampson, R. J., & Laub, J. H. (1995). Understanding variability in lives through time: Contributions of life course criminology. *Studies on Crime and Crime Prevention, 4*, 143–158.

Sampson, R. J., & Laub, J. H. (2005). A general age-graded theory of crime: Lessons learned and the future of life-course criminology. In D. P. Farrington (Ed.), *Advances in criminology: Testing integrated developmental/life-course theories of offending* (Vol. 14, pp. 165–182). New Brunswick, NJ: Transaction.

Sánchez-Jankowski, M. (1991). *Islands in the street. Gangs and American urban society.* Berkeley, CA: University of California Press.

Sánchez-Jankowski, M. (2003). Gangs and social change. *Theoretical Criminology, 7*(2), 191–216. doi:10.1177/1362480603007002413

Sanchez, R. (2000). *My bloody life: The making of a Latin King.* Chicago: Chicago Review Press.

Sandberg, S. (2009). A narrative search for respect. *Deviant Behavior, 30*(6), 478–510. doi:10.1080/01639620802296394

Sanders, G. S., & Baron, R. S. (1977). Is social comparison irrelevant for producing choice shifts? *Journal of Experimental Social Psychology, 13*(4), 303–314. doi:10.1016/0022-1031(77)90001-4

Santos, R. B. (2014). The Effectiveness of Crime Analysis for Crime Reduction: Cure or Diagnosis? *Journal of Contemporary Criminal Justice, 30*(2), 147–168. doi:10.1177/1043986214525080

Saviano, R. (2006). *Gomorrah* (V. Jewiss, Trans.). MacMillan Publishers.

Savvy PR. (2014, August 30). *Savvy PR campaign has lured many to fight in Syria's civil war.* National Public Radio.

Sayer, A. (1999). *Realism and social science.* Thousand Oaks, CA: Sage.

Schafer, J. R., & Navarro, J. (2003) The seven stage hate model: The psychopathology of hate groups. *FBI Law Enforcement Bulletin.*

Scheper-Hughes, N., & Bourgois, P. (Eds.). (2004). *Violence in War and Peace: An Anthology.* Oxford, UK: Blackwell.

Schimel, J., Simon, L., Greenberg, J., Pyszczynski, T., Solomon, S., Waxmonsky, J., & Arndt, J. (1999). Stereotypes and terror management: Evidence that mortality salience enhances stereotypic thinking and preferences. *Journal of Personality and Social Psychology, 77*(5), 905–936. doi:10.1037/0022-3514.77.5.905 PMID:10573872

Schinkel, W. (2004). The Will to Violence. *Theoretical Criminology, 8*(1), 5–32. doi:10.1177/1362480604039739

Schreck, C. J., & Miller, J. (2003). Sources of fear of crime at school: What is the relative contribution of disorder, individual characteristics, and school security? *Journal of School Violence, 2*(4), 57–79. doi:10.1300/J202v02n04_04

Schrock, D., & Schwalbe, M. (2009). Men, Masculinity, and Manhood Acts. *Annual Review of Sociology, 35*(1), 277–295. doi:10.1146/annurev-soc-070308-115933

Schubert, M., Mulvey, E. P., & Glasheen, C. (2011). Influence of mental health and substance use problems and criminogenic risk on outcomes in serious juvenile offenders. *Journal of the American Academy of Child and Adolescent Psychiatry, 50*(9), 925–937. doi:10.1016/j.jaac.2011.06.006 PMID:21871374

Schwartzman, Fineman, Slavkin, Mieszala, Thomas, Gross, Spurlin, & Baer. (1999). *Juvenile Firesetter Mental Health Intervention: A Comprehensive Discussion Of Treatment.* Service Delivery, And Training Of Providers (Report).

Scott, G. (2004). "It's a sucker's outfit": How urban gangs enable and impede the integration of ex-convicts. *Ethnography, 5*(1), 107–140. doi:10.1177/1466138104041590

Scott, K. (1993). *Monster: The Autobiography of an L.A. Gang Member Sanyika Shakur A.K.A Monster Kody Scott.* New York: The Atlantic Monthly Press.

Searle, J. R. (1995). *The construction of social reality.* New York: The Free Press.

Searle, J. R. (2006). Social ontology: Some basic principles. *Anthropological Theory, 6*(1), 12–29. doi:10.1177/1463499606061731

Sefali, P. (2014a). *Gang violence in Khayelitsha.* Cape Town: University of Cape Town Safety and Violence Initiative and Cape Town.

Sefali, P. (2014c, September 18). The rise of female township gangs. *GroundUp.*

Sefali, P. (2014b). *Khayelitsha ruled by teenage gangsters.* Cape Town: GroundUp June.

Segal, L. (1995). *Slow Motion: Changing Masculinities, Changing Men.* New Brunswick, NJ: Rutgers University Press.

Sela-Shayovitz, R. (2009). Dealing with school violence: The effect of school violence prevention training on teachers' perceived self-efficacy in dealing with violent events. *Teaching and Teacher Education, 25*(8), 1061–1066. doi:10.1016/j.tate.2009.04.010

Shade, P. (2006). Educating hopes. *Studies in Philosophy and Education, 25*(3), 191–225. doi:10.1007/s11217-005-1251-2

Shakur, T., Young, Cocker, Cunningham, Durham, Hooks, Hudson, … Troutman. (1995). *California love.* (Recorded by T. Shakur, Dr. Dre, & L. Troutman). Los Angeles, CA: Death Row Records.

Shaw, M. (1997) State Responses to Organized Crime in South Africa. *Transnational Organized Crime, 3*(2).

Shaw, M., & Reitano, T. (2013). *The evolution of organised crime in Africa: Towards a new response.* Pretoria: Institute for Security Studies.

Shaw, M. (1999). The development and control of organized crime in post-apartheid South Africa. In *Organized crime: Uncertainties and dilemmas.* University of Illinois Press.

Shelden, R. G., Tracy, S. K., & Brown, W. B. (2013). *Youth Gangs in American Society* (4th ed.). Wadsworth Publishing. (Original work published 2004)

Sheldon, W. (1940). *Varieties of Human Physique.* New York: Harper & Row.

Shen, A., & Hall, S. (2015). The same the whole world over? A review essay on youth offending from the 1980s and youth justice in contemporary China. *International Journal of Law, Crime and Justice.*

Sherif, M. (1966). *In common predicament.* Boston: Houghton Mifflin.

Sherif, M., Harvey, O. J., White, B. J., Hood, W. R., & Sherif, C. W. (1961). *The robbers cave experiment: Intergroup conflict and cooperation.* Middletown, CT: Wesleyan University Press.

Sherif, M., & Sherif, C. W. (1982). Production of intergroup conflict and its resolution – Robbers Cave experiment. In J. W. Reigh (Ed.), *Experimenting in society: Issues and examples in applied social psychology.* Glenview, IL: Scott, Foresman.

Sherman, L. W. (1970). *Youth Workers, Police and the Gangs: Chicago 1956-1970.* (Master's Thesis). Division of Social Sciences, University of Chicago.

Shihadeh, E. S., & Barranco, R. (2010). Latino employment and black violence: The unintended consequences of U.S. immigration policy. *Social Forces, 88*(3), 1393–1420. doi:10.1353/sof.0.0286

Shihadeh, E. S., & Ousey, G. C. (1998). Industrial restructuring and violence: The link between entry-level jobs, economic deprivation, and Black and White homicide. *Social Forces, 77*(1), 185–207. doi:10.1093/sf/77.1.185

Shilling, C. (1991). Educating the Body: Physical Capital and the Production of Social Inequalities. *Sociology, 25*(4), 653–672. doi:10.1177/0038038591025004006

Short, J. F. (1974). Youth, Gangs and Society: Micro and Macrosociological Processes. *The Sociological Quarterly, 15*(1), 3–19. doi:10.1111/j.1533-8525.1974.tb02122.x

Shuman, A. (1986). *Storytelling rights: The uses of oral and written texts by urban adolescents.* New York: Cambridge University Press. doi:10.1017/CBO9780511983252

Simpkins, S. D., Bouffard, S. M., Dearing, E., Kreider, H., Wimer, C., Caronongan, P., & Weiss, H. B. (2009). Adolescent adjustment and patterns of parents' behaviors in early and middle adolescence. *Journal of Research on Adolescence, 19*(3), 530–555. doi:10.1111/j.1532-7795.2009.00606.x

Skarbek, D. (2014). *The social order of the underground: How prison gangs govern the American penal system.* New York: Oxford University Press. doi:10.1093/acprof:oso/9780199328499.001.0001

Skiba, R. J., & Peterson. (2000) School discipline at a crossroads: From zero tolerance to early response. *Exceptional Children, 66*(3), 335-47.

Skywalker, L. L. (2014). *Politics of the Number: an account of predominant South African Prison gang influences* (MA Thesis). University of Cape Town.

Slavkin, M. L. (2000). Juvenile fire setters: A report of the juvenile fire setter intervention project. *Journal of Psychosocial Nursing, 38,* 6–17.

Smart, D., Vassallo, S., Sanson, A., & Dussuyer, I. (2004). *Patterns of Antisocial Behaviour from Early to Late Adolescence. Trends and Issues in Crime and Criminal Justice, No.290.* Canberra: Australian Institute of Criminology.

Smashing the Shamrock. (2012). Intelligence Report. Southern Poverty Law Center.

Smith, H. (2014, June 7). SS Songs and anti-Semitism. *The Guardian.*

Smith, C. (2010). *What is a person?* Chicago: University of Chicago Press. doi:10.7208/chicago/9780226765938.001.0001

Smith, D. L., & Smith, B. J. (2006). Perception of violence: The views of teachers who left urban schools. *High School Journal*, *89*(3), 34–42. doi:10.1353/hsj.2006.0004

Snyder, C. R., Lassegard, M. A., & El Ford, C. (1986). Distancing after group success and failure: Basking in reflected glory and cutting off reflected failure. *Journal of Personality and Social Psychology*, *51*(2), 382–388. doi:10.1037/0022-3514.51.2.382

Sobel, R. S., & Osoba, B. J. (2009). Youth gangs as pseudo-governments: Implications for violent crime. *Southern Economic Journal*, *75*(4), 996–1019.

Solomon, S., Greenberg, J., & Pyszczynski, T. (1991). Article. In M. P. Zanna (Ed.), A terror management theory of social behavior: The psychological functions of self-esteem and cultural worldviews (pp. 91–159). San Diego, CA: Academic Press.

Solomon, S., Greenberg, J., & Pyszczynski, T. (2004). The cultural animal: Twenty years of terror management theory and research. In J. Greenberg, S. L. Koole, & T. Pyszczynski (Eds.), *Handbook of experimental existential psychology* (pp. 13–34). New York: Guilford Press.

Song, J. H. L. (1996). The Asian Factor: Methodological barriers to the study of Asian Gangs and Organised crime. *American Journal of Criminal Justice*, *21*(1), 1996.

Song, J., & Dombrink, J. (1994). Asian emerging crime groups: Examining the definition of organised crime. *Criminal Justice Review*, *19*(2), 228–243. doi:10.1177/073401689401900204

South China Morning Post. (2004, January 17). Soaring Crime Rate Dims Shenzhen's Luster. *South China Morning Post.*

South China Morning Post. (2006, May 10). Shenzhen is Key Gateway for illegal Drugs trade. *South China Morning Post.*

Spaaij, R. (2008). Men Like Us, Boys Like Them: Violence, Masculinity, and Collective Identity in Football Hooliganism. *Journal of Sport and Social Issues*, *32*(4), 369–392. doi:10.1177/0193723508324082

Spergel, I. (1961, March). An exploratory research in delinquent subcultures. *The Social Service Review*, *35*(1), 33–47. doi:10.1086/640985

Spergel, I. A. (1995). *The youth gang problem*. New York, NY: Oxford University Press.

Spergel, I. A., & Grossman, S. F. (1997). The Little Village Project: A community approach to the gang problem. *Social Work*, *42*(5), 456–470. doi:10.1093/sw/42.5.456 PMID:9311304

Sprott, J. B. (2004). The development of early delinquency: Can classroom and school climates make a difference? *Canadian Journal of Criminology and Criminal Justice*, *46*(5), 553–572. doi:10.3138/cjccj.46.5.553

St. Cyr, J. L. (2003). The folk devil reacts: Gangs and moral panics. *Criminal Justice Review*, *28*(1), 26–46. doi:10.1177/073401680302800103

Stack, L. (2015, May 3). *Texas police kill gunmen at exhibit featuring cartoons of Muhammad*. Retrieved on May 5, 2015 from http://www.nytimes.com/2015/05/04/us/gunmen-killed-after-firing-on-anti-islam-groups-event.html

Stadolnik, R. F. (2000). Drawn To The Flame: Assessment And Treatment Of Juvenile Firesetting Behavior. Professional Resource Exchange. Retrieved from.http://www.amazon.com/dp/1568870639

Staff, S. (2014). *The end of tolerance? Anti Muslim movement rattles Germany*. Retrieved from http://www.spiegel.de/international/germany/anti-muslim-pegida-movement-rattles-germany-a-1009245.html

Standing, A. (2005). *The threat of gangs and anti-gangs policy*. Pretoria: Institute for Conflict Studies.

Standing, A. (2006). *Organised crime: A study from the Cape Flats*. Pretoria: Institute of Security Studies.

Stanley, S. M. (1996). School uniforms and safety. *Education and Urban Society*, *28*(4), 424–435. doi:10.1177/0013124596028004003

State v. Moreno et al. (2011). Washington, King County. *Information*. Retrieved October 29, 2014 from http://blog.seattlepi.com/seattle911/files/2011/09/Kent Car-Show-Charges.pdf

State vs. Patten. (2010). Indiana, Marion. *Probable Cause Affidavit*. Retrieved October 29, 2014 from http://media2.wishtv.com/_local/pdf/pattonPC.pdf

Steinberg, J. (2004). *Nongoloza's Children: Western Cape prison gangs during and after apartheid*. Johannesburg: Centre for the Study of Violence and Reconciliation.

Steinberg, J. (2004). *The Number*. Cape Town: Jonathan Ball.

Steinberg, L., & Cauffman, E. (1996). Maturity of judgment in adolescence: Psychosocial factors in adolescent decision making. *Law and Human Behavior*, *20*(3), 249–272. doi:10.1007/BF01499023

Stein, D., Ellis, G., Meintjies, E., & Thomas, K. (2012). Introduction: substance use and abuse in South Africa. In *Substance use and abuse in South Africa*. Cape Town: University of Cape Town Press.

Stelfox, P. (1998). Policing Lower Levels of Crime in England and Wales. *Howard Journal of Criminal Justice*, *37*(4), 393–406. doi:10.1111/1468-2311.00108

Sternberg, R. J. (1986). A triangular theory of love. *Psychological Review*, *93*(2), 119–135. doi:10.1037/0033-295X.93.2.119

Sternberg, R. J. (2003). A duplex theory of hate and its development and its application to terrorism, massacres, and genocides. *Review of General Psychology*, *7*(3), 299–328. doi:10.1037/1089-2680.7.3.299

Sternberg, R. J. (2005). From Plato to Putnam: Four ways to think about hate. In R. J. Sternberg (Ed.), *The psychology of hate* (pp. 3–35). Washington, DC: American Psychological Association. doi:10.1037/10930-000

Sternberg, R. J. (2006). A duplex theory of love. In R. J. Sternberg & K. Weis (Eds.), *The new psychology of love* (pp. 184–199). New Haven, CT: Yale University Press.

Stets, J. E., & Burke, P. J. (2000). Identity theory and social identity theory. *Social Psychology Quarterly*, *63*(3), 224–237. doi:10.2307/2695870

Stinchcomb, J. B. (2002). Promising (and not so promising) gang prevention and intervention strategies: A comprehensive literature review. *Journal of Gang Research*, *10*, 27–45.

Stoll, D. (2013) Book review: Gangsters without borders: An ethnography of a Salvadoran gang. *Social Forces, 91*(4), 1549-1551.

Stolzoff, N. C. (2000). *Wake the town and tell the people: Dancehall culture in Jamaica*. Duke University Press.

Stone, L. (2014, December 31). Ottawa gun violence reaches record 48 shootings: It's heartbreaking. *Global News*. Retrieved from http://globalnews.ca/news/1749129/ottawa-gun-violence-reaches-record-48-shootings-its-heartbreaking/

Stretesky, P. B., & Pogrebin, M. R. (2007). Gun-related gun violence: Socialization, identity, and self. *Journal of Contemporary Ethnography, 36*(1), 85–114. doi:10.1177/0891241606287416

Struch, N., & Schwartz, S. H. (1989). Intergroup aggression: Its predictors and distinctness from in-group bias. *Journal of Personality and Social Psychology, 56*(3), 364–373. doi:10.1037/0022-3514.56.3.364 PMID:2926634

Stryker, S. (1980). *Symbolic Interactionism: A social structural version*. Menlo Park, CA: The Benjamin/Cummings Publishing Company.

Sullivan, J. P., & Logan, S. (2009). *Mexico's 'Divine Justice'*. International Relations and Security Network. Retrieved June 21, 2012 from http://www.isn.ethz.ch/isn/Current-Affairs/Security-Watch/Detail/?lng=en&id=104677

Sullivan, P. M., & Knutson, J. F. (1998). The association between child maltreatment and disabilities in a hospital-based epidemiological study. *Child Abuse & Neglect, 22*, 271–288.

Suls, J., Martin, R., & Wheeler, L. (2002). Social comparison: Why, with whom, and with what effect? *Current Directions in Psychological Science, 11*(5), 159–163. doi:10.1111/1467-8721.00191

Sumner, W. G. (1906). *Folkways*. New York: Ginn.

Sun, I., Hu, R., & Wu, Y. (2012). Social Capital, political participation, and trust in the police in urban China. *Australian and New Zealand Journal of Criminology, 45*(1), 87–105. doi:10.1177/0004865811431329

Sutherland, E. H. (1947). *Principles of criminology*. Philadelphia: J.B. Lippincott Co.

Sutherland, E. H., & Cressey, D. R. (1960). *A theory of differential association. Principles of criminology* (6th ed.). Chicago, IL: Lippincott.

Swahn, M. H., Bossarte, R. M., West, B., & Topalli, V. (2010). Alcohol and drug use among gang members: Experiences of adolescents who attend school. *The Journal of School Health, 80*(7), 353–360. doi:10.1111/j.1746-1561.2010.00513.x PMID:20591101

Sweatt, L. C., Harding, Knight-Lynn, Rasheed, & Carter. (2002). Talking about the silent fear: Adolescent's experiences of violence in an urban high-rise community. *Adolescence, 37*(145), 109–121. PMID:12003284

Sweet, S. J. (1999). Understanding fraternity hazing: Insights from symbolic interactionist theory. *Journal of College Student Development, 40*(4), 355–364.

Sykes, G. M. (1958). *The Society of Captives: A Study of a Maximum Security Prison*. Princeton University Press.

Taheri-Keramati, Y. (2014). *Drugs, police inefficiencies, and gangsterism in violently impoverished communities like Overcome* (MA Thesis). Cape Town: University of Cape Town.

Tajfel, H., & Turner, J. C. (1979). An integrative theory of intergroup conflict. *The Social Psychology of Intergroup Relations, 33*(47), 74.

Tajfel, H., & Turner, J. C. (1986). An integrative theory of social conflict. In Psychology of intergroup relations. Chicago, IL: Nelson Hall.

Tajfel, H. (1982). Social psychology of intergroup relations. *Annual Review of Psychology, 33*(1), 1–39. doi:10.1146/annurev.ps.33.020182.000245

Tajfel, H., & Billig, M. (1974). Familiarity and categorization in intergroup behavior. *Journal of Experimental Social Psychology, 10*(2), 159–170. doi:10.1016/0022-1031(74)90064-X

Tajfel, H., Billig, M. G., Bundy, R. P., & Flament, C. (1971). Social categorization and intergroup behavior. *The Journal of Social Psychology, 1*, 149–178.

Tanioka, I., & Glasier. (1991). School uniforms, routine activities, and social control of delinquency in Japan. *Youth and Society, 23*(1), 50-75.

Tannenbaum, F. (1938). *Crime and the Community*. New York: University of Columbia Press.

Taylor, C. S. (1993). *Girls, Gangs and Drugs*. Michigan State University Press.

Taylor, D. (1997). *Disappearing Acts: Spectacles of Gender and Nationalism in Argentina's "Dirty War"*. Durham, NC: Duke University Press.

Taylor, S. S. (2009). How street gangs recruit and socialize members. *Journal of Gang Research, 17*, 1–27.

Telles, E. E., & Ortiz, V. (2008). *Generations of exclusion*. New York: Russell Sage.

Terlato, P. (2014, September 23). ISIS Calls For Australian Killings: The Chilling Statement That One Expert Says Is A 'Game-Changer'. *Business Insider Australia*.

Thoits, & Virshup. (1997). Me's and We's: Forms and functions of social identities. In R. D. Ashmore & L. J. Jussim (Eds.), *Self and Identity: Fundamental Issues* (pp. 106-133). Academic Press.

Thomas, S. (2012). Revisiting Brixton: The War on Babylon 1981. In D. Briggs (Ed.), *The English Riots of 2011: A Summer of Discontent*. Waterside Press.

Thornberry, T. P., Krohn, M. D., Lizotte, A. J., Smith, C. A., & Tobin, K. (2003). *Gangs and delinquency in developmental perspective*. New York, NY: Cambridge University Press.

Thornberry, T. P., Krohn, M. D., Lizotte, A. J., Smith, C. A., & Tobin, K. (2003). *Gangs and Delinquency in Developmental Perspective*. New York: Cambridge University Press.

Thornberry, T. P., Lizotte, A. J., Krohn, M. D., Farnworth, M., & Jang, S. J. (1994). Delinquent peers, beliefs, and delinquent behaviour: A longitudinal test of interactional theory. *Criminology, 32*(1), 47–84. doi:10.1111/j.1745-9125.1994.tb01146.x

Thornton, S. (1995). The social logic of subcultural capital. In *The Subcultures Reader*. London: Routledge.

Thrasher, F. M. (1927/2000). *The gang: A study of 1,313 gangs in Chicago*. Chicago: New Chicago School Press.

Thrasher, F. M. (1927). *The Gang*. Chicago: The University of Chicago Press.

Thrasher, F. M. (1927). *The gang: A study of 1,313 gangs in Chicago*. Chicago, IL: University of Chicago Press.

Thrasher, F. M. (1927). *The Gang: A study of 1,313 gangs in Chicago*. Chicago: University of Chicago Press.

Thrasher, F. M. (1927). *The Gang: A Study of 1,313 Gangs in Chicago*. Chicago: University of Chicago Press.

Tikkanen, R., Sjöberg, R. L., Ducci, F., Goldman, D., Holi, M., Tiihonen, J., & Virkkunen, M. (2009). Effects of MAOA-Genotype, Alcohol Consumption, and Aging on Violent Behavior. *Alcoholism, Clinical and Experimental Research, 33*(3), 428–434. doi:10.1111/j.1530-0277.2008.00853.x PMID:19120058

Tomsen, S. (1997). A Top Night: Social Protest, Masculinity and the Culture of Drinking Violence. *The British Journal of Criminology, 37*(1), 90–102. doi:10.1093/oxfordjournals.bjc.a014152

Tomsen, S. (2008). Masculinities, Crime and Criminalisation. In T. Anthony & C. Cunneen (Eds.), *The Critical Criminology Companion*. Sydney: Hawkins Press.

Topp, L., Degenhardt, L., Kaye, S., & Darke, S. (2002). The Emergence of Potent forms of Methamphetamine in Sydney Australia: A Case Study of the IDRS as a Strategic Early Warning. *Drug and Alcohol Review, 21*(4), 341–348. doi:10.1080/09595230210000231 99 PMID:12537703

Totten, M. (2000). *Guys, gangs and girlfriend abuse*. Peterborough, ON: Broadview Press.

Totten, M. (2012). *Nasty, brutish, and short: The lives of gang members in Canada*. Toronto, ON: James Lorimer & Company.

Townsend, M. (2014). Gangs draw up lists of girls to rape as proxy attacks on rivals: Gangs assault rivals' sisters and girlfriends as a 'low risk' method of asserting dominance. *The Guardian*. Accessed August 30, 2014, from http://www.theguardian.com/society/2014/jul/19/gangs-rape-lists-sex-assault

Trulson, C. R., & Marquant, J. W. (2009). *First Available Cell: Desegregation of the Texas Prison System*. Austin, TX: University of Texas Press.

Trump, K. S. (1993). *Youth gangs and schools: The need for intervention and prevention strategies*. Cleveland, OH: Urban Child Research Center.

Tshwete, S. (2001). Legislative responses to organised crime in the SADC region. In C. Goredema (Ed.), *Organised crime in South Africa: Assessing legislation*. Pretoria: Institute for Security Studies.

Turner, T., & Cross, C. (2014). *Ireland, Spain, and Greece see biggest change in attitudes to immigrants*. Retrieved November 1, 2014 from http://www.irishtimes.com/news/world/ireland-spain-and-greece-see-biggest-change-in-attitudes-to-immigrants-1.1776615

Tyler, K. A. (2006). A Qualitative Study of Early Family Histories and Transitions of Homeless Youth. *Journal of Interpersonal Violence, 21*(10), 1385–1393. doi:10.1177/0886260506291650 PMID:16940403

U.S. Census Bureau. (2008). 2006-2008 American Community Survey. Washington, DC: Author.

U.S. Census Bureau. (2009). Census Bureau Estimates Nearly Half of Children Under Age 5 Are Minorities. Washington, DC: Author.

U.S. Department of Education. (2013). *Student reports of bullying and cyber-bullying: Results from the 2011 School Crime Supplement to the National Crime Victimization Survey. NCES Publication No. 329*. Washington, DC: National Center for Education Statistics.

U.S. Department of Justice. (1998). *Pulling Levers: Getting Deterrence Right*. Washington, DC: U.S. Department of Justice.

U.S. Fire Administration Structure Fire Cause Methodology. (2014). Retrieved from http://www.usfa.fema.gov/fireservice/nfirs/tools/fire_cause_category_matrix.shtm

Uggen, C. (1996). *Age, employment and the duration structure of recidivism: Estimating the "true effect" of work on crime*. Paper presented at the American Sociology Association Conference, New York, NY.

Uggen, C., Manza, J., & Thompson, M. (2006). Citizenship, democracy, and the civic reintegration of criminal offenders. *Annals AAPSS, 605*(1), 281–310. doi:10.1177/0002716206286898

Umemoto, K. (2006). *The truce: Lessons from an LA gang war*. Ithaca, NY: Cornell University.

UNECE. (2010). Retrieved 18 February 2010 from: www.unece.org

United Nations. (2011). *Global Study on Homicide.* United Nations Office on Drugs and Crime.

Unnever, J. D., Cullen, F. T., & Agnew, R. (2006). Why is "bad" parenting criminogenic? Implications rival theories. *Youth Violence and Juvenile Justice, 4*(1), 3–33. doi:10.1177/1541204005282310

Valdez, A. (2007). Machismo.Encyclopedia of Race and Racism, 2(G-R), 271-274.

Valdez, A. (2003). Toward a typology of contemporary Mexican American youth gangs. In L. Kontos, D. Brotherton, & L. Barrios (Eds.), *Gangs and society: Alternative perspectives.* New York: Columbia University Press.

Valdez, A. (2005). Mexican American Youth and Adult Prison Gangs in a Changing Heroin Market. *Journal of Drug Issues, 35*(4), 842–867. doi:10.1177/002204260503500409 PMID:21614143

Valdez, A. (2007). *Mexican American Girls and Gang Violence: Beyond Risk.* New York, NY: Palgrave Macmillan. doi:10.1057/9780230601833

Valdez, A., Cepeda, A., & Kaplan, D. (2009). Homicidal Events among Mexican American Street Gangs: A Situational Analysis. *Homicide Studies, 13*(3), 288–306.

Valdez, A., Cepeda, A., Parrish, D., Horowitz, R., & Kaplan, C. D. (2013). An adapted brief strategic family therapy for gang affiliated Mexican American adolescents. *Research on Social Work Practice, 23*(4), 383–396. doi:10.1177/1049731513481389

Valdez, A., Kaplan, C. D., & Cepeda, A. (2006). The Drugs-Violence Nexus among Mexican-American Gang Members. *Journal of Psychoactive Drugs, 38*(2), 109–121. doi:10.1080/02791072.2006.10399835 PMID:16903450

Valeri, R., & Borgeson. (2005). Identifying the face of hate. *Journal of Applied Sociology, 22*, 91–104.

Valeri, R., & Borgeson. (2007). Reframing affirmative action: Examining the impact on white Americans. *Michigan Sociological Review, 21*, 193–209.

Vanneman, R. D., & Pettigrew, T. F. (1972). Race and relative deprivation in the urban United States. *Race, 13*(4), 431–486. doi:10.1177/030639687201300404

Varese, F. (2006). How Mafias Migrate. *Law & Society Review, 40*(2), 411–444. doi:10.1111/j.1540-5893.2006.00260.x

Vaughn, M. G. (2006). Do prior trauma and victimization predict weapon carrying among delinquent youth? *Youth Violence and Juvenile Justice, 4*(4), 314–327. doi:10.1177/1541204006292665

Vaughn, M. G., Fu, Q., Delisi, M., Wright, J. P., Beaver, K. M., Perron, B. E., & Howard, M. O. L. (2010). Prevalence and correlates of fire-setting in the United States: Results from the National Epidemiological Survey on Alcohol and Related Conditions. *Comprehensive Psychiatry, 51*(3), 217–223. doi:10.1016/j.comppsych.2009.06.002 PMID:20399330

Vearey, J. (2015). *Civilian Secretariat for police workshop: The development of a framework for interdepartmental anti-gang strategy in South Africa.* Cape Town Workshop.

Vearey, J. (n.d.). Nongoloza's legacy – prison and street gangs in the Western Cape. *Confidential South African Police Service Report.*

Venkatesh, S. A. (2008). *Gang Leader for a Day: A Rogue Sociologist Takes to the Streets.* Penguin Press HC.

Vigil, J. D. (1988). *Barrio Gangs: Street Life and Identity in Southern California.* Austin, TX: University of Texas Press.

Vigil, J. D. (1988). Group processes and street identity: Adolescent Chicano gang members. *Ethos (Berkeley, Calif.), 14*(4), 421–445. doi:10.1525/eth.1988.16.4.02a00040

Vigil, J. D. (1991). *Barrio gangs: Street life and identity in Southern California*. Austin: University of Texas Press.

Vigil, J. D. (1996). Street baptism: Chicago gang initiation. *Human Organization, 55*(2), 149–152. doi:10.17730/humo.55.2.3358547x86552mg4

Vinokur, A., & Burnstein, E. (1974). Effects of partially shared persuasive arguments on group-induced shifts: A group problem solving approach. *Journal of Personality and Social Psychology, 29*(3), 305–315. doi:10.1037/h0036010

Von Lampe, K. (n.d.). *Definitions of Organized Crime*. Retrieved from www.organized-crime.de/organizedcrimedefinitions.htm

Vrugt, A., & Koenis, S. (2002). Perceived self-efficacy, personal goals, social comparison, and scientific productivity. *Applied Psychology, 51*(4), 593–607. doi:10.1111/1464-0597.00110

Wacquant, L. (1998). Negative social capital: State breakdown and social destitution in America's urban core. *Netherlands Journal of Housing and the Built Environment., 13*(1), 25–40. doi:10.1007/BF02496932

Wacquant, L. (2004). *Deadly Symbiosis*. Cambridge, MA: Polity Press.

Wacquant, L. (2005). Carnal Connections: On Embodiment, Apprenticeship, and Membership. *Qualitative Sociology, 28*(4), 445–474. doi:10.1007/s11133-005-8367-0

Wacquant, L. (2007). *Body & Soul: Notebooks of an Apprentice Boxer*. OUP USA.

Wallace, K. (2013). 6-year-old suspended for kissing girl, accused of sexual harassment. *CNN*. Retrieved from: http://www.cnn.com/2013/12/11/living/6-year-old-suspended-kissing-girl/

Waller, I. (2006). *Less Law, More Order: The Truth about Reducing Crime*. Westport, CT: Praeger.

Walsh, P. (2003). *Gang War: The Inside Story of Manchester's Gangs*. Milo Books.

Walters, J. (2001). *One Aryan Nation under God*. Naperville, IL: Sourcebooks.

Wang, G. T., Qiao, H., Wei, S., & Zhang, J. (2002). Adolescent social bond, self-control and deviant behaviour in China. *International Journal of Contemporary Sociology, 39*(1), 52–68.

Wang, P. (2013). The increasing threat of Chinese organised crime: National, regional and international perspective. *The RUSI Journal, 158*(4), 6–18. doi:10.1080/03071847.2013.826492

Wang, P., & Antonopoulos, G. (2015). Organised Crime and illegal gambling: How do illegal gambling enterprises respond to the challenges posed by their illegality in china? *Australian and New Zealand Journal of Criminology, 0*(0), 1–23.

Wangshu, L. (2015, April 21). Migrant life may lead to youth crime. *China Daily*.

Webb, V. J., Ren, L., Zhao, J., He, N., & Marshall, I. H. (2011). A comparative study of youth gangs in China and the United States: Definition, offending and victimisation. *International Criminal Justice Review, 21*(3), 225–242. doi:10.1177/1057567711418825

Weiner, M. D., Sussman, S., Sun, P., & Dent, C. (2005). Explaining the link between violence perpetration, victimization and drug use. *Addictive Behaviors, 30*(6), 1261–1266. doi:10.1016/j.addbeh.2004.12.007 PMID:15925136

Westmacott, R., Stys, Y., & Brown, S. L. (2005). *Selected annotated bibliography: Evaluation of gang intervention programs (Research Brief B-36)*. Ottawa, ON: Correctional Service of Canada.

Whalen, W. J. (1966). *Handbook of secret organizations*. Milwaukee, WI: Bruce Publishing Co.

White, R. (2002). 'Social and Political Aspects of Men's Health'. *Health, 6*(3), 267–285. doi:10.1177/136345930200600301

White, R. (2006). In J. Short & L. Hughes (Eds.), *Youth Gang Research in Australia* (pp. 161–179). Studying Youth Gangs, New York: AltaMira Press.

White, R. (2008). Australian Youth Gangs and the Social Dynamics of Ethnicity. In F. van Gemert, D. Peterson, & I.-L. Lien (Eds.), *Youth Gangs, Migration, and Ethnicity*. Devon: Willan.

White, R. (2008). Disputed definitions and fluid identities: The limitations of social profiling in relation to ethnic youth gangs. *Youth Justice, 8*(2), 149–161. doi:10.1177/1473225408091375

White, R. (2011). The Challenges of Doing Collaborative Research. In L. Bartels & K. Richards (Eds.), *Qualitative Criminology: Stories from the Field*. Sydney: Federation Press.

White, R. (2013). *Youth Gangs, Violence and Social Respect: Exploring the Nature of Provocations and Punch-Ups*. Basingstoke: Palgrave Macmillan. doi:10.1057/9781137333858

White, R., Haines, F., & Asquith, N. (2012). *Crime & Criminology*. Melbourne: Oxford University Press.

White, R., & Mason, R. (2006). Youth Gangs and Youth Violence: Charting the Key Dimensions. *Australian and New Zealand Journal of Criminology, 39*(1), 54–70. doi:10.1375/acri.39.1.54

White, R., & Perrone, S. (2001). Racism, Ethnicity and Hate Crime. *Communal/Plural, 9*(2), 161–181. doi:10.1080/13207870120081479

White, R., Perrone, S., Guerra, C., & Lampugnani, R. (1999). *Ethnic Youth Gangs in Australia: Do They Exist?*. Melbourne: Australian Multicultural Foundation.

White, R., & Wyn, J. (2013). *Youth and Society: Exploring the Social Dynamics of Youth Experience*. Melbourne: Oxford University Press.

Whitwell, T. (2014, June 13). Inside Shenzhen: China's Silicon Valley. *The Guardian.*

WHO. (2010). Retrieved 18 February 2010 from: www.who.int

Wiemann, C. M., Agurcia, C. A., Berenson, A. B., Volk, R. J., & Rickert, V. L. (2000). Pregnant adolescents: Experiences and behaviors associated with physical assault by an intimate partner. *Maternal and Child Health Journal, 4*(2), 93–101. doi:10.1023/A:1009518220331 PMID:10994577

Wiggins, O., & Bui, L. (2014, October 22). Rumors about possible violence at Fright Fest prompt principal to send warning. *The Washington Post*. Retrieved from: http://www.washingtonpost.com/local/education/rumors-about-possible-violence-at-fright-fest-prompts-principal-to-send-warning/2014/10/22/c4ecfd56-5a23-11e4-bd61-346aee66ba29_story.html

Wilkinson, D. L. (2001). Violent events and social identity: Specifying the relationship between respect and masculinity in inner city youth violence. *Sociological Studies of Children and Youth, 8*, 231–265. doi:10.1016/S1537-4661(01)80011-8

Williams, J., Dunning, E., & Murphy, P. (1989). *Hooligans Abroad* (2nd ed.). Routledge.

Wilson, J. M., & Chermak, S. (2011). Community-driven violence reduction programs: Examining Pittsburgh's One Vision One Life. *Criminology & Public Policy, 10*(4), 993–1027. doi:10.1111/j.1745-9133.2011.00763.x

Wilson, W. J. (1987). *The Truly Disadvantaged: The Inner City, the Underclass and Public Policy.* Chicago: University of Chicago Press.

Wilson, W. J. (1996). *When Work Disappears: The World of the New Urban Poor.* Knopf.

Winlow, S., & Hall, S. (2006). *Violent Night: Urban Leisure and Contemporary Culture.* Berg.

Wolff, K. H. (1950). *The sociology of Georg Simmel.* New York: The Free Press.

Wong, D. S. (1999, April). Delinquency Control and Juvenile Justice in China. *Australian and New Zealand Journal of Criminology, 32*(1), 27–41. doi:10.1177/000486589903200104

Wong, D. S. (2004, December). Juvenile Protection and Delinquency Prevention Policies in China. *Australian and New Zealand Journal of Criminology, 37*(1), 52–66. doi:10.1177/00048658040370S104

Wong, S. K. (1999). Delinquency of Chinese-Canadian youth: A test of opportunity, control and intergenerational conflict theories. *Youth & Society, 29*(1), 112–133. doi:10.1177/0044118X97029001005

Wong, S. S. W. (2001). Pathways to delinquency in Hong Kong and Guangzhou (south China). *International Journal of Adolescence and Youth, 10*(1/2), 91–115. doi:10.1080/02673843.2001.9747893

Wood, J. (2006). Gang Activity in English Prisons: The Prisoners' Perspective. *Psychology, Crime & Law, 12*(6), 605–617. doi:10.1080/10683160500337667

Wood, J. L. (2014). Understanding gang membership: The significance of group processes.[in press, online first]. *Group Processes & Intergroup Relations, 17*(6), 710–729. doi:10.1177/1368430214550344

Wood, J. V. (1989). Theory and research concerning social comparison of personal attributes. *Psychological Bulletin, 106*(2), 231–248. doi:10.1037/0033-2909.106.2.231

Wood, J. V., Taylor, S. E., & Lichtman, R. R. (1985). Social comparison in adjustment to breast cancer. *Journal of Personality and Social Psychology, 49*(5), 1169–1183. doi:10.1037/0022-3514.49.5.1169 PMID:4078672

Wood, J., & Alder, J. (2001). Gang activity in English prisons: The staff perspective. *Psychology, Crime & Law, 7*(1), 167–192. doi:10.1080/10683160108401793

Wood, J., & Alleyne, E. (2010). Street gang theory and research: Where are we now and where do we go from here? *Aggression and Violent Behavior, 15*(2), 100–111. doi:10.1016/j.avb.2009.08.005

Wood, J., Moir, A., & James, M. (2009). Prisoners' gang-related activity: The importance of bullying and moral disengagement. *Psychology, Crime & Law, 15*(6), 569–581. doi:10.1080/10683160802427786

World Health Organization. (2009). *Changing Cultural and Social Norms that Support Violence.* Retrieved August 29, 2014 from http://www.who.int/violence_injury_prevention/violence/norms.pdf

Wortley, S., & Tanner, J. (2004). Social groups or criminal organizations? The extent and nature of youth gang activity in Toronto. In B. Kidd & J. Philips (Eds.), *From enforcement and prevention to civic engagement: Research on community safety* (pp. 59–80). Toronto, ON: Centre of Criminology, University of Toronto.

Wu, Y., Sun, I., & Hu, R. (2015). Public Trust in the Chinese police: The impact of ethnicity, class and Hukou. *Australian and New Zealand Journal of Criminology,* (Jan), 21.

Xiang, G. (1999). Delinquency and its prevention in China. *International Journal of Offender Therapy and Comparative Criminology, 43*(1), 61–70. doi:10.1177/0306624X99431006

Xi, J. (2001). *Research reports on China's Youth*. Beijing, China: China Youth.

Yablonsky, L. (1997). *Gangsters: Fifty Years of Madness, Drugs and Death on the Streets of America*. New York University Press.

Yoder, K. A., Whitbeck, K. B., & Hoyt, O. R. (2003). Gang involvement and membership among homeless and runaway youth. *Youth & Society*, *34*(4), 441–467. doi:10.1177/0044118X03034004003

Young, M. A., & Gonzalez, V. (2013). *Getting out of gangs, staying out of gangs: Gang intervention and desistance strategies*. Retrieved October 15, 2014, from http://www.nationalgangcenter.gov/Content/Documents/Getting-Out-Staying-Out.pdf

Young, J. (1999). *The Exclusive Society: Social Exclusion, Crime and Difference in Late Modernity*. SAGE Publications.

Zaitchik, A. (2010, August 20). Paul Fromm: The lonely voice of Canadian Hate. *Hate Watch*. Posted in the Southern Poverty Law Center's Anti Immigrant.

Zamble, E., & Porporino, E. (1988). *Coping behavior and adaptation in prison inmates*. New York: Springer-Verlag. doi:10.1007/978-1-4613-8757-2

Zatz, M. (1987). Chicano youth gangs and crime: The creation of a moral panic. *Contemporary Crises*, *11*(2), 129–158. doi:10.1007/BF00728588

Zellner, W. W. (1995). *Countercultures: A Sociological Analysis*. New York: St. Martin's Press.

Zhang, L., Messner, S. F., & Liu, J. (2008). A Critical Review of Recent Literature on Crime and Criminal Justice in China: Research Findings, Challenges and Prospects (Introduction). *Crime, Law and Social Change: An Interdisciplinary Journal, 50*, 125-130.

Zhang, Z., & Huang, W. (1984). The role of recidivists in Delinquent Gangs. In Yearbook on Chinese Juvenile Delinquency Studies. Association of Chinese Juvenile Delinquency Study.

Zhang, B. (2001). The Characteristics of Youth Gangs. *Journal of Fu Jain Police College, 62*, 40–95.

Zhang, L. (2008). Juvenile delinquency and justice in contemporary China: A critical review of the literature over 15 years. *Crime, Law, and Social Change*, *50*(3), 149–160. doi:10.1007/s10611-008-9137-1

Zhang, L. (2014). Of Marginality and 'Little Emperors': The changing Reality of Chinese Youth Gangs. In *Global Gangs: Street Violence across the world*. Minneapolis, MN: University of Minnesota Press. doi:10.5749/minnesota/9780816691470.003.0005

Zhang, L., & Messner, S. F. (1996). School attachment and official delinquency status in the People's Republic of China. *Sociological Forum*, *11*(2), 285–303. doi:10.1007/BF02408368

Zhang, L., Messner, S. F., Lu, Z., & Deng, X. (1997). Gang crime and its punishment in china. *Journal of Criminal Justice*, *25*(4), 289–302. doi:10.1016/S0047-2352(97)00014-7

Zhang, L., Wieczorek, W. F., & Welte, J. W. (1997). The nexus between alcohol and violent crime. *Alcoholism, Clinical and Experimental Research*, *21*(7), 1264–1271. doi:10.1111/j.1530-0277.1997.tb04447.x PMID:9347088

Zhang, L., Zhang, L., & Lei, X. (1993). *China's Juvenile Delinquency and Justice*. Beijing, China: World Knowledge.

Zhang, S. X. (2002). Chinese Gangs: Familial and cultural dynamics. In C. R. Huff (Ed.), *Gangs in America III*. Newbury Park, CA: Sage. doi:10.4135/9781452232201.n14

Zhou, L., Liu, W., & Wang, Z. (2004). *Contemporary Positivist Criminology: A Study of Crime Patterns*. Beijing: Publishing House of People's Courts.

Zie, Z. (2008, December 22). China planning special unit to tackle gangs. *China Daily*.

Zorick, T., Nestor, L., Miotto, K., Sugar, C., Hellemann, G., Scanlon, G., & London, E. D. et al. (2010). Withdrawal Symptoms in Abstinent Methamphetamine-Dependent Subjects. *Addiction (Abingdon, England)*, *105*(10), 1809–1818. doi:10.1111/j.1360-0443.2010.03066.x PMID:20840201

Zu-Yuan, H. (1988). China: Juvenile delinquency and its prevention. *CJ International*, *4*(5), 5–10.

About the Contributors

Simon Harding is a senior lecturer at Middlesex University and joint Head of the Urban Neighbourhoods Research Unit (UNRU). He has extensive practitioner and professional experience in crime reduction and community safety including working for the Home Office as Regional Crime Advisor (London). He is the author of numerous community safety audits, strategies and award winning projects. Simon's recent work has focussed on urban street gangs in the UK. In 2005-08 he organised the Lambeth Gangs Commission and managed London's largest anti-gangs project (The Phoenix Project). Since 2012 Simon has published three books, *Unleashed: the phenomena of status dogs and weapon dogs* (2012); *Unleashed* (2014) reprinted with new chapter; and his latest theoretical exposition on gang crime, *The Street Casino: Survival in Violent Street Gangs* (2014). This latest work has just been awarded the Frederick Milton Thrasher Award for 2014 for Superior Gang Research.

Marek Palasinski is a lecturer in psychology at Liverpool John Moores University in the UK. He specializes in forensic and social psychology. His research interests include juvenile delinquency, cybercrime and security in general. He gained his PhD from the Department of Psychology at the University of Lancaster. He uses both qualitative and quantitative research methods, serving as a reviewer for scientific journals, like Psychology, Crime & Law, Computers in Human Behavior and Cyberpsychology, Behavior & Social Networking, where he published some of his research. He also gives conference presentations and collaborates extensively with institutions in the UK and overseas.

* * *

Kevin Borgeson is associate professor in the Criminal Justice Department at Salem State University, Salem, Massachusetts, where he teaches courses in crime scene investigation, profiling, and bias crimes. Borgeson's work has appeared in Journal of Applied Sociology, Michigan Sociological Review, and American Behavioral Science.

Ami Carpenter (Ph.D., George Mason University) is Associate Professor of Conflict Analysis and Resolution. Carpenter has worked on numerous initiatives as a mediator, facilitator, trainer, and conflict resolution consultant including United States Agency for International Development (USAID) and the United States Navy. She is a member of Interpeace's Advisory Group for Assessing Resilience, and is a founding member of San Diego County's Advisory Council on Human and Child Sex Trafficking. Her research focuses on resilience to violence, particularly in conflict zones in which criminal and political networks are tightly interconnected. Currently, she is researching the connection between transnational gangs and criminal networks in Central America, and is the Principal Investigator of a Dept. of Justice study on gangs and human trafficking in the US-Mexico border region.

Alice Cepeda is currently Associate Professor in the School of Social Work at the University of Southern California. She received her PhD in Sociology from the City University of New York, Graduate Center. Her research examines the complex of social determinants that influence the development of drug abuse health disparities across generations of Mexican-origin populations. Dr. Cepeda has been a recipient of several National Institutes of Health federal grants. Her most recent National Institute on Drug Abuse funded study is following up a cohort of Mexican American adolescent females who were affiliated with male gang members during their adolescence.

Sarah Daly is a Ph.D. student at Rutgers University-Newark. She has spent much of her career working with at-risk students as a teacher and counsellor. Her areas of research and teaching include mass shootings, juvenile gang membership, and victimization.

Melissa Freitag graduated with her undergraduate degree from Hobart and William Smith Colleges in 2014. She is currently a graduate student in sociology at Bowling Green State University, Ohio. During the summer of 2014, she volunteered to work with Dr. Hansen on data collection on gang initiation rituals. In the process, Ms. Freitag was instrumental in creating a coding scheme that fit well with the grounded theory approach envisioned by Dr. Hansen for this project. Her current research interests include criminology and gender.

Jarrod Gilbert is considered to be New Zealand's leading gang expert. Dr Gilbert is a sociologist at the University of Canterbury and the Lead Researcher at Independent Research Solutions. He undertook an extensive ethnographic study into Gangs in New Zealand which led to *Patched: The History of Gangs in New Zealand* and he has won a number of writing awards. His research interests include criminal justice, gang culture and murder. Dr Gilbert has conducted large-scale studies on youth desistance, as well as the relationship between alcohol and crime. He is currently working on a book about murder as a sociological history of New Zealand. He specialises in research with practical applications.

Laura Dunbar is a PhD Candidate in the Department of Criminology at the University of Ottawa. Her doctoral research focuses on youth gangs and, more specifically, on the factors associated with success in exiting from gang involvement, especially for youth involved in the criminal justice system.

Laura L. Hansen is an Associate Professor in Criminal Justice teaching at Western New England University in Springfield, MA., U.S.A. She received her Ph.D. in Sociology at the University of California, Riverside, where she studied primarily white-collar crime and social networks. In the course of studying elite criminal networks, she began to see parallels with street gangs, leading to applied work in prevention of gang recruitment. As well as teaching criminal justice courses, Dr. Hansen is currently a research partner for The City of Holyoke and the South Holyoke Safe Neighborhood Initiative.

Ronn Johnson, Ph.D., is an Associate Professor in the School of Leadership and Educational Sciences at the University of San Diego. He is a licensed and board certified psychologist with extensive experience in academic and clinical settings. An examiner for the American Board of Professional Psychology he has served as a staff psychologist in community mental health clinics, hospitals, VA hospitals, schools and university counselling centers. His previous academic appointments include the Universitity of Iowa, University of Nebraska-Lincoln, University of Central Oklahoma, and San Diego State University. He is an adjunct professor in the Homeland Security Department at San Diego State and the School of Forensic Studies at AIU. His clinical, research, and teaching interests include forensic psychology, psychological assessment; ethical and legal issues associated with professional practice; and trauma. He crafted the DSM-5 Quadrant which is used in forensic cases and has several seminal articles on expert witnesses for police pre-employment and fitness-for-duty evaluations.

Charles Kaplan received his PhD from the University of California, Los Angeles in sociology in 1973. He is currently, the Associate Dean of Research and Research Professor at the School of Social Work at the University of Southern California. He is an active member of the NIDA National Hispanic Science Network. His research emphasizes the linking of drug abuse epidemiology with experimental approaches to drug prevention and treatment suitable for emerging special populations from an international comparative perspective. Recently, he is developing exploratory research in emerging patterns of cannabis use and abuse in the changing policy context of legalization and medicalization in the United States and Europe.

Timothy R. Lauger is an Assistant Professor of Criminology and Criminal Justice at Niagara University. He received his Ph.D. in criminal justice from Indiana University. He is the author of *'Real Gangstas: Legitimacy, Reputation, and Violence in the Intergang Environment'*, which was published by Rutgers University Press in 2012.

Dev Maitra is a third-year PhD student at the Institute of Criminology, University of Cambridge. His doctoral research is funded by the ESRC, and focuses on prison gangs, street gangs and organised crime in the North of England. His research interests also include drug-dealing networks, and the role of religious extremism in high-security English prisons. Dev is a member of Cambridge University's Prisons Research Centre, where he received an MPhil in Criminological Research funded by the ESRC. He also holds an LL.B. from the University of Bristol and was called to the Bar of England and Wales at Lincoln's Inn.

Andrej Naterer is a lecturer at the University of Maribor. Slovenia. He specialises in research on youth offending. Andrej has previously worked in the Faculty of Social Sciences, University of Ljubljana; the Faculty of Educational Sciences, University of Maribor, the Faculty of Arts, University of Maribor and on various National and international research projects. His recent work has focussed on Street children and life outside the traditional framework of socialisation and also an anthropological study of the street children subculture in Makeevka, eastern Ukraine. Andrej has published a range of monographs and articles on the issue of Street Children and has recently undertaken extensive fieldwork research in India and Zambia on this topic.

Kathryn M. Nowotny is a Chancellor's Fellow and PhD Candidate in the Department of Sociology and Population Program, Institute of Behavioral Science at the University of Colorado Boulder. Her research lies at the intersection of criminology, medical sociology, and social demography to examine the health of inmates and other criminally-involved populations. She received a NIH Ruth L Kirschstein National Research Service Award Fellowship and a NSF Doctoral Dissertation Research Improvement Grant in support of her dissertation examining health and healthcare in U.S. prisons.

Don Pinnock is an investigative journalist and photographer whose assignments have taken him to five continents. He has written 17 books, hundreds of articles and held two photographic exhibitions. He has degrees in criminology, political science and African history and has been a travel writer, lecturer, engineer, professional yachtsman and cable car operator on the Rock of Gibraltar. He is an honorary research associate of the Centre of Criminology and the Safety and Violence Initiative at the University of Cape Town, a founding member of the Usiko Trust working with high-risk youths and is a trustee of the Chrysalis Academy for young men and women from disadvantaged backgrounds. He is married to the novelist and poet Patricia Schonstein and they have two children. They all live at the foot of Table Mountain.

Avelardo Valdez is currently a professor at the USC School of Social Work and Sociology. He obtained his Ph.D. in Sociology at the University of California, Los Angeles. A primary focus of his research has been on the relationship between substance abuse and violence and health issues among high-risk groups. His research projects have been among "hidden populations" such as youth and prison gang members, heroin users, and sex workers on the U.S./Mexico border. He has published over 100 journal articles and chapters and academic publications including two books. He is a recipient of numerous federal grant awards from the National Institutes of Health (NIH), National Institute on Drug Abuse (NIDA), Centers for Disease Control and Prevention (CDC), and Substance Abuse and Mental Health Services Administration (SAMHSA). He recently finished a NIH NIDA international funded study on the diffusion of crack cocaine in Mexico City. He is currently a member of the U.S.A. Department of Justice, Office of Justice Programs, Science Advisory Board.

Robin Maria Valeri is Professor of Psychology at. St. Bonaventure University. Dr. Valeri has published on a variety of topics including hate groups, skin heads, terrorism, pets and laughter, and cigarette advertisements. Dr. Valeri's work has appeared in the American Behavioural Scientist, Journal of Applied Social Psychology, Journal of Applied Sociology, Journal of Men's Studies, and the Michigan Sociological Review. Valeri is co-editor of the book Terrorism in America (Jones & Bartlett Publishing, 2008) and co-author of Skinheads, an entry in The Blackwell Encyclopaedia of Race, Ethnicity and Nationalism (Wiley-Blackwell, forthcoming).

Rob White is Professor of Criminology at the University of Tasmania, Australia. He has published widely in the areas of youth studies, criminology and is recognised for his work in green criminology. Among his recent books are *'Youth and Society'* (with Johanna Wyn) and *'Youth Gangs, Violence and Social Respect'*.

Qianwei Zhao is a doctoral student at the University of Southern California (USC)'s School of Social Work, and is a mentee of Drs. Avelardo Valdez and Alice Cepeda. Her research mainly focuses on the reintegration process of female ex-prisoners. She earned her Bachelor of Law degree in China and her Master of Social Work (MSW) from the University of Pennsylvania. In China, she worked with elderly women facing domestic violence and children with autism. She also worked at the University of Pennsylvania for one year as a Research Assistant. In addition, Zhao conducted independent research on the educational experience of children of sex workers in Kolkata, India during an overseas research program through the University of Pennsylvania.

Index

Become an IRMA Member

Members of the **Information Resources Management Association (IRMA)** understand the importance of community within their field of study. The Information Resources Management Association is an ideal venue through which professionals, students, and academicians can convene and share the latest industry innovations and scholarly research that is changing the field of information science and technology. Become a member today and enjoy the benefits of membership as well as the opportunity to collaborate and network with fellow experts in the field.

IRMA Membership Benefits:

- **One FREE Journal Subscription**

- **30% Off Additional Journal Subscriptions**

- **20% Off Book Purchases**

- Updates on the latest events and research on Information Resources Management through the IRMA-L listserv.

- Updates on new open access and downloadable content added to Research IRM.

- A copy of the Information Technology Management Newsletter twice a year.

- A certificate of membership.

IRMA Membership $195

Scan code to visit irma-international.org and begin by selecting your free journal subscription.

Membership is good for one full year.

CPSIA information can be obtained at www.ICGtesting.com
Printed in the USA
BVOW04*1841290216

438509BV00002B/6/P